Reading Critically Writing Well

NINTH EDITION

A Reader and Guide

RISE B. AXELROD

CHARLES R. COOPER

ALISON M. WARRINER

What do you need for class today?

We want to make sure you're the first to hear about the things we do to help teachers: resources for professional development and the classroom, workshops, and symposia.

Sign up for updates, and we'll send you these professional resources:

> *Writing and Community Engagement: A Critical Sourcebook*, by Thomas Deans, Barbara Roswell, and Adrian J. Wurr

> *How Has Composition Changed?*, a report based on a comparative survey of over 3,000 writing teachers

We want to hear your feedback on new projects, ideas, revisions, and media. Help make our resources better. Tell us what kind of projects you're interested in reviewing.

Sign up for news and opportunities to review.
bedfordstmartins.com/englishupdates

Reading Critically Writing Well

A READER AND GUIDE

NINTH EDITION

Reading Critically Writing Well

A READER AND GUIDE

Rise B. Axelrod
University of California, Riverside

Charles R. Cooper
University of California, San Diego

Alison M. Warriner
California State University, East Bay

Bedford / St. Martin's
Boston • New York

For Bedford/St. Martin's

Senior Developmental Editor: John Elliott
Senior Production Editor: Bill Imbornoni
Senior Production Supervisor: Dennis J. Conroy
Senior Marketing Manager: Molly Parke
Editorial Assistant: Karrin Varucene
Copy Editor: Diana P. George
Indexer: Kirsten Kite
Photo Researcher: Linda Finigan
Permissions Manager: Kalina Ingham Hintz
Art Director: Lucy Krikorian
Text Design: Nesbitt Graphics, Inc.
Cover Design: Marine Miller
Cover Art: The cover shows a detail from Terry Frost's *Halzephron* (2001),
  © The Frost Estate/Beaux Arts, London.
Composition: MPS Limited, a Macmillan Company
Printing and Binding: RR Donnelley and Sons

President: Joan E. Feinberg
Editorial Director: Denise B. Wydra
Editor in Chief: Karen S. Henry
Director of Development: Erica T. Appel
Director of Marketing: Karen R. Soeltz
Director of Production: Susan W. Brown
Associate Director, Editorial Production: Elise S. Kaiser
Managing Editor: Shuli Traub

Library of Congress Control Number: 2010939974

Manufactured in the United States of America.

5 4 3 2 1 0
f e d c b a

For information, write: Bedford/St. Martin's, 75 Arlington Street, Boston, MA 02116
  (617-399-4000)

ISBN: 978-0-312-60761-6

Acknowledgments

Preface

Read, read, read . . . Just like a carpenter who works as an apprentice and studies the master. Read!

—WILLIAM FAULKNER

I went back to the good nature books that I had read. And I analyzed them. I wrote outlines of whole books—outlines of chapters—so that I could see their structure. And I copied down their transitional sentences or their main sentences or their closing sentences or their lead sentences. I especially paid attention to how these writers made transitions between paragraphs and scenes.

—ANNIE DILLARD

In these quotations, the Nobel Prize–winning novelist William Faulkner and the Pulitzer Prize–winning essayist Annie Dillard tell us what many authors know intuitively—that reading critically helps writers learn to write well. Reading closely and critically also helps students become analytical thinkers.

Now in its ninth edition, *Reading Critically, Writing Well* helps students see the connection between reading closely and critically and writing thoughtfully and effectively. By using the book's approach, students learn how texts work rhetorically to achieve their purposes with particular readers. They also learn an array of strategies for critical reading and thinking—strategies that contribute to enhanced comprehension of a text, inspire active engagement with it, and stimulate analysis of the text's as well as the reader's own assumptions, values, and beliefs. As the title of the book's new Chapter 1 suggests, they learn to develop the "academic habits of mind" they need to succeed both in their college work and in their careers.

This book brings critical reading and writing together by engaging students in two fundamental ways of reading: reading for meaning and reading like a writer. While Reading for Meaning activities give students insight into how readers construct meanings from what they read, Reading like a Writer activities teach students how to construct their own texts rhetorically to influence their readers' understanding and critical response. The two strategies are introduced in the Guide to Reading at the beginning of each assignment chapter and then applied to every reading selection throughout the text. Through continued use of these two critical reading strategies, students gain confidence in their ability to read with a critical eye and to write effectively in different rhetorical situations.

FEATURES

The special features of *Reading Critically, Writing Well* include the following:

Engaging Readings Demonstrating Eight Different Types of Real-World Writing

Reading Critically, Writing Well includes forty-eight readings—four published essays and two student essays in each assignment chapter (Chapters 2–9). Each of these chapters focuses on a specific type of writing that students will encounter during college or on the job, including four expository genres (autobiography, observation, reflection, and explanation of concepts) and four argument genres (evaluation, position paper on a controversial issue, speculation about causes or effects, and proposal to solve a problem.) Chosen to stimulate lively class discussion and to illustrate a variety of writing strategies, the readings provide students with provocative perspectives on many important topics. You will find many tried and true essays by distinguished professional and academic writers such as Annie Dillard, Brent Staples, Susan Orlean, Saira Shah, Deborah Tannen, Stephen King, Amitai Etzioni, Luis J. Rodriguez, Karen Stabiner, Brian Greene, Nicholas Carr, Firoozeh Dumas, and Cass Sunstein.

Throughout the book, pairs of essays or other pieces of writing engage with each other on various topics. These topically linked readings—and the accompanying activity that focuses attention on the connections and differences between them—stimulate students to respond less passively and more critically to what they read. For example, students are asked to compare two reviews of the film *Avatar* and two versions of Brent Staples's reflections on how his mere presence as a black man changes public space.

Uniquely Thorough Instruction in the Reading-Writing Connection

Reading Critically, Writing Well teaches students how to analyze the content and craft of successful writing and how to apply what they have learned to their own writing. Each assignment chapter begins with a Guide to Reading and ends with a Guide to Writing, both tailored to the distinctive features of the chapter's genre. These guides provide a set of flexible activities designed to help students learn to read a specific kind of writing with a critical eye and write in that genre with a clear purpose for their own readers. Using the chapter's first reading selection as a model, the Guide to Reading introduces the two overall strategies for critical reading—Reading for Meaning and Reading like a Writer—that are then applied to the other five selections. The Guide to Writing scaffolds the composing process, using concepts students have learned in their Reading like a Writer activities. These major structural elements of the book provide guidance for students in moving from critical reading to effective writing. In addition, Appendix 1, A Catalog of Critical Reading Strategies, explains and applies to Martin Luther King Jr.'s "Letter from Birmingham Jail" seventeen additional strategies for critical reading—ranging from annotating and summarizing to exploring the significance of figurative language and judging the writer's credibility.

"Reading for Meaning" Activities That Teach Students to Read Deeply and Critically

Three class-tested Reading for Meaning activities following each selection give students three different kinds of help in understanding and interpreting what they are reading. The first activity, Read to Comprehend, asks them to summarize their understanding of the main point of the reading and to identify and look up any words they do not understand. The second activity, Read to Respond, asks them to explore an aspect of the reading that they personally found noteworthy for any reason. The third activity, Read to Analyze Assumptions, leads students to think more critically about the beliefs and values implicit in the reading's word choices and assertions and also to examine the bases for their own assumptions as readers. Each of these three Reading for Meaning activities concludes with a list of additional critical reading strategies from Appendix 1 that would most productively enhance the student's continued efforts to read for meaning.

"Reading like a Writer" Activities That Teach Students to Read Rhetorically

The Reading like a Writer activities help students learn how to examine and assess the effectiveness of a writer's choices in light of the purpose and audience—that is, to read rhetorically. The Guide to Reading at the beginning of each assignment chapter presents several Reading like a Writer activities that each introduce a rhetorical strategy typical of the genre, such as describing people and places in observation and asserting an overall judgment in evaluation. Each subsequent essay in a chapter is followed by a Reading like a Writer activity inviting students to learn more about one of these strategies. Altogether, each chapter invites students to complete nine or ten focused rhetorical analyses of readings in the same genre.

Every Reading like a Writer activity directs students to a specific part of a reading—a few sentences or paragraphs—so that students lose no time wondering where to begin their analysis. Many activities show students the first step to take. Because they are focused and accessible, these activities make it possible for even the most inexperienced readers to complete them and engage in a serious program of rhetorical learning.

Guides to Writing That Support Students' Composing

As writing instructors, we know that students need help writing essays. To provide this support, each assignment chapter concludes with a comprehensive Guide to Writing that escorts students through their process of writing in that particular genre—from choosing a topic to editing and proofreading the essay. In our experience, all students, from the most anxious to the most confident writers, benefit in some way from the Guides to Writing.

Grounded in research on composing as well as in genre and learning theory, each Guide to Writing scaffolds student learning about a genre, coaching students by asking questions designed to help them analyze, generate, and synthesize information and ideas about their topic. Thus the Guide to Writing teaches students the kinds of questions they need to learn to ask themselves as they write. It also helps them apply the rhetorical knowledge they have gleaned from the model readings in the chapter as they compose an essay of their own in the same genre.

Along with general advice about invention, research, planning, drafting, and revising, each Guide to Writing includes four specific sections that provide students with detailed, practical help for various aspects of composing, using examples from the chapter's readings where appropriate. To increase students' grammatical facility and rhetorical prowess, a section called Considering a Useful Sentence Strategy explains a specific sentence pattern that writers typically use when composing in that genre, such as rhetorical questions in proposals and appositives in explanations of concepts. Because using sources effectively is essential to academic writing, a Working with Sources section gives advice on a specific way that sources are typically used in the genre, such as integrating quotations from interviews in observational essays and citing statistics in proposals. Reinforcing what students are learning about the connection between reading critically and writing well, a Reading a Draft Critically chart tailored to the genre helps them engage in constructive critique of their classmates'—as well as their own—writing. And finally, to make revision more efficient, a Troubleshooting Your Draft chart lists typical problems students confront in their drafts and specific solutions for each one.

Intensive Coverage of Strategies for Research and Documentation

The Guides to Writing and the comprehensive discussions of strategies for research and documentation in Appendix 2 provide students with clear, helpful guidelines for evaluating sources, integrating them into their writing, and citing them using the most current MLA and APA styles. With eight different genres, students have an opportunity to practice the full gamut of research strategies, from memory search to the field research methods of observation and interview to library and Internet research.

Activities That Ask Students to Reflect on Their Learning

Research has shown that when students reflect on their learning, they clarify their understanding and remember what they have learned longer. Reflecting also enables students to think critically about what they have learned and how they have learned it. *Reading Critically, Writing Well* provides three opportunities in each chapter for students to reflect on their learning and also to discuss what they have learned with others: Reflecting on Your Experience, Reviewing What Makes an Essay Effective, and Reflecting on What You Have Learned. These activities are placed at important transitions in each chapter, at points when looking back at what they have learned will help students move forward more productively.

NEW TO THIS EDITION

Twenty-One New Readings on Engaging Topics

Almost half of the reading selections—twenty-one of forty-eight—are new, including five new student essays and sixteen pieces by award-winning writers such as Susan Orlean and Nicholas Carr; social critics such as Kathleen A. Bogle and Claudia Wallis; and distinguished professors and researchers such Brian Greene and Cass Sunstein. The new readings engage students with current topics close to their daily lives, such as evaluations of the movie *Avatar* and an essay on the origins of hip-hop, as well as position papers and proposals about the role of science in education and modern culture, regulation of energy drinks, and the effects of Google on human intelligence. New paired essays by Wallis and Christine Rosen offer fresh perspectives on multitasking.

A New Introduction on the "Academic Habits of Mind" Students Need to Develop

A completely new Chapter 1 helps students begin to understand the skills of academic literacy—the distinctive kinds of thinking, reading, and writing they will need to do for their college courses and eventual careers. Using brief examples from different genres of texts on a topic familiar to all students—bullying in school—the chapter guides students through each essential habit of mind, ranging from exhibiting curiosity and seeing other points of view to using appropriate vocabulary and synthesizing material from several sources. A series of activities helps them discover which habits they have already cultivated and which they will need to develop and practice. The chapter also refers students to other sections of the book that will help them further develop these crucial habits.

New Guidance and Practice in Critical Analysis of Visuals

A new Appendix 3, Strategies for Analyzing Visuals, explains to students how to critically read and then write about photos, ads, works of art, and other image-based texts. The appendix concludes with a student's analysis of and essay about a photo by Gordon Parks. In addition, each assignment chapter now includes an "Analyzing Visuals" activity following one of the reading selections, in which students are asked to write a paragraph analyzing an image (or sometimes more than one) included with the selection and explaining how it illuminates the verbal text.

More Help with Critical Reading

To reduce duplication of information in the Guide to Reading and engage students more actively in the close, critical reading they need to learn to do, the annotated essay in each assignment chapter is now the second selection, and the annotations now take the form of questions; the questions prompt students not only to notice features of the genre and rhetorical elements such as transitions and topic sentences but also to think about why the writer made particular choices and how effective they are. In addition, the Read to Analyze Assumptions activity that is part of the Reading for Meaning apparatus after each essay now provides more specific references to the texts along with focused questions to remind students of issues they need to think about in analyzing assumptions in any text.

A New Sequence for the Argument Chapters

The chapter on Arguing a Position has been moved ahead of the chapters on Speculating on Causes or Effects and Making a Proposal because students usually learn and practice the general features of argument essays before they study and write specialized forms of argument. (The chapter on Evaluation remains ahead of all these chapters because often evaluations do not consider opposing views and therefore do not use the strategies of counterarguing that are so central to other kinds of argument essays.)

A New Design for Improved Navigation

Marginal tabs, a sans serif font for reading selections, the addition of chapter numbers to running heads, and varied designs for different kinds of boxed activities help instructors and students orient themselves more easily within the assignment chapters. The lists of revision suggestions in each assignment chapter have been reworked into "Troubleshooting Your Draft" charts that are easier for students to reference and use.

MORE DIGITAL CHOICES

Reading Critically, Writing Well doesn't stop with a book. Online, you'll find both free and affordable premium resources to help students get even more out of the book and your course. You'll also find convenient instructor resources, such as downloadable sample syllabi, classroom activities, and even a nationwide community of teachers. To learn more about or order any of the products below, contact your Bedford/St. Martin's sales representative, e-mail sales support (**sales_support@bfwpub.com**), or visit the Web site at **bedfordstmartins .com/readingcritically.**

Student Resources

Send students to free and open resources, upgrade to an expanding collection of innovative digital content, or package a standalone CD-ROM for free with *Reading Critically, Writing Well.*

Re:Writing, the best free collection of online resources for the writing class, offers clear advice on citing sources in *Research and Documentation Online* by Diana Hacker, thirty sample papers and designed documents, and over nine thousand writing and grammar exercises with immediate feedback and reporting in *Exercise Central.* Updated and redesigned, *Re:Writing* also features five free videos from *VideoCentral* and three new visual tutorials from our popular *ix visual exercises* by Cheryl Ball and Kristin Arola. *Re:Writing* is completely free and open (no codes required) to ensure access to all students. Visit **bedfordstmartins.com/rewriting.**

VideoCentral is a growing collection of videos for the writing class that captures real-world, academic, and student writers talking about how and why they write. Writer and teacher Peter Berkow interviewed hundreds of people—from Michael Moore to Cynthia Selfe—to produce fifty brief videos about topics such as revising and getting feedback. *VideoCentral* can be packaged with *Reading Critically, Writing Well* at a significant discount. An activation code is required. To learn more, visit **bedfordstmartins.com/videocentral.** To order *VideoCentral* packaged with the print book, use **ISBN 978-0-312-58830-4.**

Re:Writing Plus gathers all of Bedford/St. Martin's premium digital content for composition into one online collection. It includes hundreds of model documents, the first ever peer review game, and *VideoCentral. Re:Writing Plus* can be purchased separately or packaged with the print book at a significant discount. An activation code is required. To learn more, visit **bedfordstmartins .com/rewriting.** To order *Re:Writing Plus* packaged with the print book, use **ISBN 978-0-312-58829-8.**

i-series on CD-ROM presents multimedia tutorials in a flexible format—because there are things you cannot do in a book. To learn more, visit **bedfordstmartins.com/readingcritically.**

- *ix visual exercises* helps students put into practice key rhetorical and visual concepts. To order *ix visual exercises* packaged with the print book, use **ISBN 978-0-312-58828-1.**

- *i-claim: visualizing argument* offers a new way to see argument—with six tutorials, an illustrated glossary, and over seventy multimedia arguments. To order *i-claim: visualizing argument* packaged with the print book, use **ISBN 978-0-312-58826-7.**

- *i-cite: visualizing sources* brings research to life through an animated introduction, four tutorials, and hands-on source practice. To order *i-cite: visualizing sources* packaged with the print book, use **ISBN 978-0-312-58825-0.**

Instructor Resources

You have a lot to do in your course. Bedford/St. Martin's wants to make it easy for you to find the support you need—and to get it quickly. To find everything available with *Reading Critically, Writing Well,* visit **bedfordstmartins.com /readingcritically.**

The Instructor's Manual for Reading Critically, Writing Well is available either bound into the student book as an *Instructor's Edition* or in PDF that can be downloaded from the Bedford/St. Martin's online catalog. In addition to chapter overviews and teaching tips, the Instructor's Manual includes sample syllabi and suggestions for classroom activities.

TeachingCentral offers the entire list of Bedford/St. Martin's print and online professional resources in one place. You will find landmark reference works, sourcebooks on pedagogical issues, award-winning collections, and practical advice for the classroom—all free for instructors.

Bits collects creative ideas for teaching a range of composition topics in an easily searchable blog. A community of teachers—leading scholars, authors, and editors—discuss revision, research, grammar and style, technology, peer review, and much more. Take, use, adapt, and pass the ideas around. Then, come back to the site to comment or share your own suggestion.

Content cartridges for the most common course management systems—Blackboard, WebCT, Angel, and Desire2Learn—allow you to easily download digital materials from Bedford/St. Martin's for your course.

ACKNOWLEDGMENTS

We first want to thank our students and colleagues at the University of California, Riverside, and the University of California, San Diego; California State University, East Bay, and California State University, San Bernardino; and the University of Nevada, Reno, who have taught us so much about reading, writing, and teaching.

We also owe a debt of gratitude to the many reviewers who made suggestions for this revision. They include Sean Bernard, University of La Verne; S. V. Buffamanti, Niagara County Community College; Gwendolyn Diponio, Crafton Hills College; Jeannine Edwards, University of Memphis; Cheryl Easly, Central Texas College; Terry Engel, Harding University; Paul Haeder, Spokane Falls Community College; Fayeza Hasanat, University of Central Florida; Elizabeth Imafuji, Anderson University; Deanna M. Jessup, Clark State Community College; Robert Johnson, Midwestern State University; Stanley W. Johnson, Southside Virginia Community College; Sara M. King, George Mason University; Carol Miller, University of Texas at El Paso; Lance K. Morita, Leeward Community College; Kirsten Ogden, Pasadena City College; Mark Reynolds, Jefferson Davis Community College; Jenny Russell, Berkshire Community College; Sherry Steward, Rollins College; Robert Tinajero, Tarrant County College South; Mary F. Tohill, University of Akron—Wayne College; Stacia Watkins, Middle Tennessee State University; Susan Wood, Leeward Community College; and Sarah Yoder, Westmont College.

We want especially to thank our developmental editor, John Elliott. This book could not have been written without his insightful criticism, skillful editing, cheerful persistence, and good humor. Working with John all these years has been an unalloyed pleasure and wonderful learning experience. We also want to thank Joan Feinberg, Karen Henry, Denise Wydra, and Erica Appel for their leadership and support. Our deepest appreciation goes out to Nancy Perry, who has been our mainstay at Bedford/St.Martin's lo these many years; thank you, Nancy, for your wise guidance and kind friendship. We are grateful for Bill Imbornoni's seamless coordination of the production process, Diana Puglisi George's skillful copy editing, Jerilyn Bockorick's attractive new design, Diane Kraut's and Linda Finigan's work on permissions and art research, and Molly Parke's help in marketing.

Rise dedicates this book to Jeremiah Axelrod and Lil Delcampo, her son and daughter-in-law, wishing that their new life together be full of love and joy, as hers has been with her husband, Steven. Alison dedicates this book with love to her sister, Jean Warriner McLemore, whose frequent e-mails provided support and encouragement, and to her husband, Jeremiah, and her daughter, Dawn.

Rise B. Axelrod
Charles R. Cooper
Alison M. Warriner

Contents

3 OBSERVATION — 81

4 REFLECTION   147

5 EXPLAINING CONCEPTS   207

6 EVALUATION 281

7 POSITION PAPER 345

8 SPECULATING ABOUT CAUSES OR EFFECTS   410

9 PROPOSAL TO SOLVE A PROBLEM 483

APPENDIX 2

STRATEGIES FOR RESEARCH AND DOCUMENTATION   603

APPENDIX 3

STRATEGIES FOR ANALYZING VISUALS   667

Paired Readings

One of the readings in each of the following pairs is followed by an activity inviting students to compare and contrast the readings. In each pair, the page numbers in parentheses indicate the first pages of the readings; the boldface number at the end indicates the first page of the activity.

Reading Critically Writing Well

A READER AND GUIDE

CHAPTER 1

Academic Habits of Mind: Thinking, Reading, and Writing in College

Imagine yourself on a journey to a part of your country where you have never been. It's not like visiting another country, because you already know the language and have some background in common with the people, but it's a place where some of the traditions, customs, and laws may be different from what you're accustomed to. When you arrive, you are immersed in a new job with people you haven't met before, but even though you're new, you are expected to know the law of the land and the rules that pertain to your new job. These rules include knowing how to communicate, how to produce the products the job involves, and how to deal with difficulties or emergencies. Some of you may have had some experience with a culture similar to the one in this place, but others of you will feel as though you are in a foreign land. It takes some getting used to.

This new place is college. Sure, you've been through high school and you've completed academic assignments before, and you've been accepted into your college, so presumably you have the background you need to succeed. Chances are good that you have what it takes to do well in your courses. What you might not know, though, is that the world of college has its own special requirements and demands, and that in order to be successful, it helps for you to know what they are and how to respond to them.

Reading Critically, Writing Well is designed to prepare you for the special demands of thinking, reading, and writing in college. The skills you have already developed will enable you to adjust to the more intense college experience. This book will give you additional approaches to learning that will make the process more accessible to you and will help you develop the *habits of mind* that successful learners practice. It will help you develop skills for *critical thinking* and *critical reading*, activities that will be useful in all of your college courses. In addition, you will discover many strategies that lead to *writing well*, assuring that you will be successful in college and in your career and other activities afterwards.

All of your professors will assume you already have these skills—if you think of college as a new job in an unfamiliar place, they have been living there and doing the job for a long time, and they often forget what it was like when they first arrived and started working—so you have to take the initiative to develop the skills and begin to incorporate them into your daily behavior. Once you do, not only will you be comfortable in this new place, but you will also have acquired strategies that help you wherever else you go, no matter what you choose as a career. Each chapter of this book introduces additional approaches to the work of college, and three appendices—A *Catalog of Critical Reading Strategies, Strategies for Research and Documentation,* and *Strategies for Analyzing Visuals,* will further reinforce your academic literacy.

In this introductory chapter, we explore the habits of mind practiced by successful students, as well as by professors and people in many different careers. "Habits of mind" refer to the ways of thinking, investigating, and inquiring typical of people in the process of learning. They are also reflected in the products of learners: in the writing, speaking, or performing that result from certain habits. As the word "habit" suggests, these practices can be cultivated: You can acquire them by trying them on, making them work for you, and repeating them until you have internalized them.

You are probably familiar with many of the habits of mind typical of successful students. For example, you already know that you need to come to class prepared, be attentive in class, complete assignments on time, ask the teacher for clarification if an assignment isn't clear to you, and contribute to class discussions. In addition to those habits, though, there are many with which you might not be as familiar—habits of mind this chapter will invite you to try out. As you do the activities in it, you may find some of them easy—those about habits with which you are familiar—and some of them difficult—those about habits you have yet to learn. Don't be discouraged if you find yourself struggling. Just do the activity to get a feel for it, and know that as you work through the book and consult the appendices, you will become more adept at the habits of mind explored here.

Before reading further, consider what you may already know about your own habits of mind.

ACTIVITY 1

What habits of mind do you already possess as you approach this course? Think about how you studied in high school, or how you followed up on something—inside or outside of school—that inspired you, such as a sport, a craft, a dance, a school subject like English or science, or playing a musical instrument. Write down your answers to the following questions: What sparked your interest in this field in the first place? What kinds of questions about it did you have? How did you go about finding out more information? What did you do with your information? When you look back on your experience, what habits of mind did you form as you satisfied your curiosity and followed through on your interest?

Hold in your mind (and on screen or on paper) these habits of mind you have acquired; you may see as you read on that you have a head start on the habits of mind expected of college students. At the end of this chapter, you will revisit this activity.

THINKING CRITICALLY

Critical thinking doesn't mean thinking about something negatively—as if you were criticizing it—but rather thinking through ideas with a questioning and sometimes skeptical mind. When you think critically, you raise questions about what you have been reading, writing, discussing, or thinking, and you try to explore answers to questions you and others have raised. Critical reading and writing well involve the same skills as critical thinking, along with some additional ones that you need when you are actively reading a passage or when you are writing. You will work more on these skills as you make your way through this chapter and through this book.

In order to begin working on the habits of mind required for critical thinking, read the following four passages on the topic of bullying in schools. All of these passages come from texts that are in the *genre* of speculating about causes and effects (chapter 7 in *Reading Critically, Writing Well*). Here, *genre* means a kind or category of writing seeking to achieve a particular purpose with readers and following certain conventions or rules of form and content expected by readers. In this case, all of the excerpts assert that bullying is a problem; they formally define bullying; and then they try to determine the effects the problem causes—in other words, the *consequences* of bullying. As you read these excerpts for the first time, bear in mind one of the habits of mind expected of critical thinkers is **being curious.**

What in these texts indicates that the writers are curious? What questions do you think they asked themselves in order to write these texts? Note that these questions are not usually written down; they are only *implied* by assertions the authors make in response to their unwritten questions.

1. Ron Banks, "Bullying in Schools"

As established by studies in Scandinavian countries, a strong correlation appears to exist between bullying other students during the school years and experiencing legal or criminal troubles as adults. In one study, 60 percent of those characterized as bullies in grades 6–9 had at least one criminal conviction by age 24 (Olweus 1993). Chronic bullies seem to maintain their behaviors into adulthood, negatively influencing their ability to develop and maintain positive relationships (Oliver, Hoover, and Hazler 1994).

Victims often fear school and consider school to be an unsafe and unhappy place. As many as 7 percent of America's eighth-graders stay home at least once a month because of bullies. The act of being bullied tends to increase some students' isolation because their peers do not want to lose status by associating with them or because they do not want to increase the risks of being bullied themselves. Being bullied leads to depression and low self-esteem, problems that can carry into adulthood (Olweus 1993; Batsche and Knoff 1994).

2. Tara L. Kuther, "Understanding Bullying"

Bullying is not a normal part of growing up. Victims of bullying suffer psychological and sometimes physical scars that last a lifetime. Victims report greater fear and anxiety, feel less accepted, suffer from more health problems, and score lower on measures of academic achievement and self-esteem than students who are not bullied. Victims often turn their anger inward, which may lead to depression, anxiety, and even suicide. The experience of bullying is also linked with violence, as the fatal school shootings in Littleton, Colorado, and Jonesborough, Arkansas, have illustrated.

However, it's not just victims who are hurt by bullying. Bullies fail to learn how to cope, manage their emotions, and communicate effectively—skills vital to success in the adult world. Without intervention, bullies suffer stunted emotional growth and fail to develop empathy. Since bullies are accustomed to achieving their immediate goals by pushing others around, they don't learn how to have genuine relationships with other people. Instead, they externalize and blame others for their problems, never taking responsibility, nor learning how to care for another's needs. Bullies who don't learn other ways of getting what they want develop into adult bullies who are more likely to experience criminal troubles, be abusive toward their spouses, and have more aggressive children, perhaps continuing the cycle of bullying into the next generation.

3. Michael D. Lemonick, "The Bully Blight"

Whatever the reason for bullying, the consequences are clear. Nishina [Adrienne Nishina, a postdoctoral scholar at the UCLA Graduate School of Education and Information Studies] found that victims feel sick more often than their classmates do, are absent more often and tend to have lower grades. They are also more depressed and withdrawn—a natural reaction, says Nishina, but one that "can subsequently lead to more victimization." The studies also indicate that schools take too narrow a view of what constitutes bullying. Physical aggression is forbidden, as are such forms of verbal bullying as sexual harassment and racial slurs. But the rules are generally silent about less incendiary name calling. "You're probably not going to get into trouble if you call someone fat or stupid," Nishina says. "But our research suggests victimized students felt equally bad."

She also classifies nonphysical, nonverbal behaviors, including gestures and making faces, as bullying. "They happen quite a bit and can have an effect as well," Nishina says. "But they're very subtle and very difficult for us to capture and assess well." Even tougher to assess is the growing phenomenon of cyberbullying—vicious text messages or e-mails, or websites on which kids post degrading rumors. A recent survey of more than 5,500 teens found that 72% of them said online bullying was just as distressing as the face-to-face kind.

The damage from bullying doesn't stop after graduation. According to Dr. William Coleman, professor of pediatrics at the University of North Carolina School of Medicine, bullies are four times as likely as the average child to have engaged in criminal behavior by age 24; they also grow up deficient in social, coping, and negotiating skills and are more likely to engage in substance abuse. Victims have similar problems; they also have fewer friends and are more likely to be depressed.

4. **Tonja R. Nansel, Mary Overpeck, Ramani S. Pilla, W. June Ruan, Bruce Simons-Morton, and Peter Scheidt, "Bullying Behaviors among US Youth: Prevalence and Association with Psychosocial Adjustment"**

Both bullying and being bullied were associated with poorer psychosocial adjustment; however, there were notable differences among those bullied, bullies, and those reporting both behaviors. Those bullied demonstrated poorer social and emotional adjustment, reporting greater difficulty making friends, poorer relationships with classmates, and great loneliness. Youth who are socially isolated and lack social skills may be more likely targets for being bullied. This is consonant with the finding by Hoover and colleagues[32,33] that the most frequent reason cited by youth for persons being bullied is that they "didn't fit in." At the same time, youth who are bullied may well be avoided by other youth, for fear of being bullied themselves or losing social status among their peers. . . . Interestingly, being bullied was associated with less frequency of alcohol use and had a nonlinear relationship with smoking. This is not altogether surprising, given Farrington's[34,35] finding that socially inept youth were less likely to be involved in delinquency than other youth.

Persons who bullied others were more likely to be involved in other problem behaviors such as drinking alcohol and smoking. They showed poorer school adjustment, both in terms of academic achievement and perceived school climate. Yet they reported greater ease of making friends, indicating that bullies are not socially isolated. Considering their greater involvement in other problem behaviors, it is likely that these youths have friends who endorse bullying and other problem behaviors, and who may be involved in bullying as well.

Those youth who reported both bullying and being bullied demonstrated poorer adjustment across both social/emotional dimensions and problem behaviors. Considering the combination of social isolation, lack of success in school, and involvement in problem behaviors, youth who both bully others and are bullied may represent an especially high-risk group.*

ACTIVITY 2

You can see that even though the authors of the four excerpts above did not directly ask questions in their texts, all of them had questions about the long-term effects of bullying, especially on people who later committed crimes or who suffered from difficult psychological adjustments to adult life. Write down questions of your own that are prompted either by reading or rereading these excerpts on bullying or just by your own curiosity. Your own experience with bullying may suggest other questions about its effects that have not been addressed. Or you may have questions about how writers reach conclusions about effects. For example, you might wonder what else may have caused the effects being written about—such as how such factors as social and economic background or cultural values and attitudes may play a role.

In doing Activity 2, you have practiced another habit of mind: **asking provocative questions.** In the college setting, "provocative" does not usually mean asking questions that provoke irritation; instead it means asking questions to promote further inquiry and perhaps lead to more questions that probe more deeply into the subject. In this activity, you have also practiced a skill that is important in academic work and in your work and life after college: figuring out what is unwritten as well as written—what is implied in a text. This skill will help you understand the perspective of authors, whatever they write.

In *Reading Critically, Writing Well*, each reading in each chapter is followed by a section called *Reading for Meaning*, divided into three activities based on different kinds of questions you ask of the text you've just read. First you *read to comprehend*, which involves asking yourself what the main point of the reading is and discovering the meaning of words you don't know. Then you *read to respond,* exploring your reactions to the text, bringing to it your own knowledge and experience. Finally, you *read to analyze assumptions* you find in the reading—along with your own assumptions: This activity involves discovering the authors' perspectives, values, and beliefs, as well as probing your own values and beliefs to see how they shape your reading and interpretation of the text. Often these

---

*A listing of the sources of texts 1–4 can be found at the end of the chapter.

assumptions are unwritten and you have to figure them out from the questions you ask. (There is more about "Questioning to Understand and Remember" in Appendix 1, A Catalog of Critical Reading Strategies.)

The habit of asking questions about what you read also extends to asking questions about the *methods* of the authors, along with their *strategies*. For example, in the excerpts about the effects of bullying in later life, you also might question whether the evidence provided is sufficient or appropriate. Look again at excerpt 1. As you read, think about the statistics offered in evidence: "In Scandinavian countries, . . . 60 percent of those characterized as bullies in grades 6–9 had at least one criminal conviction by age 24 (Olweus 1993)." And: "As many as 7 percent of America's eighth-graders stay home at least once a month because of bullies."

In the first case, the author gives the source for his statistic—Olweus—whom you can look up in the bibliography at the conclusion of the article. (All of the sources for the excerpts are listed at the end of this chapter, p. 18.) In addition to checking Olweus's article for information, you might also consider whether the culture in middle schools in Scandinavia is similar enough to the one in the United States to draw the conclusion that the bullying problem is as serious here, which in this case would mean our middle school bullies also are likely to get at least one criminal conviction by age 24. You also might question whether 7 percent of eighth-graders' staying home because of bullies is a significant percentage. How many stay home because they haven't done their homework, or because they don't feel well? The statistic of 7 percent has little meaning unless it can be compared and judged in context. (See "Contextualizing" in Appendix 1, A Catalog of Critical Reading Strategies.)

ACTIVITY 3

Reread excerpt 3 by Michael D. Lemonick. Lemonick also uses statistics, but unlike the author of excerpt 1, he does not specifically cite his sources because he is writing for *Time* magazine, a publication whose readers do not necessarily expect writers to do so. But *Time* does hire fact-checkers in an effort to ensure its information is accurate. Assuming, then, that the information is accurate, what additional questions would you pose for Lemonick? For example, after reading the first paragraph, you might like to know what "more often" means in these cases of bullied students who are sick, absent, have lower grades, or are more depressed and withdrawn *more often* than their classmates. Is it a significant number or amount of time—and what constitutes "significant"? How do you know it's only the bullied students who suffer like this? Also, you might want to know more about the sources, even though the facts have been checked. Does the information here come from a source that might have an interest in creating public awareness of bullying—such as a book to sell? It's important to think about writers' motives when you are asking questions.

Now look at paragraph 2 or 3 from excerpt 3 and write down your own questions about it. Then compare your questions with those of a classmate. What do you learn from these questions? How do you think they could help your critical reading—and, ultimately, your writing well?

In *Reading Critically, Writing Well*, the final activity for each reading is *Reading like a Writer*. Here you have the opportunity to ask questions about the strategies and methods of the author. Reading like a writer, you look closely at *rhetoric*—the ways that writers make their ideas understandable and seek to influence readers.

UNDERSTANDING ACADEMIC DISCOURSE

You may have noticed that the excerpts above are written in different styles from one another, even though they are on the same topic. Two of them are written for a general audience, whereas the other two are written specifically for an *academic* audience. Such an audience is composed of students and faculty in colleges and universities, or readers of journals in one of the disciplines studied in college, such as history, anthropology, or biology. When you are in college, you usually major in a discipline, and part of your education in that discipline is learning its *discourse*—its ways of communication, such as terminology, ways of establishing authority, and formats for presenting ideas. You learn how to read *journals* in the discipline, such as the *Journal of the American Medical Association* if you're a pre-med student, or the *History Review* if you're studying history or anthropology.

When authors use academic discourse, they assume an audience who is familiar with the language and ideas of their discipline, and with the *genres* of writing practiced in that discipline. Depending on how specialized the genre they are working in is, writers can include or exclude material according to how knowledgeable their audience is. Often such writing includes evidence of research, and both this evidence and the piece of writing in general follow the formatting conventions of the discipline, which means they adhere to certain rules for formal writing practiced by all writers in the discipline. For example, academic writers in the field of English literature who are citing material from another text usually follow MLA format, the style used by the **M**odern **L**anguage **A**ssociation, and likewise, most academic writers in psychology follow APA style, used by the **A**merican **P**sychological **A**ssociation. You can learn about these styles in Appendix 2: Strategies for Research and Documentation, pp. 644–66.

ACTIVITY 4

Review the excerpts about bullying and decide which two are written in academic discourse. Pay special attention to vocabulary, sentence structure, and the ways sources are cited. Think about how the writers establish their authority. Note any features you find that indicate these excerpts are written for an academic community.

Then note any features you find that indicate the other two excerpts are not written in academic discourse, but for a general audience or an audience outside the academy.

Do you feel as though you are a member of the intended audience for any of these excerpts? Why or why not? What effect does the writing style of each excerpt have on you? Why do you feel this way?

In doing Activity 4, you have practiced another habit of mind expected of college students: **reading with awareness of yourself and others.** When you read with awareness, you analyze as you read, asking questions of the text, and you also note the strategies the authors use to reach the audience and to establish their credibility. At the same time, you note your own reactions to these strategies. Another term for reading with awareness is *reading critically*, and it is a skill important in all kinds of writing, academic or not. The activities in the *Reading for Meaning* sections following each reading selection in this book will help you hone your critical reading skill, as will "Judging the Writer's Credibility" in Appendix 1, A Catalog of Critical Reading Strategies.

READING CRITICALLY

You may already know how to read critically, having practiced critical reading in high school or in previous reading situations. For example, if you read and discussed literary works in your English classes, you may have discussed the significance and effectiveness of the *figurative language*—metaphors, similes, and symbols—in a given work (see "Exploring the Significance of Figurative Language" in Appendix 1, A Catalog of Critical Reading Strategies) or of the development of particular characters. In your history classes, you may have read analyses of the causes of the Civil War from several different and perhaps opposing viewpoints. In college, you will deepen and extend those skills by reading a variety of texts that may expose you to wholly new ideas, make you question your own value system, and help you see different points of view. You'll also often have opportunities to discuss what you read with your professors and classmates, and doing so will introduce you to additional critical reading strategies that can enhance your existing habits of mind.

ACTIVITY 5

Read the two excerpts below on the prevalence and definitions of bullying in schools. The first is from the same article as excerpt 4 on page 5, written for the *Journal of the American Medical Association,* and the second is from a recent book on bullying, written for the general public and for people who work in schools. As you read, make notes about the following:

1. Any ideas that are new to you, especially those that challenge what you currently think about bullying.

2. Any references to assumptions that are contrary to the writers' beliefs. Look especially for references by the authors to the beliefs other people might have that differ from the authors', or to values that may be currently accepted but are open to question.

3. How the writers handle the assumptions that are contrary to their own.

Tonja R. Nansel, Mary Overpeck, Ramani S. Pilla, June Ruan, Bruce Simons-Morton, and Peter Scheidt, "Bullying Behaviors among US Youth: Prevalence and Association with Psychosocial Adjustment":

> Bullying among school-aged youth is increasingly being recognized as an important problem affecting well-being and social functioning. While a certain amount of conflict and harassment is typical of youth peer relations, bullying presents a potentially more serious threat to healthy youth development. The definition of bullying is widely agreed on in literature on bullying.[1-4] Bullying is a specific type of aggression in which (1) the behavior is intended to harm or disturb, (2) the behavior occurs repeatedly over time, and (3) there is an imbalance of power, with a more powerful person or group attacking a less powerful one. This asymmetry of power may be physical or psychological, and the aggressive behavior may be verbal (eg, name-calling, threats), physical (eg, hitting), or psychological (eg, rumors, shunning/exclusion). . . .
>
> Bullying takes many forms, and findings about the types of bullying that occur are fairly similar across countries. A British study involving 23 schools found that direct verbal aggression was the most common form of bullying, occurring with similar frequency in both sexes.[13] Direct physical aggression was more common among boys, while indirect forms were more common among girls. Similarly, in a study of several middle schools in Rome, the most common types of bullying reported by boys were threats, physical harm, rejection, and name-calling.[14] The most common forms for girls were name-calling, teasing, rumors, rejection, and taking of personal belongings. . . .

Barbara Coloroso, "The Bully, the Bullied, and the Bystander":

> In a study conducted in 2001 by the Kaiser Foundation, a U.S. health care philanthropy organization, in conjunction with the Nickelodeon TV network and Children Now, a youth advocacy group, almost three-quarters of pre-teens interviewed said bullying is a regular occurrence at school and that it becomes even more pervasive as kids start high school; 86 percent of the children between the ages of twelve and fifteen said that they get teased or bullied at school—making bullying more prevalent than smoking, alcohol, drugs, or sex among the same age group. More than half of children between the ages of eight and eleven said that bullying is a "big problem" at school. "It's a big concern on kids' minds. It's something they're dealing with every day," reports Lauren Asher of the Kaiser Foundation . . . (p. 12).
>
> Individual incidents of verbal, physical, or relational bullying can appear trivial or insignificant, nothing to be overly concerned about, part of the school culture. But it is the imbalance of power, the intent to harm, the threat of further aggression, and the creation of an atmosphere of terror that should raise red flags and signal a need for intervention. Sadly, even when the[se] four markers of bullying are clearly in evidence, adults have been known to minimize or dismiss the bullying, underestimate its seriousness, blame the bullied child, and/or heap on additional insult to injury (p. 22).

Once you have made your notes about ideas that are new to you, think about what you expect from the authors after they have raised these ideas. Do you want more information about what *causes* bullying? About *where* it happens? About *what to do about it*? Do you need more evidence of the problem before you can be convinced of its importance?

Whatever you jotted down in Activity 5, you have practiced other habits of mind expected of college students, including **experimenting with new ideas and challenging your own beliefs.** In addition, in responding to items 2 and 3, you have learned to see where and how authors deal with *counterarguments*, the statements and assumptions of people with whom they disagree. (See "Looking for Patterns of Opposition" in Appendix 1, A Catalog of Critical Reading Strategies.) When you consider what others think about an issue and how to respond to those who disagree with you, you are practicing the habit of **seeing other points of view and showing respect for them.**

Perhaps you noted that Nansel and her coauthors acknowledged the common idea that "boys must be boys" or that "all kids tease each other" when they write "While a certain amount of conflict and harassment is typical of youth peer relations, bullying presents a potentially more serious threat to healthy youth development." By granting that some aggressive behavior among young people is to be expected, these authors let their audience know that they have considered this factor in their thinking, but that they believe bullying is more serious. As a reader, you can decide whether their mention of this other point of view is enough, along with their definitions of bullying, or whether you need more evidence to convince you (see "Evaluating the Logic of an Argument" in Appendix 1, A Catalog of Critical Reading Strategies). Similarly, you can see Coloroso dealing with the same issue in the beginning and end of the second paragraph of her excerpt, and again, you can see how she approaches other points of view and decide whether you agree with her strategies.

Once you have completed this activity, you might be asked or decide to talk about bullying with your classmates, friends, or family, and you may start to develop your own ideas about what defines bullying, what causes it, or what schools could do about it. By discussing your reading about the problem and speculating about other ways of looking at it, you engage in the following habits of mind: **engaging in intellectual discussions and generating hypotheses.** In fact, college offers you many opportunities to practice both of these habits of mind, because you are in situations where others are reading the same material, and discussion is an effective means to think through your ideas about both the content and the methods of the material you read. You can test your own hypotheses—again, about the content or the methods—by discussing them with your classmates and professors and getting rich feedback that will help you develop these skills further.

WRITING WELL

It's an adage among teachers and writers that "the more you read, the better you write." All college students have experience with writing for school, and many of you have extensive experience with informal writing as well, especially in technology-based forums such as blogs, Twitter, or Facebook. This kind of online writing can make you more comfortable with the written word, and may even take away the dreaded blank-page or blank-screen syndrome: how on earth should I begin? It also helps you become more aware of who your audience is, because your writing is directed to a variety of people other than your teachers.

In college much of your submitted writing will be more formal, with specific guidelines: much of it will be academic discourse. Even so, you will still practice a great deal of informal writing in getting ready for your formal writing, and the Guides to Writing in *Reading Critically, Writing Well* provide a variety of activities that help you learn to write formal essays. As you make your way through these activities, remember that writing is *recursive*: that it does not proceed smoothly in a straight line from beginning to end, but rather is a fairly chaotic process. As writers, we rarely if ever begin with a complete understanding of our subject or a clear, detailed plan for writing about it. We put together some information and ideas, start writing, and let the writing lead us to understanding. While writing helps us achieve greater understanding, it also raises questions and unexpected complexities, which, in turn, can inspire more writing and, nearly always, generate further ideas and insights. As you work through a writing task, you may find yourself rearranging and rewriting much of your original text.

To understand how writing can be generative, try the following activity.

ACTIVITY 6

For fifteen minutes, write nonstop—keep your pen on the paper or your fingers on the keyboard—in response to the following questions about your own experiences with bullying. Don't take time to make corrections or revisions—just keep writing as ideas occur to you. You can respond to the questions in any order.

Note that you need not share your responses with anyone else, including your instructor or classmates, although you may choose to do so. You can write exactly what occurs to you—uncensored—because no one else will see it.

- Have you ever been bullied?
- How would you define the bullying that happened to you?
- How did you deal with it? What were the consequences?
- Have you ever bullied anyone?
- What did you do?
- Why did you do it?
- What did the person you bullied do in response?
- What happened afterward?

Write down anything more you can think of about these experiences with bullying. Now reread what you have written. Does anything surprise you—did you write anything that you hadn't planned to write, but that emerged from the experience of writing? If so, you've now seen how writing itself can be generative. If not, keep trying—the more you write, the more likely you will discover new ideas.

Experienced writers have learned to trust this fascinating discovery process, sometimes called "freewriting" because they know that writing is an unsurpassed way of thinking. Writing helps you discover, explore, develop, and refine your ideas in a way that cannot compare with just sitting around and thinking about a subject. Because writing leaves a record of your thinking, it reduces the burden of remembering and allows you to direct all your mental energy toward other tasks. By rereading what you have written, you can figure out where you became derailed or recall points that you forgot were important or see new possibilities you did not notice before.

The specific kind of writing you have done in Activity 6 illustrates another habit of mind that college writers need to master: **reporting facts and narrating events.** You probably already do both of these in your informal writing, but even the most sophisticated formal academic discourse calls on reporting and narrating, in part because reporting is necessary to provide background information, and in part because narration is usually highly interesting. For an example of straight reporting without any narrative, look at the excerpts from Nansel et al. (on pp. 5–6). You can see that their discourse is limited to "just the facts." To personalize otherwise dry prose with human interest, engaging readers deeply in the topic, writers often turn to narration. See how Michael D. Lemonick opens his article "The Bully Blight," from which excerpt 3 (pp. 4–5) is taken:

> Like most of her classmates at Washington High School in Milwaukee, Wis., La Shanda Trimble, 18, is attentive to fashion trends; it's the particular trend she chooses that sets her apart. She's a Goth, wearing black lipstick and nail polish, listening to bands like Linkin Park and Rob Zombie rather than rapper Nelly or R&B star Ciara. She likes to wear her hair in pigtails instead of the more popularly accepted braids. The other kids don't approve. "They think I should act like them," says the 11th-grader. "They like me to listen to rap and pop and wear, like, brand-new shoes."
>
> For these stylistic transgressions, Trimble is routinely punished. "I'd be walking down to a class, and I'd hear murmuring, and somebody would say, 'She's going to put a spell on you.'" One boy rode a broom into class to mock her; another called her ugly and crazy. Finally, one day last month, she couldn't take it anymore. "I started crying uncontrollably," she says. She's behind in her classwork now because she avoids going to school whenever she can.
>
> Bullies have lurked in hallways and on playgrounds ever since history's first day of school, and until recently, dealing with them was considered just another painfully useful life lesson. But that attitude is changing. In 2002 the American Medical Association warned that bullying is a public-health issue with long-term mental-health consequences for both bullies and their victims. Just last month UCLA researchers published two new studies showing that bullying is much more widespread and harmful than anyone knew.

By telling an anecdote about a young woman who was bullied, and by using dialogue, Lemonick draws in the reader with personal, detailed information about firsthand experience with bullying.

In his third paragraph, Lemonick follows his anecdote by acknowledging a counterargument to the argument his article is going to make, but then briefly summarizes two studies that support his own position. In doing so, he practices another habit of mind important to college writers: **summarizing ideas or information contained in a text.**

The two final sentences summarize the *ideas* that "bullying is a public-health issue with long-term mental-health consequences" and that it is much more damaging than had been suspected as well as the *information* that it is also much more common. A more detailed example of summarized *information* can be found in the excerpt from Coloroso's book (p. 11): "almost three-quarters of pre-teens interviewed said bullying is a regular occurrence at school and that it becomes even more pervasive as kids start high school; 86 percent of the children between the ages of twelve and fifteen said that they get teased or bullied at school—making bullying more prevalent than smoking, alcohol, drugs, or sex among the same age group. More than half of children between the ages of eight and eleven said that bullying is a 'big problem' at school."

ACTIVITY 7

Choose any one of the seven excerpts you have read in this chapter and examine the text to find summaries of ideas and summaries of information. Mark them accordingly, and then write a few sentences explaining which summaries are of ideas and which are of information and why. Then write a few more sentences exploring your reactions to these different kinds of summaries. Do both kinds seem equally valid and reliable (or equally questionable) to you? Or do you trust the summarized information but question the summarized ideas, or vice versa? Or do you have some other response?

To learn more about how to summarize in any given situation, turn to "Summarizing" in Appendix 1: A Catalog of Critical Reading Strategies, pp. 564–65.

As you have been reading these excerpts, noticing how they report, narrate, and summarize, you may also have noticed the variety of texts from which the authors get their ideas and information. Authors like Nansel et al. use firsthand research that they report or summarize. Authors like Kuther and Coloroso use evidence from several sources, some of which are their own work (primary research) and others of which are studies conducted by other researchers (secondary research). Banks and Lemonick report, narrate, and summarize information almost entirely from secondary sources. Whatever the stance of their sources, these published authors have examined the topic of bullying through several lenses, examining their sources for validity, checking on statistics, questioning conclusions, cross-checking references, comparing information and ideas, and reading everything with a critical eye. They are practicing two habits of mind that you have been practicing in this chapter: **critically assessing the authority and value of research materials that have been located** and **critically analyzing the ideas or arguments of others.**

For example, the source for the British study that Nansel et al. cite is a British journal, *Aggressive Behaviour*, which reports on primary (firsthand) research, and the study they cite on bullying in Italian middle-school students was published in *School Psychology International*. Both of these journals are "peer-reviewed," which means that all of the articles published in them are reviewed by experts—peers of the authors—in the field. (See Appendix 2, Strategies for Research and Documentation, pp. 603–66.) Clearly, Nansel et al. critically analyzed the studies and the methods of a number of other researchers in order to reach their own conclusions and to determine what to include in their articles. And researchers often not only cite other sources to support their arguments but also question or challenge sources they find unconvincing. For example, one of the authors cited in the Banks excerpt (p. 3), Olweus, concludes in his own article that while girls suffer from bullying and bully others too, they do not do *more* bullying than boys: "Our research data . . . clearly contradict the view that girls are the most frequent and worst bullies, a view suggested by such recent books as *Queen Bees and Wannabes* (Wiseman 2002) and *Odd Girl Out* (Simmons 2002)."

This critical reading and thinking, this critical analysis of the ideas and arguments of others, eventually leads writers to practice yet another habit of mind: **synthesizing ideas from several sources.** Whenever you see evidence that an idea (or a piece of information) cited by a writer is based on more than one specific source—such as in attributions (providing the name of the person whose research is being cited), citations, footnotes, or endnotes—you know that the authors have *synthesized* material. All of the excerpts in this chapter synthesize material; each one provides an example of combining material from several sources. For instance, note that in excerpt 1, Ron Banks cites studies by Olweus, research by Batsche and Knoff, and another work by Oliver, Hoover, and Hazler. In excerpt 3, you can see that Lemonick depends on postdoctoral scholar Adrienne Nishina's research for two paragraphs, and then uses the research of pediatrician William Coleman.

You can also see from the first sentence of Nansel et al.'s article (p. 5), that the writers would have had to read several sources to make such a broad assertion: "Bullying among school-aged youth is increasingly being recognized as an important problem affecting well-being and social functioning." Because this article is published in *JAMA* (the *Journal of the American Medical Association*), you can assume it is written for an American—or at least an English-speaking—audience, so you already know that the authors are probably referring to bullying in schools in the United States, but in their second paragraph you learn the full sweep of their research:

> Bullying takes many forms, and findings about the types of bullying that occur are fairly similar across countries. A British study involving 23 schools found that direct verbal aggression was the most common form of bullying, occurring with similar frequency in both sexes.[13] Direct physical aggression was more common among boys, while indirect forms were more common among girls. Similarly, in a study of several middle schools in Rome, the most common types of bullying reported by boys were threats, physical harm, rejection, and name-calling.[14] The most common forms for girls were name-calling, teasing, rumors, rejection, and taking of personal belongings.

ACTIVITY 8

To develop the habit of mind of *synthesizing*—using ideas and information from several sources to support a broader point in your own work, write a paragraph about bullying with the purpose of informing the principal of the high school you attended about the problem. For this activity, all you need to do is *attribute* your borrowed information to the correct source; you do not need to document it with formal source citations (see Appendix 2, Strategies for Research and Documentation, pp. 603–66, for information on attribution). Use as many sources as you need (from those in this chapter) to make your point. Feel free to also use anecdotes from your own writing on bullying for Activity 6 if they are appropriate.

(For more information on *synthesis,* see Appendix 1, A Catalog of Critical Reading Strategies, pp. 567–68.)

You may have noticed that all of the excerpts in this chapter are in final, polished form, with correct spelling, grammar, and punctuation, and with vocabulary appropriate to the genre in which they are written. In general, publishers do their best to make all their products error-free in content and appropriate in style. Academic and professional authors, too, try to ensure that their written work is as perfect as they can achieve when they submit it to publishers. Most authors revise several times until their writing satisfies them, and often they give it to a friend, family member, or colleague—sometimes to several people—for review. Their care and attention to detail are reflected in habits of mind that yield writing deserving the careful consideration of those reading it—whether publishers, the general public, or, in the case of student writing, professors. They **use vocabulary appropriate to college-level work and the discipline, use correct grammar and punctuation,** and **spell accurately.** These may seem like less important considerations than those discussed earlier, but they are essential to establishing yourself as a credible author who deserves the time of a thoughtful reader. They warrant just as much attention as you give to citing sources properly and to following the conventions of the genre in which you are writing. (See "Editing and Proofreading" near the end of every chapter.)

ACTIVITY 9

Look back at what you wrote for Activity 1, where you speculated about the habits of mind you already practice. Think now about what you have learned about the habits of mind that lead to successful thinking, reading, and writing, whether in school, at work, or in other areas of your life. Write a note to a younger person—a friend, a sibling, one of your own children—who is in his or her junior year of high school and is thinking about college. In two or three pages, describe the habits of mind you think this person should start (or continue) practicing to assure his or her success in college and in careers and life after college. Feel free to use examples from this chapter as well as from your own experience to support your assertions.

Sources for Texts on pp. 3–6

Banks, Ron. "Bullying in Schools." ERIC Clearinghouse on Elementary and Early Childhood Education, 1997. *Infotrac.* Web. 15 Aug. 2003.

Coloroso, Barbara. *The Bully, the Bullied, and the Bystander.* New York: Harper/Quill, 2004. Print.

Kuther, Tara L. "Understanding Bullying." Parent Teacher Association. n.d. <www.pta.org/1160.htm> Web. 3 May 2010.

Lemonick, Michael D. "The Bully Blight." *Time Magazine* 18 Apr. 2005, 144–145. Print.

Nansel, Tonja R., Mary Overpeck, Ramani S. Pilla, W. June Ruan, Bruce Simons-Morton, and Peter Scheidt. "Bullying Behaviors among US Youth: Prevalence and Association with Psychosocial Adjustment." *Journal of the American Medical Association* 25 (Apr. 2001): 2094–2100. Print.

Olweus, Dan. "A Profile of Bullying at School." *Educational Leadership.* Mar. 2003. *Academic Search Premier.* Web. 14 Feb. 2005.

Autobiography

Autobiography involves telling stories about key events in your life and describing people who have played important roles in it. Whether writing about an exhilarating childhood game or a difficult relationship, you should evoke for readers a vivid impression to help them see what you saw, hear what you heard, and feel what you felt. To write autobiography, therefore, you need to revisit the past, immersing yourself in the sights, sounds, and other sensations of memory. You also need to think deeply about the meaning of your experience—why it was and still is significant to you. Thinking deeply about the significance of important events and people in your life can help you discover something about the forces within yourself and within society that have helped to shape who you are and what is important to you.

While writing about your own life can be both enjoyable and instructive, so too can reading about other people's lives. As readers, we often take pleasure in seeing reflections of our own experience in other people's autobiographical writing. We enjoy recognizing similarities between the people and the events we have known and those that we read about. But sometimes the differences can be far more thought-provoking. For example, we may see how certain conditions — such as whether we grew up in the suburbs or the city; whether we are male or female; whether we are of African, European, Asian, Middle Eastern, or other descent—can profoundly affect our lives and perspectives. Autobiography sometimes affirms our preconceptions, but it is most effective when it leads us to question our certainties, challenging us to see ourselves and others in a new light.

Whether you are reading or writing autobiography, it is important to remember that autobiography is public, not private. While it involves self-presentation and contributes to self-knowledge, it does not require writers to make unwanted self-disclosures. Autobiographers compose themselves for readers; they fashion a self in words, much as a novelist creates a character. As readers, we come to "know" the people we read about by the way they are portrayed. Consequently, when you write autobiography, you have to decide how to portray yourself. This decision depends on whom you expect to read your essay (your audience) and what you want to communicate to readers (your purpose).

As you work through this chapter, you will learn more about autobiography by reading several different examples of it. You will see that some autobiographical essays center on a single event that occurred over a brief period of hours or days, while other essays focus on a person who played a significant role in the writer's life. Whether you decide to tell a story about a remembered event or to write about another person, you will practice two of the most basic writing strategies — narration and description. As you will see in later chapters of this book, narration and description can play roles not only in autobiography but also in providing explanations and advancing arguments.

The readings in this chapter will help you learn a lot about autobiography. From the readings and from the suggestions for writing that follow each reading, you will get ideas for your own autobiographical essay. As you read and write about the selections, keep in mind the following assignment, which sets out the goals for writing an autobiographical essay. To support your writing of this assignment, the chapter concludes with a Guide to Writing Autobiography.

THE WRITING ASSIGNMENT

Write an autobiographical essay about a significant event or person in your life. Choose the event or person with your readers in mind. The subject should be one that you feel comfortable presenting to others and that will lead readers to reflect on their own lives or on the differences between your personal experiences and their own. Present your experience dramatically and vividly so that readers can imagine what it was like for you. Through a careful choice of words and details, convey the meaning and importance in your life — what we call the *autobiographical significance* — of the event or person you've chosen to write about.

WRITING SITUATIONS FOR AUTOBIOGRAPHY

You may think that only politicians, scientists, novelists, and celebrities write their autobiographies. But autobiographical writing is much more widespread, as the following examples indicate:

- As part of her college application, a high-school senior includes an auto-biographical essay that conveys why she wants to study medical science. In the essay, she recalls what happened when she did her first scientific experiment on the nutritional effects on mice of different breakfast cereals and was forced to stop the experiment because the mice eating cereals like Count Chocula and Fruit Loops, and not eating anything else, were dying. She indicates that the experiment aroused her interest in science and the ethics of research on living creatures.

- Asked to recall a significant early childhood memory for an assignment in a psychology class, a college student writes about a fishing trip he took as a nine-year-old. He reflects on the significance of the trip. It was the first trip he took alone with his father, and it began a new stage in their relationship.

- As part of a workshop on management skills, a business executive writes about a person who influenced his ideas about leadership. As he explores his memory and feelings, he realizes that he mistook fear for admiration. He recognizes that he has been emulating the wrong model, an autocratic leader who got people to perform by intimidating them.

Thinking about Your Experience

Autobiography

Before studying a type of writing, it is useful to spend some time thinking about what you already know about it. You have almost certainly told stories about events in your life and described memorable people you have known, even if you have not written down these stories. When you tell such stories, you are composing autobiography. You also may have written autobiographically for school assignments, for a college application, and in letters or e-mails to family and friends.

- Recall one particular story you told orally or in writing, and then consider questions like these: What did you want your audience members to think and feel? How did they react to your story?

- Reflect also on the autobiographical stories that have been told to you or that you have read or seen in films or on television. What made these stories interesting?

- Write at least a page about your experience with autobiography.

A GUIDE TO READING AUTOBIOGRAPHY

This guide introduces you to the basic features and strategies typical of autobiographical writing by looking closely at a brief but powerful autobiographical essay by Annie Dillard. Focus first on *reading for meaning*, seeking to grasp the event's significance for Dillard — what the incident meant to her both at the time she experienced it and years later when she wrote about it — as well as the meanings you find in Dillard's story (for example, what it suggests about how childhood has or has not changed, the games children play, a child's idea of what is exciting and heroic). Then, to learn about how Dillard makes her story exciting and suspenseful, try *reading like a writer* by analyzing her writing strategies. These two activities — reading for meaning and reading like a writer — follow every reading in this chapter.

Annie Dillard

An American Childhood

Annie Dillard (b. 1945) is a prolific writer whose first book, Pilgrim at Tinker Creek *(1974), won the Pulitzer Prize for nonfiction writing. Since then, she has written eleven other books in a variety of genres. They include* Teaching a Stone to Talk *(1988),* The Writing Life *(1989),* Mornings Like This *(1996), and* The Maytrees *(2007). Dillard has also written an autobiography of her early years,* An American Childhood *(1987), from which the following selection comes.*

This reading relates an event that occurred one winter morning when the seven-year-old Dillard and a friend were chased relentlessly by an adult stranger at whose car they had been throwing snowballs. Dillard admits that she was terrified at the time, and yet paradoxically she asserts that she has "seldom been happier since." As you read, think about how this paradox helps you grasp the autobiographical significance of the experience for Dillard.

1   Some boys taught me to play football. This was fine sport. You thought up a new strategy for every play and whispered it to the others. You went out for a pass, fooling everyone. Best, you got to throw yourself mightily at someone's running legs. Either you brought him down or you hit the ground flat out on your chin, with your arms empty before you. It was all or nothing. If you hesitated in fear, you would miss and get hurt: you would take a hard fall while the kid got away, or you would get kicked in the face while the kid got away. But if you flung yourself wholeheartedly at the back of his knees — if you gathered and joined body and soul and pointed them diving fearlessly — then you likely wouldn't get hurt, and

you'd stop the ball. Your fate, and your team's score, depended on your concentration and courage. Nothing girls did could compare with it.

Boys welcomed me at baseball, too, for I had, through enthusiastic practice, what was weirdly known as a boy's arm. In winter, in the snow, there was neither baseball nor football, so the boys and I threw snowballs at passing cars. I got in trouble throwing snowballs, and have seldom been happier since.

On one weekday morning after Christmas, six inches of new snow had just fallen. We were standing up to our boot tops in snow on a front yard on trafficked Reynolds Street, waiting for cars. The cars traveled Reynolds Street slowly and evenly; they were targets all but wrapped in red ribbons, cream puffs. We couldn't miss.

I was seven; the boys were eight, nine, and ten. The oldest two Fahey boys were there—Mikey and Peter—polite blond boys who lived near me on Lloyd Street, and who already had four brothers and sisters. My parents approved Mikey and Peter Fahey. Chickie McBride was there, a tough kid, and Billy Paul and Mackie Kean too, from across Reynolds, where the boys grew up dark and furious, grew up skinny, knowing, and skilled. We had all drifted from our houses that morning looking for action, and had found it here on Reynolds Street.

It was cloudy but cold. The cars' tires laid behind them on the snowy street a complex trail of beige chunks like crenellated castle walls. I had stepped on some earlier; they squeaked. We could not have wished for more traffic. When a car came, we all popped it one. In the intervals between cars we reverted to the natural solitude of children.

I started making an iceball—a perfect iceball, from perfectly white snow, perfectly spherical, and squeezed perfectly translucent so no snow remained all the way through. (The Fahey boys and I considered it unfair actually to throw an iceball at somebody, but it had been known to happen.)

I had just embarked on the iceball project when we heard tire chains come clanking from afar. A black Buick was moving toward us down the street. We all spread out, banged together some regular snowballs, took aim, and, when the Buick drew nigh, fired.

A soft snowball hit the driver's windshield right before the driver's face. It made a smashed star with a hump in the middle.

Often, of course, we hit our target, but this time, the only time in all of life, the car pulled over and stopped. Its wide black door opened; a man got out of it, running. He didn't even close the car door.

He ran after us, and we ran away from him, up the snowy Reynolds sidewalk. At the corner, I looked back; incredibly, he was still after us. He was in city clothes: a suit and tie, street shoes. Any normal adult would have quit, having sprung us into flight and made his point. This man was gaining on us. He was a thin man, all action. All of a sudden, we were running for our lives.

11   Wordless, we split up. We were on our turf; we could lose ourselves in the neighborhood backyards, everyone for himself. I paused and considered. Everyone had vanished except Mikey Fahey, who was just rounding the corner of a yellow brick house. Poor Mikey, I trailed him. The driver of the Buick sensibly picked the two of us to follow. The man apparently had all day.

12   He chased Mikey and me around the yellow house and up a backyard path we knew by heart: under a low tree, up a bank, through a hedge, down some snowy steps, and across the grocery store's delivery driveway. We smashed through a gap in another hedge, entered a scruffy backyard and ran around its back porch and tight between houses to Edgerton Avenue; we ran across Edgerton to an alley and up our own sliding woodpile to the Halls' front yard; he kept coming. We ran up Lloyd Street and wound through mazy backyards toward the steep hilltop at Willard and Lang.

13   He chased us silently, block after block. He chased us silently over picket fences, through thorny hedges, between houses, around garbage cans, and across streets. Every time I glanced back, choking for breath, I expected he would have quit. He must have been as breathless as we were. His jacket strained over his body. It was an immense discovery, pounding into my hot head with every sliding, joyous step, that this ordinary adult evidently knew what I thought only children who trained at football knew: that you have to fling yourself at what you're doing, you have to point yourself, forget yourself, aim, dive.

14   Mikey and I had nowhere to go, in our own neighborhood or out of it, but away from this man who was chasing us. He impelled us forward; we compelled him to follow our route. The air was cold; every breath tore my throat. We kept running, block after block; we kept improvising, backyard after backyard, running a frantic course and choosing it simultaneously, failing always to find small places or hard places to slow him down, and discovering always, exhilarated, dismayed, that only bare speed could save us—for he would never give up, this man—and we were losing speed.

15   He chased us through the backyard labyrinths of ten blocks before he caught us by our jackets. He caught us and we all stopped.

16   We three stood staggering, half blinded, coughing, in an obscure hilltop backyard: a man in his twenties, a boy, a girl. He had released our jackets, our pursuer, our captor, our hero: he knew we weren't going anywhere. We all played by the rules. Mikey and I unzipped our jackets. I pulled off my sopping mittens. Our tracks multiplied in the backyard's new snow. We had been breaking new snow all morning. We didn't look at each other. I was cherishing my excitement. The man's lower pants legs were wet; his cuffs were full of snow, and there was a prow of snow beneath them on his shoes and socks. Some trees bordered the little flat backyard, some messy winter trees. There was no one around: a clearing in a grove, and we the only players.

It was a long time before he could speak. I had some difficulty at first 17 recalling why we were there. My lips felt swollen; I couldn't see out of the sides of my eyes; I kept coughing.

"You stupid kids," he began perfunctorily. 18

We listened perfunctorily indeed, if we listened at all, for the chew- 19 ing out was redundant, a mere formality, and beside the point. The point was that he had chased us passionately without giving up, and so he had caught us. Now he came down to earth. I wanted the glory to last forever.

But how could the glory have lasted forever? We could have run 20 through every backyard in North America until we got to Panama. But when he trapped us at the lip of the Panama Canal, what precisely could he have done to prolong the drama of the chase and cap its glory? I brooded about this for the next few years. He could only have fried Mikey Fahey and me in boiling oil, say, or dismembered us piecemeal, or staked us to anthills. None of which I really wanted, and none of which any adult was likely to do, even in the spirit of fun. He could only chew us out there in the Panamanian jungle, after months or years of exalt-ing pursuit. He could only begin, "You stupid kids," and continue in his ordinary Pittsburgh accent with his normal righteous anger and the usual common sense.

If in that snowy backyard the driver of the black Buick had cut off 21 our heads, Mikey's and mine, I would have died happy, for nothing has required so much of me since as being chased all over Pittsburgh in the middle of winter—running terrified, exhausted—by this sainted, skinny, furious redheaded man who wished to have a word with us. I don't know how he found his way back to his car.

READING FOR MEANING

This section presents three activities that will help you think about the mean-ings in Dillard's autobiographical story.

Read to Comprehend

Write a few sentences briefly explaining what happened that winter morning when Dillard was seven years old.

Identify any words with meanings you are unsure of — such as *perfunctorily* (paragraph 18) and *righteous* (20) — and find the dictionary definition for each word that makes the best sense in the context.

To help you understand the essay better, also consider trying one of these critical reading strategies, explained in Appendix 1: *outlining, paraphrasing,* or *questioning to understand and remember.*

Read to Respond

Write a paragraph or two exploring your initial thoughts and feelings about Dillard's autobiographical narrative. Focus on anything that stands out for you, perhaps because it resonates with your own experience or because you find a statement puzzling. For example, consider writing about one of the following:

- how a particular scene — such as the iceballing (paragraphs 6–7) or the confrontation (15–21) scene — contributes to your understanding of the event's significance for Dillard; or

- why you think Dillard uses such words as "hero" (16) and "sainted" (21) to describe the man who chased her, even though she dismisses what he said when he finally caught her as "redundant, a mere formality, and beside the point" (19).

To help develop your response, also consider trying one of these critical reading strategies, explained in Appendix 1: *contextualizing, recognizing emotional manipulation,* or *judging the writer's credibility.*

Read to Analyze Assumptions

All writing contains *assumptions* — ideas and attitudes that are taken for granted as commonly accepted truths. Personal or individual assumptions also tend to reflect the values and beliefs of a particular community, which help shape the way those in the group think, act, and understand the world. All writing reflects assumptions held by the writer, but assumptions held by others, such as readers or sources cited by the writer, may also be present. Sometimes assumptions are stated explicitly, but often they are only implied, so you may have to search for underlying assumptions in the word choices and examples.

Why go to the effort to analyze assumptions in a reading? Assumptions have powerful effects. They influence our opinions and judgments by leading us to value some things and devalue others. These effects are even more powerful because they are taken for granted, often accepted without question by those who hold them. To understand a reading on a deep level, then, it is necessary to bring its assumptions to the surface and to question them. To think critically about assumptions, here are some kinds of questions you could ask: Who holds this assumption (the writer, readers, and/or others cited in the essay)? What are the effects of the assumption in the context of the essay specifically or in society more generally? What do you think about the assumption, and is there anything in the essay that raises doubts about it? How does the assumption reinforce or critique commonly held views, and are there any alternative ideas, beliefs, or values that would challenge this assumption?

Write a paragraph or two analyzing an assumption in Dillard's essay. You might choose an assumption from the list below, using the questions accompanying it in addition to the ones above to help you get started. Or you can choose another assumption in the essay to explore.

- **assumptions about the value of rules and fair play.** Dillard asserts proudly that "[w]e all played by the rules" (paragraph 16) and that she and the Fahey boys "considered it unfair actually to throw an iceball at somebody" (6). Words like *rules* and *unfair* suggest there are principles of conduct or ethics that determine what is considered fair or right.

  To think critically about the assumptions in this essay related to rules and fairness, ask yourself questions like these: What rule do you think the man assumes the kids have broken? Who (the kids, the adult writer, readers at the time or today) would agree he is right to reprimand them for breaking this rule? Even though the young Dillard admires him for chasing them down, is there any reason to question the propriety of his behavior?

- **assumptions about the superiority of boys' play.** Dillard describes the way the neighborhood boys taught her to play football, claiming that "[n]othing girls did could compare with it" (paragraph 1). To think critically about the assumptions in this essay related to the different ways boys and girls play, ask yourself questions like these: What does Dillard seem to be saying about social expectations regarding gender at the time (1950s) and place (Pittsburgh) that she is describing? How have assumptions about girls and boys changed in mainstream American culture today, if at all? To what extent do you share these assumptions? Why?

- **assumptions about the desirability of committing yourself "whole-heartedly."** When she describes learning to play football, Dillard stresses the value of going all out and "diving fearlessly" into whatever it is you are doing (paragraph 1).

  To think critically about the assumptions in the essay related to committing yourself wholeheartedly, ask yourself questions like these: Dillard says that in football, at least, the result of "diving fearlessly" is that you are not likely to get hurt "and you'd stop the ball" (paragraph 1). But is this true even in football? Dillard admires the man for chasing them "passionately without giving up," using words like "glory" and "sainted" to describe him (paragraphs 19–21). But when he starts reprimanding them, she describes him quite differently: "his normal righteous anger and the usual common sense" (20). Why does she pose this opposition between passionate behavior and common sense? For what goals and under what circumstances do you throw yourself wholeheartedly into something? And when, if ever, do you act with "normal" caution and "the usual common sense"? How do you decide?

To help you analyze assumptions in Dillard's essay, also consider trying one of these critical reading strategies, explained in Appendix 1: *reflecting on challenges to your beliefs and values, exploring the significance of figurative language,* or *looking for patterns of opposition.*

READING LIKE A WRITER

This section leads you through an analysis of Dillard's autobiographical writing strategies: *narrating the story, presenting people, describing places,* and *conveying the autobiographical significance.* For each strategy, you will be asked to reread and annotate part of Dillard's essay to see how she uses the strategy to accomplish her particular purpose.

When you study the selections later in this chapter, you will see how different autobiographers use these same strategies for different purposes. The Guide to Writing Autobiography near the end of the chapter suggests ways you can use these strategies in your own writing.

Narrating the Story

Whether focusing on a single event or a person, writers nearly always tell a story or several brief stories called *anecdotes.* Stories are so pervasive in our culture, indeed in most cultures, that we are all familiar with what makes a story effective. A well-told story draws readers in by arousing their curiosity and often keeps them reading by building suspense or drama, making them want to know what will happen next.

Dillard's essay focuses on a single incident that occurred in a relatively short span of time. A chase is nearly always dramatic because it is suspenseful. Readers want to know whether the man will catch the kids and, if he does, what will happen. Dillard heightens the drama in several ways. One strategy she uses is *identification,* letting us into her point of view. In addition, she uses *surprise.* In fact, Dillard surprises us from beginning to end. The first surprise is that the man gets out of the car. But when he chases the kids and then continues to chase them beyond the point that most reasonable people would do so, the suspense increases. We simply cannot know what such a man is capable of doing.

Dillard also primarily uses *action verb forms.* Here is a sentence with several action verbs (underlined): "We all <u>spread</u> out, <u>banged</u> together some regular snowballs, <u>took</u> aim, and, when the Buick drew nigh, <u>fired</u>" (paragraph 7). These verbs describe vividly a series of actions. Now look at the verbs in these two sentences: "This man was gaining on us. He was a thin man, all action" (10). Both sentences use the verb *was,* but only the first sentence has an action verb (by combining *was* with the *-ing* form: "was gaining"). The verb in the second sentence is not an action verb; instead, it serves as a kind of equal sign describing a quality or characteristic of the subject ("a thin man"). As writers, we use both kinds of verbs, but in narrative writing action verbs tend to predominate. This activity will help you see how Dillard uses action verbs.

Analyze

1. Reread paragraphs 11 to 15, underlining as many of the action verbs as you can find. Do not worry if you miss some.

2. Also underline as many verbals as you can. Verbals are verb forms that usually end in *-ing,* as in "staggering" and "coughing" (paragraph 16), or *-ed,* as in "blinded" (16) and "smashed" (8), or that begin with *to,* as in "to fling" and "to point" (13).

3. Identify two or three sentences in which the action verbs and verbals are especially vivid, helping you imagine the drama of the chase.

Write

Write several sentences explaining what you have learned about Dillard's use of verbs and verbals to represent action and to make her narrative dramatic. Use examples from paragraphs 11 and 15 to support your explanation.

Presenting People

Autobiographers describe people by depicting what they look like, by letting readers hear how they speak, and by characterizing their behavior and personality. Often, one or two specific details about the way a person looks, dresses, talks, or acts will be sufficient to give readers a vivid impression of the person. As you will see when you read the essays later in this chapter by Aleksandra Crapanzano and Brad Benioff, even autobiographical essays that focus on a person rather than a single event tend to use only a few well-chosen details to present the person.

To see how Dillard presents people, look at the descriptions of the neighborhood boys in paragraph 4. Notice that she gives each boy a brief descriptive tag: "Mikey and Peter — polite blond boys who lived near me on Lloyd Street" and "Chickie McBride . . . a tough kid, and Billy Paul and Mackie Kean too, from across Reynolds, where the boys grew up dark and furious, grew up skinny, knowing, and skilled." The details "blond" and "skinny" create a visual image, whereas "polite," "tough," and "knowing" convey Dillard's characterizations or evaluations of the boys. These characterizations or evaluations contribute not only to the impression we get of each boy but also to our understanding of his significance in the writer's life. (As you will see later in the chapter, such characterizations are one way writers convey autobiographical significance.)

Analyze

1. In paragraphs 10, 16, and 21, find and underline words and phrases that visually describe the man. Also put brackets around words and phrases that characterize or evaluate the man.

2. Look at paragraph 18 and the last sentence of paragraph 20, where Dillard presents the man through dialogue. Underline the details used to describe how the man looks and sounds. Also put brackets around words and phrases used to characterize or evaluate what the man says and how he says it.

3. Think about how Dillard's presentation of the man in these five paragraphs helps you see him in your mind's eye and understand his role in the chase.

Write

Write several sentences examining Dillard's use of descriptive details and characterizations to present the man. Use examples from the words and phrases you underlined and bracketed to support your ideas.

Describing Places

Whether autobiography centers on an event or a person, it nearly always includes some description of places. Writers make a remembered place vivid by naming memorable objects they want readers to see there and by detailing these objects. For examples of *naming* and *detailing,* look at paragraph 3, where Dillard describes what it looked like on that particular morning after Christmas. Notice that Dillard uses naming to point out the snow, Reynolds Street, and the cars. She also adds details that give information about these objects: "*six inches* of *new* snow," "*trafficked* Reynolds Street," "cars traveled . . . *slowly* and *evenly.*"

To make her description evocative as well as vivid, Dillard adds a third describing strategy: *comparing.* In paragraph 5, for example, she describes the trail made by car tires in the snow as being "like crenellated castle walls." The word *like* makes the comparison explicit and identifies it as a simile. Dillard also uses implicit comparisons, called metaphors, such as when she calls the cars "targets all but wrapped in red ribbons, cream puffs" (3).

Analyze

1. Examine how Dillard uses naming and detailing to describe a "perfect iceball" in paragraph 6. What does she name it, and what details does she add to specify the qualities that make an iceball "perfect"?

2. Look closely at the two comparisons in paragraphs 3 and 5. Notice also the following comparisons in other paragraphs: "smashed star" (8), "sprung us into flight" (10), "mazy backyards" (12), "every breath tore my throat" (14), and "backyard labyrinths" (15). Choose any single comparison — simile or metaphor — in the reading, and think about how it helps you imagine what the place was like for Dillard on that day.

Write

Write a few sentences explaining how Dillard uses the describing strategies of *naming, detailing,* and *comparing* to help you imagine what the places she presents seemed like during the chase. Give at least one example from the reading of each describing strategy.

Conveying the Autobiographical Significance

Autobiographers convey the significance of an event or a person in two ways: by *showing* and by *telling.* Through your analysis of how Dillard narrates the story, presents people, and describes places, you have looked at some of the ways she *shows* the event's significance. This activity focuses on what Dillard *tells* readers.

When Dillard writes in the opening paragraphs about boys teaching her to play football and baseball, she is telling why these experiences were memorable and important. Autobiographers usually tell both what they remember thinking and feeling *at the time* and what they think and feel now *as they write about the past.* Readers must infer from the ideas and the writer's choice of words whether a phrase or sentence conveys the writer's past or present perspective, remembered feelings and thoughts or current ones.

For example, look at the following sentences from paragraph 1: "You thought up a new strategy for every play and whispered it to the others. You went out for a pass, fooling everyone." The words "whispered" and "fooling" suggest that here Dillard is trying to reconstruct a seven-year-old child's way of speaking and thinking. In contrast, when she tells us that football was a "fine sport" and what was fine about it — "Your fate, and your team's score, depended on your concentration and courage" — we can infer from words such as *fate, concentration,* and *courage* that Dillard is speaking from her present adult perspective, telling us what she may have sensed as a child but now can more fully understand and articulate.

To determine the autobiographical significance of the remembered event or person, Dillard's readers need to pay attention to what she tells them about the significance — both her remembered feelings and thoughts and her present perspective.

Analyze

1. Reread paragraphs 19 to 21, where Dillard comments on the chase and the man's "chewing out." Put brackets around words and phrases that tell what the adult Dillard is thinking as she writes about this event from her past. For example, in the first sentence of paragraph 19, the words *perfunctorily* and *redundant* may seem to you to be examples of adult language, rather than words a seven-year-old would use.

2. Underline words and phrases in the same paragraphs that seem to convey thoughts and feelings that Dillard remembers from when she was a child.

Write

Write several sentences explaining what you have learned about the event's significance for Dillard. What does she tell readers about the thoughts and feelings she had as a child as well as the thoughts and feelings she has now as an adult looking back on the experience? Quote selected words and phrases from your underlining and bracketing, indicating what identifies them as either remembered or present-perspective thoughts and feelings.

A Special Reading Strategy

Comparing and Contrasting Related Readings: Dillard's "An American Childhood" and Rodriguez's "Always Running"

Comparing and contrasting related readings is a critical reading strategy useful both in reading for meaning and in reading like a writer. This strategy is particularly applicable when writers present similar subjects, as is the case in the autobiographical narratives in this chapter by Annie Dillard (p. 22) and Luis J. Rodriguez (p. 39). Both writers tell what happened when they broke the rules and were chased by adults. In both instances, their transgressions are relatively minor; however, the chase is viewed very differently by each writer and its results also differ dramatically. To compare and contrast these two autobiographies, think about issues such as these:

- Compare these essays in terms of their cultural and historical contexts. What seems to you to be most significant about the two versions of an American childhood represented in these essays?

- Compare how the two writers make their narratives dramatic. Compare the strategies Dillard uses in presenting the chase (paragraphs 11–14) with those Rodriguez uses (paragraphs 27–32). In addition to looking at the kinds of verbs each writer employs, you might also analyze how they construct sentences to push the action forward or slow it down. Notice also the length of the sentences and how much information the writers pack into sentences.

See Appendix 1 (pp. 596–601) for detailed guidelines on comparing and contrasting related readings.

READINGS

Saira Shah

Longing to Belong

Saira Shah (b. 1964) is a journalist and documentary filmmaker. The daughter of an Afghan father and Indian mother, she was born and educated in England. After graduating from the School of Oriental and African Studies at London University, Shah began her career as a freelance journalist in the 1980s, reporting on the Afghan guerrillas who were fighting the Soviet occupation; eventually she became a war correspondent for Britain's Channel 4 News. She is the recipient of the Courage under Fire and Television Journalist of the Year awards for her risky reporting on conflicts in some of the world's most troubled areas, including the Persian Gulf and Kosovo. She is best known in the United States for her undercover documentary films about the Taliban rule in Afghanistan, Beneath the Veil *(2001) and* Unholy War *(2002).*

"Longing to Belong," originally published in the New York Times Magazine *in 2003, is adapted from Shah's autobiography,* The Storyteller's Daughter *(2003), which relates her search to understand her father's homeland of Afghanistan. In this essay, Shah tells what happened when, at the age of seventeen, she visited her father's Afghan relatives living in Pakistan. As she explained in an interview, "I wanted this kind of romantic vision. This is the exile's condition, though, isn't it? If you grow up outside the place that you think of as your home, you want it to be impossibly marvelous. There is also the question of how Afghan I am. When I was growing up, I had this secret doubt—which I couldn't even admit to myself—that I was not at all an Afghan because I was born in Britain to a mixed family."*

As you read, think about Shah's search for her ethnic identity and the sense of cultural dislocation she experiences.

1   The day he disclosed his matrimonial ambitions for me, my uncle sat me at his right during lunch. This was a sign of special favor, as it allowed him to feed me choice tidbits from his own plate. It was by no means an unadulterated pleasure. He would often generously withdraw a half-chewed delicacy from his mouth and lovingly cram it into mine—an Afghan habit with which I have since tried to come to terms. It was his way of telling me that I was valued, part of the family.

2   My brother and sister, Tahir and Safia, and my elderly aunt Amina and I were all attending the wedding of my uncle's son. Although my uncle's home was closer than I'd ever been, I was not yet inside Afghanistan. This branch of my family lived in Peshawar, Pakistan.

Why do you think Shah saves this information, rather than beginning the essay with it? What does her opening paragraph accomplish?

On seeing two unmarried daughters in the company of a female chaperone, my uncle obviously concluded that we had been sent to be married. I was taken aback by the visceral longing I felt to be part of this world. I had never realized that I had been starved of anything. Now, at 17, I discovered that like a princess in a fairy tale, I had been cut off from my origins. This was the point in the tale where, simply by walking through a magical door, I could recover my gardens and palaces. If I allowed my uncle to arrange a marriage for me, I would belong.

Over the next few days, the man my family wished me to marry was introduced into the inner sanctum. He was a distant cousin. His luxuriant black mustache was generally considered to compensate for his lack of height. I was told breathlessly that he was a fighter pilot in the Pakistani Air Force. As an outsider, he wouldn't have been permitted to meet an unmarried girl. But as a relative, he had free run of the house. Whenever I appeared, a female cousin would fling a child into his arms. He'd pose with it, whiskers twitching, while the women cooed their admiration.

A huge cast of relatives had assembled to see my uncle's son marry. The wedding lasted nearly 14 days and ended with a reception. The bride and groom sat on an elevated stage to receive greetings. While the groom was permitted to laugh and chat, the bride was required to sit perfectly still, her eyes demurely lowered. I didn't see her move for four hours.

Watching this *tableau vivant* of a submissive Afghan bride, I knew that marriage would never be my easy route to the East. I could live in my father's mythological homeland only through the eyes of the storyteller. In my desire to experience the fairy tale, I had overlooked the staggeringly obvious: the storyteller was a man. If I wanted freedom, I would have to cut my own path. I began to understand why my uncle's wife had resorted to using religion to regain some control—at least in her own home. Her piety gave her license to impose her will on others.

My putative fiancé returned to Quetta, from where he sent a constant flow of lavish gifts. I was busy examining my hoard when my uncle's wife announced that he was on the phone. My intended was a favorite of hers; she had taken it upon herself to promote the match. As she handed me the receiver, he delivered a line culled straight from a Hindi movie: "We shall have a

3

4

5

6

What do you learn about Shah from her remembered thoughts and feelings here? What do the highlighted phrases suggest about her present perspective?

What do these descriptive details—and the way Shah presents them—tell you about the family's choice of fiancé and Shah's attitude toward him?

How does this image of the wedding couple help you understand Shah's change of mind?

love-match, *ach-cha*?" Enough was enough. I slammed
down the phone and went to find Aunt Amina. When
she had heard me out, she said: "I'm glad that finally
you've stopped this silly wild goose chase for your
roots. I'll have to extricate you from this mess. Wait
here while I put on something more impressive." As a
piece of Islamic one-upmanship, she returned wearing
not one but three head scarves of different colors.

Why do you think Shah
quotes what the "fiancé"
and Aunt Amina said,
instead of summarizing it?

7   My uncle's wife was sitting on her prayer platform in
the drawing room. Amina stormed in, scattering servants
before her like chaff. "Your relative . . . ," was Amina's
opening salvo, ". . . has been making obscene remarks
to my niece." Her mouth opened, but before she could
find her voice, Amina fired her heaviest guns: "Over the
telephone!"

8   "How dare you!" her rival began.

9   It gave Amina exactly the opportunity she needed to
move in for the kill. "What? Do you support this lewd
conduct? Are we living in an American movie? Since
when have young people of mixed sexes been permitted to speak to each other *on the telephone*? Let alone
to talk—as I regret to inform you your nephew did—of
love! Since when has love had anything to do with marriage? What a dangerous and absurd concept!"

10   My Peshawari aunt was not only outclassed; she was
out-Islamed too. "My niece is a rose that hasn't been
plucked," Amina said. "It is my task as her chaperone to
ensure that this happy state of affairs continues. A match
under such circumstances is quite out of the question.
The engagement is off." My uncle's wife lost her battle
for moral supremacy and, it seemed, her battle for sanity
as well. In a gruff, slack-jawed way that I found unap-
pealing, she made a sharp, inhuman sound that sounded
almost like a bark.

How does Shah make
this confrontation scene
dramatic and funny at the
same time?

READING FOR MEANING

This section presents three activities that will help you think about the meanings in Shah's autobiographical essay.

Read to Comprehend

Write a few sentences briefly explaining what happened during Shah's visit
with relatives in Pakistan.

Identify any words with meanings you are unsure of — such as *unadulterated* (paragraph 1) and *tableau vivant* (5) — and find the dictionary definition for each word that makes the best sense in the context.

To help you understand the essay better, also consider trying one of these critical reading strategies, explained in Appendix 1: *summarizing* or *questioning to understand and remember*.

Read to Respond

Write several paragraphs exploring your initial thoughts and feelings about Shah's autobiographical story. Focus on anything that stands out for you, perhaps because it resonates with your own experience or because you find a statement puzzling. For example, consider writing about one of the following:

- Shah's "longing to belong" — perhaps in relation to your own experience;

- her uncle's assumption that Shah and her sister were sent to Pakistan "to be married" (paragraph 2); or

- Shah's realization that "[i]f I wanted freedom, I would have to cut my own path" (5).

To help develop your response, also consider trying one of these critical reading strategies, explained in Appendix 1: *contextualizing* or *reflecting on challenges to your beliefs and values*.

Read to Analyze Assumptions

Write a paragraph or two analyzing an assumption in Shah's essay. To think critically about assumptions, here are some kinds of questions you could ask: Who holds this assumption (the writer, readers, and/or others cited in the essay)? What are the effects of the assumption in the context of the essay specifically or in society more generally? What do you think about the assumption, and is there anything in the essay that raises doubts about it? How does the assumption reinforce or critique commonly held views, and are there any alternative ideas, beliefs, or values that would challenge this assumption?

You might choose an assumption from the list below, using the questions accompanying it in addition to the ones above to help you get started. Or you can choose another assumption in the essay to explore.

- **assumptions about the values underlying cultural differences.** Shah begins her story by describing how her uncle "would often generously withdraw a half-chewed delicacy from his mouth and lovingly cram it into mine" (paragraph 1). Shah seems ambivalent about this "Afghan habit" — expressing distaste as well as gratitude.

  To think critically about the assumptions in this essay related to cultural differences, ask yourself questions like these: What do you think are the beliefs or values underlying Shah's mixed feelings about her uncle's "Afghan habit"? Where in this essay do you find evidence of Shah's ambivalence about any other Afghan custom, and what underlies her attitude toward it? If you have experienced cultural difference, what was your attitude and what values affected your way of thinking?

- **assumptions about the influence of fairy tales.** Shah describes herself as "a princess in a fairy tale" (paragraph 2). She refers specifically to her father's stories about his "mythological homeland" (5), but romantic stories about princesses such as *Cinderella, Sleeping Beauty,* and *The Little Mermaid* are also popular in America. For example, the Walt Disney Company hosts a Princess Web site, and girls visiting Disney World can be a fairy-tale princess for a day.

  To think critically about the assumptions in this essay regarding the influence of fairy tales, ask yourself questions like these: What are girls — and perhaps also boys — taught by the fairy tales with which you are familiar? Considering your own experience with fairy tales, what attitudes or ideas do they seem to encourage? How does Shah achieve a critical perspective toward her own "desire to experience the fairy tale" (5)?

To help you analyze assumptions in Shah's essay, also consider trying one of these critical reading strategies, explained in Appendix 1: *reflecting on challenges to your beliefs and values, exploring the significance of figurative language,* or *looking for patterns of opposition.*

READING LIKE A WRITER

CONVEYING AUTOBIOGRAPHICAL SIGNIFICANCE

Shah conveys the autobiographical significance of the event through a combination of showing and telling. She begins the essay with a vivid image of her uncle: "He would often generously withdraw a half-chewed delicacy from his mouth and lovingly cram it into mine" (paragraph 1). This image conveys dramatically how she felt at the time, especially to Western readers who, like her, are inclined to be repelled by this particular cultural practice. The choice of the word *cram,* because it implies force, conveys a sense not only of disgust but also of violation. Yet by modifying *cram* with the adverb *lovingly,* Shah makes clear the ambivalence of her feelings. When she calls her uncle's behavior "an Afghan habit," she suggests to her Western readers that it should be read not as a sign of domination but of love and acceptance. In effect, by taking food from his own mouth, he is extending to her his protection and treating her as if she were his own daughter.

Analyze

1. Shah uses a vivid image to convey her remembered feelings when she describes herself as "a princess in a fairy tale" (paragraph 2). Reread paragraphs 2 and

3 to see how she imagines this fairy tale and what she feels about the reality of her experience. Underline the words or phrases that show or tell you how Shah feels about the man with whom she has been matched.

2. Reread paragraphs 4 and 5 to see how the image of her uncle's son and his bride affect her fairy-tale fantasy. Underline words or phrases that show or tell how Shah feels about the role in which she has cast herself.

Write

Write several sentences explaining what you have learned about the auto-biographical significance of this event for Shah. Give two or three examples from your underlining to support your explanation.

CONSIDERING IDEAS FOR YOUR OWN WRITING

Like Shah, consider writing about an event that you were looking forward to but that turned out differently than you had expected—perhaps a dreadful disappointment, a delightful surprise, or more likely a surprising combination of disappointment and delight. You might write about a time when you had thought you wanted something but then realized your desires were more complicated, when you were trying to fit in and discovered something about yourself or about the group to which you wanted to belong, or when you tried to conform to someone else's expectations for you or decided not to try to conform, but to rebel and go your own way. If, like Shah's, your experience involves a clash of cultures, you might write about that aspect of your experience and how it has affected you.

Luis J. Rodriguez

Always Running

Luis J. Rodriguez (b. 1954) is an award-winning writer who has published many books, including the short-story collection The Republic of East L.A.: Stories *(2002), the novel* Music of the Mill *(2005), a children's book, a book of poems, and the best-selling autobiography* Always Running: La Vida Loca, Gang Days in L.A. *(1993), from which this selection is excerpted. Among the many honors bestowed upon Rodriguez are the Chicago Sun-Times Book Award, a New York Times Notable Book Award, the Lila Wallace–Reader's Digest Writers' Award, and the Hispanic Heritage Award for Literature. Rodriguez also occasionally writes essays for* The Nation, Los Angeles Weekly, *and* Americas Review. *In addition to writing, Rodriguez has helped found several arts organizations in Chicago and Los Angeles and a nonprofit community group that works with gang members and other young people. If you want to learn more about Rodriguez, visit his official Web site at http://www.luisjrodriguez.com.*

In this excerpt from his autobiography, which he began writing when he was fifteen years old, Rodriguez tells what happened at the age of ten when he trespassed to play basketball in a school yard. As you read, put yourself in the young Rodriguez's place. Would you have climbed the fence? When you were a child, where could you go to play? If you were caught breaking the rules, how do you think you would have responded?

One evening dusk came early in South San Gabriel, with wind and cold 1
spinning to earth. People who had been sitting on porches or on metal
chairs near fold-up tables topped with cards and beer bottles collected
their things to go inside. Others put on sweaters or jackets. A storm gathered beyond the trees.

Tino and I strolled past the stucco and wood-frame homes of the neigh- 2
borhood consisting mostly of Mexicans with a sprinkling of poor white
families (usually from Oklahoma, Arkansas and Texas). *Ranchera* music
did battle with Country & Western songs as we continued toward the local
elementary school, an oil-and-grime stained basketball under my arm.

We stopped in front of a chain-link fence which surrounded the school. An 3
old brick building cast elongated shadows over a basketball court of concrete
on the other side of the fence. Leaves and paper swirled in tiny tornadoes.

"Let's go over," Tino proposed. 4

I looked up and across the fence. A sign above us read: NO ONE ALLOWED 5
AFTER 4:30 PM, BY ORDER OF THE LOS ANGELES COUNTY SHERIFF'S DEPARTMENT. Tino
turned toward me, shrugged his shoulders and gave me a who-cares look.

"Help me up, man, then throw the ball over." 6

I cupped my hands and lifted Tino up while the boy scaled the fence, 7
jumped over and landed on sneakered feet.

"Come on, Luis, let's go," Tino shouted from the other side. 8

9   I threw over the basketball, walked back a ways, then ran and jumped on the fence, only to fall back. Although we were both 10 years old, I cut a shorter shadow.

10   "Forget you, man," Tino said. "I'm going to play without you."

11   "Wait!" I yelled, while walking further back. I crouched low to the ground, then took off, jumped up and placed torn sneakers in the steel mesh. I made it over with a big thud.

12   Wiping the grass and dirt from my pants, I casually walked up to the ball on the ground, picked it up, and continued past Tino toward the courts.

13   "Hey Tino, what are you waiting for?"

14   The gusts proved no obstacle for a half-court game of B-ball, even as dark clouds smothered the sky.

15   Boy voices interspersed with ball cracking on asphalt. Tino's lanky figure seemed to float across the court, as if he had wings under his thin arms. Just then, a black-and-white squad car cruised down the street. A searchlight sprayed across the school yard. The vehicle slowed to a halt. The light shone toward the courts and caught Tino in mid-flight of a lay-up.

16   The dribbling and laughter stopped.

17   "All right, this is the sheriff's," a voice commanded. Two deputies stood by the fence, batons and flashlights in hand.

18   "Let's get out of here," Tino responded.

19   "What do you mean?" I countered. "Why don't we just stay here?"

20   "You nuts! We trespassing, man," Tino replied. "When they get a hold of us, they going to beat the crap out of us."

21   "Are you sure?"

22   "I know, believe me, I know."

23   "So where do we go?"

24   By then one of the deputies shouted back: "You boys get over here by the fence—now!"

25   But Tino dropped the ball and ran. I heard the deputies yell for Tino to stop. One of them began climbing the fence. I decided to take off too.

26   It never stopped, this running. We were constant prey, and the hunters soon became big blurs: the police, the gangs, the junkies, the dudes on Garvey Boulevard who took our money, all smudged into one. Sometimes they were teachers who jumped on us Mexicans as if we were born with a hideous stain. We were always afraid. Always running.

27   Tino and I raced toward the dark boxes called classrooms. The rooms lay there, hauntingly still without the voices of children, the commands of irate teachers or the clapping sounds of books as they were closed. The rooms were empty, forbidden places at night. We scurried around the structures toward a courtyard filled with benches next to the cafeteria building.

28   Tino hopped on a bench, then pulled himself over a high fence. He walked a foot or two on top of it, stopped, and proceeded to climb over to the cafeteria's rooftop. I looked over my shoulder. The deputies weren't far behind, their guns drawn. I grabbed hold of the fence on the side of the

cafeteria. I looked up and saw Tino's perspiring face over the roof's edge, his arm extended down toward me.

I tried to climb up, my feet dangling. But then a firm hand seized a foot 29 and pulled at it.

"They got me!" I yelled. 30

Tino looked below. A deputy spied the boy and called out: "Get down 31 here . . . you *greaser!*"

Tino straightened up and disappeared. I heard a flood of footsteps on 32 the roof—then a crash. Soon an awful calm covered us.

"Tino!" I cried out. 33

A deputy restrained me as the other one climbed onto the roof. He 34 stopped at a skylight, jagged edges on one of its sides. Shining a flashlight inside the building, the officer spotted Tino's misshapen body on the floor, sprinkled over with shards of glass.

READING FOR MEANING

This section presents three activities that will help you think about the meanings in Rodriguez's autobiographical story.

Read to Comprehend

Write a few sentences briefly explaining what happened when Rodriguez and his friend Tino tried to play basketball in the school yard.

Identify any words with meanings you are unsure of—such as *elongated* (paragraph 3) or *irate* (27)—and find the dictionary definition for each word that makes the best sense in the context.

To help you understand the essay better, also consider trying one of these critical reading strategies, explained in Appendix 1: *outlining, summarizing, paraphrasing,* or *questioning to understand and remember.*

Read to Respond

Write several paragraphs exploring your initial thoughts and feelings about Rodriguez's autobiographical story. Focus on anything that stands out for you, perhaps because it resonates with your own experience or because you find a statement puzzling. For example, consider writing about one of the following:

- the shocking conclusion;

- the relationship between Rodriguez and Tino—perhaps reflecting on relationships you have had with friends;

- the sign posted on the school yard fence and the boys' reaction to it; or

- the behavior of the police and of the boys when the police arrive.

To help develop your response, also consider trying one of these critical reading strategies, explained in Appendix 1: *contextualizing* or *reflecting on challenges to your beliefs and values.*

Read to Analyze Assumptions

Write a paragraph or two analyzing an assumption in Rodriguez's essay. To think critically about assumptions, here are some kinds of questions you could ask: Who holds this assumption (the writer, readers, and/or others cited in the essay)? What are the effects of the assumption in the context of the essay specifically or in society more generally? What do you think about the assumption, and is there anything in the essay that raises doubts about it? How does the assumption reinforce or critique commonly held views, and are there any alternative ideas, beliefs, or values that would challenge this assumption?

You might choose an assumption from the list below, using the questions accompanying it in addition to the ones above to help you get started. Or you can choose another assumption in the essay to explore.

- **assumptions about stereotyping.** When Tino tells Luis that he won't do what the deputies ask because they will "beat the crap out of us" (paragraph 20), he assures Luis that he knows what he's talking about: "'I know, believe me, I know'" (22). Predicting how an individual will act based on how he or she has behaved in the past under similar circumstances may be fairly reliable. But it is much less reliable to predict how members of a group will act based on how others in that group have behaved in the past. Making this kind of assumption about members of a group is stereotyping.

  To think critically about the assumptions in this essay regarding stereotyping, ask yourself questions like these: In addition to Tino, who else in the essay stereotypes others? What seems to drive people's tendency to stereotype others — in the essay or in your own experience and observation? How, if at all, does this story attempt to influence readers and possibly lead them to resist the destructive cycle of stereotyping and prejudice?

- **assumptions about the role schools should play in society.** Rodriguez shows us that the neighborhood kids are clearly not welcome at the school after hours, and perhaps even during regular school hours.

  To think critically about the assumptions in this essay related to school, ask yourself questions like these: What are the young Rodriguez's feelings about the school? What does the writer seem to assume about the way neighborhood schools should treat their students? To what extent does Rodriguez's experience parallel either your own experience or your observation?

To help you analyze assumptions in Rodriguez's essay, also consider trying one of these critical reading strategies, explained in Appendix 1: *reflecting on challenges to your beliefs and values, exploring the significance of figurative language,* or *looking for patterns of opposition.*

A Special Reading Strategy

Contextualizing

Contextualizing is a special critical reading strategy. You can use it to read for meaning, to develop your analysis of the assumptions underlying "Always Running," and to compare your own assumptions with those of Rodriguez. To contextualize an autobiographical essay like "Always Running," you need to explore the event's contexts:

- *When* the event occurred and how the historical moment influenced what happened: paragraph 9 indicates that the event occurred when Rodriguez was ten years old. According to Rodriguez's official Web site, he was born in 1954. So the event he is writing about occurred in 1964 or 1965. You could do further Internet research to learn what was happening during this historical period.

- *Where* the event occurred and how the location played a role: paragraph 1 identifies the location as "South San Gabriel," an area of Los Angeles, California. In paragraph 2, Rodriguez briefly describes the neighborhood. If you wanted to know more about this location during this period, you could read more of Rodriguez's autobiography or do further Internet research. If you do a Google search for "1960s Los Angeles ethnic," for example, you would learn about the area's ethnic makeup and political tensions, including the Watts riots of 1965.

- *Who* was involved and how the power relationships among those involved affected what happened: Rodriguez identifies himself and Tino as "Mexicans" (26). He does not identify the officers' ethnicity, but the fact that one of them calls Tino "'you *greaser*'" (31) suggests his attitude toward people of Mexican descent and may help explain Tino's assumption that if he didn't run away, the police would beat him.

See Appendix 1 (pp. 570–71) for detailed guidelines on using contextualizing as a critical reading strategy.

READING LIKE A WRITER

PRESENTING PLACES AND PEOPLE

Autobiographers typically use a combination of *naming* and *detailing* along with *comparing* to present people and places. These descriptive strategies create vivid images that enable readers to imagine what the experience was like for the writer, and they also create a dominant impression that helps readers understand the autobiographical significance.

In paragraph 3, for example, Rodriguez describes the school yard this way:

> We stopped in front of a chain-link fence which surrounded the school. An old brick building cast elongated shadows over a basketball court of concrete on the other side of the fence. Leaves and paper swirled in tiny tornadoes.

Rodriguez names features such as the "fence," "building," and "basketball court" that he wants readers to notice about the scene. He also adds details to give readers information about these features. Descriptive details usually provide sensory information indicating what the place looks, sounds, smells, tastes, and feels like. Notice that Rodriguez chooses details like the "chain-link" of the fence, the "brick" of the building, and the "concrete" of the basketball court that give visual and tactile information. The brick and concrete suggest the hardness of these surfaces, an impression that is reinforced when we see how difficult it is for the young Rodriguez to get over the chain-link fence.

Rodriguez also uses comparison when he metaphorically describes the swirling leaves and papers as "tiny tornadoes." The word *tornadoes* reinforces other descriptive language in this selection. For example, the opening paragraph ends with a reference to a gathering storm, and the "gusts" and "dark clouds" of the gathering storm are mentioned again in paragraph 14. The storm is literal in that the weather actually is changing. But the storm is also figurative or symbolic — that is, it stands for the tragedy of Tino's death. It may also suggest the social upheaval that was building toward the cataclysm of the Watts riots.

Analyze

1. Reread the selection, underlining the naming, detailing, and comparing used to describe Tino's body language (paragraph 5), the ease with which he scales the fence (7), his body in motion as he plays basketball (15), his actions as he runs away (28), and finally his body fallen to the floor (34).

2. Notice, in paragraph 15, that Rodriguez describes Tino figuratively as if he were flying: seeming "to float across the court, as if he had wings." Review the descriptive language you have underlined to see where this image of Tino flying, or not being weighed down by gravity, is reinforced. Contrast this image of Tino with the way the young Rodriguez is described; in paragraphs 9 to 12, for example, Rodriguez struggles to scale the fence that Tino seems to climb so effortlessly.

Write

Write several sentences explaining what you have discovered about Rodriguez's description of Tino. What dominant impression do these images of Tino suggest to you? How do they help you understand the significance of what happened? Give two or three examples from your underlining to support your explanation.

CONSIDERING IDEAS FOR YOUR OWN WRITING

In this autobiographical essay, Rodriguez writes about a traumatic event. If you feel comfortable sharing your memories of a traumatic experience with your instructor and classmates, consider writing about it for this occasion. Instead of writing about something that turned out worse than you had expected, you could also consider something that turned out better or just differently. Rodriguez's essay also suggests the possibility of writing about a time when you did something uncharacteristic or when you followed someone else's lead. You might also think about people — like Tino — whom you knew as a child or as an early adolescent and the reasons that those people were significant in your life.

Aleksandra Crapanzano

Lobster Lessons

Aleksandra Crapanzano has written screenplays, including an adapta- tion of Reading Lolita in Tehran, *and also writes about food for the* New York Times Magazine *The Way We Eat column. She won the MFK Fisher Distinguished Writing Award for an article in* Gourmet *magazine, in which this reading originally appeared. As you read, notice how Margaret changes as a result of her relationship with Crapanzano and also how Crapanzano changes as well.*

1   Rituals are at once burdens and gifts; this is what makes them worth doing, and having, and keeping. It was a remarkable old woman who taught me this lesson—and how, along the way, not to cook a lobster—and I will never forget it.

2   John and I had been together a year. I had met his parents and he'd met mine. We had moved in together, traveled together, eaten great meals together, but we had not yet settled into (how could we have?) any enduring rituals. Then when summer arrived, it was time to get seri- ous. Serious, for John, meant introducing me to a tiny beach cottage on the east coast of Nantucket, where he'd spent at least a part of every summer of his life; serious meant our spending a few weeks there with his permanent Other Woman, his great-aunt Margaret, whose cottage it was.

3   Eighty-two years old and a legend in children's book publishing, Margaret, John had warned me, was a creature of habit. To be precise, dietary habit. I'd already heard tales of her spartan daily regimen, which consisted largely of grapefruit (three), skim milk (two tall glasses), and a tuna-fish sandwich. Dinner was, without variation and without fail, a cold chicken leg (boiled), two red potatoes (also boiled), and a pile of grayish green beans (ditto). I was 21 that summer, already something of a food snob, and spartan wasn't really in my repertoire.

4   The first sign of a new world order came on the day we were supposed to pick Margaret up at the ferry terminal. John, who had never before shown the least interest in cooking, suddenly declared, in the voice of an anxious sergeant, that he knew what his aunt liked to eat and how she liked to eat it—and that while we were all cohabiting, he would take charge of the meals, if that was all right with me. I watched in horror as he filled an entire shopping cart at the A&P with water-packed tuna and low- fat mayonnaise. When I reached for a head of garlic, he simply shook his head in dismay, sensing perhaps the inevitable clash of palates in two of

Nantucket, 2002: Novelist John Burnham Schwartz with his great-aunt Margaret K. McElderry, the legendary children's book publisher.

the women he loved best. But it was the margarine that almost brought our relationship to an early end. It would be months before we again crossed the threshold of a supermarket together.

From that first dinner with Margaret in her cottage, I remember her 5 smiling at me as the three of us clinked glasses over the table, making me feel wonderfully welcome. But the food itself? Let's just say that, as with any real trauma, the details are buried deep in my psyche.

The following day, I walked up from the beach to find John waiting for 6 me in Margaret's cherry-red 1967 Buick convertible. "Let's go get the lobsters," he called out over the noisy engine. This was promising. I hopped in. Lobsters, corn on the cob, and baked potatoes: It would be messy and buttery and fun. That evening, I was digging out an old T-shirt, knowing I'd be sprayed and stained by dinner's end, when I looked up and caught sight of John through the window. He was stumbling up from the ocean, through the beach grass, weighted down by an enormous black lobster pot, the water sloshing out by the gallon and running down his legs. As he came up the porch steps, I asked him what he was doing. "If you want your lobsters to taste of the ocean, you have to cook them in ocean water," he explained. Margaret, I learned, had been cooking lobsters this way all her life, as had her parents. It was hard to think of refuting the idea, even when John described the hours and boxes of Brillo it would take to scrub the pot clean.

7   The smell of boiling brine brought me into the kitchen, where I found Margaret and John standing at the stove. John was holding the lid down on the steaming pot so the lobsters, despite their desperate tail-banging, couldn't escape. Margaret had her hand on top of his and was pressing down with her frail fingers. Years ago, when John was a boy, it would have been Margaret's strength that kept the lid in place. Roles had reversed, but they were still a team. Yet something was terribly wrong. The minutes were ticking by, and the lobsters were still boiling away in the pot. I waited and waited, biting my tongue. After a full 23 minutes—not a second more nor less by the stovetop timer—Margaret gave the word and John removed the ruined creatures with a long pair of tongs.

8   As I silently mourned the soggy creature on my plate, Margaret washed hers down with plenty of white wine and began telling marvelous stories. She'd been coming to Nantucket since the 1920s and told of riding her bicycle as a girl to fetch ice for her mother's icebox, five miles each way. On sunny days, the ice would start to melt and drip from the basket down her legs and between her toes. She told of the winter when the kitchen—an old farmer's shed—had been drawn by sled all the way across a frozen Sesachacha Pond and attached to the cottage. She told of volunteering in London during the Blitz, when food was rationed, and of the magical day a friend brought a dozen fresh eggs to her as a rare gift. So rare that all her friends and neighbors showed up for a spontaneous "fresh eggs party." As Margaret scrambled them over a makeshift stove, an air-raid siren wailed, but no one left to take shelter. Not before savoring a taste of peace. Not before remembering a better time.

9   Now, more than 50 years later, at the end of our dinner, Margaret dabbed her lips dry, set down her checkered napkin, and heartily proclaimed: "These lobsters are the best I've ever had." Cheeks rosy from the sun, a glass of wine in hand, her merry blue eyes full of wonder, she seemed impossibly young—and I was smitten.

10   The thought of those scrambled eggs kept me awake that night. For 50 years, Margaret had held their taste in her memory. Clearly she had an appetite for something beyond her boiled regimen. I decided to feed that hunger and, the very next day, took over the kitchen.

If my plan was to work, I reasoned, I needed to find inspiration,   11
rather than dread, in Margaret's usual fare of milk, tuna, and a narrow
range of boiled things. That first night, I simmered a loin of pork in
milk with a few sage leaves, a little lemon zest, and a hidden clove of
garlic: A dish so comforting and mild, it tasted of childhood. Margaret
was transfixed by the golden curdles of milk in the sauce and seemed
to suspect me of alchemy. I said nothing to dissuade her of this lovely
hypothesis. *Vitello tonnato* for lunch the next day satisfied her need
for her daily ration of tuna and begged for a bottle of rosé and a sleepy
afternoon. Vacation had finally begun. *Boeuf à la ficelle* had us discussing the health virtues of boiling, and John watched in disbelief as
Margaret took, with an enthusiasm bordering on compulsion, to the
cornichons I'd set out.

Dinner by dinner, I moved slowly through the classics, rewriting the   12
parameters of Margaret's diet. And while it was sometimes a burden to
cook for her, it was also a joy. She responded to good food with an appetite some 80 years in the making but still girlish in its pleasure. I had, it
seemed, opened a Pandora's box of tastes.

The following summer, an actual box arrived from Margaret's office   13
the day before her arrival—this one sent via FedEx and containing dozens of recipes that Margaret had clipped from newspapers and magazines
throughout the winter months. A short note was attached, in which she
expressed her hope that I'd want to take a crack at all of them. With no
fancy appliances, no gadgets, a single sharp knife, and a colander with
only one remaining leg, I cooked every single dish. It was the stuff of
fantasy—asparagus flan and summer pudding, oyster chowder and
strawberry soup. Margaret kept religious track of them all, noting the ones

The author, left, with the Other Woman in her husband's life.

she particularly liked and filing them away for future summers. It never occurred to her that she might take a recipe home to New York and try it over the winter. Habits might be broken on holiday, but Labor Day returned life to its proper austerity. Still, the thought of Margaret clipping away — dreaming, really — through the long, cold months conjured the irrepressible hope of a love affair.

14   The years went by and Margaret's age finally took its long-delayed toll. There was the first summer she could no longer walk the 50 feet to the beach. She'd sit on the porch steps staring at that small, insurmountable distance. And then the summer when her hands were no longer strong enough to crack a lobster shell. John tenderly took the lobster from her, cracked it, and gave it back, continuing the conversation all the while. At the end of dinner, with undiminished fervor, she declared it the best lobster she'd had yet. By then, I'd learned that she graced every lobster dinner with those same words.

15   Margaret's impatience with her weakening body inevitably turned outward. At five o'clock sharp, she would stomp her cane and call out from the porch: "It's time for a drink!" John and I would scurry, leaving computers, work, sentences half-written — John to get white wine from the fridge, me to get the requisite peanuts. We were older, our obligations had multiplied, summers no longer stretched into fall. Our own frustrations occasionally began to simmer.

16   One night in particular has stayed with me. Margaret had just arrived, and we were to have our annual lobster feast. It had taken me ten years to scale the boiling time down to a palatable 12 or 13 minutes, and I'd permanently replaced the dreaded margarine with actual butter. But change is not always a friend. John was in the throes of finishing a new novel and had been at his desk, writing, a solid ten hours by the time he broke for the day. Showered, eager for a glass of wine, he'd already put on fresh khakis, uncorked a good bottle, and settled into the Kennedy Rocker when Margaret appeared with the lobster pot.

17   The wind was up and we could all hear the ocean roaring on the beach. John asked if this once we might use salted tap water. Margaret's response was a simple enough "No," but the indignation in her voice was unmistakable. John was silent — and as angry as I'd ever seen him. "It just won't do," added Margaret, impatiently tapping her cane on the floor. But John was already rolling up his pants to perform his time-honored chore.

18   The water was freezing and the sky steel-gray that evening. Margaret sat down on the porch steps and watched John disappear over the dune. I observed her from a few feet away. Far from victorious, she seemed to be questioning herself, wondering, no doubt, if time had made her ways too fixed, irrelevant. I took a seat next to her. Stupidly, I tried to tell her that

she was right, even Jasper White, the great New England chef, called for cooking lobsters in ocean water. But that was hardly the point. It was, of course, the ritual, in all its effort, that mattered. It set the meal squarely in her history, some 90 years of it, by then, and set it apart from other days and other meals.

John came up the porch steps, bent over his burden. Margaret, sur- 19
prising us mightily, conceded that next time we might try tap water, but John shook his head. It wouldn't be the same. And seeing him standing there, soaking wet but smiling, his arms trembling under the weight of the huge lobster pot filled with fresh seawater from the Atlantic Ocean, I couldn't help but agree. At the end of dinner, Margaret, true to herself, rose to the occasion — she declared her lobster the very best she'd ever eaten.

This summer Margaret will be 97. She'll come to Nantucket with a 20
caretaker, an oxygen tank, and a wheelchair. Her short-term memory is under assault, but the past she remembers with intense feeling. Traditions are more important to her than ever. They connect our family. John and I now have a little boy and a large dog. When it's time to collect the ocean water, I imagine I'll give our son a bucket and Margaret and I will watch him traipse after his father, learning the way we have always cooked lobsters.

READING FOR MEANING

This section presents three activities that will help you think about the meanings in Crapanzano's autobiographical essay.

Read to Comprehend

Write a few sentences briefly summarizing what you learn about Margaret from reading this portrait of her.

Identify any words with meanings you are unsure of — such as *palate* (paragraph 3) and *smitten* (9) — and find the dictionary definition for each word that makes the best sense in the context.

To help you understand the essay better, also consider trying one of these critical reading strategies, explained in Appendix 1: *outlining* or *questioning to understand and remember*.

Read to Respond

Write several paragraphs exploring your initial thoughts and feelings about Crapanzano's autobiographical portrait of Margaret. Focus on anything that stands out for you, perhaps because it resonates with your own experience or because you find a statement puzzling. For example, consider writing about one of the following:

- the opening assertion that "rituals are at once burdens and gifts" (paragraph 1);

- Margaret's story about volunteering in London during the Blitz (8); or

- the idea that traditions — maybe especially traditions around food — connect families (20).

To help develop your response, also consider trying one of these critical reading strategies, explained in Appendix 1: *contextualizing* or *reflecting on challenges to your beliefs and values.*

Read to Analyze Assumptions

Write a paragraph or two analyzing an assumption in Crapanzano's essay. To think critically about assumptions, here are some kinds of questions you could ask: Who holds this assumption (the writer, readers, and/ or others cited in the essay)? What are the effects of the assumption in the context of the essay specifically or in society more generally? What do you think about the assumption, and is there anything in the essay that raises doubts about it? How does the assumption reinforce or critique commonly held views, and are there any alternative ideas, beliefs, or values that would challenge this assumption?

You might choose an assumption from the list below, using the questions accompanying it in addition to the ones above to help you get started. Or you can choose another assumption in the essay to explore.

- **assumptions about the value of rituals.** Crapanzano opens her essay with the statement "Rituals are at once burdens and gifts; this is what makes them worth doing, and having and keeping" (paragraph 1).

    To think critically about the assumptions in this essay about the value of rituals, ask yourself questions like these: What does Crapanzano mean when she calls them *burdens* and *gifts*? What rituals does she refer to that fall into either category? How does the essay show that rituals are worth keeping? When she sees John and Margaret holding the pot's lid down, she seems to appreciate ritual; but that certainly is not her attitude about Margaret's family ritual of boiling lobsters in salt water for 23 minutes until they're soggy. How does the essay deal with this ambiguity?

- **assumptions about eating and pleasure.** Reflecting on Margaret's story about the "fresh eggs party" she enjoyed during the London Blitz, Crapanzano recognizes that even though Margaret has followed a limited and austere diet, deep down she associates eating with pleasure. So when Crapanzano begins cooking for Margaret, it is as if she had "opened a Pandora's box of tastes" (12).

To think critically about the assumptions in this essay related to the pleasures of food, ask yourself questions like these: Why do you think the fresh eggs party was so memorable for Margaret? Do you have any memories of special meals, and if so, why are your memories so strong? Why do you imagine Margaret took such pleasure in clipping recipes during the winter months but never thought to try any of the recipes herself during the winter?

To help you analyze assumptions in Crapanzano's essay, also consider trying one of these critical reading strategies, explained in Appendix 1: *reflecting on challenges to your beliefs and values* or *looking for patterns of opposition.*

READING LIKE A WRITER

PRESENTING A PERSON THROUGH ANECDOTES AND RECURRING ACTIVITIES

Autobiography uses narrative in various ways. Some autobiographies, like those in this chapter by Annie Dillard, Saira Shah, Luis J. Rodriguez, and Jean Brandt, focus on a single memorable event that occurred within a few hours or days, whereas others, like those by Aleksandra Crapanzano and Brad Benioff, focus on a person with whom the writer had an important relationship. Autobiographies that focus on a person may use two narrating strategies — anecdotes and recurring activities. *Anecdotes* present experiences that are one-time occurrences. Like a snapshot, an anecdote catches the person at a particular place and time, giving the reader a sense of what the person did and said on that occasion, such as one time when someone tripped and dropped the cake at a birthday party. *Recurring activities,* in contrast, present experiences that are typical and occur more than once, often on a regular basis with only a little variation over a period of time, such as several occasions when the same person tripped and dropped things, suggesting the person's clumsiness or nervousness. As you analyze Crapanzano's use of anecdotes and recurring activities, you will see how they differ and what each contributes to the portrait of Margaret.

Analyze

1. Reread paragraphs 4 to 9, where Crapanzano presents two anecdotes — one describing herself and John shopping at the A&P and the other relating the

first lobster dinner with Margaret. Note how she narrates these anecdotes, specifically the kinds of information she provides.

2. Reread paragraphs 11 to 13, where Crapanzano presents recurring activities — the various dishes she cooked to entice Margaret. Note that in these paragraphs, Crapanzano does not go into detail but simply identifies the dishes she cooked. Also, she tells us what Margaret typically did.

Write

Write a sentence or two describing how the anecdotes and recurring activities differ, pointing to specific ways that Crapanzano presents these experiences. Then consider why she begins with detailed anecdotes but then switches to quick recurring activities, lists of dishes she made and Margaret's reactions to them.

ANALYZING VISUALS

Write a paragraph analyzing the photographs included in Crapanzano's autobiographical essay and explaining what they contribute to the essay. To do the analysis, you can use the criteria chart for the Analysis of Visuals in Appendix 3 on pp. 670–72. Don't feel you have to answer all of the questions in the chart; focus on those that seem most productive in helping you write a paragraph-length analysis. To help you get started, consider adding these questions that specifically refer to Crapanzano's photographs:

- What do you learn about the relationships depicted in these two photographs?

- What do you learn about the people from the way they are dressed? From the direction in which they are looking?

- What do you make of the fact that both photographs are taken on the deck with the water in the background and that neither shows people sitting at the table or preparing a meal?

- What does the caption underneath each photograph add to your understanding?

For additional help, refer to Appendix 3: Analyzing Visuals.

CONSIDERING IDEAS FOR YOUR OWN WRITING

Autobiographers often write about people with whom they have close and somewhat complicated relationships. Like Crapanzano, you might choose to present a person you are trying to figure out, perhaps a close friend or family member. Or you might consider writing about a person for whom you felt (and maybe still feel) strong and perhaps conflicting emotions. Try to recall particular events or conversations with the person that you could use to help readers understand your relationship with the person. Another possibility is to write about a teacher, mentor, counselor, religious leader, or some other older person who influenced you deeply, for good or ill. Consider also someone who passed on to you a sense of your family history or culture.

Brad Benioff

Rick

Brad Benioff was a first-year college student when he wrote the following essay for an assignment in his composition class. Like Aleksandra Crapanzano in the preceding selection, Benioff focuses his essay on a memorable person: his high-school water-polo coach, Rick Rezinas.

As you read, notice how Benioff uses dialogue to dramatize his relationship with Rick.

1   I walked through the dawn chill, shivering as much from nervousness as from the cold. Steam curled up from the water in the pool and disappeared in the ocher morning light. Athletes spread themselves about on the deck, lazily stretching and whispering to each other as if the stillness were sacred. It was to be my first practice with the high school water polo team. I knew nothing about the game, but a friend had pushed me to play, arguing, "It's the most fun of any sport. Trust me." He had awakened me that morning long before daylight, forced me into a bathing suit, and driven me to the pool.

2   "Relax," he said. "Rick is the greatest of coaches. You'll like him. You'll have fun."

3   The mythical Rick. I had heard of him many times before. All the older players knew him by his first name and always spoke of him as a friend rather than a coach. He was a math teacher at our school, and his classes were very popular. Whenever class schedules came out, everyone hoped to be placed in Mr. Rezinas's class. He had been known to throw parties for the team or take them on weekend excursions skiing or backpacking. To be Rick's friend was to be part of an exclusive club, and I was being invited to join. And so I looked forward with nervous anticipation to meeting this man.

4   My friend walked me out to the pool deck and steered me toward a man standing beside the pool.

5   "Rick," announced my friend, "I'd like you to meet your newest player."

6   Rick was not a friendly looking man. He wore only swim trunks, and his short, powerful legs rose up to meet a bulging torso. His big belly was solid. His shoulders, as if to offset his front-heaviness, were thrown back, creating a deep crease of excess muscle from his sides around the small of his back, a crease like a huge frown. His arms were crossed, two medieval maces placed carefully on their racks, ready to be swung at any moment. His round cheeks and chin were darkened by traces of black whiskers. His hair was sparse. Huge, black, mirrored sunglasses replaced his eyes. Below his prominent nose was a thin, sinister mustache. I couldn't believe this menacing-looking man was the legendary jovial Rick.

He said nothing at first. In those moments of silence, I felt more inadequate than ever before in my life. My reflection in his glasses stared back at me, accusing me of being too skinny, too young, too stupid, too weak to be on his team. Where did I get the nerve to approach him with such a ridiculous body and ask to play water polo, a man's game? Finally, he broke the silence, having finished appraising my meager body. "We'll fatten him up," he growled. 7

Thus began a week of torture. For four hours a day, the coach stood beside the pool scowling down at me. I could do nothing right. 8

"No! No! No!" He shook his head in disgust. "Throw the damn ball with your whole arm! Get your goddamn elbow out of the water!" 9

Any failure on my part brought down his full wrath. He bellowed at my incompetence and punished me with push-ups and wind sprints. Even when I was close to utter exhaustion, I found no sympathy. "What the hell are you doing on the wall?" he would bellow. "Coach . . . my side, it's cramped." 10

"Swim on it! If you can't take a little pain, then you don't play!" With this, he would push me off the wall. 11

He seemed to enjoy playing me against the older, stronger players. "Goddamn it, Brad! If someone elbows or hits you, don't look out at me and cry, 'It's not fair.' Push back! Don't be so weak!" I got elbowed around until it seemed that none of my internal organs was unscathed. He worked me until my muscles wouldn't respond, and then he demanded more. 12

"You're not trying! Push it!" 13

"Would you move? You're too slow! Swim!" 14

"Damn it! Get out and give me twenty!" 15

It took little time for me to hate both the game and the man who ruled it. 16

I reacted by working as hard as I could. I decided to deprive him of the pleasure of finding fault with me. I learned quickly and started playing as flawlessly as possible. I dispensed with looking tired, showing pain, or complaining of cramps. I pushed, hit, and elbowed back at the biggest of players. No matter how flawless or aggressive my performance, though, he would find fault and let me know it. He was never critical of other players. He would laugh and joke with the other players; but whenever he saw me, he frowned. 17

I decided to quit. 18

After a particularly demanding practice, I walked up to this tyrant. I tried to hold his gaze, but the black glasses forced me to look down. 19

"Coach Rezinas," I blurted, "I've decided that I don't want to play water polo." His scowl deepened. Then after a moment he said, "You can't quit. Not until after the first game." And he walked away. The dictator had issued his command. 20

There was no rule to keep me from quitting. Anger flushed through me. Somehow I would get revenge on this awful man. After the first game? 21

Okay. I would play. I would show him what a valuable player I was. He would miss my talents when I quit. I worked myself up before the first game by imagining the hated face: the black glasses, the thin mustache, the open, snarling mouth. I was not surprised that he placed me in the starting lineup because I was certain he would take me out soon. I played furiously. The ball, the goal, the opposition, even the water seemed to be extensions of Rick, his face glaring from every angle, his words echoing loudly in my ears. Time and time again I would get the ball and, thinking of his tortures, fire it toward the goal with a strength to kill. I forgot that he might take me out. No defender could stand up to me. I would swim by them or over them. Anger and the need for vengeance gave me energy. I didn't notice the time slipping by, the quarters ending.

22   Then, the game ended. My teammates rushed out to me, congratulating and cheering me. I had scored five goals, a school record for one game, and shut out the other team with several key defensive plays. Now I could get revenge. Now I could quit. I stepped out of the pool prepared with the words I would spit into his face: "I QUIT!"

23   As I approached him, I stopped dead. He was smiling at me, his glasses off. He reached out with his right hand and shook mine with exuberance.

24   "I knew you had it in you! I knew it!" he laughed.

25   Through his laughter, I gained a new understanding of the man. He had pushed me to my fullest potential, tapping into the talent I may never have found in myself. He was responsible for the way I played that day. My glory was his. He never hated me. On the contrary, I was his apprentice, his favored pupil. He had brought out my best. Could I really hate someone who had done that much for me? He had done what he had promised: he had fattened me up mentally as well as physically. All this hit me in a second and left me completely confused. I tried to speak, but only managed to croak, "Coach . . . uh . . . I, uh. . . ." He cut me off with another burst of laughter. He still shook my hand.

26   "Call me Rick," he said.

READING FOR MEANING

This section presents three activities that will help you think about the meanings in Benioff's autobiographical essay.

Read to Comprehend

Write a few sentences briefly explaining what you think Benioff wants readers to understand about Rick and why he was so important in Benioff's life.

Identify any words with meanings you are unsure of — such as *ocher* (paragraph 1) and *unscathed* (12) — and find the dictionary definition for each word that makes the best sense in the context.

To help you understand the essay better, also consider trying one of these critical reading strategies, explained in Appendix 1: *summarizing* or *questioning to understand and remember*.

Read to Respond

Write several paragraphs exploring your initial thoughts and feelings about Benioff's autobiographical essay about his relationship with Rick. Focus on anything that stands out for you, perhaps because it resonates with your own experience or because you find a statement puzzling. For example, consider writing about one of the following:

- Rick's coaching style, perhaps comparing it with other styles of coaching or teaching with which you are familiar;

- the fact that Rick found fault with Benioff "[n]o matter how flawless or aggressive [his] performance" (paragraph 17); or

- the high-school students' desire to be "Rick's friend" and thus "part of an exclusive club" (3), perhaps in relation to your experience with exclusive groups in high school or college.

To help develop your response, also consider trying one of these critical reading strategies, explained in Appendix 1: *contextualizing* or *reflecting on challenges to your beliefs and values*.

Read to Analyze Assumptions

Write a paragraph or two analyzing an assumption in Benioff's essay. To think critically about assumptions, here are some kinds of questions you could ask: Who holds this assumption (the writer, readers, and/or others cited in the essay)? What are the effects of the assumption in the context of the essay specifically or in society more generally? What do you think about the assumption, and is there anything in the essay that raises doubts about it? How does the assumption reinforce or critique commonly held views, and are there any alternative ideas, beliefs, or values that would challenge this assumption?

You might choose an assumption from the list below, using the questions accompanying it, in addition to the ones above to help you get started. Or you can choose another assumption in the essay to explore.

- **assumptions about the good and bad qualities of coaching.** Benioff's friend describes Rick as "the greatest of coaches" (paragraph 2) and Benioff writes that "the older players . . . always spoke of him as a friend rather than a coach" (3). But Benioff calls Rick a "tyrant" (19) and a "dictator" (20). He complains that Rick demands too much of him and works him too hard, always finding fault and never giving him praise — at least, until Benioff proves himself to be worthy.

To think critically about the assumptions in this essay related to coaching, ask yourself questions like these: What does Benioff assume are the good and the bad qualities of coaching? Why does his attitude change after the game? In your experience, are coaches like Rick or other authority figures (such as parents, teachers, bosses) expected to be tough and critical rather than sympathetic and encouraging? Why would one style of leadership or authority be preferred to another? Should it be?

- **assumptions about the male body and masculinity.** Benioff calls water polo "a man's game" and seems delighted that Rick "fattened [him] up mentally as well as physically" (25). For example, Benioff describes his own body before undergoing Rick's makeover as "too skinny . . . too weak," "ridiculous," and "meager" (7). These images are in sharp contrast to those he uses to describe Rick's "powerful," "bulging," "solid" muscular body (6).

  To think critically about the assumptions in this essay related to the male body and masculinity, ask yourself questions like these: What qualities of the male body does Benioff come to share with Rick? Where do you see evidence that our culture celebrates the same physical qualities that Benioff does? If you think of masculinity, or manliness, as a set of attitudes and behavior that may change over time and vary among different communities and cultural traditions, what does Benioff's admiration of Rick suggest about American ideas of manliness early in the twenty-first century? Where, if anywhere, does Benioff question the kind of masculinity Rick represents? What other qualities, if any, does our culture (or another culture of which you are aware) associate with masculinity?

To help you analyze assumptions in Benioff's essay, also consider trying one of these critical reading strategies, explained in Appendix 1: *exploring the significance of figurative language* or *looking for patterns of opposition.*

READING LIKE A WRITER

DESCRIBING A PERSON THROUGH VISUAL DETAILS

Visual description enables readers to see a person and to get a sense of how that person appears to others. For example, providing vivid details of someone's facial features could show whether a person looks others directly in the eye or avoids eye contact. This activity will help you see how Benioff uses visual description to give readers a picture of Rick as well as an understanding of his significance to the writer.

Analyze

1. Reread paragraph 6, where Benioff describes Rick. Notice that the writer makes only two general statements characterizing Rick, in the first and last sentences of the paragraph. The remaining sentences in this paragraph

offer visual details and images describing Rick's appearance. Because Rick is wearing only swim trunks and sunglasses, Benioff concentrates on the appearance of Rick's body.

2. Underline the parts of Rick's body that Benioff singles out, beginning with "legs" and "torso" in the second sentence. Then put a wavy line under each visual detail Benioff uses to describe the parts of Rick's body, beginning with "short, powerful" and "bulging" in sentence 2.

3. Put a star by the two comparisons: a simile in sentence 4 (a *simile* makes an explicit comparison by using the word *like* or *as*) and a metaphor in sentence 5 (a *metaphor* implicitly compares two items by describing one in terms of the other).

Write

Write several sentences explaining the impression you get of Rick as seen through Benioff's eyes. Quote the visual details and comparisons that contribute most to this impression.

CONSIDERING IDEAS FOR YOUR OWN WRITING

Think about the coaches, teachers, employers, and other mentors who have influenced your life. Choose one of these people, and consider how you can describe what that person taught you and how he or she went about doing it. As a writer aiming to describe this individual's significance in your life, how would you reveal what you learned about the person and about yourself ? Or as an alternative, you might consider someone with whom you have had continuing disagreements or conflicts and then speculate on how you can describe your relationship with that person.

Jean Brandt

Calling Home

Jean Brandt wrote this essay as a first-year college student. In it, she tells about a memorable event that occurred when she was thirteen. Reflecting on how she felt at the time, Brandt writes, "I was afraid, embarrassed, worried, mad." As you read, make your own marginal notes indicating where the writer's tumultuous and contradictory remembered feelings are expressed in the essay.

The other readings in this chapter are followed by reading and writing activities. Following this reading, however, you are on your own to decide how to read for meaning and read like a writer.

1   As we all piled into the car, I knew it was going to be a fabulous day. My grandmother was visiting for the holidays; and she and I, along with my older brother and sister, Louis and Susan, were setting off for a day of last-minute Christmas shopping. On the way to the mall, we sang Christmas carols, chattered, and laughed. With Christmas only two days away, we were caught up with holiday spirit. I felt light-headed and full of joy. I loved shopping—especially at Christmas.

2   The shopping center was swarming with frantic last-minute shoppers like ourselves. We went first to the General Store, my favorite. It carried mostly knickknacks and other useless items which nobody needs but buys anyway. I was thirteen years old at the time, and things like buttons and calendars and posters would catch my fancy. This day was no different. The object of my desire was a 75-cent Snoopy button. Snoopy was the latest. If you owned anything with the Peanuts on it, you were "in." But since I was supposed to be shopping for gifts for other people and not myself, I couldn't decide what to do. I went in search of my sister for her opinion. I pushed my way through throngs of people to the back of the store where I found Susan. I asked her if she thought I should buy the button. She said it was cute and if I wanted it to go ahead and buy it.

3   When I got back to the Snoopy section, I took one look at the lines at the cashiers and knew I didn't want to wait thirty minutes to buy an item worth less than one dollar. I walked back to the basket where I found the button and was about to drop it when suddenly, instead, I took a quick glance around, assured myself no one could see, and slipped the button into the pocket of my sweatshirt. I hesitated for a moment, but once the item was in my pocket, there was no turning back. I had never before stolen anything; but what was done was done. A few seconds later, my sister appeared and asked, "So, did you decide to buy the button?"

4   "No, I guess not." I hoped my voice didn't quaver. As we headed for the entrance, my heart began to race. I just had to get out of that store. Only a few more yards to go and I'd be safe. As we crossed the threshold, I heaved

a sigh of relief. I was home free. I thought about how sly I had been, and I felt proud of my accomplishment.

An unexpected tap on my shoulder startled me. I whirled around to find a middle-aged man, dressed in street clothes, flashing some type of badge and politely asking me to empty my pockets. Where did this man come from? How did he know? I was so sure that no one had seen me! On the verge of panicking, I told myself that all I had to do was give this man his button back, say I was sorry, and go on my way. After all, it was only a 75-cent item.

Next thing I knew, he was talking about calling the police and having me arrested and thrown in jail, as if he had just nabbed a professional thief instead of a terrified kid. I couldn't believe what he was saying.

"Jean, what's going on?"

The sound of my sister's voice eased the pressure a bit. She always managed to get me out of trouble. She would come through this time too.

"Excuse me. Are you a relative of this young girl?"

"Yes, I'm her sister. What's the problem?"

"Well, I just caught her shoplifting, and I'm afraid I'll have to call the police."

"What did she take?"

"This button."

"A button? You are having a thirteen-year-old arrested for stealing a button?"

"I'm sorry, but she broke the law."

The man led us through the store and into an office, where we waited for the police officers to arrive. Susan had found my grandmother and brother, who, still shocked, didn't say a word. The thought of going to jail terrified me, not because of jail itself but because of the encounter with my parents afterward. Not more than ten minutes later, two officers arrived and placed me under arrest. They said that I was to be taken to the station alone. Then they handcuffed me and led me out of the store. I felt alone and scared. I had counted on my sister being with me, but now I had to muster up the courage to face this ordeal all by myself.

As the officers led me through the mall, I sensed a hundred pairs of eyes staring at me. My face flushed, and I broke out in a sweat. Now everyone knew I was a criminal. In their eyes, I was a juvenile delinquent, and thank God the cops were getting me off the streets. The worst part was thinking my grandmother might be having the same thoughts. The humiliation at that moment was overwhelming. I felt like Hester Prynne being put on public display for everyone to ridicule.

That short walk through the mall seemed to take hours. But once we reached the squad car, time raced by. I was read my rights and questioned. We were at the police station within minutes. Everything happened so fast I didn't have a chance to feel remorse for my crime. Instead, I viewed what was happening to me as if it were a movie. Being searched, although embarrassing, somehow seemed to be exciting. All the movies and television programs I had seen were actually coming to life. This is what it was really like. But why were criminals always portrayed as frightened and regretful? I was having fun. I thought I had nothing to fear—until I was allowed my one phone call. I was trembling as I dialed home. I didn't know what I was going to say to my parents, especially my mother.

19   "Hi, Dad, this is Jean."

20   "We've been waiting for you to call."

21   "Did Susie tell you what happened?"

22   "Yeah, but we haven't told your mother. I think you should tell her what you did and where you are."

23   "You mean she doesn't even know where I am?"

24   "No, I want you to explain it to her."

25   There was a pause as he called my mother to the phone. For the first time that night, I was close to tears. I wished I had never stolen that stupid pin. I wanted to give the phone to one of the officers because I was too ashamed to tell my mother the truth, but I had no choice.

26   "Jean, where are you?"

27   "I'm, umm, in jail."

28   "Why? What for?"

29   "Shoplifting."

30   "Oh no, Jean. Why? Why did you do it?"

31   "I don't know. No reason. I just did it."

32   "I don't understand. What did you take? Why did you do it? You had plenty of money with you."

33   "I know but I just did it. I can't explain why. Mom, I'm sorry."

34   "I'm afraid sorry isn't enough. I'm horribly disappointed in you."

35   Long after we got off the phone, while I sat in an empty jail cell waiting for my parents to pick me up, I could still distinctly hear the disappointment and hurt in my mother's voice. I cried. The tears weren't for me but for her and the pain I had put her through. I felt like a terrible human being. I would rather have stayed in jail than confront my mom right then. I dreaded each passing minute that brought our encounter closer. When the officer came to release me, I hesitated, actually not wanting to leave. We went to the front desk, where I had to sign a form to retrieve my belongings. I saw my parents a few yards away, and my heart raced. A large knot formed in my stomach. I fought back the tears.

36   Not a word was spoken as we walked to the car. Slowly, I sank into the back seat anticipating the scolding. Expecting harsh tones, I was relieved to hear almost the opposite from my father.

37   "I'm not going to punish you, and I'll tell you why. Although I think what you did was wrong, I think what the police did was more wrong. There's no excuse for locking a thirteen-year-old behind bars. That doesn't mean I condone what you did, but I think you've been punished enough already."

As I looked from my father's eyes to my mother's, I knew this ordeal was   38
over. Although it would never be forgotten, the incident was not mentioned
again.

READING FOR MEANING

Reading for meaning involves three activities:

- reading to comprehend,
- reading to respond, and
- reading to analyze assumptions.

Write a page or so explaining your understanding of the meaning of
Brandt's story, a personal response you have to it, and one of its assumptions.

READING LIKE A WRITER

Autobiographers who are focusing on a remembered event or person

- narrate the event or anecdotes,
- present people,
- present places, and
- convey autobiographical significance.

Choose one of these strategies in Brandt's story, and analyze it carefully through close rereading and annotating. Then write several sentences
explaining what you have learned, giving specific examples from the reading
to support your explanation. Add a few sentences evaluating how successfully Brandt uses the strategy to dramatize the experience for her readers.

Reviewing What Makes an Effective Essay

Autobiography

Analyze

Choose one reading from this chapter that seems to you especially effective. Before rereading the selection, jot down one or two reasons you remember it as an example of good autobiographical writing.

Reread your chosen selection, and add further notes about what makes it a particularly successful example of autobiography. Consider the selection's purpose and how well it achieves that purpose for its intended readers. (You can make an informed guess about the intended readers and their expectations by noting the publication source of the essay.) Then assess how well the essay uses the writing strategies of narrating events or anecdotes, presenting people and places, and conveying autobiographical significance. You can review these strategies in the Guide to Reading Autobiography (p. 22).

Write

Write at least a page supporting your choice of this reading as an example of effective autobiographical writing. Refer to details and specific parts of the essay as you explain how it works as autobiography and as you justify your evaluation of its effectiveness. You need not argue that it is the best reading in the chapter or that it is flawless, only that it is, in your view, a strong example of the genre.

A GUIDE TO WRITING AUTOBIOGRAPHY

The readings in this chapter have helped you learn a great deal about autobiographical writing. You have seen that some autobiographies tell dramatic stories, while others present vivid portraits of people who played a significant role in the writer's life. Whether the focus is on events or people, you have discovered that the overall purpose for writers of autobiography is to convey the significance — both the meaning and the importance — of their past experience. In so doing, autobiographers often present themselves as individuals affected by social and cultural influences.

As a reader of autobiography, you have examined how autobiographers convey through their writing drama and vividness as well as significance. But you may have also found that different readers interpret the significance of an autobiographical selection differently. In other words, you have seen how the meanings readers make are affected by their personal experience as well as their social and cultural contexts.

Having learned how autobiographers invest their writing with drama, vividness, and significance and how readers interpret and respond to autobiographical writing, you can now approach autobiography more confidently as a writer. You can more readily imagine the problems you must solve as a writer of autobiography, the materials and possibilities you have to work with, the choices and decisions you must make. This Guide to Writing offers detailed suggestions for writing autobiographical essays and resources to help you meet the special challenges this kind of writing presents.

INVENTION AND RESEARCH

The following activities will help you choose a memorable *event* or an important *person* to write about, recall details about your subject, and explore its significance in your life. Completing these activities will produce a record of remembered details and thoughts that will be invaluable as you draft your essay.

Choosing a Subject

List the most promising subjects you can think of, beginning with any you listed for the Considering Ideas for Your Own Writing activities following the readings in this chapter. Rather than limiting yourself to the first subject that comes to mind, take a few minutes to consider your options and list as many subjects as you can. Below are some criteria that can help you choose a promising subject, followed by additional suggestions for the types of events and people you might consider writing about.

Criteria for Choosing a Subject

- Writing about the event or relationship with the person should reveal something significant about you, something you are willing to disclose to your readers.

- The event should take place over a short period of time, but the relationship with the person could extend over a long period of time and include several anecdotes.

- Your writing about the event or relationship should center on some kind of conflict (for example, a power struggle between you and the person, an obstacle you faced together, a confrontation with others or with an institution).

- Your writing about the event or relationship should reveal complex or ambivalent feelings (rather than superficial or sentimental ones that oversimplify the subject or make it predictable).

- Your writing about the event or relationship should lead readers to think about their own experience and about the cultural forces that shape their lives and yours.

Events

- a difficult situation (for example, when you had to make a tough choice, or when you struggled to perform a challenging task)

- an incident that shaped you in a particular way or revealed an aspect of your personality you had not seen before (for example, independence, insecurity, ambition, jealousy, or heroism)

- an occasion when something did not turn out as you thought it would (for example, when you expected to be criticized but were praised or ignored instead, or when you were convinced you would succeed but failed)

- an encounter with another person that changed you (for example, altered how you see yourself, changed your ideas about other people, or led you to understand someone else's point of view)

People

- someone who made you feel you were part of a larger community or had something worthwhile to contribute or someone who made you feel alienated or like an outsider

- someone who helped you develop a previously unknown or undeveloped side of yourself, or led you to question assumptions or stereotypes you had about other people

- someone who surprised, pleased, or disappointed you (for example, someone you admired who let you down or someone you did not appreciate who turned out to be admirable)

- someone in a position of power over you or someone over whom you had power

Developing Your Subject

The following activities will help you develop your subject by recalling actions that happened during the event or by telling anecdotes that reveal something about the person. These activities will also help you recall details of the place and people.

Recalling the Event or Person

Event.   Write a quick sketch telling what happened. Don't worry about what you're leaving out or about making your narrative dramatic; later you can fill in the details and shape the story.

Person.   List anecdotes you could tell about the person, choose one, and write a quick sketch telling what happened. If more than one promising anecdote comes to mind, go ahead and write about each of them. Later, you can decide whether to include all of these anecdotes. Exploring them now will help you understand what you want readers to know about the person and your relationship.

Followup.   Read your sketch looking for surprise, confrontation, crisis, change, or discovery that might suggest why the event or relationship is significant for you. Try dramatizing that part of your sketch by adding dialogue, your thoughts and feelings at the time, and/or your present perspective on what happened. (See below for advice on reconstructing dialogue as well as recalling feelings and exploring present perspectives.)

Presenting Important People

Event.   Recall other people who were involved, and write a brief description of each person.

Person.   List aspects of the person's appearance and dress, ways of walking and gesturing, tone of voice and mannerisms — anything that would help readers see the person as you remember her or him.

Reconstructing Dialogue.   Write a few lines of dialogue that you could use to convey something important about the event or to give readers an impression of the person you have chosen to write about. You may use direct quotation, enclosing the words you remember being spoken in quotation marks, or you may use indirect quotation, paraphrasing and summarizing what was said. Try to re-create the give-and-take quality of normal conversation in the dialogue.

Describing Important Places. Identify the place where the event happened or a place you associate with the person, and detail what you see in the scene as you visualize it. Try to recall specific sensory details — size, shape, color, condition, and texture of the scene or memorable objects in it. Imagine the place from the front and from the side, from a distance and from close up.

Considering Visuals. Think about whether visuals — photographs, postcards, ticket stubs — would strengthen your presentation of the event or person. If you submit your essay electronically to other students and your instructor or if you post it on a Web site, consider including snippets of film or sound as well as photographs or other memorabilia that might give readers a more vivid sense of the time, place, and people about which you are writing. Visual and audio materials are not a requirement of an effective autobiographical essay, as you can tell from the readings in this chapter, but they could add a new dimension to your writing. If you want to use photographs or recordings of people, though, be sure to request their permission.

Reflecting on Your Subject

The following activities will help you think about the significance of your subject by recalling your remembered feelings and thoughts as well as exploring your present perspective. The activities will also help you consider your purpose in writing about this subject and formulate a tentative thesis statement.

Recalling Your Feelings and Thoughts. Write for a few minutes, trying to recall your thoughts and feelings when the event was occurring or when you knew the person. What did you feel — in control or powerless, proud or embarrassed, vulnerable, detached, judgmental? How did you show or express your feelings? What did you want others to think of you at the time? What did you think of yourself? What were the immediate consequences for you personally?

Exploring Your Present Perspective. Write for a few minutes, trying to express your present thoughts and feelings as you look back on the event or person. How have your feelings changed? What insights do you now have? What does your present perspective reveal about what you were like at the time? Try looking at the event or person in broad cultural or social terms. For example, consider whether you or anyone else upset gender expectations or felt out of place in some way.

Considering Your Purpose. Write for several minutes exploring what you want your readers to understand about the significance of the event or person. Use the following questions to help clarify your thoughts:

- What will writing about this event or person enable you to suggest about yourself as an individual? What will it let you suggest about the social and cultural forces that helped shape you — for example, how people exercise power over one another, how family and community values and attitudes affect individuals, or how economic and social conditions influence our sense of self?

- What do you not understand about the event or relationship? What about it still puzzles you or seems contradictory? What do you feel ambivalent about?

- What about your subject do you expect will seem familiar to your readers? What do you think will surprise them, perhaps getting them to think in new ways or to question some of their assumptions and stereotypes?

Formulating a Tentative Thesis Statement.   Review what you wrote for Considering Your Purpose, and add another two or three sentences that will help you convey to readers the significance of the event or person in your life. Try to write sentences that do not just summarize what you have written but that also extend your insights and reflections. These sentences may be contradictory because they express ambivalent feelings. They also must necessarily be partial and speculative because you may never understand fully the event's or person's significance.

Keep in mind that readers do not expect you to begin your essay with the kind of explicit introductory thesis statement typical of argumentative essays. None of the readings in this chapter offers to readers an explicit thesis statement explaining the significance of the event or person. Instead, the readings convey the significance by combining showing with telling in their narration of events and descriptions of people and places. And yet it is possible for readers to infer from each reading an implied thesis or impression of the significance.

For example, some readers might decide that Dillard wants readers to think that what was most significant and memorable about the event was the way the man threw himself into the chase, showing that childlike enthusiasm sometimes can survive into adulthood. Other readers might focus on the idea that what was significant was that the man as well as the children "all played by the rules" (paragraph 16) and that when people play by the rules they act with honor and nobility. If, like you, Dillard had tried to write a few sentences about the significance she hoped to convey in writing about this small but memorable event in her life, she might have written sentences like these.

Nearly all first attempts at stating a thesis are eventually revised once drafting gets underway. Writing the first draft helps autobiographers discover what they think and feel about their subject and find ways to convey its significance without ever spelling it out directly. Just because there is no explicit thesis statement in an autobiography does not mean that the essay lacks focus or fails to convey significance.

DRAFTING

The following guidelines will help you set goals for your draft, plan its organization, choose relevant details, think about a useful sentence strategy, and decide how to begin.

Setting Goals

Establishing goals for your draft before you begin writing will enable you to make decisions and work more confidently. Consider the following questions now, and keep them in mind as you draft. They will help you set goals for drafting as well as recall how the writers you have read in this chapter tried to achieve similar goals.

- *How can I present my subject vividly and memorably to readers?* Should I rely on dialogue to present people and relationships, as so many of the writers in this chapter do, especially Brandt? Or should I concentrate on presenting action rather than dialogue, like Dillard and Rodriguez? Can I use visual or other sensory details, as Shah, Rodriguez, and Benioff do, to give readers a vivid impression of the person and place while also establishing the significance of my subject?

- *How can I help readers understand the meaning and importance of the event or person?* Can I build the suspense, as all of the writers do? Can I show how I changed, as Shah and Benioff do?

- *How can I avoid superficial or one-dimensional presentations of my experience and my relations with others?* Knowing that my readers will not expect easy answers about what makes the event or person significant, how can I satisfy their expectations for writing that has some depth and complexity? How might I employ one or more of the strategies illustrated by the writers I have read in this chapter — the paradox in Dillard's feeling both terror and pleasure as she is chased by the man from the black Buick? Benioff's love-hate relationship with his coach? What contradictions, paradoxes, or ironies exist in my own story?

Organizing Your Draft

With these goals in mind, plan your draft by making a tentative outline. Although your plan may change as you write and revise your draft, outlining before you begin drafting can help you get organized. If you are uncertain about how to organize your material, review how some of the writers in this chapter organize their autobiographical essays.

For an *event,* outline the sequence of main actions, from the beginning to the end of the event.

For a *person,* outline the order of the recurring activities, or anecdotes you will use to present the person, interspersing relevant character traits, physical details, and dialogue.

Working with Sources

Using Memory and Memorabilia

In the essays that you will write in later chapters of this book, you will rely on interviews, observation, and print and online sources to support your explanations or arguments. In writing about a remembered event or person, however, you will rely almost entirely on memory—your own memory and that of others. You may also refer to memorabilia such as pictures, videos, letters, and documents. Aleksandra Crapanzano uses a variety of such sources to present Margaret in "Lobster Lessons."

Crapanzano's primary source is her own memory, as she makes explicit in the following sentences: "From that first dinner with Margaret in her cottage, I remember her smiling at me . . . " (paragraph 5). None of the other writers is as direct as Crapanzano is. Although they all relate what they remember, they do not say so because they present their memories in specific terms, often referring to a particular time and place, as we can see in these brief examples: "On one weekday morning after Christmas" (Dillard, paragraph 3) and "One evening dusk came early in South San Gabriel" (Rodriguez, paragraph 1).

In addition to recounting firsthand memory, writers may also relay what others have told them. Benioff, for example, introduces Rick as "The mythical Rick. I had heard of him many times before. All the older players knew him by his first name and always spoke of him as a friend" (paragraph 3). Similarly, Crapanzano tells us that "John had warned" her about his great-aunt's diet; she had "already heard tales of her spartan daily regimen" before meeting Margaret (paragraph 3).

Crapanzano is the only writer in this chapter who uses memorabilia to enhance her narrative. For example, she includes two photographs, and although she doesn't refer to them specifically, the photo of John wearing khakis with a good bottle of wine in hand corresponds to how she describes their pre-dinner routine (paragraphs 15–16). She also refers to the box of recipes Margaret "had clipped from newspapers and magazines throughout the winter months" (paragraph 13). It is not clear if Crapanzano still has the box of recipes with Margaret's notes about which ones "she particularly liked" (13). Including visuals and, in online texts, other media such as audio and video can help bring memory to life.

Choosing Relevant Details

The invention and research activities helped you generate many details, probably more than you can use. To decide which details to include in your draft and which to leave out, consider how well each detail contributes to the overall impression you want to create. But before you discard any details that seem irrelevant, think again about what they might suggest about the significance of your subject. Sometimes, seemingly irrelevant details or ones that do not fit neatly can lead you to new insights.

Considering a Useful Sentence Strategy

As you draft your essay, you will need to present the details you have chosen in ways that help readers imagine the people, places, and events. One effective way to do so is to use sentences with participial phrases. These phrases are based on verb forms called participles: either present participles, ending in -*ing* (*being, longing, grasping, drinking*), or past participles, usually ending in *ed, d, en, n,* or *t* (*baked, found, driven, torn, sent*). Participial phrases help you show simultaneous actions, make an action or image more specific or vivid, and relate what you or someone else was thinking or feeling at the time of an action.

- To show simultaneous actions:

  Every time I glanced back, *choking for breath,* I expected he would have quit. (Dillard, paragraph 13)

  I whirled around to find a middle-aged man, dressed in street clothes, *flashing some type of badge* and *politely asking me to empty my pockets.* (Brandt, paragraph 5)

- To make a previously mentioned action or image more specific and vivid:

  Shining a flashlight inside the building, the officer spotted Tino's misshapen body on the floor, *sprinkled over with shards of glass.* (Rodriguez, paragraph 34)

  Amina stormed in, *scattering servants before her like chaff.* (Shah, paragraph 7)

- To relate what you or someone else was thinking or feeling at the time:

  Slowly, I sank into the back seat *anticipating the scolding.* (Brandt, paragraph 36)

  I waited and waited, *biting my tongue.* (Crapanzano, paragraph 7)

  When I reached for a head of garlic, he simply shook his head in dismay, *sensing perhaps the inevitable clash of palates in two of the women he loved best.* (Crapanzano, paragraph 4)

From that first dinner with Margaret in her cottage, I remember her smiling at me as the three of us clinked glasses over the table, *making me feel wonderfully welcome.* (Crapanzano, paragraph 5)

Participial phrases are not required for a successful autobiographical essay, yet they do provide writers an effective sentence option. For another sentence strategy that can strengthen your autobiographical writing, the use of absolute phrases to help readers imagine actions and objects, see Chapter 3, pages 81–146.

Writing the Beginning

To engage your readers' interest from the start, consider beginning with a compelling graphic description (as Rodriguez and Benioff do), a startling action (as Dillard does), or a vivid memory (as Shah does) or by creating a sense of expectation (as Brandt does). You might have to try two or three different beginnings before finding a promising way to start, but do not agonize for too long over the first sentence. Try out any possible beginning, and see where it takes you.

READING A DRAFT CRITICALLY

Getting a critical reading of your draft will help you see how to improve it. Your instructor may schedule class time for reading drafts, or you may want to ask a classmate or a tutor in the writing center to read your draft. Ask your reader to use the following guidelines and to write out a response for you to consult during your revision.

Read for a First Impression

1. **Read the draft without stopping, and then write a few sentences giving your general impression.**

2. **Identify one aspect of the draft that seems especially effective.**

Read Again to Suggest Improvements

1. **Recommend ways to make the narrative more dramatic and telling:**

   For a draft presenting an *event:*

   - Point to any scenes where the action seems to drag or become confusing.

- Suggest places where the drama might be intensified — by using more active verbs, or shifting the placement of background information or descriptive detail, for example.

- Indicate where dialogue could add drama to a confrontation scene.

For a draft presenting a *person:*

- Note which anecdotes and recurring activities seem especially effective in illustrating something important about the person or the relationship.

- Point to one weak anecdote or recurring activity, and suggest how it could be made more effective, such as by adding graphic details and dialogue or by telling how it relates to the person's significance.

- Indicate any passages where direct quotations could be more effectively presented indirectly by paraphrasing, summarizing, or combining a striking quotation with a summary.

2. **Suggest ways to make the description more vivid or to convey more effectively the dominant impression of the essay:**

- Describe the impression you get from the writer's description of the event or person.

- Identify one or two passages where you think the description is especially vivid (for example, where the visual details and images help you picture the event or person).

- Point to any passages where the description could be made more vivid or where it seems to contradict the impression you get from other parts of the essay.

3. **Suggest how the autobiographical significance could be better developed:**

- Briefly explain your understanding of the significance, indicating anything that puzzles or surprises you about the event or person.

- Note any word choice, contradiction, or irony — in the way people and places are described or in the way the story is told — that alerts you to a deeper meaning that the writer could develop.

- Point to any passages where the writer needs to clarify the historical, social, or cultural dimensions of the experience or relationship.

4. **Suggest how the organization could be improved. Consider the overall plan of the essay, perhaps by making a scratch outline (see Appendix 1 for an example):**

   - For an *event,* indicate any passages where narrative transitions or verb tense markers are needed to make the story unfold more logically and clearly.

   - For a *person,* suggest where topic sentences or transitions could be added to indicate more clearly what impression of the person the anecdotes or recurring activities are intended to convey.

5. **Evaluate the effectiveness of visuals:**

   - If any visuals do not seem relevant, or if there seem to be too many visuals, identify the ones that the writer could consider dropping, explaining your thinking.

   - If a visual does not seem to be appropriately placed, suggest a better place for it.

REVISING

This section offers suggestions for revising your draft. Revising means reenvisioning your draft, trying to see it in a new way, given your purpose and readers, in order to develop a more engaging, coherent autobiography.

The biggest mistake you can make while revising is to focus initially on words or sentences. Instead, first try to see your draft as a whole to assess its likely impact on your readers. Think imaginatively and boldly about cutting unconvincing material, adding new material, and moving material around. Your computer makes even drastic revisions physically easy, but you still need to make the mental effort and decisions that will improve your draft.

You may have received help with this challenge from a classmate or tutor who gave your draft a critical reading. If so, keep this feedback in mind as you decide which parts of your draft need revising and what specific changes you could make. The following suggestions will help you solve problems and strengthen your essay.

TROUBLESHOOTING YOUR DRAFT

To Make the Narrative More Dramatic and Telling

Problem	Suggestions for Revising
The story or anecdote meanders and seems to have no point or significance.	• Focus the action so that it builds more directly toward the climax. • Make the significance explicit by adding remembered or present thoughts and feelings.
The narrative drags or tension slackens.	• Use more active verbs. • Use shorter sentences or participial phrases to show simultaneous actions. • Dramatize the conflict with dialogue. • Add transitions to propel the story through time.
Background information or descriptive detail interrupts the drama.	• Cut the information or detail or scale it back. • Move the information or detail to somewhere else in the essay.
The dialogue does not seem interesting or important.	• Use indirect instead of direct dialogue or combine the two. • Paraphrase or summarize what was said, quoting only memorable or significant words or phrases.

To Present People Vividly

Problem	Suggestions for Revising
The description of a person is vague or sketchy.	• Add details showing what the person looks like or how he or she gestures, moves, or talks.
Some of the detail seems inconsistent or contradictory.	• Cut the inconsistent or contradictory parts. • Use the inconsistencies to develop the significance of the story.
The description does not convey the impression you intended.	• Cut some descriptive details and add others. • Rethink the impression you want your writing to convey and the significance it suggests.

To Describe Places Vividly

Problem	Suggestions for Revising
Details about a place do not contribute to the dominant impression you want to convey.	• Cut unnecessary details. • Consider whether contradictory details suggest ways to deepen the significance.

To Describe Places Vividly

Problem	Suggestions for Revising
Readers cannot imagine the place.	• Add more sensory detail to evoke the sense of sight, touch, smell, taste, and/or hearing. • Identify items in the place by name using specific nouns and descriptive adjectives.
The point of view is inconsistent or confusing.	• Change or simplify it to make it consistent and clear.

To Convey the Autobiographical Significance

Problem	Suggestions for Revising
Readers may not understand the significance to you of the person or event.	• Expand or add passages where you convey the significance more directly. • Use participial phrases to reveal what you were thinking or feeling as the event occurred or as you interacted with the person. • Add your current thoughts and feelings as you look back on the event or person.
The significance seems too pat or simplistic.	• Explore and develop contradictions and complexities in how you view the significance. • Express ambivalent feelings.
Readers may not understand the importance of the social, cultural, or historical context.	• Give background information to reveal important influences.

To Make the Organizational Plan More Effective

Problem	Suggestions for Revising
Readers may be confused about what happened when.	• Add or clarify transitions. • Add verb tense markers.
Readers may not see clearly how the anecdotes or recurring activities contribute to the portrait of the person.	• Add forecasting statements. • Add topic sentences.

EDITING AND PROOFREADING

After you have revised your essay, be sure to spend some time checking for errors in usage, punctuation, and mechanics and considering matters of style. If you keep a list of errors you typically make, begin by checking your draft against this list. Ask someone else to proofread your essay before you print out a copy for your instructor or send it electronically.

From our research on student writing, we know that essays dealing with autobiographical subjects have a high percentage of errors in verb tense and punctuation. You should proofread your narration for verb tense errors and your description for punctuation errors — such as comma splices and missing commas after introductory elements. Check a writer's handbook for help with these potential problems.

Reflecting on What You Have Learned

Autobiography

In this chapter, you have read critically several pieces of autobiography and have written one of your own. To better remember what you have learned, pause now to reflect on the reading and writing activities you completed in this chapter.

1. Write a page or so reflecting on what you have learned. Begin by describing what you are most pleased with in your essay. Then explain what you think contributed to your achievement. Be specific about this contribution.

   - If it was something you learned from the readings, indicate which readings and specifically what you learned from them.

   - If it came from your invention writing, point out the section or sections that helped you most.

   - If you got good advice from a critical reader, explain exactly how the person helped you — perhaps by helping you understand a particular problem in your draft or by helping you add a new dimension to your writing.

   - Try to write about your achievement in terms of what you have learned about the genre.

2. Reflect more generally on how you tend to interpret autobiographical writing, your own as well as other writers'. Consider some of the following questions: In reading for meaning, do you tend to find yourself interpreting the significance of the event or person in terms of the writer's personal feelings, sense of self-esteem, or psychological well-being? Or do you more often think of significance in terms of larger social or economic influences — for example, whether the writer is male or female, rich or poor, suburban or urban, African American or Anglo? Where do you think you learned to interpret the significance of people's stories about themselves and their relationships — from your family, friends, television, school?

Observation

Certain kinds of writing are based on fresh observation or direct investigation. Travel writers, for example, profile places they have visited; naturalists describe phenomena they have observed undisturbed in nature. Investigative reporters or clinical psychologists write up interviews with individuals, while cultural anthropologists and educational researchers write ethnographies of groups they have studied in depth. Much of what we know about people and the world we learn from this kind of writing.

Writing about your own observations offers special challenges and rewards. It requires you to pay more attention than you normally do to everyday activities. You need to look with all your senses and give your curiosity free rein. Taking a questioning stance will enable you to make discoveries in even the most mundane settings. In addition, it helps to take voluminous notes because you might not know what is significant until you begin to sort through the observations, information, and quotations you have collected. That way, after the work of observing and interviewing is done, another kind of equally challenging and rewarding work can begin—making meaning of the bits and pieces you have gathered. Analyzing and synthesizing your notes, you interpret your subject and decide what you want to tell your readers about it. These activities of close observation and careful note-taking, combined with thoughtful analysis and imaginative synthesis, form the basic strategies of researching and learning in many areas of college study.

When writing about your observations, you will have an immediate advantage if you choose a place, an activity, or a person unfamiliar to readers. But even if the subject is familiar, you can still intrigue and inform readers by presenting it in a new light or by focusing on a little noticed or poorly understood aspect of the subject. By focusing on certain details, you help readers imagine what the place looks, sounds, and smells like; picture how the people dress, gesture, and talk; and understand your idea about or interpretation of the subject.

The readings in this chapter will help you learn a lot about observational writing. From the readings and from the ideas for writing that follow each reading, you will get ideas for your own observational essay. As you read and write about the selections, keep in mind the following assignment, which sets out the goals for writing an observational essay. To support your writing of this assignment, the chapter concludes with a Guide to Writing Observational Essays.

THE WRITING ASSIGNMENT

Write an observational essay about an intriguing place, person, or activity in your community. Your essay may be a brief profile of an individual based on one or two interviews; a description of a place or activity observed once or twice; or a longer, more fully developed profile of a person, place, or activity based on observational visits and interviews conducted over several days. Observe your subject closely, and then present what you have learned in a way that both informs and engages readers.

WRITING SITUATIONS FOR OBSERVATIONAL ESSAYS

As we indicated earlier, many people—including travel writers, investigative reporters, clinical psychologists, and cultural anthropologists—write essays based on observations and interviews. In your other college courses, you may have an opportunity to write an observational essay like one of the following:

- For an art history course, a student writes about a local artist recently commissioned to paint outdoor murals for the city. The student visits the artist's studio and talks with him about the process of painting murals, large pictures painted on walls or the sides of buildings. The artist invites the student to spend the following day as a part of a team of local art students and neighborhood volunteers working on the mural under the artist's direction. This firsthand experience helps the student profile the artist, present some of the students, and give readers a clear impression of the process of collaboration involved in mural painting.

- For a journalism course, a student profiles a typical day in the life of an award-winning scientist. He spends a day observing the scientist at home and at work, and he interviews colleagues, students, and family, as well as the scientist herself. Her daily life, he learns, is very much like that of other working mothers—a constant effort to balance the demands of her career against the needs of her family. He conveys this idea in his essay by alternating between details about the scientist's work and those about her family life.

- For a sociology class, a student writes about a controversial urban renewal project to replace decaying houses with a library and park. To learn about the history of the project, she reads newspaper reports and interviews people who helped plan the project as well as some neighborhood residents and activists who oppose it. She also tours the site with the project manager to see what is actually being done. In addition to presenting different points of view about the project, her essay describes the library and park in detail, including pictures of the neighborhood before the project and drawings of what it will look like afterward.

Thinking about Your Experience

Observation

Before studying a type of writing, it is useful to spend some time thinking about what you already know about it. You may have written about your firsthand observations, describing what you saw or heard, for a school assignment or during a trip. If you haven't written observational essays or reports, you have certainly made them orally to friends and family.

- Recall one occasion when you reported your observations orally or in writing, and then consider questions like these: Why were you communicating what you saw and heard to members of this particular audience? Did you make your report primarily to teach them something, to show that you had learned something yourself, to entertain them, or for some other reason? What did you choose to emphasize? Why?

- Reflect also on observational reports you have read, heard, or seen on television. If you recall one such report in some detail, try to identify what made it interesting to you. What tone did the narrator adopt? What descriptive details, dialogue, or commentary stood out for you?

- Write at least a page about your experience with observational writing.

A GUIDE TO READING OBSERVATIONAL ESSAYS

This guide introduces you to the basic features and strategies typical of observational writing by looking closely at a brief but intriguing profile of Albert Yeganeh and his unique New York City restaurant, Soup Kitchen International. Focus first on *reading for meaning*, looking closely at the essay's content and ideas. Then, to learn about how the unnamed *New Yorker* writer crafts the essay, try *reading like a writer* by analyzing the strategies that make the essay vivid and informative. These two activities—reading for meaning and reading like a writer—follow every reading in this chapter.

The *New Yorker*

Soup

"Soup" was published anonymously in a 1989 issue of the New Yorker, *a magazine read by many people across the country who enjoy its cartoons, short stories, music and art reviews, political and social commentary, and profiles of people and places. The subject of this essay is Albert Yeganeh, the creative and demanding owner/chef of a small take-out restaurant that serves only soup. In 1995, Yeganeh's restaurant inspired an episode of the then-popular television program* Seinfeld.

The writer of "Soup" relies extensively on dialogue quoted from the interview to keep the focus on Yeganeh's personality and ideas. Readers can readily imagine the reporter interviewing Yeganeh, writing down soup names and ingredients, observing people in line, and even standing in line for a bowl of soup. As you read, notice the prominence given to reporting what Yeganeh told the writer.

1   When Albert Yeganeh says "Soup is my lifeblood," he means it. And when he says "I am extremely hard to please," he means that, too. Working like a demon alchemist in a tiny storefront kitchen at 259-A West Fifty-fifth Street, Mr. Yeganeh creates anywhere from eight to seventeen soups every weekday. His concoctions are so popular that a wait of half an hour at the lunchtime peak is not uncommon, although there are strict rules for conduct in line. But more on that later.

2   "I am psychologically kind of a health freak," Mr. Yeganeh said the other day, in a lisping staccato of Armenian origin. "And I know that soup is the greatest meal in the world. It's very good for your digestive system. And I use only the best, the freshest ingredients. I am a perfectionist. When I make a clam soup, I use three different kinds of clams. Every other place uses canned clams. I'm called crazy. I am not crazy. People don't realize why I get so upset. It's because if the soup is not perfect and I'm still selling it, it's a torture. It's *my* soup, and that's why I'm so upset. First you clean and then you cook. I don't believe that ninety-nine per cent of the restaurants in New York know how to clean a tomato. I tell my crew to wash the parsley *eight* times. If they wash it five or six times, I scare them. I tell them they'll go to jail if there is sand in the parsley. One time, I found a mushroom on the floor, and I fired that guy who left it there." He spread

his arms and added, "This place is the only one like it in . . . in . . . the whole earth! One day, I hope to learn something from the other places, but so far I haven't. For example, the other day I went to a very fancy restaurant and had borscht. I had to send it back. It was *junk*. I could see all the chemicals in it. I never use chemicals. Last weekend, I had lobster bisque in Brooklyn, a very well-known place. It was *junk*. When I make a lobster bisque, I use a whole lobster. You know, I never advertise. I don't have to. All the big-shot chefs and the kings of the hotels come here to see what *I'm* doing."

As you approach Mr. Yeganeh's Soup Kitchen International from a dis-   3
tance, the first thing you notice about it is the awning, which proclaims "Homemade Hot, Cold, Diet Soups." The second thing you notice is an aroma so delicious that it makes you want to take a bite out of the air. The third thing you notice, in front of the kitchen, is an electric signboard that flashes, saying, "Today's Soups . . . Chicken Vegetable . . . Mexican Beef Chili . . . Cream of Watercress . . . Italian Sausage . . . Clam Bisque . . . Beef Barley . . . Due to Cold Weather . . . For Most Efficient and Fastest Service the Line Must . . . Be Kept Moving . . . Please . . . Have Your Money . . . Ready . . . Pick the Soup of Your Choice . . . Move to Your Extreme . . . Left After Ordering."

"I am not prejudiced against color or religion," Mr. Yeganeh told us,   4
and he jabbed an index finger at the flashing sign. "Whoever follows that I treat very well. My regular customers don't say anything. They are very intelligent and well educated. They know I'm just trying to move the line. The New York cop is very smart—he sees everything but says nothing. But the young girl who wants to stop and tell you how nice you look and hold everyone up—*yah*!" He made a guillotining motion with his hand. "I tell you, I hate to work with the public. They treat me like a slave. My philosophy is: The customer is always wrong and I'm always right. I raised my prices to try to get rid of some of these people, but it didn't work."

The other day, Mr. Yeganeh was dressed in chef's whites with orange   5
smears across his chest, which may have been some of the carrot soup cooking in a huge pot on a little stove in one corner. A three-foot-long handheld mixer from France sat on the sink, looking like an overgrown gardening tool. Mr. Yeganeh spoke to two young helpers in a twisted Armenian-Spanish barrage, then said to us, "I have no overhead, no trained waitresses, and I have the cashier here." He pointed to himself theatrically. Beside the doorway, a glass case with fresh green celery, red and yellow peppers, and purple eggplant was topped by five big gray soup urns. According to a piece of cardboard taped to the door, you can buy Mr. Yeganeh's soups in three sizes, costing from four to fifteen dollars. The order of any well-behaved customer is accompanied by little waxpaper packets of bread, fresh vegetables (such as scallions and radishes), fresh

fruit (such as cherries or an orange), a chocolate mint, and a plastic spoon. No coffee, tea, or other drinks are served.

6   "I get my recipes from books and theories and my own taste," Mr. Yeganeh said. "At home, I have several hundreds of books. When I do research, I find that I don't know anything. Like cabbage is a cancer fighter, and some fish is good for your heart but some is bad. Every day, I should have one sweet, one spicy, one cream, one vegetable soup—and they *must* change, they should always taste a little different." He added that he wasn't sure how extensive his repertoire was, but that it probably includes at least eighty soups, among them African peanut butter, Greek moussaka, hamburger, Reuben, B.L.T., asparagus and caviar, Japanese shrimp miso, chicken chili, Irish corned beef and cabbage, Swiss chocolate, French calf's brain, Korean beef ball, Italian shrimp and eggplant Parmesan, buffalo, ham and egg, short rib, Russian beef Stroganoff, turkey cacciatore, and Indian mulligatawny. "The chicken and the seafood are an addiction, and when I have French garlic soup I let people have only one small container each," he said. "The doctors and nurses love that one."

7   A lunch line of thirty people stretched down the block from Mr. Yeganeh's doorway. Behind a construction worker was a man in expensive leather, who was in front of a woman in a fur hat. Few people spoke. Most had their money out and their orders ready.

8   At the front of the line, a woman in a brown coat couldn't decide which soup to get and started to complain about the prices.

9   "You talk too much, dear," Mr. Yeganeh said, and motioned her to move to the left. "Next!"

10   "Just don't talk. Do what he says," a man huddled in a blue parka warned.

11   "He's downright rude," said a blond woman in a blue coat. "Even abusive. But you can't deny it, his soup is the best."

READING FOR MEANING

This section presents three activities that will help you think about the meanings in "Soup."

Read to Comprehend

Write a few sentences briefly explaining what you learned about Mr. Yeganeh and his views about running a restaurant.

Identify any words with meanings you are unsure of—such as *staccato* (paragraph 2) and *barrage* (5)—and find the dictionary definition for each word that makes the best sense in the context.

To help you understand the essay better, also consider trying one of these critical reading strategies, explained in Appendix 1: *summarizing* or *questioning to understand and remember.*

Read to Respond

Write a paragraph or two exploring your initial thoughts and feelings about the observational essay "Soup." Focus on anything that stands out for you, perhaps because it resonates with your own experience or because you find a statement puzzling. For example, consider writing about one of the following:

- Yeganeh's ideas about food quality and health, perhaps in comparison to the quality at fast-food restaurants with which you are familiar;

- Yeganeh's work ethic for himself and his employees, perhaps in relation to your experience as an employee or a manager; or

- his customers' willingness to follow Yeganeh's strict rules and tolerate his rudeness.

To help develop your response, also consider trying one of these critical reading strategies, explained in Appendix 1: *contextualizing* or *reflecting on challenges to your beliefs and values.*

Read to Analyze Assumptions

All writing contains *assumptions*—ideas and attitudes that are taken for granted as commonly accepted truths. Personal or individual assumptions also tend to reflect the values and beliefs of a particular community, which help shape the way those in the group think, act, and understand the world. All writing reflects assumptions held by the writer, but assumptions held by others, such as readers or sources cited by the writer, may also be present. Sometimes assumptions are stated explicitly, but often they are only implied, so you may have to search for underlying assumptions in the word choices and examples.

Why go to the effort to analyze assumptions in a reading? Assumptions have powerful effects. They influence our opinions and judgments by leading us to value some things and devalue others. These effects are even more powerful because they are taken for granted, often accepted without question by those who hold them. To understand a reading on a deep level, then, it is necessary to bring its assumptions to the surface and to question them. To think critically about assumptions, here are some kinds of questions you could ask: Who holds this assumption (the writer, readers, and/or others cited in the essay)? What are the effects of the assumption in the context of the essay specifically or in society more generally? What do you think about the assumption, and is there anything in the essay that raises doubts about it? How does the assumption reinforce or critique commonly held views, and are there any alternative ideas, beliefs, or values that would challenge this assumption?

Write a paragraph or two analyzing an assumption in "Soup." You might choose an assumption from the list below, using the questions accompanying it in addition to the ones above to help you get started. Or you can choose another assumption in the essay to explore.

- **assumptions about power**. Yeganeh describes himself as "a perfectionist" (paragraph 2) and admits he's "extremely hard to please" (1). He brags about scaring his employees and tells how he fired someone for leaving a mushroom on the floor. In addition, he defends his rules and right to deny service to anyone who does not follow them.

  To think critically about the assumptions in this essay related to power, ask yourself questions like these: When Yeganeh scares and fires his employees, how much is he holding them to a high standard, and how much is he just showing off? Why does he tell the customer that she talks too much? Because she is disrupting the efficiency of his operation? Because she is complaining about his prices? Do you think Yeganeh is a tyrant who abuses power, or does he use his power appropriately?

- **assumptions about customer service**. When Yeganeh says, "The customer is always wrong and I'm always right" (4), he is reversing the popular saying that the customer is always right.

  To think critically about assumptions in this essay related to customer service, ask yourself questions like these: What expectations do you think customers typically have about service in take-out establishments like Yeganeh's? What about in sit-down restaurants? For example, do customers expect servers to wait patiently while they read the menu, or the chef to make changes in menu items just for them? How about servers' assumptions regarding customers—for example, do they expect customers to stop talking when the server arrives to take the order? If the food is not cooked properly or the wrong order arrives at the table, what do customers and servers assume should be done, if anything? How are these assumptions about service affected by the type of restaurant involved? What seem to be the assumptions of the writer and of Yeganeh's customers about service? What are yours?

To help you analyze assumptions in "Soup," also consider trying one of these critical reading strategies, explained in Appendix 1: *reflecting on challenges to your beliefs and values* or *looking for patterns of opposition*.

READING LIKE A WRITER

This section leads you through an analysis of the observational writing strategies illustrated in "Soup": *describing people and places, organizing information from various sources, adopting an authorial role,* and *conveying a dominant impression of the subject.* For each strategy, you will be asked to reread and annotate part of the essay to see how that particular strategy works in "Soup."

When you study the selections later in this chapter, you will see how different writers use these same strategies to achieve their various purposes. The Guide to Writing Observational Essays near the end of the chapter suggests ways you can use these strategies in your own writing.

Describing People and Places

Observational writing, like autobiography (Chapter 2), succeeds by presenting the subject vividly and concretely. Writers of observation usually describe both people and places, although they may emphasize one over the other. Visual details usually predominate in an observational essay, but some writers complement these by describing sounds, smells, tastes, and even textures and temperatures.

Observational writers present people through visual details and action—how they look, dress, gesture, as well as what they do and how they do it. Notice, for example, that the author of "Soup" briefly describes the people waiting in line with a few choice visual details, mainly about their clothing—"a man in expensive leather" (paragraph 7), "a man huddled in a blue parka" (10), "a blond woman in a blue coat" (11). Writers also show how people talk and interact with one another, often including both direct quotations from their notes and paraphrases of what people have said. See, for example, the warning offered by the man in the parka and the blond woman's response. To gain a sense of an individual's personality, readers usually need only a few details indicating the person's tone of voice, facial expression, style of dress, or movements.

Analyze

1. Reread paragraphs 1, 2, and 4 to 6, and underline the words and phrases that enable you to imagine what Albert Yeganeh looks and sounds like. Do not underline what he says, but do underline descriptions of how he looks and sounds as he says it. Reflect on how the description of Yeganeh's gestures and motions help you envision him as he talks.

2. Also reread paragraphs 3 and 5, and put brackets around the words and phrases that enable you to imagine the Soup Kitchen International. Which senses do these descriptions bring to mind?

Write

Write several sentences explaining how the author describes Yeganeh and his restaurant. Give examples from your analysis of the descriptive language to indicate how the writer helps you envision Yeganeh and the Soup Kitchen International.

Organizing Information from Various Sources

In addition to describing their firsthand observations, writers often present information derived from interviews, and they may also collect materials at the site and do some background Internet or library research.

Readers of observational writing are usually comfortable not knowing the exact source of information that is summarized or paraphrased, although they do expect the writer to identify the source of direct quotations. This informal way of using sources typical of observational writing differs from the more formal conventions of writing in academic and professional scholarship, where it is expected that all of the sources will be clearly identified (in the text itself as well as in a works cited or reference list) so that readers can follow up with their own research.

Deciding which details of this diverse information to include in the essay and organizing all of it in a way that is easy to follow and that interests readers as it informs them can be quite challenging. Writers typically rely on two basic organizational plans: *topical* and *narrative*. Topically arranged essays group together logically related bits of information, such as those about specific parts of the subject. Narratively organized essays arrange information chronologically, combining bits of information into a story. Most observational essays use one or the other kind of organization, but sometimes writers combine elements of both. "Soup" is a good example of topical organization, but it also concludes with a brief narrative.

Analyze

1. Make a scratch outline of paragraphs 1 to 6 of "Soup," listing the topics or kinds of information presented. Notice that some paragraphs include more than one topic. Paragraph 2, for instance, raises several topics: the health benefits of soup, Yeganeh's perfectionism, his emphasis on cleanliness, and the ways that his restaurant compares to others. You do not have to list every topic, but try to identify the most important ones in the other paragraphs. (For an example of scratch outlining, see Appendix 1, p. 561.)

2. Reread paragraphs 7 to 11, where the writer presents a little narrative. Consider what relation, if any, this concluding narrative has to the topics that were presented in earlier paragraphs.

Write

Write a few sentences discussing whether you think the concluding narrative is related to any of the topics presented in earlier paragraphs, and if so how it is related. In other words, what do you learn from the narrative that illuminates or adds to what you learned from the earlier paragraphs?

Adopting an Authorial Role

In making observations and writing them up, writers have a choice of roles to perform: as a *detached spectator* or as a *participant observer*. In the spectator role, the writer acts as an independent reporter, watching and listening but remaining outside of the activity. In contrast, the participant observer becomes an insider, at least for a short time, joining in the activity with the people being interviewed and observed.

Both roles have potential advantages and disadvantages. One benefit of the spectator role is that readers can easily identify with the spectator's point of view because as readers they are in a similar position. A possible disadvantage is that as an outsider, the writer has to depend on what people say in interviews and what can be learned from observation. Consequently, the writer may miss or misinterpret important details. The participant-observer role has the advantage of enabling the writer to reveal insider knowledge gained from intimate experience with the subject. But possible disadvantages of being so close to the subject are that the essay turns into a personal narrative or the writer doesn't anticipate what readers who are unfamiliar with the subject need to know.

The author of "Soup" chose to remain in the spectator role throughout the essay. He or she easily could have sampled the soups and included in the essay firsthand impressions of the taste and texture of different ones. The author might also have worked for a time in Yeganeh's kitchen, participating in the soup preparation, and written about the experience of working under Mr. Yeganeh rather than only describing his behavior toward his workers and quoting his criticism of them. But instead, the author chose to remain an outsider looking in, getting information only from interviews and observations instead of from personal insider experience as well.

Analyze

Reread the essay and look for any places where the writer could have included insider knowledge derived from taking the role of participant observer. What advantages or disadvantages do you see in the role the writer chose to take?

Write

Write a few sentences discussing the role the writer chose to adopt, indicating what you think are the role's advantages or disadvantages for this particular subject.

Conveying a Dominant Impression of the Subject

Readers want observational essays to communicate any insights into the subject that the writer gained by observing a place and interviewing people. But they do not expect such essays to make an argument asserting the writer's interpretation or evaluation of the subject. In fact, they would be surprised if the writer's ideas were more prominent than the presentation of people and places.

In this regard, observational writing resembles autobiographical writing. In both genres, writers convey their perspective on what is significant and interesting about the subject primarily through showing, with some telling interspersed. That is, the writer's word choices and selection of details and quotations create a dominant impression of the subject. Any explicit statements interpreting or evaluating the subject or expressing the writer's attitude toward it reinforce the dominant impression. For example, writers sometimes indicate what they had expected prior to observing the subject. They may also react to something that was said or done while they were on the scene.

The author of "Soup" does not state a judgment about Yeganeh or analyze him, but as a careful reader you can infer what the writer thinks from the writer's word choices as well as from the details he or she decided to include in the essay.

Analyze

1. Underline any words or phrases that suggest the author's attitudes toward or feelings about Yeganeh as a human being, cook, and businessman.

2. Note in the margin any interpretation or evaluation of Yeganeh and his way of doing business that might be implied by what he says and does.

Write

Write several sentences identifying the dominant impression you have of Yeganeh and his Soup Kitchen International. Quote two or three phrases or sentences from the essay that convey this impression most strongly, and identify briefly the attitude, interpretation, or evaluation you see in each phrase or sentence.

READINGS

Susan Orlean

Show Dog

Susan Orlean is a staff writer for the New Yorker *and widely recognized as a master of observational writing. Some of her* New Yorker *essays have been reprinted in books including* The Bullfighter Checks Her Makeup: My Encounters with Extraordinary People *(2001) and* My Kind of Place: Travel Stories from a Woman Who's Been Everywhere *(2004). The 2002 Academy Award–nominated film* Adaptation *was based on Orlean's novel* The Orchid Thief, *which began as a* New Yorker *profile, "Orchid Fever," which like "Show Dog" was originally published in 1995. A dog lover, Orlean claims to have cowritten* Throw Me a Bone: 50 Healthy, Canine Taste-Tested Recipes for Snacks, Meals, and Treats *(2003) with her Welsh springer spaniel, Cooper. She is currently writing a biography of Rin Tin Tin. As you read "Show Dog," notice how Orlean interweaves information from direct observation, interview, and background library or Internet research.*

1   If I were a bitch, I'd be in love with Biff Truesdale. Biff is perfect. He's friendly, good-looking, rich, famous, and in excellent physical condition. He almost never drools. He's not afraid of commitment. He wants children—actually, he already has children and wants a lot more. He works hard and is a consummate professional, but he also knows how to have fun.

What is Orlean trying to do in this opening, and how well does she do it?

2   What Biff likes most is food and sex. This makes him sound boorish, which he is not—he's just elemental. Food he likes even better than sex. His favorite things to eat are cookies, mints, and hotel soap, but he will eat just about anything. Richard Krieger, a friend of Biff's who occasionally drives him to appointments, said not long ago, "When we're driving on 1-95, we'll usually pull over at McDonald's. Even if Biff is napping, he always wakes up when we're getting close. I get him a few plain hamburgers with buns—no ketchup, no mustard, and no pickles. He loves hamburgers. I don't get him his own French fries, but if I get myself fries I always flip a few for him into the back."

3   If you're ever around Biff while you're eating something he wants to taste—cold roast beef, a Wheatables cracker, chocolate, pasta, aspirin, whatever—he will

What impression of Biff
does this description make?

stare at you across the pleated bridge of his nose and
let his eyes sag and his lips tremble and allow a little
bead of drool to percolate at the edge of his mouth until
you feel so crummy that you give him some. This routine
puts the people who know him in a quandary, because
Biff has to watch his weight. Usually, he is as skinny as
Kate Moss, but he can put on three pounds in an instant.
The holidays can be tough. He takes time off at Christmas
and spends it at home, in Attleboro, Massachusetts, where
there's a lot of food around and no pressure and no
schedule and it's easy to eat all day. The extra weight
goes to his neck. Luckily, Biff likes working out. He runs
for fifteen or twenty minutes twice a day, either outside
or on his Jog-Master. When he's feeling heavy, he runs
longer, and skips snacks, until he's back down to his
ideal weight of seventy-five pounds.

Biff is a boxer. He is a show dog—he performs under   4
the name Champion Hi-Tech's Arbitrage—and so looking good is not mere vanity; it's business. A show dog's
career is short, and judges are unforgiving. Each breed is
judged by an explicit standard for appearance and tem-
perament, and then there's the incalculable element of
charisma in the ring. When a show dog is fat or lazy or
sullen, he doesn't win; when he doesn't win, he doesn't
enjoy the ancillary benefits of being a winner, like
appearing as the celebrity spokesmodel on packages of
Pedigree Mealtime with Lamb and Rice, which Biff will
be doing soon, or picking the best-looking bitches and
charging them six hundred dollars or so for his sexual
favors, which Biff does three or four times a month.
Another ancillary benefit of being a winner is that almost
every single weekend of the year, as he travels to shows
around the country, he gets to hear people applaud for
him and yell his name and tell him what a good boy
he is, which is something he seems to enjoy at least as
much as eating a bar of soap.

How well does Orlean
transition to reporting information about Biff's career
as a show dog? Where
do you think she learned
it from—background
research, interview,
observation?

Pretty soon, Biff won't have to be so vigilant about   5
his diet. After he appears at the Westminster Kennel
Club's show, this week, he will retire from active show
life and work full time as a stud. It's a good moment for
him to retire. Last year, he won more shows than any
other boxer, and also more than any other dog in the
purebred category known as Working Dogs, which also
includes Akitas, Alaskan malamutes, Bernese mountain

dogs, bullmastiffs, Doberman pinschers, giant schnauzers, Great Danes, Great Pyrenees, komondors, kuvaszok, mastiffs, Newfoundlands, Portuguese water dogs, Rottweilers, St. Bernards, Samoyeds, Siberian huskies, and standard schnauzers. Boxers were named for their habit of standing on their hind legs and punching with their front paws when they fight. They were originally bred to be chaperones— to look forbidding while being pleasant to spend time with. Except for show dogs like Biff, most boxers lead a life of relative leisure. Last year at Westminster, Biff was named Best Boxer and Best Working Dog, and he was a serious contender for Best in Show, the highest honor any show dog can hope for. He is a contender to win his breed and group again this year, and is a serious contender once again for Best in Show, although the odds are against him, because this year's judge is known as a poodle person.

Why do you think Orlean tells us about the category of Working Dogs and the history of boxers?

6   Biff is four years old. He's in his prime. He could stay on the circuit for a few more years, but by stepping aside now he is making room for his sons Trent and Rex, who are just getting into the business, and he's leaving while he's still on top. He'll also spend less time in airplanes, which is the one part of show life he doesn't like, and more time with his owners, William and Tina Truesdale, who might be persuaded to waive his snacking rules.

7   Biff has a short, tight coat of fox-colored fur, white feet and ankles, and a patch of white on his chest roughly the shape of Maine. His muscles are plainly sketched under his skin, but he isn't bulgy. His face is turned up and pushed in, and has a dark mask, spongy lips, a wishbone-shaped white blaze, and the earnest and slightly careworn expression of a small-town mayor. Someone once told me that he thought Biff looked a little bit like President Clinton. Biff's face is his fortune. There are plenty of people who like boxers with bigger bones and a stockier body and taller shoulders— boxers who look less like marathon runners and more like weight-lifters—but almost everyone agrees that Biff has a nearly perfect head.

How do the comparisons (highlighted) help you picture Biff?

8   "Biff's head is his father's," William Truesdale, a veterinarian, explained to me one day. We were in the Truesdales' living room in Attleboro, which overlooks acres of hilly fenced-in fields. Their house is a big, sunny ranch with a stylish pastel kitchen and boxerabilia on

Notice the shift here from observation to interview. How does Orlean make the transition? Is it effective? Why or why not?

every wall. The Truesdales don't have children, but at any given moment they share their quarters with at least a half-dozen dogs. If you watch a lot of dog-food commercials, you may have seen William—he's the young, handsome, dark-haired veterinarian declaring his enthusiasm for Pedigree Mealtime while his boxers gallop around.

"Biff has a masculine but elegant head," William went on. "It's not too wet around the muzzle. It's just about ideal. Of course, his forte is right here." He pointed to Biff's withers, and explained that Biff's shoulder-humerus articulation was optimally angled, and bracketed his superb brisket and forelegs, or something like that. While William was talking, Biff climbed onto the couch and sat on top of Brian, his companion, who was hiding under a pillow. Brian is an English toy Prince Charles spaniel who is about the size of a teakettle and has the composure of a hummingbird. As a young competitor, he once bit a judge—a mistake Tina Truesdale says he made because at the time he had been going through a little mind problem about being touched. Brian, whose show name is Champion Cragmor's Hi-Tech Man, will soon go back on the circuit, but now he mostly serves as Biff's regular escort. When Biff sat on him, he started to quiver. Biff batted at him with his front leg. Brian gave him an adoring look.

"Biff's body is from his mother," Tina was saying. "She had a lot of substance."

"She was even a little extreme for a bitch," William said. "She was rather buxom. I would call her zaftig."

"Biff's father needed that, though," Tina said. "His name was Tailo, and he was fabulous. Tailo had a very beautiful head, but he was a bit fine, I think. A bit slender."

"Even a little feminine," William said, with feeling. "Actually, he would have been a really awesome bitch."

How does Orlean signal to readers that she is about to relate an anecdote?

The first time I met Biff, he sniffed my pants, stood up on his hind legs and stared into my face, and then trotted off to the kitchen, where someone was cooking macaroni. We were in Westbury, Long Island, where Biff lives with Kimberly Pastella, a twenty-nine-year-old professional handler, when he's working. Last year, Kim and Biff went to at least one show every weekend. If they drove, they took Kim's van. If they flew, she went coach and he went cargo. They always shared a hotel room.

15   While Kim was telling me all this, I could hear Biff rummaging around in the kitchen. "Biffers!" Kim called out. Biff jogged back into the room with a phony look of surprise on his face. His tail was ticking back and forth. It is cropped so that it is about the size and shape of a half-smoked stogie. Kim said that there was a bitch downstairs who had been sent from Pennsylvania to be bred to one of Kim's other clients, and that Biff could smell her and was a little out of sorts. "Let's go," she said to him. "Biff, let's go jog." We went into the garage, where a treadmill was set up with Biff's collar suspended from a metal arm. Biff hopped on and held his head out so that Kim could buckle his collar. As soon as she leaned toward the power switch, he started to jog. His nails clicked a light tattoo on the rubber belt.

16   Except for a son of his named Biffle, Biff gets along with everybody. Matt Stander, one of the founders of *Dog News*, said recently, "Biff is just very, very personable. He has a *je ne sais quoi* that's really special. He gives of himself all the time." One afternoon, the Truesdales were telling me about the psychology that went into making Biff who he is. "Boxers are real communicators," William was saying. "We had to really take that into consideration in his upbringing. He seems tough, but there's a fragile ego inside there. The profound reaction and hurt when you would raise your voice at him was really something."

What topic do you think holds the information in this paragraph together?

17   "I *made* him," Tina said. "I made Biff who he is. He had an overbearing personality when he was small, but I consider that a prerequisite for a great performer. He had such an *attitude*! He was like this miniature man!" She shimmied her shoulders back and forth and thrust out her chin. She is a dainty, chic woman with wide-set eyes and the neck of a ballerina. She grew up on a farm in Costa Rica, where dogs were considered just another form of livestock. In 1987, William got her a Rottweiler for a watchdog, and a boxer, because he had always loved boxers, and Tina decided to dabble with them in shows. Now she makes a monogrammed Christmas stocking for each animal in their house, and she watches the tape of Biff winning at Westminster approximately once a week. "Right from the beginning, I made Biff think he was the most fabulous dog in the world," Tina said.

How effectively does Orlean weave description into this bit of dialogue?

Why do you think Orlean includes this information about Tina?

"He doesn't take after me very much," William said. 18
"I'm more of a golden retriever."

"Oh, he has my nature," Tina said. "I'm very strong- 19
willed. I'm brassy. And Biff is an egotistical, self-centered,
selfish person. He thinks he's very important and special,
and he doesn't like to share."

Why do you think William
and Tina talk about Biff this
way? Does it surprise you?

Biff is priceless. If you beg the Truesdales to name a 20
figure, they might say that Biff is worth around a hundred thousand dollars, but they will also point out that
a Japanese dog fancier recently handed Tina a blank
check for Biff. (She immediately threw it away.) That
check notwithstanding, campaigning a show dog is a
money-losing proposition for the owner. A good handler gets three or four hundred dollars a day, plus travel
expenses, to show a dog, and any dog aiming for the
top will have to be on the road at least a hundred days
a year. A dog photographer charges hundreds of dollars
for a portrait, and a portrait is something that every serious owner commissions, and then runs as a full-page
ad in several dog-show magazines. Advertising a show
dog is standard procedure if you want your dog or your
presence on the show circuit to get well known. There
are also such ongoing show-dog expenses as entry fees,
hair-care products, food, health care, and toys. Biff's
stud fee is six hundred dollars. Now that he will not be
at shows, he can be bred several times a month. Breeding him would have been a good way for him to make
money in the past, except that whenever the Truesdales
were enthusiastic about a mating they bartered Biff's service for the pick of the litter. As a result, they now have
more Biff puppies than Biff earnings. "We're doing this
for posterity," Tina says. "We're doing it for the good of
all boxers. You simply can't think about the cost."

What do you learn about
the show dog business from
this paragraph?

On a recent Sunday, I went to watch Biff work at one 21
of the last shows he would attend before his retirement.
The show was sponsored by the Lehigh Valley Kennel
Club and was held in a big, windy field house on the campus of Lehigh University, in Bethlehem, Pennsylvania.
The parking lot was filled with motor homes pasted with
life-size decals of dogs. On my way to the field house,
I passed someone walking an Afghan hound wearing
a snood, and someone else wiping down a Saluki with a
Flintstones beach towel. Biff was napping in his crate—a
fancy-looking brass box with bright silver hardware and

What do you learn about
Biff and his life from this
anecdote that you didn't
learn from the information
that came before?

with luggage tags from Delta, USAir, and Continental hanging on the door. Dogs in crates can look woeful, but Biff actually likes spending time in his. When he was growing up, the Truesdales decided they would never reprimand him, because of his delicate ego. Whenever he got rambunctious, Tina wouldn't scold him— she would just invite him to sit in his crate and have a time-out.

22   On this particular day, Biff was in the crate with a bowl of water and a gourmet Oinkeroll. The boxer judging was already over. There had been thirty-three in competition, and Biff had won Best in Breed. Now he had to wait for several hours . . . for Best in Show. . . .

23   While he was napping, I pawed through his suitcase. In it was some dog food; towels; an electric nail grinder; a whisker trimmer; a wool jacket in a lively pattern that looked sort of Southwestern; an apron; some antibiotics; baby oil; coconut-oil coat polish; boxer chalk powder; a copy of *Dog News;* an issue of *Showsight* magazine, featuring an article subtitled "Frozen Semen—Boon or Bain?" and a two-page ad for Biff, with a full-page, full-color photograph of him and Kim posed in front of a human-size toy soldier; a spray bottle of fur cleanser; another Oinkeroll; a rope ball; and something called a Booda Bone. The apron was for Kim. The baby oil was to make Biff's nose and feet glossy when he went into the ring. Boxer chalk powder—as distinct from, say, West Highland-white-terrier chalk powder—is formulated to cling to short, sleek boxer hair and whiten boxers' white markings. . . .

> Here's another list (like the list of breeds in the Working Dogs category). Why do you think Orlean includes so many details?

24   Typically, dog contestants first circle the ring together; then each contestant poses individually for the judge, trying to look perfect as the judge lifts its lips for a dental exam, rocks its hindquarters, and strokes its back and thighs. The judge at Lehigh was a chesty, mustached man with watery eyes and a grave expression. He directed the group with hand signals that made him appear to be roping cattle. The Rottweiler looked good, and so did the giant schnauzer. I started to worry. Biff had a distracted look on his face, as if he'd forgotten something back at the house. Finally, it was his turn. He pranced to the center of the ring. The judge stroked him and then waved his hand in a circle and stepped out of the way. Several people near me began clapping.

How does Orlean make this little narrative dramatic?

A flashbulb flared. Biff held his position for a moment, and then he and Kim bounded across the ring, his feet moving so fast that they blurred into an oily sparkle, even though he really didn't have very far to go. He got a cookie when he finished the performance, and another a few minutes later, when the judge wagged his finger at him, indicating that Biff had won again.

You can't help wondering whether Biff will experi- 25 ence the depressing letdown that retired competitors face. At least, he has a lot of stud work to look forward to, although William Truesdale complained to me once that the Truesdales' standards for a mate are so high—they require a clean bill of health and a substantial pedigree—that "there just aren't that many right bitches out there." Nonetheless, he and Tina are optimistic that Biff will find enough suitable mates to become one of the most influential boxer sires of all time. "We'd like to be remembered as the boxer people of the nineties," Tina said, "Anyway, we can't wait to have him home." . . .

Just then, Biff, who had been on the couch, jumped 26 down and began pacing. "Going somewhere, honey?" Tina asked.

Why do you think Orlean ends with this description of Biff? How would the essay be different if it ended with his winning perfor-mance (paragraph 24) or Tina's comment about how they want to be remem-bered (25)?

He wanted to go out, so Tina opened the back door, 27 and Biff ran into the back yard. After a few minutes, he noticed a ball on the lawn. The ball was slippery and a little too big to fit in his mouth, but he kept scrambling and trying to grab it. In the meantime, the Truesdales and I sat, stayed for a moment, fetched ourselves turkey sandwiches, and then curled up on the couch. Half an hour passed, and Biff was still happily pursuing the ball. He probably has a very short memory, but he acted as if it were the most fun he'd ever had.

READING FOR MEANING

This section presents three activities that will help you think about the mean-ings in Orlean's observational essay.

Read to Comprehend

Write a few sentences briefly explaining what you think is the main idea Orlean wants her readers to understand about Biff and his entourage, indicating where in the essay you see that idea expressed.

Identify any words with meanings you are unsure of—such as *boorish* (paragraph 2) and *brisket* (9)—and find the dictionary definition for each word that makes the best sense in the context.

To help you understand the essay better, also consider trying one of these critical reading strategies, explained in Appendix 1: *summarizing* or *questioning to understand and remember.*

Read to Respond

Write several paragraphs exploring your initial thoughts and feelings about Orlean's observational essay. Focus on anything that stands out for you, perhaps because it resonates with your own experience or because you find a statement puzzling. For example, consider writing about one of the following:

- Orlean's way of opening or closing the essay;

- the Truesdales and their relationship to Biff; or

- how the essay resonates with your own experience with dogs or other pets.

To help develop your response, also consider trying one of these critical reading strategies, explained in Appendix 1: *contextualizing* or *reflecting on challenges to your beliefs and values.*

Read to Analyze Assumptions

Write a paragraph or two analyzing an assumption in Orlean's essay. To think critically about assumptions, here are some kinds of questions you could ask: Who holds this assumption (the writer, readers, and/or others cited in the essay)? What are the effects of the assumption in the context of the essay specifically or in society more generally? What do you think about the assumption, and is there anything in the essay that raises doubts about it? How does the assumption reinforce or critique commonly held views, and are there any alternative ideas, beliefs, or values that would challenge this assumption?

You might choose an assumption from the list below, using the questions accompanying it in addition to the ones above to help you get started. Or you can choose another assumption in the essay to explore.

- **assumptions about pets.** Orlean quotes William and Tina Truesdale talking about Biff as if they were his natural, rather than adoptive, parents: "'He doesn't take after me very much,' William said. . . . 'Oh, he has my nature,' Tina said" (paragraphs 18–19). Referring to an animal as if it were a human being is called *anthropomorphism*. Tina and William anthropomorphize Biff so thoroughly that the differences between the species seems to evaporate for them.

  To think critically about the assumptions in this essay related to pets, ask yourself questions like these: How do William and Tina anthropomorphize Biff in their comments elsewhere in the essay? Does Orlean do so as well? If you have or have had a pet, have you also spoken or thought about it as if it was a human being? Why do you think people tend to treat their pets this way? How do you think people reconcile their feelings for their own pets with their (in)different treatment of other animals of the same or other species?

- **assumptions about the show dog business.** In addition to being a member of the family, Biff is big business for the Truesdales. Orlean makes the point that "Biff is priceless" (paragraph 20). But she also explains that caring for a show dog is very expensive, and that the money is earned from the dog's celebrity in the form of both endorsements and stud fees. In describing Biff's life, Orlean points out that he lives with his trainer, not the Truesdales, and competes nearly every weekend. She also lets us see that during a show, dogs spend a lot of time in crates looking "woeful" or "napping" (paragraph 21).

  To think critically about the assumptions in this essay related to the business of showing and breeding dogs, ask yourself questions like these: What does Orlean seem to assume about the quality of life of a working show dog? What beliefs and values are the Truesdales expressing in showing Biff and using him for highly selective mating with other purebred boxers? What are your own assumptions about these issues?

To help you analyze assumptions in Orlean's essay, also consider trying one of these critical reading strategies, explained in Appendix 1: *reflecting on challenges to your beliefs and values* or *looking for patterns of opposition.*

READING LIKE A WRITER

ORGANIZING INFORMATION FROM VARIOUS SOURCES

Like the author of "Soup," Orlean relies primarily on topical organization. Observational writers who use topical organization often omit transitions between topics. Instead, they may use a device similar to jump cuts in film—making abrupt shifts from one scene or topic to another. For example, the topic of paragraph 2 is Biff's eating habits. This topic continues into paragraph 3 with additional examples of foods he likes, and paragraph 3 concludes by describing how Biff maintains "his ideal weight" (3). Beginning with "Biff is a boxer. He is a show dog," paragraph 4 seems to jump to another topic entirely. Although Orlean does not provide an explicit transition connecting this new topic to the one that went before, readers can easily supply the logical cause-effect relationship between the topics of exercising to maintain an ideal weight and performing as a show dog. In fact, Orlean implies that even Biff sees the logical connection between overeating, exercising, and enjoying the perks of winning.

Sometimes, Orlean uses a device like repeating a key word or a related word to serve as a transitional bridge. Look, for example, at the way the word *head* is repeated in paragraphs 7 to 13. It first appears at the end of paragraph 7, and is repeated at the beginning of paragraphs 8 and 9. The topic is elaborated on further in paragraphs 10 to 13 and connected by the related word *body* (10) and repeated word *head* (12). In narrative sections of the essay, Orlean uses more familiar time markers to provide clear transitions. For example, paragraph 5 opens with the phrase "Pretty soon," a temporal transition that looks forward in time to Biff's coming retirement, the paragraph's topic.

Analyze

1. Examine the jump cut–like transitions between paragraphs 6 and 7, 15 and 16, or 19 and 20. Consider how you react as a reader to these abrupt topic shifts.

2. Reread paragraphs 21 to 25, where Orlean narrates what she observed during a dog show, and highlight the transitional words and phrases.

Write

Write a few sentences assessing how Orlean's use—or omission—of transitions in the paragraphs you analyzed affects your ability to follow the information she presents.

CONSIDERING IDEAS FOR YOUR OWN WRITING

Some observational essays are about a particular individual who has an unusual job or hobby, or has accomplished something special. In profiling Biff, Orlean is writing this kind of profile. Even though she can't interview Biff, she spends time with him in several different locations and interviews people who live and work with him. You might consider writing about somebody you find intriguing, perhaps someone who does the kind of work you are interested in learning more about—for example, a police officer, attorney, or judge; a high-school or college coach; an independent contractor or small business owner; a newspaper editor, blogger, or poet; a performance artist, graffiti artist, or musician.

John T. Edge

I'm Not Leaving until I Eat This Thing

John T. Edge (b. 1962) is director of the Southern Foodways Alliance at the University of Mississippi, where he coordinates an annual conference on Southern food. A food writer for publications including Oxford American, Saveur, *and the* New York Times, *he has also contributed to NPR's* All Things Considered. *Edge's essays are regularly included in* Best Food Writing *anthologies, and he has coedited several cookbooks and travel guides. He has published many books of his own:* A Gracious Plenty: Recipes and Recollections from the American South *(1999);* Southern Belly *(2007), a portrait of Southern food told through profiles of people and places; and a series on iconic American foods, including* Hamburgers and Fries: An American Story *(2005) and* Donuts: An American Passion *(2006).*

This reading first appeared in a 1999 issue of Oxford American *(where the illustration on page 105 appeared) and was reprinted in 2000 in* Utne Reader. *Edge focuses his considerable observational writing skills on an unusual manufacturing business in rural Louisiana—Farm Fresh Food Supplier. He introduces readers to the company's workers and its pig products, a best-seller being pickled pig lips, which are sometimes bottled in vivid patriotic and special-events colors. Unlike the author of the previous reading, Edge participates in his subject—not by joining in the activities at Farm Fresh but by attempting to eat a pig lip at Jesse's Place, a nearby "juke" bar. You will see that the reading begins and ends with this personal experience. As you read, enjoy Edge's struggle to eat a pig lip, and pay attention to the information Edge offers about the history and manufacture of pickled pig lips at Farm Fresh.*

1 It's just past 4:00 on a Thursday afternoon in June at Jesse's Place, a country juke 17 miles south of the Mississippi line and three miles west of Amite, Louisiana. The air conditioner hacks and spits forth torrents of Arctic air, but the heat of summer can't be kept at bay. It seeps around the splintered doorjambs and settles in, transforming the squat particleboard-plastered roadhouse into a sauna. Slowly, the dank barroom fills with grease-smeared mechanics from the truck stop up the road and farmers straight from the fields, the soles of their brogans thick with dirt clods. A few weary souls make their way over from the nearby sawmill. I sit alone at the bar, one empty bottle of Bud in front of me, a second in my hand. I drain the beer, order a third, and stare down at the pink juice spreading outward from a crumpled foil pouch and onto the bar.

2 *I'm not leaving until I eat this thing,* I tell myself.

3 Half a mile down the road, behind a fence coiled with razor wire, Lionel Dufour, proprietor of Farm Fresh Food Supplier, is loading up the last truck of the day, wheeling case after case of pickled pork offal out of his

cinder-block processing plant and into a semitrailer bound for Hattiesburg, Mississippi.

His crew packed lips today. Yesterday, it was pickled sausage; the day before that, pig feet. Tomorrow, it's pickled pig lips again. Lionel has been on the job since 2:45 in the morning, when he came in to light the boilers. Damon Landry, chief cook and maintenance man, came in at 4:30. By 7:30, the production line was at full tilt: six women in white smocks and blue bouffant caps, slicing ragged white fat from the lips, tossing the good parts in glass jars, the bad parts in barrels bound for the rendering plant. Across the aisle, filled jars clatter by on a conveyor belt as a worker tops them off with a Kool-Aid-red slurry of hot sauce, vinegar, salt, and food coloring. Around the corner, the jars are capped, affixed with a label, and stored in pasteboard boxes to await shipping. 4

Unlike most offal—euphemistically called "variety meats"—lips belie their provenance. Brains, milky white and globular, look like brains. Feet, the ghosts of their cloven hoofs protruding, look like feet. Testicles look like, well, testicles. But lips are different. Loosed from the snout, trimmed of their fat, and dyed a preternatural pink, they look more like candy than like carrion. 5

At Farm Fresh, no swine root in an adjacent feedlot. No viscera-strewn killing floor lurks just out of sight, down a darkened hallway. These pigs died long ago at some Midwestern abattoir. By the time the lips arrive in Amite, they are, in essence, pig Popsicles, 50-pound blocks of offal and ice. 6

7   "Lips are all meat," Lionel told me earlier in the day. "No gristle, no bone, no nothing. They're bar food, hot and vinegary, great with a beer. Used to be the lips ended up in sausages, headcheese, those sorts of things. A lot of them still do."

8   Lionel, a 50-year-old father of three with quick, intelligent eyes set deep in a face the color of cordovan, is a veteran of nearly 40 years in the pickled pig lips business. "I started out with my daddy when I wasn't much more than 10," Lionel told me, his shy smile framed by a coarse black mustache flecked with whispers of gray. "The meatpacking business he owned had gone broke back when I was 6, and he was peddling out of the back of his car, selling dried shrimp, napkins, straws, tubes of plastic cups, pig feet, pig lips, whatever the bar owners needed. He sold to black bars, white bars, sweet shops, snowball stands, you name it. We made the rounds together after I got out of school, sometimes staying out till two or three in the morning. I remember bringing my toy cars to this one joint and racing them around the floor with the bar owner's son while my daddy and his father did business."

9   For years after the demise of that first meatpacking company, the Dufour family sold someone else's product. "We used to buy lips from Dennis Di Salvo's company down in Belle Chasse," recalled Lionel. "As far as I can tell, his mother was the one who came up with the idea to pickle and pack lips back in the '50s, back when she was working for a company called Three Little Pigs over in Houma. But pretty soon, we were selling so many lips that we had to almost beg Di Salvo's for product. That's when we started cooking up our own," he told me, gesturing toward the cast-iron kettle that hangs from the rafters by the front door of the plant. "My daddy started cooking lips in that very pot."

10   Lionel now cooks lips in 11 retrofitted milk tanks, dull stainless-steel cauldrons shaped like oversized cradles. But little else has changed. Though Lionel's father has passed away, Farm Fresh remains a family-focused company. His wife, Kathy, keeps the books. His daughter, Dana, a button-cute college student who has won numerous beauty titles, takes to the road in the summer, selling lips to convenience stores and wholesalers. Soon, after he graduates from business school, Lionel's younger son, Matt, will take over operations at the plant. And his older son, a veterinarian, lent his name to one of Farm Fresh's top sellers, Jason's Pickled Pig Lips.

11   "We do our best to corner the market on lips," Lionel told me, his voice tinged with bravado."Sometimes they're hard to get from the packing houses. You gotta kill a lot of pigs to get enough lips to keep us going. I've got new customers calling every day; it's all I can do to keep up with demand, but I bust my ass to keep up. I do what I can for my family—and for my customers.

12   "When my customers tell me something," he continued, "just like when my daddy told me something, I listen. If my customers wanted me to dye

the lips green, I'd ask, 'What shade?' As it is, every few years we'll do some red and some blue for the Fourth of July. This year we did jars full of Mardi Gras lips—half purple, half gold," Lionel recalled with a chuckle. "I guess we'd had a few beers when we came up with that one."

Meanwhile, back at Jesse's Place, I finish my third Bud, order my fourth. *Now,* I tell myself, my courage bolstered by booze, *I'm ready to eat a lip.*   13

They may have looked like candy in the plant, but in the barroom   14 they're carrion once again. I poke and prod the six-inch arc of pink flesh, peering up from my reverie just in time to catch the barkeep's wife, Audrey, staring straight at me. She fixes me with a look just this side of pity and asks, "You gonna eat that thing or make love to it?"

Her nephew, Jerry, sidles up to a bar stool on my left. "A lot of people   15 like 'em with chips," he says with a nod toward the pink juice pooling on the bar in front of me. I offer to buy him a lip, and Audrey fishes one from a jar behind the counter, wraps it in tinfoil, and places the whole affair on a paper towel in front of him.

I take stock of my own cowardice, and, following Jerry's lead, reach for   16 a bag of potato chips, tear open the top with my teeth, and toss the quivering hunk of hog flesh into the shiny interior of the bag, slick with grease and dusted with salt. Vinegar vapors tickle my nostrils. I stifle a gag that rolls from the back of my throat, swallow hard, and pray that the urge to vomit passes.

With a smash of my hand, the potato chips are reduced to a pulp,   17 and I feel the cold lump of the lip beneath my fist. I clasp the bag shut and shake it hard in an effort to ensure chip coverage in all the nooks and crannies of the lip. The technique that Jerry uses—and I mimic—is not unlike that employed by home cooks mixing up a mess of Shake 'n Bake chicken.

I pull from the bag a coral crescent of meat now crusted with blond   18 bits of potato chips. When I chomp down, the soft flesh dissolves between my teeth. It tastes like a flaccid cracklin', unmistakably porcine, and not altogether bad. The chips help, providing texture where there was none. Slowly, my brow unfurrows, my stomach ceases its fluttering.

Sensing my relief, Jerry leans over and peers into my bag. "Kind of look   19 like Frosted Flakes, don't they?" he says, by way of describing the chips rapidly turning to mush in the pickling juice. I offer the bag to Jerry, order yet another beer, and turn to eye the pig feet floating in a murky jar by the cash register, their blunt tips bobbing up through a pasty white film.

READING FOR MEANING

This section presents three activities that will help you think about the meanings in Edge's observational essay.

Read to Comprehend

Write a few sentences briefly explaining what you think is the main idea Edge wants his readers to understand about the Dufour family business, Farm Fresh Food Supplier, indicating where in the essay you see that idea expressed.

Identify any words with meanings you are unsure of—such as *euphemistically* (paragraph 5) and *abattoir* (6)—and find the dictionary definition for each word that makes the best sense in the context.

To help you understand the essay better, also consider trying one of these critical reading strategies, explained in Appendix 1: *summarizing* or *questioning to understand and remember.*

Read to Respond

Write several paragraphs exploring your initial thoughts and feelings about Edge's observational essay. Focus on anything that stands out for you, perhaps because it resonates with your own experience or because you find a statement puzzling. For example, consider writing about one of the following:

- Edge's description of the production line at Farm Fresh Food Supplier (paragraph 4), perhaps in relation to your own work experience;

- Lionel Dufour's story about how he "made the rounds" with his father after school (8), perhaps in relation to your own experience learning from a relative or mentor; or

- your reaction to Edge's attempt to eat the pig lip, possibly in relation to your own experience trying an unusual food.

To help develop your response, also consider trying one of these critical reading strategies, explained in Appendix 1: *contextualizing* or *reflecting on challenges to your beliefs and values.*

Read to Analyze Assumptions

Write a paragraph or two analyzing an assumption in Edge's essay. To think critically about assumptions, here are some kinds of questions you could ask: Who holds this assumption (the writer, readers, and/or others cited in the essay)? What are the effects of the assumption in the context of the essay specifically or in society more generally? What do you think about the assumption, and is there anything in the essay that raises doubts about it? How does the assumption reinforce or critique commonly held views, and are there any alternative ideas, beliefs, or values that would challenge this assumption?

You might choose an assumption from the list below, using the questions accompanying it in addition to the ones above to help you get started. Or you can choose another assumption in the essay to explore.

- **assumptions about culture and food.** For many people, foods that they did not eat as children seem strange and sometimes even repulsive. Even though he is a Southerner, Edge is squeamish about eating a popular southern delicacy, pickled pig lips.

  To think critically about assumptions regarding culture and food, ask yourself questions like these: Why do you suppose Edge uses the words *courage* (paragraph 13) and *cowardice* (16) to describe his hesitancy to try a new food? What might he assume about pig lips that makes him fearful? Remember that he has already visited Farm Fresh, so he knows a lot about pig lips and their production. Think of food anxieties that you or people you know have. What do you think causes them? What kinds of personal and cultural beliefs and values influence people's food preferences—and anxieties?

- **assumptions about work.** In describing Jesse's Place, "a country juke" where locals come after work to drink and socialize (paragraph 1), and Farm Fresh Supplier, a factory where pig parts are cooked and prepared for shipping, Edge mentions many jobs that involve tiring physical labor—such as mechanics, farmers, sawmill workers, and assembly-line workers.

  To think critically about the assumptions in this essay related to work, ask yourself questions like these: Lionel Dufour, the factory owner who gets to work at 2:45 a.m. and does "blue-collar" jobs such as loading trucks, seems to represent the work ethic for Edge. But unlike his employees, Dufour makes a lot of money. Why are manual laborers not paid well or given much respect in our culture, while a strong work ethic is celebrated as a great American virtue? Why do you suppose Edge does not interview one of the factory workers or the other customers at the bar?

To help you analyze assumptions in the essay, also consider trying one of these critical reading strategies, explained in Appendix 1: *reflecting on challenges to your beliefs and values, exploring the significance of figurative language,* or *looking for patterns of opposition.*

READING LIKE A WRITER

CHOOSING A ROLE AND ORGANIZING THE INFORMATION

Whereas most writers of observational essays choose to adopt either the role of a detached spectator or the role of a participant observer, Edge chose to use both roles. He acted as a spectator during his visit to Farm Fresh Food Supplier and as a participant when he tried to eat a pickled pig lip produced by Farm Fresh.

Another choice that writers have is to organize their information topically or narratively. Again, Edge uses both methods. He organizes the information that he gleaned from visiting Farm Fresh under several topics and the information that he gained from trying to eat a pig lip as a narrative. Not all narratively organized profiles also involve participant observation (see, for example, Peggy

Orenstein's "The Daily Grind: Lessons in the Hidden Curriculum" on p. 113).
But if telling the story of the writer's participation would give the essay added
interest and drama, writers should consider using a narrative plan or a combination of narrative and topical organization.

Analyze

1. Reread paragraphs 1 and 2, where Edge begins telling the story of his attempt
   to eat a pig lip. Notice how he sets up the time and place, describes the bar,
   and creates suspense.

2. Skim paragraphs 3 to 12, highlighting each new topic that is introduced.

3. Reread paragraphs 13 to 19, where Edge returns to his story about eating the
   pig lip. Reflect on the relation of the bar story to the report of Edge's visit to
   Farm Fresh. What, if anything, do you learn from Edge's story about trying
   to eat a pig lip that you cannot find out from paragraphs 3 to 12?

Write

Write several sentences explaining how Edge's use of both roles—
spectator and participant—contributes to the effectiveness of his observational
essay.

ANALYZING VISUALS

Write a paragraph analyzing the photograph included in Edge's essay
and explaining what it contributes to the essay.

To do the analysis, you can use the criteria chart for the Analysis of
Visuals in Appendix 3 on pp. 670–72. Don't feel you have to answer all
of the questions in the chart; focus on those that seem most productive
in helping you write a paragraph-length analysis. To help you get started,
consider adding these questions that specifically refer to Edge's visual:

- Edge could have included a full-body photograph of a pig, a picture of
  pigs at play, or some other composition. Why do you think he chose a
  close-up of a pig's face taken from one particular angle?

- Given his purpose and audience, why do you think Edge chose a
  photograph of a pig instead of a photograph of pig lips in a jar or
  being eaten at a site like Jesse's Place? Or why didn't he choose a
  photograph of the Farm Fresh company or the DuFour family? What
  does the choice of visual suggest about the subject and the writer's
  perspective?

CONSIDERING IDEAS FOR YOUR OWN WRITING

Consider writing about a place that serves, produces, or sells something unusual, perhaps something that, like Edge, you could try yourself to discover more about for the purpose of informing and engaging your readers. If no such place comes to mind, you could browse the online Yellow Pages of your local phone directory for ideas, for example, a company that produces or packages some special ethnic or regional food or a local café that serves it. There are many other possibilities—acupuncture clinic, caterer, novelty toy and balloon store, microbrewery, chain-saw dealer, boatbuilder, talent agency, ornamental iron manufacturer, bead store, hair or nail salon, aquarium and pet fish supplier, auto-detailing shop, tattoo parlor, scrap-metal recycler, fly-fishing shop, handwriting analyst, dog- or cat-sitting service, photo restorer, burglar alarm installer, Christmas tree farm, wedding specialist, reweaving specialist, wig salon. You need not evaluate the quality of work at the place as part of your observational essay. Instead, keep the focus on informing readers about the service or product the place offers. Relating a personal experience with the service or product is a good idea but not a requirement of an observational essay.

A Special Reading Strategy

Comparing and Contrasting Related Readings: "Soup" and Edge's "I'm Not Leaving until I Eat This Thing"

Comparing and contrasting related readings is a special critical reading strategy that is useful both in reading for meaning and in reading like a writer. This strategy is particularly applicable when writers present similar subjects, as is the case in the observational essays in this chapter by the *New Yorker* writer (p. 84) and John T. Edge (p. 104). Both writers describe a business they observed and report on their interview with the business owner. In both instances, the business involves food products and their preparation; however, Edge adopts the role of participant observer, whereas the author of "Soup" maintains a more "objective" distance. To compare and contrast these two observational essays, think about issues such as these:

- Compare these essays in terms of their cultural contexts. What seems to you to be most significant about the two business philosophies represented in these essays?

- Compare how the two writers organize the information derived from interview and observation. Highlight the places in each essay where information from interviews is quoted or summarized and places where information from direct observation is presented.

- Compare Edge's alternation between the participant-observer and spectator-observer roles with the *New Yorker* writer's consistent spectator role. Note any places in "Soup" where you get a sense of the writer's point of view or judgment. What do the participant's observations add to Edge's essay?

See Appendix 1 (pp. 596–601) for detailed guidelines on comparing and contrasting related readings.

Peggy Orenstein

The Daily Grind: Lessons in the Hidden Curriculum

Peggy Orenstein has been a managing editor of Mother Jones *and a member of the editorial board of* Esquire, *and is now a contributing writer for the* New York Times Magazine. *Her essays have appeared in the* New Yorker, Vogue, *and many other nationally known publications and in many anthologies, including* The Best American Science Writing *(2004). Among her books are* Flux: Women on Sex, Work, Kids, Love, and Life in a Half-Changed World *(2002) and* Waiting for Daisy: A Tale of Two Continents, Three Religions, Five Infertility Doctors, an Oscar, an Atomic Bomb, a Romantic Night and One Woman's Quest to Become a Mother *(2007). Orenstein also was featured in the documentary films* Crumb *(1994) and* Searching for Asian America *(2003) and was the executive producer of the Oscar-nominated documentary* The Mushroom Club *(2006).*

This observational essay, profiling an eighth-grade math class, comes from the opening chapter of Orenstein's book, School Girls: Young Women, Self-Esteem, and the Confidence Gap *(1994). She undertook the extensive research for this book after reading a study conducted by the American Association of University Women in 1991 that identified a gender gap in the achievements of male and female students in America. Her research concentrated on the ways in which some schools and teachers—often unwittingly—may inhibit girls' classroom experiences and constrain their opportunities to participate. As you read the essay, think about whether the story it tells is one you have witnessed firsthand.*

Amy Wilkinson has looked forward to being an eighth grader forever— 1
at least for the last two years, which, when you're thirteen, seems like the same thing. By the second week of September she's settled comfortably into her role as one of the school's reigning elite. Each morning before class, she lounges with a group of about twenty other eighth-grade girls and boys in the most visible spot on campus: at the base of the schoolyard, between one of the portable classrooms that was constructed in the late 1970s and the old oak tree in the overflow parking lot. The group trades gossip, flirts, or simply stands around, basking in its own importance and killing time before the morning bell.

At 8:15 on Tuesday the crowd has already convened, and Amy is stand- 2
ing among a knot of girls, laughing. She is fuller-figured than she'd like to be, wide-hipped and heavy-limbed with curly blond hair, cornflower-blue eyes, and a sharply upturned nose. With the help of her mother, who is a drama coach, she has become the school's star actress: last year she played Eliza in Weston's production of *My Fair Lady*. Although she

earns solid grades in all of her subjects—she'll make the honor roll this fall—drama is her passion, she says, because "I love entertaining people, and I love putting on characters."

3   Also, no doubt, because she loves the spotlight: this morning, when she mentions a boy I haven't met, Amy turns, puts her hands on her hips, anchors her feet shoulder width apart, and bellows across the schoolyard, "Greg! Get over here! You have to meet Peggy."

4   She smiles wryly as Greg, looking startled, begins to make his way across the schoolyard for an introduction. "I'm not exactly shy," she says, her hands still on her hips. "I'm bold."

5   Amy is bold. And brassy, and strong-willed. Like any teenager, she tries on and discards different selves as if they were so many pairs of Girbaud jeans, searching ruthlessly for a perfect fit. During a morning chat just before the school year began, she told me that her parents tried to coach her on how to respond to my questions. "They told me to tell you that they want me to be my own person," she complained. "My mother *told* me to tell you that. I do want to be my own person, but it's like, you're interviewing me about who I am and she's telling me what to say—that's not my own person, is it?"

6   When the morning bell rings, Amy and her friends cut off their conversations, scoop up their books, and jostle toward the school's entrance. Inside, Weston's hallways smell chalky, papery, and a little sweaty from gym class. The wood-railed staircases at either end of the two-story main building are worn thin in the middle from the scuffle of hundreds of pairs of sneakers pounding them at forty-eight-minute intervals for nearly seventy-five years. Amy's mother, Sharon, and her grandmother both attended this school. So will her two younger sisters. Her father, a mechanic who works on big rigs, is a more recent Weston recruit: he grew up in Georgia and came here after he and Sharon were married.

7   Amy grabs my hand, pulling me along like a small child or a slightly addled new student: within three minutes we have threaded our way through the dull-yellow hallways to her locker and then upstairs to room 238, Mrs. Richter's math class.

8   The twenty-two students that stream through the door with us run the gamut of physical maturity. Some of the boys are as small and compact as fourth graders, their legs sticking out of their shorts like pipe cleaners. A few are trapped in the agony of a growth spurt, and still others cultivate downy beards. The girls' physiques are less extreme: most are nearly their full height, and all but a few have already weathered the brunt of puberty. They wear topknots or ponytails, and their shirts are tucked neatly into their jeans.

9   Mrs. Richter, a ruddy, athletic woman with a powerful voice, has arranged the chairs in a three-sided square, two rows deep. Amy walks to the far side of the room and, as she takes her seat, falls into a typically feminine pose: she

crosses her legs, folds her arms across her chest, and hunches forward toward her desk, seeming to shrink into herself. The sauciness of the playground disappears, and, in fact, she says hardly a word during class. Meanwhile, the boys, especially those who are more physically mature, sprawl in their chairs, stretching their legs long, expanding into the available space.

Nate, a gawky, sanguine boy who has shaved his head except for a   10
small thatch that's hidden under an Oakland A's cap, leans his chair back on two legs and, although the bell has already rung, begins a noisy conversation with his friend, Kyle.

Mrs. Richter turns to him. "What's all the discussion about, Nate?" she   11
asks.

"*He's* talking to *me*," Nate answers, pointing to Kyle. Mrs. Richter   12
writes Nate's name on the chalkboard as a warning toward detention and he yells out in protest. They begin to quibble over the justice of her decision, their first—but certainly not their last—power struggle of the day. As they argue, Allison, a tall, angular girl who once told me, "My goal is to be the best wife and mother I can be," raises her hand to ask a question.

Mrs. Richter, finishing up with Nate, doesn't notice.   13

"Get your homework out, everyone!" the teacher booms, and walks   14
among the students, checking to make sure no one has shirked on her or his assignment. Allison, who sits in the front row nearest both the blackboard and the teacher, waits patiently for another moment, then, realizing she's not getting results, puts her hand down. When Mrs. Richter walks toward her, Allison tries another tack, calling out her question. Still, she gets no response, so she gives up.

As a homework assignment, the students have divided their papers into   15
one hundred squares, color-coding each square prime or composite—prime being those numbers which are divisible only by one and themselves, and composite being everything else. Mrs. Richter asks them to call out the prime numbers they've found, starting with the tens.

Nate is the first to shout, "Eleven!" The rest of the class chimes in a sec-   16
ond later. As they move through the twenties and thirties, Nate, Kyle, and Kevin, who sit near one another at the back of the class, call out louder and louder, casually competing for both quickest response and the highest decibel level. Mrs. Richter lets the boys' behavior slide, although they are intimidating other students.

"Okay," Mrs. Richter says when they've reached one hundred. "Now,   17
what do you think of one hundred and three? Prime or composite?"

Kyle, who is skinny and a little pop-eyed, yells out, "Prime!" but Mrs.   18
Richter turns away from him to give someone else a turn. Unlike Allison, who gave up when she was ignored, Kyle isn't willing to cede his teacher's attention. He begins to bounce in his chair and chant, *"Prime! Prime! Prime!"* Then, when he turns out to be right, he rebukes the teacher, saying, "See, I told you."

19   When the girls in Mrs. Richter's class do speak, they follow the rules. When Allison has another question, she raises her hand again and waits her turn; this time, the teacher responds. When Amy volunteers her sole answer of the period, she raises her hand, too. She gives the wrong answer to an easy multiplication problem, turns crimson, and flips her head forward so her hair falls over her face.

20   Occasionally, the girls shout out answers, but generally they are to the easiest, lowest-risk questions, such as the factors of four or six. And their stabs at public recognition depend on the boys' largesse: when the girls venture responses to more complex questions, the boys quickly become territorial, shouting them down with their own answers. Nate and Kyle are particularly adept at overpowering Renee, who, I've been told by the teacher, is the brightest girl in the class. (On a subsequent visit, I will see her lay her head on her desk when Nate overwhelms her and mutter, "I hate this class.")

21   Mrs. Richter doesn't say anything to condone the boys' aggressiveness, but she doesn't have to: they insist on—and receive—her attention even when she consciously tries to shift it elsewhere in order to make the class more equitable.

22   After the previous day's homework is corrected, Mrs. Richter begins a new lesson, on the use of exponents.

23   "What does three to the third power mean?" she asks the class.

24   "*I know!*" shouts Kyle.

25   Instead of calling on Kyle, who has already answered more than his share of questions, the teacher turns to Dawn, a somewhat more voluble girl who has plucked her eyebrows down to a few hairs.

26   "Do you know, Dawn?"

27   Dawn hesitates, and begins "Well, you count the number of threes and. . . ."

28   "*But I know!*" interrupts Kyle. "*I know!*"

29   Mrs. Richter deliberately ignores him, but Dawn is rattled: she never finishes her sentence, she just stops.

30   "*I know! ME!*" Kyle shouts again, and then before Dawn recovers herself he blurts, "*It's three times three times three!*"

31   At this point, Mrs. Richter gives in. She turns away from Dawn, who is staring blankly, and nods at Kyle. "Yes," she says. "Three times three times three. Does everyone get it?"

32   "*YES!*" shouts Kyle; Dawn says nothing.

33   Mrs. Richter picks up the chalk. "Let's do some others," she says.

34   "Let me!" says Kyle.

35   "I'll pick on whoever raises their hand," she tells him.

36   Nate, Kyle, and two other boys immediately shoot up their hands, fingers squeezed tight and straight in what looks like a salute.

37   "Don't you want to wait and hear the problem first?" she asks, laughing.

They drop their hands briefly. She writes "8⁴" on the board. "Okay, what would that look like written out?"   38

Although a third of the class raise their hands to answer, including a number of students who haven't yet said a word, she calls on Kyle anyway.   39

"Eight times eight times eight times eight," he says triumphantly, as the other students drop their hands.   40

When the bell rings, I ask Amy about the mistake she made in class and the embarrassment it caused her. She blushes again.   41

"Oh yeah," she says. "That's about the only time I ever talked in there. I'll never do that again."   42

READING FOR MEANING

This section presents three activities that will help you think about the meanings in Orenstein's observational essay.

Read to Comprehend

Write a few sentences briefly explaining what you think is the main idea Orenstein wants her readers to understand about Mrs. Richter's class, indicating where in the essay you see that idea expressed.

Identify any words with meanings you are unsure of—such as *sanguine* (paragraph 10) and *shirked* (14)—and find the dictionary definition for each word that makes the best sense in the context.

To help you understand the essay better, also consider trying one of these critical reading strategies, explained in Appendix 1: *summarizing* or *questioning to understand and remember.*

Read to Respond

Write several paragraphs exploring your initial thoughts and feelings about Orenstein's observational essay. Focus on anything that stands out for you, perhaps because it resonates with your own experience or because you find a statement puzzling. For example, consider writing about one of the following:

- cliques like the one Amy belongs to and which Orenstein describes as "the school's reigning elite" (paragraph 1);

- the contradictory images of Amy—the "bold," "brassy, and strong-willed" Amy (5), who is an honor roll student and actress, in contrast to the Amy in math class, "seeming to shrink into herself" and "say[ing] hardly a word" (9); or

- the ways that your own school experiences add to your understanding of and response to the essay.

To help develop your response, you might consider trying one of these critical reading strategies, explained in Appendix 1: *reflecting on challenges to your beliefs and values* or *judging the writer's credibility.*

Read to Analyze Assumptions

Write a paragraph or two analyzing an assumption in Orenstein's essay. To think critically about assumptions, here are some kinds of questions you could ask: Who holds this assumption (the writer, readers, and/or others cited in the essay)? What are the effects of the assumption in the context of the essay specifically or in society more generally? What do you think about the assumption, and is there anything in the essay that raises doubts about it? How does the assumption reinforce or critique commonly held views, and are there any alternative ideas, beliefs, or values that would challenge this assumption?

You might choose an assumption from the list below, using the questions accompanying it in addition to the ones above to help you get started. Or you can choose another assumption in the essay to explore.

- **assumptions about power struggles.** Orenstein describes Mrs. Richter's math class as the site of power struggles—between some boys and girls and between the teacher and two boys, Nate and Kyle. Even though she is the only adult and teacher in the room and presumably possesses power (she sets the rules and can send students to detention), Mrs. Richter seems unable to exercise it effectively or fairly.

  To think critically about the assumptions in this essay related to power struggles, ask yourself questions like these: In what ways do Mrs. Richter, Nate and Kyle, and even the girls assert power in the classroom? For example, how do you interpret the fact that the boys raise their hands most of the time or that Mrs. Richter is the one asking questions and presumably determining which answers are correct? How do the behaviors of Mrs. Richter and girls like Allison and Dawn create a space for Nate and Kyle to exercise power? What assumptions about power do you think Orenstein, Mrs. Richter, the boys, and the girls hold? What were your assumptions about power in the classroom before you read this essay? Did reading it affect those assumptions? If so, how?

- **assumptions about gender differences.** In Mrs. Richter's math class, the boys seem to know all the answers. In the 1980s, standardized test scores showed that (at least in the United States) girls were significantly behind boys in math, but in recent years the gap seems to be narrowing. Nevertheless, many people continue to assume that boys are better than girls at math and science. Several theories have been put forward to explain this apparent gender difference: (1) boys are naturally endowed with better spatial abilities and logical thinking skills than girls; (2) boys are more interested in math and science careers; (3) boys, unlike girls, typically play games such as baseball that help them develop math skills; and (4) parents and teachers tend to treat girls stereotypically as weaker in math and therefore create a self-fulfilling prophecy.

To think critically about assumptions in this essay related to gender differences, ask yourself questions like these: What do Orenstein, Mrs. Richter, the boys, and the girls seem to assume about who will be able to answer Mrs. Richter's questions? When you were in elementary or middle school, how common was the assumption that boys would do better in math and science than girls? Which of the four theories listed above do you think you or your teachers would have accepted? What are your assumptions about this issue now?

To help you analyze assumptions in the essay, also consider trying one of these critical reading strategies, explained in Appendix 1: *contextualizing, reflecting on challenges to your beliefs and values,* or *looking for patterns of opposition.*

READING LIKE A WRITER

DESCRIBING PEOPLE

Writers of observational essays often focus their observations on people, whether alone or interacting with others. To present people, writers can choose from a repertoire of describing strategies. They may show us how people look and dress as well as how they gesture and move. They also may let us hear people talk, either to the interviewer or with other people. In this essay, we hear Amy talk to Orenstein, and we overhear the students and teacher talking with one another in the classroom. Dialogue functions in observational writing both to present people and to inform readers about a subject. To present the Weston School students' interactions and the teacher's role in the eighth-grade math classroom, Orenstein relies increasingly on dialogue beginning in paragraph 11. From paragraph 22 to the end, she relies mainly on dialogue.

Analyze

1. Reread paragraphs 1 to 5, 8 to 10, and 18, and underline the details that enable you to visualize Amy, Mrs. Richter, Nate, and Kyle.

2. Reread paragraphs 22 to 41, focusing on the dialogue (the material within quotation marks) and the descriptive speaker tags (*she asks, shouts Kyle*). Think about what you learn about the teacher and the students from this dialogue, and make notes about what you discover.

Write

Write several sentences explaining the kinds of details that Orenstein uses to describe people, giving examples from your annotations. Add another sentence or two explaining what the dialogue adds to your understanding of the people.

CONSIDERING IDEAS FOR YOUR OWN WRITING

Consider writing an observational essay about a group of people who interact with each other for a specific purpose. The essay might be about a teacher and students interacting in a classroom to learn a specific concept or practice a skill; a group of actors rehearsing for a play; a basketball team practicing for an upcoming game; employees working collaboratively on a project; committee members, businesspeople, or politicians debating a policy or proposal; or members of a club, sports team, or other interest group meeting to resolve a crisis.

A Special Reading Strategy

Looking for Patterns of Opposition

Looking for patterns of opposition can be an especially useful strategy for reading observational essays like Peggy Orenstein's "The Daily Grind: Lessons in the Hidden Curriculum." Following the instructions in Appendix 1, pp. 575–79, you will see that the first thing you need to do is reread the essay and mark the oppositions you find. "The Daily Grind," like the "Letter from Birmingham Jail" excerpt that we use to illustrate this strategy, is teeming with oppositions or binaries. In many instances, two opposing terms are obvious, such as *girls* versus *boys*. A less obvious opposition is the contrasting description *feminine pose . . . seeming to shrink into herself* versus *boys . . . expanding into the available space* (paragraph 9). Sometimes, one of the opposing terms is not introduced until later in the essay. For example, Amy is described in paragraph 5 as *bold*, but later, in paragraph 9, she is described as *say[ing] hardly a word during class*. You may even find instances where only one of the terms appears in the essay and you need to supply the missing opposite term. For example, Amy is described in paragraph 3 as someone who *loves the spotlight*, but in Mrs. Richter's class it is clear from her behavior that she doesn't want to be noticed. So you could present the opposition as *loves the spotlight* versus *tries to disappear* (or you could use the description *flips her head forward so her hair falls over her face* [paragraph 19]).

See Appendix 1 for detailed guidelines on using the looking for patterns of opposition strategy.

Brian Cable

The Last Stop

Brian Cable wrote the following observational essay when he was a first-year college student. His observations are based on a visit to a mortuary, or funeral home, a subject he views with both seriousness and humor. Hoping as he enters the mortuary not to end up as a participant that day, he records what he sees and interviews two key people, the funeral director and the embalmer. In reporting his observations, he seems equally concerned with the burial process—from the purchase of a casket to the display of the body—and the people who manage this process.

As you read, notice how the writer presents the place and people and how he attempts to heighten readers' interest in the mortuary by considering it in the larger social context of people's beliefs about death and burial.

Let us endeavor so to live that when we come to die even the undertaker will be sorry.

—MARK TWAIN

Death is a subject largely ignored by the living. We don't discuss it much, not as children (when Grandpa dies, he is said to be "going away"), not as adults, not even as senior citizens. Throughout our lives, death remains intensely private. The death of a loved one can be very painful, partly because of the sense of loss, but also because someone else's mortality reminds us all too vividly of our own. 1

Thus did I notice more than a few people avert their eyes as they walked past the dusty-pink building that houses the Goodbody Mortuaries. It looked a bit like a church—tall, with gothic arches and stained glass—and somewhat like an apartment complex—low, with many windows stamped out of red brick. 2

It wasn't at all what I had expected. I thought it would be more like Forest Lawn, serene with lush green lawns and meticulously groomed gardens, a place set apart from the hustle of day-to-day life. Here instead was an odd pink structure set in the middle of a business district. On top of the Goodbody Mortuaries sign was a large electric clock. What the hell, I thought, mortuaries are concerned with time, too. 3

I was apprehensive as I climbed the stone steps to the entrance. I feared rejection or, worse, an invitation to come and stay. The door was massive, yet it swung open easily on well-oiled hinges. "Come in," said the sign. "We're always open." Inside was a cool and quiet reception room. Curtains were drawn against the outside glare, cutting the light down to a soft glow. 4

I found the funeral director in the main lobby, adjacent to the reception room. Like most people, I had preconceptions about what an undertaker 5 looked like. Mr. Deaver fulfilled my expectations entirely. Tall and thin, he even had beady eyes and a bony face. A low, slanted forehead gave way to a beaked nose. His skin, scrubbed of all color, contrasted sharply with his jet black hair. He was wearing a starched white shirt, gray pants, and black shoes. Indeed, he looked like death on two legs.

6   He proved an amiable sort, however, and was easy to talk to. As funeral director, Mr. Deaver ("call me Howard") was responsible for a wide range of services. Goodbody Mortuaries, upon notification of someone's death, will remove the remains from the hospital or home. They then prepare the body for viewing, whereupon features distorted by illness or accident are restored to their natural condition. The body is embalmed and then placed in a casket selected by the family of the deceased. Services are held in one of three chapels at the mortuary, and afterward the casket is placed in a "visitation room," where family and friends can pay their last respects. Goodbody also makes arrangements for the purchase of a burial site and transports the body there for burial.

7   All this information Howard related in a well-practiced, professional manner. It was obvious he was used to explaining the specifics of his profession. We sat alone in the lobby. His desk was bone clean, no pencils or paper, nothing—just a telephone. He did all his paperwork at home; as it turned out, he and his wife lived right upstairs. The phone rang. As he listened, he bit his lips and squeezed his Adam's apple somewhat nervously.

8   "I think we'll be able to get him in by Friday. No, no, the family wants him cremated."

9   His tone was that of a broker conferring on the Dow Jones. Directly behind him was a sign announcing "Visa and Master Charge Welcome Here." It was tacked to the wall, right next to a crucifix.

10   "Some people have the idea that we are bereavement specialists, that we can handle the emotional problems which follow a death: Only a trained therapist can do that. We provide services for the dead, not counseling for the living."

11   Physical comfort was the one thing they did provide for the living. The lobby was modestly but comfortably furnished. There were several couches, in colors ranging from earth brown to pastel blue, and a coffee table in front of each one. On one table lay some magazines and a vase of flowers. Another supported an aquarium. Paintings of pastoral scenes hung on every wall. The lobby looked more or less like that of an old hotel. Nothing seemed to match, but it had a homey, lived-in look.

12   "The last time the Goodbodies decorated was in '59, I believe. It still makes people feel welcome."

13   And so "Goodbody" was not a name made up to attract customers but the owners' family name. The Goodbody family started the business way back in 1915. Today, they do over five hundred services a year.

"We're in *Ripley's Believe It or Not*, along with another funeral home 14
whose owners' names are Baggit and Sackit," Howard told me, without
cracking a smile.

I followed him through an arched doorway into a chapel that smelled 15
musty and old. The only illumination came from sunlight filtered through a
stained glass ceiling. Ahead of us lay a casket. I could see that it contained
a man dressed in a black suit. Wooden benches ran on either side of an
aisle that led to the body. I got no closer. From the red roses across the
dead man's chest, it was apparent that services had already been held.

"It was a large service," remarked Howard. "Look at that casket—a 16
beautiful work of craftsmanship."

I guess it was. Death may be the great leveler, but one's coffin quickly 17
reestablishes one's status.

We passed into a bright, fluorescent-lit "display room." Inside were 18
thirty coffins, lids open, patiently awaiting inspection. Like new cars on
the showroom floor, they gleamed with high-gloss finishes.

"We have models for every price range." 19

Indeed, there was a wide variety. They came in all colors and various 20
materials. Some were little more than cloth-covered cardboard boxes, others were made of wood, and a few were made of steel, copper, or bronze.
Prices started at $400 and averaged about $1,800. Howard motioned
toward the center of the room: "The top of the line."

This was a solid bronze casket, its seams electronically welded to resist 21
corrosion. Moisture-proof and air-tight, it could be hermetically sealed off
from all outside elements. Its handles were plated with 14-karat gold. The
price: a cool $5,000.

A proper funeral remains a measure of respect for the deceased. But it 22
is expensive. In the United States the amount spent annually on funerals
is about $2 billion. Among ceremonial expenditures, funerals are second
only to weddings. As a result, practices are changing. Howard has been
in this business for forty years. He remembers a time when everyone
was buried. Nowadays, with burials costing $2,000 a shot, people often
opt instead for cremation—as Howard put it, "a cheap, quick, and easy
means of disposal." In some areas of the country, the cremation rate is
now over 60 percent. Observing this trend, one might wonder whether
burials are becoming obsolete. Do burials serve an important role in
society?

For Tim, Goodbody's licensed mortician, the answer is very definitely 23
yes. Burials will remain in common practice, according to the slender
embalmer with the disarming smile, because they allow family and friends
to view the deceased. Painful as it may be, such an experience brings
home the finality of death. "Something deep within us demands a confrontation with death," Tim explained. "A last look assures us that the person
we loved is, indeed, gone forever."

24   Apparently, we also need to be assured that the body will be laid to rest in comfort and peace. The average casket, with its inner-spring mattress and pleated satin lining, is surprisingly roomy and luxurious. Perhaps such an air of comfort makes it easier for the family to give up their loved one. In addition, the burial site fixes the deceased in the survivors' memory, like a new address. Cremation provides none of these comforts.

25   Tim started out as a clerk in a funeral home but then studied to become a mortician. "It was a profession I could live with," he told me with a sly grin. Mortuary science might be described as a cross between pre-med and cosmetology, with courses in anatomy and embalming as well as in restorative art.

26   Tim let me see the preparation, or embalming, room, a white-walled chamber about the size of an operating room. Against the wall was a large sink with elbow taps and a draining board. In the center of the room stood a table with equipment for preparing the arterial embalming fluid, which consists primarily of formaldehyde, a preservative, and phenol, a disinfectant. This mixture sanitizes and also gives better color to the skin. Facial features can then be "set" to achieve a restful expression. Missing eyes, ears, and even noses can be replaced.

27   I asked Tim if his job ever depressed him. He bridled at the question: "No, it doesn't depress me at all. I do what I can for people and take satisfaction in enabling relatives to see their loved ones as they were in life." He said that he felt people were becoming more aware of the public service his profession provides. Grade-school classes now visit funeral homes as often as they do police stations and museums. The mortician is no longer regarded as a minister of death.

28   Before leaving, I wanted to see a body up close. I thought I could be indifferent after all I had seen and heard, but I wasn't sure. Cautiously, I reached out and touched the skin. It felt cold and firm, not unlike clay. As I walked out, I felt glad to have satisfied my curiosity about dead bodies, but all too happy to let someone else handle them.

READING FOR MEANING

This section presents three activities that will help you think about the meanings in Cable's observational essay.

Read to Comprehend

Write a few sentences briefly explaining what you think is the main idea Cable wants his readers to understand about the Goodbody Mortuary, indicating where in the essay you see that idea expressed.

Identify any words with meanings you are unsure of— such as *avert* (paragraph 2) and *pastoral* (11)—and find the dictionary definition for each word that makes the best sense in the context.

To help you understand the essay better, also consider trying one of these critical reading strategies, explained in Appendix 1: *summarizing* or *questioning to understand and remember.*

Read to Respond

Write several paragraphs exploring your initial thoughts and feelings about Cable's observational essay. Focus on anything that stands out for you, perhaps because it resonates with your own experience or because you find a statement puzzling. For example, consider writing about one of the following:

- Cable's preconceptions about what an undertaker would look like (paragraph 5), perhaps in relation to fictional representations with which you are familiar;

- the information that "[g]rade-school classes now visit funeral homes as often as they do police stations and museums" (27), perhaps in relation to the field trips you took in grade school; or

- Cable's "curiosity about dead bodies" and what one feels like (28), in relation to your own firsthand experience of death.

To help develop your response, also consider trying one of these critical reading strategies, explained in Appendix 1: *contextualizing* or *reflecting on challenges to your beliefs and values.*

Read to Analyze Assumptions

Write a paragraph or two analyzing an assumption in Cable's essay. To think critically about assumptions, here are some kinds of questions you could ask: Who holds this assumption (the writer, readers, and/or others cited in the essay)? What are the effects of the assumption in the context of the essay specifically or in society more generally? What do you think about the assumption, and is there anything in the essay that raises doubts about it? How does the assumption reinforce or critique commonly held views, and are there any alternative ideas, beliefs, or values that would challenge this assumption?

You might choose an assumption from the list below, using the questions accompanying it in addition to the ones above to help you get started. Or you can choose another assumption in the essay to explore.

- **assumptions about death.** Cable begins his essay by suggesting that we tend not to talk directly and openly about death and that the painfulness of a loved one's death may be in part "because someone else's mortality reminds us all too vividly of our own" (paragraph 1). Later, he also reports Tim's different idea that "[s]omething deep within us demands a confrontation with death" (23).

  To think critically about the assumptions in this essay related to death, ask yourself questions like these: How are Cable's and Tim's beliefs reflected in their comments elsewhere in the essay? Which attitude best represents your own? What cultural, family, and religious traditions affect your thinking about death? As you compare your assumptions with those of other students in your class, particularly students brought up with different traditions, what important differences do you see in the way people view death?

- **assumptions about funerals as a status symbol.** Comparing the coffin "display room" to a new car "showroom" (paragraph 18) and describing the top-of-the-line $5,000 "solid bronze casket" with "14-karat gold" handles (21), Cable suggests that "[d]eath may be the great leveler, but one's coffin quickly reestablishes one's status" (17).

     To think critically about the assumptions in this essay related to funerals as a status symbol, ask yourself questions like these: It is fairly obvious why someone would want an expensive car (because of its luxury and performance, for example) or an expensive home (for its accommodations and location, for example), but why do you suppose so many people buy expensive caskets, cemetery plots, and newspaper death notices and spend as much money on a funeral as they do on a wedding? What messages does an expensive funeral send to the people who attend? What other kinds of assumptions besides those about status might motivate people to spend a lot of money for this purpose?

To help you analyze assumptions in the essay, also consider trying one of these critical reading strategies, explained in Appendix 1: *reflecting on challenges to your beliefs and values, exploring the significance of figurative language,* or *looking for patterns of opposition.*

READING LIKE A WRITER

CONVEYING A DOMINANT IMPRESSION OF THE SUBJECT

Writers of observational essays seek to inform readers about a subject, but they go further to convey to readers their impression of the subject. The observational essay's dominant impression is comparable to the autobiographical essay's autobiographical significance. It brings the many details into focus, letting readers know what the writer considers important and interesting about the subject. Writers create a dominant impression in several ways—by the attitude or preconceptions they reveal, by the information they include and leave out, and by the way they describe the subject. Readers may not find a sentence beginning "My impression is . . . ," but they will nevertheless get a distinct impression of the subject.

Analyze

1. Underline words and phrases in the essay that most clearly or strongly suggest Cable's attitudes toward or feelings about Goodbody Mortuaries. Be

selective. In a successful essay, every detail reveals the author's attitude, but certain details will be especially revealing.

2. Note in the margin what your annotations seem to reveal about Cable's attitude toward his subject.

Write

Write several sentences explaining the impression you get about Goodbody Mortuaries, supporting your explanation with examples from the reading. Then add a few sentences evaluating how successful you think Cable is in conveying an impression of the funeral home.

CONSIDERING IDEAS FOR YOUR OWN WRITING

Think of places or activities that you have strong preconceptions about or that you have had little or no experience with and yet have been curious about or perhaps even put off by. Maybe in your neighborhood there is an upscale gym where you assume participants are interested primarily in posing for and competing with each other, a day-care center where you assume the teachers are idealistic and devoted to the children, a tattoo parlor where you assume all the clients are young, an acupuncture clinic where you doubt there is any scientific basis for the treatments, or a fast-food place where you expect that nearly all employees find their jobs onerous and unrewarding. Or perhaps on your campus there is a tutoring center where you assume tutors do students' work for them, a student counseling center where you have been led to believe that students are not treated with sympathy and understanding, or an office that seems to schedule campus events at times that make it difficult for commuter students to participate. Because many readers would likely share your preconceptions and curiosity, you would have a relatively easy time engaging their interest in the subject. How would you test your preconceptions through your observations and interviews? How might you use your preconceptions to capture readers' attention, as Cable does?

Juan Diego Arellano

A Trip to the Dentist

Juan Diego Arellano was a first-year college student when he wrote the following essay for an assignment in his composition class. Like Brian Cable in the preceding selection, Arellano writes about a particular place and some of the people who work there.

As you read, notice how Arellano focuses his observations on Dr. Piedra's handling of Molly and think about the impression this anecdote creates.

The other readings in this chapter are followed by reading and writing activities. Following this reading, however, you are on your own to decide how to read for meaning and read like a writer.

1   The buildings surrounding the Children's Dentistry of Rancho Cucamonga were virtually identical—tan walls, a few windows, and a suite number above each entrance. The dentistry, however, was set apart by a giant poster of a smiling purple hippo (the logo) attached to its double doors, immediately giving the office a "kid-friendly" appeal. Still, I was apprehensive; not only was this the first interview that I had ever done, but I also had not visited a pediatric dentistry in years and I had no idea what to expect.

2   I pushed open the doors and was greeted not by the lackluster waiting room I expected but instead by color and liveliness—it didn't even look like a dentist's office. A jungle theme was obvious from the detailed wall mural of exotic creatures: A panda bear snacked on bamboo next to the entrance, a colorful toucan rested under the shade of an enormous tree in the corner of the lobby, and a trail of ladybugs surrounded the orange shuttered windows of the receptionist's desk. A woman sat behind the desk, busily typing information into her computer. As I approached, she looked up with a smile and said, "May I help you?" I explained that I had an appointment with Dr. Isabella Piedra; I was here to learn about her work as a pediatric dentist. She introduced herself as Mirtha, the office manager, and informed me that the doctor was with a patient but that I should "please take a seat" and she would show me around the office in a few moments while I waited to speak to Dr. Piedra.

3   I sat down in one of the waiting room chairs, watching the children interact as they waited for their names to be called. Two boys played vigorously on the Playstation, while a mother played a touch-screen game on the wall with her toddler. Other parents sat quietly in the jungle-themed faux bamboo chairs, some reading magazines, others amusing themselves by watching *Finding Nemo* on the flat-screen TV at the opposite end of the room. I was surprised to see the extent to which the dentist had created a welcoming and relaxing environment for the parents and their children, even making *me* more at ease as I apprehensively waited for the interview.

Mirtha walked from behind her desk and into the lobby, saying "Let me   4
show you around." Her assistant buzzed us through to the back where the
procedures took place. As soon as we walked through the doors, the vig-
orous cries of a child startled me. I was even more astonished by Mirtha's
tranquil demeanor in the midst of such a frenzied atmosphere.

"It's normal for the kids to react this way," she said. "It's not because   5
they are in pain, but because they misbehave." She continued by explaining that the loudest, "most uncooperative kids" are usually with their
parents, who unintentionally encourage them to act out by sympathizing
with them. I wondered why she assumed the kids were not really in pain
or at least scared, but I thought it best not to ask.

I followed her into a narrow, nearly empty cleaning room and was   6
overpowered by the antiseptic smell of disinfectant. Every instrument in
the dentistry must undergo an extensive sterilizing process, which begins
with a boiling bath in an ultrasonic machine that removes debris from the
tools. This is followed by a cold rinse with cleaning agents and other anti-
septics, after which the tools are sealed, vacuum-packed and reheated to
230 degrees before they can be reused.

Mirtha demonstrated this procedure as she explained each of the steps,   7
reiterating to me the high standards of dentistry. As she was finishing, we
could hear Dr. Piedra escorting a little boy to the lobby, telling his parents
that he needed to come back in six months for a checkup. We abruptly
concluded our tour, and I was ushered into Dr. Piedra's office, where we
found her filling out charts from her last procedure.

Dr. Piedra was of medium height, thin, with shoulder-length hair tied   8
into a perky ponytail. Under her starched white lab coat she wore pink
and white scrubs with tennis shoes.

"Take a seat," she invited me; "it's great to meet you!" She had a   9
thick Spanish accent with a warm tone that instantly made me feel less
anxious—a great bedside manner, I thought. Her desk was covered with
a clutter of pens, papers, charts, and framed family photos, but despite the
mess it was clear that Dr. Piedra had everything under control.

We sat across from each other in comfortable chairs, and she told me   10
why she had chosen pediatric over general dentistry. Her answer was simple: "The main difference is that children are just less complicated. I love
the kids; they complain less, and unlike most adults they don't tell me how
to do my job." As we conversed, I was impressed by Dr. Piedra's passion
for her profession and enthusiasm for her patients despite her hilarious stories of patients who had thrown up on her, spit on her, and even bitten her.
"The best part about the job is seeing patients that I've had for over twelve
years," she said with conviction. "It's amazing to see them grow up."

A typical day for Dr. Piedra starts at 8 a.m., treating the "emergency   11
patients." She then attends to the surgical patients, who take up most of the
day. The last hours are generally dedicated to the treatment of new patients

and other appointments. Telling me this schedule led her to another point about why she chose dentistry over other medical professions: "The hours are more regulated; I have practically a nine to five job, so I can spend more time with my own kids."

12   Her compelling stories were cut short as the intercom sounded: "Dr. Piedra, your patient is ready in room two." She rose from her chair, asking, "Would you like to see one of my procedures as part of your interview?" Excited, I trailed behind her into the exam room, the walls of which matched the exotic mural that I had seen in the waiting room. The dentist's chair was in the center of the room, surrounded by an X-ray machine and trays with instruments perfectly lined up in neat rows. A flat-screen TV on the ceiling played a movie for the patient to watch during the procedure.

13   We entered and a small girl (about five years old), whom the doctor introduced as Molly, lay pouting on the chair, arms crossed, and determined. I was surprised at the child's attitude, especially after all the positive things that Dr. Piedra had told me about her patients. I wondered if this was what Mirtha meant when she described some of the patients as misbehaving.

14   The doctor walked toward Molly, asked how she was doing, and remarked on how much the girl had grown since the last time she'd seen her. Molly glared at her but said nothing. The doctor put on latex gloves, picked up one of her tools, and sweetly asked Molly to open her mouth—a request that was firmly refused. The mood instantly changed; the tension in the room was obvious. Dr. Piedra attempted to gently open Molly's mouth, and as soon as she did the little girl's teeth chomped down on the dentist's fingers. Apparently unaffected by her patient's behavior, the doctor calmly pressed the intercom on the wall: "Jill, can you come to room two, please?"

15   Jill entered the room a few seconds later. She was tall, big and muscular—she meant business. Molly sat in her seat, still cold and uncooperative. I sat in the corner of the room with horrified anticipation, as if I were about to watch a wrestling match. Jill wasted no time. She swiftly applied light pressure to Molly's jaw, forcing her to open her mouth just long enough for Dr. Piedra to insert a type of wedge that made it impossible for Molly to close her mouth. Molly tried to fight back by kicking and yelling, but both the doctor and the assistant remained unmoved. The event unfolding in front of me was a complete contrast with what I had previously thought about the doctor—I hadn't expected her to use physical force to restrain her patients. Eventually, though, Molly grew tired of fighting back and allowed Dr. Piedra to examine her.

16   Ten minutes later, Dr. Piedra removed her hands from the girl's mouth, took off her gloves and said triumphantly, "OK, sweetie, we're all done!" She nodded at Jill, who released the girl from her death grip. Ironically, the minute the procedure was over, Molly stopped crying and followed Jill to

the lobby to meet her mom and to receive a handful of stickers. As soon as they left, I asked Dr. Piedra if this was often a common problem. In answering, she acknowledged my surprise at the mismatch between her friendly bedside manner and the forceful way she deals with problem patients like Molly: "It may seem like I'm rough with the patients, but I enjoy them so much because I know that eventually they will grow out of their behavior."

I walked out, feeling confused about Molly's behavior and disturbed that Dr. Piedra resorted to force without trying less radical solutions. I wondered if Molly could have been cajoled into cooperating or if her mother could have helped calm her. I know that many adults have anxiety about dental procedures and take pills to calm themselves. Would pills work for kids too? As I walked out, the smiling jungle animals frolicking on the walls took on new meaning. It was a jungle in there. I was glad I was neither a patient nor planning to become a pediatric dentist.

17

READING FOR MEANING

Reading for meaning involves three activities:

- reading to comprehend,
- reading to respond, and
- reading to analyze assumptions.

Reread Arellano's essay, and then write a page or so explaining your understanding of its basic meaning or main point, a personal response you have to it, and what you see as one of its underlying assumptions.

READING LIKE A WRITER

Writers of observational essays

- describe places and people,
- organize information from various sources,
- adopt an authorial role, and
- convey a dominant impression of the subject.

Focus on one of these strategies in Arellano's essay, and analyze it carefully through close rereading and annotating. Then write several sentences explaining what you have learned, giving specific examples from the reading to support your explanation. Add a few sentences evaluating how successfully Arellano uses the strategy to help readers understand what goes on behind the scenes in a children's dental office.

Reviewing What Makes an Effective Essay

Observation

Analyze

Choose one reading from this chapter that seems to you especially effective. Before rereading the selection, jot down one or two reasons you remember it as an example of good observational writing.

Reread your chosen selection, and add further notes about what makes it a particularly successful example. Consider the selection's purpose and how well it achieves that purpose for its intended readers. (You can make an informed guess about the intended readers and their expectations by noting the publication source of the essay.) Then assess how well the essay uses the writing strategies of describing people and places, organizing information from various sources, adopting an authorial role, and conveying a dominant impression of the subject.

Write

Write at least a page supporting your choice of this reading as an example of effective observational writing. Refer to details and specific parts of the essay as you explain how it works as observation and as you justify your evaluation of its effectiveness. You need not argue that it is the best reading in the chapter or that it is flawless, only that it is, in your view, a strong example of the genre.

A GUIDE TO WRITING
OBSERVATIONAL ESSAYS

The readings in this chapter have helped you learn a great deal about observational writing. You have seen that writers of observational essays present unfamiliar places, people, and activities. You have also seen that they collect large amounts of information and ideas from visits and interviews, which must be sorted, organized, and integrated into a readable draft. As a reader of observational writing, you have examined how writers convey a dominant impression through their selection and organization of information about the subject. Having learned how writers present their subject in a way that interests and informs readers, and seen how readers interpret and respond to observational writing, you can now approach observation more confidently as a writer. You can more readily imagine the problems you must solve as a writer of observation, the materials and possibilities you have to work with, the choices and decisions you must make. This Guide to Writing offers detailed suggestions for writing observational essays and resources to help you solve the special challenges this kind of writing presents.

INVENTION AND RESEARCH

The following activities will help you choose a subject, research and reflect on your subject, and decide on the impression you want your essay to convey to readers. Keep a written record of your work on these activities to use later when you draft and revise the essay.

Choosing a Subject

List the most promising subjects you can think of, beginning with any you listed for the Considering Ideas for Your Own Writing activities following the readings in this chapter. Rather than limiting yourself to the first subject that comes to mind, take a few minutes to consider your options and list as many subjects as you can. Below are some criteria that can help you choose a promising subject, followed by additional suggestions for the types of people, places, and activities you might consider writing about.

Criteria for Choosing a Subject

Whether your subject is a person, a group of people, a place, or an activity, it should be

- a subject that you can gain access to in the time allowed for researching the essay, allowing you to make detailed observations;

- a subject about which (or with whom) you can conduct in-depth interviews;

- a subject about which/whom you can find background information (if required by your instructor);

- a subject about which/whom you have ideas or at least strong curiosity;

- a subject your readers will find interesting and informative.

People

- anyone doing work that you might want to do—city council member, police officer, lab technician, computer programmer, attorney, salesperson

- anyone with an unusual job or hobby—dog trainer, private detective, ham radio operator, race car driver, novelist

- a campus personality—coach, distinguished teacher, newspaper editor, oldest or youngest student

- someone recently recognized for community service or achievement

Places

- small-claims court, consumer fraud office, city planner's office

- bodybuilding gym, weight-reduction clinic, martial arts school

- hospital emergency room, campus health center, hospice, psychiatric unit

- recycling center, airport control tower, theater, museum, sports arena

Activities

- tutoring, registering voters, rehearsing for a play, repairing a car

- an unconventional sports event—dogs' Frisbee tournament, chess match, amateur wrestling or boxing meet, dog sledding, log sawing and splitting, ice-fishing contest, Olympics for people with disabilities

- a team practicing a sport or other activity (one you can observe as a curious outsider, not as an experienced participant)

- a community improvement project—graffiti cleaning, tree planting, house repairing, church painting, road or highway litter collecting

- special courses—rock climbing, folk dancing, dog training, truck driving

Researching Your Subject

The writing and research activities that follow will enable you to gather information and ideas about your subject.

Considering Your Own Role. Decide tentatively whether you will adopt a detached spectator or participant-observer role to present your observations. As a detached spectator, you would present what you learn from visiting the place and interviewing people there. As a participant-observer, you would conduct interviews and also take part in an activity at the place for a brief period to gain firsthand experience you can insert into your essay. To become a participant, you will need to ask permission and possibly arrange more than one visit.

Making a Schedule. Set up a tentative schedule for your observational and interview visits. If you could and want to participate in the activity you are writing about, schedule that, too. Figure out first the amount of time you have to complete your essay. Then determine the scope of your project—a one-time observation, an interview with follow-up, or multiple observations and interviews. Decide what visits you will need to make, whom you will need to interview, and what library or Internet work you might want to do to get background information about your subject. Estimate the time necessary for each, knowing you might need to schedule more time than anticipated. Then use phone calls or e-mails to schedule visits or arrange interviews. (Consult the Field Research section in Appendix 2, pp. 603–07, for helpful guidelines on observing, interviewing, and taking notes.)

Exploring Readers' and Your Own Preconceptions. Write for several minutes about your readers' as well as your own assumptions and expectations. For example, ask questions like these about your readers: Who are they? What are they likely to think about the subject? What would they want to know about it?

Also reflect on yourself: Why do you want to research this subject? What do you expect to find out about it? What aspects of it do you expect to be interesting or entertaining?

Visiting a Place. During your visit, take notes on what you observe. Do not try to impose order on your notes at this stage; simply record whatever you notice. Pay special attention to visual details and other kinds of details (sounds, smells) as well as overheard conversations that you can draw on later to describe the place and people.

Interviewing a Person. Prepare for the interview by writing out some preliminary questions. But do not be afraid of abandoning your script during the interview. Listen carefully to what is said and ask follow-up questions. Take notes; if you like and your subject agrees, you may also tape-record the interview.

Gathering Information. If you do background reading, take careful notes and keep accurate bibliographic records of your sources. Try to pick up relevant fliers, brochures, or reports at the place you observe. In addition, you might conduct research on the Internet or in your college library. (For more information, see Appendix 2 on Library and Internet Research.)

Reflecting on Your Subject

After you research your subject, consider your purpose in writing about it and formulate a tentative thesis statement.

Considering Your Purpose.   Write for several minutes about the impression of the subject you want to convey to your readers. As you write, try to answer this question: What makes this subject worth observing? Your answer to this question might change as you write, but a preliminary answer will give your writing a direction to follow, or what journalists commonly call an "angle," on the subject. This angle will help you choose what to include as well as what to emphasize in your draft. Use the following questions to help clarify the dominant impression you want your essay to convey:

- What visual images or other sensory details of the subject stand out in your memory? Think about the feelings these images evoke in you. If they evoke contradictory feelings, consider how you could use these details to convey to readers the complexity of your feelings about the place, people, or activities you observed.

- What is most surprising about your observations? Compare the preconceptions you listed earlier with what you actually saw or heard.

- What interests you the most about the people you interviewed? Compare the direct observations you made about them with the indirect or secondhand information you gathered about them.

Formulating a Tentative Thesis Statement.   Review what you wrote for Considering Your Purpose, and add two or three sentences that will bring into focus the dominant impression you want to give readers about the person, place, or activity you observed. This impression is based on an insight into, interpretation of, or idea about the person, place, or activity you have gained while observing it. Try to write sentences that do not summarize what you have already written but that convey a deeper understanding of the dominant impression you want to make on your readers.

Keep in mind that readers do not expect you to begin your observational essay with the kind of explicit thesis statement typical of argumentative essays. None of the readings in this chapter offers to readers an explicit statement of the dominant impression the writer hopes to convey about the subject. Instead, the writers convey an impression through the ways they describe their subjects, select information to share with readers, or narrate the story of their experiences with the subject. And yet it is possible for readers to infer from each reading a dominant impression of the subject.

Nearly all first attempts to state a dominant impression or a thesis are eventually revised once drafting gets under way. Writing the first draft helps writers of observational essays discover their main impression and find ways to convey that impression without ever stating it directly. Just because there is no explicit thesis statement in an observational essay does not mean that it lacks focus or fails to convey an impression of its subject.

Considering Visuals. Think about whether visuals—photographs you take, drawings you make, copies of revealing illustrative materials you picked up at the place you observed—would strengthen your observational essay. If you submit your essay electronically to other students and your instructor or if you post it to a Web site, consider including snippets of your interviews or sounds from the place (if you make use of a tape recorder in your project) or your own digital photographs or video. Remember to ask permission to make visual or audio records. Some people may be willing to be interviewed or share printed material but reluctant to allow photographs or recordings. Visual and audio materials are not at all a requirement of an effective observational essay, as you can tell from the readings in this chapter, but they could add a new dimension to your writing.

DRAFTING

The following guidelines will help you set goals for your draft, plan its organization, and think about a useful sentence strategy.

Setting Goals

Establishing goals for your draft before you begin writing will enable you to make decisions and work more confidently. Consider the following questions now, and keep them in mind as you draft. They will help you set goals for drafting as well as recall how the writers you have read in this chapter tried to achieve similar goals.

- *How can I help my readers imagine the subject?* In addition to describing visual details, as all of the authors in this chapter do, should I evoke other senses, in the way that Edge describes how a pig lip smells and tastes and what its unusual texture is? Should I characterize people by their clothes, facial expressions, and talk, as Orlean, Orenstein, Cable, and Arellano do? Should I use surprising metaphors or similes, as the author of "Soup" does in describing Yeganeh's "working like a demon alchemist" (paragraph 1)?

- *How can I engage my readers?* Should I begin with a surprising statement, as the author of "Soup," Orlean, and Cable do? Should I begin by setting the stage, as Edge, Orenstein, and Arellano do? Should I introduce the person, as Orenstein, Orlean, and the author of "Soup" do? Can I use my experience as a participant observer to engage readers' interest, as Edge does? Can I use humor, as Edge, Orlean, and Cable do?

- *How can I present and distribute the information?* Should I present some information through dialogue from interviews, as all the writers do? Can I also present overheard conversation, as in "Soup" and Orenstein's essay? Should I present information I gathered from direct observations, as all the authors do, as well as from secondary research in the library and on the Internet, as Orlean may do?

- *How can I organize and present the information?* Should I organize it topically in groups of related information, as the author of "Soup," Orlean, and Cable do? Should I arrange it in a chronological narrative order, as Arellano does? Should I alternate between a narrative and a topical organization, as Edge does?

- *How can I convey a dominant impression?* Should I select information that focuses on one primary aspect of the subject, as the author of "Soup" does? Should I use my experience as a participant observer or as a guide to focus on what I think is important, as Edge, Orlean, and Orenstein do? Should I insert my own insights, as Orenstein, Cable, and Arellano do?

Organizing Your Draft

With your goals in mind, reread the notes you took about the place and people, and decide how to organize them—grouped into topics or put in chronological order. If you think a topical organization would work best, try grouping your observations and naming the topic of each group. If you think narrating what happened would help you organize your observations, make a time line and note where the information would go. You might want to try different kinds of outlines before settling on a plan and drafting your essay.

Writers who use a narrative structure usually follow a simple, straightforward chronology to present activities observed over a limited period—a few hours or a few days—in the order in which they occurred. Orenstein, for example, recounts what happened during a single class period.

Writers who organize their observations topically must limit the number of topics they cover. The author of "Soup," for example, focuses on Yeganeh's ideas about soup and his attitudes toward customers. In the topically organized section of his essay, Edge concentrates on the history and process of bottling and selling pig lips at Farm Fresh Food Supplier.

Writing the Beginning

To engage your readers' interest from the start, consider beginning by describing the place from the outside and as you enter (as Cable and Arellano do), by quoting the subject (as the author of "Soup" does), by setting the time and place (as Edge does), by relating something interesting about the subject (as Orenstein does), or by expressing your own amusing reaction to the subject (as Orlean does). You might have to try two or three different beginnings before finding a promising way to start, but do not agonize for too long over the first sentence. Try out any possible beginning, and see where it takes you.

Using Your Role

Whether you choose to adopt a participant-observer or a detached spectator role, you need to think about how you can use your role to engage readers and present the information you've chosen to include. Either role can be used to help readers identify with you. For example, if you are entering a place most of us avoid (as Cable does when he enters the mortuary), you can take us with you as you learn about the place and look over other people's shoulders to see what they're doing. Or if you act as a participant trying to learn how to do what others routinely do (as Edge does when he tries to eat a pickled pig lip), readers can imagine themselves in your shoes.

Regardless of your role, also consider whether to refer to yourself in your draft. Here are some possibilities:

- Place yourself at the scene. (For example, "I followed him through an arched doorway into a chapel that smelled musty and old" [Cable, paragraph 15].)

- Refer to your own actions. (For example, "Amy grabs my hand, pulling me along like a small child or a slightly addled new student" [Orenstein, paragraph 7].)

- Share your thoughts and feelings. (For example, "I walked out, feeling confused about Molly's behavior and disturbed that Dr. Piedra resorted to force without trying less radical solutions" [Arellano, paragraph 17].)

Considering a Useful Sentence Strategy

As you draft your observation essay, you will need to help your readers imagine actions and objects. A sentence strategy called an *absolute phrase* enables writers to show simultaneous parts of a complex action or to detail observations of a person or object.

Here is an example, with the absolute phrase in italics:

> Some of the boys are as small and compact as fourth graders, *their legs sticking out of their shorts like pipe cleaners.* (Orenstein, paragraph 8)

Orenstein could have presented her observation of the boys' skinny legs in a separate sentence, but the absolute phrase gives a visual image showing just how skinny they are. Here's another example:

> I offer the bag to Jerry, order yet another beer, and turn to eye the pig feet floating in a murky jar by the cash register, *their blunt tips bobbing up through a pasty white film.* (Edge, paragraph 19)

Working with Sources

Integrating Quotations from Interviews

In addition to describing people, your observational essay will also quote them. These quotations can be revealing because they let readers hear different people speaking for themselves rather than being presented through your voice. Nevertheless, the writer decides which quotations to use and how to use them. Therefore, one major task you face in drafting and revising your essay is to choose quotations from your notes, to present them in a way that reveals the character of the people you interviewed and the important information you learned from them, and to integrate these quotations smoothly into your sentences.

When you quote directly (rather than paraphrase or summarize) what someone said or wrote, you will usually need to identify the speaker. The principal way to do so is to create what is called a *speaker tag*. You may rely on a general or all-purpose speaker tag, using the forms of *say* and *tell*:

"I am not prejudiced against color or religion," Mr. Yeganeh *told* us. . . . ("Soup," paragraph 4)

"She was even a little extreme for a bitch," William *said*. "She was rather buxom. I would call her zaftig." (Orlean, paragraph 11)

Other speaker tags more precisely describe the speaker's tone or attitude:

"They told me to tell you that they want me to be my own person," she *complained*. (Orenstein, paragraph 5)

Kyle, who is skinny and a little pop-eyed, *yells out*, "Prime!" . . . (Orenstein, paragraph 18)

"It was a large service," *remarked* Howard. (Cable, paragraph 16)

"Biff's head is his father's," William Truesdale, a veterinarian, *explained* to me one day. (Orlean, paragraph 8)

Whether you use specific or general speaker tags, consider adding a word or phrase to identify or describe the speaker or to reveal more about *how, where, when,* or *why* the speaker speaks:

"The best part about the job is seeing patients that I've had for over twelve years," she *said with conviction*. "It's amazing to see them grow up." (Arellano, paragraph 10)

> "We do our best to corner the market on lips," Lionel *told me, his voice tinged with bravado.* (Edge, paragraph 11)
>
> "I'm not exactly shy," she *says, her hands still on her hips.* "I'm bold." (Orenstein, paragraph 4)
>
> "It was a profession I could live with," he *told me with a sly grin.* (Cable, paragraph 25)
>
> "I *made* him," Tina said. "I made Biff who he is. He had an overbearing personality when he was small, but I consider that a prerequisite for a great performer. He had such an *attitude*! He was like this miniature man!" She *shimmied her shoulders back and forth and thrust out her chin.* (Orlean, paragraph 17)
>
> "Take a seat," she *invited me*; "it's great to meet you!" *She had a thick Spanish accent with a warm tone* that instantly made me feel less anxious—a great bedside manner, I thought. (Arellano, paragraph 9)
>
> Don't forget to enclose all quotations in quotation marks and to separate the quotation from its speaker tag with appropriate punctuation, usually a comma.

Again, Edge could have presented his observation in a separate sentence, but the absolute phrase lets him bring together his turning and looking with what he actually saw, emphasizing the at-a-glance instant of another possible stomach flutter.

Absolute phrases nearly always are attached to the end of a main clause, adding various kinds of details to it to create a more complex, informative sentence. They are made up of two main parts: a noun or a pronoun followed by a word or phrase that modifies the noun or pronoun and usually includes a present participle (ending in *-ing*) or a past participle (usually ending in *-ed*). Following are additional examples of absolute phrases from this chapter's readings. (Notice that the third example does not include a participle.)

> Biff held his position for a moment, and then he and Kim bounded across the ring, *his feet moving so fast that they blurred into an oily sparkle*, even though he really didn't have very far to go. (Orlean, paragraph 24)
>
> This was a solid bronze casket, *its seams electronically welded to resist corrosion.* (Cable, paragraph 21)

"I'm not exactly shy," she says, *her hands still on her hips*. (Orenstein, paragraph 4).

Absolute phrases are certainly not required for a successful observation essay—experienced writers use them only occasionally—yet they do offer writers an effective sentence option. Try them out in your own writing.

READING A DRAFT CRITICALLY

Getting a critical reading of your draft will help you see how to improve it. Your instructor may schedule class time for reading drafts, or you may want to ask a classmate or a tutor in the writing center to read your draft. Ask your reader to use the following guidelines and to write out a response for you to consult during your revision.

Read for a First Impression

1. **Read the draft without stopping, and then write a few sentences giving your general impression.**

2. **Identify one aspect of the draft that seems particularly effective.**

Read Again to Suggest Improvements

1. **Suggest ways of making descriptions of places and people more vivid.**

   - Find a description of a place, and suggest what details could be added to objects in the scene (location, size, color, and shape) or what sensory information (look, sound, smell, taste, and touch) could be included to help you picture the place.

   - Find a description of a person, and indicate what else you would like to know about the person's dress, facial expression, tone of voice, and gestures.

   - Find reported conversation, and note whether any of the quotes could be paraphrased or summarized without losing impact.

   - Find passages where additional reported conversation could enhance the drama or help bring a person to life.

2. **Recommend ways of making the organization clearer or more effective.**

   - If the essay is organized chronologically, look for passages where the narrative seems to wander pointlessly or leaves out important information.

Also suggest cues that could be added to indicate time sequence (*initially, then, afterward*).

- If the essay is organized topically, mark topics that get too much or too little attention, transitions between topics that need to be added or clarified, and topics that should be placed elsewhere.

- If the essay alternates narration with topical information, suggest where transitions could be made smoother or sequencing could be improved.

3. **Suggest how the essay could be made more engaging and informative.**

- If the essay seems boring or you feel overwhelmed by too much information, suggest how the information could alternate with vivid description or lively narration. Also consider whether any of the information could be cut or simplified.

- List any questions you still have about the subject.

4. **Suggest ways to make the impression conveyed to you more focused and coherent.**

- Tell the writer what dominant impression you get of the subject.

- Point to key information that supports this dominant impression, so that the writer knows how you arrived at it.

- Point to any information that makes you doubt or question your impression.

5. **Evaluate the effectiveness of visuals.**

- If any visuals do not seem relevant, or if there seem to be too many visuals, identify the ones that the writer could consider dropping, explaining your thinking.

- If a visual does not seem to be appropriately placed, suggest a better place for it.

REVISING

This section offers suggestions for revising your draft. Revising means reenvisioning your draft, trying to see it in a new way, given your purpose and readers, in order to develop a more vivid, informative observational essay.

The biggest mistake you can make while revising is to focus initially on words or sentences. Instead, first try to see your draft as a whole to assess its likely impact on your readers. Think imaginatively and boldly about cutting unconvincing material, adding new material, and moving material around. Your computer makes even drastic revisions physically easy, but you still need to make the mental effort and decisions that will improve your draft.

You may have received help with this challenge from a classmate or tutor who gave your draft a critical reading. If so, keep this feedback in mind as you decide which parts of your draft need revising and what specific changes you could make. The following suggestions will help you solve problems and strengthen your essay.

TROUBLESHOOTING YOUR DRAFT

To Make Your Description of Places and People More Vivid	
Problem	**Suggestions for Revising**
People do not come alive.	• Show people interacting with each other by talking, moving, or gesturing. • Add speaker tags to characterize how people talk. • Directly quote only the language that conveys personality or essential information, and paraphrase or summarize other parts.
The place is hard to visualize.	• Identify items in the place by name using specific nouns and descriptive adjectives. • Add sensory detail—sight, sound, smell, taste, touch. • Say what the place is like or unlike. • Consider adding a visual — photograph or sketch.

To Make the Organization Clearer and More Effective	
Problem	**Suggestions for Revising**
The narrative drags or rambles.	• Try adding drama through dialogue or more action. • Give the narrative shape — for example, by building suspense or tension.
A topically arranged essay seems disorganized or out of balance, with too much about some topics and too little about others.	• Try rearranging topics to see whether another order makes more sense. • Add clearer, more explicit transitions or topic sentences. • Move, cut, or condense information to restore balance.
The essay seems disjointed, with abrupt shifts or confusing transitions.	• Add appropriate logical, spatial, or temporal transitional words or phrases. • Use repeated or related words as a transitional bridge.

To Make the Essay More Engaging and Informative

Problem	Suggestions for Revising
The opening fails to engage readers' attention.	• Consider alternatives. Think of questions you could open with, or look for an engaging image or dialogue later in the essay to move to the beginning. • Go back to your notes for other ideas. • Recall how the writers in this chapter open their essays.
The essay bores or overwhelms readers with too much information about the subject.	• Cut obvious or extraneous information. • Consider alternating blocks of information with descriptive or narrative materials. • Try presenting more of the information through lively dialogue.
Readers have questions about the subject.	• Look over your research notes to see if you can answer their questions. • If you have time, do follow-up research to find out answers to their questions.

To Strengthen the Essay's Dominant Impression

Problem	Suggestions for Revising
Readers get an impression you did not expect.	• Look at what gave them this impression and whether it could be used to enrich the impression you intended. • Cut or revise the language that gave a wrong impression.
The dominant impression is unclear or too simplistic.	• Add language or details that strengthen and clarify the dominant impression. • Express ambivalent feelings about the subject. • Discuss more directly the contradictions or complexities you see in the subject.
Readers may not understand the importance of the social, cultural, or historical context.	• Add background information to reveal important influences on the subject.

EDITING AND PROOFREADING

After you have revised your essay, be sure to spend some time checking for errors in usage, punctuation, and mechanics and considering matters of style. If you keep a list of errors you typically make, begin by checking your draft against this list. Ask someone else to proofread your essay before you print out a copy for your instructor or send it electronically.

From our research on student writing, we know that observational essays tend to have errors in the use of quotation marks, when writers quote the exact words of people they have interviewed. Check a writer's handbook for help with this problem.

Reflecting on What You Have Learned

Observation

In this chapter, you have read critically several observational essays and have written one of your own. To better remember what you have learned, pause now to reflect on the reading and writing activities you completed in this chapter.

1. Write a page or so reflecting on what you have learned. Begin by describing what you are most pleased with in your essay. Then explain what you think contributed to your achievement. Be specific about this contribution.

   - If it was something you learned from the readings, indicate which readings and specifically what you learned from them.

   - If it came from your invention writing, interviews, or observations, point out the parts that helped you most.

   - If you got good advice from a critical reader, explain exactly how the person helped you—perhaps by helping you understand a particular problem in your draft or by helping you add a new dimension to your writing.

   - Try to write about your achievement in terms of what you have learned about the genre.

2. Reflect more generally on how you tend to interpret observational writing. Observational essays may seem impartial and objective, but they inevitably reflect the writer's interests and values, especially in creating a dominant impression of the subject. Consider the following questions about your own project: How did your interests and values influence your choice of subject, which details you included or emphasized, the kinds of questions you asked in interviews, and how you responded to what you were told and what you observed? In your essay itself, how do these influences show through? How could these influences be made more visible in your essay, and do you wish you had made them more visible?

4

Reflection

Like autobiographical and observational writing, reflective writing is based on the writer's personal experience. Reflective writers present something they did, saw, heard, or read. They try to make their writing vivid so that the reader can imagine what they experienced. But unlike writers of autobiography and observation, their goal is not primarily to present their experience so that the reader can imagine it. Instead, reflective writers present their experience in order to explore its possible meanings. They use events in their lives and people and places they have observed as the occasions or springboards for thinking about society—how people live and what people believe.

In this chapter, for example, one writer tells what happened one evening when he was taking a walk and he noticed a woman react to him with evident fear. This experience, and others like it, leads him to think about popular stereotypes concerning gender and race. Another writer, scanning the scars on his body, ponders their significance and the stories they tell. Still another writer muses about the objects he has found on the sidewalks of his city and how they represent the signs of our times.

As you can see from these few examples, reflective essays explore wide-ranging subjects. Reflective writers may think about social change with its many opportunities and challenges (such as changes in scientific knowledge, in the environment, and in ways to perfect the body). They may examine customs in our culturally diverse society (such as those related to eating and dating). They may explore traditional virtues and vices (pride, jealousy, and compassion) or common hopes and fears (the desire for an ecologically balanced world).

These subjects may seem far reaching, but writers of reflections have relatively modest goals. They do not attempt to exhaust their subjects, nor do they set themselves up as experts. They simply try out their ideas. One meaning of the word "essay," in fact, is "to try out." Reflective essays are exercises, experiments, and opportunities to explore ideas informally and tentatively.

Reflective writing is enjoyable to write and read precisely because it is exploratory and creative. It can be as stimulating as a lively conversation. It often surprises us with its insights and unlikely connections and encourages us to look in new ways at even the most familiar things, examining with a critical eye what we usually take for granted.

The readings in this chapter will help you learn about reflective writing. From the readings and from the suggestions for writing that follow each reading, you will get ideas for your own reflective essay. As you read and write about the selections, keep in mind the following assignment, which sets out the goals for writing a reflective essay. To support your writing of this assignment, the chapter concludes with a Guide to Writing Reflective Essays.

THE WRITING ASSIGNMENT

Write a reflective essay based on something you experienced or observed. Describe this occasion vividly so that readers can understand what happened and will care about what you have to say about it. In reflecting on the particular occasion, make some general statements exploring its possible meanings or cultural significance. Consider what the occasion might imply about how people in our society behave toward one another, what they value, and what assumptions or stereotypes they may hold consciously or unconsciously. Think of reflective writing as a stimulating conversation in which you seek to expose—and perhaps question—your readers' attitudes and beliefs as well as your own.

WRITING SITUATIONS FOR REFLECTIVE ESSAYS

Writers use a wide range of particular occasions to launch their reflections. These occasions nearly always lead them to reflect on some aspect of contemporary culture, as the following examples indicate:

- A former football player writes a reflective essay for his college alumni magazine about his experience playing professional sports. He recounts a specific occasion when he sustained a serious injury but continued to play because he knew that playing with pain was regarded as a sign of manliness. As he reflects on what happened, he recalls that he first learned the custom of playing with pain from his father but that the lesson was reinforced later by coaches and other players. He wonders why boys playing sports are taught not to show pain but encouraged to show other feelings like aggression and competitiveness. Taking an anthropological view, he sees contemporary sports as equivalent to the kind of training Native American boys traditionally went through to become warriors. This comparison leads him to question whether sports training today prepares boys (and perhaps girls, too) for the kinds of roles they need to play in contemporary society.

- Writing for a political science course, a student reflects on her first experience voting in a presidential election. She begins by describing a recent conversation with friends about how people decide to vote for one presidential candidate over another. They agreed that most people they know seem to base their decisions on trivial, even bizarre, reasons, rather than on a candidate's experience, voting record in previous offices, character, or even campaign promises. For example, one friend knew someone who voted for a presidential candidate because he reminded her of her grandfather, while another friend knew someone who voted against a candidate because he did not like the way the candidate dressed. The writer then reflects on the humorous as well as the serious implications of such voting decisions.

- A first-year college student, in an essay for his composition course, reflects on a performance of his high-school chorus that far surpassed the members' expectations. He describes their trip to the statewide competition and their anxious rehearsals before the performance and, during the competition, their unexpected feelings of confidence, their precision and control, and the exuberance of the performance. He considers factors that led to their success, such as fear of embarrassment, affection for their teacher, the excitement of a trip to the state capital, and the fact that they had rehearsed especially attentively for weeks because the music was so challenging and the competition so fierce. After considering possible reasons for their success, the writer concludes with some ideas about the special pleasures of success where cooperation and individual creativity are essential.

Thinking about Your Experience

Reflection

Before studying a type of writing, it is useful to spend some time thinking about what you already know about it. You may have written about your reflections as you explored your ideas and reactions to things you have seen, heard, or read by corresponding with friends or by writing for school.

- Recall a time when you communicated your reflections in writing or orally, and then consider questions like these: What was the particular occasion that triggered your reflections? Was it something you observed firsthand, saw online, heard on the radio, or overheard on the street? Why did this particular occasion seem interesting or significant to you? Were you surprised by the ideas it stimulated?

- Recall also reflections you have read, heard, or seen on television or online. What made them interesting?

- Write at least a page about your experience with reflective writing.

A GUIDE TO READING REFLECTIVE ESSAYS

This guide introduces you to the basic features and strategies typical of reflective writing by looking closely at a powerful reflective essay by Brent Staples. Focus first on *reading for meaning*, seeking to grasp the occasion's significance to Staples as well as the meanings you find in the essay (for example, your own feelings about stereotyping and fearful occasions). Then, to learn how Staples makes his essay thoughtful and engaging to readers, try *reading like a writer* by analyzing his writing strategies. These two activities—reading for meaning and reading like a writer—follow every reading in this chapter.

Brent Staples

Black Men and Public Space

Brent Staples (b. 1951) earned his PhD in psychology from the University of Chicago and went on to become a journalist, writing for several magazines and newspapers, including the Chicago Sun-Times. *In 1985, he became assistant metropolitan editor of the* New York Times, *where he is now a member of the editorial board. His autobiography,* Parallel Time: Growing Up in Black and White *(1994), won the Anisfield Wolff Book Award.*

The following essay originally appeared in Ms. *magazine in 1986 under the title "Just Walk On By." Staples revised it slightly for publication in* Harper's *a year later under the present title. The particular occasion for Staples's reflections is an incident that occurred for the first time in the mid-1970s, when he discovered that his mere presence on the street late at night was enough to frighten a young white woman. Recalling this incident leads him to reflect on issues of race, gender, and class in the United States. As you read, think about why Staples chose the new title, "Black Men and Public Space."*

1   My first victim was a woman—white, well dressed, probably in her early twenties. I came upon her late one evening on a deserted street in Hyde Park, a relatively affluent neighborhood in an otherwise mean, impoverished section of Chicago. As I swung onto the avenue behind her,

there seemed to be a discreet, uninflammatory distance between us. Not so. She cast back a worried glance. To her, the youngish black man—a broad six feet two inches with a beard and billowing hair, both hands shoved into the pockets of a bulky military jacket—seemed menacingly close. After a few more quick glimpses, she picked up her pace and was soon running in earnest. Within seconds she disappeared into a cross street.

That was more than a decade ago, I was twenty-two years old, a graduate student newly arrived at the University of Chicago. It was in the echo of that terrified woman's footfalls that I first began to know the unwieldy inheritance I'd come into—the ability to alter public space in ugly ways. It was clear that she thought herself the quarry of a mugger, a rapist, or worse. Suffering a bout of insomnia, however, I was stalking sleep, not defenseless wayfarers. As a softy who is scarcely able to take a knife to a raw chicken—let alone hold one to a person's throat—I was surprised, embarrassed, and dismayed all at once. Her flight made me feel like an accomplice in tyranny. It also made it clear that I was indistinguishable from the muggers who occasionally seeped into the area from the surrounding ghetto. That first encounter, and those that followed, signified that a vast, unnerving gulf lay between nighttime pedestrians—particularly women—and me. And I soon gathered that being perceived as dangerous is a hazard in itself. I only needed to turn a corner into a dicey situation, or crowd some frightened, armed person in a foyer somewhere, or make an errant move after being pulled over by a policeman. Where fear and weapons meet—and they often do in urban America—there is always the possibility of death.

In that first year, my first away from my hometown, I was to become thoroughly familiar with the language of fear. At dark, shadowy intersections, I could cross in front of a car stopped at a traffic light and elicit the thunk, thunk, thunk of the driver—black, white, male, or female—hammering down the door locks. On less traveled streets after dark, I grew accustomed to but never comfortable with people crossing to the other side of the street rather than pass me. Then there were the standard unpleasantries with policemen, doormen, bouncers, cabdrivers, and others whose business it is to screen out troublesome individuals before there is any nastiness.

I moved to New York nearly two years ago and I have remained an avid night walker. In central Manhattan, the near-constant crowd cover minimizes tense one-on-one street encounters. Elsewhere—in SoHo, for example, where sidewalks are narrow and tightly spaced buildings shut out the sky—things can get very taut indeed.

After dark, on the warrenlike streets of Brooklyn where I live, I often see women who fear the worst from me. They seem to have set their faces on neutral, and with their purse straps strung across their chests bandolier-style, they forge ahead as though bracing themselves against being tackled. I understand, of course, that the danger they perceive is not a hallucination. Women are particularly vulnerable to street violence, and young black males are drastically overrepresented among the perpetrators of that violence. Yet these truths are no solace against the kind of alienation that comes of being ever the suspect, a fearsome entity with whom pedestrians avoid making eye contact.

6 It is not altogether clear to me how I reached the ripe old age of twenty-two without being conscious of the lethality nighttime pedestrians attributed to me. Perhaps it was because in Chester, Pennsylvania, the small, angry industrial town where I came of age in the 1960s, I was scarcely noticeable against a backdrop of gang warfare, street knifings, and murders. I grew up one of the good boys, had perhaps a half-dozen fistfights. In retrospect, my shyness of combat has clear sources.

7 As a boy, I saw countless tough guys locked away; I have since buried several, too. They were babies, really—a teenage cousin, a brother of twenty-two, a childhood friend in his mid-twenties—all gone down in episodes of bravado played out in the streets. I came to doubt the virtues of intimidation early on. I chose, perhaps unconsciously, to remain a shadow—timid, but a survivor.

8 The fearsomeness mistakenly attributed to me in public places often has a perilous flavor. The most frightening of these confusions occurred in the late 1970s and early 1980s, when I worked as a journalist in Chicago. One day, rushing into the office of a magazine I was writing for with a deadline story in hand, I was mistaken for a burglar. The office manager called security and, with an ad hoc posse, pursued me through the labyrinthine halls, nearly to my editor's door. I had no way of proving who I was. I could only move briskly toward the company of someone who knew me.

9 Another time I was on assignment for a local paper and killing time before an interview. I entered a jewelry store on the city's affluent Near North Side. The proprietor excused herself and returned with an enormous red Doberman pinscher straining at the end of a leash. She stood, the dog extended toward me, silent to my questions, her eyes bulging nearly out of her head. I took a cursory look around, nodded, and bade her good night.

10 Relatively speaking, however, I never fared as badly as another black male journalist. He went to nearby Waukegan, Illinois, a couple of summers ago to work on a story about a murderer who was born there. Mistaking the reporter for the killer, police officers hauled him from his car at gunpoint and but for his press credentials would probably have tried to book him. Such episodes are not uncommon. Black men trade tales like this all the time.

11 Over the years, I learned to smother the rage I felt at so often being taken for a criminal. Not to do so would surely have led to madness. I now take precautions to make myself less threatening. I move about with care, particularly late in the evening. I give a wide berth to nervous

people on subway platforms during the wee hours, particularly when I have exchanged business clothes for jeans. If I happen to be entering a building behind some people who appear skittish, I may walk by, letting them clear the lobby before I return, so as not to seem to be following them. I have been calm and extremely congenial on those rare occasions when I've been pulled over by the police.

And on late-evening constitutionals I employ what has proved to be an   12 excellent tension-reducing measure: I whistle melodies from Beethoven and Vivaldi and the more popular classical composers. Even steely New Yorkers hunching toward nighttime destinations seem to relax, and occasionally they even join in the tune. Virtually everybody seems to sense that a mugger wouldn't be warbling bright, sunny selections from Vivaldi's *Four Seasons*. It is my equivalent of the cow-bell that hikers wear when they know they are in bear country.

READING FOR MEANING

This section presents three activities that will help you think about the meanings in Staples's reflective essay.

Read to Comprehend

Write a few sentences briefly explaining some of the occasions that prompted Staples's reflection and how Staples explores the actions he took to address these occasions.

Identify any words with meanings you are unsure of—such as *discreet* (paragraph 1) and *constitutionals* (12)—and find the dictionary definition for each word that makes the best sense in the context.

To help you understand the essay better, also consider trying one of these critical reading strategies, explained in Appendix 1: *summarizing* or *paraphrasing*.

Read to Respond

Write several paragraphs exploring your initial thoughts and feelings about Staples's reflective essay. Focus on anything that stands out for you, perhaps because it resonates with your own experience or because you find a statement puzzling. For example, consider writing about one of the following:

- Staples's reactions to being seen as threatening, perhaps in relation to how you think you would react if you were in his position;

- an experience you have had in which racial, gender, age, or other differences caused tension, comparing your experience with that of Staples or one of the people he encountered.

To help develop your response, also consider trying one of these critical reading strategies, explained in Appendix 1: *reflecting on challenges to your beliefs and values, recognizing emotional manipulation,* or *judging the writer's credibility.*

Read to Analyze Assumptions

All writing contains *assumptions*—ideas and attitudes that are taken for granted as commonly accepted truths. Personal or individual assumptions also tend to reflect the values and beliefs of a particular community, which help shape the way those in the group think, act, and understand the world. All writing reflects assumptions held by the writer, but assumptions held by others, such as readers or sources cited by the writer, may also be present. Sometimes assumptions are stated explicitly, but often they are only implied, so you may have to search for underlying assumptions in the word choices and examples.

Why go to the effort to analyze assumptions in a reading? Assumptions have powerful effects. They influence our opinions and judgments by leading us to value some things and devalue others. These effects are even more powerful because they are taken for granted, often accepted without question by those who hold them. To understand a reading on a deep level, then, it is necessary to bring its assumptions to the surface and to question them. To think critically about assumptions, here are some kinds of questions you could ask: Who holds this assumption (the writer, readers, and/or others cited in the essay)? What are the effects of the assumption in the context of the essay specifically or in society more generally? What do you think about the assumption, and is there anything in the essay that raises doubts about it? How does the assumption reinforce or critique commonly held views, and are there any alternative ideas, beliefs, or values that would challenge this assumption?

Write a paragraph or two analyzing an assumption in Staples's essay. You might choose one from the list below, using the questions accompanying it in addition to the ones above to help you get started. Or you can choose another assumption in the essay to explore.

- **assumptions about the unfairness and danger of racial profiling.** The examples Staples uses to develop his reflection—starting with the young woman who suddenly becomes frightened of him out late on a deserted street in Chicago (paragraph 1), and ending with the story of how the black male journalist was hauled from his car at gunpoint (10) by police who assumed he was the criminal—illustrate how often he and other black men assume they are the object of racial profiling. A "softy" (2) according to himself, he realizes that another pedestrian could see him as a "mugger, a rapist, or worse" when all he is doing is "stalking sleep." He sees that this initial faulty perception by others can be a danger to him and to all black men because frightened people can behave violently.

To think critically about the assumptions in this essay related to racial profiling, ask yourself questions like these: How did Staples become aware of racial profiling and its consequences? (Reread paragraph 3 before you respond). Why does he acknowledge that "women are particularly vulnerable to street violence, and young black males are drastically overrepresented among the perpetrators of that violence" (5) and then follow this acknowledgment with "[y]et those truths are no solace against the kind of alienation that comes of being ever the suspect, a fearsome entity with whom pedestrians avoid making eye contact" (5). To what extent, if any, are the pedestrians who react in this way aware of the effects on black men of their behavior? Is Staples right in his assumption that he has been racially profiled? Are there any other possible explanations? Is there any usefulness in racial profiling?

- **assumptions about the effects of smothering anger**. Staples mentions his anger only once, in paragraph 11: "I learned to smother the rage I felt at so often being taken for a criminal. Not to do so would surely have led to madness."

  To think critically about the assumptions in this essay related to how one should deal with anger, ask yourself questions like these: What meanings could the term "madness" have in the context of this essay? Why do you suppose Staples follows this strategy of smothering his rage? When an American feels angry, how does he or she behave, in your experience? What happens when anger goes unchecked, or, alternatively, when it is smothered? What assumptions do you have about anger—how do you feel you should deal with it and how do you expect others to deal with it?

- **assumptions about how musical choices affect others**. Staples concludes by writing that to reduce tension on his late-night walks, he whistles Beethoven and Vivaldi along with works of other "classical" composers. "Virtually everybody seems to sense that a mugger wouldn't be warbling bright, sunny selections from Vivaldi's *Four Seasons*" (12).

  To think critically about the assumptions in this essay related to the effects of one's musical choices, ask yourself questions like these: Why is a classical piece more effective at reducing fear than other kinds of music such as rock, country, or rap? Why is a "sunny selection" more effective than, say, blues? Do you share Staples's assumption that classical music calms fearful people, or do you think there could be another explanation for how they react to his whistling? For example, could it be that the music calms Staples himself and therefore he sends out a different message?

To help you analyze assumptions in Staples's essay, also consider trying one of these critical reading strategies, explained in Appendix 1: *contextualizing*, or *reflecting on challenges to your beliefs and values*.

READING LIKE A WRITER

This section guides you through an analysis of Staples's reflective writing strategies: *presenting the particular occasion, developing the reflections, maintaining topical coherence,* and *engaging readers.* For each strategy, you will be asked to reread and annotate part of Staples's essay to see how he uses the strategy.

When you study the selections later in this chapter, you will see how different writers use these same strategies for different purposes. The Guide to Writing Reflective Essays near the end of the chapter suggests ways you can use these strategies in your own writing.

Presenting the Particular Occasion

Reflective writers present a particular occasion—something they experienced or observed—to introduce their general reflections. They may describe the occasion in detail, or they may sketch it out quickly. The key in either case is to present the occasion in a vivid and suggestive way that encourages readers to want to know more about the writer's thoughts. To succeed at presenting the occasion vividly, writers rely on the same narrating and describing strategies you practiced in Chapter 2 (Autobiography) and Chapter 3 (Observation).

Staples lets readers know from the word "first" in the introductory phrase ("My first victim") that what happened on this occasion happened again later. But he focuses in the opening paragraph on this first occasion. Staples presents this first event in vivid detail, trying to give readers a sense of the surprise and anxiety he felt at the time. In addition to helping readers imagine what happened, Staples presents the event in a way that suggests the larger meanings he will develop in subsequent paragraphs.

Analyze

1. Reread the opening sentence of paragraph 1, where Staples describes the person he encountered. Notice that even before he identifies her by gender, he uses the word "victim" to name her. Underline the details he gives to describe this person and the actions she takes.

2. Turn to the places in paragraph 1 where Staples describes himself as the woman saw him. Put brackets around the names used to identify him, and underline the details used to describe him physically as well as the actions he takes.

3. Choose three or four details that you think help make this particular occasion especially vivid and dramatic.

Write

Write several sentences explaining what you have learned about how Staples uses this event to create a dramatic occasion that helps to introduce his reflections. Support your explanation with some of the details you singled out.

Developing the Reflections

While the particular occasion introduces the subject, the reflections explore the subject by developing the writer's ideas. For example, Staples begins with an occasion when his mere presence on the street frightened a woman into running away from him. He uses this event to introduce the general subject: fear resulting from racial profiling. As he explains, "It was in the echo of that terrified woman's footfalls that I first began to know the unwieldy inheritance I'd come into" (paragraph 2).

Throughout the rest of the essay, Staples examines this "inheritance" from various angles, using a range of reflective writing strategies. He expresses his feelings (at being misperceived as a threat); he explains (the effects of racial profiling, including the danger to himself); he gives examples (of other occasions when people reacted to him with fear or hostility); and finally, he explains again (the "precautions" he takes to make himself appear "less threatening") (11). These are just some of the strategies writers use to develop their reflections. This activity will help you see how Staples uses examples to illustrate and explain his ideas.

Analyze

1. Read the opening sentence of paragraph 3, where Staples introduces the idea that there is a "language of fear." Reread the rest of the paragraph to see how he uses examples to help readers understand what he means.

2. Look at paragraphs 11 and 12, where Staples writes about the "precautions" he takes to make himself seem "less threatening." Choose one or two examples that you think work especially well to help readers understand what he means.

Write

Write several sentences explaining what you have learned about Staples's use of examples, pointing to the examples you think are especially effective.

Maintaining Topical Coherence

Reflective essays explore ideas on a subject by turning them this way and that, examining them first from one perspective and then from another, and sometimes piling up examples to illustrate the ideas. Such essays may seem rambling, with one idea or example added to another in a casual way. It is not always clear where the writer is going, and the essay may not seem to end conclusively. This apparently casual organization is deceptive, however, because in fact the reflective writer has arranged the parts carefully to give the appearance of a mind at work. While each new idea or example may seem to turn the essay in an unexpected new direction, reflective writers use what we call *topical coherence* to make the parts of a reflective essay connect to the central subject.

An important way of achieving topical coherence is to refer to the subject at various points in the essay by repeating certain key words or phrases associated with it. In the opening anecdote presenting the particular occasion, Staples dramatizes the woman's fear of him. He does not use the word "fear," however, until the end of paragraph 2. He then repeats that word twice: at the beginning of paragraph 3, in the phrase "language of fear," and at the beginning of paragraph 5. He also concludes paragraph 5 with a phrase that indicates how others, particularly women, see him: as "a fearsome entity." In addition, Staples uses several related words, such as "terrified" and "frightened" (paragraph 2) as well as "nervous" and "skittish" (11). By repeating the word "fear" and words related to it, Staples highlights the subject of his reflections.

Another way reflective writers achieve topical coherence is through carefully placed transitions. Staples, as you will see in this activity, uses time and place markers to introduce a series of examples illustrating the fear he engenders in others simply because of his race and gender.

Analyze

1. Skim paragraphs 2 to 4, 7 to 9, and 11, and put brackets around the time and place markers. Begin by bracketing the time marker "more than a decade ago" and the place marker "at the University of Chicago" in the opening sentence of paragraph 2.

2. Notice how many different times and places Staples refers to with these markers.

Write

Write several sentences explaining how Staples uses time and place markers to help maintain topical coherence. Support your explanation with examples from the reading.

Engaging Readers

Readers of reflective essays, like readers of autobiographical and observational writing, expect writers to engage their interest. In fact, most readers have no pressing reason to read reflective writing. They choose to read an essay because something about it catches their eye—a familiar author's name, an intriguing title, an interesting graphic or drop quote. Journalists typically begin feature articles, ones that do not deal with "hard" news, with what they call a *hook*, designed to catch readers' attention. The particular occasion that opens many reflective essays often serves this purpose. Staples's opening phrase, "My first victim," certainly grabs attention.

But once "caught," readers have to be kept reading. One of the ways reflective writers keep readers engaged is by projecting an image of themselves—sometimes called the *writer's persona* or *voice*—that readers can identify with or at least find interesting. Staples, for example, uses the first-person pronouns *my* and *I* to present himself in his writing and to speak directly to readers. In paragraph 2, for example, he describes himself as "a softy" and explains how he felt when he realized that the woman was so frightened by him that she ran for her life. Like most reflective writers, Staples tries to make himself sympathetic to readers so that they will listen to what he has to say.

Analyze

1. Look for places in the essay where you get a sense of Staples as a person, and in the margin briefly describe the impression you get.

2. Think about what engages you or draws you into the essay.

Write

Write several sentences about the impressions you get of Staples from reading this essay, exploring how these impressions affect your interest in his ideas.

A Special Reading Strategy

Comparing and Contrasting Related Readings: Brent Staples's "Black Men and Public Space" and an excerpt from his autobiography, *Parallel Time*.

Comparing and contrasting related readings is a critical reading strategy useful both in reading for meaning and in reading like a writer. This strategy is particularly applicable when writers present similar subjects, as is the case in the two reflective readings by Brent Staples that are compared here. The first, "Black Men and Public Space," the essay you have just read, was first published in 1986. The second, the excerpt below from Staples's autobiography, *Parallel Time*, was published in 1994. Both readings deal with the same occasion—when Staples encountered his "first victim" (paragraph 1 in both). But you will notice that the details of this first encounter, as well as Staples's reflections about it, differ significantly in the two readings. As you read, notice what Staples keeps from the original and what he changes. To compare and contrast these two reflective readings, think about issues such as these:

- Compare these readings in terms of the way the particular occasion is described. What seems to you to be most significant about these two descriptions? Note, for example, the details about the location and the woman's appearance as well as how Staples describes his immediate reaction.

- Compare how Staples describes what he calls "the language of fear" in these readings (paragraph 3 in both). Highlight the places in each reading where the language of fear is described. In what ways is his description similar and different? How does he explain its causes?

- Compare these readings to see what Staples thinks and feels about the situation he finds himself in and what actions he decides to take. What are the main differences in his reactions? Speculate on why he decided to make so radical a revision of his earlier reflections in his autobiography published nearly a decade after his original essay was published. What do you think might have changed (in Staples's feelings, in the broader cultural climate, or in some other way) during that period that led Staples to share with readers his angry response rather than leaving readers with the image of himself he projects at the end of the original version?

See Appendix 1 (pp. 596–601) for detailed guidelines on comparing and contrasting related readings.

From *Parallel Time*

1   At night, I walked to the lakefront whenever the weather permitted. I was headed home from the lake when I took my first victim. It was late fall, and the wind was cutting. I was wearing my navy pea jacket, the collar turned up, my hands snug in the pockets. Dead leaves scuttled in shoals along the streets. I turned out of Blackstone Avenue and headed west on 57th Street, and there she was, a few yards ahead of me, dressed in business clothes and carrying a briefcase. She looked back at me once, then again, and picked up her pace. She looked back again and started to run. I stopped where I was and looked up at the surrounding windows. What did this look like to people peeking out through their blinds? I was out walking. But what if someone had thought they'd seen something they hadn't and called the police. I held back the urge to run. Instead, I walked south to The Midway, plunged into its darkness, and remained on The Midway until I reached the foot of my street.

I'd been a fool. I'd been walking the streets grinning good eve- 2
ning at people who were frightened to death of me. I did violence to
them by just being. How had I missed this? I kept walking at night,
but from then on I paid attention.

I became expert in the language of fear. Couples locked arms or 3
reached for each other's hand when they saw me. Some crossed to
the other side of the street. People who were carrying on conversations went mute and stared straight ahead, as though avoiding my
eyes would save them. This reminded me of an old wives' tale: that
rabid dogs didn't bite if you avoided their eyes. The determination
to avoid my eyes made me invisible to classmates and professors
whom I passed on the street.

It occurred to me for the first time that I was big. I was 6 feet 1½ 4
inches tall, and my long hair made me look bigger. I weighed only
170 pounds. But the navy pea jacket that Brian had given me was
broad at the shoulders, high at the collar, making me look bigger
and more fearsome than I was.

I tried to be innocuous but didn't know how. The more I thought 5
about how I moved, the less my body belonged to me; I became
a false character riding along inside it. I began to avoid people. I
turned out of my way into side streets to spare them the sense that
they were being stalked. I let them clear the lobbies of buildings
before I entered, so they wouldn't feel trapped. Out of nervousness
I began to whistle and discovered I was good at it. My whistle was
pure and sweet—and also in tune. On the street at night I whistled
popular tunes from the Beatles and Vivaldi's *Four Seasons*. The tension drained from people's bodies when they heard me. A few even
smiled as they passed me in the dark.

Then I changed. I don't know why, but I remember when. I was 6
walking west on 57th Street, after dark, coming home from the
lake. The man and the woman walking toward me were laughing
and talking but clammed up when they saw me. The man touched
the woman's elbow, guiding her toward the curb. Normally I'd
have given way and begun to whistle, but not this time. This time
I veered toward them and aimed myself so that they'd have to part
to avoid walking into me. The man stiffened, threw back his head
and assumed the stare: eyes dead ahead, mouth open. His face took
on a bluish hue under the sodium vapor streetlamps. I suppressed
the urge to scream into his face. Instead I glided between them, my
shoulder nearly brushing his. A few steps beyond them I stopped
and howled with laughter. I called this game Scatter the Pigeons.

Fifty-seventh Street was too well lit for the game to be much fun; 7
people didn't feel quite vulnerable enough. Along The Midway were
heart-stopping strips of dark sidewalk, but these were so frightening

that few people traveled them. The stretch of Blackstone between 57th and 55th provided better hunting. The block was long and lined with young trees that blocked out the streetlight and obscured the heads of people coming toward you.

8   One night I stooped beneath the branches and came up on the other side, just as a couple was stepping from their car into their town house. The woman pulled her purse close with one hand and reached for her husband with the other. The two of them stood frozen as I bore down on them. I felt a surge of power: these people were mine; I could do with them as I wished. If I'd been younger with less to lose, I'd have robbed them, and it would have been easy. All I'd have to do was stand silently before them until they surrendered their money. I thundered, "Good evening!" into their bleached-out faces and cruised away laughing.

9   I held a special contempt for people who cowered in their cars as they waited for the light to change at 57th and Woodlawn. The intersection was always deserted at night, except for a car or two stuck at the red. Thunk! Thunk! Thunk! They hammered down the door locks when I came into view. Once I had hustled across the street, head down, trying to seem harmless. Now I turned brazenly into the headlights and laughed. Once across, I paced the sidewalk, glaring until the light changed. They'd made me terrifying. Now I'd show them how terrifying I could be.

READINGS

Dana Jennings

Our Scars Tell the Stories of Our Lives

Dana Jennings (b. 1957) is a journalist who has written for the Manchester Union Leader *and the* Wall Street Journal *and is now an editor at the* New York Times. *He is best known for his novel,* Lonesome Standard Time *(1996); his non-fiction,* Sing Me Back Home: Love, Death and Country Music *(2008); and his blog for the* New York Times *Well section in which he writes about prostate cancer, with which he was diagnosed in 2008. You can find his blog by typing his name into "search" at http://well.blogs.nytimes.com/.*

The following essay appeared in the Times *on July 21, 2009. Pondering the scars on his own body, Jennings notes that scars tell stories. He develops his reflection by relating some of the stories prompted by his scars, and speculates about their larger meaning. As you read, think about your own scars and what they mean to you, and whether your understanding of scars is enlarged by reading this essay.*

1 Our scars tell stories. Sometimes they're stark tales of life-threatening catastrophes, but more often they're just footnotes to the ordinary but bloody detours that befall us on the roadways of life. When I parse my body's motley parade of scars, I see them as personal runes and conversation starters. When I wear shorts, the footlong surgical scar on my right knee rarely fails to draw a comment. And in their railroad-track-like appearance, my scars remind me of the startling journeys that my body has taken—often enough to the hospital or the emergency room.

What is the particular occasion (or two) that prompts Jennings to think about the meaning of scars?

2 The ones that intrigue me most are those from childhood that I can't account for. The one on my right eyebrow, for example, and a couple of ancient pockmarks and starbursts on my knees. I'm not shocked by them. To be honest, I wonder why there aren't more.

3 I had a full and active boyhood, one that raged with scabs and scrapes, mashed and bloody knees, bumps and lumps, gashes and slashes, cats' claws and dogs' teeth, jagged glass, ragged steel, knots, knobs and shiners. Which raises this question: How do any of us get out of childhood alive?

How does this paragraph help the reader identify with Jennings?

4 My stubborn chin has sustained a fair bit of damage over the years. On close examination, there's a faint

delta of scars that brings back memories of my teenage war on acne. Those frustrating days of tetracycline and gritty soaps left my face not clean and glowing but red and raw. The acne also ravaged my back, scoring the skin there so that it still looks scorched and lunar.

I further cratered my chin as an adult. First, I 5 sprinted into a cast-iron lamppost while chasing a fly ball in a park in Washington; I actually saw a chorus line of stars dance before my eyes as I crumpled to the ground. Second, I hooked one of those old acne potholes with my razor and created an instant dueling scar.

How do these stories help you see how scars have different effects on memory?

Scanning down from the jut of my chin to the tips 6 of my toes, I've even managed to brand my feet. In high school and college I worked at Kingston Steel Drum, a factory in my New Hampshire hometown that scoured some of the 55-gallon steel drums it cleaned with acid and scalding water. The factory was eventually shut down by the federal government and became a Superfund hazardous waste site, but not before a spigot malfunctioned one day and soaked my feet in acid.

7   Then there are the heavy hitters, the stitched whips and serpents that make my other scars seem like dimples on a golf ball.

8   There's that mighty scar on my right knee from when I was 12 years old and had a benign tumor cut out. Then there are the scars on my abdomen from when my colon (devoured by ulcerative colitis) was removed in 1984, and from my radical open prostatectomy last summer to take out my cancerous prostate. (If I ever front a heavy metal band, I think I'll call it Radical Open Prostatectomy.)

9   But for all the potential tales of woe that they suggest, scars are also signposts of optimism. If your body is game enough to knit itself back together after a hard physical lesson, to make scar tissue, that means you're still alive, means you're on the path toward healing.

10   Scars, perhaps, were the primal tattoos, marks of distinction that showed you had been tried and had survived the test. And like tattoos, they also fade, though the one from my surgery last summer is still a fierce and deep purple.

11   There's also something talismanic about them. I rub my scars the way other people fret a rabbit's foot or burnish a lucky penny. Scars feel smooth and dry, the same way the scales of a snake feel smooth and dry.

12   I find my abdominal scars to be the most profound. They vividly remind me that skilled surgeons unlocked me with their scalpels, took out what had to be taken, sewed me back up and saved my life. It's almost as if they left their life-giving signatures on my flawed flesh.

13   The scars remind me, too, that in this vain culture our vanity sometimes needs to be punctured and deflated—and that's not such a bad thing. To paraphrase Ecclesiastes, better to be a scarred and living dog than to be a dead lion.

14   It's not that I'm proud of my scars—they are what they are, born of accident and necessity—but I'm not embarrassed by them, either. More than anything, I relish the stories they tell. Then again, I've always believed in the power of stories, and I certainly believe in the power of scars.

Why do you suppose Jennings makes this paragraph only one sentence long?

What kind of shift is indicated by this paragraph? How does it affect you?

What is the purpose of these more general descriptions of scars?

Here Jennings reminds us that scars are often seen as defacing. Where else does Jennings address this issue? Is Jennings being truthful when he says he's not proud of his scars? Could his reflection be interpreted in another way?

READING FOR MEANING

This section presents three activities that will help you think about the meanings in Jennings's reflective essay.

Read to Comprehend

Write a few sentences briefly explaining some of the occasions that prompted Jennings's reflection and the history of the scars he observes.

Identify any words with meanings you are unsure of—such as *runes* (paragraph 1) and *talismanic* (11)—and find the dictionary definition for each word that makes the best sense in the context.

To help you understand the essay, also consider trying one of these critical reading strategies, explained in Appendix 1: *summarizing* or *paraphrasing*.

Read to Respond

Write several paragraphs exploring your initial thoughts and feelings about Jennings's reflective essay. Focus on anything that stands out for you, perhaps because it resonates with your own experience or because you find a statement puzzling. For example, consider writing about one of the following:

- your response to Jennings's assertion that "scars, perhaps, were the primal tattoos, marks of distinction that showed you had been tried and had survived the test" (10).

- what you think Jennings means when he concludes with "I've always believed in the power of stories, and I certainly believe in the power of scars" (14).

- how you feel about any scars you might have, and what they might mean to other people.

To help develop your response, also consider trying one of these critical reading strategies, explained in Appendix 1: *reflecting on challenges to your beliefs and values, recognizing emotional manipulation,* or *judging the writer's credibility*.

Read to Analyze Assumptions

Write a paragraph or two analyzing an assumption in Jennings's essay. To think critically about assumptions, here are some kinds of questions you could ask: Who holds this assumption (the writer, readers, and/or others cited in the essay)? What are the effects of the assumption in the context of the essay specifically or in society more generally? What do you think about the assumption, and is there anything in the essay that raises doubts about it? How does the assumption reinforce or critique commonly held views, and are there any alternative ideas, beliefs, or values that would challenge this assumption?

You might choose an assumption from the list below, using the questions accompanying it along with the ones above to help you get started. Or you can choose another assumption in the essay to explore.

- **assumptions about the role of scars in memories.** In the first eight paragraphs, Jennings details accidents and illnesses that led to many of his scars, from a minor shaving scar to radical surgical scars. Then in paragraph 9, he writes: "But for all the potential tales of woe that they suggest, scars are also signposts of optimism." Not only do scars mean healing, but Jennings goes on to say that they are "primal tattoos, marks of distinction that showed you had been tried and had survived the test" (10). These statements seem to contradict his assertion that he is not proud of his scars (14).

  To think critically about the assumptions in this essay related to the role of scars in memories, ask yourself questions like these: How do you account for these contradictions? Could scars play more than one role in a person's memories? How does the text support the ideas both that scars bring back memories of triumph and survival and that they remind us of unhappy times? Is there a way to reconcile these two views? If so, what is it?

- **assumptions about the power of stories.** Clearly Jennings values stories—the word "stories" is in his title and in his first sentence, and in his final paragraph, he says about his scars "I relish the stories they tell" and "I've always believed in the power of stories" (14). As he scans the scars on his body, he tells brief stories to illustrate how he got many of them.

  To think critically about the assumptions in this essay related to the power of stories, ask yourself questions like these: What effect does the story about each scar have on you as a reader? How do the stories differ from each other, and what difference does that make to your reading experience? How do the stories help you understand the kind of person Jennings is? Do the stories help you rethink your beliefs about scars?

To help you analyze assumptions in the essay, also consider trying one of these critical reading strategies, explained in Appendix 1: *reflecting on challenges to your beliefs and values*, or *exploring the significance of figurative language*.

A Special Reading Strategy

Exploring the Significance of Figurative Language

Figurative language adds color and richness to writing by taking words literally associated with one thing and applying them to something else, often in an unexpected or unconventional way, to create a vivid image or other sensory impression in readers' minds. For example, in this essay Jennings refers to his scars as "footnotes to the ordinary but bloody detours that befall us on the roadways of life" (1), and adds that his scars, in their "railroad-track-like appearance" remind him of the "journeys [his] body has taken" (1). To explore the significance of figurative language in this essay:

1. List and label all the figures of speech—metaphors, similes (metaphors that use "like" or "as"), and symbols—that you find in "Our Scars Tell the Stories of Our Lives."

2. Look for patterns. Then, group the figures of speech according to similar feelings and attitudes and label them.

3. Write for ten minutes to explore the themes you discovered in step 2. What meanings emerge from the patterns and your writing?

   See Appendix 1 (pp. 573–75) for detailed guidelines on exploring the significance of figurative language.

READING LIKE A WRITER

PRESENTING THE PARTICULAR OCCASION

Reflections are often triggered by a one-time event or observation. In the previous reading, for example, you saw how Brent Staples started thinking about his subject as a result of a particular event and how he uses the time marker "late one evening" (paragraph 1) to let readers know this was a one-time event. Later in his essay, however, Staples refers to other occasions to make the point that the event on that particular night became an unhappily frequent occurrence.

Jennings chooses to begin his reflection with a conclusion he has drawn from thinking about his scars: "Our scars tell stories" (paragraph 1). Often reflective essays are the result of such pondering, and Jennings tells us how his particular occasion came about: "When I parse my body's motley parade of scars, I see them as personal runes and conversation starters" (1). Then he adds: "When I wear shorts, the footlong surgical scar on my right knee rarely fails to draw a comment" (1). He travels over his body, narrating the story that each scar brings up, grouping them according to their significance, and making meaning out of his memories. The following activity will help you analyze the strategies Jennings uses to present his particular occasion—in this case, the tracing of the scars on his body—and his reflections that resulted from it.

Analyze

1. *Look closely* at Jennings's narratives in paragraphs 4, 5, 6, and 8.

2. Next *observe* in the paragraphs that follow (9–13) how Jennings uses the stories of his scars to draw conclusions about their meanings.

Write

Write several sentences explaining how Jennings's descriptive details and narrative give the occasion its impact. Support your explanation with examples from your observations.

CONSIDERING IDEAS FOR YOUR OWN WRITING

Jennings's essay suggests many subjects for reflection. His stories could prompt you to think about experiences from which you have scars, or about other topics he mentions, such as the meaning of tattoos, or experiences you've had with surgery or other medical issues. He even opens up the subject of vanity in our culture for consideration.

Consider whether a particular occasion ever prompted you to think about subjects that made you ponder something more deeply, and that might also be interesting to other readers. How did you become the person you are? Were there events in your childhood that shaped your worldview? How did you form your own sense of what is beautiful, or of right and wrong? Was there a particular occasion where your sense was challenged or reinforced? Your reflection could be about your own personal experiences, or it could be about your culture, your family, your job, or your schooling. Any occasion that spurs thinking deeply about a subject would work as a prompt for your reflective essay.

ANALYZING VISUALS

Write a paragraph analyzing the drawing included with Jennings's reflective essay and explaining what it contributes to the essay. To do the analysis, you can use the criteria chart for the Analysis of Visuals in Appendix 3 on pp. 670–72. Don't feel you have to answer all the questions on the chart: focus on those that seem most productive in helping you write a paragraph-length analysis. To help you get started, consider adding these questions that specifically refer to the drawing:

- Why do you suppose the artist depicted some of Jennings's scars but not others — why cut off part of his head and show only portions of his arms and legs?

- Why would the artist show stitches on so many of the scars, even though the stitch marks probably do not still show on Jennings's body?

Steven Doloff

A Universe Lies on the Sidewalks of New York

Steven Doloff is a professor of humanities and media studies at the Pratt Institute in New York City, where he won a Distinguished Teacher Award in 2001. His writing has been published in scholarly journals like the James Joyce Quarterly *and the* Shakespeare Quarterly *as well as in the* Washington Post *and the* New York Times.

"A Universe Lies on the Sidewalks of New York" was first published in 2002 in Newsday, *a newspaper based on Long Island in the New York metropolitan area, as part of a series called "City Life." As you read, think about any daily activity that might lead you to reflect on its meaning to your life as a whole.*

1   In an oversized brandy snifter on my kitchen counter I keep a dozen bullets I have picked up off the sidewalks in my neighborhood. Along the northern edge of Greenwich Village, I have found, over the last 10 years or so, mashed .45 caliber slugs, cute little .22 caliber shells that look like they fell off a charm bracelet, and inch-long snub-nosed other things that could smack down a refrigerator.

2   With every one I have picked up, I've wondered the same things: How did this get here? If it was a slug, did it miss someone? If it was a shell, did it hit someone? Was it from a cop's gun or a felon's? (I ruled out licensed animal hunters on 14th Street.) I haven't found any loose ordnance lately, and homicide rates are currently way down. I guess there's a connection.

3   Some urban sociologists study the contents of garbage cans, and others mull over graffiti. As both a student and a member of the passing parade, I look down to consider what we step on and over as we march along to our various drummers. One could say that New York's sidewalks make up a kind of endless concrete newspaper from which we can read, in the minute flotsam and jetsam at our feet, news of the mass of people who walk them.

4   For instance, about 10 years ago, I noticed almost every day (but did not pick up) dozens of party-colored crack vials scattered about my neighborhood. They are now, I am happy to report, gone (at least from my sidewalks), and crack abuse is also much diminished. Two years ago, I actually found a crumpled hundred-dollar bill in the street. That, too, perhaps, was a sign of the times—wafted uptown from a stockbroker's window after the Dow Jones Industrial Average leapt to some record-breaking bullish height.

5   And how about those devalued pennies everywhere that almost nobody bothers to bend over for anymore? (I pick up the shiny ones.) I wonder if the fluctuating number of pennies to be found on some carefully selected stretch of sidewalk, say near Wall Street, might not be useful as

a kind of economic indicator of imminent stock market movements (the "PDI—penny density index").

Perhaps most intriguing are the gum spots—you know, those little black cir-   6
cles, ranging in size from nickels to drink coasters, that speckle the sidewalks and subway platforms from one end of our city to the other. While evenly distributed in most places, they tend to cluster like asteroid belts around phone booths, bus stops, litter baskets and building entrances. And they do not wear, fade or scrape away, ever. I once watched a building-maintenance worker with a steam hose trying to clear these chicle pox from a tiny patch of sidewalk near a doorway. I watched because I was amazed by his wonderfully futile gesture. It took him nearly 15 minutes to get rid of one stain. He was standing in a nest of hundreds.

We may not be able to see many stars in Manhattan, but there is this   7
whole universe of gum spots before our eyes that most of us never even notice. If travelers from another planet ever visited New York City, I'm sure they would marvel at the trillions of spat, dropped and flicked lumps of flattened chewing gum that cover our metropolis, and wonder what kind of tree-sap chomping maniacs lived here.

Once in a while I come across spots in the making—small, pink baby   8
circles, not yet stomped into wider, blackened, hardened spots. I almost feel sorry for these untrammeled innocents, these newly attached freckles to the concrete skin of our city. But then I remember they will outlive me and that the future belongs to them.

It's not all good news on the sidewalk, but it's the truth.   9

READING FOR MEANING

This section presents three activities that will help you think about the meanings in Doloff's reflective essay.

Read to Comprehend

Write a few sentences briefly explaining what Doloff sees in the sidewalks of New York.

Identify any words with meanings you are unsure of—such as *felon* (paragraph 2) and *chicle* (6) — and find the dictionary definition for each word that makes the best sense in the context.

To help you understand the essay better, also consider trying one of these critical reading strategies, explained in Appendix 1: *outlining* or *summarizing*.

Read to Respond

Write several paragraphs exploring your initial thoughts and feelings about Doloff's reflective essay. Focus on anything that stands out for you, perhaps because it resonates with your own experience or because you find a statement puzzling. For example, consider writing about the following:

- sidewalks that you use (or whatever you walk on right outside where you live) and the things that you have found there;

- something that you have picked up from the ground in a public place and kept and its significance for you; or

- your response to Doloff's last sentence: "It's not all good news on the sidewalk, but it's the truth" (9).

To help develop your response, also consider trying one of these critical reading strategies, explained in Appendix 1: *reflecting on challenges to your beliefs and values, recognizing emotional manipulation,* or *judging the writer's credibility.*

Read to Analyze Assumptions

Write a paragraph or two analyzing an assumption in Doloff's essay. To think critically about assumptions, here are some kinds of questions you could ask: Who holds this assumption (the writer, readers, and/or others cited in the essay)? What are the effects of the assumption in the context of the essay specifically or in society more generally? What do you think about the assumption, and is there anything in the essay that raises doubts about it? How does the assumption reinforce or critique commonly held views, and are there any alternative ideas, beliefs, or values that would challenge this assumption?

You might choose one assumption from the list below, using the questions accompanying it in addition to the ones above to help you get started. Or you can choose another assumption to explore.

- **assumptions about the meaning of artifacts**. In each of his paragraphs, Doloff makes an assumption about the meaning of an artifact he has seen on the street, much as an archaeologist would make if discovering artifacts in a ruin. (An artifact is any object produced or shaped by human craft, especially a tool, weapon, or ornament of archaeological or historical interest.) What is your response to the conclusions he draws from his artifacts? Would you draw the same conclusions or perhaps different ones? Doloff also ponders what "travelers from another planet" (paragraph 7) would think if they saw all the gum splats on the sidewalks of New York.

  To think critically about the assumptions in this essay related to artifacts, ask yourself questions like these: What truths about humanity (or perhaps just New Yorkers) do you derive from Doloff's reflection?

- **assumptions about our future and immortality**. In paragraph 8, Doloff considers the new "small, pink baby circles, not yet stomped into wider, blackened, hardened spots." He almost feels "sorry" for them, until he remembers the "future belongs to them" (8).

To think critically about the assumptions in this essay related to how we might be perceived by future generations, ask yourself questions like these: What larger concern is Doloff hinting at by making gum spots and their immortality the last artifact he reflects on?

To help you analyze assumptions in Doloff's essay, also consider trying one of these critical reading strategies, explained in Appendix 1: *exploring the significance of figurative language* or *judging the writer's credibility.*

READING LIKE A WRITER

ENGAGING READERS

Reflective writers use an array of strategies early in an essay to engage readers' interest. They often craft an attention-grabbing title—"Black Men and Public Space," "Our Scars Tell the Stories of Our Lives," "A Universe Lies on the Sidewalks of New York"—and work to make their opening sentences intriguing. For example, Brent Staples opens his essay with a shocking confession ("My first victim was a woman"), and Wendy Lee (see p. 182) begins with a mysterious statement ("When my friend told me that her father had once compared her to a banana, I stared at her blankly"). Reflective writers sometimes try to establish a tone or project a voice that will engage readers—by using humor or exaggeration, for instance.

Analyze

1. Review Doloff's title, and recall its initial impact on you. How well did it engage your interest? What did you expect?

2. Reread the first two paragraphs, and notice the strategies Doloff uses to interest readers, such as referring to bullet shells as "cute" and to "[bullet-sized] other things that could smack down a refrigerator." In the second paragraph, he makes a joke about ruling out "licensed animal hunters on 14th Street."

Write

Write several sentences explaining the strategies that Doloff uses to engage readers and their effectiveness for you as a reader.

CONSIDERING IDEAS FOR YOUR OWN WRITING

Steven Doloff's particular occasion was simply staring into a brandy snifter full of bullets he had collected over the years, which made him ponder where he got them and think about other things he had found on the sidewalks of

New York. Reflective essays can be about almost anything, even something that is in front of you every day. Look around your room, your home, your school, and your neighborhood to see if any sight or object makes you think deeply or sends your mind into new places. How would you interpret your object? What does it symbolize for you?

If you don't see anything that provokes thought, try hearing, feeling, or even tasting: our senses can often provide us with an entryway into intriguing topics. Think about how a song, a cooking smell, or a taste can trigger memories, and reflect on how and why those memories made a lasting impression on you. For some people, just the smell of chlorine can bring back a summer camp experience that changed their way of thinking, or the sweet taste of Halloween candy can remind them of a childhood experience worthy of reflection.

Firoozeh Dumas

The "F Word"

Firoozeh Dumas (b. 1965) is an Iranian-American writer. She is best known for her memoir Funny in Farsi: A Memoir of Growing Up Iranian in America *(2003), from which the excerpt below is taken. (Farsi is another name for the Persian language, which is the most widely spoken language in Iran.) Dumas has also written another memoir,* Laughing without an Accent *(2008).*

"The 'F Word'" is Dumas's account of what happens when languages and cultures collide, as they often do for the children of immigrants. As she describes how Americans in general deal (or fail to deal) with names from languages unfamiliar to them, Dumas explains how dealing with this situation is part of the immigrant experience for those from many language backgrounds. As you read, think about your own experience with unfamiliar kinds of names, and note how Dumas employs humor.

My cousin's name, Farbod, means "Greatness." When he moved to   1
America, all the kids called him "Farthead." My brother Farshid ("He Who
Enlightens") became "Fartshit." The name of my friend Neggar means
"Beloved," although it can be more accurately translated as "She Whose
Name Almost Incites Riots." Her brother Arash ("Giver") initially couldn't
understand why every time he'd say his name, people would laugh and
ask him if it itched.

All of us immigrants knew that moving to America would be fraught   2
with challenges, but none of us thought that our names would be such an
obstacle. How could our parents have ever imagined that someday we
would end up in a country where monosyllabic names reign supreme,
a land where "William" is shortened to "Bill," where "Susan" becomes
"Sue," and "Richard" somehow evolves into "Dick"? America is a great
country, but nobody without a mask and a cape has a *z* in his name.
And have Americans ever realized the great scope of the guttural sounds
they're missing? Okay, so it has to do with linguistic roots, but I do believe
this would be a richer country if all Americans could do a little tongue
aerobics and learn to pronounce "kh," a sound more commonly associated in this culture with phlegm, or "gh," the sound usually made by actors
in the final moments of a choking scene. It's like adding a few new spices
to the kitchen pantry. Move over, cinnamon and nutmeg, make way for
cardamom and sumac.

Exotic analogies aside, having a foreign name in this land of Joes and   3
Marys is a pain in the spice cabinet. When I was twelve, I decided to sim-
plify my life by adding an American middle name. This decision serves as
proof that sometimes simplifying one's life in the short run only compli-
cates it in the long run.

4   My name, Firoozeh, chosen by my mother, means "Turquoise" in Farsi. In America, it means "Unpronounceable" or "I'm Not Going to Talk to You Because I Cannot Possibly Learn Your Name and I Just Don't Want to Have to Ask You Again and Again Because You'll Think I'm Dumb or You Might Get Upset or Something." My father, incidentally, had wanted to name me Sara. I do wish he had won that argument.

5   To strengthen my decision to add an American name, I had just finished fifth grade in Whittier, where all the kids incessantly called me "Ferocious." That summer, my family moved to Newport Beach, where I looked forward to starting a new life. I wanted to be a kid with a name that didn't draw so much attention, a name that didn't come with a built-in inquisition as to when and why I had moved to America and how was it that I spoke English without an accent and was I planning on going back and what did I think of America?

6   My last name didn't help any. I can't mention my maiden name, because:

7   "Dad, I'm writing a memoir."

8   "Great! Just don't mention our name."

9   Suffice it to say that, with eight letters, including a *z*, and four syllables, my last name is as difficult and foreign as my first. My first and last name together generally served the same purpose as a high brick wall. There was one exception to this rule. In Berkeley, and only in Berkeley, my name drew people like flies to baklava. These were usually people named Amaryllis or Chrysanthemum, types who vacationed in Costa Rica and to whom lentils described a type of burger. These folks were probably not the pride of Poughkeepsie, but they were refreshingly nonjudgmental.

10   When I announced to my family that I wanted to add an American name, they reacted with their usual laughter. Never one to let mockery or good judgment stand in my way, I proceeded to ask for suggestions. My father suggested "Fifi." Had I had a special affinity for French poodles or been considering a career in prostitution, I would've gone with that one. My mom suggested "Farah," a name easier than "Firoozeh" yet still Iranian. Her reasoning made sense, except that Farrah Fawcett was at the height of her popularity and I didn't want to be associated with somebody whose poster hung in every postpubescent boy's bedroom. We couldn't think of any American names beginning with *F*, so we moved on to *J*, the first letter of our last name. I don't know why we limited ourselves to names beginning with my initials, but it made sense at that moment, perhaps by the logic employed moments before bungee jumping. I finally chose the name "Julie" mainly for its simplicity. My brothers, Farid and Farshid, thought that adding an American name was totally stupid. They later became Fred and Sean.

11   That same afternoon, our doorbell rang. It was our new next-door neighbor, a friendly girl my age named Julie. She asked me my name and after a

moment of hesitation, I introduced myself as Julie. "What a coincidence!" she said. I didn't mention that I had been Julie for only half an hour.

Thus I started sixth grade with my new, easy name and life became   12
infinitely simpler. People actually remembered my name, which was an entirely refreshing new sensation. All was well until the Iranian Revolution, when I found myself with a new set of problems. Because I spoke English without an accent and was known as Julie, people assumed I was American. This meant that I was often privy to their real feelings about those "damn I-raynians." It was like having those X-ray glasses that let you see people undressed, except that what I was seeing was far uglier than people's underwear. It dawned on me that these people would have probably never invited me to their house had they known me as Firoozeh. I felt like a fake.

When I went to college, I eventually went back to using my real name.   13
All was well until I graduated and started looking for a job. Even though I had graduated with honors from UC Berkeley, I couldn't get a single interview. I was guilty of being a humanities major, but I began to suspect that there was more to my problems. After three months of rejections, I added "Julie" to my résumé. Call it coincidence, but the job offers started coming in. Perhaps it's the same kind of coincidence that keeps African Americans from getting cabs in New York.

Once I got married, my name became Julie Dumas. I went from having   14
an identifiably "ethnic" name to having ancestors who wore clogs. My family and non-American friends continued calling me Firoozeh, while my coworkers and American friends called me Julie. My life became one big knot, especially when friends who knew me as Julie met friends who knew me as Firoozeh. I felt like those characters in soap operas who have an evil twin. The two, of course, can never be in the same room, since they're played by the same person, a struggling actress who wears a wig to play one of the twins and dreams of moving on to bigger and better roles. I couldn't blame my mess on a screenwriter; it was my own doing.

I decided to untangle the knot once and for all by going back to my real   15
name. By then, I was a stay-at-home mom, so I really didn't care whether people remembered my name or gave me job interviews. Besides, most of the people I dealt with were in diapers and were in no position to judge. I was also living in Silicon Valley, an area filled with people named Rajeev, Avishai, and Insook.

Every once in a while, though, somebody comes up with a new per-   16
mutation and I am once again reminded that I am an immigrant with a foreign name. I recently went to have blood drawn for a physical exam. The waiting room for blood work at our local medical clinic is in the basement of the building, and no matter how early one arrives for an appointment, forty coughing, wheezing people have gotten there first. Apart from reading *Golf Digest* and *Popular Mechanics*, there isn't much to do except guess the number of contagious diseases represented in the windowless

room. Every ten minutes, a name is called and everyone looks to see which cough matches that name. As I waited patiently, the receptionist called out, "Fritzy, Fritzy!" Everyone looked around, but no one stood up. Usually, if I'm waiting to be called by someone who doesn't know me, I will respond to just about any name starting with an *F*. Having been called Froozy, Frizzy, Fiorucci, and Frooz and just plain "Uhhhh . . . ," I am highly accommodating. I did not, however, respond to "Fritzy" because there is, as far as I know, no "t" in my name. The receptionist tried again, "Fritzy, Fritzy DumbAss." As I stood up to this most linguistically original version of my name, I could feel all eyes upon me. The room was momentarily silent as all of these sick people sat united in a moment of gratitude for their own names.

17   Despite a few exceptions, I have found that Americans are now far more willing to learn new names, just as they're far more willing to try new ethnic foods. Of course, some people just don't like to learn. One mom at my children's school adamantly refused to learn my "impossible" name and instead settled on calling me "F Word." She was recently transferred to New York where, from what I've heard, she might meet an immigrant or two and, who knows, she just might have to make some room in her spice cabinet.

READING FOR MEANING

This section presents three activities that will help you think about the meanings in Dumas's reflective essay.

Read to Comprehend

Write a few sentences identifying the occasion for Dumas's reflection and listing two or three experiences that keep reminding her of the problems with her name.

Identify any words whose meanings you are unsure of—such as *incessantly* (paragraph 5) and *privy* (12)—and find the dictionary definition for each word that makes the best sense in the context.

To help you understand the essay better, also consider trying one of these critical reading strategies, explained in Appendix 1: *outlining* or *paraphrasing*.

Read to Respond

Write several paragraphs exploring your initial thoughts and feelings about Dumas's reflective essay. Focus on anything that stands out for you, perhaps because it resonates with your own experience or because you find a statement puzzling. For example, consider writing about the following:

- any immigrant experiences that the essay reminds you of, either as an immigrant yourself or with an immigrant you know;

- Dumas's statement that she "couldn't get a single interview" (paragraph 13) when she looked for jobs using her real name;

- your response to Dumas's analogy between language and food when she wishes Americans would broaden their naming repertoire: "It's like adding a few new spices to the kitchen pantry. Move over, cinnamon and nutmeg, make way for cardamom and sumac" (2); or

- what in the essay made you laugh.

To help develop your response to the essay, also consider trying one of these critical reading strategies explained in Appendix 1: *outlining, contextualizing,* or *exploring the significance of figurative language.*

Read to Analyze Assumptions

Write a paragraph or two analyzing an assumption in Dumas's essay. To think critically about assumptions, here are some kinds of questions you could ask: Who holds this assumption (the writer, readers, and/or others cited in the essay)? What are the effects of the assumption in the context of the essay specifically or in society more generally? What do you think about the assumption, and is there anything in the essay that raises doubts about it? How does the assumption reinforce or critique commonly held views, and are there any alternative ideas, beliefs, or values that would challenge this assumption?

You might choose one assumption from the list below, using the questions accompanying it in addition to the ones above to help you get started. Or you can choose another assumption to explore.

- **assumptions about the effects of names**. In the first few paragraphs, Dumas explains that the mispronunciation or complete mangling of her name motivates her to find a simple, "American" name that everyone can pronounce and understand. In paragraph 10, however, she shows a more complicated view of naming. Asking for suggestions from her family for a new name, she rejects her father's choice of "Fifi" because she has no "special affinity for French poodles" and was not "considering a career in prostitution." She rejects "Farah" because she doesn't want to be a reminder of Farrah Fawcett. In paragraph 13, she speculates that her Iranian name prevented job offers, because when she switched to "Julie," the offers started.

  To think critically about the assumptions in this essay related to the effects of names, ask yourself questions like these: What does a name tell us about the background of a person? Why does a name associated in the public mind with a certain person make that name unsuitable for someone else? If the people who did not offer Dumas a job were rejecting her on the basis of her Iranian name, what assumptions were they making about her and perhaps about her culture? Do you think these assumptions are widely shared in America?

- **assumptions about the power of humor in writing.** In almost every paragraph of this essay there is humor in some form: a throwaway line at the end of the paragraph, a poke by Dumas at herself as author, hilarious mangled names, and funny behavior from her characters. Yet the essay is about serious subjects: the power of names to hurt; prejudice against a culture; the innate seriousness of a medical facility.

  To think critically about the assumptions in this essay related to the power of humor in writing, ask yourself questions like these: Why does Dumas include so much humor? What function does her humor serve? Humor isn't often generic—it usually depends on a particular context—yet Dumas seems to be able to cross cultural boundaries with her humor. Why is her humor funny for Americans and also for people from other cultures who might read her essay? Does her humor detract from the seriousness of her message, or does it advance it? Why?

To help you analyze assumptions in the essay, also consider trying one of these critical reading strategies, explained in Appendix 1: *reflecting on challenges to your beliefs and values* or *judging the writer's credibility.*

READING LIKE A WRITER

MAINTAINING TOPICAL COHERENCE

Because reflective essays are exploratory, often trying out several ideas, they may appear to be only loosely organized, following a "first I had this idea and then I had another idea" principle of organization. Yet readers seldom become confused because writers are careful to maintain topical coherence and to provide cues to help readers follow the writer's train of thought. One of the main ways that writers establish logical coherence is by repeating a key word or phrase related to the essay's general subject. Recall that Brent Staples repeats the key word *fear* to help readers keep track of his reflections. Dana Jennings also uses repetition in this way. As you reread Dumas's essay, you will see that the key word for the general subject of her essay, *name*, is introduced in the first sentence, and is carried through in some form or other in virtually every paragraph in her essay. This repetition of an important word from one paragraph to the next serves as a chain that makes her paragraphs flow coherently from one to the next.

Analyze

1. Skim the essay, and notice the contexts for the repeated word *name*.

2. Examine the differences in these contexts.

Write

Write several sentences explaining what you have learned about Dumas's use of word repetition to maintain topical coherence and help readers follow her thinking.

CONSIDERING IDEAS FOR YOUR OWN WRITING

Dumas's essay suggests several ideas for writing your own reflection. Hers was prompted by her decision just before entering sixth grade to change her name because she was moving to a new school. In doing so, she was rejecting not only her peers for mocking her, but also the heritage reflected in her name. You could write an essay that explores what your heritage means to you (and what particular occasion led you to know what it means). Such an exploration might include not only aspects of your heritage that you find problematic (as Dumas found her name to be) but also those about which you have positive or mixed feelings.

The more specific topic of problematic names is another possibility for an essay. Has your own name ever been ridiculed, whether for the reasons Dumas's was or others, and how did you react? Have you ever thought about changing your name, using one of your given names rather than another, or switching from a nickname to your actual name or vice versa when you were entering a new setting in your life, such as starting college? If so, why?

The end of Dumas's essay also suggests likely topics for reflection: "Despite a few exceptions, I have found that Americans are now far more willing to learn new names, just as they're far more willing to try new ethnic foods" (17). Think of particular occasions where you saw evidence of changes in the way Americans—or people of another nationality—think about new things, whatever they might be. These changes might be in the direction either of greater acceptance, such as Dumas finds, or of resistance to or rejection of change.

Wendy Lee

Peeling Bananas

*Wendy Lee wrote the following essay when she was a high-school stu-
dent, and it was published in* Chinese American Forum, *a quarterly journal of news and opinion. In the essay, Lee reflects on growing up in America
as the child of parents born in China. While she focuses mainly on going to
school, her interest is larger—to discover how she can be American without
losing the knowledge and experience of her Chinese heritage.*

*As you read, reflect on how you might hold on to the special qualities
of your family or ethnic group while at the same time becoming part of a
larger, more diverse community.*

1   When my friend told me that her father had once compared her to a
banana, I stared at her blankly. Then I realized that her father must have
meant that outside she had the yellow skin of a Chinese, but inside she
was white like an American. In other words, her appearance was Chinese,
but her thoughts and values were American. Looking at my friend in her
American clothes with her perfectly straight black hair and facial features
so much like my own, I laughed. Her skin was no more yellow than mine.

2   In kindergarten, we colored paper dolls: red was for Indians, black for
Afro-Americans, yellow was for Chinese. The dolls that we didn't color at
all—the white ones—were left to be Americans. But the class wanted to
know where were the green, blue or purple people? With the paper dolls,
our well-meaning teacher intended to emphasize that everyone is basically the same, despite skin color. Secretly I wondered why the color of my
skin wasn't the shade of my yellow Crayola. After we colored the dolls, we
stamped each one with the same vacant, smiley face. The world, according
to our teacher, is populated by happy, epidermically diverse people.

3   What does it mean to be a Chinese in an American school? One thing
is to share a last name with a dozen other students, so that you invariably
squirm when roll-call is taken. It means never believing that the fairy-tales
the teacher read during story time could ever happen to you, because you
don't have skin as white as snow or long golden hair. "You're Chinese?"
I remember one classmate saying. "Oh, I really like Chinese food." In
the depths of her overfriendly eyes I saw fried egg-rolls and chow mein.
Once, for show-and-tell, a girl proudly told the class that one of her ancestors was in the picture of George Washington crossing the Delaware. I
promptly countered that by thinking to myself, "Well, my grandfather was
Sun Yat-sen's[1] physician, so THERE."

[1]*Sun Yat-sen* (1866–1925): Revolutionary leader of China and first president of
the Chinese Republic (1911–1912). [Ed.]

In my home, there is always a rather haphazard combination of the   4
past and present. Next to the scrolls of black ink calligraphy on the dining
room wall is a calendar depicting scenes from the midwest; underneath
the stacked Chinese newspapers, the *L.A. Times*. In the refrigerator, next
to the milk and butter, are tofu and bok choy from the weekly trips to the
local Chinese supermarket. Spoons are used for soup, forks for salad, but
chopsticks are reserved for the main course. I never noticed the disparity
between my lifestyle and that of white Americans—until I began school.
There, I became acquainted with children of strictly Caucasian heritage
and was invited to their homes. Mentally I always compared the interiors
of their homes to my own and to those of my mother's Chinese friends.
What struck me was that their homes seemed to have no trace of their
heritages at all. But nearly all Chinese-American homes retain aspects of
the Chinese culture; aspects that reflect the yearning for returning home
Chinese immigrants always have.

Chinese immigrants like my parents have an unwavering faith in China's   5
potential to truly become the "middle kingdom," the literal translation of
the Chinese words for China. They don't want their first-generation children to forget the way their ancestors lived. They don't want their children to forget that China has a heritage spanning thousands of years, while
America has only a paltry two hundred. My mother used to tape Chinese
characters over the words in our picture books. Ungratefully my sister
and I tore them off because we were more interested in seeing how the
story turned out. When she showed us her satin Chinese dresses, we were
more interested in playing dress-up than in the stories behind the dresses;
when she taught us how to use chopsticks, we were more concentrated on
eating the Chinese delicacies she had prepared. (Incidentally, I still have
to remind myself how to hold my chopsticks properly, though this may
merely be a personal fault; I can't hold a pencil properly either.)

After those endless sessions with taped-over books and flash-cards, my   6
mother packed us off to Chinese School. There, we were to benefit from
interaction with other Chinese-American children in the same predica-
ment—unable to speak, read, or write Chinese nicely. There, we were
supposed to make the same progress we made in our American schools.
But in its own way, Chinese School is as much of a banana as are Chinese-Americans. A Chinese School day starts and ends with a bow to the
teacher to show proper reverence. In the intervening three hours, the students keep one eye on the mysterious symbols of Chinese characters on
the blackboard and the other on the clock. Their voices may be obedi-
ently reciting a lesson, but silently they are urging the minute hand to go
faster. Chinese is taught through the American way, with workbooks and
homework and tests. Without distinctive methods to make the experience
memorable and worthwhile for its students, Chinese School, too, is in
danger of becoming completely Americanized. Chinese-American kids,

especially those in their teens, have become bewitched by the American ideal of obtaining a career that makes lots and lots of money. Their Chinese heritage probably doesn't play a big part in their futures. Many Chinese-Americans are even willing to shed their skins in favor of becoming completely American. Certainly it is easier to go forward and become completely American than to regress and become completely Chinese in America.

7   Sometimes I imagine what it would be like to go back to Taiwan or mainland China. Through eyes misty with romantic sentiment, I can look down a crooked, stone-paved street where a sea of black-haired and slanted-eyed people are bicycling in tandem. I see factories where people are hunch-backed over tables to manufacture plastic toys and American flags. I see fog-enshrouded mountains of Guilin, the yellow mud of the Yangtze River, and the Great Wall of China snaking across the landscape as it does in the pages of a *National Geographic* magazine. When I look up at the moon, I don't see the pale, impersonal sphere that I see here in America. Instead, I see the plaintive face of Chang-Oh, the moon goddess. When I look up at the moon, I may miss my homeland like the famous poet Li Bai did in the poem that every Chinese School student can recite. But will that homeland be America or China?

8   When the crooked street is empty with no bicycles, I see a girl standing across from me on the other side of the street. I see mirrored in her the same perfectly straight black hair and facial features that my Chinese-American friend has, or the same that I have. We cannot communicate, for I only know pidgin Mandarin whereas she speaks fluent Cantonese, a dialect of southern China. Not only is the difference of language a barrier, but the differences in the way we were brought up and the way we live. Though we look the same, we actually are of different cultures, and I may cross the street into her world but only as a visitor. However, I also realize that as a hybrid of two cultures, I am unique, and perhaps that uniqueness should be preserved.

READING FOR MEANING

This section presents three activities that will help you think about the meanings in Lee's reflective essay.

Read to Comprehend

Write a few sentences identifying the occasion for Lee's reflections and listing two or three experiences by which Lee remains aware of her Chinese ethnicity.

Identify any words with meanings you are unsure of—such as *haphazard* (paragraph 4) and *paltry* (5)—and find the dictionary definition for each word that makes the best sense in the context.

To help you understand the essay better, also consider trying one of these critical reading strategies, explained in Appendix 1: *summarizing* or *questioning to understand and remember*.

Read to Respond

Write several paragraphs exploring your initial thoughts and feelings about Lee's reflective essay. Focus on anything that stands out for you, perhaps because it resonates with your own experience or because you find a statement puzzling. For example, consider writing about one of the following:

- the implications of calling someone a banana or an Oreo;

- Lee's thoughts about her kindergarten teacher's decision to have students color paper dolls (paragraph 2), perhaps in connection to your own experience of well-meaning but misguided teachers; or

- your response to Lee's observation that the homes of her Caucasian friends "seemed to have no trace of their heritages at all" (4).

To help develop your response, also consider trying one of these critical reading strategies, explained in Appendix 1: *contextualizing, reflecting on challenges to your beliefs and values*, or *recognizing emotional manipulation*.

Read to Analyze Assumptions

Write a paragraph or two analyzing an assumption in Lee's essay. To think critically about assumptions, here are some kinds of questions you could ask: Who holds this assumption (the writer, readers, and/or others cited in the essay)? What are the effects of the assumption in the context of the essay specifically or in society more generally? What do you think about the assumption, and is there anything in the essay that raises doubts about it? How does the assumption reinforce or critique commonly held views, and are there any alternative ideas, beliefs, or values that would challenge this assumption?

You might choose an assumption from the list below, using the questions accompanying it in addition to the ones above to help you get started. Or you can choose another assumption in the essay to explore.

- **assumptions about the cultural effects of school**. Lee writes that it was only when she began school that she "noticed the disparity between my lifestyle and that of white Americans" (paragraph 4). She has already referred to school experiences that awakened her to her "difference"—the colors of paper dolls and the stereotypes that other children had of Chinese people. What effect does school have on children that home does not?

To think critically about the assumptions in this essay related to school and its functions in America—which seem to go beyond learning subjects in classes—ask yourself questions like these: How does school shape you, compared to how your family or home shapes you? When Lee goes to "Chinese School," she complains that "Chinese is taught through the American way, with workbooks and homework and tests" (6). What does she offer as an alternative to the American way, and what does she assume about how learning occurs?

- **assumptions about the importance of heritage**. Lee notes that American homes "seemed to have no trace of their heritages at all. But nearly all Chinese-American homes retain aspects of the Chinese culture" (4). She adds in the next paragraph that China has a "heritage spanning thousands of years, while America has only a paltry two hundred" (5).

  To think critically about the assumptions in this essay related to heritage, ask yourself questions like these: What does Lee seem to be assuming about the expression of one's ethnic or national heritage? About the length of that heritage? Do you agree with these assumptions? Why or why not? Does your home, or do the homes of your friends, reflect a distinctive heritage? Is that heritage long or short, and does it seem to make a difference? What positives and negatives about heritage is Lee perhaps not considering? What are your assumptions about the place of heritage in a person's home and, by implication, in his or her life?

To help you analyze assumptions in Lee's essay, also consider trying one of these critical reading strategies, explained in Appendix 1: *reflecting on challenges to your beliefs and values* or *looking for patterns of opposition.*

READING LIKE A WRITER

DEVELOPING REFLECTIONS THROUGH COMPARISON AND CONTRAST

In reflective writing, insights and ideas are central. Yet writers cannot merely list ideas, regardless of how fresh and daring their ideas might be. Instead, writers must work imaginatively to develop their ideas, to explain and elaborate them, and to view them from one angle and then another. One well-established way to develop ideas is through comparison and contrast.

Analyze

1. Review the comparisons and contrasts in paragraphs 4, 6, and 8 of Lee's essay.

2. Choose one of these paragraphs to analyze more closely. What exactly is being compared or contrasted? Underline details that highlight the comparisons and contrasts.

Write

Write several sentences describing how Lee uses comparisons and contrasts to develop her ideas. From the one paragraph you chose to analyze, identify the terms (the items being compared) of the comparison or contrast and the ideas they enable Lee to develop.

CONSIDERING IDEAS FOR YOUR OWN WRITING

Consider reflecting on your own ethnicity, beginning your essay, as Lee does, with a concrete occasion. If you are among the "white Caucasians" Lee mentions, you may doubt that you have an ethnicity in the sense that Lee has one. Consider, however, that Asians do not comprise a single ethnicity. Among Asian Americans, there are many distinctly different ethnicities, as defined by their countries or regions of origin: Chinese, Japanese, Korean, Cambodian, Vietnamese, and Philippine, among others. "White Caucasians" also represent many national origins: German, Swedish, Russian, Polish, Irish, Italian, British, Greek, and French, to mention a few. In all of these immigrant groups, as well as others, intermarriage and acculturation to whatever is uniquely American have blurred many of the original ethnic distinctions. Nevertheless, Lee's reflections remind us of the likelihood that in nearly every American family there remain remnants of one or more national or regional ethnicities. This idea for writing invites you to reflect on whatever meanings remain for you personally in your ethnic identities.

A Special Reading Strategy

Comparing and Contrasting Related Readings: Dumas's "The 'F Word'" and Lee's "Peeling Bananas"

Comparing and contrasting related readings is a special critical reading strategy useful both in reading for meaning and in reading like a writer. This strategy is particularly applicable when writers present similar subjects, as in the reflective essays in this chapter by Firoozeh Dumas (p. 175) and Wendy Lee (p. 182). Both writers reflect about their ethnic heritage. To compare and contrast these two reflective essays, think about issues such as these:

- Compare these essays in terms of their authors' beliefs about identity. What aspects of identity do these two essays focus on? What do you learn about the influence of ethnic or racial background from reading them side by side?

- Compare how these two writers use material to develop their reflections. What material is external to them, and what is internal? What attitude or tone does each writer take toward the material? How do their different approaches affect you as a reader?

See Appendix 1 (pp. 596–601) for detailed guidelines on comparing and contrasting related readings.

Katherine Haines

Whose Body Is This?

Katherine Haines wrote this essay for an assignment in her first-year college composition course. As the title suggests, the writer reflects on her dismay and anger about American society's obsession with the perfect body—especially the perfect female body. As you read, note the many kinds of details Haines uses to develop her reflections.

The other readings in this chapter are followed by reading and writing activities. Following this reading, however, you are on your own to decide how to read for meaning and read like a writer.

"Hey Rox, what's up? Do you wanna go down to the pool with me? It's 1 a gorgeous day."

"No thanks, you go ahead without me." 2

"What? Why don't you want to go? You've got the day off work, and 3 what else are you going to do?"

"Well, I've got a bunch of stuff to do around the house . . . pay the bills, 4 clean the bathroom, you know. Besides, I don't want to have to see myself in a bathing suit—I'm so fat."

Why do so many women seem obsessed with their weight and body 5 shape? Are they really that unhappy and dissatisfied with themselves? Or are these women continually hearing from other people that their bodies are not acceptable?

In today's society, the expectations for women and their bodies are 6 all too evident. Fashion, magazines, talk shows, "lite" and fat-free food in stores and restaurants, and diet centers are all daily reminders of these expectations. For instance, the latest fashions for women reveal more and more skin: shorts have become shorter, to the point of being scarcely larger than a pair of underpants, and the bustier, which covers only a little more skin than a bra, is making a comeback. These styles are flattering on only the slimmest of bodies, and many women who were previously happy with their bodies may emerge from the dressing room after a run-in with these styles and decide that it must be diet time again. Instead of coming to the realization that these clothes are unflattering for most women, how many women will simply look for different and more flattering styles, and how many women will end up heading for the gym to burn off some more calories or to the bookstore to buy the latest diet book?

When I was in junior high, about two-thirds of the girls I knew were 7 on diets. Everyone was obsessed with fitting into the smallest-size miniskirt possible. One of my friends would eat a carrot stick, a celery stick, and two rice cakes for lunch. Junior high (and the onset of adolescence) seemed to be the beginning of the pressure for most women. It is at this age that appearance suddenly becomes important, especially for those girls who want to be "popular" and those who are cheerleaders or on the drill team. The pressure is intense; some girls believe no one will like them or accept them if they are "overweight," even by a pound or two. The measures these girls will take to attain the body that they think will make them acceptable are often debilitating and life threatening.

8   My sister was on the drill team in junior high. My sister wanted to fit in with the right crowd—and my sister drove herself to the edge of becoming anorexic. I watched as she came home from school, having eaten nothing for breakfast and at lunch only a bag of pretzels and an apple (and she didn't always finish that), and began pacing the Oriental carpet that was in our living room. Around and around and around, without a break, from four o'clock until dinnertime, which was usually at six or seven o'clock. And then at dinner, she would take minute portions and only pick at her food. After several months of this, she became much paler and thinner but not in any sort of attractive sense. Finally, after catching a cold and having to stay in bed for three days because she was so weak, she was forced to go to the doctor. The doctor said she was suffering from malnourishment and was to stay in bed until she regained some of her strength. He advised her to eat lots of fruits and vegetables until the bruises all over her body had healed (these were a result of vitamin deficiency). Although my sister did not develop anorexia, it was frightening to see what she had done to herself. She had little strength, and the bruises she had made her look like an abused child.

9   This mania to lose weight and have the "ideal" body is not easily avoided in our society. It is created by television and magazines as they flaunt their models and latest diet crazes in front of our faces. And then there are the Nutri-System and Jenny Craig commercials, which show hideous "before" pictures and glamorous "after" pictures and have smiling, happy people dancing around and talking about how their lives have been transformed simply because they have lost weight. This propaganda that happiness is in large part based on having the "perfect" body shape is a message that the media constantly sends to the public. No one seems to be able to escape it.

10   My mother and father were even sucked in by this idea. One evening, when I was in the fifth grade, I heard Mom and Dad calling me into the kitchen. Oh no, what had I done now? It was never good news when you got summoned into the kitchen alone. As I walked into the kitchen, Mom looked up at me with an anxious expression; Dad was sitting at the head of the table with a pen in hand and a yellow legal pad in front of him. They informed me that I was going on a diet. A diet!? I wanted to scream at them, "I'm only ten years old, why do I have to be on a diet?" I was so embarrassed, and I felt so guilty. Was I really fat? I guess so, I thought, otherwise why would my parents do this to me?

It seems that this obsession with the perfect body and a woman's   11
appearance has grown to monumental heights. It is ironic, however, that
now many people feel that this problem is disappearing. People have
begun to assume that women want to be thin because they just want to
be "healthy." But what has happened is that the sickness slips in under the
guise of wanting a "healthy" body. The demand for thin bodies is anything
but "healthy." How many anorexics or bulimics have you seen that are
healthy?

It is strange that women do not come out and object to society's pres-   12
sure to become thin. Or maybe women feel that they really do want to be
thin and so go on dieting endlessly (they call it "eating sensibly"), thinking
this is what they really want. I think if these women carefully examined
their reasons for wanting to lose weight—and were not allowed to include
reasons that relate to society's demands, such as a weight chart, a question-
naire in a magazine, a certain size in a pair of shorts, or even a scale—they
would find that they are being ruled by what society wants, not what
they want. So why do women not break free from these standards? Why
do they not demand an end to being judged in such a demeaning and
senseless way?

Self-esteem plays a large part in determining whether women succumb   13
to the will of society or whether they are independent and self-assured
enough to make their own decisions. Lack of self-esteem is one of the
things the women's movement has had to fight the hardest against. If
women didn't think they were worthy, then how could they even begin
to fight for their own rights? The same is true with the issue of body size.
If women do not feel their body is worthy, then how can they believe
that it is okay to just let it stay that way? Without self-esteem, women will
be swayed by society and will continue to make themselves unhappy by
trying to maintain whatever weight or body shape society is dictating for
them. It is ironic that many of the popular women's magazines (*Cosmo-
politan, Mademoiselle, Glamour*) often feature articles on self-esteem, how
essential it is, and how to improve it—and then in the same issue give the
latest diet tips. This mixed message will never give women the power they
deserve over their bodies and will never enable them to make their own
decisions about what type of body they want.

"Rox, why do you think you're fat? You work out all the time, and you   14
just bought that new suit. Why don't you just come down to the pool for a
little while?"

"No, I really don't want to. I feel so self-conscious with all those people   15
around. It makes me want to run and put on a big, baggy dress so no one
can tell what size I am!"

"Ah, Rox, that's really sad. You have to learn to believe in yourself and   16
your own judgment, not other people's."

READING FOR MEANING

Reading for meaning involves three activities:

- reading to comprehend,
- reading to respond, and
- reading to analyze assumptions.

Write a page or so explaining your understanding of the meaning of Haines's essay, a personal response you have to it, and one of its assumptions.

READING LIKE A WRITER

Writers of reflective essays

- present the particular occasion,
- develop the reflections,
- maintain topical coherence, and
- engage readers.

Choose one of these strategies in Haines's essay, and analyze it carefully through close rereading and annotating. Then write several sentences explaining what you have learned, giving specific examples from the reading to support your explanation. Add a few sentences evaluating how successfully Haines uses the strategy to reflect on society's obsession with the perfect body.

A Special Reading Strategy ──────────────────────

Comparing and Contrasting Related Readings: Haines's "Whose Body Is This?" and Khella's "The Route to American Obesity"

Comparing and contrasting related readings is a critical reading strategy useful both in reading for meaning and in reading like a writer. This strategy is particularly applicable when writers present similar subjects, as is the case in the essays by Katherine Haines (p. 189) and Jeremy Khella (p. 456), both of whom are writing about body weight. To compare and contrast these two readings, think about issues such as these:

- Compare how the two writers feel about body weight. What are their main concerns in writing their essays? Do they take into consideration some of the points made by each other (even though they have not read each other's essays)?

- Compare the assumptions each writer has about the relationship between body weight and health.

- Compare the assumptions each writer has about the relationship between body weight and self-esteem.

See Appendix 1 (pp. 596–601) for detailed guidelines on comparing and contrasting related readings.

Reviewing What Makes an Effective Essay

Reflection

Analyze

Choose one reading from this chapter that seems to you especially effective. Before rereading the selection, jot down one or two reasons you remember it as an example of good reflective writing.

Reread your chosen selection, and add further annotations about what makes it a particularly successful example. Consider the selection's purpose and how well it achieves that purpose for its intended readers. (You can make an informed guess about the intended readers and their expectations by noting the publication source of the essay.) Then assess how well the essay uses the writing strategies of presenting the particular occasion, developing the reflections, maintaining topical coherence, and engaging readers. You can review these strategies in the A Guide to Reading Essays Explaining Concepts (p. 209).

Write

Write at least a page supporting your choice of this reading as an example of effective reflective writing. Refer to details and specific parts of the essay as you explain how it works as reflection and as you justify your evaluation of its effectiveness. You need not argue that it is the best reading in the chapter or that it is flawless, only that it is, in your view, a strong example of the genre.

A GUIDE TO WRITING REFLECTIVE ESSAYS

The readings in this chapter have helped you learn a great deal about reflective writing. At its best, the reflective essay is interesting, lively, insightful, and engaging—much like good conversation—and it avoids sounding pretentious or preachy in its focus on basic human and social issues that concern us all. Writers of reflection are not reluctant to say what they think or to express their most personal observations.

As you develop your reflective essay, you can review the readings to see how other writers use various strategies to solve problems you might also encounter. This Guide to Writing is designed to help you through the various decisions you will need to make as you plan, draft, and revise your reflective essay.

INVENTION AND RESEARCH

The following activities will help you find a particular occasion and a general subject, test your choices, present the particular occasion, and develop your reflections.

Finding a Particular Occasion and a General Subject

As the readings in this chapter illustrate, writers of reflection usually center their essays on one (or more than one) event or occasion. They connect this occasion to a subject they want to reflect on. In the process of invention, however, the choice of a particular occasion does not always come before the choice of a general subject. Sometimes writers set out to reflect on a general subject (such as envy or friendship) and must search for the right occasion (an image or anecdote) with which to particularize it.

Start by listing several possible occasions and the general subjects they suggest in a two-column chart, as shown in the following example:

Particular Occasions	*General Subjects*
I met someone covered with tattoos.	Body art or self-mutilation
I am amazed by people's personal revelations on talk shows.	Desire for celebrity status
While shopping for clothes, I couldn't decide what to buy and let the salesperson pressure me.	Indecisiveness and low self-esteem

For particular occasions, consider conversations you have had or overheard; memorable scenes you observed, read about, or saw in a movie or on television;

and other incidents in your own or someone else's life that might lead you to reflect more generally. Then consider the general subjects suggested by the particular occasions—human qualities such as compassion, vanity, jealousy, and faithfulness; social customs for dating, eating, and working; abstract notions such as fate, free will, and imagination.

In making your chart, you will find that a single occasion might suggest several subjects and that a subject might be particularized by a variety of occasions. Each entry will surely suggest other possibilities for you to consider. Do not be concerned if your chart starts to look messy. A full and rich exploration of possible topics will give you confidence in the subject you finally choose and in your ability to write about it. If you have trouble getting started, review the Considering Ideas for Your Own Writing activities following the readings in this chapter. As further occasions and subjects occur to you over the next two or three days, add them to your chart.

Testing Your Choices

Review your chart, and choose a particular occasion and a general subject you now think look promising. To test whether your choices will work, write for fifteen minutes or so, exploring your thoughts. Do not make any special demands on yourself to be profound or even coherent. Just write your ideas as they come to mind, letting one idea suggest another. Your aims are to determine whether you have enough to say about the occasion and subject and whether they hold your interest. If you discover that you do not have much to say about the occasion or that you quickly lose interest in the subject, choose another set of possibilities and try again. It might take a few preliminary explorations to find the right occasion and subject.

Presenting the Particular Occasion

The following activities will help you recall details about the particular occasion for your reflection. Depending on the occasion you have decided to write about, choose Narrating an Event or Describing What You Observed.

Narrating an Event.   Write for five to ten minutes narrating what happened during the event. Try to make your story vivid so that readers can imagine what it was like. Describe the people involved in the event—what they looked like, how they acted, what they said—and the place where it occurred.

Describing What You Observed.   Write for five or ten minutes describing what you observed. Include as many details as you can recall so that your readers can imagine what you experienced.

Developing Your Reflections

To explore your ideas about the subject, try an invention strategy called *cubing*. Based on the six sides of a cube, this strategy leads you to turn over your subject as you would a cube, looking at it in six different ways. Read the instructions for the following activities, and then write for five minutes on each one. Your goal is to invent new ways of considering your subject.

Generalizing.   Consider what you have learned from the event or experience that will be the occasion for your reflections. What ideas does it suggest to you? What does it suggest about people in general or about the society in which you live?

Giving Examples.   Illustrate your ideas with specific examples. What examples would best help your readers understand your ideas?

Comparing and Contrasting.   Think of a subject that could be compared with yours, and explore the similarities and the differences.

Extending.   Take your subject to its logical limits, and speculate about its implications. Where does it lead?

Analyzing.   Take apart your subject. What is it made of? How are the parts related to one another? Are they all of equal importance?

Applying.   Think about your subject in practical terms. How can you use it or act on it? What difference would it make to you and to others?

Considering Your Purpose.   Write for several minutes about your purpose for writing this essay. As you write, try to answer the question: What do I want my readers to think about the subject after reading my essay? Your answer to this question may change as you write, but thinking about your purpose now may help you decide which of your ideas to include in the essay. Use the following questions to help clarify your purpose:

- Which of your ideas are most important to you? Why?

- How do your ideas relate to one another? If your ideas seem contradictory, consider how you could use the contradictions to convey to readers the complexity of your ideas and feelings on the subject.

- Which of your ideas do you think will most surprise your readers? Which are most likely to be familiar?

- Is the particular occasion for your reflections likely to resonate with your readers' experience and observation? If not, consider how you can make the particular occasion vivid or dramatic for readers.

Formulating a Tentative Thesis Statement.   Review what you wrote for Considering Your Purpose and add another two or three sentences that will bring into focus your reflections. What do they seem to be about? Try to write sentences that indicate what you think is most important or most interesting about the subject, what you want readers to understand from reading your essay.

Keep in mind that readers do not expect you to begin your reflective essay with the kind of thesis statement typical of an argumentative essay, which asserts an opinion the writer then goes on to support. None of the readings in this chapter begins with an explicit statement of the writer's main idea. They all begin with a particular occasion followed by ideas suggested by the occasion. Brent Staples, for example, follows the particular occasion with a general statement of his main idea: "It was in the echo of that terrified woman's footfalls that I first began to know the unwieldy inheritance I'd come into—the ability to alter public space in ugly ways" (paragraph 2). He then explores this rather abstract idea, indicating that his "unwieldy inheritance" is racial stereotyping and the fear it engenders in others. Similarly, Steven Doloff follows the particular occasion with the reflection that "New York's sidewalks make up a kind of endless concrete newspaper from which we can read, in the minute flotsam and jetsam at our feet, news of the mass of people who walk them" (paragraph 3). Katherine Haines also introduces her main idea after presenting the particular occasion: "In today's society, the expectations for women and their bodies are all too evident. Fashion, magazines, talk shows, 'lite' and fat-free food in stores and restaurants, and diet centers are all daily reminders of these expectations" (paragraph 6).

As you explore your ideas and think about the particular occasion for your reflections, you can expect your ideas to change. The fun of writing a reflective essay is that you can share with readers your thinking process, taking them along for the ride.

Considering Visuals.   Think about whether visuals—cartoons, photographs, drawings—would help readers understand and appreciate your reflections. If you submit your essay electronically to other students and your instructor, or if you post it on a Web site, consider including photographs and snippets of film or sound. You could construct your own visuals, scan materials from books and magazines, or download them from the Internet. Visual and audio materials are not at all a requirement of an effective reflective essay, as you can tell from the readings in this chapter, but they could add a new dimension to your writing. If you want to use photographs or recordings of people, though, be sure to obtain their permission.

DRAFTING

The following guidelines will help you set goals for your draft, plan its organization, and think about a useful sentence strategy.

Setting Goals

Establishing goals for your draft before you begin writing will enable you to make decisions and work more confidently. Consider the following questions now, and keep them in mind as you draft. They will help you set goals for drafting as well as recall how the writers you have read in this chapter tried to achieve similar goals.

- *How can I present the particular occasion vividly and in a way that anticipates my reflections?* Should I narrate the event, as Staples does? Refer to a surprising perspective, like Jennings? Create an imaginary dialogue, like Haines?

- *How can I best develop my reflections?* Should I include brief and extended examples, as all of the writers in this chapter do? Should I use comparisons and contrasts, like Lee? Take an imaginary tour, like Jennings? Refer to previous times, like Dumas? Create an imaginary or conversational scene, like Lee and Haines?

- *How can I maintain topical coherence?* Like Staples, can I use topic sentences to make clear the connections between my ideas or insights and the examples that develop them? Can I use word repetition, like Dumas and Haines, to keep my readers on track as they follow the course of my reflections?

- *How can I engage and hold my readers' interest?* Should I reveal the human interest and social significance of my subject by opening my essay with a dramatic event, as Staples does? Should I start with a personal observation, as Jennings, Doloff, and Dumas do? A familiar dialogue, like Haines? An ethnic stereotype, like Staples and Lee? Like all the writers in this chapter, should I reveal my personal commitment to the subject, and should I attempt to inspire my readers to think deeply about their own lives?

Organizing Your Draft

You might find it paradoxical to plan a type of essay that does not aim to reach conclusions or that seeks to give readers the impression that it is finding its way as it goes. And yet you have seen in the readings in this chapter that reflective essays, at least after they have been carefully revised with readers in mind, are usually easy to follow. Part of what makes a reflective essay easy to read is its topical coherence, such as the repetition of key words and phrases that keep the reader's focus on the subject that is being explored in the essay. Writers often develop coherence as they draft and revise their essays, but there are some ways in which planning can also help.

For example, one approach to planning is to begin with the particular occasion, outlining the sequence of events in a way that emphasizes the main point you want the occasion to make. After figuring out how you will present the particular occasion, you could choose one idea you want to develop in detail or list several ideas you think your essay will touch on, possibly indicating how each idea relates to the one that follows. Sometimes when writers go this far in planning, they are actually drafting segments of the essay, discovering a tentative plan as they write.

Another approach to planning begins with the ideas you want to discuss. You could consider various ways of sequencing your ideas. For example, you could start with an obvious idea, one you expect most readers would think of. Then you could develop the idea in unexpected ways or build a train of ideas that leads in a surprising direction. Yet another approach is to pair ideas with examples and develop a sequence of pairs that explores different aspects of your subject or tries out different points of view on it.

Remember that the goal of planning is to discover what you want to say and a possible way of organizing your ideas. Planning a reflective essay can be especially challenging because the process of reflecting is itself a process of discovery: you won't really know what you want your essay to say until you've drafted and revised it. But if you think of planning simply as a way of getting started and remember that you will have a lot of opportunity to reorganize your ideas and develop them further, planning can become an extremely pleasurable and creative activity.

Working with Sources

Using Time Cues to Orient Readers

In the essays that you will write in later chapters of this book, you will rely on interviews, observations, and print or visual sources to support your explanations or arguments. In writing a reflection, however, you will rely almost entirely on your memory, as you did with autobiography. As you complete the invention work, your memory will provide you with several pages of notes, and these notes will stimulate your memory further and lead to further notes. As you draft and revise, still more memories may flood in for you to incorporate in your essay.

Among these rich, varied mental and written sources are ones related to the particular occasion that prompted your reflection. Telling about this occasion will often require you to tell a story. As you develop your reflection, you will be exploring the consequences of that occasion, and you may need to continue the story. Your readers will expect you to keep them oriented to any story you tell by giving them explicit cues about time—cues about the decade, year, season, and time of day; about the pace at which events unfolded; and about the sequence in which the various events took place. Sometimes the occasion is not mentioned in the beginning but later (as with Dumas's occasion, which she holds until the fifth paragraph), so it is especially important to keep your readers oriented.

When experienced writers of reflection use these cues, they nearly always place them at the beginnings of sentences or paragraphs, as Dumas does in "The 'F Word'":

When I was twelve . . . (paragraph 3)

I had just finished fifth grade . . . (5)
Thus I started sixth grade . . . (12)
When I went to college . . . (13)
Once I got married . . . (14)

Placing these important time cues—time of day, time of year, or, as in these examples, time of life—at the beginning of a sentence or paragraph may not seem noteworthy, but the effect changes depending on where time cues are placed. Experienced writers of reflection give high priority to keeping readers oriented to time, including the overall time frame of the particular occasion as well as the sequence of consequences that result from the particular occasion. To do so, they can rely on words or phrases as well as clauses:

For instance, *about 10 years ago*, I noticed almost every day (but did not pick up) dozens of party-colored crack vials scattered about my neighborhood. They are *now*, I am happy to report, gone (at least from my sidewalks), and crack abuse is also much diminished. *Two years ago*, I actually found a crumpled hundred-dollar bill in the street. (Doloff, paragraph 4)

As you draft and revise, look to locating your time cues at the beginnings of your sentences or paragraphs. It is easy to do, and your readers will follow you more easily.

Considering a Useful Sentence Strategy

In addition to planning the sequence of your ideas and repeating key words and phrases, you can enhance the topical coherence of your reflective essay by using parallel grammatical structures to connect related ideas or examples. In the first paragraph of Jennings's essay, he uses two different kinds of parallel structure. In his second sentence, *Sometimes they're stark tales of life-threatening catastrophes, but more often they're just footnotes . . .* he uses a parallel structure that mimics "on the one hand, *this*, and on the other hand, *that*." In the third and fourth sentences, he begins each one with *When I* plus a verb: *When I parse my body's . . . When I wear shorts. . . .*

Now look at this sentence from his paragraph 3:

I had a full and active boyhood, one that raged with scabs and scrapes, mashed and bloody knees, bumps and lumps, gashes and slashes, cats' claws and dogs' teeth, jagged glass, ragged steel, knots, knobs and shiners.

Here he uses parallel grammatical structure ("X and Y") as well as words that rhyme or that look and sound similar ("scabs and scrapes," "knots" and "knobs") to convey the wide range of his scars and the occasions that produced them.

Finally, in the last sentence of the essay, Jennings leaves readers with another powerful parallel phrasing that sums up his reflection: "I've always believed in the power of stories, and I certainly believe in the power of scars" (14).

Here are two more similar uses of parallel form to signal related ideas or examples from other essays in this chapter:

> If it was a slug, did it miss someone? If it was a shell, did it hit someone? (Doloff, paragraph 2)

> They don't want their first-generation children to forget. . . . They don't want their children to forget. . . . (Lee, paragraph 5)

While there are many ways to signal that a group of ideas is related, writers of reflective essays tend to rely on parallel form because it is highly visible; readers notice it at a glance. Parallel form also creates a pleasant rhythm that engages readers and keeps them reading. Moreover, it is very flexible; the variations are endless. Clearly, parallelism is not required for a successful reflective essay, yet it provides you with an effective sentence option to try out in your own essay.

READING A DRAFT CRITICALLY

Getting a critical reading of your draft will help you see how to improve it. Your instructor may schedule class time for reading drafts, or you may want to ask a classmate or a tutor in the writing center to read your draft. Ask your reader to use the following guidelines and to write out a response for you to consult during your revision.

Read for a First Impression

1. **Read the draft without stopping, and then write a few sentences giving your general impression.**

2. **Identify one aspect of the draft that seems especially effective.**

Read Again to Suggest Improvements

1. **Suggest ways of presenting the occasion more effectively.**

   - Read the paragraphs that present the occasion for the reflections, and tell the writer if the occasion dominates the essay, taking up an unjustified amount of space, or if it needs more development.

   - Note whether this occasion suggests the significance or importance of the subject, and consider how well it prepares readers for the reflections by providing a context for them.

- Tell the writer what in the occasion works well and what needs improvement.

2. **Help the writer develop the reflections.**

   - Look for two or three ideas that strike you as especially interesting, insightful, or surprising, and tell the writer what interests you about them. Then, most important, suggest ways these ideas might be developed further through examples, comparisons or contrasts, social implications, connections to other ideas, and so on.

   - Identify any ideas you find uninteresting, explaining briefly why you find them so.

3. **Recommend ways to strengthen topical coherence.**

   - Skim the essay, looking for gaps between sentences and paragraphs, those places where the meaning does not carry forward smoothly. Mark each gap, and try to recommend a way to make the meaning clear.

   - Skim the essay again, looking for irrelevant or unnecessary material that disrupts coherence and diverts the reader's attention. Mark this material, and explain to the writer why it seems to you irrelevant or unnecessary.

   - Consider the essay as a sequence of sections. Ask yourself whether some of the sections could be moved to make the essay easier to follow. Mark any section that seems out of place, and suggest where it might be better located.

4. **Suggest ways to further engage readers.**

   - Point out parts of the essay that draw you in, hold your interest, inspire you to think, challenge your attitudes or values, or keep you wanting to read to the end.

   - Try to suggest ways the writer might engage readers more fully. Consider the essay in light of what is most engaging for you in the essays you have read in this chapter.

   - Look at any visuals in the essay, and tell the writer what, if anything, they contribute to the writer's reflections.

REVISING

This section offers suggestions for revising your draft. Revising means reenvisioning your draft, trying to see it in a new way, given your purpose and readers, in order to develop an engaging, coherent reflective essay.

The biggest mistake you can make while revising is to focus initially on words or sentences. Instead, first try to see your draft as a whole in order to assess its likely impact on your readers. Think imaginatively and boldly about cutting unconvincing material, adding new material, and moving material around. Your computer makes even drastic revisions physically easy, but you still need to make the mental effort and decisions that will improve your draft.

You may have received help with this challenge from a classmate or tutor who gave your draft a critical reading. If so, keep this feedback in mind as you decide which parts of your draft need revising and what specific changes you could make. The following suggestions will help you solve problems and strengthen your essay.

TROUBLESHOOTING YOUR DRAFT

To Present the Particular Occasion More Effectively

Problem	Suggestions for Revising
The occasion seems uninteresting or too general and abstract.	• Add details to make it more dramatic or less predictable. • Make it into a story.
The occasion is not clearly related to the reflections that follow.	• Revise it to be more relevant. • Choose another occasion that is more relevant.

To Develop the Reflections More Fully

Problem	Suggestions for Revising
Promising ideas are not fully developed.	• Provide further examples. • Provide more explanation of the ideas.
Some ideas seem too predictable.	• Drop them. • Try to come up with more insightful ideas.
The reflections do not move beyond personal association.	• Extend them into the social realm. • Comment on their larger implications—what they mean for people in general.

To Strengthen Topical Coherence

Problem	Suggestions for Revising
There are distracting gaps between sentences or paragraphs.	• Try reordering the sequence of action. • Add explicit transitions. • If there are pairs or series of related ideas or examples, revise into parallel form.

To Strengthen Topical Coherence

Problem	Suggestions for Revising
The reflection seems scattered and disorganized.	• Look for words and phrases whose repetition would help readers follow your reflections. • See if there is a time line you could develop more clearly.

To Better Engage Readers

Problem	Suggestions for Revising
The reflection doesn't encourage readers to reflect on their own lives.	• Expand beyond the personal with more generalized stories or anecdotes. • Express the significance more directly.

EDITING AND PROOFREADING

After you have revised your essay, be sure to spend some time checking for errors in usage, punctuation, and mechanics and considering matters of style. If you keep a list of errors you typically make, begin by checking your draft against this list. Ask someone else to proofread your essay before you print out a copy for your instructor or send it electronically.

From our research on student writing, we know that reflective essays have a relatively high frequency of unnecessary shifts in verb tense and mood. Consult a writer's handbook for information on unnecessary verb shifts, and then edit your essay to correct any shifts that you find.

Reflecting on What You Have Learned

Reflection

In this chapter, you have read critically several reflective essays and have written one of your own. To better remember what you have learned, pause now to reflect on the reading and writing activities you completed in this chapter.

1. Write a page or so reflecting on what you have learned. Begin by describing what you are most pleased with in your essay. Then explain what you think contributed to your achievement. Be specific about this contribution.

- If it was something you learned from the readings, indicate which readings and specifically what you learned from them.

- If it came from your invention writing, point out the section or sections that helped you most.

- If you got good advice from a critical reader, explain exactly how the person helped you—perhaps by helping you understand a particular problem in your draft or by helping you add a new dimension to your writing.

- Try to write about your achievement in terms of what you have learned about the genre.

2. Reflect more generally on reflective essays, a genre of writing that has been important for centuries and is still practiced in our society today. Consider some of the following questions: How comfortable do you feel relying on your own experiences or observations as a basis for developing ideas about general subjects or for developing ideas about the way people are and the ways they interact? How comfortable are you with merely trying out your own personal ideas on a subject rather than researching it or interviewing people to collect their ideas? How comfortable do you feel adopting a conversational rather than a formal tone? How would you explain your level of comfort? How might your gender, social class, or ethnic group have influenced the ideas you came up with for your essay? What contribution might reflective essays make to our society that other genres cannot make?

Explaining Concepts

Essays explaining concepts feature a kind of explanatory writing that is especially important for college students to understand. Each of the essays you will analyze in this chapter explains a single concept, including the business concept of *the long tail*, the sociological and psychological concepts of *markedness, dating,* and *hooking up,* and the musical concept of *hip-hop.* For your own explanatory essay, you will choose a concept from your current studies or special interests.

For you as a college student, a better understanding of how to read and write explanations of concepts is useful in several ways. It gives you strategies for critically reading the textbooks and other concept-centered material in your college courses. It helps give you confidence to write a common type of essay exam and paper assignment. And it acquaints you with the basic strategies or modes of development common to all types of explanatory writing—definition, classification or division, comparison and contrast, process narration, illustration, and causal explanation.

A *concept* is a major idea. Every field of study has its concepts: physics has quantum theory, subatomic particles, the Heisenberg principle; psychiatry has neurosis, schizophrenia, narcissism; composition has invention, heuristics, recursiveness; business management has corporate culture, micromanagement, direct marketing; and music has harmony and counterpoint. Concepts include abstract ideas, phenomena, and processes. Concepts are central to the understanding of virtually every subject—we create concepts, name them, communicate them, and think with them.

As you work through this chapter, keep in mind that we learn a new concept by connecting it to what we have previously learned. Good explanatory writing, therefore, must be incremental, adding bit by bit to the reader's knowledge. Explanatory writing goes wrong when the flow of new information is either too fast or too slow for the intended readers, when the information is too difficult or too simple, or when the writing is rambling or just plain dull.

The readings in this chapter will help you see what makes explanatory writing interesting and informative. From the readings and from the ideas for writing that follow each reading, you will get ideas for writing your own essay about a concept. As you read and write about the selections, keep in mind the following assignment, which sets out the goals for writing an essay explaining a concept. To support your writing of this assignment, the chapter concludes with a Guide to Writing Essays Explaining Concepts.

THE WRITING ASSIGNMENT

Choose a concept that interests you enough to study further. Write an essay explaining the concept. Consider carefully what your readers already know about the concept and how your essay can add to their knowledge.

WRITING SITUATIONS FOR ESSAYS EXPLAINING CONCEPTS

Writing that explains concepts is familiar in college and professional life, as the following examples show:

- For a presentation at the annual convention of the American Medical Association, an anesthesiologist writes a report on the concept of *awareness during surgery*. He presents evidence that patients under anesthesia, as in hypnosis, can hear, and he reviews research demonstrating that they can perceive and carry out instructions that speed their recovery. He describes briefly how he applies the concept in his own work—how he prepares patients before surgery, what he tells them while they are under anesthesia, and what happens as they recover.

- A business reporter for a newspaper writes an article about *virtual reality*. She describes the lifelike, three-dimensional experience created by wearing gloves and video goggles wired to a computer. To help readers understand this new concept, she contrasts it with television. For investors, she describes which corporations have shown an interest in the commercial possibilities of virtual reality.

- As part of a group assignment, a college student at a summer biology camp in the Sierra Nevada mountains reads about the condition of mammals at birth. She discovers the distinction between infant mammals that are *altricial* (born nude and helpless within a protective nest) and those that are *precocial* (born well formed with eyes open and ears erect). In her part of a group report, she develops this contrast point by point, giving many examples of specific mammals but focusing in detail on altricial mice and precocial porcupines. Domestic cats, she points out, are an intermediate example—born with some fur but with eyes and ears closed.

Thinking about Your Experience

Explaining Concepts

Before studying a type of writing, it is useful to spend some time thinking about what you already know on the subject. In school, you have probably written numerous explanations of concepts for exams and papers. In and out of school, you may have also had extensive experience explaining concepts to friends and family.

- Recall an occasion when you tried to explain a concept to others and then consider questions like these: What were you trying to explain? Why was it important? What difficulties were you able to anticipate? What strategies did you use? For example, did you think of examples to make your explanation more understandable or compare your subject to something more familiar?

- Recall also explanations you have heard or read in school, on the Internet, on television, or elsewhere. What made them successful?

- Write at least a page about your experience with explanatory writing.

A GUIDE TO READING ESSAYS EXPLAINING CONCEPTS

This guide introduces you to the basic features and strategies typical of explanatory writing by looking closely at an engaging essay by Chris Anderson, the editor-in-chief of *Wired* magazine. Focus first on *reading for meaning,* seeking to grasp the topic's significance to Anderson as well as the meanings you find in the essay—for example, your own feelings about marketing strategies and how people are affected by marketing. Then, to learn how Anderson makes his essay thoughtful and engaging to readers, try *reading like a writer* by analyzing his writing strategies. These two activities—reading for meaning and reading like a writer—follow every reading in this chapter.

Chris Anderson

The Long Tail

Chris Anderson (b. 1961) has a degree in physics from George Washington University and has worked at the magazines the Economist, Nature, *and the* Scientist. *Currently he is editor-in-chief of* Wired, *which won a National Magazine Award under his tenure. His book,* The Long Tail: Why the Future of Business Is Selling Less of More *(2006), is an expansion of the article below, which was first published in* Wired *in 2004. Anderson's most recent book is* Free *(2009). Anderson posts online at: http://twitter.com/chr1sa and http://diydrones.com.*

As you read, think about your own experience in obtaining books, music, or movies. Do you buy them new? Used? Do you download them from free sites? Do you follow recommendations from the sites where you obtain them? How do you feel about the idea of marketing directed specifically to your individual tastes?

1   In 1988, a British mountain climber named Joe Simpson wrote a book called *Touching the Void,* a harrowing account of near death in the Peruvian Andes. It got good reviews but, only a modest success, it was soon forgotten. Then, a decade later, a strange thing happened. Jon Krakauer wrote *Into Thin Air,* another book about a mountain-climbing tragedy, which became a publishing sensation. Suddenly *Touching the Void* started to sell again.

2   Random House rushed out a new edition to keep up with demand. Booksellers began to promote it next to their *Into Thin Air* displays, and sales rose further. A revised paperback edition, which came out in January, spent 14 weeks on the *New York Times* bestseller list. That same month, IFC Films released a docudrama of the story to critical acclaim. Now *Touching the Void* outsells *Into Thin Air* more than two to one.

3   What happened? In short, Amazon.com recommendations. The online bookseller's software noted patterns in buying behavior and suggested that readers who liked *Into Thin Air* would also like *Touching the Void.* People took the suggestion, agreed wholeheartedly, wrote rhapsodic reviews. More sales, more algorithm-fueled recommendations, and the positive feedback loop kicked in.

4   Particularly notable is that when Krakauer's book hit shelves, Simpson's was nearly out of print. A few years ago, readers of Krakauer would never even have learned about Simpson's book—and if they had, they wouldn't have been able to find it. Amazon changed that. It created the *Touching the Void* phenomenon by combining infinite shelf space with real-time information about buying trends and public opinion. The result: rising demand for an obscure book.

5   This is not just a virtue of online booksellers; it is an example of an entirely new economic model for the media and entertainment industries,

one that is just beginning to show its power. Unlimited selection is revealing truths about what consumers want and how they want to get it in service after service, from DVDs at Netflix to music videos on Yahoo! Launch to songs in the iTunes Music Store and Rhapsody. People are going deep into the cata-log, down the long, long list of available titles, far past what's available at Blockbuster Video, Tower Records, and Barnes & Noble. And the more they find, the more they like. As they wander further from the beaten path, they discover their taste is not as mainstream as they thought (or as they had been led to believe by marketing, a lack of alternatives, and a hit-driven culture).

An analysis of the sales data and trends from these services and others 6 like them shows that the emerging digital entertainment economy is going to be radically different from today's mass market. If the 20th-century enter-tainment industry was about hits, the 21st will be equally about misses. . . .

[T]he industry has a poor sense of what people want. Indeed, we have 7 a poor sense of what we want. We assume, for instance, that there is little demand for the stuff that isn't carried by Wal-Mart and other major retailers; if people wanted it, surely it would be sold. The rest, the bottom 80 percent, must be subcommercial at best.

But as egalitarian as Wal-Mart may seem, it is actually extraordinarily 8 elitist. Wal-Mart must sell at least 100,000 copies of a CD to cover its retail overhead and make a sufficient profit; less than 1 percent of CDs do that kind of volume. What about the 60,000 people who would like to buy the latest Fountains of Wayne or Crystal Method album, or any other nonmain-stream fare? They have to go somewhere else. Bookstores, the megaplex, radio, and network TV can be equally demanding. We equate mass market with quality and demand, when in fact it often just represents familiarity, savvy advertising, and broad if somewhat shallow appeal. What do we really want? We're only just discovering, but it clearly starts with *more*.

To get a sense of our true taste, unfiltered by the economics of scarcity, 9 look at Rhapsody, a subscription-based streaming music service (owned by RealNetworks) that currently offers more than 735,000 tracks.

Chart Rhapsody's monthly statistics and you get a "power law" demand 10 curve that looks much like any record store's, with huge appeal for the top tracks, tailing off quickly for less popular ones. But a really interesting thing happens once you dig below the top 40,000 tracks, which is about the amount of the fluid inventory (the albums carried that will eventually be sold) of the average real-world record store. Here, the Wal-Marts of the world go to zero—either they don't carry any more CDs, or the few poten-tial local takers for such fringy fare never find it or never even enter the store.

The Rhapsody demand, however, keeps going. Not only is every one 11 of Rhapsody's top 100,000 tracks streamed at least once each month, the same is true for its top 200,000, top 300,000, and top 400,000. As fast as Rhapsody adds tracks to its library, those songs find an audience, even if it's just a few people a month, somewhere in the country.

12   This is the Long Tail.

13   You can find everything out there on the Long Tail. There's the back catalog, older albums still fondly remembered by longtime fans or redis-covered by new ones.

14   There are live tracks, B-sides, remixes, even (gasp) covers. There are niches by the thousands, genre within genre within genre: Imagine an entire Tower Records devoted to '80s hair bands or ambient dub. There are foreign bands, once priced out of reach in the Import aisle, and obscure bands on even more obscure labels, many of which don't have the distri-bution clout to get into Tower at all.

15   Oh sure, there's also a lot of crap. But there's a lot of crap hiding between the radio tracks on hit albums, too. People have to skip over it on CDs, but they can more easily avoid it online, since the collaborative filters typically won't steer you to it. Unlike the CD, where each crap track costs perhaps one-twelfth of a $15 album price, online it just sits harm-lessly on some server, ignored in a market that sells by the song and evalu-ates tracks on their own merit.

16   What's really amazing about the Long Tail is the sheer size of it. Com-bine enough nonhits on the Long Tail and you've got a market bigger than the hits. Take books: The average Barnes & Noble carries 130,000 titles. Yet more than half of Amazon's book sales come from *outside* its top 130,000 titles. Consider the implication: If the Amazon statistics are any guide, the market for books that are not even sold in the average bookstore is larger than the market for those that are (see "Anatomy of the Long Tail," below). In other words, the potential book market may be twice as big as

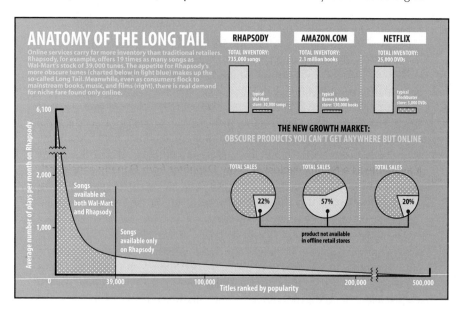

ANATOMY OF THE LONG TAIL

Online services carry far more inventory than traditional retailers. Rhapsody, for example, offers 19 times as many songs as Wal-Mart's stock of 39,000 tunes. The appetite for Rhapsody's more obscure tunes (charted below in light blue) makes up the so-called Long Tail. Meanwhile, even as consumers flock to mainstream books, music, and films (right), there is real demand for niche fare found only online.

RHAPSODY	AMAZON.COM	NETFLIX
TOTAL INVENTORY: 735,000 songs	TOTAL INVENTORY: 2.3 million books	TOTAL INVENTORY: 25,000 DVDs
typical Wal-Mart store: 30,000 songs	typical Barnes & Noble store: 130,000 books	typical Blockbuster store: 3,000 DVDs

THE NEW GROWTH MARKET:
OBSCURE PRODUCTS YOU CAN'T GET ANYWHERE BUT ONLINE

TOTAL SALES 22% | TOTAL SALES 57% | TOTAL SALES 20%

product not available in offline retail stores

Average number of plays per month on Rhapsody

6,100

2,000

Songs available at both Wal-Mart and Rhapsody

1,000

Songs available only on Rhapsody

0   39,000   100,000   200,000   500,000

Titles ranked by popularity

it appears to be, if only we can get over the economics of scarcity. Venture capitalist and former music industry consultant Kevin Laws puts it this way: "The biggest money is in the smallest sales."

The same is true for all other aspects of the entertainment business, to 17 one degree or another. Just compare online and offline businesses: The average Blockbuster carries fewer than 3,000 DVDs. Yet a fifth of Netflix rentals are outside its top 3,000 titles. Rhapsody streams more songs each month *beyond* its top 10,000 than it does its top 10,000. In each case, the market that lies outside the reach of the physical retailer is big and getting bigger.

When you think about it, most successful businesses on the Internet 18 are about aggregating the Long Tail in one way or another. Google, for instance, makes most of its money off small advertisers (the long tail of advertising), and eBay is mostly tail as well—niche and one-off products. By overcoming the limitations of geography and scale, just as Rhapsody and Amazon have, Google and eBay have discovered new markets and expanded existing ones.

This is the power of the Long Tail. The companies at the vanguard of it 19 are showing the way with three big lessons. Call them the new rules for the new entertainment economy.

Rule 1: Make everything available

If you love documentaries, Blockbuster is not for you. Nor is any other 20 video store—there are too many documentaries, and they sell too poorly to justify stocking more than a few dozen of them on physical shelves. Instead, you'll want to join Netflix, which offers more than a thousand documentaries—because it can. Such profligacy is giving a boost to the documentary business; last year, Netflix accounted for half of all US rental revenue for *Capturing the Friedmans*, a documentary about a family destroyed by allegations of pedophilia.

Netflix CEO Reed Hastings, who's something of a documentary buff, 21 took this newfound clout to PBS, which had produced *Daughter from Danang*, a documentary about the children of US soldiers and Vietnamese women. In 2002, the film was nominated for an Oscar and was named best documentary at Sundance, but PBS had no plans to release it on DVD. Hastings offered to handle the manufacturing and distribution if PBS would make it available as a Netflix exclusive. Now *Daughter from Danang* consistently ranks in the top 15 on Netflix documentary charts. That amounts to a market of tens of thousands of documentary renters that did not otherwise exist.

There are any number of equally attractive genres and subgenres 22 neglected by the traditional DVD channels: foreign films, anime, independent movies, British television dramas, old American TV sitcoms. These underserved markets make up a big chunk of Netflix rentals. Bollywood alone accounts for nearly 100,000 rentals each month. The availability of offbeat content drives new customers to Netflix—and anything that cuts the cost of customer acquisition is gold for a subscription business. Thus the company's first lesson: Embrace niches.

23   Netflix has made a good business out of what's unprofitable fare in movie theaters and video rental shops because it can aggregate dispersed audiences. It doesn't matter if the several thousand people who rent *Doctor Who* episodes each month are in one city or spread, one per town, across the country—the economics are the same to Netflix. It has, in short, broken the tyranny of physical space. What matters is not where customers are, or even how many of them are seeking a particular title, but only that some number of them exist, anywhere.

24   As a result, almost anything is worth offering on the off chance it will find a buyer. This is the opposite of the way the entertainment industry now thinks. Today, the decision about whether or when to release an old film on DVD is based on estimates of demand, availability of extras such as commentary and additional material, and marketing opportunities such as anniversaries, awards, and generational windows (Disney briefly rereleases its classics every 10 years or so as a new wave of kids come of age). It's a high bar, which is why only a fraction of movies ever made are available on DVD.

25   That model may make sense for the true classics, but it's way too much fuss for everything else. The Long Tail approach, by contrast, is to simply dump huge chunks of the archive onto bare-bones DVDs, without any extras or marketing. Call it the Silver Series and charge half the price. Same for independent films. This year, nearly 6,000 movies were submitted to the Sundance Film Festival. Of those, 255 were accepted, and just two dozen have been picked up for distribution; to see the others, you had to be there. Why not release all 255 on DVD each year as part of a discount Sundance Series? In a Long Tail economy, it's more expensive to evaluate than to release. Just do it!

26   The same is true for the music industry. It should be securing the rights to release all the titles in all the back catalogs as quickly as it can— thoughtlessly, automatically, and at industrial scale. (This is one of those rare moments where the world needs more lawyers, not fewer.) So too for videogames. Retro gaming, including simulators of classic game consoles that run on modern PCs, is a growing phenomenon driven by the nostalgia of the first joystick generation. Game publishers could release every title as a 99-cent download three years after its release—no support, no guarantees, no packaging.

27   All this, of course, applies equally to books. Already, we're seeing a blurring of the line between in and out of print. Amazon and other networks of used booksellers have made it almost as easy to find and buy a second-hand book as it is a new one. By divorcing bookselling from geography, these networks create a liquid market at low volume, dramatically increasing both their own business and the overall demand for used books. Combine that with the rapidly dropping costs of print-on-demand technologies and it's clear why any book should always be available.

Indeed, it is a fair bet that children today will grow up never knowing the meaning of out of print.

Rule 2: Cut the price in half. Now lower it.

Thanks to the success of Apple's iTunes, we now have a standard price   28
for a downloaded track: 99 cents. But is it the right one?

Ask the labels and they'll tell you it's too low: Even though 99 cents   29
per track works out to about the same price as a CD, most consumers just
buy a track or two from an album online, rather than the full CD. In effect,
online music has seen a return to the singles-driven business of the 1950s.
So from a label perspective, consumers should pay more for the privilege
of purchasing à la carte to compensate for the lost album revenue.

THE REAL COST OF MUSIC

Online music services don't incur packaging, distribution, and retail fees – and they should charge accordingly.

CREATION COSTS
Artist $1.50
Marketing and profit $5.00
Publishing $0.96
= $7.46

divided by
12 tracks
=
62¢/track
+
17¢ online
delivery cost

+

PRODUCTION COSTS
Packaging $0.75
Distribution $2.00
Retail markup $5.00
= $7.76

$15.21 per CD

79¢ per song

Source: Jonathan Daniel and Joe Fleischer, Crush Music Media Management

30   Ask consumers, on the other hand, and they'll tell you that 99 cents is too high. It is, for starters, 99 cents more than Kazaa. But piracy aside, 99 cents violates our innate sense of economic justice: If it clearly costs less for a record label to deliver a song online, with no packaging, manufacturing, distribution, or shelf space overheads, why shouldn't the price be less, too?

31   Surprisingly enough, there's been little good economic analysis on what the right price for online music should be. The main reason for this is that pricing isn't set by the market today but by the record label demi-cartel. Record companies charge a wholesale price of around 65 cents per track, leaving little room for price experimentation by the retailers.

32   That wholesale price is set to roughly match the price of CDs, to avoid dreaded "channel conflict." The labels fear that if they price online music lower, their CD retailers (still the vast majority of the business) will revolt or, more likely, go out of business even more quickly than they already are. In either case, it would be a serious disruption of the status quo, which terrifies the already spooked record companies. No wonder they're doing price calculations with an eye on the downsides in their traditional CD business rather than the upside in their new online business.

33   But what if the record labels stopped playing defense? A brave new look at the economics of music would calculate what it really costs to simply put a song on an iTunes server and adjust pricing accordingly. The results are surprising.

34   Take away the unnecessary costs of the retail channel—CD manufacturing, distribution, and retail overheads. That leaves the costs of finding, making, and marketing music. Keep them as they are, to ensure that the people on the creative and label side of the business make as much as they currently do. For a popular album that sells 300,000 copies, the creative costs work out to about $7.50 per disc, or around 60 cents a track. Add to that the actual cost of delivering music online, which is mostly the cost of building and maintaining the online service rather than the negligible storage and bandwidth costs. Current price tag: around 17 cents a track. By this calculation, hit music is overpriced by 25 percent online—it should cost just 79 cents a track, reflecting the savings of digital delivery.

35   Putting channel conflict aside for the moment, if the incremental cost of making content that was originally produced for physical distribution available online is low, the price should be, too. Price according to digital costs, not physical ones.

36   All this good news for consumers doesn't have to hurt the industry. When you lower prices, people tend to buy more. Last year, Rhapsody did an experiment in elastic demand that suggested it could be a lot more. For a brief period, the service offered tracks at 99 cents, 79 cents, and 49 cents. Although the 49-cent tracks were only half the price of the 99-cent tracks, Rhapsody sold three times as many of them.

Since the record companies still charged 65 cents a track—and Rhapsody   37
paid another 8 cents per track to the copyright-holding publishers—
Rhapsody lost money on that experiment (but, as the old joke goes, made
it up in volume). Yet much of the content on the Long Tail is older material
that has already made back its money (or been written off for failing to
do so): music from bands that had little record company investment and
was thus cheap to make, or live recordings, remixes, and other material
that came at low cost.

Such "misses" cost less to make available than hits, so why not charge   38
even less for them? Imagine if prices declined the further you went down
the Tail, with popularity (the market) effectively dictating pricing. All it
would take is for the labels to lower the wholesale price for the vast majority of their content not in heavy rotation; even a two- or three-tiered pricing structure could work wonders. And because so much of that content is
not available in record stores, the risk of channel conflict is greatly diminished. The lesson: Pull consumers down the Tail with lower prices.

How low should the labels go? The answer comes by examining the   39
psychology of the music consumer. The choice facing fans is not how
many songs to buy from iTunes and Rhapsody, but how many songs to
buy rather than download for free from Kazaa and other peer-to-peer networks. Intuitively, consumers know that free music is not really free: Aside
from any legal risks, it's a time-consuming hassle to build a collection that
way. Labeling is inconsistent, quality varies, and an estimated 30 percent
of tracks are defective in one way or another. As Steve Jobs put it at the
iTunes Music Store launch, you may save a little money downloading
from Kazaa, but "you're working for under minimum wage." And what's
true for music is doubly true for movies and games, where the quality of
pirated products can be even more dismal, viruses are a risk, and down-
loads take so much longer.

So free has a cost: the psychological value of convenience. This is the   40
"not worth it" moment where the wallet opens. The exact amount is an
impossible calculus involving the bank balance of the average college student multiplied by their available free time. But imagine that for music,
at least, it's around 20 cents a track. That, in effect, is the dividing line
between the commercial world of the Long Tail and the underground.
Both worlds will continue to exist in parallel, but it's crucial for Long Tail
thinkers to exploit the opportunities between 20 and 99 cents to maximize
their share. By offering fair pricing, ease of use, and consistent quality, you
can compete with free.

Perhaps the best way to do that is to stop charging for individual tracks   41
at all. Danny Stein, whose private equity firm owns eMusic, thinks the
future of the business is to move away from the ownership model entirely.
With ubiquitous broadband, both wired and wireless, more consumers
will turn to the celestial jukebox of music services that offer every track

ever made, playable on demand. Some of those tracks will be free to listeners and advertising-supported, like radio. Others, like eMusic and Rhapsody, will be subscription services. Today, digital music economics are dominated by the iPod, with its notion of a paid-up library of personal tracks. But as the networks improve, the comparative economic advantages of unlimited streamed music, either financed by advertising or a flat fee (infinite choice for $9.99 a month), may shift the market that way. And drive another nail in the coffin of the retail music model.

Rule 3: Help me find it

42   In 1997, an entrepreneur named Michael Robertson started what looked like a classic Long Tail business. Called MP3.com, it let anyone upload music files that would be available to all. The idea was the service would bypass the record labels, allowing artists to connect directly to listeners. MP3.com would make its money in fees paid by bands to have their music promoted on the site. The tyranny of the labels would be broken, and a thousand flowers would bloom.

43   Putting aside the fact that many people actually used the service to illegally upload and share commercial tracks, leading the labels to sue MP3.com, the model failed at its intended purpose, too. Struggling bands did not, as a rule, find new audiences, and independent music was not transformed. Indeed, MP3.com got a reputation for being exactly what it was: an undifferentiated mass of mostly bad music that deserved its obscurity.

44   The problem with MP3.com was that it was *only* Long Tail. It didn't have license agreements with the labels to offer mainstream fare or much popular commercial music at all. Therefore, there was no familiar point of entry for consumers, no known quantity from which further exploring could begin.

45   Offering only hits is no better. Think of the struggling video-on-demand services of the cable companies. Or think of Movielink, the feeble video download service run by the studios. Due to overcontrolling providers and high costs, they suffer from limited content: in most cases just a few hundred recent releases. There's not enough choice to change consumer behavior, to become a real force in the entertainment economy.

46   By contrast, the success of Netflix, Amazon, and the commercial music services shows that you need *both* ends of the curve. Their huge libraries of less-mainstream fare set them apart, but hits still matter in attracting consumers in the first place. Great Long Tail businesses can then guide consumers further afield by following the contours of their likes and dislikes, easing their exploration of the unknown.

47   For instance, the front screen of Rhapsody features Britney Spears, unsurprisingly. Next to the listings of her work is a box of "similar artists." Among them is Pink. If you click on that and are pleased with what you

hear, you may do the same for Pink's similar artists, which include No Doubt. And on No Doubt's page, the list includes a few "followers" and "influencers," the last of which includes the Selecter, a 1980s ska band from Coventry, England. In three clicks, Rhapsody may have enticed a Britney Spears fan to try an album that can hardly be found in a record store.

Rhapsody does this with a combination of human editors and genre 48 guides. But Netflix, where 60 percent of rentals come from recommendations, and Amazon do this with collaborative filtering, which uses the browsing and purchasing patterns of users to guide those who follow them ("Customers who bought this also bought . . ."). In each, the aim is the same: Use recommendations to drive demand down the Long Tail.

This is the difference between push and pull, between broadcast and 49 personalized taste. Long Tail business can treat consumers as individuals, offering mass customization as an alternative to mass-market fare.

The advantages are spread widely. For the entertainment industry itself, 50 recommendations are a remarkably efficient form of marketing, allowing smaller films and less-mainstream music to find an audience. For consumers, the improved signal-to-noise ratio that comes from following a good recommendation encourages exploration and can reawaken a passion for music and film, potentially creating a far larger entertainment market overall. (The average Netflix customer rents seven DVDs a month, three times the rate at brick-and-mortar stores.) And the cultural benefit of all of this is much more diversity, reversing the blanding effects of a century of distribution scarcity and ending the tyranny of the hit.

Such is the power of the Long Tail. Its time has come. 51

READING FOR MEANING

This section presents three activities that will help you think about the meanings in Anderson's explanatory essay.

Read to Comprehend

Write a few sentences briefly explaining the concept of the economic model of the *Long Tail* and its significance.

Identify any words with meanings you are unsure of—such as *aggregating* (paragraph 18) and *niches* (22)—and find the dictionary definition for each word that makes the best sense in the context.

To help you understand the essay better, also consider trying one of these critical reading strategies, explained in Appendix 1: *outlining* or *summarizing*.

Read to Respond

Write several paragraphs exploring your initial thoughts and feelings about Anderson's explanation of a concept. Focus on anything that stands out for you, perhaps because it resonates with your own experience or because you find a statement puzzling. For example, consider writing about one of the following:

- your own experience with buying or downloading a book, a song, or a movie that you learned about from a vendor who said "people who bought this also bought...."

- what you think of the three "new rules for the new entertainment economy" (paragraph 19).

- Anderson's assertion that "most successful businesses on the Internet are about aggregating the Long Tail in one way or another" (18).

To help develop your response, also consider trying one of these critical reading strategies, explained in Appendix 1: *questioning to understand and remember* or *judging the writer's credibility.*

Read to Analyze Assumptions

All writing contains *assumptions*—ideas and attitudes that are taken for granted as commonly accepted truths. Personal or individual assumptions also tend to reflect the values and beliefs of a particular community, which help shape the way those in the group think, act, and understand the world. All writing reflects assumptions held by the writer, but assumptions held by others, such as readers or sources cited by the writer, may also be present. Sometimes assumptions are stated explicitly, but often they are only implied, so you may have to search for underlying assumptions in the word choices and examples.

Why go to the effort to analyze assumptions in a reading? Assumptions have powerful effects. They influence our opinions and judgments by leading us to value some things and devalue others. These effects are even more powerful because they are taken for granted, often accepted without question by those who hold them. To understand a reading on a deep level, then, it is necessary to bring its assumptions to the surface and to question them. To think critically about assumptions, here are some kinds of questions you could ask: Who holds this assumption (the writer, readers, and/or others cited in the essay)? What are the effects of the assumption in the context of the essay specifically or in society more generally? What do you think about the assumption, and is there anything in the essay that raises doubts about it? How does the assumption reinforce or critique commonly held views, and are there any alternative ideas, beliefs, or values that would challenge this assumption?

Write a paragraph or two analyzing an assumption in Anderson's essay. You might choose an assumption from the list below, using the questions accompanying it in addition to the ones above to help you get started. Or you can choose another assumption in the essay to explore.

- **the assumption that for consumers, more choice is better.** Anderson writes that the deeper people can go into a catalog, "down the long, long list of available titles. . . . the more they find, the more they like" (paragraph 5). Later, he writes that "[w]e equate mass market with quality and demand, when in fact it often just represents familiarity, savvy advertising, and broad if somewhat shallow appeal. What do we really want? We're only just discovering, but it clearly starts with *more*" (8).

  To think critically about the assumptions in this essay related to consumers preferring more choice, ask yourself questions like these: why would more choice be appealing to consumers? What are the advantages of more choice? What could be the disadvantages? Does more choice necessarily imply that there would be more items available that consumers would like? Is pleasing consumers the best policy for a company to adopt?

- **the assumption that a "niche" taste is superior to "mainstream" taste.** Anderson asserts that "[u]nlimited selection is revealing truths about what consumers want and how they want to get it. . . . As they wander further from the beaten path, they discover their taste is not as mainstream as they thought (or as they had been led to believe by marketing, a lack of alternatives, and a hit-driven culture)" (paragraph 5). He adds that "the industry has a poor sense of what people want. Indeed, we have a poor sense of what we want" (7).

  To think critically about the assumptions in this essay about "mainstream" taste, ask yourself questions like these: How accurate is the assumption that people have a poor sense of what they want? What determines a person's taste in books, movies, music, and so on? How does wandering from the beaten path guarantee one will develop a superior taste? Do you believe that mainstream media determine the taste of most people, including yourself?

To help you analyze assumptions in Anderson's essay, also consider trying one of these critical reading strategies, explained in Appendix 1: *reflecting on challenges to your beliefs and values* or *recognizing emotional manipulation*.

READING LIKE A WRITER

This section guides you through an analysis of Anderson's explanatory writing strategies: *devising a readable plan, using appropriate explanatory strategies, integrating sources smoothly*, and *engaging readers' interest*. For each strategy you will be asked to reread and annotate part of Anderson's essay to see how he uses the strategy in "The Long Tail."

When you study the selections later in this chapter, you will see how different writers use these same strategies. The Guide to Writing Essays Explaining

Guide
to
Reading

CHAPTER 5 Explaining Concepts

Concepts near the end of the chapter suggests ways you can use these strategies in your own writing.

Devising a Readable Plan

Experienced writers of explanation know that readers often have a hard time making their way through new and difficult material and sometimes give up in frustration. Writers who want to avoid this scenario construct a reader-friendly plan by dividing the information into clearly distinguishable topics. They also give readers road signs—forecasting statements, topic sentences, transitions, and summaries—to guide them through the explanation.

Writers often provide a forecasting statement early in the essay to let readers know where they are heading. Forecasting statements can also appear at the beginnings of major sections of the essay. Topic sentences announce each segment of information as it comes up, transitions (such as *in contrast* and *another*) relate what is coming to what came before, and summaries remind readers what has been explained already. Anderson effectively deploys all of these strategies.

Analyze

Mark those sentences that forecast, announce topics, make transitions, and offer brief summaries. (These strategies are defined in the preceding paragraph. Look especially at paragraph 18 in the essay.)

Write

Write several sentences explaining how Anderson makes use of forecasting statements, transitions, brief summaries, and topic sentences to reveal his overall plan to readers. Give examples from the reading to support your explanation. Then, considering yourself among Anderson's intended readers, write a few more sentences evaluating how successful the writer's efforts are for you.

Using Appropriate Explanatory Strategies

When writers organize and present information, they rely on strategies we call the building blocks of explanatory essays—defining, classifying or dividing, comparing and contrasting, narrating a process, illustrating, and reporting causes or effects. The strategies a writer chooses are determined by the topics covered, the kinds of information available, and the writer's assessment of readers' knowledge about the concept. Following are brief descriptions of the writing strategies that are particularly useful in explaining concepts:

Defining: briefly stating the meaning of the concept or any other word likely to be unfamiliar to readers.

Classifying or dividing: grouping related information about a concept into two or more separate groups and labeling each group, or dividing a concept into parts to consider each part separately.

Comparing and contrasting: pointing out how the concept is similar to and different from a related concept.

Narrating a process: presenting procedures or a sequence of steps as they unfold over time to show the concept in practice.

Illustrating: giving examples, relating anecdotes, listing facts and details, and quoting sources to help readers understand a concept.

Reporting causes or effects: identifying the known causes or effects related to a concept.

Anderson makes good use of all these fundamentally important explanatory strategies. Here are a few examples of where you can find them: defining in paragraphs 5, 8, and 13; classifying in paragraphs 17 and 22; comparing and contrasting in paragraphs 15 to 17; narrating a process in paragraphs 1 to 4; illustrating in paragraphs 16, 17, and 21; and reporting known effects in paragraphs 5, 10 to 11, and 34. These strategies are found in many other paragraphs throughout the essay.

Analyze

1. Review Anderson's use of each explanatory strategy described in the preceding paragraph, and select one to analyze more closely.

2. Make notes in the margin about how Anderson uses that one strategy and what special contribution it makes to your understanding of the Long Tail within the context of the whole reading.

Write

Write several sentences explaining how the strategy you have analyzed works in this essay to help readers understand the Long Tail.

Integrating Sources Smoothly

In addition to drawing on personal knowledge and fresh observations, writers often do additional research about the concepts they are trying to explain. Doing research in the library and on the Internet, writers immediately confront the ethical responsibility to their readers of locating relevant sources, evaluating them critically, and representing them without distortion. You will find advice on meeting this responsibility in Appendix 2 (pp. 603–66).

Developing an explanation sentence by sentence on the page or the screen, writers confront a different challenge in using sources. They need to know how to integrate source material smoothly into their own sentences and to cite the sources of those materials accurately, sometimes using formal citation styles that point readers to a full description of each source in a list of works cited at the end of the essay.

How writers cite or refer to research sources depends on the writing situation they find themselves in. Certain formal situations, such as college assignments or scholarly publications, have prescribed rules for citing sources. As a student, you may be expected to cite your sources formally because your writing will be judged in part by what you have read and how you have used your reading. For more informal writing—newspaper and magazine articles, for example—readers do not expect writers to include page references or publication information, only to identify their sources. In this chapter, Beth L. Bailey, Linh Kieu Ngo, and Justin Ton cite their sources formally; Chris Anderson, Deborah Tannen, and Kathleen Bogle cite their sources informally.

Writers may quote, summarize, or paraphrase their sources—quoting when they want to capture the exact wording of the original source; summarizing to convey only the gist or main points; and paraphrasing when they want to include most of the details in some part of the original. Whether they quote, summarize, or paraphrase, writers try to integrate source material smoothly into their writing. For example, they deliberately vary the way they introduce borrowed material, avoiding repetition of the same signal phrases (X *said, as* Y *put it*) or sentence pattern (a *that* clause, use of the colon).

Analyze

1. Look closely at paragraph 16, where Anderson quotes a source directly. Now look at the rest of the paragraph and see how Anderson incorporates source material without quoting the source.

2. Put brackets around the signal phrase or key part of a sentence pattern that he uses to introduce the quotation, noticing how he integrates the quotation into his sentence. Notice how he integrates statistics and other information without quoting into the rest of the paragraph.

Write

Write a few sentences describing how Anderson introduces and integrates quotations into his writing. Give examples from your annotations in paragraph 16.

Engaging Readers' Interest

Most people read explanations of concepts because they are helpful for work or school. Readers do not generally expect the writing to entertain but simply to inform. Nevertheless, explanations that keep readers engaged with lively writing are usually appreciated. Writers explaining concepts may engage readers' interest in a variety of ways. For example, they may remind readers of what they already know about the concept. They may show readers a new way of using a familiar concept or dramatize that the concept has greater importance than readers had realized. They can connect the concept, sometimes through metaphor or analogy, to common human experiences. They may present the concept in a humorous way to convince readers that learning about a concept can be painless or even pleasurable.

Anderson relies on many of these strategies to engage his readers' interest. Keep in mind that his original readers could either read or skip his article. Those who had enjoyed and learned from his earlier articles would be more likely to try out the first few paragraphs of this one, but Anderson could not count on their having any special interest in the Long Tail. He has to try to generate that interest—and rather quickly, in the first few sentences or paragraphs.

Analyze

Reread paragraphs 1 to 5, and note in the margin the various ways Anderson reaches out to interest readers in his subject.

Write

Write several sentences explaining how Anderson attempts to engage his readers' interest in the Long Tail. To support your explanation, give examples from your annotations in paragraphs 1 to 5. What parts seem most effective to you? Least effective?

ANALYZING VISUALS

Write a paragraph analyzing the two charts included in Anderson's "The Long Tail" and explaining what they contribute to the essay. To do the analysis, you can use the criteria chart for the Analysis of Visuals in Appendix 3 on pp. 670–72. Don't feel you have to answer all of the questions on the chart: focus on those that seem most productive in helping you write a paragraph-length analysis. To help you get started, consider adding these questions that specifically refer to Anderson's visuals:

- How does "Anatomy of the Long Tail" illustrate Kevin Laws's assertion that "[t]he biggest money is in the smallest sales"? How does it illustrate Anderson's comparison of online and offline business: "In each case, the market that lies outside the reach of the physical retailer is big and getting bigger"?

- Why do you suppose Rhapsody, Amazon.com, and Netflix are the three representative companies chosen for "Anatomy of the Long Tail"?

- How does the pie chart in "Anatomy of the Long Tail" help you understand the concept of the long tail?

- The second "big lesson" of the companies at the vanguard of the long tail (paragraph 28) is: "Cut the price in half. Now lower it." How does the chart "The Real Cost of Music" help you understand the economics of the long tail regarding music? Does understanding this chart help you understand Anderson's speculation that eventually most streamed music will be unlimited, financed by advertising or a subscription (41)? If so, how? If not, how would you design a chart to show this possibility?

READINGS

Deborah Tannen

Marked Women

Deborah Tannen (b. 1945), who is university professor in linguistics at Georgetown University, has written more than twenty books and scores of articles. Although she does write technical works on linguistics, she also writes for a more general audience on the ways that language reflects the society in which it develops, particularly the society's attitudes about gender. Both her 1986 book, That's Not What I Meant! How Conversational Style Makes or Breaks Your Relations with Others, *and her 1990 book,* You Just Don't Understand: Women and Men in Conversation, *were best-sellers. Her most recent books include* The Argument Culture: Moving from Debate to Dialogue *(1998),* I Only Say This Because I Love You: Talking to Your Parents, Partner, Sibs, and Kids When You're All Adults *(2002), and* You're Wearing THAT? Understanding Mothers and Daughters in Conversation *(2007). In addition, Tannen writes poetry, plays, and reflective essays.*

In the following selection, originally published in the New York Times Magazine *in 1993, Tannen explains the concept of markedness, a "staple of linguistic theory." Linguistics—the study of language as a system for making meaning—has given birth to a new discipline called* semiology, *the study of any system for making meaning. Tannen's essay embodies this shift, as it starts with a verbal principle (the marking of words) and applies it to the visual world (the marking of hairstyle and clothing). As you read, note places where Tannen unpacks the meaning of what various conference participants are wearing. Does Tannen's experience illuminate your own?*

1   Some years ago I was at a small working conference of four women and eight men. Instead of concentrating on the discussion I found myself looking at the three other women at the table, thinking how each had a different style and how each style was coherent.

2   One woman had dark brown hair in a classic style, a cross between Cleopatra and Plain Jane. The severity of her straight hair was softened by wavy bangs and ends that turned under. Because she was beautiful, the effect was more Cleopatra than plain.

How do these opening paragraphs engage the reader's interest?

3   The second woman was older, full of dignity and composure. Her hair was cut in a fashionable style that left her with only one eye, thanks to a side part that let a curtain of hair fall across half her face. As she looked

In paragraphs 1–7, what are the main explanatory strategies Tannen employs? What is the effect of these strategies?

down to read her prepared paper, the hair robbed her of bifocal vision and created a barrier between her and the listeners.

The third woman's hair was wild, a frosted blond avalanche falling over and beyond her shoulders. When she spoke she frequently tossed her head, calling attention to her hair and away from her lecture.   4

Then there was makeup. The first woman wore facial cover that made her skin smooth and pale, a black line under each eye and mascara that darkened already dark lashes. The second wore only a light gloss on her lips and a hint of shadow on her eyes. The third had blue bands under her eyes, dark blue shadow, mascara, bright red lipstick and rouge; her fingernails flashed red.   5

I considered the clothes each woman had worn during the three days of the conference: In the first case, man-tailored suits in primary colors with solid-color blouses. In the second, casual but stylish black T-shirts, a floppy collarless jacket and baggy slacks or a skirt in neutral colors. The third wore a sexy jump suit; tight sleeveless jersey and tight yellow slacks; a dress with gaping armholes and an indulged tendency to fall off one shoulder.   6

Shoes? No. 1 wore string sandals with medium heels; No. 2, sensible, comfortable walking shoes; No. 3, pumps with spike heels. You can fill in the jewelry, scarves, shawls, sweaters—or lack of them.   7

As I amused myself finding coherence in these styles, I suddenly wondered why I was scrutinizing only the women. I scanned the eight men at the table. And then I knew why I wasn't studying them. The men's styles were unmarked.   8

Why does Tannen wait until now to introduce linguistic theory?

The term "marked" is a staple of linguistic theory. It refers to the way language alters the base meaning of a word by adding a linguistic particle that has no meaning on its own. The unmarked form of a word carries the meaning that goes without saying—what you think of when you're not thinking anything special.   9

The unmarked tense of verbs in English is the present — for example, *visit*. To indicate past, you mark the verb by adding *ed* to yield *visited*. For future, you add a word: *will visit*. Nouns are presumed to be singular until marked for plural, typically by adding *s* or *es*, so *visit* becomes *visits* and *dish* becomes *dishes*.   10

11   The unmarked forms of most English words also convey "male." Being male is the unmarked case. Endings like *ess* and *ette* mark words as "female." Unfortunately, they also tend to mark them for frivolousness. Would you feel safe entrusting your life to a doctorette? Alfre Woodard, who was an Oscar nominee for best supporting actress, says she identifies herself as an actor because "actresses worry about eyelashes and cellulite, and women who are actors worry about the characters we are playing." Gender markers pick up extra meanings that reflect common association with the female gender: not quite serious, often sexual.

How does this paragraph prepare you for Tannen's assertion in paragraph 29 that she may be marked as a feminist?

12   Each of the women at the conference had to make decisions about hair, clothing, makeup and accessories, and each decision carried meaning. Every style available to us was marked. The men in our group had made decisions, too, but the range from which they chose was incomparably narrower. Men can choose styles that are marked, but they don't have to, and in this group none did. Unlike the women, they had the option of being unmarked.

What does this paragraph suggest about the organizational plan Tannen will follow in the rest of the essay?

13   Take the men's hair styles. There was no marine crew cut or oily longish hair falling into eyes, no asymmetrical, two-tiered construction to swirl over a bald top. One man was unabashedly bald; the others had hair of standard length, parted on one side, in natural shades of brown or gray or graying. Their hair obstructed no views, left little to toss or push back or run fingers through and, consequently, needed and attracted no attention. A few men had beards. In a business setting, beards might be marked. In this academic gathering, they weren't.

14   There could have been a cowboy shirt with string tie or a three-piece suit or a necklaced hippie in jeans. But there wasn't. All eight men wore brown or blue slacks and nondescript shirts of light colors. No man wore sandals or boots; their shoes were dark, closed, comfortable, and flat. In short, unmarked.

What is the purpose of pointing out the men's appearance in paragraphs 13–15? Together with the description of the women's appearance in paragraphs 2–7, what explanatory strategy does this represent?

15   Although no man wore makeup, you couldn't say the men didn't wear makeup in the sense that you could say a woman didn't wear makeup. For men, no makeup is unmarked.

16   I asked myself what style we women could have adopted that would have been unmarked, like the men's. The answer was none. There is no unmarked woman.

Why do you think Tannen does not describe her own appearance as part of this discussion?

There is no woman's hair style that can be called standard, that says nothing about her. The range of women's hair styles is staggering, but a woman whose hair has no particular style is perceived as not caring about how she looks, which can disqualify her from many positions, and will subtly diminish her as a person in the eyes of some. 17

Women must choose between attractive shoes and comfortable shoes. When our group made an unexpected trek, the woman who wore flat, laced shoes arrived first. Last to arrive was the woman in spike heels, shoes in hand and a handful of men around her. 18

What is the effect of piling up so many examples and illustrations of the ways women's appearance is marked?

If a woman's clothing is tight or revealing (in other words, sexy), it sends a message—an intended one of wanting to be attractive, but also a possibly unintended one of availability. If her clothes are not sexy, that too sends a message, lent meaning by the knowledge that they could have been. There are thousands of cosmetic products from which women can choose and myriad ways of applying them. Yet no makeup at all is anything but unmarked. Some men see it as a hostile refusal to please them. 19

Women can't even fill out a form without telling stories about themselves. Most forms give four titles to choose from. "Mr." carries no meaning other than that the respondent is male. But a woman who checks "Mrs." or "Miss" communicates not only whether she has been married but also whether she has conservative tastes in forms of address—and probably other conservative values as well. Checking "Ms." declines to let on about marriage (checking "Mr." declines nothing since nothing was asked), but it also marks her as either liberated or rebellious, depending on the observer's attitudes and assumptions. 20

Here Tannen does use herself as an example. Why here and not elsewhere?

I sometimes try to duck these variously marked choices by giving my title as "Dr."—and in so doing risk marking myself as either uppity (hence sarcastic responses like "Excuse *me!*") or an over-achiever (hence reactions of congratulatory surprise like "Good for you!"). 21

All married women's surnames are marked. If a woman takes her husband's name, she announces to the world that she is married and has traditional values. To some it will indicate that she is less herself, more identified by her husband's identity. If she does not take her husband's name, this too is marked, seen as worthy of comment: She has *done* something; she has "kept her own name." A man is never said to have "kept his own name" because it 22 never occurs to anyone that he might have given it up. For him using his own name is unmarked.

23   A married woman who wants to have her cake and eat it too may use her surname plus his, with or without a hyphen. But this too announces her marital status and often results in a tongue-tying string. In a list (Harvey O'Donovan, Jonathan Feldman, Stephanie Woodbury McGillicutty), the woman's multiple name stands out. It is marked.

24   I have never been inclined toward biological explanations of gender differences in language, but I was intrigued to see Ralph Fasold bring biological phenomena to bear on the question of linguistic marking in his book *The Sociolinguistics of Language*. Fasold stresses that language and culture are particularly unfair in treating women as the marked case because biologically it is the male that is marked. While two X chromosomes make a female, two Y chromosomes make nothing. Like the linguistic markers *s*, *es*, or *ess*, the Y chromosome doesn't "mean" anything unless it is attached to a root form—an X chromosome.

Why does Tannen bring in a source here? What do you notice about the way she introduces it?

25   Developing this idea elsewhere Fasold points out that girls are born with full female bodies, while boys are born with modified female bodies. He invites men who doubt this to lift up their shirts and contemplate why they have nipples.

26   In his book, Fasold notes "a wide range of facts which demonstrates that female is the unmarked sex." For example, he observes that there are a few species that produce only females, like the whiptail lizard. Thanks to parthenogenesis, they have no trouble having as many daughters as they like. There are no species, however, that produce only males. This is no surprise, since any such species would become extinct in its first generation.

Tannen reminds readers that the female is the source of birth—and therefore life. Why bring that up here?

27   Fasold is also intrigued by species that produce individuals not involved in reproduction, like honeybees and leaf-cutter ants. Reproduction is handled by the queen and a relatively few males; the workers are sterile females. "Since they do not reproduce," Fasold said, "there is no reason for them to be one sex or the other, so they default, so to speak, to female."

28   Fasold ends his discussion of these matters by pointing out that if language reflected biology, grammar books would direct us to use "she" to include males and females and "he" only for specifically male referents. But they don't. They tell us that "he" means "he or she," and that "she" is

used only if the referent is specifically female. This use of "he" as the sex-indefinite pronoun is an innovation introduced into English by grammarians in the eighteenth and nineteenth centuries, according to Peter Mühlhäusler and Rom Harré in *Pronouns and People*. From at least about 1500, the correct sex-indefinite pronoun was "they," as it still is in casual spoken English. In other words, the female was declared by grammarians to be the marked case.

29   Writing this article may mark me not as a writer, not as a linguist, not as an analyst of human behavior, but as a feminist—which will have positive or negative, but in any case powerful, connotations for readers. Yet I doubt that anyone reading Ralph Fasold's book would put that label on him.

30   I discovered the markedness inherent in the very topic of gender after writing a book on differences in conversational style based on geographical region, ethnicity, class, age, and gender. When I was interviewed, the vast majority of journalists wanted to talk about the differences between women and men. While I thought I was simply describing what I observed—something I had learned to do as a researcher—merely mentioning women and men marked me as a feminist for some.

Is Tannen fully objective in this essay, or do you think that sometimes she is not? What evidence do you have for your answer?

31   When I wrote a book devoted to gender differences in ways of speaking, I sent the manuscript to five male colleagues, asking them to alert me to any interpretation, phrasing, or wording that might seem unfairly negative toward men. Even so, when the book came out, I encountered responses like that of the television talk show host who, after interviewing me, turned to the audience and asked if they thought I was male-bashing.

What explanatory strategy is Tannen using in paragraphs 31 and 32? How effective do you find it?

32   Leaping upon a poor fellow who affably nodded in agreement, she made him stand and asked, "Did what she said accurately describe you?" "Oh, yes," he answered. "That's me exactly." "And what she said about women—does that sound like your wife?" "Oh, yes," he responded. "That's her exactly." "Then why do you think she's male-bashing?" He answered, with disarming honesty, "Because she's a woman and she's saying things about men."

33   To say anything about women and men without marking oneself as either feminist or anti-feminist, male-basher or apologist for men seems as impossible for a woman as trying to get dressed in the morning without inviting interpretations of her character.

34   Sitting at the conference table musing on these matters, I felt sad to think that we women didn't have the freedom to be unmarked that the men sitting next to us had. Some days you just want to get dressed and go about your business. But if you're a woman, you can't, because there is no unmarked woman.

Do you agree with this conclusion? Why or why not?

READING FOR MEANING

This section presents three activities that will help you think about the meanings in Tannen's explanation of the concept of "marking."

Read to Comprehend

Write a few sentences briefly explaining the concept of being "marked" as Deborah Tannen sees it.

Identify any words with meanings you are unsure of—such as *coherent* (paragraph 1) and *coherence* (8), *referents* (28), and *inherent* (30)—and find the dictionary definition for each word that makes the best sense in the context.

To help you understand the essay better, also consider trying one of these critical reading strategies, explained in Appendix 1: *outlining* or *paraphrasing*.

Read to Respond

Write several paragraphs exploring your initial thoughts and feelings about Tannen's explanatory essay. Focus on anything that stands out for you, perhaps because it resonates with your own experience or because you find a statement puzzling. For example, consider writing about one of the following:

- the idea that men have a choice of whether to be marked or unmarked but women are always marked no matter what they do, perhaps in relation to your own experience;

- your response to the assertion that how a choice like checking "Ms." on a form is understood depends on the interpreter's "attitudes and assumptions" (paragraph 20), considering what might influence such attitudes and assumptions; or

- your view of Tannen in light of her assertion that "this article may mark me not as a writer, not as a linguist, not as an analyst of human behavior, but as a feminist—which will have positive or negative, but in any case powerful, connotations for readers" (29).

To help develop your response, also consider trying one of these critical reading strategies, explained in Appendix 1: *contextualizing, recognizing emotional manipulation*, or *judging the writer's credibility*.

Read to Analyze Assumptions

Write a paragraph or two analyzing an assumption in Tannen's essay. To think critically about assumptions in Tannen's essay, here are some kinds of questions you could ask: Who holds this assumption (the writer, readers, and/or others cited in the essay)? What are the effects of the assumption in the context of the essay specifically or in society more generally? What do you think about the assumption, and is there anything in the essay that raises doubts about it? How does the assumption reinforce or critique commonly held views, and are there any alternative ideas, beliefs, or values that would challenge this assumption?

You might choose an assumption from the list below, using the questions accompanying it in addition to the ones above to help you get started. Or you can choose another assumption in the essay to explore.

- **assumptions about the value of biologically based evidence.** Tannen is a linguist and therefore looks at "markers" through a linguist's eyes. For example, she provides a comparison to word forms that are "unmarked" and "marked"—such as the present and past forms of a verb and the plural form of a noun—to help her readers understand the concept of being "marked" (10). But near the end of her essay, she cites Ralph Fasold, who "bring[s] biological phenomena to bear on the question of linguistic marking" (24), and she explains his evidence that the "unmarked" gender should really be female rather than male.

  To think critically about the assumptions in this essay related to the value of scientifically based evidence, ask yourself questions like these: Why do you think Tannen steps out of her field of expertise to support her thesis that women in our culture are marked and men are not? Is biologically based evidence particularly convincing to readers in our culture, or is there perhaps another reason she brings in Fasold's theories? If so, what might that reason be?

- **assumptions about the effects of being "marked."** In her final paragraph, Tannen says she feels "sad" that "women didn't have the freedom to be unmarked. . . . Some days you just want to get dressed and go about your business. But if you're a woman, you can't, because there is no unmarked woman" (34).

  To think critically about the assumptions in this essay related to the effects of being "marked," ask yourself: Do you share Tannen's view that being marked is a burden? Can you think of ways in which being unmarked might be limiting or perhaps boring—or being marked could be liberating or creative?

To help you analyze assumptions in Tannen's essay, also consider trying one of these critical reading strategies, explained in Appendix 1: *reflecting on challenges to your beliefs and values* or *looking for patterns of opposition.*

READING LIKE A WRITER

ENGAGING READERS' INTEREST

Explanatory writing aimed at nonspecialist readers usually makes an effort to engage those readers' interest in the information offered. Chris Anderson, for example, writing for a popular magazine, exerts himself to be engaging, even entertaining. Also writing for a magazine read by an educated but nonspecialist audience, Tannen likewise attempts to engage and hold her readers' interest. Like Anderson, she weaves these attempts to engage readers into the flow of information. While they are not separate from the information—for information itself, even dryly presented, can interest readers—direct attempts to engage are nevertheless a recognizable feature of Tannen's explanatory essay. For example, she opens the essay in an inviting way, with several intriguing descriptions, which later serve as examples of the concept. In addition, she adopts an informal conversational tone by using the first-person pronoun *I*, and she comments on her own thinking process.

Analyze

1. Reread paragraphs 1 to 8, and look for places where you are aware of Tannen's tone or voice.

2. Skim the rest of the essay, focusing on paragraphs 13 to 16, 21, 24, and 29 to 34, where Tannen uses the first-person *I* or other conversational devices, such as "Take the men's hair styles" as an opener for paragraph 13. Make notes about these devices and their effect on you as a reader.

Write

Write several sentences describing Tannen's tone and some of the strategies she uses to create it. Give examples from the reading to illustrate your analysis.

CONSIDERING IDEAS FOR YOUR OWN WRITING

If you are taking a course concerned with language and society, you might want to learn about and then explain another linguistic concept, such as semantics, language acquisition, connotation, or discourse community; or a semiotic concept, such as signification, code, iconography, ideology, or popular culture. Related fields with interesting concepts to learn and write about are gender studies and sociology. Gender studies is concerned with such concepts as gender, femininity, masculinity, identity formation, objectification, intersubjectivity, nonsexist language, androgyny, domesticity, patriarchy, and the construction of desire. Sociology studies group dynamics and social patterns using such concepts as socialization, the family, role model, community, cohort, social stratification, positivism, dysfunctional families, and status.

B e t h   L .   B a i l e y

Dating

Beth L. Bailey (b. 1957) is professor of history at Temple University. She has also taught at Barnard College, at the University of New Mexico, and at the University of Indonesia. Bailey has written several scholarly books on nineteenth- and twentieth-century American culture, including Sex in the Heartland *(1999), and cowritten others, including* A People and a Nation *(2008). She has also served as a coeditor of* The Columbia Guide to America in the 1960s *(2001),* America in the Seventies *(2004), and* A History of Our Time *(6th edition 2003; 7th edition 2007). Her most recent book is* America's Army: Making the All-Volunteer Force *(2009). "Dating" comes from Bailey's first book,* From Front Porch to Back Seat: Courtship in Twentieth-Century America *(1988).*

Bailey first became interested in studying courtship attitudes and behavior when, as a college senior, she appeared on a television talk show to defend coed dorms, which were then relatively new and controversial. She was surprised when many people in the audience objected to coed dorms not on moral grounds but out of fear that too much intimacy between young men and women would hasten "the dissolution of the dating system and the death of romance."

As you read Bailey's historical explanation of dating, think about the attitudes and behavior of people your own age in regard to courtship and romance. Note how Bailey uses the features of explanatory writing, including integrating sources smoothly and using appropriate explanatory strategies, such as defining, comparing and contrasting, illustrating, and reporting causes or effects.

1   One day, the 1920s story goes, a young man asked a city girl if he might call on her (Black, 1924, p. 340). We know nothing else about the man or the girl—only that, when he arrived, she had her hat on. Not much of a story to us, but any American born before 1910 would have gotten the punch line. "She had her hat on": those five words were rich in meaning to early twentieth-century Americans. The hat signaled that she expected to leave the house. He came on a "call," expecting to be received in her family's parlor, to talk, to meet her mother, perhaps to have some refreshments or to listen to her play the piano. She expected a "date," to be taken "out" somewhere and entertained. He ended up spending four weeks' savings fulfilling her expectations.

2   In the early twentieth century this new style of courtship, dating, had begun to supplant the old. Born primarily of the limits and opportunities of urban life, dating had almost completely replaced the old system of calling by the mid-1920s—and, in so doing, had transformed American courtship. Dating moved courtship into the public world, relocating it from family

parlors and community events to restaurants, theaters, and dance halls. At the same time, it removed couples from the implied supervision of the private sphere—from the watchful eyes of family and local community—to the anonymity of the public sphere. Courtship among strangers offered couples new freedom. But access to the public world of the city required money. One had to buy entertainment, or even access to a place to sit and talk. Money—men's money—became the basis of the dating system and, thus, of courtship. This new dating system, as it shifted courtship from the private to the public sphere and increasingly centered around money, fundamentally altered the balance of power between men and women in courtship.

The transition from calling to dating was as complete as it was fundamental. By the 1950s and 1960s, social scientists who studied American courtship found it necessary to remind the American public that dating was a "recent American innovation and not a traditional or universal custom" (Cavin, as cited in "Some," 1961, p. 125). Some of the many commentators who wrote about courtship believed dating was the best thing that had ever happened to relations between the sexes; others blamed the dating system for all the problems of American youth and American marriage. But virtually everyone portrayed the system dating replaced as infinitely simpler, sweeter, more innocent, and more graceful. Hardheaded social scientists waxed sentimental about the "horse-and-buggy days," when a young man's offer of a ride home from church was tantamount to a proposal and when young men came calling in the evenings and courtship took place safely within the warm bosom of the family. "The courtship which grew out of the sturdy social roots [of the nineteenth century]," one author wrote, "comes through to us for what it was—a gracious ritual, with clearly defined roles for man and woman, in which everyone knew the measured music and the steps" (Moss, 1963, p. 151). 3

Certainly a less idealized version of this model of courtship had existed in America, but it was not this model that dating was supplanting. Although only about 45 percent of Americans lived in urban areas by 1910, few of them were so untouched by the sweeping changes of the late nineteenth century that they could live that dream of rural simplicity. Conventions of courtship at that time were not set by simple yeoman farmers and their families but by the rising middle class, often in imitation of the ways of "society." . . . 4

The call itself was a complicated event. A myriad of rules governed everything: the proper amount of time between invitation and visit (a fortnight or less); whether or not refreshments should be served (not if one belonged to a fashionable or semi-fashionable circle, but outside of "smart" groups in cities like New York and Boston, girls *might* serve iced drinks with little cakes or tiny cups of coffee or hot chocolate and sandwiches); chaperonage (the first call must be made on daughter and mother, but excessive chaperonage would indicate to the man that his attentions 5 were unwelcome); appropriate topics of conversation (the man's interests, but never too personal); how leave should be taken (on no account should the woman "accompany [her caller] to the door nor stand talking while he struggles into his coat") ("Lady," 1904, p. 255).

6   Each of these "measured steps," as the mid-twentieth century author nostalgically called them, was a test of suitability, breeding, and back-ground. Advice columns and etiquette books emphasized that these were the manners of any "well-bred" person—and conversely implied that deviations revealed a lack of breeding. However, around the turn of the century, many people who did lack this narrow "breeding" aspired to politeness. Advice columns in women's magazines regularly printed ques-tions from "Country Girl" and "Ignoramus" on the fine points of calling etiquette. Young men must have felt the pressure of girls' expectations, for they wrote to the same advisers with questions about calling. In 1907, *Harper's Bazaar* ran a major article titled "Etiquette for Men," explaining the ins and outs of the calling system (Hall, 1907, pp. 1095–97). In the first decade of the twentieth century, this rigid system of calling was the convention not only of the "respectable" but also of those who aspired to respectability.

7   At the same time, however, the new system of dating was emerging. By the mid-1910s, the word *date* had entered the vocabulary of the middle-class public. In 1914, the *Ladies' Home Journal*, a bastion of middle-class respectability, used the term (safely enclosed in quotation marks but with no explanation of its meaning) several times. The word was always spoken by that exotica, the college sorority girl—a character marginal in her exot-icness but nevertheless a solid product of the middle class. "One beautiful evening of the spring term," one such article begins, "when I was a college girl of eighteen, the boy whom, because of his popularity in every phase of college life, I had been proud gradually to allow the monopoly of my 'dates,' took me unexpectedly into his arms. As he kissed me impetuously I was glad, from the bottom of my heart, for the training of that mother who had taught me to hold myself aloof from all personal familiarities of boys and men" ("How," 1914, p. 9).

8   Sugarcoated with a tribute to motherhood and virtue, the dates—and the kiss—were unmistakably presented for a middle-class audience. By 1924, ten years later, when the story of the unfortunate young man who went to call on the city girl was current, dating had essentially replaced calling in middle-class culture. The knowing smiles of the story's listen-ers had probably started with the word *call*—and not every hearer would have been sympathetic to the man's plight. By 1924, he really should have known better. . . .

9   Dating, which to the privileged and protected would seem a system of increased freedom and possibility, stemmed originally from the lack of opportunities. Calling, or even just visiting, was not a practicable system

for young people whose families lived crowded into one or two rooms. For even the more established or independent working-class girls, the parlor and the piano often simply didn't exist. Some "factory girls" struggled to find a way to receive callers. The *Ladies' Home Journal* approvingly reported the case of six girls, workers in a box factory, who had formed a club and pooled part of their wages to pay the "janitress of a tenement house" to let them use her front room two evenings a week. It had a piano. One of the girls explained their system: "We ask the boys to come when they like and spend the evening. We haven't any place at home to see them, and I hate seeing them on the street" (Preston, 1907, p. 31).

Many other working girls, however, couldn't have done this even had   10
they wanted to. They had no extra wages to pool, or they had no notions of middle-class respectability. Some, especially girls of ethnic families, were kept secluded—chaperoned according to the customs of the old country. But many others fled the squalor, drabness, and crowdedness of their homes to seek amusement and intimacy elsewhere. And a "good time" increasingly became identified with public places and commercial amusements, making young women whose wages would not even cover the necessities of life dependent on men's "treats" (Peiss, 1986, pp. 51–52, 75). Still, many poor and working-class couples did not so much escape from the home as they were pushed from it.

These couples courted on the streets, sometimes at cheap dance halls   11
or eventually at the movies. These were not respectable places, and women could enter them only so far as they, themselves, were not considered respectable. Respectable young women did, of course, enter the public world, but their excursions into the public were cushioned. Public courtship of middle-class and upper-class youth was at least *supposed* to be chaperoned; those with money and social position went to private dances with carefully controlled guest lists, to theater parties where they were a private group within the public. As rebels would soon complain, the supervision of society made the private parlor seem almost free by contrast. Women who were not respectable did have relative freedom of action—but the trade-off was not necessarily a happy one for them.

The negative factors were important, but dating rose equally from the   12
possibilities offered by urban life. Privileged youth, as Lewis Erenberg shows in his study of New York nightlife, came to see the possibility of privacy in the anonymous public, in the excitement and freedom the city offered (1981, pp. 60–87, 139–42). They looked to lower-class models of freedom—to those beyond the constraints of respectability. As a society girl informed the readers of the *Ladies' Home Journal* in 1914: "Nowadays it is considered 'smart' to go to the low order of dance halls, and not only be a looker-on, but also to dance among all sorts and conditions of men and women. . . . Nowadays when we enter a restaurant and dance place it is hard to know who is who" ("A Girl," 1914, p. 7). In 1907, the same

magazine had warned unmarried women never to go alone to a "public restaurant" with any man, even a relative. There was no impropriety in the act, the adviser had conceded, but it still "lays [women] open to misunderstanding and to being classed with women of undesirable reputation by the strangers present" (Kingsland, May 1907, p. 48). Rebellious and adventurous young people sought that confusion, and the gradual loosening of proprieties they engendered helped to change courtship. Young men and women went out into the world *together*, enjoying a new kind of companionship and the intimacy of a new kind of freedom from adult supervision.

13   The new freedom that led to dating came from other sources as well. Many more serious (and certainly respectable) young women were taking advantage of opportunities to enter the public world—going to college, taking jobs, entering and creating new urban professions. Women who belonged to the public world by day began to demand fuller access to the public world in general. . . .

14   Between 1890 and 1925, dating—in practice and in name—had gradually, almost imperceptibly, become a universal custom in America. By the 1930s it had transcended its origins: Middle America associated dating with neither upper-class rebellion nor the urban lower classes. The rise of dating was usually explained, quite simply, by the invention of the automobile. Cars had given youth mobility and privacy, and so had brought about the system. This explanation—perhaps not consciously but definitely not coincidentally—revised history. The automobile certainly contributed to the rise of dating as a *national* practice, especially in rural and suburban areas, but it was simply accelerating and extending a process already well under way. Once its origins were located firmly in Middle America, however, and not in the extremes of urban upper- and lower-class life, dating had become an American institution.

15   Dating not only transformed the outward modes and conventions of American courtship, it also changed the distribution of control and power in courtship. One change was generational: the dating system lessened parental control and gave young men and women more freedom. The dating system also shifted power from women to men. Calling, either as a simple visit or as the elaborate late nineteenth-century ritual, gave women a large portion of control. First of all, courtship took place within the girl's home—in women's "sphere," as it was called in the nineteenth century—or at entertainments largely devised and presided over by women. Dating moved courtship out of the home and into man's sphere—the world outside the home. Female controls and conventions lost much of their power outside women's sphere. And while many of the conventions of female propriety were restrictive and repressive, they had allowed women (young women and their mothers) a great deal of immediate control over courtship. The transfer of spheres thoroughly undercut that control.

Second, in the calling system, the woman took the initiative. Etiquette 16
books and columns were adamant on that point: it was the "girl's privilege" to ask a young man to call. Furthermore, it was highly improper for
the man to take the initiative. In 1909 a young man wrote to the *Ladies'
Home Journal* adviser asking, "May I call upon a young woman whom
I greatly admire, although she had not given me the permission? Would
she be flattered at my eagerness, even to the setting aside of conventions, or would she think me impertinent?" Mrs. Kingsland replied: "I
think that you would risk her just displeasure and frustrate your object of
finding favor with her." Softening the prohibition, she then suggested an
invitation might be secured through a mutual friend (Kingsland, 1909,
p. 58). . . .

Contrast these strictures with advice on dating etiquette from the 1940s 17
and 1950s: An advice book for men and women warns that "girls who
[try] to usurp the right of boys to choose their own dates" will "ruin a
good dating career. . . . Fair or not, it is the way of life. From the Stone
Age, when men chased and captured their women, comes the yen of a
boy to do the pursuing. You will control your impatience, therefore, and
respect the time-honored custom of boys to take the first step" (Richmond,
1958, p. 11). . . .

This absolute reversal of roles almost necessarily accompanied 18
courtship's move from woman's sphere to man's sphere. Although the
convention-setters commended the custom of woman's initiative because it
allowed greater exclusivity (it might be "difficult for a girl to refuse the permission to call, no matter how unwelcome or unsuitable an acquaintance
of the man might be"), the custom was based on a broader principle of
etiquette (Hart and Brown, 1944, p. 89). The host or hostess issued any
invitation; the guest did not invite himself or herself. An invitation to call
was an invitation to visit in a woman's home.

An invitation to go out on a date, on the other hand, was an invita- 19
tion into man's world—not simply because dating took place in the public
sphere (commonly defined as belonging to men), though that was part of
it, but because dating moved courtship into the world of the economy.
Money—men's money—was at the center of the dating system. Thus, on
two counts, men became the hosts and assumed the control that came
with that position.

There was some confusion caused by this reversal of initiative, espe- 20
cially during the twenty years or so when going out and calling coex-
isted as systems. (The unfortunate young man in the apocryphal story, for
example, had asked the city girl if he might call on her, so perhaps she
was conventionally correct to assume he meant to play the host.) Confusions generally were sorted out around the issue of money. One young
woman, "Henrietta L.," wrote to the *Ladies' Home Journal* to inquire
whether a girl might "suggest to a friend going to any entertainment or

place of amusement where there will be any expense to the young man." The reply: "Never, under any circumstances." The adviser explained that the invitation to go out must "always" come from the man, for he was the one "responsible for the expense" (Kingsland, Oct. 1907, p. 60). This same adviser insisted that the woman must "always" invite the man to call; clearly she realized that money was the central issue.

21   The centrality of money in dating had serious implications for court-ship. Not only did money shift control and initiative to men by making them the "hosts," it led contemporaries to see dating as a system of exchange best understood through economic analogies or as an economic system pure and simple. Of course, people did recognize in marriage a similar economic dimension—the man undertakes to support his wife in exchange for her filling various roles important to him—but marriage was a permanent relationship. Dating was situational, with no long-term commitments implied, and when a man, in a highly visible ritual, spent money on a woman in public, it seemed much more clearly an economic act.

22   In fact, the term *date* was associated with the direct economic exchange of prostitution at an early time. A prostitute called "Maimie," in letters written to a middle-class benefactor/friend in the late nineteenth century, described how men made "dates" with her (Peiss, 1986, p. 54). And a former waitress turned prostitute described the process to the Illinois Senate Committee on Vice this way: "You wait on a man and he smiles at you. You see a chance to get a tip and you smile back. Next day he returns and you try harder than ever to please him. Then right away he wants to make a date, and offer you money and presents if you'll be a good fellow and go out with him" (Rosen, 1982, p. 151). These men, quite clearly, were buying sexual favors—but the occasion of the exchange was called a "date."

23   Courtship in America had always turned somewhat on money (or background). A poor clerk or stockyards worker would not have called upon the daughter of a well-off family, and men were expected to be economically secure before they married. But in the dating system money entered directly into the relationship between a man and a woman as the symbolic currency of exchange in even casual dating.

24   Dating, like prostitution, made access to women directly dependent on money. . . . In dating, though, the exchange was less direct and less clear than in prostitution. One author, in 1924, made sense of it this way. In dating, he reasoned, a man is responsible for all expenses. The woman is responsible for nothing—she contributes only her company. Of course, the man contributes his company, too, but since he must "add money to balance the bargain" his company must be worth less than hers. Thus, according to this economic understanding, she is selling her company to him. In his eyes, dating didn't even involve an exchange; it was a direct

purchase. The moral "subtleties" of a woman's position in dating, the author concluded, were complicated even further by the fact that young men,"discovering that she must be bought, [like] to buy her when [they] happen] to have the money" (Black, 1924, p. 342).

Yet another young man, the same year, publicly called a halt to such 25 "promiscuous buying." Writing anonymously (for good reason) in *American Magazine*, the author declared a "one-man buyer's strike." This man estimated that, as a "buyer of feminine companionship" for the previous five years, he had "invested" about $20 a week—a grand total of over $5,000. Finally, he wrote, he had realized that "there is a point at which any commodity—even such a delightful commodity as feminine companionship—costs more than it is worth" ("Too-high," 1924, pp. 27, 145–50). The commodity he had bought with his $5,000 had been priced beyond its "real value" and he had had enough. This man said "enough" not out of principle, not because he rejected the implications of the economic model of courtship, but because he felt he wasn't receiving value for money.

In . . . these economic analyses, the men are complaining about the 26 new dating system, lamenting the passing of the mythic good old days when "a man without a quarter in his pocket could call on a girl and not be embarrassed," the days before a woman had to be "bought" ("Too-high," 1924, pp. 145–50). In recognizing so clearly the economic model on which dating operated, they also clearly saw that the model was a bad one—in purely economic terms. The exchange was not equitable; the commodity was overpriced. Men were operating at a loss.

Here, however, they didn't understand their model completely. True, the 27 equation (male companionship plus money equals female companionship) was imbalanced. But what men were buying in the dating system was not just female companionship, not just entertainment—but power. Money purchased obligation; money purchased inequality; money purchased control.

The conventions that grew up to govern dating codified women's 28 inequality and ratified men's power. Men asked women out; women were condemned as "aggressive" if they expressed interest in a man too directly. Men paid for everything, but often with the implication that women "owed" sexual favors in return. The dating system required men always to assume control, and women to act as men's dependents.

Yet women were not without power in the system, and they were will- 29 ing to contest men with their "feminine" power. Much of the public discourse on courtship in twentieth-century America was concerned with this contestation. Thousands of sources chronicled the struggles of, and between, men and women—struggles mediated by the "experts" and arbiters of convention—to create a balance of power, to gain or retain control of the dating system. These struggles, played out most clearly in the fields of sex, science, and etiquette, made ever more explicit the complicated relations between men and women in a changing society.

References

Black, A. (1924, August). Is the young person coming back? *Harper's*, 340, 342.

Erenberg, L. (1981). *Steppin' out*. Westport, Conn.: Greenwood Press.

A Girl. (1914, July). Believe me. *Ladies' Home Journal*, 7.

Hall, F. H. (1907, November). Etiquette for men. *Harper's Bazaar*, 1095–97.

Hart, S., & Brown, L. (1944). *How to get your man and hold him*. New York: New Power Publications.

How may a girl know? (1914, January). *Ladies' Home Journal*, 9.

Kingsland. (1907, May). *Ladies' Home Journal*, 48.

———. (1907, October). *Ladies' Home Journal*, 60.

———. (1909, May). *Ladies' Home Journal*, 58.

Lady from Philadelphia. (1904, February). *Ladies' Home Journal*, 255.

Moss, A. (1963, April). Whatever happened to courtship? *Mademoiselle*, 151.

Peiss, K. (1986). *Cheap amusements: Working women and leisure in turn-of-the-century New York*. Philadelphia: Temple University Press.

Preston, A. (1907, February). After business hours—what? *Ladies' Home Journal*, 31.

Richmond, C. (1958). *Handbook of dating*. Philadelphia: Westminster Press.

Rosen, R. (1982). *The lost sisterhood: Prostitution in America, 1900–1918*. Baltimore: Johns Hopkins University Press, 1982.

Some expert opinions on dating. (1961, August). *McCall's*, 125.

Too-high cost of courting. (1924, September). *American Magazine*, 27, 145–50.

READING FOR MEANING

This section presents three activities that will help you think about the meanings in Bailey's explanation of the concept of dating.

Read to Comprehend

Write a few sentences briefly explaining some of the occasions that prompted Bailey's explanation of a concept and how Bailey explores the actions she took to address these occasions.

Identify any words with meanings you are unsure of—such as *supplant* (paragraph 2), *chaperonage* (5), and *arbiters* (29)—and find the dictionary definition for each word that makes the best sense in the context.

To help you understand the essay better, also consider trying one of these critical reading strategies, explained in Appendix 1: *outlining* or *questioning to understand and remember*.

Read to Respond

Write several paragraphs exploring your initial thoughts and feelings about Bailey's explanation of a concept. Focus on anything that stands out for you, perhaps because it resonates with your own experience or because you find a statement puzzling. For example, consider writing about one of the following:

- the contrasts between the dating system in the early decades of the twentieth century (as described by Bailey) and the courtship system you know today, connecting your contrasts to specific features of the early system;

- the identification of a "good time" with "public places and commercial amusements" (paragraph 10), perhaps in relation to your own view of what constitutes a good time; or

- the "centrality of money in dating" (21).

To help develop your response also consider trying one of these critical reading strategies, explained in Appendix 1: *contextualizing, recognizing emotional manipulation,* or *judging the writer's credibility.*

Read to Analyze Assumptions

Write a paragraph or two analyzing an assumption in Bailey's essay. To think critically about assumptions, here are some kinds of questions you could ask: Who holds this assumption (the writer, readers, and/or others cited in the essay)? What are the effects of the assumption in the context of the essay specifically or in society more generally? What do you think about the assumption, and is there anything in the essay that raises doubts about it? How does the assumption reinforce or critique commonly held views, and are there any alternative ideas, beliefs, or values that would challenge this assumption?

You might choose an assumption from the list below, using the questions accompanying it in addition to the ones above to help you get started. Or you can choose another assumption in the essay to explore.

- **assumptions about who has control in courtship.** Bailey writes that the transformation from "calling" to "dating" in the twentieth century "changed the distribution of control and power in courtship" (paragraph 15). Under calling, she argues, women had control; under dating, men had control.

  To think critically about the assumptions in this reading related to who has control in courtship, ask yourself questions like these: To what extent do you agree with Bailey on this issue? Are there other power dynamics involved in calling or dating that she is ignoring? What assumptions about rules or rituals of courtship do you see in play in our current society, and where does the power lie now? Who decides how to initiate intimacy? Are power and economics the only or even the main factors involved in courtship and intimacy between the sexes? How do love, affection, physical chemistry, or even simple pleasure in companionship complicate the picture—either in the period Bailey is writing about or today?

- **assumptions about the role of the media in courtship.** Throughout her essay, Bailey uses examples from magazines, journals, and manuals to support her assertions about "calling" and "dating." She seems to assume that the information in these publications reflects accurately the customs of the time, but she also suggests that it may have helped to bring about the *changes* in these customs.

  To think critically about the assumptions in this essay related to the role of the media in courtship, ask yourself questions like these: If someone were to write about the rituals of courtship in early twenty-first-century America, what would be the best sources of information? How accurately do you think they would represent what actually happens in American culture? To what extent do media (such as magazine articles, television shows, or Web sites like FaceBook) *create* cultural assumptions—about courtship or anything else—as well as reflect them?

To help you analyze assumptions in Bailey's essay, also consider trying one of these critical reading strategies, explained in Appendix 1: *reflecting on challenges to your beliefs and values* or *looking for patterns of opposition.*

READING LIKE A WRITER

EXPLAINING THROUGH COMPARISON/CONTRAST

One of the best ways of explaining something new is to relate it, through comparison or contrast, to something that is familiar or well known. A *comparison* points out similarities between items; a *contrast* points out differences. Sometimes writers use both comparison and contrast; sometimes they use only one or the other. Bailey uses comparison and contrast a little differently. She is not explaining something new to readers by relating it to something already known to them. Instead, she is explaining something already known—dating—by relating it to something that is unknown to most readers—calling, an earlier type of courtship. Since she is studying dating as a sociologist, this historical perspective enables her to consider the changing relationship between men and women and the things that it tells us about changing social and cultural expectations and practices.

Analyze

1. Reread paragraphs 15 to 19, and underline the sentences that assert the points of the contrast Bailey develops in these paragraphs. To get started, underline the first and last sentences in paragraph 15. Except for paragraph 17, you will find one or two sentences in the other paragraphs that assert the points.
2. Examine the other sentences to discover how Bailey develops or illustrates each of the points of the contrast between calling and dating.

Write

Write *several sentences* reporting what you have learned about how Bailey develops the contrast between calling and dating. Give examples from paragraphs 15 to 19 to support your explanation. Write a few more sentences evaluating how informative you find Bailey's contrast given your own knowledge of dating. What parts are least and most informative? What makes the most informative part so successful?

CONSIDERING IDEAS FOR YOUR OWN WRITING

Like Bailey, you might choose a concept that tells something about current or historical social values, behaviors, or attitudes. To look at changing attitudes toward immigration and assimilation, for example, you could write about the concept of the melting pot and the alternatives that have been suggested. Some related concepts you might consider are multiculturalism, race, ethnicity, masculinity or femininity, heterosexuality or homosexuality, and affirmative action.

Kathleen A. Bogle

"Hooking Up": What Educators Need to Know

Kathleen A. Bogle is an assistant professor of sociology and criminal justice at La Salle University in Philadelphia. She received her master's degree in criminal justice from Saint Joseph's University, where she also taught and was granted the Faculty Merit Award for Teaching. She received her doctoral degree in sociology from the University of Delaware. Her major areas of research include gender, sexual behavior, and intimate relationships.

Bogle's book, Hooking Up: Sex, Dating, and Relationships on Campus, *was published in 2008.* Hooking Up *is based on interviews with students and young alumni from two east coast universities that were conducted to understand why dating has declined in favor of a new script for sexual relations. Bogle says she "wrote this book with several audiences in mind, including college administrators, parents and college students" (Inside Higher Ed, Jan. 29, 2008). Her audience for the article below, published in the* Chronicle of Higher Education *shortly after the book was published, is professionals—administrators and teachers—in colleges and universities.*

As you read, think about your own experiences with dating and/or hooking up, and pay attention to the strategies Bogle uses to help her audience follow her reasoning and understand her explanation of this relatively new (from a historical perspective) concept.

1   In 2001 the longtime student practice of "hooking up" gained national attention when the Institute for American Values released a report titled "Hooking Up, Hanging Out, and Hoping for Mr. Right: College Women on Mating and Dating Today." Subsequent news-media coverage claimed that dating had declined in popularity among college students, in favor of casual sex. Despite most commentators' lamentations about the death of courtship and their concern over students' "new," morally questionable sexual activity, the term "hooking up" has become commonplace and the practice an accepted part of the college experience. For campus administrators, counselors, and professors, whose only exposure to hooking up has been media accounts or pop-culture references, it is important to know what hooking up really involves. Understanding the hookup culture on college campuses is the first step toward addressing two of the biggest residence-life issues: student alcohol abuse and sexual assaults.

2   Hooking up is not new. It has been an entrenched part of campus culture for decades. In fact, the shift from dating to hooking up is the result of many social changes, which began in the mid-1960s. During this period, many colleges became coeducational, enrollments rose, and a greater proportion of students began living on campuses. Additionally, students began rebelling against the rules monitoring their behavior, especially those that

restricted contact between the sexes; this forced many administrators to relax or abolish the policies. The campus became a place where droves of 18- to 22- year-old men and women lived in close proximity to one another, sometimes in coed dormitories, where *in loco parentis* was collapsing.

Changes also began to take root among students themselves. Following the sexual revolution, students delayed marriage and other adult responsibilities; they had a more liberal view of sex before marriage and often considered their college years a time to party. Increasingly, college years became a time when men and women could engage in casual relationships. So hooking up began and has flourished because students now have unfettered access to each other, and because casual relationships have become socially acceptable.

Hooking up is not synonymous with casual sex or one-night stands. Rather, hooking up, like dating, is a system for socializing with the opposite sex and finding sexual and romantic partners. But while dating called for a couple to get to know each other en route to sexual intimacy, with hooking up the sex comes first. A typical hookup scenario begins at a party or bar where two classmates — who either just met or are longtime friends — pair off at the end of the evening for a sexual encounter, which could involve a range of activity from kissing to intercourse.

Although there are no strings attached between partners, hooking up is not just about sex. It's also a way for students to find relationships. After an initial hookup, partners may develop a relationship in which they hang out and hook up again. Some even become exclusive couples. Finding boyfriends or girlfriends via hooking up is possible, although it is not the most likely outcome. Most hookups do not evolve into anything more. Yet the hooking-up system stays intact because students believe there are no clear alternatives. Because hooking up dominates the social scene on campuses, most students consider it the only available route to sexual encounters and romantic relationships.

The demise of dating on campuses goes beyond just a change in how students mate and relate. In the dating era, drinking was not typically a central activity for couples out for the evening; in fact, it was considered wrong for a dating partner to drink excessively. This is not to say that college students who dated never drank; rather, in the hookup era, alcohol has taken on a more central role. As the Friday-night or Saturday-night date became a thing of the past, the focus of student socializing became partying with groups of friends. Mingling begins with groups at parties or bars, and hooking up generally occurs toward the end of the night, when students are under the influence of alcohol.

Some observers have suggested that alcohol consumption is what leads to hooking up. The widely accepted explanation assumes that drinking reduces inhibitions, which leads to risky sexual behavior. A student drinks too much, hooks up as a result, and in some cases regrets the encounter.

However, the link between alcohol and hooking up should perhaps be understood differently. It may be that the hookup system drives student alcohol consumption rather than the other way around. One reason that hooking up requires alcohol is that students need it to alleviate anxiety. Drinking provides liquid courage with which to express interest, initiate a hookup, and allay fear of rejection. Alcohol also helps to dismiss—temporarily, at least—concerns over the sexual aspects of hooking up: deciding how far the encounter should go or being sexually intimate outside of an exclusive relationship. Another reason that hooking up calls for alcohol use is that students can use it to justify their behavior. Alcohol gives them permission to be out of control and is a handy excuse for poor decisions. If students regret their choices later, or have misgivings about going too far, they can tell themselves and others, "I was drunk" or "I had beer goggles on."

9   The shift from dating to hooking up has also changed the nature of the sexual-assault problem. Most sexual assaults no longer take the form of a typical date-rape scenario. Instead incidents occur during or after campus parties where many students are drinking heavily and hooking up. Given that alcohol-fueled (consensual) hookup encounters are common, it can be difficult for students, as well as administrators, to distinguish between a hookup and a sexual encounter that crosses the line and becomes rape. As a result, victim-blaming and underreporting remain rampant, despite decades of work by women's advocacy groups.

10   Part of the confusion surrounding sexual assault on the college campus stems from the ambiguity of the "unable to consent" provision of state rape laws. A sexual encounter is considered rape if a person is deemed too intoxicated or too high on drugs to consent to sex. Among those immersed in the hookup culture on contemporary college campuses, judging how drunk is too drunk to consent is not a simple task. Most reasonable people agree that if someone is "passed-out drunk," then he or she cannot consent to sex. But many cases are not so clear-cut.

11   Misperceptions, too, can make sexual assaults difficult for some students to identify in the age of hooking up. Although the practice encompasses a wide range of behavior, activities at one end of the spectrum—say, anonymous sex between strangers—receive a disproportionate amount of attention. As a result, students often think that their classmates have more hookup partners and go farther sexually than they actually do. The mentality that "everybody is doing it" and "anything goes" makes it believable that nearly every scenario, no matter how outrageous, could be consensual sex. That leads to a climate in which lines are blurred and students have trouble differentiating a drunken hookup from a sexual assault. That distorted perception affects almost every aspect of sexual assault on campuses. It increases the likelihood that students will engage in abusive behavior, reduces the likelihood of a victim's coming forward, and affects whether a victim will be believed by classmates and administrators.

12   College administrators cannot change the fact that hooking up dominates campus culture. They should not denounce it, given that it has been going on for decades and encompasses a wide range of behavior. But by

striving to understand it better, they can help to educate students. Most programs seem to deal with alcohol abuse and sexual assaults without putting them in context. Just as no one could understand date rape without first understanding dating, campus sexual assaults must be examined in light of hooking up. Likewise, efforts to reduce alcohol-related incidents and binge drinking that do not include educating students about the connection between alcohol use and hooking up will continue to be ineffective.

Colleges need new strategies that recognize the impact of the hookup 13 culture on both sexual assaults and alcohol consumption. Residence-life programs must open a more honest dialogue with students about hooking up, deal with their misperceptions, and acknowledge the complex social world that students face. Only when administrators develop a clearer understanding of the hookup culture can they begin to design programs that will reduce campus drinking and sexual assaults.

READING FOR MEANING

This section presents three activities that will help you think about the meanings in Bogle's explanation of the concept of "hooking up."

Read to Comprehend

Write a few sentences briefly explaining the concept of "hooking up."

Identify any words with meanings you are unsure of—such as *demise* (paragraph 6) and *denounce* (12)—and find the dictionary definition for each word that makes the best sense in the context.

To help you understand the essay better, also consider trying one of these critical reading strategies, explained in Appendix 1: *paraphrasing* or *questioning to understand and remember.*

Read to Respond

Write a paragraph or two exploring your initial thoughts and feelings about Bogle's explanation of a concept. Focus on anything that stands out for you, perhaps because it resonates with your own experience or because you find a statement puzzling. For example, consider writing about one of the following:

- what you see as the relationship, if any, between hooking up and alcohol or hooking up and sexual assault.

- your opinion of Bogle's statement that "[a]lthough there are no strings attached between partners, hooking up is not just about sex. It's also a way for students to find relationships" (paragraph 5).

To help develop your response, also consider trying one of these critical reading strategies, explained in Appendix 1: *contextualizing* or *reflecting on challenges to your beliefs and values.*

Read to Analyze Assumptions

Write a paragraph or two analyzing an assumption in Bogle's essay. To think critically about assumptions, here are some kinds of questions you could ask: Who holds this assumption (the writer, readers, and/or others cited in the essay)? What are the effects of the assumption in the context of the essay specifically or in society more generally? What do you think about the assumption, and is there anything in the essay that raises doubts about it? How does the assumption reinforce or critique commonly held views, and are there any alternative ideas, beliefs, or values that would challenge this assumption?

You might choose an assumption from the list below, using the questions accompanying it in addition to the ones above to help you get started. Or you can choose another assumption in the essay to explore.

- **the assumption that hooking up is a widely accepted practice.** In her opening paragraph, Bogle says that "the term 'hooking up' has become commonplace and the practice an accepted part of the college experience." She adds that "hooking up began and has flourished because students now have unfettered access to each other, and because casual relationships have become socially acceptable" (paragraph 3).

  To think critically about the assumptions in this essay related to the acceptance of hooking up in college, ask yourself questions like these: Does Bogle provide enough evidence to convince you that hooking up is widely practiced? Does the assumption that hooking up is widely practiced and accepted square with your own experience and that of your friends, including those who attend other colleges?

- **assumptions about the responsibilities of college personnel.** Bogle says that "[u]nderstanding the hookup culture on college campuses is the first step toward addressing two of the biggest residence-life issues: student alcohol abuse and sexual assaults" (paragraph 1). She seems to believe that "administrators, counselors, and professors" should address these student-life issues but "cannot change the fact that hooking up dominates campus culture" and therefore "should not denounce" it (12).

  To think critically about the assumptions in this essay related to responsibilities of college personnel, ask yourself questions like these: To what extent should college personnel be responsible for students' behavior and the consequences of that behavior? Should colleges have rules to try to reduce alcohol consumption and sexual assault? What beliefs or values sustain the idea that college personnel are responsible for setting up a structure to help students with their social lives? Does this idea conflict with Bogle's assumption that because hooking up itself is "entrenched" on campuses (2), it cannot be replaced or reduced by another system for social and sexual interaction and should not be criticized? Why or why not?

To help you analyze assumptions in Bogle's essay, also consider trying one of these critical reading strategies, explained in Appendix 1: *looking for patterns of opposition* or *evaluating the logic of an argument*.

READING LIKE A WRITER

DEVISING A READABLE PLAN

Think of a readable plan as a logical, interrelated sequence of topics. Each topic or main idea follows the preceding topic in a way that makes sense to readers. In addition, as you may have noticed in analyzing Chris Anderson's explanatory essay about the Long Tail, readers appreciate a sequence of topics that is visibly cued by forecasting statements, topic sentences, transitions, and brief summaries. We see all of these cueing devices in Bogle's essay. Note how she places material by using time markers "In 2001 . . ." (paragraph 1), "During this period . . . [the mid-1960s]" (2), and "Following the sexual revolution" (3). She also guides the reader with strong transitions in the first sentence of every paragraph.

These transitions refer back to the content of the previous paragraph, often including brief summaries, and forecast the content of the upcoming paragraph, often including the topic sentence. For example, look at the last sentence of paragraph 3:

> So hooking up began and has flourished because students now have unfettered access to each other, and because casual relationships have become socially acceptable.

Then look at the beginning of paragraph 4:

> Hooking up is not synonymous with casual sex or one-night stands. Rather, hooking up, like dating, is a system for socializing with the opposite sex and finding sexual and romantic partners.

You can see that Bogle helps her readers see the relationship between each paragraph as part of her readable plan. In this case she does not want readers to think that a "casual relationship" is the same as casual sex or a one-night stand, so after she notes that casual *relationships* have become socially acceptable in paragraph 3, she reminds the reader at the beginning of paragraph 4 that this is different from *casual sex*, and points the reader to her next topic, how hooking up is a system for socializing and finding partners.

These important cueing strategies can do nothing to rescue an illogical sequence of topics, however. That is, they can only point out logical connections; they cannot *create* such connections. You can learn more about how writers devise readable plans by outlining their essays.

Analyze

1. Skim the essay, and notice how transitions present the topics in a logical sequence. Make an outline of these transitions.

2. Examine the way these transitions are constructed.

3. Point to any places where Bogle forecasts the topics that come next or summarizes what came before.

Write

Write several sentences describing the main strategies that Bogle uses to construct a readable plan for her essay.

CONSIDERING IDEAS FOR YOUR OWN WRITING

Bogle's essay may prompt you to think about several campus issues that are important to you, from sexual behavior to classroom behavior. For more material, thumb through your college texts to get a sampling of ideas that have become important to various disciplines, and think about explaining one of those concepts—such as acculturation, ethnocentrism, or kinship in anthropology; social construction of identity, socialization, or stratification in sociology; torque, aerodynamics, or ergonomics in automotive design; or nanotechnology, stem-cell research, or genetic engineering in biology.

A Special Reading Strategy

Comparing and Contrasting Related Readings: Bailey's "Dating" and Bogle's "Hooking Up"

Comparing and contrasting related readings is a critical reading strategy useful both in reading for meaning and in reading like a writer. This strategy is particularly applicable when writers present similar subjects, as is the case in the explanatory readings in this chapter by Beth L. Bailey (p. 236) and by Kathleen A. Bogle (p. 248). Both readings seek to define the concept of dating and similar rituals. To compare and contrast these two readings explaining concepts, think about issues such as these:

- Compare these readings in terms of their explanatory strategies. What strategies do they share? How are their strategies different?

- Compare these readings in terms of their purposes and formats. Bailey's is an excerpt from her first book, and Bogle's is an article based on her book but written for a college journal. Both share a historical perspective, but Bogle has additional reasons for writing.

- Compare these readings in terms of how well they explain their concept—Bailey of dating, and Bogle of hooking up. Which one gives you the best sense of the concept, and why?

See Appendix 1 (pp. 596–601) for detailed guidelines on comparing and contrasting related readings.

Linh Kieu Ngo

Cannibalism: It Still Exists

Linh Kieu Ngo wrote this essay when he was a first-year college student. In it, he explains a concept of importance in anthropology and of wide general interest—cannibalism, the eating of human flesh by other humans. Most Americans may know about survival cannibalism, but few may know about the importance historically of dietary and ritual cannibalism. Ngo explains all of these types in his essay.

As you read, think about any examples of survival cannibalism you may have read about. Note also the strategies that Ngo employs for his explanation, such as classifying or dividing, comparing and contrasting, or others you find interesting.

Fifty-five Vietnamese refugees fled to Malaysia on a small fishing boat to escape communist rule in their country following the Vietnam War. During their escape attempt, the captain was shot by the coast guard. The boat and its passengers managed to outrun the coast guard to the open sea, but they had lost the only person who knew the way to Malaysia, the captain.

The men onboard tried to navigate the boat, but after a week fuel ran out and they drifted farther out to sea. Their supply of food and water was gone; people were starving, and some of the elderly were near death. The men managed to produce a small amount of drinking water by boiling salt water, using dispensable wood from the boat to create a small fire near the stern. They also tried to fish, but had little success.

A month went by, and the old and weak died. At first, the crew threw the dead overboard, but later, out of desperation, the crew turned to human flesh as a source of food. Some people vomited as they attempted to eat it, while others refused to resort to cannibalism and see the bodies of their loved ones sacrificed for food. Those who did not eat died of starvation, and their bodies in turn became food for others. Human flesh was cut out, washed in salt water, and hung to dry for preservation. The liquids inside the cranium were eaten to quench thirst. The livers, kidneys, heart, stomach, and intestines were boiled and eaten.

Five months passed before a whaling vessel discovered the drifting boat, looking like a graveyard of bones. There was only one survivor.

Cannibalism, the act of human beings eating human flesh (Sagan 2), has a long history and continues to hold interest and create controversy. Many books and research reports offer examples of cannibalism, but a few scholars have questioned whether cannibalism was ever practiced anywhere, except in cases of ensuring survival in times of famine or isolation (Askenasy 43–54). Recently, some scholars have tried to understand why people in the West have been so eager to attribute cannibalism to non-Westerners (Barker, Hulme, and Iversen). Cannibalism has long been a part of American popular culture. For example, Mark Twain's "Cannibalism in the Cars" tells a humorous story about cannibalism by well-to-do travelers on a train stranded in a snowstorm, and cannibalism is still a popular subject for jokes ("Cannibals").

6   If we assume there is some reality to the reports about cannibalism, how can we best understand this concept? Cannibalism can be broken down into two main categories: exocannibalism, the eating of outsiders or foreigners, and endocannibalism, the eating of members of one's own social group (Shipman 70). Within these categories are several functional types of cannibalism, three of the most common being survival cannibalism, dietary cannibalism, and religious and ritual cannibalism.

7   Survival cannibalism occurs when people trapped without food have to decide "whether to starve or eat fellow humans" (Shipman 70). In the case of the Vietnamese refugees, the crew and passengers on the boat ate human flesh to stay alive. They did not kill people to get human flesh for nourishment, but instead waited until the people had died. Even after human carcasses were sacrificed as food, the boat people ate only enough to survive. Another case of survival cannibalism occurred in 1945, when General Douglas MacArthur's forces cut supply lines to Japanese troops stationed in the Pacific Islands. In one incident, Japanese troops were reported to have sacrificed the Arapesh people of northeastern New Guinea for food in order to avoid death by starvation (Tuzin 63). The most famous example of survival cannibalism in American history comes from the diaries, letters, and interviews of survivors of the California-bound Donner Party, who in the winter of 1846 were snowbound in the Sierra Nevada Mountains for five months. Thirty-five of eighty-seven adults and children died, and some of them were eaten (Hart 116–17; Johnson).

8   Unlike survival cannibalism, in which human flesh is eaten as a last resort after a person has died, in dietary cannibalism, humans are purchased or trapped for food and then eaten as a part of a culture's traditions. In addition, survival cannibalism often involves people eating other people of the same origins, whereas dietary cannibalism usually involves people eating foreigners.

9   In the Miyanmin society of the west Sepik interior of Papua New Guinea, villagers do not value human flesh over that of pigs or marsupials because human flesh is part of their diet (Poole 17). The Miyanmin people observe no differences in "gender, kinship, ritual status, and bodily substance"; they eat anyone, even their own dead. In this respect, then, they practice both endocannibalism and exocannibalism; and to ensure a constant supply of human flesh for food, they raid neighboring tribes and drag their victims back to their village to be eaten (Poole 11). Perhaps, in

the history of this society, there was at one time a shortage of wild game to be hunted for food, and because people were more plentiful than fish, deer, rabbits, pigs, or cows, survival cannibalism was adopted as a last resort. Then, as their culture developed, the Miyanmin may have retained the practice of dietary cannibalism, which has endured as a part of their culture.

Similar to the Miyanmin, the people of the Leopard and Alligator societies in South America eat human flesh as part of their cultural tradition. Practicing dietary exocannibalism, the Leopard people hunt in groups, with one member wearing the skin of a leopard to conceal the face. They ambush their victims in the forest and carry their victims back to their village to be eaten. The Alligator people also hunt in groups, but they hide themselves under a canoelike submarine that resembles an alligator, then swim close to a fisherman's or trader's canoe to overturn it and catch their victims (MacCormack 54). 10

Religious or ritual cannibalism is different from survival and dietary cannibalism in that it has a ceremonial purpose rather than one of nourishment. Sometimes only a single victim is sacrificed in a ritual, while at other times many are sacrificed. For example, the Bangala tribe of the Congo River in central Africa honors a deceased chief or leader by purchasing, sacrificing, and feasting on slaves (Sagan 53). The number of slaves sacrificed is determined by how highly the tribe members revered the deceased leader. 11

Ritual cannibalism among South American Indians often serves as revenge for the dead. Like the Bangalas, some South American tribes kill their victims to be served as part of funeral rituals, with human sacrifices denoting that the deceased was held in high honor. Also like the Bangalas, these tribes use outsiders as victims. Unlike the Bangalas, however, the Indians sacrifice only one victim instead of many in a single ritual. For example, when a warrior of a tribe is killed in battle, the family of the warrior forces a victim to take the identity of the warrior. The family adorns the victim with the deceased warrior's belongings and may even force him to marry the deceased warrior's wives. But once the family believes the victim has assumed the spiritual identity of the deceased warrior, the family kills him. The children in the tribe soak their hands in the victim's blood to symbolize their revenge of the warrior's death. Elderly women from the tribe drink the victim's blood and then cut up his body for roasting and eating (Sagan 53–54). By sacrificing a victim, the people of the tribe believe that the death of the warrior has been avenged and the soul of the deceased can rest in peace. 12

In the villages of certain African tribes, only a small part of a dead body is used in ritual cannibalism. In these tribes, where the childbearing capacity of women is highly valued, women are obligated to eat small, raw 13 fragments of genital parts during fertility rites. Elders of the tribe supervise this ritual to ensure that the women will be fertile. In the Bimin-Kuskusmin tribe, for instance, a widow eats a small, raw fragment of flesh from the penis of her deceased husband in order to enhance her future fertility and reproductive capacity. Similarly, a widower may eat a raw fragment of flesh from his deceased wife's vagina along with a piece of her bone marrow; by eating her flesh, he hopes to strengthen the fertility capacity of his daughters borne by his dead wife, and by eating her bone marrow, he honors her reproductive capacity. Also, when an elder woman of the village who has shown great reproductive capacity dies, her uterus and the interior parts of her vagina are eaten by other women who hope to further benefit from her reproductive power (Poole 16–17).

14   Members of developed societies in general practice none of these forms of cannibalism, with the occasional exception of survival cannibalism when the only alternative is starvation. It is possible, however, that our distant-past ancestors were cannibals who through the eons turned away from the practice. We are, after all, descended from the same ancestors as the Miyanmin, the Alligator, and the Leopard people, and survival cannibalism shows that people are capable of eating human flesh when they have no other choice.

Works Cited

Askenasy, Hans. *Cannibalism: From Sacrifice to Survival*. Amherst: Prometheus, 1994. Print.

Barker, Francis, Peter Hulme, and Margaret Iversen, eds. *Cannibalism and the New World*. Cambridge: Cambridge UP, 1998. Print.

Brown, Paula, and Donald Tuzin, eds. *The Ethnography of Cannibalism*. Washington: Society of Psychological Anthropology, 1983. Print.

"Cannibals." *Jokes and Funny Stories*. N.p. 2006. Web. 4 Apr. 2009.

Hart, James D. *A Companion to California*. Berkeley: U of California P, 1987. Print.

Johnson, Kristin. "New Light on the Donner Party." Kristin Johnson, 31 Jan. 2006. Web. 4 Apr. 2009.

MacCormack, Carol. "Human Leopard and Crocodile." Brown and Tuzin 54–55.

Poole, Fitz John Porter. "Cannibals, Tricksters, and Witches." Brown and Tuzin 11, 16–17.

Sagan, Eli. *Cannibalism*. New York: Harper, 1976. Print.

Shipman, Pat. "The Myths and Perturbing Realities of Cannibalism." *Discover* Mar. 1987: 70+. Print.

Tuzin, Donald. "Cannibalism and Arapesh Cosmology." Brown and Tuzin 61–63.

Twain, Mark. "Cannibalism in the Cars." *The Complete Short Stories of Mark Twain*. Ed. Charles Neider. New York: Doubleday, 1957. 9–16. Print.

READING FOR MEANING

This section presents three activities that will help you think about the meanings in Ngo's explanation of cannibalism.

Read to Comprehend

Write a few sentences briefly explaining the different types of cannibalism, according to Ngo.

Identify any words with meanings you are unsure of—such as *kinship* (paragraph 9) and *eons* (14)—and find the dictionary definition for each word that makes the best sense in the context.

To help you understand the essay better, also consider trying one of these critical reading strategies, explained in Appendix 1: *previewing* or *outlining*.

Read to Respond

Write a paragraph or two exploring your initial thoughts and feelings about Ngo's explanatory essay. Focus on anything that stands out for you, perhaps because it resonates with your own experience or because you find a statement puzzling. For example, consider writing about one of the following:

- your response to the anecdotes about the Vietnamese refugees (paragraphs 1–4) and the Donner Party in California (7).

- your response to the idea that cannibalism may be performed for ceremonial or ritual purposes

- whether you think you would resort to cannibalism to survive.

To help develop your response, also consider trying one of these critical reading strategies, explained in Appendix 1: *recognizing emotional manipulation* or *judging the writer's credibility*.

Read to Analyze Assumptions

Write a paragraph or two analyzing an assumption in Ngo's essay. To think critically about assumptions, here are some kinds of questions you could ask: Who holds this assumption (the writer, readers, and/or others cited in the essay)? What are the effects of the assumption in the context of the essay specifically or in society more generally? What do you think about the assumption, and is there anything in the essay that raises doubts about it? How does the assumption reinforce or critique commonly held views, and are there any alternative ideas, beliefs, or values that would challenge this assumption?

You might choose an assumption from the list below, using the questions accompanying it in addition to the ones above to help you get started. Or you can choose another assumption in the essay to explore.

- **assumptions about how to deal with the dead.** Ngo discusses several tribes that practice cannibalism in some form to honor the dead or to take on the good traits of the dead (paragraphs 11–13). The people in these tribes believe that even a small portion of a human being can carry the meaning of the whole person. Many cultures and religions of the world practice a form of this belief, although they may substitute another substance to represent the human. Yet as Ngo reports, the practice of cannibalism, even of people who are already dead, is controversial (5).

  To think critically about assumptions in this essay related to how people deal with their dead, ask yourself questions like these: Why does cannibalism create such controversy? What beliefs and values come into play among those who find cannibalism disgusting? How and why do people comfort themselves with portions or symbols of the bodies of the dead?

- **assumptions about what constitutes "developed societies."** Ngo does not define "developed societies" (paragraph 14), so he must assume that readers know what he means. Members of the tribes he describes, though, might think our society is anything but "developed."

  To think critically about assumptions in this essay related to "development," ask yourself: What might Western industrialized societies do that would make "undeveloped societies" uncomfortable? How do you feel about the assumptions behind the idea of some societies' being "developed" while others are not?

  To help you analyze assumptions in Ngo's essay, also consider trying one of these critical reading strategies, explained in Appendix 1: *reflecting on challenges to your beliefs and values*, or *looking for patterns of opposition*.

READING LIKE A WRITER

INTEGRATING SOURCES SMOOTHLY

When writers explain concepts to their readers, they nearly always rely in part on information gleaned from sources in a library or on the Internet. When they do so, they must acknowledge these sources. Within their essays, writers must find ways to integrate smoothly into their own sentences the information borrowed from each source and to acknowledge or cite each source. When you analyzed Chris Anderson's essay, you learned that writers rely on certain signal phrases and sentence structures to integrate quoted materials smoothly into their essays. Sometimes, however, writers do not quote a source but instead summarize or paraphrase it. (See Appendix 1, pp. 564–66, for examples of summarizing and paraphrasing.) When they do so, they may acknowledge the source of the summarized or paraphrased material through signal phrases or special sentence structures, or they may use a formal style of parenthetical citation. Ngo relies on both these strategies. (Ngo's parenthetical citations refer to sources in the Works Cited list at the end of his essay.)

Analyze

1. In paragraphs 7 and 9, notice how Ngo sets up a sentence to integrate the quoted phrases.

2. Put a check mark in the margin by each instance of parenthetical citation in paragraphs 5, 6, and 9 to 13. Notice where these citations are located in Ngo's sentences and the different forms they take.

3. Make notes in the margin about similarities and differences you observe in Ngo's use of parenthetical citations.

Write

Write a few sentences explaining how Ngo integrates quoted phrases into his sentences and makes use of parenthetical citations. Support your explanation with examples from the reading.

CONSIDERING IDEAS FOR YOUR OWN WRITING

Consider writing about some other well-established human taboo or practice, such as ostracism, incest, pedophilia, murder, circumcision, celibacy or virginity, caste systems, a particular religion's dietary restrictions, adultery, stealing, gourmandism, or divorce.

A Special Reading Strategy

Summarizing

Summarizing, a potent reading-for-meaning strategy, is also a kind of writing you will encounter in your college classes and on the job. By rereading Ngo's essay on cannibalism with an eye toward finding its main ideas, you can do the groundwork for writing a summary of it. Taking the time to write a summary will help you remember what you have read and could help you explain to others the important ideas in Ngo's essay. For detailed guidelines on writing an extended summary, see Appendix 1 (pp. 564–65).

Justin Ton

Hip-Hop You Don't Stop

Justin Ton wrote the following essay when he was a college student. He explains the concept of hip-hop, which he enjoys and researched carefully.

As you read, think about what you know (or don't know) about hip-hop, and see if this essay expands your understanding. You may want to annotate the text, paying special attention to the features of explanatory writing, such as a readable plan, appropriate strategies (defining, classifying or dividing, comparing and contrasting, narrating, illustrating, and reporting causes or effects), integrating sources smoothly, and engaging readers' interest.

Hip-Hop is supposed to uplift and create, to educate people on a larger level and to make a change.

—DOUG E. FRESH, RAPPER, RECORD PRODUCER, AND BEAT BOXER

1   In the past thirty years, hip-hop culture has spread throughout the globe. It can be found in television commercials, on the radio, in movies, and even in sports. What many people do not know, however, is where the roots of hip-hop lie. Where did it come from? Who started it? How did it come about? With hip-hop's permeating presence, it is essential to understand its roots to see its expansion. Like most cultures, hip-hop has evolved over time but has maintained several constants, known as its four pillars, or elements. These pillars can be traced back to the origins of hip-hop and show how it was created. The four elements of hip-hop are the Disc Jockey (DJ), the Master of Ceremonies (MC, also known as emcee), dance, and graffiti (Kugelberg 17).

2   Hip-hop was born during the 1970s in the South Bronx area of New York City (Newman). According to a *History Detectives* show on PBS, while DJing one of his dance parties at his place on Sedgewick Avenue, DJ Kool Herc "extended an instrumental beat (breaking or scratching) to let people dance longer and began MCing during the extended breakdancing" ("Birthplace"). Kool Herc chose parts of songs that the crowd reacted best to and extended them. He even linked the break to songs with similar breaks (Newman). This led to the creation of breakbeat DJing and rapping over such beats. The parties that Kool Herc threw brought a positive, fun atmosphere to inner-city New York, taking the focus away from gangs and violence. Later on, as hip-hop grew within popular music, it became a symbol of independence and an outlet for people to voice their opinions.

3   Being the father of this music genre and culture, the DJ is the most important person in hip-hop. The DJ chooses what music to play, how to play it, and often which rapper to promote. Kool Herc created the

model for a DJ, and other legendary DJs like Afrika Bambaataa, Grand-master Flash, and The Grand Wizard Theodore built on it. Grand Wizard Theodore created what is now called scratching: rubbing the vinyl record back and forth on the turntable to create scratching noises ("The Birth of Rap"). This led to DJs having not only breaks to sample music, but also the power to create their own sounds and beats. Grandmaster Flash fur-ther developed DJing by inventing the crossfader, which allowed DJs to smoothly transition from one turntable to the other or mix both sources together seamlessly (Hansen). The technique of scratching and the inven-tion of the crossfader gave DJs even more tools to create and mix music, and they are still staples of DJing today.

The DJ is also the predecessor of the MC. Between songs, the DJ would   4
talk over a beat to interact with the crowd ("The Birth of Rap"). This tech-nique was later divided into two distinct roles: the DJ spun the music and the MC spoke over the beat between songs. Eventually, the MC began to rap—to create rhyming statements in the rhythm of the beat ("The Birth of Rap"). The pairing of the rapper and the DJ seems integral to hip-hop, as evident from popular groups throughout its history—Grandmaster Flash and the Furious Five of the '70s, Run DMC of the '80s, and A Tribe Called Quest of the '90s.

Rapping has evolved from simply talking over a beat to become a dis-   5
tinctive form of spoken language. The first major rap group, The Last Poets, created the mold for rappers (Powell 246). The Harlem rappers Omar Ben Hassen, Alafia Pudim, Abiodun Oyewole, and Nilaja formed the group, which rapped about social issues relevant to the black community (Powell 246). This was the first major instance of using rap as a tool for speak-ing out on social issues, but it is most definitely not the last. In the last thirty years, rap has been a prominent outlet for this purpose. Examples range from Kanye West rapping about materialism, to Ice Cube discuss-ing police violence, to Jay-Z questioning the relief efforts for Hurricane Katrina. People in the inner cities of America have found a new weapon and craft: their voices.

The style of rapping has changed with the times. The basic repertoire of   6
rhyming couplets has expanded to include many other literary techniques like alliteration, assonance, wordplay, metaphors and similes, and variet-ies of meter. For example, the 1979 song "Rapper's Delight" featured lines such as, "Because they say that miracles never cease / I've created a dev-astating masterpiece" (Sugarhill Gang). This line features rhyming couplets in "cease" and "masterpiece," and the line follows the meter of the beat. In the 2008 song "Time," the rapper Gemini (whose real name is Demarco Castle) raps as if he is talking to time: "I'll never kill you again, put my faith in your hands / I only race with you because being late is not in the plans /And if I wasted you, I had too much on my hands / Is it true they say you wait for no man?" These particular four bars use metaphors and

personification to compare time to a person. The complex bars of the 2008 verse show how rap has grown into a style of complex poetry with music.

7   If rap is poetry over music, then hip-hop dance is poetry in motion. Beginning at the dance parties of Kool Herc, people danced to the breaks created by the DJ ("Birthplace"). Break-dancing, also known as breaking or b-boying, has grown from a dance party staple to full routines and battles. B-boying is now not only a way to dance at a party, but also a visual art. In his review of Joseph Schloss's book *FOUNDATION: B-Boys, B-Girls, and Hip-Hop Culture in New York*, Adam Mansbach describes, with the help of Schloss's own words, a standard b-boy routine: "rhythmic, upright 'toprock' introduces a dancer, who then executes a 'drop' to the floor and performs 'footwork'—'disciplined, flowing moves that display rhythm, finesse, and creativity'—followed by strength-based 'power moves' and acrobatic 'air moves,' and concluding with a 'freeze,' 'a concluding pose that summarizes his or her statement.'" This foundation for a b-boy routine allows a dancer to improvise with different moves, creating variety.

8   The fourth pillar of hip-hop, graffiti, is much different from the other three pillars, as it is the only element not based on music,. Tagging, marking one's territory with graffiti (Bowen 24), is a way that graffiti has manifested hip-hop culture. Writers, or graffiti artists, go through the community, tagging their signature on various places (Bowen 24). Although viewed by most of the general public as vandalism, graffiti is a means of self-promotion, marking territory, art, or addressing social issues. Tagging grew from signatures on subways, lamp posts, and mailboxes to large pieces on sides of buildings (Bowen 24). Stemming from the inner cities and practiced by those who participate in hip-hop, graffiti is linked to hip-hop culture. It has become an art form, adding color to neighborhoods. In her article about graffiti art in Toronto, Tracey Bowen says that graffiti "enlivens the city's derelict areas," and "borders on a form of public mural making" (22–24). Just like hip-hop, graffiti has "crossed the boundaries of street culture, youth culture, and the art community" (Bowen 22). Because hip-hop and graffiti reach a similar audience and have similar origins, the two will forever be connected.

9   As many pastimes or hobbies contain an element of competition, the four pillars of hip-hop have also found ways to create a contest: battling. Dance battles have been the most prominent form of hip-hop dance in mainstream media. Dance battles first entered the mainstream in 1981, when the Rock Steady Crew battled the Dynamic Rockers at Lincoln Center in New York City ("Hip-Hop Dance History"). Even today, movies like *You Got Served* and *Stomp the Yard* have focused on the battle aspect of hip-hop dance. Large-scale rap battles like The Iron Mic, DJ competitions like the DMC World DJ Championships, and the ongoing territorial battles of graffiti artists have also cemented to the competition aspect of hip-hop.

Hip-hop is not only a music genre; it is a culture. The four pillars—the   10
DJ, the MC, dance, and graffiti—come together to create a lifestyle that
has successfully adapted to generations of youth. These pillars have been
used as a means of preventing violence in the inner cities of America, all
while creating a fun and positive atmosphere. Whether via a rap or dance
battle or expressing emotions through a visual art like graffiti, hip-hop has
been a way for people to channel their negative energy into something
positive, or nonviolent. As hip-hop grows and changes, the four elements
will remain constant in the culture.

Works Cited

"The Birth of Rap: A Look Back." *World Cafe*. WXPN, Philadelphia, 22 Feb.
  2007. Radio.

"Birthplace of Hip-Hop." Narr. Tukufu Zuberi. *History Detectives*. PBS,
  23 Feb. 2008. Television.

Bowen, Tracey. "Graffiti Art: A Contemporary Study of Toronto Artists."
  Studies in Art Education 41.1 (1999): 22–39. *JSTOR*. Web. 2 Nov. 2009.

Castle, Demarco. "Time." *The Testimony of Gemstones*. 1st and 15th,
  2008. CD.

Hansen, Kjetil. *Turntable Music*. The Music Group at the Department of
  Speech, Music and Hearing, KTH. 2000. Web. 9 Nov. 2009.

"Hip-Hop Dance History." *dance here*. 7 July 2008. Web. 9 Nov. 2009.

Kugelberg, Johan. *Born in the Bronx*. New York: Oxford UP, 2007. Print.

Mansbach, Adam. "The Ascent of Hip-Hop: A Historical, Cultural, and
  Aesthetic Study of B-boying." *Boston Globe* 24 May 2009, Books: 2.
  Web. 2 Nov. 2009.

Newman, Mark. "History of Turntablism." *pedestrian*. 3 Jan. 2003. Web. 9
  Nov. 2009.

Powell, Catherine. "Rap Music: An Education with a Beat from the Street."
  The Journal of Negro Education 60.3 (1991): 245–259. *JSTOR*. Web. 2
  Nov. 2009.

Sugarhill Gang. "Rapper's Delight." *Sugarhill Gang*. Sugar Hill Studios,
  1979. CD.

READING FOR MEANING

Reading for meaning involves three activities:

- reading to comprehend,
- reading to respond, and
- reading to analyze assumptions.

Write a page or so explaining your understanding of the basic meaning of
Ton's essay, a personal response you have to it, and one of its assumptions.

READING LIKE A WRITER

Writers of essays explaining concepts

- devise a readable plan,
- use appropriate explanatory strategies,
- integrate sources smoothly into the writing, and
- engage readers' interest.

Choose one of these strategies in Ton's essay, and analyze it carefully through close rereading and annotating. Then write several sentences explaining what you have learned, giving specific examples from the reading to support your explanation. Add a few sentences evaluating how successfully Ton uses the strategy to explain hip-hop.

Explaining Concepts

Analyze

Choose one reading from this chapter that seems to you especially effective. Before rereading the selection, jot down one or two reasons you remember it as an example of good explanatory writing.

Reread your chosen selection and add further notes about what makes it a particularly successful example of explaining a concept. Consider the selection's purpose and how well it achieves that purpose for its intended readers. (You can make an informed guess about the intended readers and their expectations by noting the publication source of the essay.)

Then assess how well the essay uses the writing strategies of devising a readable plan, using appropriate explanatory strategies, integrating sources smoothly into the writing, and engaging readers' interest. You can review these strategies in A Guide to Reading Essays Explaining Concepts (p. 209).

Write

Write at least a page supporting your choice of this reading as an example of effective explanatory writing. Refer to details and specific parts of the essay as you explain how it works as an explanation of a concept and as you justify your evaluation of its effectiveness. You need not argue that it is the best reading in the chapter or that it is flawless, only that it is, in your view, a strong example of the genre.

A GUIDE TO WRITING ESSAYS EXPLAINING CONCEPTS

The readings in this chapter have helped you learn a great deal about essays explaining concepts. The readings also have helped you understand new concepts and learn more about concepts with which you are already familiar. Now that you have seen how writers use explanatory strategies that are appropriate for their readers, anticipating what their readers are likely to know, you can approach this type of writing confidently. This Guide to Writing is designed to help you through the various decisions you will need to make as you plan, draft, and revise your essay explaining a concept.

INVENTION AND RESEARCH

The following activities will help you choose a concept, consider what your readers need to know, explore what you already know, and gather and sort through your information.

Choosing a Concept

List the most promising concepts you could explain, beginning with any you listed for the Considering Ideas for Your Own Writing activities following the readings in this chapter. Rather than limiting yourself to the first subject that comes to mind, take a few minutes to consider your options and list as many concepts as you can. Below are some concepts from various fields of study for you to consider:

- *Literature:* representation, figurative language, canon, postcolonialism, modernism, irony, epic

- *Philosophy:* Platonic forms, causality, syllogism, existentialism, nihilism, logical positivism, determinism, phenomenology

- *Business management:* autonomous work group, quality circle, management by objectives, zero-based budgeting, benchmarking, focus group

- *Psychology:* phobia, narcissism, fetish, emotional intelligence, divergent and convergent thinking, behaviorism, Jungian archetype

- *Government:* one person/one vote, federalism, socialism, theocracy, separation of church and state, exclusionary rule, political machine, political action committee, Astroturfing

- *Biology:* photosynthesis, ecosystem, plasmolysis, phagocytosis, DNA, species, punctuated evolution, homozygosity, diffusion

- *Art:* composition, cubism, iconography, pop art, conceptual art, performance art, graffiti, Dadaism, surrealism, expressionism

- *Math:* Mobius transformation, boundedness, null space, eigenvalue, complex numbers, integral, exponent, polynomial, factoring, Pythagorean theorem, continuity, derivative, infinity

- *Physical sciences:* gravity, mass, weight, energy, quantum theory, law of definite proportions, osmotic pressure, first law of thermodynamics, entropy, free energy, fusion

- *Public health:* alcoholism, epidemic, vaccination, drug abuse, contraception, prenatal care, AIDS education, disability, autism

- *Environmental studies:* acid rain, recycling, ozone depletion, sewage treatment, toxic waste, endangered species, greenhouse effect

- *Sports psychology:* Ringelman effect, leadership, cohesiveness, competitiveness, anxiety management, aggression, visualization, runner's high

- *Law:* arbitration, strike, minimum wage, liability, reasonable doubt, sexual harassment, nondisclosure agreement, assumption of evidence

- *Meteorology:* jet stream, hydrologic cycle, El Niño, Coriolis effect, Chinook or Santa Ana wind, standard time system, tsunami

- *Nutrition and health:* vegetarianism, bulimia, diabetes, food allergy, aerobic exercise, obesity, Maillard reaction, sustainability, locavore

Choose a concept that interests you and that you think would interest your readers. You might not know very much about the concept now, but the guidelines that follow will help you learn more about it so that you can explain it to others.

Analyzing Your Readers

Write for a few minutes, analyzing your potential readers. Begin by identifying your readers and what you want them to know. Even if you are writing only for your instructor, you should consider what he or she knows about your concept. Ask yourself the following questions to stimulate your thinking: What might my potential readers already know about the concept or about the field of study to which it applies? What new, useful, or interesting information about the concept could I provide for them? What questions might they ask?

Researching the Concept

Even if you know quite a bit about the concept, you may want to do additional library or Internet research or consult an expert. Before you begin, check with your instructor for special requirements, such as submitting photocopies or printouts of your sources or using a particular documentation style.

Exploring What You Already Know about the Concept.   Write for a few minutes about the concept to discover what you know about it. Pose any questions you now have about the concept, and try to answer questions you expect your readers would have.

Finding More Information.   Before embarking on research, review any materials you already have at hand that explain your concept. If you are considering a concept from one of your courses, find explanatory material in your textbook and lecture notes. To learn more, find sources on your concept at the library or on the Internet, take notes on or make copies of relevant material, and keep a working bibliography. (See Appendix 2, Strategies for Research and Documentation, for detailed guidance on finding information at a library and on the Internet.)

Consulting Experts.   Identify one or more people knowledgeable about the concept or the field of study in which it is used, and request information from them. If you are writing about a concept from a course, consult the professor, teaching assistant, or other students. If the concept relates to your job, consider asking your supervisor. If it relates to a subject you have encountered on television, on the Internet, or in other media, you might e-mail the author or post a query on a blog or at a relevant Web site. Consulting experts can answer your questions as well as lead you to other sources—Web sites, other blogs, chatrooms, articles, and books.

Focusing Your Explanation.   With your own knowledge of the concept and that of your readers in mind, consider how you might focus your explanation. Determine how the information you have gathered so far could be divided. For example, if you were writing about the concept of schizophrenia, you might focus on the history of its diagnosis and treatment, its symptoms, its effects on families, the current debate about its causes, or the current preferred methods of treatment. If you were writing a book, you might want to cover all these aspects of the concept, but in a relatively brief essay you can focus on only one or two of them.

Confirming Your Focus.   Choose a focus for your explanation, and write several sentences justifying the focus you have chosen. Why do you think this focus will appeal to your readers? What interests you about it? Do you have enough information to plan and draft your explanation? Do you know where you can find any additional information you need?

Formulating a Working Thesis.   Draft a thesis statement. A working thesis—as opposed to a final, revised thesis—will help you begin drafting your essay purposefully. The thesis in an essay explaining a concept simply announces the concept and focus of the explanation. Here are four examples from the readings.

- "Each of the women at the conference had to make decisions about hair, clothing, makeup and accessories, and each decision carried meaning. Every style available to us was marked. The men in our group had made decisions, too, but the range from which they chose was incomparably narrower. Men can choose styles that are marked, but they don't have to, and in this group none did. Unlike the women, they had the option of being unmarked" (Tannen, paragraph 12).

- "Understanding the hookup culture on college campuses is the first step toward addressing two of the biggest residence-life issues: student alcohol abuse and sexual assaults" (Bogle, paragraph 1).

- "Cannibalism can be broken down into two main categories: exocannibalism, the eating of outsiders or foreigners, and endocannibalism, the eating of members of one's own social group (Shipman 70). Within these categories are several functional types of cannibalism, three of the most common being survival cannibalism, dietary cannibalism, and religious and ritual cannibalism" (Ngo, paragraph 6).

- "Like most cultures, hip-hop has evolved over time but has maintained several constants, known as its four pillars, or elements. These pillars can be traced back to the origins of hip-hop and show how it was created. The four elements of hip-hop are the Disc Jockey (DJ), the Master of Ceremonies (MC, also known as emcee), dance, and graffiti (Kugelberg 17)" (Ton, paragraph 1).

Notice that Bogle's, Ngo's, and Ton's thesis statements announce the concept and also forecast the main topics they will take up in the essay. Forecasts, though not required, can be helpful to readers, especially when the concept is unfamiliar or the explanation is complicated.

Considering Visuals.   Think about whether visuals—tables, graphs, drawings, photographs—would make your explanation clearer. You could construct your own visuals, download materials from the Internet, copy images from print sources (like books, magazines, and newspapers), or scan into your essay visuals from books and magazines. Visuals are not a requirement of an essay explaining a concept, as you can tell from the readings in this chapter, but they sometimes can add a new dimension to your writing, as you can see from analyzing the visuals in "The Long Tail." Be sure to cite the source(s) for your visuals.

DRAFTING

The following guidelines will help you set goals for your draft, plan its organization, and think about a useful sentence strategy.

Setting Goals

Establishing goals for your draft before you begin writing will enable you to make decisions and work more confidently. Consider the following questions now, and keep them in mind as you draft. They will help you set goals for drafting as well as recall how the writers you have read in this chapter tried to achieve similar goals.

- *How can I begin engagingly so as to capture my readers' attention?* Should I begin with an anecdote (as Anderson, Tannen, Bailey, and Ngo do), or with a reference to the surprising information that prompted the essay (as Bogle does)? Should I begin by asking rhetorical questions?

- *How can I orient readers so they do not get confused?* Should I provide an explicit forecasting statement (as Bogle, Ngo, and Ton do)? Should I add transitions to help readers see how the parts of my essay relate to one another (as Bailey, Bogle, and Ngo do)? Should I use rhetorical questions and summary statements (as Anderson and Ton do)? Or should I use all of these cueing devices, together with headings and subheadings?

- *How should I conclude my explanation?* Should I frame the essay by echoing the opening at the end (as Tannen and Bogle do)? Should I summarize my explanation and discuss the implications (as Anderson, Ngo, and Ton do)?

Organizing Your Draft

With goals in mind, make a tentative outline of the topics you now think you want to cover as you give readers information about the concept. You might want to make two or three different outlines before choosing the one that looks most promising. Try to introduce new material in stages, so that readers' understanding of the concept builds slowly but steadily. Keep in mind that an essay explaining a concept is made up of four basic parts:

1. an attempt to engage readers' interest in the explanation,

2. the thesis statement, announcing the concept and the way it will be focused and perhaps also forecasting the sequence of topics,

3. an orientation to the concept, which may include a description or definition of it, and

4. the information about the concept, organized around a series of topics that reflect how the information has been divided up.

An attempt to gain readers' interest could take as little space as two or three sentences or as much as four or five paragraphs. The thesis statement and orientation are usually quite brief, sometimes only a few sentences. One topic may require one or several paragraphs, and there can be few or many topics, depending on how the information has been divided up.

Consider tentative any outline you do before you begin drafting. Never be a slave to an outline. As you draft, you will usually see ways to improve on your original plan. Be ready to revise your outline, shift parts around, or drop or add parts as you draft.

Working with Sources

Introducing Sources Carefully and Precisely

When explaining concepts, writers usually need to present information from different sources, and they have many ways to introduce the information they quote or summarize. Here are a few examples from the concept essays in this chapter (the introductory words and phrases are in italics):

> Venture capitalist and former music industry consultant Kevin Laws *puts it this way*: "The biggest money is in the smallest sales." (Anderson, paragraph 16)

> In his book, Fasold *notes* "a wide range of facts which demonstrates that female is the unmarked sex." (Tannen, paragraph 26)

> "The courtship which grew out of the sturdy social roots [of the nineteenth century]," one author *wrote*, "comes through to us for what it was—a gracious ritual, with clearly defined roles for man and woman, in which everyone knew the measured music and the steps." (Bailey, paragraph 3)

By using the phrase *puts it this way*, Anderson takes a neutral stance toward the information he got from Kevin Laws. Similarly, Tannen's *notes* and Bailey's *wrote* indicate that the authors are not characterizing or judging their sources but simply reporting them.

Often, however, writers are more descriptive—even opinionated—when they introduce information from sources, as these examples demonstrate:

> Fasold *stresses* that language and culture are particularly unfair in treating women as the marked case because biologically it is the male that is marked. (Tannen, paragraph 24)

> Fasold ends his discussion of these matters by *pointing out* that if language reflected biology, grammar books would direct us to use "she" to include males and females and "he" only for specifically male referents. (Tannen, paragraph 28)

> By the 1950s and 1960s, social scientists who studied American courtship *found it necessary to remind* the American public that dating was a "recent American innovation and not a traditional or universal custom." (Bailey, paragraph 3)

> The *Ladies' Home Journal approvingly reported* the case of six girls, workers in a box factory, who had formed a club and pooled part of their wages to pay the "janitress of a tenement house" to let them use her front room two evenings a week. (Bailey, paragraph 9)

> In . . . these economic analyses, the men *are complaining* about the new dating system, *lamenting* the passing of the mythic good old days when "a man without a quarter in his pocket could call on a girl and not be embarrassed," the days before a woman had to be "bought." (Bailey, paragraph 26)

The verbs and verb phrases in these examples—*stresses, pointing out, found it necessary to remind, approvingly reported, are complaining, lamenting*—do not neutrally report the source material but describe the particular role played by the source in explaining the concept. Verbs like *found, showed, discovered,* and *presented* are used to introduce information resulting from scientific research. When Bogle wants to draw your attention to the title of a report, she simply uses the verb *released* to describe what the Institute for American Values did with the report (paragraph 1). In contrast, verbs like *emphasize* and *stresses* may suggest that what is being reported is an interpretation that others may disagree with. Verbs like *approvingly report* and *complain* or *lament* suggest the state of mind of the person being quoted—or the writer's interpretation of it.

As you refer to sources in your concept explanation, you will want to choose carefully among a wide variety of precise verbs. When you are introducing sources in an argumentative essay, you also will want to draw from another set of verbs that suggest agreement or disagreement with a position, such as *argues, contends, asserts, claims, supports, refutes, repudiates, advocates, contradicts, rejects, corroborates,* and *acknowledges.*

Notice that Linh Kieu Ngo does not introduce his sources in the body of "Cannibalism: It Still Exists." Instead, he simply integrates the information from them into his sentences, and readers can see where he got it from the parenthetical citation and the Works Cited list. Here is an example from paragraph 9, in which Ngo includes a quotation together with information he paraphrases from his source:

> The Miyanmin people observe no differences in "gender, kinship, ritual status, and bodily substance"; they eat anyone, even their own dead. In this respect, then, they practice both endocannibalism and exocannibalism; and to ensure a constant supply of human flesh for food, they raid neighboring tribes and drag their victims back to their village to be eaten (Poole, 11).

This strategy of integrating but not introducing source material is useful when you want to emphasize the information and play down the source.

Considering a Useful Sentence Strategy

As you draft your essay, you will need to identify people, introduce terms, and present details to help readers understand the concept you are explaining. One way to accomplish these goals is to use sentences with appositives. An appositive is made up of a group of words, usually based on a noun or a pronoun, that identifies or gives more information about another noun or pronoun just preceding it. Appositives come in many forms and may be introduced by a comma, dash, parenthesis, or colon, as shown in these examples (the appositives appear in bold type):

> Jon Krakauer wrote *Into Thin Air*, **another book about a mountain-climbing tragedy**, . . . (Anderson, paragraph 1)

> [A]nd eBay is mostly tail as well—**niche and one-off products . . .** (Anderson, paragraph 18)

> this new style of courtship, **dating**, . . . (Bailey, paragraph 2)

> True, the equation (**male companionship plus money equals female companionship**) was imbalanced. (Bailey, paragraph 27)

All of this chapter's readings use appositives. Writers explaining concepts rely on appositives because they serve many different purposes, as shown in the following examples.

- To identify a thing or person and establish a source's authority:

  In 1914, the *Ladies' Home Journal*, **a bastion of middle-class respectability**, used . . . (Bailey, paragraph 7)

- To introduce and define a new term:

  Eventually, the MC began to rap—**to create rhyming statements in the rhythm of the beat** ("The Birth of Rap"). (Ton, paragraph 4)

- To give examples or more specific information:

  The third woman's hair was wild, **a frosted blond avalanche falling over and beyond her shoulders**. (Tannen, paragraph 4)

  Although the practice encompasses a wide range of behavior, activities at one end of the spectrum—**say, anonymous sex between strangers**—receive a disproportionate amount of attention. (Bogle, paragraph 11)

Appositives accomplish these and other purposes efficiently by enabling the writer to put related bits of information next to each other in the same sentence, thereby merging two potential sentences into one or shrinking a potential clause to a phrase. For example, Ngo uses an appositive in this sentence:

> Cannibalism, **the act of human beings eating human flesh . . .** , has a long history and continues to hold interest and create controversy. (Ngo, paragraph 5)

But he could have conveyed the same information in either of the following ways:

Cannibalism can be defined as the act of human beings eating human flesh. It has a long history and continues to hold interest and create controversy.

Cannibalism, which can be defined as the act of human beings eating human flesh, has a long history and continues to hold interest and create controversy.

Both of these versions are readable and clear. By using an appositive, however, Ngo saves four or five words, subordinates the definition of cannibalism to his main idea about history and controversy, and yet locates the definition exactly where readers need to see it, right after the word being defined.

In addition to using appositives, you can strengthen your concept explanation with other kinds of sentence strategies. For example, you may want to review the information in Chapter 6 on sentences that express comparison and contrast (pp. 337–39).

READING A DRAFT CRITICALLY

Getting a critical reading of your draft will help you see how to improve it. Your instructor may schedule class time for reading drafts, or you may want to ask a classmate or a tutor in the writing center to read your draft. Ask your reader to use the following guidelines and to write out a response for you to consult during your revision.

Read for a First Impression

1. **Read the draft without stopping, and then write a few sentences giving your general impression.**

2. **Identify one aspect of the draft that seems particularly effective.**

Read Again to Suggest Improvements

1. **Consider whether the concept is clearly explained and focused.**

   - Restate briefly what you understand the concept to mean, indicating if you have any uncertainty or confusion about its meaning.

   - Identify the focus of the explanation and assess whether the focus seems appropriate, too broad, or too narrow for the intended readers.

   - If you can, suggest another, possibly more interesting, way to focus the explanation.

2. **Recommend ways of making the organization clearer or more effective.**

   - Indicate whether a forecasting statement, topic sentences, or transitions could be added or improved.

   - Point to any place where you become confused or do not know how something relates to what went before.

   - Comment on whether the conclusion gives you a sense of closure or leaves you hanging.

3. **Consider whether the content is appropriate for the intended readers.**

   - Point to any place where the information might seem obvious to readers or too elementary for them.

   - Indicate any terms that the writer should define or define more clearly, as well as any that the writer has defined but you do not think need to be defined.

   - Think of unanswered questions readers might have about the concept. Try to suggest additional information that should be included.

   - Recommend new strategies the writer could usefully adopt—comparing the concept to a concept more familiar to readers, dividing some of the information into smaller or larger topics, reporting known causes or effects of the concept, giving further facts or examples, or narrating how a part of the concept actually works. Explain how the writer could make use of the strategy.

4. **Assess whether quotations are integrated smoothly and acknowledged properly.**

   - Point to any place where a quotation is not smoothly integrated into the writer's sentence and offer a revision.

   - Indicate any quotations that would have been just as effective if put in the writer's own words.

   - If sources are not acknowledged correctly, remind the writer to consult Appendix 2.

5. **Evaluate the effectiveness of visuals.**

   - Look at any visuals in the essay, and tell the writer what, if anything, they contribute to your understanding of the concept explanation.

   - If any visuals do not seem relevant, explain your thinking.

REVISING

This section offers suggestions for revising your draft. Revising means reenvisioning your draft, trying to see it in a new way, given your purpose and readers, in order to develop a more lively, engaging, and informative essay explaining a concept.

The biggest mistake you can make while revising is to focus initially on words or sentences. Instead, first try to see your draft as a whole to assess its likely impact on your readers. Think imaginatively and boldly about cutting unconvincing material, adding new material, and moving material around. Your computer makes even drastic revisions physically easy, but you still need to make the mental effort and decisions that will improve your draft.

You may have received help with this challenge from a classmate or tutor who gave your draft a critical reading. If so, keep this feedback in mind as you decide which parts of your draft need revising and what specific changes you could make. The following suggestions will help you solve problems and strengthen your essay.

TROUBLESHOOTING YOUR DRAFT

To Make the Concept Clearer and More Focused

Problem	Suggestions for Revising
The concept's meaning is confusing or unclear.	• Define the concept more precisely. • Give concrete examples. • Use an appositive to introduce and define new terms or give specific details.
The focus seems too broad or too narrow.	• Concentrate on one aspect of the concept. • Review your invention and research notes for a larger or more significant aspect of the concept to focus on.

To Improve the Organization

Problem	Suggestions for Revising
The essay as a whole is difficult to follow.	• Forecast at the beginning of the essay by listing the topics in the order they will appear. • Rearrange your topics for clarity.
Connections from one sentence or paragraph to the next are vague or unclear.	• Make the connections clearer by improving or adding transitions. • Revise or add topic sentences to make connections between paragraphs clear.
The essay is long and complicated.	• Consider using headings and subheadings to orient readers. • Outline your essay to see if the connections between parts are clear.

To Strengthen the Explanatory Strategies

Problem	Suggestion for Revising
The content seems thin.	• Consider adding other explanatory strategies. • Consider developing your strategies more fully.
Some words are new to most readers.	• Define them; consider using an appositive. • Explain how they relate to more familiar terms. • Add analogies and examples to make them less abstract.
The information is categorized in an unusual or unclear way.	• Add a sentence or two making your categories explicit.
The concept seems vague.	• Compare it to something familiar. • Apply it to a real-world experience.

To Integrate Quotations Smoothly and Acknowledge Sources Properly

Problem	Suggestions for Revising
Quotations are not smoothly integrated into the text.	• Add appropriate signal phrases. • Rewrite the text to attach the quotations to the sentences before or after them.
Some quotations could just as effectively be expressed in your own words.	• Try paraphrasing the quote. • Try summarizing the material.
Sources are not acknowledged properly.	• Check Appendix 2 for the correct citation form. • Use an appositive to identify the source and establish its authority.

EDITING AND PROOFREADING

After you have revised your essay, be sure to spend some time checking for errors in usage, punctuation, and mechanics and considering matters of style. If you keep a list of errors you typically make, begin by checking your draft against this list. Ask someone else to proofread your essay before you print out a copy for your instructor or send it electronically.

From our research on student writing, we know that essays explaining concepts tend to have errors in essential or nonessential clauses beginning with *who*, *which*, or *that*, as well as errors in the use of commas to set off phrases that interrupt the flow of the sentence. Check a writer's handbook for help with these potential problems.

Reflecting on What You Have Learned

Explaining Concepts

In this chapter, you have read critically several pieces explaining a concept and have written one of your own. To better remember what you have learned, pause now to reflect on the reading and writing activities you completed in this chapter.

1. Write a page or so reflecting on what you have learned. Begin by describing what you are most pleased with in your essay. Then explain what you think contributed to your achievement. Be specific about this contribution.

   - If it was something you learned from the readings, indicate which readings and specifically what you learned from them.

   - If it came from your invention writing, point out the section or sections that helped you most.

   - If you got good advice from a critical reader, explain exactly how the person helped you—perhaps by helping you understand a particular problem in your draft or by helping you add a new dimension to your writing.

   - Try to write about your achievement in terms of what you have learned about the genre.

2. Reflect more generally on explaining concepts, a genre of writing important in education and in society. Consider some of the following questions: When doing research, did you discover that some of the information on concepts was challenged by experts? What were the grounds for the challenge? Did you think your readers might question your information? How did you decide what information might seem new or surprising to readers? Did you feel comfortable in your roles as the selector and giver of knowledge? Describe how you felt in these roles.

CHAPTER 6

Evaluation

We make evaluations every day, stating judgments about such things as food, clothes, books, classes, teachers, political candidates, television programs, performers, and films. Most of our everyday judgments simply express our personal preference: "I liked it" or "I didn't like it." But as soon as someone asks "Why?," we realize that evaluation goes beyond individual taste and needs to present an argument to support our judgment.

If you want others to take your judgment seriously, you have to give reasons for it, and your reasons must be based on shared criteria that readers recognize as appropriate for evaluating a particular type of subject. For example, in writing a review of an action film like *Mission Impossible III*, you would want to show that you are judging the film according to standards most people would use to evaluate other action films, including the first two films in the Mission Impossible series. In his ReelViews review, James Berardinelli places the film in a general category ("if you're yearning for a flashy, leave-your-brain-at-the-door summer movie"). Then he goes on to argue that even though it has all the characteristics of a summer blockbuster ("It's loud, raucous, frenetic, and blows things up real good"), he found the film disappointing because "it's testosterone without adrenaline, danger without suspense."

Berardinelli shows readers that he understands that they expect him to judge the film as an example of its genre, so he bases his judgment on qualities such as the film's special effects, its action sequences, and, most important, its ability to generate excitement—to be a thrilling cinematic roller-coaster ride. He even makes a point of saying that he is not criticizing the film's "plot contrivances" because "they go with the territory."

Readers would think Berardinelli is suffering shell shock from seeing too many action films if the reasons he gave for his judgment were that the seats in the theater were uncomfortable or that the popcorn was stale. These reasons are inappropriate for judging the quality of a film, but they are excellent criteria for judging the quality of a movie theater. For reasons to be considered appropriate, they must reflect the values or standards typically used in evaluating the kind of thing under consideration, such as a film or a car. The criteria you would use for evaluating a film obviously differ from those you would use for evaluating a car. Acting, direction, and story are common standards for judging films. Handling, safety, and styling are some of the standards used for judging cars.

Readers expect writers of evaluations both to offer appropriate reasons and to support their reasons. If one of your reasons for liking the all electric Tesla Roadster Sport is its quick acceleration, you could cite road-test results (0 to 60 mph in 3.7 seconds) as evidence. (Statistical support like this makes sense only when Tesla's rate is compared with the acceleration rates of other comparable gasoline-powered cars, such as the Porsche 911 at 0 to 60 in 4.3 seconds.) Similarly, if one of your reasons for liking a particular song is the wit and insight of the lyrics, you could quote lines as examples to show readers how witty and insightful the lyrics are. Support is important because it deals in specifics, showing exactly what value terms like *witty* and *insightful* mean to you.

As you can see, evaluation of the kind you will read and write in this chapter is intellectually rigorous. In college, you will have many opportunities to write evaluations. You may be asked to critique a book or a journal article, judge a scientific hypothesis against the results of an experiment, assess the value of conflicting interpretations of a historical event or a short story, or evaluate a class you have taken. You will also undoubtedly read evaluative writing in your courses and be tested on what you have read.

Written evaluations will almost certainly play an important part in your work life as well. On the job, you will probably be evaluated periodically and may have to evaluate people whom you supervise. It is also likely that you will be asked your opinion of various plans or proposals under consideration, and your ability to make reasonable, well-supported evaluations will affect your chances for promotion.

As the word *evaluation* suggests, evaluative arguments are basically about values, about what each of us thinks is important. Reading and writing evaluations will help you understand your own values as well as those of others. You will learn that when your basic values conflict with your readers' values, you may not be able to convince readers to accept a judgment different from their own. In such cases, you will usually want to try to give reasons to justify why you value particular criteria over others—for example, why an action film's exciting direction is more important than the plausability of its plot.

The readings in this chapter will help you learn a good deal about evaluative writing. From the readings and from the ideas for writing that follow each reading, you will get ideas for your own evaluative essay. As you read and write about the selections, keep in mind the following assignment, which sets out the goals for writing an evaluative essay. To support your writing of this assignment, the chapter concludes with a Guide to Writing Evaluations.

THE WRITING ASSIGNMENT

Evaluation

Choose a subject that you can both evaluate and make a confident judgment about. Write an essay evaluating this subject. State your judgment clearly, and back it up with reasons and support. Describe the subject for readers unfamiliar with it, and give them a context for understanding it. Your purpose is to convince readers that your judgment is informed and based on generally accepted criteria for judging this kind of subject.

WRITING SITUATIONS FOR EVALUATIONS

Following are a few examples to suggest the range of situations that may call for evaluative writing, including academic and work-related situations:

- For a conference on innovation in education, an elementary schoolteacher evaluates *Schoolhouse Rock*, an animated television series developed in the 1970s and reinvented in several new formats: books, CD-ROM learning games, and DVDs. She praises the original series as an entertaining way of presenting information, giving two reasons the series remains an effective teaching tool. Witty lyrics and catchy tunes make the information memorable, and cartoonlike visuals make the lessons pleasurable. She supports each reason by showing and discussing examples of popular *Schoolhouse Rock* segments, such as "Conjunction Junction," "We the People," and "Three Is a Magic Number." She ends by expressing her hope that teachers and developers of educational multimedia will learn from the example of *Schoolhouse Rock*.

- A supervisor reviews the work of a probationary employee. She judges the employee's performance as being adequate overall but still needing improvement in several key areas, particularly completing projects on time and communicating clearly with others. To support her judgment, she describes several problems that the employee has had over the six-month probationary period.

- An older brother, a college junior, sends an e-mail message to his younger brother, a high-school senior who is trying to decide which college to attend. Because the older brother attends one of the colleges being considered and has friends at another, he feels competent to offer advice. He centers his message on the question of what standards to use in evaluating colleges. He argues that if playing football is the primary goal, then college number one is the clear choice. But if having the opportunity to work in an award-winning scientist's genetics lab is more important, then the second college is the better choice.

Thinking about Your Experience

Evaluations

Before studying a type of writing, it is useful to spend some time thinking about what you already know about it. You may have discussed with friends or family members why a particular movie or diet is good or bad, successful or unsuccessful. You might have written evaluative essays for school about a literary text, a theatrical performance, or a scientific report.

- Recall a time when you were evaluating—orally or in writing—something you had seen, heard, read, or tried, such as a movie, performance, book, sports team, restaurant, television show, video game, or cell phone. Was your judgment all positive or all negative, or a mixture? What were your criteria for evaluation—the standards on which you based your judgment? How did you know your audience would share your criteria?

- Reflect on the evaluations you have read, heard, or seen on television or online. If you recall one of them in some detail, try to identify what made it interesting for you. How did the author try to make the evaluation convincing?

- Write at least a page about your experience with evaluations.

A GUIDE TO READING EVALUATIONS

This guide introduces you to the basic features and strategies typical of evaluative writing by looking closely at a brief but intriguing evaluation by Amitai Etzioni, a sociologist. Focus first on *reading for meaning*, looking closely at the essay's content and ideas. Then, to learn about how Etzioni tries to makes his evaluation convincing, *read like a writer* by analyzing how Etzioni crafts his essay. These two activities—reading for meaning and reading like a writer—follow every reading in this chapter.

Amitai Etzioni

Working at McDonald's

Amitai Etzioni (b. 1929) is a sociologist who has taught at Columbia, Harvard, and George Washington universities. Etzioni is a respected scholar—he served as president of the American Sociological Association as well as founding president of the Society for the Advancement of

Socio-Economics—and he is a highly visible public intellectual whose writing is read by many people outside of academia. He has written numerous articles and more than two dozen books—for example, about overcoming excessive individualism (The Spirit of Community, *1983*); *limiting the erosion of privacy in an age of technological surveillance* (The Limits of Privacy, *2004*); *and most recently, rethinking foreign policy in an age of terrorism* (Security First: For a Muscular, Moral Foreign Policy, *2007*). *Among his many awards are the Simon Wiesenthal Center's 1997 Tolerance Book Award and the Conference on Value Inquiry's award for Extraordinary Contributions to the Appreciation and Advancement of Human Values.*

The following essay was originally published in 1986 in the Miami Herald, *a major newspaper that circulates in South Florida. The original headnote identifies Etzioni as the father of five sons, including three teenagers, and points out that his son Dari helped Etzioni write this essay—although it does not say what Dari contributed.*

Before you read, think about the paying jobs you held during high school or hold now in college—not just summer jobs but those you worked during the months when school was in session. Think about what you learned that might have made you a better student and prepared you for college or for the kind of work you hope to do in the future. As you read, think about how the standards or criteria that Etzioni uses to evaluate jobs at fast-food restaurants would apply to the kinds of jobs you have held.

McDonald's is bad for your kids. I do not mean the flat patties and the white-flour buns; I refer to the jobs teen-agers undertake, mass-producing these choice items. 1

As many as two-thirds of America's high school juniors and seniors now hold down part-time paying jobs, according to studies. Many of these are in fast-food chains, of which McDonald's is the pioneer, trend-setter, and symbol. 2

At first, such jobs may seem right out of the Founding Fathers' educational manual for how to bring up self-reliant, work-ethic-driven, productive youngsters. But in fact, these jobs undermine school attendance and involvement, impart few skills that will be useful in later life, and simultaneously skew the values of teen-agers—especially their ideas about the worth of a dollar. 3

It has been a longstanding American tradition that youngsters ought to get paying jobs. In folklore, few pursuits are more deeply revered than the newspaper route and the sidewalk lemonade stand. Here the youngsters are to learn how sweet are the fruits of labor and self-discipline (papers are delivered early in the morning, rain or shine), and the ways of trade (if you price your lemonade too high or too low . . .). 4

Roy Rogers, Baskin Robbins, Kentucky Fried Chicken, et al. may at first seem nothing but a vast extension of the lemonade stand. They provide very large numbers of teen jobs, provide regular employment, pay quite well compared to many other teen jobs, and, in the modern equivalent of toiling over a hot stove, test one's stamina. 5

6   Closer examination, however, finds the McDonald's kind of job highly uneducational in several ways. Far from providing opportunities for entre-preneurship (the lemonade stand) or self-discipline, self-supervision, and self-scheduling (the paper route), most teen jobs these days are highly structured—what social scientists call "highly routinized."

7   True, you still have to have the gumption to get yourself over to the hamburger stand, but once you don the prescribed uniform, your task is spelled out in minute detail. The franchise prescribes the shape of the coffee cups; the weight, size, shape, and color of the patties; and the texture of the napkins (if any). Fresh coffee is to be made every eight minutes. And so on. There is no room for initiative, creativity, or even elementary rearrangements. These are breeding grounds for robots working for yesterday's assembly lines, not tomorrow's high-tech posts.

8   There are very few studies of the matter. One of the few is a 1984 study by Ivan Charper and Bryan Shore Fraser. The study relies mainly on what teen-agers write in response to questionnaires rather than actual obser-vations of fast-food jobs. The authors argue that the employees develop many skills such as how to operate a food-preparation machine and a cash register. However, little attention is paid to how long it takes to acquire such a skill, or what its significance is.

9   What does it matter if you spend 20 minutes to learn to use a cash register, and then—"operate" it? What skill have you acquired? It is a long way from learning to work with a lathe or carpenter tools in the olden days or to program computers in the modern age.

10   A 1980 study by A. V. Harrell and P. W. Wirtz found that, among those students who worked at least 25 hours per week while in school, their unemployment rate four years later was half of that of seniors who did not work. This is an impressive statistic. It must be seen, though, together with the finding that many who begin as part-time employees in fast-food chains drop out of high school and are gobbled up in the world of low-skill jobs.

11   Some say that while these jobs are rather unsuited for college-bound, white, middle-class youngsters, they are "ideal" for lower-class, "non-academic," minority youngsters. Indeed, minorities are "over-represented" in these jobs (21 percent of fast-food employees). While it is true that these places provide income, work, and even some training to such youngsters, they also tend to perpetuate their disadvantaged status. They provide no career ladders, few marketable skills, and undermine school attendance and involvement.

12   The hours are often long. Among those 14 to 17, a third of fast-food employees (including some school dropouts) labor more than 30 hours per week, according to the Charper-Fraser study. Only 20 percent work 15 hours or less. The rest: between 15 and 30 hours.

13   Often the stores close late, and after closing one must clean up and tally up. In affluent Montgomery County, Md., where child labor would

not seem to be a widespread economic necessity, 24 percent of the seniors at one high school in 1985 worked as much as five to seven days a week; 27 percent, three to five. There is just no way such amounts of work will not interfere with school work, especially homework. In an informal survey published in the most recent yearbook of the high school, 58 percent of the seniors acknowledged that their jobs interfere with their school work.

The Charper-Fraser study sees merit in learning teamwork and working 14 under supervision. The authors have a point here. However, it must be noted that such learning is not automatically educational or wholesome. For example, much of the supervision in fast-food places leans toward teaching one the wrong kinds of compliance: blind obedience, or shared alienation with the "boss."

Supervision is often both tight and woefully inappropriate. Today, fast- 15 food chains and other such places of work (record shops, bowling alleys) keep costs down by having teens supervise teens with often no adult on the premises.

There is no father or mother figure with which to identify, to emulate, 16 to provide a role model and guidance. The work-culture varies from one place to another: Sometimes it is a tightly run shop (must keep the cash registers ringing); sometimes a rather loose pot party interrupted by customers. However, only rarely is there a master to learn from, or much worth learning. Indeed, far from being places where solid adult work values are being transmitted, these are places where all too often delinquent teen values dominate. Typically, when my son Oren was dishing out ice cream for Baskin Robbins in upper Manhattan, his fellow teen-workers considered him a sucker for not helping himself to the till. Most youngsters felt they were entitled to $50 severance "pay" on their last day on the job.

The pay, oddly, is the part of the teen work-world that is most diffi- 17 cult to evaluate. The lemonade stand or paper route money was for your allowance. In the old days, apprentices learning a trade from a master contributed most, if not all, of their income to their parents' household. Today, the teen pay may be low by adult standards, but it is often, especially in the middle class, spent largely or wholly by the teens. That is, the youngsters live free at home ("after all, they are high school kids") and are left with very substantial sums of money.

Where this money goes is not quite clear. Some use it to sup- 18 port themselves, especially among the poor. More middle-class kids set some money aside to help pay for college, or save it for a major purchase—often a car. But large amounts seem to flow to pay for an early introduction into the most trite aspects of American consumerism: flimsy punk clothes, trinkets, and whatever else is the last fast-moving teen craze.

19   One may say that this is only fair and square; they are being good American consumers and spend their money on what turns them on. At least, a cynic might add, these funds do not go into illicit drugs and booze. On the other hand, an educator might bemoan that these young, yet unformed individuals, so early in life driven to buy objects of no intrinsic educational, cultural, or social merit, learn so quickly the dubious merit of keeping up with the Joneses in ever-changing fads, promoted by mass merchandising.

20   Many teens find the instant reward of money, and the youth status symbols it buys, much more alluring than credits in calculus courses, European history, or foreign languages. No wonder quite a few would rather skip school—and certainly homework—and instead work longer at a Burger King. Thus, most teen work these days is not providing early lessons in work ethic; it fosters escape from school and responsibilities, quick gratification, and a short cut to the consumeristic aspects of adult life.

21   Thus, parents should look at teen employment not as automatically educational. It is an activity—like sports—that can be turned into an educational opportunity. But it can also easily be abused. Youngsters must learn to balance the quest for income with the needs to keep growing and pursue other endeavors that do not pay off instantly—above all education.

22   Go back to school.

READING FOR MEANING

This section presents three activities that will help you think about the meanings in "Working at McDonald's."

Read to Comprehend

Write a few sentences briefly summarizing Etzioni's argument about the value of part-time jobs for teenagers.

Identify any words with meanings you are unsure of—such as *skew* (paragraph 3), *intrinsic* (paragraph 19), and *dubious* (19)—and find the dictionary definition for each word that makes the best sense in the context.

To help you understand the essay better, also consider trying one of these critical reading strategies, explained in Appendix 1: *outlining* or *summarizing*.

Read to Respond

Write a paragraph or two exploring your initial thoughts and feelings about Etzioni's evaluation. Focus on anything that stands out for you, perhaps because it resonates with your own experience or because you find a statement puzzling. For example, consider writing about one of the following:

- Etzioni's assertion that McDonald's-type jobs "skew the values of teen-agers—especially their ideas about the worth of a dollar" (paragraph 3);

- the "longstanding American tradition that youngsters ought to get paying jobs" (4)—considering the reasons for this tradition or whether it is a tradition that other cultures with which you are familiar share;

- Etzioni's argument that working while attending school interferes with school work (13), perhaps in relation to your own work and school experience; or

- how Etzioni's description of McDonald's-type jobs reminds you of the kind of work you have done.

To help develop your response, also consider trying one of these critical reading strategies, explained in Appendix 1: *contextualizing, recognizing emotional manipulation*, or *judging the writer's credibility*.

Read to Analyze Assumptions

All writing contains *assumptions*—ideas and attitudes that are taken for granted as commonly accepted truths. Personal or individual assumptions also tend to reflect the values and beliefs of a particular community, which help shape the way those in the group think, act, and understand the world. All writing reflects assumptions held by the writer, but assumptions held by others, such as readers or sources cited by the writer, may also be present. Sometimes assumptions are stated explicitly, but often they are only implied, so you may have to search for underlying assumptions in the word choices and examples.

Why go to the effort to analyze assumptions in a reading? Assumptions have powerful effects. They influence our opinions and judgments by leading us to value some things and devalue others. These effects are even more powerful because they are taken for granted, often accepted without question by those who hold them. To understand a reading on a deep level, then, it is necessary to bring its assumptions to the surface and to question them. To think critically about assumptions, here are some kinds of questions you could ask: Who holds this assumption (the writer, readers, and/or others cited in the essay)? What are the effects of the assumption in the context of the essay specifically or in society more generally? What do you think about the assumption, and is there anything in the essay that raises doubts about it? How does the assumption reinforce or critique commonly held views, and are there any alternative ideas, beliefs, or values that would challenge this assumption?

Write a paragraph or two analyzing an assumption in Etzioni's essay. You might choose an assumption from the list below, using the questions accompanying it in addition to the ones above to help you get started. Or you can choose another assumption in the essay to explore.

- **assumptions about the usefulness of certain skills.** Etzioni asserts that fast-food jobs "impart few skills that will be useful in later life" (paragraph 3). For example, he claims they do not provide "opportunities for entrepreneurship . . . or self-discipline, self-supervision, and self-scheduling" (6) and "[t]here is no room for initiative, creativity" (7).

  To think critically about the assumptions in this essay related to what skills are learned at fast-food jobs and how useful they are, ask yourself questions like these: How different, really, is delivering newspapers from working at McDonald's in terms of the skills learned about discipline, scheduling, and so on? Similarly, what more is a young person likely to learn about entrepreneurship by operating a lemonade stand than by working in a fast-food restaurant (4)? What other kinds of skills do teens learn when working at fast-food restaurants, and what potential use do you think these skills have in future life?

- **assumptions about the culture of consumerism.** Toward the end of the essay, Etzioni complains that the things teenagers choose to buy with the money they earn from fast-food jobs represent "the most trite aspects of American consumerism: flimsy punk clothes, trinkets, and whatever else is the last fast-moving teen craze" (18). By referring to consumerism—enthusiastic spending on material possessions such as clothes, entertainment, and other consumer goods—as "American," Etzioni makes clear he is referring to something that is not limited to teenagers. Nevertheless, his focus on teens—what they buy and why they buy it—reveals Etzioni's ideas about teenagers' indoctrination into a consumerist culture.

  To think critically about the assumptions in this essay related to American consumerism, ask yourself questions like these: Etzioni uses the words *trite, flimsy,* and *trinkets* to criticize the things teens buy, but if teens purchased items that were original, well-made, and valuable, do you think he would still object? What might he be criticizing other than teenagers' taste? In referring to "fads" and "mass merchandising," he seems to assume teens are especially vulnerable to the influence of advertising (19). To what extent, if any, do you agree?

To help you analyze assumptions in Etzioni's essay, also consider trying one of these critical reading strategies, explained Appendix 1: *reflecting on challenges to your beliefs and values* or *evaluating the logic of an argument.*

READING LIKE A WRITER

This section leads you through an analysis of Etzioni's evaluative writing strategies: *presenting the subject, asserting an overall judgment, giving reasons and support,* and *anticipating objections and alternative judgments.* For each strategy, you will be asked to reread and annotate part of Etzioni's essay to see how he uses the strategy to accomplish his particular purpose.

When you study the selections later in this chapter, you will see how different writers of evaluative essays use these same strategies. The Guide to Writing Evaluations near the end of the chapter suggests ways you can use these strategies in your own writing.

Presenting the Subject

Writers must present the subject so readers know what is being judged. Writers can simply name the subject, but usually they describe it in some detail. A film reviewer, for example, might identify the actors, describe the characters they play, and tell some of the plot. As a critical reader, you may notice that the language used to present the subject also may serve to evaluate it. Therefore, you should look closely at how the subject is presented. Note where the writer's information about the subject comes from, whether the information is reliable, and whether anything important seems to have been left out.

Analyze

1. Reread paragraphs 5 to 7, 9, 12, 15, and 16, and underline the factual details that describe the people who work at fast-food restaurants and what they do.

2. Identify the details in these paragraphs that you accept as valid as well as details you think are inaccurate or only partially true.

3. Consider whether any important information you know about fast-food jobs is missing from Etzioni's presentation of them.

Write

Write several sentences explaining what readers learn about the subject from the way Etzioni presents it, giving specific examples from the reading to support your explanation. Add another sentence or two evaluating Etzioni's presentation of the subject in terms of its accuracy and completeness.

Asserting an Overall Judgment

A writer's overall judgment of the subject is the main point of an evaluative essay, asserting that the subject is good or bad, or better or worse than something comparable. Although readers expect a definitive judgment, they also appreciate a balanced one that acknowledges, for example, any good qualities of a subject judged overall to be bad. Evaluations usually explicitly state the judgment up front in the form of a thesis and may restate it in different ways throughout the essay.

Analyze

1. Reread paragraphs 3, 20, and 21, where Etzioni states his overall judgment, and consider whether you find his statements clear.

2. Decide whether Etzioni changes his initial judgment in any way when he restates it in somewhat different language at the end of the essay. Consider why he restates his judgment.

Write

Write a few sentences describing and evaluating Etzioni's assertion of his overall judgment.

Giving Reasons and Support

Any evaluative argument must explain and justify the writer's judgment. To be convincing, the reasons given must be recognized by readers as appropriate for evaluating the type of subject under consideration. That is, the reasons must reflect the values or standards of judgment that people typically use in similar situations. The reasons also must be supported by relevant examples, quotations, facts, statistics, or personal anecdotes. This support may come from the writer's own knowledge or experience, from that of other people, and from published materials.

Analyze

1. Etzioni names three principal reasons for his judgment in the final sentence of paragraph 3. Underline these reasons, and then consider the appropriateness of each one given Etzioni's intended readers—the largely middle-class adult subscribers to the *Miami Herald*. Why do you think they would or would not likely accept each reason as appropriate for evaluating part-time jobs for teenagers? What objections, if any, might a critical reader have to Etzioni's reasoning?

2. One reason Etzioni gives to clarify his view that working at McDonald's is "bad" for students is that the jobs "impart few skills that will be useful in later life" (3). Etzioni then attempts to support (to argue for) this reason in paragraphs 4 to 9. Reread these paragraphs noticing the kinds of support Etzioni relies on.

3. Evaluate how well Etzioni supports his argument in paragraphs 4 to 9. Why do you think his readers will or will not find the argument convincing? Which supporting details might they find most convincing? Least convincing?

Write

Write several sentences reporting what you have learned about how Etzioni uses reasons and support as an evaluative writing strategy in his essay. Give examples (from paragraphs 4 to 9) of the type of support he provides for the "impart few skills" reason. Write a few more sentences explaining how convincing you think his readers will find this support.

Anticipating Objections and Alternative Judgments

Sometimes reviewers try to anticipate and respond to readers' possible objections and alternative judgments. For example, some parents with children in high school may not be persuaded by Etzioni's reasons for criticizing a readily available source of income. A relatively poor family, for instance, might firmly oppose his judgment, seeing part-time work at McDonald's as good for high-school students who must buy their own clothes and pay for their entertainment. Other parents may object to Etzioni's comparing a fast-food job unfavorably to a job selling lemonade or delivering newspapers.

Etzioni certainly is aware that some readers have objections in mind. These objections do not cause him to waver in his own judgment, as you have seen, but they do persuade him to respond by counterarguing. Aside from simply acknowledging that others disagree, there are two basic ways to counterargue. A writer can *refute* readers' objections, arguing that they are simply wrong, or *accommodate* objections, acknowledging that they are justified but do not damage the writer's overall judgment. Etzioni uses both refutation and accommodation in his counterarguments.

Analyze

1. Reread paragraphs 8 to 11, 14, and 19, where Etzioni brings up either a reader's likely objection or an alternative judgment about the worth of part-time work. (Some alternative judgments are attributed to researchers rather than readers, though it is likely some readers would have similar ideas.) Underline the alternative judgment or objection in each of these paragraphs.

2. Choose any two of these counterarguments, and then look closely at Etzioni's strategy. Decide first whether he refutes or accommodates the objection or alternative judgment. Then note how he goes about doing so.

3. Evaluate whether Etzioni's counterarguments are likely to convince skeptical readers to accept his views.

Write

Write several sentences identifying the objections and alternative judgments against which Etzioni counterargues. Describe his counterarguments, and evaluate how persuasive they are likely to be with his intended audience.

READINGS

James Berardinelli

Avatar

James Berardinelli has an unusual background for a film critic in that he earned both bachelor's and master's degrees in electrical engineering and for many years worked in that field. He became interested in film in college, and now that he is a reviewer, he sees over two hundred theatrical releases a year. He has posted on his own ReelViews *Web site over 3,300 full-length movie reviews, and he also contributes to such other film review sites as* Rotten Tomatoes. *In addition, Berardinelli writes a blog,* ReelThoughts, *in which he discusses issues such as film piracy and censorship. Collections of his* ReelViews *reviews have been published in several editions, with a foreword by Roger Ebert that calls Berardinelli "literate, opinionated, well-informed, and a good writer." This review of* Avatar *appeared originally on* ReelViews *in December 2009.*

As you read Berardinelli's review, notice that the opening paragraph reminds readers of the context in which he is writing—specifically, the high level of anticipation and hype about the film's 3D photography. Berardinelli does not assume people are reading this particular review, as they do reviews of most films, to decide whether or not to see the film. He assumes they are waiting eagerly to see it. Given that situation, why do you think he devotes so much of his essay to discussing the film's plot?

Why do you think Berardinelli begins with superlatives like *most?*

Avatar has been described as a "game-changer," and perhaps it is. I'll leave that for future historians to determine. What I can say with some assuredness is this is the most technically amazing motion picture to have arrived on screens in many years—perhaps since Peter Jackson's *The Return of the King*. It's also among the most anticipated openings of the decade. Expectations can be a double-edged sword; ask George Lucas. But when a filmmaker meets or exceeds them, the results are tremendous, and that's the case with *Avatar*. James Cameron has a lot riding on this film, his long-delayed follow-up to *Titanic* (which came out an even dozen years ago), the all-time box office champion in unadjusted dollars. Under "normal" circumstances, at stake would have been only Cameron's reputation and future autonomy with astronomical budgets. But Cameron has hitched his wagon to 3D and declared this to be the wave of the future. Watching *Avatar*, I can almost believe it. If every filmmaker could do with 3D what Cameron achieves, I'd gladly wear the uncomfortable glasses to every screening.

1

This visual is one of the original *Avatar* posters displayed in the United States. The Analyzing Visuals activity on p. 302 invites you to compare it with other posters displayed here and abroad.

2   *Avatar* is entertainment of the highest order. It's the best movie of 2009. In 3D, it's immersive (that's the buzzword everyone uses for the 3D experience), but the traditional film elements—story, character, editing, theme, emotional resonance, etc.—are presented with sufficient expertise to make even the 2D version an engrossing 2½-hour experience. Despite expending an extraordinary amount of time, money, and effort

Why do you think Berardinelli emphasizes *Avatar*'s "traditional film elements"?

perfecting the 3D elements, Cameron never lost sight of what's important. His narrative could almost be considered a science fiction version of *Dances with Wolves* (by way of *Surrogates*), and it works for many of the reasons *Dances* worked. Cameron also borrows from his own catalog. The space/military culture is reminiscent of that in *Aliens* and the cross-cultural romance recalls *Titanic*. *Avatar* doesn't have Leonardo DiCaprio but its love story is in some ways more potent than the one told in *Titanic* because the stakes are higher. From a purely visual perspective, Cameron gives us one of the most amazing presentations ever of an alien world and builds toward an epic clash that may only have been matched twice previously in movie theaters (both times by Peter Jackson).

What does referencing these other films contribute to the evaluation?

Avatar takes us to the planet Pandora in the year 2154. 3 Pandora is a jungle world at which Earthmen have arrived with the intention of performing some strip-mining. Although corporations run the show, the military, led by Colonel Miles Quaritch (Stephen Lang), is on hand to provide protection and lend support. The humans' engagements with the indigenous humanoid population, the 10-foot high, blue-skinned Na'vi, have been contentious, bordering on hostile. For a while, Dr. Grace Augustine (Sigourney Weaver) had some success interacting with the natives by using "avatars" (synthetic Na'vi remotely controlled by humans) to provide education and technological advancement, but progress slowed and Grace was closed out of Na'vi society. Now, she and her group of avatars are trying to find a way back in.

That portal comes in the unlikely person of Jake Sully 4 (Sam Worthington), a paraplegic ex-marine. Sam's journey to Pandora is a fluke. His twin brother, who had trained for years to inhabit an avatar and whose genetic identity was imprinted upon one, died unexpectedly and Jake was the only one who could take his place. He is caught between two masters: Colonel Quaritch, who wants the soldier to form a bond with the Na'vi so he can pass back valuable tactical information, and Grace, who wants to rebuild the lines of communication. A series of events in the jungle separate Jake from the other avatars and place him in mortal danger. His life is saved by Neytiri (Zoe Saldana), who distrusts him but believes he is touched by the Na'vi god. She takes him to the "home tree" where he must not only plead for his life but

Why include plot detail in a film review? Is too much given away?

for the opportunity to learn their ways. Neytiri becomes his mentor and he soon finds himself more in sympathy with his blue-skinned "brothers" than with Colonel Quaritch, who is planning a massive operation to relocate the Na'vi away from a rich load of ore.

5   Most 3D films use the technology as a gimmick—a means to prompt younger audience members to "ooh" and "aah." That's not the case here. Cameron's film is immersive because the 3D was ingrained in its cinematic DNA. He has compensated for the pervasive dimness caused by polarized lenses by increasing the brightness (the images look too bright when viewed without the glasses). He has avoided 3D "tricks" (throwing things at the audience) that might take the viewer out of the experience. *Avatar*'s visuals are so sumptuous that, perhaps as little as ten minutes into the movie, I forgot I was wearing the glasses. I'm still not as bullish as Cameron about the future of 3D, but I see potential where I had not previously perceived it.

Why do you think Berardinelli raises the question of whether Avatar's use of 3D is a "gimmick"?

6   Cameron understands how the pieces of the puzzle need to come together to form a complete motion picture, and he assembles them as only a master can. The story, although simple, resonates deeply at a time when media battles rage about whether or not humanity is destroying itself and its planet. As with *Dances with Wolves* and *The Last Samurai*, this is about a military man who finds himself transformed by the culture he adopts and ends up opposing his own people in an impossible battle. Jake's love affair with Neytiri confirms Cameron as being a romantic at heart. The Pandora menagerie is like something out of a dungeon master's wet dream: dinosaur-like creatures that are impervious to bullets, vicious carnivores that make T-Rexes look tame, scavengers that roam and attack in packs, dragon-like flying creatures that populate the skies, and vegetation that's just as alive as the animals. The blue-skinned Na'vi, clearly modeled after the Native Americans, are among the most "ordinary" of Pandora's inhabitants.

Why is it important that the story "resonates" for viewers?

7   All movies like this must have a villain; *Avatar* provides two. The first is the bureaucrat, Parker Selfridge (Giovanni Ribisi), who is devoted to the profit margin above all else. Any resemblance to the Paul Reiser character in *Aliens* is intentional. Maybe Cameron was thinking of the studio bosses controlling his budget

The highlighted phrase refers to genre conventions— expectations viewers have for particular kinds of films. How useful is it to evaluate this film in terms of genre conventions?

when he created Selfridge. Then there's Colonel Quaritch, who is brought brilliantly to life by the scene-
stealing performance of Stephen Lang. This man's a
real sonofabitch, but it's impossible not to admire him
on one level. Like Robert Duvall in *Apocalypse Now*,
he loves the smell of napalm in the morning . . . at noon,
and during the night. Quaritch is never CGI animated
but he always seems bigger than life. If there's a human
star of *Avatar*, it's Lang.

Lang may have the showiest role but he's not the   8
only actor to do a creditable job. Sam Worthington and
Sigourney Weaver are both solid, even though a good
portion of their characters' screen time is animated.
Zoe Saldana is even more challenged, since she never
appears "in the flesh." Like Andy Serkis' Gollum, she is
entirely CGI-rendered, but she accomplished her own
motion capture work and provided the voice. Michelle
Rodriguez, like Stephen Lang, is never required to become
blue. Her role is secondary but unambiguously heroic.
Weaver's presence affirms that, as bad as Cameron's
reputation as a taskmaster may be, there are actors who
appreciate his perfectionist approach. (Others in this
group include Michael Biehn, Arnold Schwarzenegger,
Bill Paxton, and Linda Hamilton.)

Why does Berardinelli bring
up others' criticism?

After the late summer 20-minute preview of *Avatar*,   9
there was some unease about the look of the Na'vi.
Such concerns are baseless. They can appear opposite
humans without the special effects being called into
question; we never view them as anything less than
three-dimensional. Like Gollum, they transcend their
pixel-based conception. We believe them. We accept
them. We care about them. That's the key to *Avatar*
being more than a hollow spectacle. In *Transformers 2*,
everything (including the humans) is soulless. Here,
there's heart and soul to spare.

Does a film review really
need to point out what's
good and bad in order to be
complete?

Any criticisms I have of *Avatar* are in the nature of nit-   10
picks, but I will mention them for completeness' sake. At
worst, they are ephemeral distractions, easily dismissed.
At best, they will not be noticed at all. Sam Worthington's performance is solid but his American accent is not.
As was evident in *Terminator: Salvation*, Worthington's
"American" sometimes comes with an Aussie twang.
Visually, *Avatar* is almost flawless, but there are some
instances when the camera moves so fast that the 3D

effect doesn't track well, resulting in a brief moment of disorientation. Finally, although James Horner's score is predominantly effective, there are instances in which he again engages in self-cannibalization. Material sounding a lot like it originated in his often-used *Star Trek II* and *Aliens* scores pops up from time-to-time.

11   *Avatar* is the most engaging and enthralling motion picture I have experienced this year—and *experience* is the appropriate word. There's a rush associated with coming to Pandora; this feels more like an interactive endeavor than a passive one. In addition to being emotionally satisfying and one hell of a wild ride, *Avatar* boasts a smart script, reminding us that would-be blockbusters don't have to be defined by the imbecility of a *Transformers 2* or a *2012*. James Cameron has been entertaining movie-goers for more than a quarter century and he is in an elite category of filmmakers who has yet to spawn a dog. For quality like this, I'm willing to wait, although hopefully his next movie will come a little more quickly than the 12 years of *Avatar*'s gestation.

How effective is this way to end the review?

READING FOR MEANING

This section presents three activities that will help you think about the meanings in Berardinelli's film review.

Read to Comprehend

Write a few sentences identifying Berardinelli's reasons for his overall judgment of the film *Avatar*.

Identify any words with meanings you are unsure of—such as *autonomy* (paragraph 1) and *immersive* (2)—and find the dictionary definition for each word that makes the best sense in the context.

To help you understand the essay better, also consider trying one of these critical reading strategies, explained in Appendix 1: *summarizing* or *questioning to understand and remember*.

Read to Respond

Write several paragraphs exploring your initial thoughts and feelings about Berardinelli's review. Focus on anything that stands out for you, perhaps because it resonates with your own experience or because you find a statement puzzling. You might consider writing about the following:

- Berardinelli's judgment that "*Avatar* is entertainment of the highest order. It's the best movie of 2009" (paragraph 2)— perhaps in relation to your own evaluation of the film, if you have seen it;

- the assertion that Cameron "has avoided 3D 'tricks' (throwing things at the audience) that might take the viewer out of the experience"(5) and instead used 3D to immerse viewers in the cinematic experience (2); or

- the idea that "although simple," *Avatar*'s story "resonates deeply," especially because the movie came out at "a time when media battles rage about whether or not humanity is destroying itself and its planet" (6).

To help develop your response, also consider trying one of these critical reading strategies, explained in Appendix 1: *contextualizing* or *reflecting on challenges to your beliefs and values*.

Read to Analyze Assumptions

Write a paragraph or two analyzing an assumption in Berardinelli's essay. To think critically about assumptions, here are some kinds of questions you could ask: Who holds this assumption (the writer, readers, and/or others cited in the essay)? What are the effects of the assumption in the context of the essay specifically or in society more generally? What do you think about the assumption, and is there anything in the essay that raises doubts about it? How does the assumption reinforce or critique commonly held views, and are there any alternative ideas, beliefs, or values that would challenge this assumption?

You might choose an assumption from the list below, using the questions accompanying it in addition to the ones above to help you get started. Or you can choose another assumption in the essay to explore.

- **assumptions about the value of being immersed in the experience.** The idea that the experience of watching *Avatar* is "immersive" is introduced in paragraph 2, repeated in paragraph 5, and reinforced using different words—*engaging, enthralling,* and *interactive* rather than *passive*—at the end of the essay in paragraph 11.

  To think critically about the assumptions in this essay related to the value of being immersed in the experience of watching a film, ask yourself questions like these: What do you think Berardinelli and others who use this "buzzword" *immersive* to describe "the 3D experience" mean by it (2)? How is the experience of watching 3D films interactive and not passive? If you have had any other media experience that you thought was also immersive, what was it? What are the advantages of being immersed in such an experience rather than remaining detached from it? What might be the dangers?

- **assumptions about morality.** "All movies like this," Berardinelli claims in paragraph 7, "must have a villain." Then he goes on to identify two villains in *Avatar*: "the bureaucrat . . . who is devoted to the profit margin above all else" and "Colonel Quaritch." Berardinelli describes *Avatar* as "an epic clash" (2) between corporate Earthmen and their military support, on the one hand, and Pandora's indigenous population and the "unlikely person of Jake Sully" (4), on the other hand.

To think critically about the assumptions in this essay regarding morality, ask yourself questions like these: What kinds of movie do you think Berardinelli is talking about when he refers to "movies like this"? How is morality typically defined in such films? Think of an example in which the moral boundaries between the good guys and the bad guys is clearly defined. Think of another example of a film where morality is presented as more ambiguous, so much so that the good guys look a lot like the bad guys, and vice versa.

To help you analyze assumptions in Berardinelli's essay, also consider trying one of these critical reading strategies, explained in Appendix 1: *reflecting on challenges to your beliefs and values* or *looking for patterns of opposition*.

READING LIKE A WRITER

PRESENTING THE SUBJECT

Writers of evaluative essays usually begin by naming and describing their subject, but often they provide only enough information to give readers a context for the judgment. However, certain kinds of evaluations—such as book, musical performance, television, and film reviews—may require more information because readers are trying to decide whether to buy the book, attend the performance, or see the film or television program. Reviewers of these kinds of subjects carefully choose details that help readers make a decision. Film reviews, for example, typically identify the actors and director, describe the setting, tell a little about the plot without giving too much away, and identify the film by genre or type. Informing readers about the genre is especially important because different genres have different criteria to meet. All films may be evaluated on the basis of the acting, directing, screenwriting, and so on. But comedies have to be funny, and action films have to be exciting. Therefore, as a critical reader, you will want to think about how Berardinelli classifies and judges *Avatar*.

Analyze

1. Underline the words in paragraph 2 that Berardinelli uses to suggest different categories or genres of films, beginning with "science fiction," to which *Avatar* could be compared. Notice that for each genre, Berardinelli also gives an example of a film that could be compared to *Avatar*.

2. What criteria or standards do people usually use when evaluating films in the various genres Berardinelli refers to, and what does *Avatar* have in common with the other films he mentions?

Write

Write a few sentences discussing how Berardinelli classifies *Avatar* and why he suggests it fits into more than one category. Add a sentence or two discussing how classifying the film in these ways affects his judgment of *Avatar*.

CONSIDERING IDEAS FOR YOUR OWN WRITING

Consider writing an evaluation of a film, a television show or series, or another visual or media event. Instead of trying to think of a particular film, try first choosing a genre (such as comedy, action, fantasy, documentary, and so on) that you know well. Familiarity with the genre will enable you to base your argument on criteria or standards that people typically apply to that genre. Moreover, you will be able to make comparisons with other examples of the genre with which your readers may be familiar. Remember that you can argue, as Berardinelli does, that the film has characteristics of several genres. The way the film combines genre features may be praiseworthy or not. Remember that you do not have to write an all-positive or all-negative evaluation. A mixed review can be just as valuable to readers.

ANALYZING VISUALS

Write a paragraph analyzing the poster Berardinelli displayed along with his review and explaining what it contributes to the essay. Alternatively, you could go online to find two or more *Avatar* posters to analyze and compare. To do the analysis, you can use the criteria chart in Appendix 3 on pp. 670–72. Don't feel you have to answer all of the questions on the chart: focus on those that seem most productive in helping you write a paragraph-length analysis. To help you get started, consider adding these questions that specifically refer to posters for *Avatar*:

- How does the poster or posters represent 3D photography?

- What does the poster or posters reveal about the story?

- What do you learn about the characters from the direction they are looking, their expressions, their relationship?

For additional help, refer to Appendix 3: Analyzing Visuals.

Tom Maurstad

Avatar

Tom Maurstad writes about entertainment, film, and media for the Dallas Morning News, *where this review of* Avatar *was originally published. As you read this review, think about how it compares with the review by Berardinelli and your own judgment of the film, if you have seen it.*

Maybe one day future film historians will point back to *Avatar* and proclaim it a crucial work. Maybe they will say that it was an early 21st-century film that signaled what would become a new kind of film experience. Maybe they will highlight it as the essential film that introduced a new synthesis of real and virtual, human and machine, video game and movie. Maybe.

But the one thing they won't do is declare *Avatar* a great movie, for the simple reason that, all buzz and hype notwithstanding, it isn't.

It's misleading to give *Avatar*, the new sci-fi action-fantasy film from writer-director James Cameron, a single thumbs-up or -down reaction when, really, it is two experiences. There is *Avatar* as an unconditionally innovative achievement providing the latest and greatest in 3-D photography and computer-generated imagery: the new. And there is *Avatar* as a clumsy and cliché-filled drama: the old. The new *Avatar* gets an A; the old *Avatar* gets an F (earning its C average).

If you go to *Avatar* to see what $300 million looks like, you won't be disappointed. Cameron knows how to get a bang for his bucks and fills the screen with dazzling sights, from the early scenes of humans floating through the high-tech cavern of their spaceship to the money-shot sequences of the alien Na'vi swooping over their jungle planet on the backs of giant flying lizards.

Speaking of the Na'vi and their jungle planet brings us to the awkward center beneath the surface dazzle—the story. *Avatar* is set in some indeterminate future (press notes say 2154, but the movie never makes that clear). Humans, in the form of some all-powerful and seemingly American corporation, are stationed on the Na'vi planet to extract some rare and fantastically valuable mineral (or metal—again, unclear). Why do they want it and what makes it so valuable? Who knows? It's this movie's MacGuffin, there to drive the actions of the characters without making any particular sense to the story.

Our hero is Jake Sully (Sam Worthington), a paraplegic soldier whose twin brother, we quickly learn, died while working on the Avatar project on the Na'vi's planet. Since Jake is his genetic double, he takes his brother's place. The Avatar project is led by a passionate but cantankerous doctor, Grace Augustine (Sigourney Weaver). She and her research team have developed a system to mix human DNA with alien DNA to create Na'vi bodies that humans can animate with their minds through a high-tech contraption that looks like a tanning bed.

7   Dr. Augustine is doing this as her Jane Goodall-like mission to learn all she can about this alien tribe; the corporation funding her is doing it as a way of getting the tribe to move off its holy homeland without resorting to wholesale slaughter. This evil imperialist agenda is represented by the heartless corporate exec (Giovanni Ribisi) intent on getting to untapped treasure one way or another. His right-hand man is the cartoonish mercenary, Col. Miles Quaritch (Stephen Lang), who is little more than an amalgam of leatherneck clichés.

8   And stuck in the middle is Jake, who quickly embraces his fleet-footed alternate reality as a Na'vi. He meets and falls in love with Neytiri (Zoe Saldana), the chief's daughter, and becomes an important leader in the tribe. Just think Kevin Costner in *Dances with Wolves*, only with blue skin and a tail.

9   So *Avatar* sets about telling you a story you already know and have seen many times before. The Na'vi natives are pure and innocent; the white-man interlopers are evil and corrupt, but the one good white man joins the natives and is determined to save them.

10   At more than 2½ hours, *Avatar* is full of overlong sequences of flying and fighting in which Cameron just can't resist showcasing all the cool things he can do with his computers and cameras. And it is cool. But all this "change the way you look at films" hype is just that. While *Avatar* is impressively seamless, you're never fooled. This doesn't look like a documentary film; it looks like a video game.

11   And if I could have been the avatar instead of watching *Avatar*, this experience would have been a lot more fun. Maybe that will be its lasting legacy. *Avatar* is the first major film pointing us to a future in which its video-game version is the bigger and better platform.

READING FOR MEANING

This section presents three activities that will help you think about the meanings in Maurstad's film review.

Read to Comprehend

Write a sentence or two explaining on what basis Maurstad is judging *Avatar*.
Identify any words with meanings you are unsure of—such as *synthesis* (paragraph 1) and *interlopers* (9)—and find the dictionary definition for each word that makes the best sense in the context.
To help you understand the essay better, also consider trying one of these critical reading strategies, explained in Appendix 1: *summarizing* or *questioning to understand and remember*.

Read to Respond

Write several paragraphs exploring your initial thoughts and feelings about Maurstad's film review. Focus on anything that stands out for you, perhaps because it resonates with your own experience or because you find a statement puzzling. You might consider writing about the following:

- Maurstad's judgment of the film—perhaps in relation to your own judgment;

- Maurstad's questioning of the film's story, in particular the use of a "MacGuffin," a cinematic device that activates the plot but may be vague and fades in importance as the story unfolds (paragraph 5); or

- Maurstad's comparison of Dr. Augustine to the real Jane Goodall, the scientist who studies chimpanzees in their natural habitat (7).

To help develop your response, also consider trying one of these critical reading strategies, explained in Appendix 1: *contextualizing* or *reflecting on challenges to your beliefs and values*.

Read to Analyze Assumptions

Write a paragraph or two analyzing an assumption in Maurstad's essay. To think critically about assumptions, here are some kinds of questions you could ask: Who holds this assumption (the writer, readers, and/or others cited in the essay)? What are the effects of the assumption in the context of the essay specifically or in society more generally? What do you think about the assumption, and is there anything in the essay that raises doubts about it? How does the assumption reinforce or critique commonly held views, and are there any alternative ideas, beliefs, or values that would challenge this assumption?

You might choose an assumption from the list below, using the questions accompanying it in addition to the ones above to help you get started. Or you can choose another assumption in the essay to explore.

- **the assumption that predictability is a fault in storytelling**. Maurstad claims that *Avatar* tells "a story you already know and have seen many times before" (paragraph 9), a description not intended as a compliment. In contrast to its technical innovations, he claims the film's plot and characters are "cliché-filled" (3).

  To think critically about this assumption that predictability is a bad thing in storytelling, ask yourself questions like these: If you have seen the film, do you agree with Maurstad that *Avatar*'s story has been told many times before? Whether or not you have seen this particular film, what do you think of Maurstad's assumption that retelling a familiar plot is not a good thing? The word *cliché* is used to indicate something is unoriginal and predictable. Is predictability in a film's story and characterization necessarily a shortcoming? Or do you think Maurstad is especially dis-appointed that James Cameron chose this particular story to retell: "The Na'vi natives are pure and innocent; the white-man interlopers are evil and corrupt, but the one good white man joins the natives and is deter-mined to save them" (9)?

- **assumptions about the value of different media.** Maurstad talks about *Avatar* being hyped as a new experience, "a new synthesis of real and virtual, human and machine, video game and movie" (paragraph 1). He concludes by asserting that *Avatar* "doesn't look like a documentary film; it looks like a video game" (10). But he adds that it would have been better as a video game: "if I could have been the avatar instead of watching *Avatar*, this experience would have been a lot more fun" (11).

  To think critically about the assumptions in this essay regarding dif-ferent media, ask yourself questions like these: How are the experiences of watching a film and playing a video game similar and different? Does Maurstad's assumption that the film *looks* like but doesn't *feel* like a video game correspond to your own experience? How is being an avatar in a video game different from watching a film about Sam's avatar?

READING LIKE A WRITER

ASSERTING AN OVERALL JUDGMENT

Readers expect an evaluative essay to make a definitive overall judgment of the subject—an assertion that the subject is good or bad or that it is better or worse than something else of the same kind. But since few subjects are perfect, readers appreciate a balanced evaluation in which the weaknesses as well as the strengths are pointed out.

Analyze

1. Reread paragraphs 1 to 3 and underline where Maurstad asserts his overall judgment of the film *Avatar*.

2. Skim the rest of the essay, noting where Maurstad evaluates the film's 3D photography and where he discusses the film's storytelling. How much space does he give to each aspect of the film? Given his overall judgment, why do you think he chose to devote so much of his essay to one aspect rather than treating them equally?

Write

Write a sentence or two explaining Maurstad's judgment of *Avatar* and why you think he devotes so much of his essay to the aspect of the film he criticizes.

CONSIDERING IDEAS FOR YOUR OWN WRITING

Consider evaluating something that involves new technology or innovations in a field. Recent innovations in media include 3D photography and high-definition television; in automobiles, hybrid and electric cars; in architecture, houses where interior walls have been replaced with electronic fields that can shield a room from view or, with a flick of a switch, allow the room to be seen. You could also write about innovations in landscaping, in museum displays, in music, in art, in computers, or in theaters or other performance spaces. For such an evaluation, you could choose something that is completely accessible to you and with which you are familiar, or you could do some research to educate yourself.

A Special Reading Strategy

Comparing and Contrasting Related Readings: Berardinelli's and Maurstad's Reviews of *Avatar*

Comparing and contrasting related readings is a critical reading strategy that is useful both in reading for meaning and in reading like a writer. This strategy is particularly applicable when writers present similar subjects, as is the case in the essays by James Berardinelli (p. 294) and Tom Maurstad (p. 303) both of whom are evaluating the same film. To compare and contrast these two reviews, think about issues such as these:

- Compare how the two writers describe the film's plot. Film reviewers normally tell readers something of the story to whet their appetite, but they are usually careful not to give away too much of the plot. How do Berardinelli and Maurstad handle this sometimes delicate balance? In addition to introducing the story, reviewers also often evaluate it. How do Berardinelli and Maurstad judge *Avatar*'s story line?

- Compare the standards or criteria on which Berardinelli and Maurstad base their judgment of the film. Film reviewers usually apply criteria that are appropriate to the genre. How do Berardinelli's and Maurstad's criteria relate to the way they classify *Avatar*?

See Appendix 1 (pp. 596–601) for detailed guidelines on comparing and contrasting related readings.

Christine Rosen

The Myth of Multitasking

Christine Rosen holds a PhD in history and is a prominent scholar and commentator on bioethics and the social effects of technology. She has written several books, including My Fundamentalist Education *(2005),* Preaching Eugenics *(2004), and* The Feminist Dilemma *(2001). She frequently appears on National Public Radio, CNN, Fox News, and other venues. Rosen's essays have appeared in such prestigious publications as the* New York Times Magazine, Washington Post, Wall Street Journal, National Review, *and* New Atlantis, *where she is a senior editor and where this essay originally appeared in 2008.*

In this essay, Rosen evaluates multitasking. As you read, think about your own experience with multitasking and what you think are its advantages and disadvantages.

1   In one of the many letters he wrote to his son in the 1740s, Lord Chesterfield offered the following advice: "There is time enough for everything in the course of the day, if you do but one thing at once, but there is not time enough in the year, if you will do two things at a time." To Chesterfield, singular focus was not merely a practical way to structure one's time; it was a mark of intelligence. "This steady and undissipated attention to one object, is a sure mark of a superior genius; as hurry, bustle, and agitation, are the never-failing symptoms of a weak and frivolous mind."

2   In modern times, hurry, bustle, and agitation have become a regular way of life for many people—so much so that we have embraced a word to describe our efforts to respond to the many pressing demands on our time: *multitasking*. Used for decades to describe the parallel processing abilities of computers, multitasking is now shorthand for the human attempt to do simultaneously as many things as possible, as quickly as possible, preferably marshalling the power of as many technologies as possible.

3   In the late 1990s and early 2000s, one sensed a kind of exuberance about the possibilities of multitasking. Advertisements for new electronic gadgets—particularly the first generation of handheld digital devices—celebrated the notion of using technology to accomplish several things at once. The word multitasking began appearing in the "skills" sections of résumés, as office workers restyled themselves as high-tech, high-performing team players. "We have always multitasked—inability to walk and chew gum is a time-honored cause for derision—but never so intensely or self-consciously as now," James Gleick wrote in his 1999 book *Faster*. "We are multitasking connoisseurs—experts in crowding, pressing, packing, and overlapping distinct activities in our all-too-finite moments." An article in the *New York Times Magazine* in 2001 asked, "Who can remember life

before multitasking? These days we all do it." The article offered advice on "How to Multitask" with suggestions about giving your brain's "multitasking hot spot" an appropriate workout.

But more recently, challenges to the ethos of multitasking have   4 begun to emerge. Numerous studies have shown the sometimes-fatal danger of using cell phones and other electronic devices while driving, for example, and several states have now made that particular form of multitasking illegal. In the business world, where concerns about time-management are perennial, warnings about workplace distractions spawned by a multitasking culture are on the rise. In 2005, the BBC reported on a research study, funded by Hewlett-Packard and conducted by the Institute of Psychiatry at the University of London, that found, "Workers distracted by e-mail and phone calls suffer a fall in IQ more than twice that found in marijuana smokers." The psychologist who led the study called this new "infomania" a serious threat to workplace productivity. One of the *Harvard Business Review*'s "Breakthrough Ideas" for 2007 was Linda Stone's notion of "continuous partial attention," which might be understood as a subspecies of multitasking: using mobile computing power and the Internet, we are "constantly scanning for opportunities and staying on top of contacts, events, and activities in an effort to miss nothing."

Dr. Edward Hallowell, a Massachusetts-based psychiatrist who   5 specializes in the treatment of attention deficit/hyperactivity disorder and has written a book with the self-explanatory title *CrazyBusy*, has been offering therapies to combat extreme multitasking for years; in his book he calls multitasking a "mythical activity in which people believe they can perform two or more tasks simultaneously." In a 2005 article, he described a new condition, "Attention Deficit Trait," which he claims is rampant in the business world. ADT is "purely a response to the hyperkinetic environment in which we live," writes Hallowell, and its hallmark symptoms mimic those of ADD. "Never in history has the human brain been asked to track so many data points," Hallowell argues, and this challenge "can be controlled only by creatively engineering one's environment and one's emotional and physical health." Limiting multitasking is essential. Best-selling business advice author Timothy Ferriss also extols the virtues of "single-tasking" in his book, *The 4-Hour Workweek*.

Multitasking might also be taking a toll on the economy. One study   6 by researchers at the University of California at Irvine monitored interruptions among office workers; they found that workers took an average of twenty-five minutes to recover from interruptions such as phone calls or answering e-mail and return to their original task. Discussing multitasking with the *New York Times* in 2007, Jonathan B. Spira, an analyst at the business research firm Basex, estimated that extreme multitasking—information overload—costs the U.S. economy $650 billion a year in lost productivity.

CHANGING OUR BRAINS

7   To better understand the multitasking phenomenon, neurologists and psychologists have studied the workings of the brain. In 1999, Jordan Grafman, chief of cognitive neuroscience at the National Institute of Neuro-logical Disorders and Stroke (part of the National Institutes of Health), used functional magnetic resonance imaging (fMRI) scans to determine that when people engage in "task-switching"—that is, multitasking behavior—the flow of blood increases to a region of the frontal cortex called Brodmann area 10. (The flow of blood to particular regions of the brain is taken as a proxy indication of activity in those regions.) "This is presumably the last part of the brain to evolve, the most mysterious and exciting part," Grafman told the *New York Times* in 2001—adding, with a touch of hyperbole, "It's what makes us most human."

8   It is also what makes multitasking a poor long-term strategy for learning. Other studies, such as those performed by psychologist René Marois of Vanderbilt University, have used fMRI to demonstrate the brain's response to handling multiple tasks. Marois found evidence of a "response selection bottleneck" that occurs when the brain is forced to respond to several stimuli at once. As a result, task-switching leads to time lost as the brain determines which task to perform. Psychologist David Meyer at the University of Michigan believes that rather than a bottleneck in the brain, a process of "adaptive executive control" takes place, which "schedules task processes appropriately to obey instruc-tions about their relative priorities and serial order," as he described to the *New Scientist*. Unlike many other researchers who study multitask-ing, Meyer is optimistic that, with training, the brain can learn to task-switch more effectively, and there is some evidence that certain simple tasks are amenable to such practice. But his research has also found that multitasking contributes to the release of stress hormones and adrena-line, which can cause long-term health problems if not controlled, and contributes to the loss of short-term memory.

9   In one recent study, Russell Poldrack, a psychology professor at the University of California, Los Angeles, found that "multitasking adversely affects how you learn. Even if you learn while multitask-ing, that learning is less flexible and more specialized, so you can-not retrieve the information as easily." His research demonstrates that people use different areas of the brain for learning and storing new information when they are distracted: brain scans of people who are distracted or multitasking show activity in the striatum, a region of the brain involved in learning new skills; brain scans of people who are

not distracted show activity in the hippocampus, a region involved in storing and recalling information. Discussing his research on National Public Radio recently, Poldrack warned, "We have to be aware that there is a cost to the way that our society is changing, that humans are not built to work this way. We're really built to focus. And when we sort of force ourselves to multitask, we're driving ourselves to perhaps be less efficient in the long run even though it sometimes feels like we're being more efficient."

If, as Poldrack concluded, "multitasking changes the way people learn," what might this mean for today's children and teens, raised with an excess of new entertainment and educational technology, and avidly multitasking at a young age? Poldrack calls this the "million-dollar question." Media multitasking—that is, the simultaneous use of several different media, such as television, the Internet, video games, text messages, telephones, and e-mail—is clearly on the rise, as a 2006 report from the Kaiser Family Foundation showed: in 1999, only 16 percent of the time people spent using any of those media was spent on multiple media at once; by 2005, 26 percent of media time was spent multitasking. "I multitask every single second I am online," confessed one study participant. "At this very moment I am watching TV, checking my e-mail every two minutes, reading a newsgroup about who shot JFK, burning some music to a CD, and writing this message." 10

The Kaiser report noted several factors that increase the likelihood of media multitasking, including "having a computer and being able to see a television from it." Also, "sensation-seeking" personality types are more likely to multitask, as are those living in "a highly TV-oriented household." The picture that emerges of these pubescent multitasking mavens is of a generation of great technical facility and intelligence but of extreme impatience, unsatisfied with slowness and uncomfortable with silence: "I get bored if it's not all going at once, because everything has gaps— waiting for a website to come up, commercials on TV, etc.," one participant said. The report concludes on a very peculiar note, perhaps intended to be optimistic: "In this media-heavy world, it is likely that brains that are more adept at media multitasking will be passed along and these changes will be naturally selected," the report states. "After all, information is power, and if one can process more information all at once, perhaps one can be more powerful." This is techno-social Darwinism, nature red in pixel and claw. 11

Other experts aren't so sure. As neurologist Jordan Grafman told *Time* magazine: "Kids that are instant messaging while doing homework, playing games online and watching TV, I predict, aren't going to do well in the long run." "I think this generation of kids is guinea pigs," educational psychologist Jane Healy told the *San Francisco Chronicle*; she worries that they might become adults who engage in "very quick but very shallow 12 thinking." Or, as the novelist Walter Kirn suggests in a deft essay in *The Atlantic*, we might be headed for an "Attention-Deficit Recession."

PAYING ATTENTION

13   When we talk about multitasking, we are really talking about attention: the art of paying attention, the ability to shift our attention, and, more broadly, to exercise judgment about what objects are worthy of our attention. People who have achieved great things often credit for their success a finely honed skill for paying attention. When asked about his particular genius, Isaac Newton responded that if he had made any discoveries, it was "owing more to patient attention than to any other talent." [. . .]

14   [To] William James, the great psychologist [who] wrote at length about the varieties of human attention [in] *The Principles of Psychology* (1890) . . . steady attention was . . . the default condition of a mature mind. . . . To readers a century later, that placid portrayal may seem alien—as though depicting a bygone world. Instead, today's multitasking adult may find something more familiar in James's description of the youthful mind: an "extreme mobility of the attention" that "makes the child seem to belong less to himself than to every object which happens to catch his notice." For some people, James noted, this challenge is never overcome; such people only get their work done "in the interstices of their mind-wandering." Like Chesterfield, James believed that the transition from youthful distraction to mature attention was in large part the result of personal mastery and discipline—and so was illustrative of character. "The faculty of voluntarily bringing back a wandering attention, over and over again," he wrote, "is the very root of judgment, character, and will."

15   Today, our collective will to pay attention seems fairly weak. We require advice books to teach us how to avoid distraction. In the not-too-distant future we may even employ new devices to help us overcome the unintended attention deficits created by today's gadgets. As one *New York Times* article recently suggested, "Further research could help create clever technology, like sensors or smart software that workers could instruct with their preferences and priorities to serve as a high tech 'time nanny' to ease the modern multitasker's plight." Perhaps we will all accept as a matter of course a computer governor—like the devices placed on engines so that people can't drive cars beyond a certain speed. Our technological governors might prompt us with reminders to set mental limits when we try to do too much, too quickly, all at once.

16   Then again, perhaps we will simply adjust and come to accept what James called "acquired inattention." E-mails pouring in, cell phones ringing, televisions blaring, podcasts streaming—all this may become background noise, like the "din of a foundry or factory" that James observed workers could scarcely avoid at first, but which eventually became just

another part of their daily routine. For the younger generation of multitaskers, the great electronic din is an expected part of everyday life. And given what neuroscience and anecdotal evidence have shown us, this state of constant intentional self-distraction could well be of profound detriment to individual and cultural well-being. When people do their work only in the "interstices of their mind-wandering," with crumbs of attention rationed out among many competing tasks, their culture may gain in information, but it will surely weaken in wisdom.

READING FOR MEANING

This section presents three activities that will help you think about the meanings in Rosen's evaluative essay.

Read to Comprehend

Write a few sentences summarizing Rosen's reasons for critiquing multitasking.

Identify any words with meanings you are unsure of—such as *undissipated* (paragraph 1) and *social Darwinism* (11)—and find the dictionary definition for each word that makes the best sense in the context.

To help you understand the essay better, also consider trying one of these critical reading strategies, explained in Appendix 1: *outlining* or *questioning to understand and remember*.

Read to Respond

Write several paragraphs exploring your initial thoughts and feelings about Rosen's argument. Focus on anything that stands out for you, perhaps because it resonates with your own experience or because you find a statement puzzling. You might consider writing about the following:

- your experience multitasking compared to "single-tasking"—and what the advantages or disadvantages are of focusing your attention on one task at a time (paragraph 5);

- the idea that with practice people can get better at learning while multitasking, but that such learning is less effective than focused learning (8–9); or

- the suggestions that multitaskers are impatient and "uncomfortable with silence," and that they quickly get bored (11).

To help develop your response, also consider trying one of these critical reading strategies, explained in Appendix 1: *contextualizing* or *reflecting on challenges to your beliefs and values*.

Read to Analyze Assumptions

Write a paragraph or two analyzing an assumption in Rosen's essay. To think critically about assumptions, here are some kinds of questions you could ask: Who holds this assumption (the writer, readers, and/or others cited in the essay)? What are the effects of the assumption in the context of the essay specifically or in society more generally? What do you think about the assumption, and is there anything in the essay that raises doubts about it? How does the assumption reinforce or critique commonly held views, and are there any alternative ideas, beliefs, or values that would challenge this assumption?

You might choose an assumption from the list below, using the questions accompanying it in addition to the ones above to help you get started. Or you can choose another assumption in the essay to explore.

- **assumptions about the causes of not focusing attention.** Quoting Lord Chesterfield's writing from the eighteenth century and William James's from the nineteenth, Rosen suggests that not focusing one's attention may indicate "a weak and frivolous mind" (paragraph 1) or the lack of "a mature mind" or of "judgment, character, and will" (14). Such language makes a moral judgment about a person's lack of seriousness or self-discipline. In contrast, quoting Dr. Edward Hallowell, Rosen suggests that not focusing attention may be a sign of illness akin to "attention deficit/hyperactivity disorder" (5).

  To think critically about the assumptions in this essay about the causes of not focusing attention, ask yourself questions like these: Why do you suppose people, particularly young people, who do not focus their attention have been labeled as lacking in character or intelligence or suffering from a medical malady? Do you think that critics are less likely today than in the past to make judgments about intelligence or character, and perhaps more likely to make medical diagnoses about the same kinds of behavior? Why or why not?

- **assumptions about the role of media in multitasking.** According to Rosen, the Kaiser Family Foundation reported a substantial increase in media multitasking: "in 1999, only 16 percent of the time people spent using" media "such as television, the Internet, video games, text messages, telephones, and e-mail" "was spent on multiple media at once; by 2005, 26 percent of media time was spent multitasking" (paragraph 10).

  To think critically about the assumptions in this essay regarding media multitasking, ask yourself questions like these: When you are multitasking, is some kind of electronic medium always involved or do you ever multitask without using media? One Kaiser survey participant suggested, "I get bored if it's not all going at once, because everything has gaps—waiting for a website to come up, commercials on TV, etc." (11). Do you primarily use media multitasking to fill or kill time, or for some other reason?

To help you analyze assumptions in Rosen's essay, also consider trying one of these critical reading strategies, explained in Appendix 1: *reflecting on challenges to your beliefs and values* or *looking for patterns of opposition.*

READING LIKE A WRITER

GIVING REASONS AND SUPPORT

Rosen relies primarily on authorities and research studies to support her argument about the value of multitasking. If she were writing for an academic audience, she would be expected to include formal citations so that other scholars could find her sources if they were also researching the subject. Instead, she is writing for a general audience, readers of the *New Atlantis,* a journal that describes itself as "meet[ing] the need for 'empirically-grounded political economy.'" Consequently, Rosen does not include a works cited list, but she sometimes provides readers with information about her sources, such as the authority's name and academic affiliation, often together with the publication in which the report originally appeared—so that scholars presumably could track down the sources if they wanted to follow up on Rosen's research.

Analyze

1. Reread paragraphs 4 to 9, and highlight the names of authorities or the research studies Rosen cites.

2. Choose two sources and determine how Rosen uses them to support her argument.

Write

Write a couple of sentences explaining how Rosen uses sources to support her evaluative argument. Add another sentence or two speculating on how convincing these sources are likely to be for Rosen's readers.

CONSIDERING IDEAS FOR YOUR OWN WRITING

You might want to consider evaluating a hobby or leisure-time activity with which you are familiar—physical activities such as skateboarding or spinning; intellectual activities such as reading or sudoko; activities people do by themselves or those that they do with others. For the activity you choose, think about which aspects of it are beneficial and which are potentially harmful. Alternatively, you might be interested in evaluating a kind of job or profession you already know a lot about or that you can research in the time available to you.

A Special Reading Strategy

Looking for Patterns of Opposition

To refute a favorable judgment she expects readers to have made about multitasking, Rosen tries to reframe the argument about its value. Reframing is a common strategy writers use to help readers see the subject in a new way. Rosen tries to set up an opposition between focused attention and multitasking that makes multitasking seem less preferable. She uses Lord Chesterfield's letters advising his son and William James's ideas about psychology to associate focused attention with maturity and intelligence, and multitasking with immaturity and a lack of intelligence or at least the inability to think properly.

- Reread paragraphs 1 to 3 and 13 to 16, highlighting the words Rosen uses to develop this opposition.

- To analyze the system of oppositions Rosen sets up, try using the critical reading strategy *looking for patterns of opposition* (see Appendix 1, pages 575–79). It simply involves making a two-column chart and placing the words Rosen associates with focused attention in one column and the words she associates with multi-tasking in the other column. Then, put an asterisk next to the word that Rosen values more highly—for example, *maturity* as opposed to *immaturity*.

- Write a couple of sentences describing the way that Rosen uses this system of oppositions to reframe readers' ideas about multitasking.

Christine Romano

Jessica Statsky's "Children Need to Play, Not Compete": An Evaluation

Christine Romano wrote the following essay when she was a first-year college student. In it, she evaluates a position paper written by another student, Jessica Statsky's "Children Need to Play, Not Compete," which appears in Chapter 7 of this book (pp. 388–93). Romano focuses not on the writing strategies Statsky uses but rather on her logic—that is, on whether Statsky's argument is likely to convince her intended readers. She evaluates the logic of the argument according to the standards presented in Appendix 1 (pp. 579–82). You might want to review these standards before you read Romano's evaluation. Also, if you have not read Statsky's essay, you might want to do so now, thinking about what seems most and least convincing to you about her argument that competitive sports can be harmful to young children.

Parents of young children have a lot to worry about and to hope for. In "Children Need to Play, Not Compete," Jessica Statsky appeals to their worries and hopes in order to convince them that organized competitive sports may harm their children physically and psychologically. Statsky states her thesis clearly and fully forecasts the reasons she will offer to justify her position: Besides causing physical and psychological harm, competitive sports discourage young people from becoming players and fans when they are older and inevitably put parents' needs and fantasies ahead of children's welfare. Statsky also carefully defines her key terms. By *sports*, for example, she means to include both contact and noncontact sports that emphasize competition. The sports may be organized locally at schools or summer sports camps or nationally, as in the examples of Peewee Football and Little League Baseball. She is concerned only with children six to twelve years of age.

In this essay, I will evaluate the logic of Statsky's argument, considering whether the support for her thesis is appropriate, believable, consistent, and complete. While her logic *is* appropriate, believable, and consistent, her argument also has weaknesses. It seems incomplete because it neglects to anticipate parents' predictable questions and objections and because it fails to support certain parts fully.

Statsky provides appropriate support for her thesis. Throughout her essay, she relies for support on different kinds of information (she cites fourteen separate sources, including books, newspapers, and Web sites). Her quotations, examples, and statistics all support the reasons she believes competitive sports are bad for children. For example, in paragraph 3, Statsky offers the reason that "overly competitive sports" may damage children's growing bodies and that contact sports, in particular, may be especially hazardous. She supports this reason by paraphrasing Koppett's statement that muscle strain or even lifelong injury may result when a twelve-year-old throws curve balls. She then quotes Tutko on the dangers of tackle football. The opinions of both experts are obviously appropriate. They are relevant to her reason, and we can easily imagine that they would worry many parents.

4   Not only is Statsky's support appropriate but it is also believable. Statsky quotes or summarizes authorities to support her argument in nearly every paragraph. The question is whether readers would find these authorities believable or credible. Since Statsky relies almost entirely on authorities to support her argument, readers must believe these authorities for her argument to succeed. I have not read Statsky's sources, but I think there are good reasons to consider them authoritative. First of all, the newspaper writers she quotes write for two of America's most respected newspapers, the *New York Times* and the *Los Angeles Times*. Both of these newspapers have sports reporters who not only report on sports events but also take a critical look at sports issues. In addition, both newspapers have reporters who specialize in children's health and education. Second, Statsky gives background information about the authorities she quotes, information intended to increase the person's believability in the eyes of parents of young children. In paragraph 3, she tells readers that Thomas Tutko is "a psychology professor at San Jose State University and coauthor of the book *Winning Is Everything and Other American Myths.*" In paragraph 6, she announces that Martin Rablovsky is "a former sports editor for the *New York Times,*" and she notes that he has watched children play organized sports for many years. Third, Statsky quotes from a number of Web sites, including the official Little League site, the site of the National Association of Sports Officials, and the Parentsknow.com database. Parents are likely to accept the authority of the Little League site and be interested in what other parents and sports officials have to say.

5   In addition to quoting authorities, Statsky relies on examples and anecdotes to support the reasons for her position. If examples and anecdotes are to be believable, they must seem representative to readers, not bizarre or highly unusual or completely unpredictable. Readers can imagine a similar event happening elsewhere. For anecdotes to be believable, they should, in addition, be specific and true to life. All of Statsky's examples and anecdotes fulfill these requirements, and her readers would likely find them believable. For example, early in her argument, in paragraph 4, Statsky reasons that fear of being hurt greatly reduces children's enjoyment of contact sports. The anecdote comes from Tosches's investigative report on Peewee Football, as does the quotation

by the mother of an eight-year-old player who says that the children become frightened and pretend to be injured in order to stay out of the game. In the anecdote, a seven-year-old makes himself vomit to avoid playing. Because these echo the familiar "I feel bad" or "I'm sick" excuse children give when they do not want to go somewhere (especially school) or do something, most parents would find them believable. They could easily imagine their own children pretending to be hurt or ill if they were fearful or depressed. The anecdote is also specific. Tosches reports what the boy said and did and what the coach said and did.

Other examples provide support for all the major reasons Statsky gives for her position: 6

- That competitive sports pose psychological dangers—children becoming serious and unplayful when the game starts (paragraph 6)

- That adults' desire to win puts children at risk—parents fighting each other at a Peewee Football game, a baseball coach setting fire to an opposing team's jersey, and the fatal beating of a man supervising a hockey game by the unhappy parent of a player (paragraph 10)

- That organized sports should emphasize cooperation and individual performance instead of winning—a coach wishing to ban scoring but finding that parents would not support him and a New York City basketball league in which all children play an equal amount of time and scoring is easier (paragraph 14)

All of these examples are appropriate to the reasons they support. They are also believable. Together, they help Statsky achieve her purpose of convincing parents that organized, competitive sports may be bad for their children and that there are alternatives.

If readers are to find an argument logical and convincing, it must be   7
consistent and complete. While there are no inconsistencies or contradictions in Statsky's argument, it is seriously incomplete because it neglects to support fully one of its reasons, it fails to anticipate many predictable questions parents would have, and it pays too little attention to noncontact competitive team sports. The most obvious example of thin support comes in paragraph 13, where Statsky asserts that many parents are ready for children's team sports that emphasize cooperation and individual performance. Yet the example of a Little League official who failed to win parents' approval to ban scores raises serious questions about just how many parents are ready to embrace noncompetitive sports teams. The other support, a brief description of City Sports for Kids in New York City, is very convincing but will only be logically compelling to those

parents who are already inclined to agree with Statsky's position. Parents inclined to disagree with Statsky would need additional evidence. Most parents know that big cities receive special federal funding for evening, weekend, and summer recreation. Brief descriptions of six or eight non-competitive teams in a variety of sports in cities, rural areas, suburban neighborhoods—some funded publicly, some funded privately—would be more likely to convince skeptics. Statsky is guilty here of failing to accept the burden of proof, a logical fallacy.

8   Statsky's argument is also incomplete in that it fails to anticipate certain objections and questions that some parents, especially those she most wants to convince, are almost sure to raise. In the first sentences of paragraphs 8 and 12, Statsky does show that she is thinking about her readers' questions. She does not go nearly far enough, however, to have a chance of influencing two types of readers: those who themselves are or were fans of and participants in competitive sports and those who want their six- to twelve-year-old children involved in mainstream sports programs despite the risks, especially the national programs that have a certain prestige. Such parents might feel that competitive team sports for young children create a sense of community with a shared purpose, build character through self-sacrifice and commitment to the group, teach children to face their fears early and learn how to deal with them through the support of coaches and team members, and introduce children to the principles of social cooperation and collaboration. Some parents are likely to believe and to know from personal experience that coaches who burn opposing teams' jerseys on the pitching mound before the game starts are the exception, not the rule. Some young children idolize teachers and coaches, and team practice and games are the brightest moments in their lives. Statsky seems not to have considered these reasonable possibilities, and as a result her argument lacks a compelling logic it might have had. By acknowledging that she was aware of many of these objections—and perhaps even accommodating more of them in her own argument, as she does in paragraph 12, while refuting other objections—she would have strengthened her argument.

9   Finally, Statsky's argument is incomplete because she overlooks examples of noncontact team sports. Track, swimming, and tennis are good examples that some readers would certainly think of. Some elementary schools compete in track meets. Public and private clubs and recreational programs organize competitive swimming and tennis competitions. In these sports, individual performance is the focus. No one gets trampled. Children exert themselves only as much as they are able to. Yet individual performances are scored, and a team score is derived. Because Statsky fails to mention any of these obvious possibilities, her argument is weakened.

The logic of Statsky's argument, then, has both strengths and weak-   10
nesses. The support she offers is appropriate, believable, and consistent.
The major weakness is incompleteness—she fails to anticipate more fully
the likely objections of a wide range of readers. Her logic would prevent parents who enjoy and advocate competitive sports from taking her
argument seriously. Such parents and their children have probably had
positive experiences with team sports, and these experiences would lead
them to believe that the gains are worth whatever risks may be involved.
Many probably think that the risks Statsky points out can be avoided by
careful monitoring. For those parents inclined to agree with her, Statsky's
logic is likely to seem sound and complete. An argument that successfully
confirms readers' beliefs is certainly valid, and Statsky succeeds admirably
at this kind of argument. Because she does not offer compelling counterarguments to the legitimate objections of those inclined not to agree with
her, however, her success is limited.

READING FOR MEANING

This section presents three activities that will help you think about the meanings in Romano's evaluation.

Read to Comprehend

Write a few sentences briefly explaining the strengths and weaknesses of
Statsky's argument, according to Romano.

Identify any words with meanings you are unsure of—such as *skeptics* and
logical fallacy (paragraph 7)—and find the dictionary definition for each word
that makes the best sense in the context.

To help you understand the essay better, also consider trying one of these
critical reading strategies, explained in Appendix 1: *summarizing* or *questioning
to understand and remember.*

Read to Respond

Write several paragraphs exploring your initial thoughts and feelings about
Romano's evaluation. Focus on anything that stands out for you, perhaps because
it resonates with your own experience or because you find a statement puzzling.
You might consider writing about the following:

- reasons that Romano finds Statsky's argument believable (paragraphs 4–6);

- further reasons that parents of six- to twelve-year-old children might find
  Statsky's argument incomplete; or

- your own experience as a member of an organized sports team for children of the same age group, comparing or contrasting it with what Romano finds believable or incomplete in Statsky's argument.

To help develop your response, also consider trying one of these critical reading strategies, explained in Appendix 1: *looking for patterns of opposition* or *evaluating the logic of an argument.*

Read to Analyze Assumptions

Write a paragraph or two analyzing an assumption in Romano's essay. To think critically about assumptions, here are some kinds of questions you could ask: Who holds this assumption (the writer, readers, and/or others cited in the essay)? What are the effects of the assumption in the context of the essay specifically or in society more generally? What do you think about the assumption, and is there anything in the essay that raises doubts about it? How does the assumption reinforce or critique commonly held views, and are there any alternative ideas, beliefs, or values that would challenge this assumption?

You might choose an assumption from the list below, using the questions accompanying it in addition to the ones above to help you get started. Or you can choose another assumption in the essay to explore.

- **assumptions about the relative value of competition or cooperation.** Romano gives an example supporting Statsky's argument that team sports for young children "should emphasize cooperation and individual performance instead of winning" (paragraph 6). In paragraph 8, however, Romano suggests that some parents believe that team sports may teach cooperation together with competition and that the two skills and attitudes may be more closely related than Statsky acknowledges.

  To think critically about the assumptions in this essay related to competition and cooperation, ask yourself questions like these: What do you think leads Romano to claim that children learn both competition and cooperation when they participate in team sports? Do you think that competition is highly valued in our society and, if so, why? Do you think that cooperation is valued as highly as competition? How is learning to cooperate and collaborate beneficial for us as individuals and as a society?

- **assumptions about the importance of facing fear.** As Romano notes in paragraph 5, "Statsky reasons that fear of being hurt greatly reduces children's enjoyment of contact sports," and as support she cites Tosches's anecdote about the child who "makes himself vomit to avoid playing." Nevertheless, Romano suggests that some parents think facing fear is a good thing—that "competitive team sports for young children . . . teach children to face their fears early and learn how to deal with them" (8).

To think critically about the assumptions in this essay related to facing fear, ask yourself questions like these: In what contexts, other than sports, do people typically experience physical or psychological fear? Why might some people think that learning "how to deal" with fear (presumably by doing something even though it causes us to be fearful) is a good thing? How do the stories we read and watch on television and film reinforce this assumption that fear should be faced and dealt with, if not overcome?

To help you analyze assumptions in Romano's essay, also consider trying one of these critical reading strategies, explained in Appendix 1: *reflecting on challenges to your beliefs and values* or *looking for patterns of opposition.*

READING LIKE A WRITER

ANTICIPATING OBJECTIONS AND ALTERNATIVE JUDGMENTS

Writers of evaluation usually try to anticipate and respond to readers' possible objections and alternative judgments. In anticipating readers, writers may simply acknowledge that others disagree, may accommodate into their argument some points that others have made, or may try to refute objections and alternative judgments. Romano's first draft of her evaluation of Statsky's essay was totally positive. It did not anticipate objections that readers might make to her evaluation or alternative judgments that they might have of Statsky's essay. Two classmates who read Romano's draft helped her understand that readers might disagree with her evaluation and see flaws in Statsky's argument. This constructive criticism led Romano to modify her essay to accommodate other views. The revised essay offers a balanced evaluation of Statsky's essay by both arguing for its apparent strengths and anticipating readers' objections and alternative judgments.

Analyze

1. Reread paragraphs 7 to 10, noting where Romano anticipates readers' possible alternative judgments of Statsky's argument.

2. Make notes in the margin about how Romano accommodates or refutes readers' criticisms of Statsky's argument.

Write

Write several sentences reporting on what you have learned about how Romano anticipates readers' objections and alternative judgments. Give examples to show how she accommodates or refutes readers' criticism.

CONSIDERING IDEAS FOR YOUR
OWN WRITING

List several texts you would consider evaluating. For example, you might include in your list an essay from one of the chapters in this book. If you choose an argument from Chapters 6 through 9, you could evaluate its logic (as Romano does), emotional appeals, or credibility, relying on the guidelines in Appendix 1. You might prefer to evaluate a children's book you read when you were younger or one you now read to your own children, a magazine for people interested in computers or cars (or another topic), or a scholarly article you read for a research paper. You need not limit yourself to texts written on paper; also consider a Web site or an article from an online magazine or newspaper. Choose one possibility from your list, and see whether you can come up with three or four reasons for why you find it a strong or weak text.

Larry Ballesteros

A Winning Formula? A Review of *Slumdog Millionaire*

Larry Ballesteros wrote this film review for his first-year composition class. As you read, look for his thesis statement, where he asserts his overall judgment of Slumdog Millionaire. *Also notice the basis or criteria on which he makes this judgment, and if you have seen the film consider whether the criteria seem appropriate.*

The other readings in this chapter are followed by reading and writing activities. Following this reading, however, you are on your own to decide how to read for meaning and read like a writer.

Few movies are able to adequately contrast the harshness of reality with the eloquence and endurance of love. *Slumdog Millionaire* does just that. It is a simple, classical romance juxtaposed with the harsh reality of life in the slums of India. More specifically, it is the story of a young man, Jamal, who finds himself as a contestant on India's popular game show equivalent to *Who Wants to Be a Millionaire*. As he answers the questions, the film flashes back to moments of his childhood and adolescence. It is in this way that the story of Jamal's challenging life as an orphan growing up in the slums of India—along with his brother, Salim, and their friend Latika, who later becomes the object of Jamal's affection—is told. Various aspects of the film's production, including acting, directing, and editing, contribute to making *Slumdog Millionaire* a great movie; although other aspects of production—a less than stellar script, for example, and plot ambiguities— lessen the magnitude of its greatness.

A key reason for the overall success of *Slumdog Millionaire* is the continuously impressive performances of the young actors playing the three main characters—Jamal, Salim, and Latika. These young actors display a charming, exuberant charisma that sets the tone for the rest of the film. Furthermore, their effortless and obvious enjoyment, conveyed through their excellent performances, allows the audience to better understand the film's context—the reality of life in India—without overdramatizing. Moreover, the adolescent as well as the adult main character portrayals continue to convey the same charm and exuberance of the younger characters. Also, the main villain, Maman, who is an example of true heartlessness, seems to embody the overall environment of life in an Indian slum. So, it suffices to say that the acting in *Slumdog Millionaire* is superb, which may be attributed in part to the many other strong aspects of the movie, such as its great directing.

The film triumphs in directing and overall composition. Danny Boyle brings a great vision to life in this beautiful composition of love and adversity. The film almost boasts of its true-life quality and raw-cut style. Boyle seems to enjoy the abundance of diversity that his chosen setting has to offer him, shooting in a variety of well-known places in India, such as the Taj Mahal and the slums of Mumbai. The film is so very dependent on the setting that its landscape seems to govern its every turn, which is good in one sense but seems to diminish Boyle's role as a director in another. However, I feel Boyle has done an excellent job and deserves every accolade bestowed on him for this marvelous film. Accordingly, the film earned many fine reviews and awards for superb directorship as well as cinematography, which the visual style of the film well contributed to.

4   The visual style of the film is emphasized through the abundant use of both warm and cool colors, reminiscent of films like *Traffic* and *Amores Perros*. This emphasis evokes a casual feeling that makes the movie seem like it's constantly in transition. For instance, the first half of the movie is centered on providing background information on the main characters, but through the use of flashbacks. The majority of the film's attention seems to be focused on the story taking place in the second half of the

film. The colors give the scenes a dreamlike quality that is very passive and fleeting but at the same time memorable. Each character has his or her own specific hue in some scenes. Latika, for example, often wears bright yellow, especially in the latter half of the film. Overall, this effect is a great attribute of the film and very much appreciated.

A major drawback to the film is the fact that the script is somewhat   5
bland at times and extremely predictable at others. For example, in the scene where Jamal finds Latika for a second time, now in their adult lives, each word spoken between them is so predictable that it almost seems like a scene from a midday soap opera. Furthermore, there are a few scenes in which there seem to be some gaps between the character's lines and their reactions. An example of this is when Jamal punches Salim in the construction building and tells him he will never forgive him but then almost immediately afterward comes to live with Salim at his apartment. However, this may be relative to cultural differences between American cinema and Indian cinema whereas, in most American movies, characters are often unforgiving. Therefore, it suffices to say that the script is somewhat poor, though less frustrating than some of the film's plot ambiguities.

Ambiguities in the plot are a major hindrance to the cohesiveness and   6
eloquence of the film. One such instance of ambiguity is the scene in which Salim kicks Jamal out of the hotel room and takes Latika, at which point it is unclear whether Salim sexually assaults Latika or is simply looking to get rid of Jamal for some other reason. Additionally, the scene in which Salim fills a bathtub with money and waits for his boss to come in and kill him is likewise ambiguous. I suppose this scene is meant to convey some sort of altruistic symbolism, possibly the triumph of love over money, but this is unclear. Overall, however, the plot does a good job of conveying a sense of heightened drama and struggle, and even though the editing at times seems somewhat lackluster, the scene-to-scene transitions are clear and distinct.

The editing has a distinct, unconventional style but is somewhat remi-   7
niscent of an amateur or low-budget film at times. Scenes are very raw and often leave in flaws like actors looking into the camera unintentionally or, as in one particular scene, interruptions by security guards. This is somewhat refreshing, in a rebellious way, but also somewhat confusing while watching the film. For example, there is a scene in which the camera is focused on the communications office Jamal works at and halfway through the scene three or four security guards walk past the camera and say, "No filming." Fortunately, it is a very quick and discrete scene and is somewhat unnoticeable considering how thick the security guard's accent is. Overall, this raw style is a unique way of further embracing the film's setting in India, though a bit too amateur for my taste.

In contrast to my own opinion, some people may find this film to be   8
too ambiguous, or too sappy. Certainly, what I consider to be the overall charm of the film—the enduring love story—could be considered the worst part by others. Some people may argue that the film is just too

unrealistic and poorly depicts how love really is, even though I do not fully agree with this notion. The film also has often shaky or rough camera work, which some people may find disturbing. Therefore, I can see why some people might not like this film.

9   In conclusion, though it has some minor flaws, *Slumdog Millionaire* seems to have the winning formula for what can be considered a great film. Most, if not all, the elements that make this film what it is are related to the beautiful and complex land of India. This film sails past most Hollywood films simply because it derives its strength from this diverse place, with the combination of all of its perilous and magnificent aspects. Such a movie is to be treasured by the avid movie fanatic because it introduces a whole new world of cinema that is both revealing and eclectic in its sources of inspiration.

Work Cited

Slumdog Millionaire. Dir. Danny Boyle. Perf. Dev Patel, Freida Pinto, and Irrfan Khan. Fox Searchlight, 2009. DVD.

READING FOR MEANING

Reading for meaning involves three activities:

- reading to comprehend,
- reading to respond, and
- reading to analyze assumptions.

Write a page or so explaining your understanding of the meaning of Ballesteros's essay, a personal response you have to it, and one of its assumptions.

READING LIKE A WRITER

Writers of evaluative essays

- present the subject,
- assert an overall judgment,
- give reasons and support, and
- anticipate objections and alternative judgments.

Choose one of these strategies in Ballesteros's film review, and analyze it carefully through close rereading and annotating. Then write several sentences explaining what you have learned, giving specific examples from the reading to support your explanation. Add a few sentences evaluating how successfully Ballesteros uses the strategy to argue effectively for his evaluation of the film.

Reviewing What Makes an Effective Essay

Evaluations

Analyze

Choose one reading from this chapter that seems to you especially effective. Before rereading the selection, jot down one or two reasons you remember it as an example of good evaluative writing.

Reread your chosen selection and add further notes about what makes it a particularly successful example. Consider the selection's purpose and how well it achieves that purpose for its intended readers. (You can make an informed guess about the intended readers and their expectations by noting the publication source of the essay.) Then assess how well the essay uses the writing strategies of presenting the subject, asserting an overall judgment, giving reasons and support, and anticipating objections and alternative judgments.

Write

Write at least a page supporting your choice of this reading as an example of effective evaluative writing. Refer to details and specific parts of the essay as you explain how it works and as you justify your evaluation of its effectiveness. You need not argue that it is the best reading in the chapter or that it is flawless, only that it is, in your view, a strong example of the genre.

A GUIDE TO WRITING EVALUATIONS

This Guide to Writing is designed to help you in writing an evaluation. Here you will find activities to help you choose a subject and discover what to say about it, organize your ideas and draft the essay, read the draft critically, revise the draft to strengthen your argument, and edit and proofread the essay to improve its readability.

INVENTION AND RESEARCH

The following activities will help you choose a subject, develop your judgment of it, and construct a convincing argument based on sound criteria, reasons, and supporting evidence.

Choosing a Subject

List the most promising subjects you can think of, beginning with any you listed for the Considering Ideas for Your Own Writing activities following the readings in this chapter. Rather than limiting yourself to the first subject that comes to mind, take a few minutes to consider your options and list as many subjects as you can. Below are some criteria that can help you choose a promising subject, followed by additional suggestions for the types of subjects you might consider writing about.

Criteria for Choosing a Subject

The subject should be

- one that has strengths and/or weaknesses you could write about;

- one that you can examine closely, that you can view and review;

- one typically evaluated according to criteria or standards of judgment that you understand;

- one you can judge confidently because you have knowledge and interest in it.

Categories from Which You Might Choose a Subject

- *Culture*: a film or group of films by a single director, a television show or series, a computer game, a song or recorded performance, an art museum or individual work of art, an amusement park

- *Written Work*: an essay in this book or another your instructor approves, a short story, Web site, magazine, campus publication, textbook in a course you've taken

- *Education*: your high school, a particular course you've taken, a laboratory you've worked in, a library or campus support service, a teacher or program

- *Government*: an elected official or candidate for public office, a proposed or existing law, an agency or program

- *Social*: a club or organized activity such as a camping trip, sports team, debate group

Developing Your Argument

The writing and research activities that follow will enable you to explore your subject, analyze your readers, and begin developing your evaluation.

Exploring Your Subject.   To find out what you already know about the subject, list the main things you now know about it and then make notes about how you will go about becoming familiar enough with your subject to write about it like an expert or insider. You may know little or much about your subject, and you may feel uncertain how to learn more about it. For now, discover what you do know.

Analyzing Your Readers.   Make notes about your readers. Who exactly are your readers? They may be your classmates, or you may want—or be asked by your instructor—to write for another audience. You could write for the general public, as most of the writers in this chapter seem to be doing. Or you could write for a more narrow audience—for example, parents considering the purchase of a children's learning game or experienced video game players. How much will your readers know about your subject and others of its type? What standards might they use to judge a subject like yours? Will you have to argue that the criteria you are applying are appropriate, perhaps by comparing your subject to other similar subjects or by citing authorities?

Considering Your Judgment.   Make a list of the good and bad qualities of your subject, and write a sentence or two asserting your overall judgment of it. Remember that your overall judgment can be mixed—arguing that your subject succeeds in certain ways and fails in others. But you should also consider which qualities are essential and which are minor distractions, shortcomings perhaps that do not diminish the larger achievement. The essential qualities should be the most important criteria on which most knowledgeable reviewers evaluate subjects of this kind.

Testing Your Choice.   Consider whether you know enough about the subject you have chosen or can learn enough in the time available. At this point, you should have a clear sense of what more you need to learn about your subject and how you can get that information. If you have not made progress in understanding your subject and do not see how you can do so right away, it is probably wise for you to consider choosing another subject.

Listing Reasons.   List at least two or three reasons you could give to persuade your readers of your judgment. Reasons answer the question "Why do you judge this aspect of the subject positively [or negatively]?" Try phrasing your reasons as *because* statements. For example, Etzioni argues that fast-food jobs are bad for high-school students because they "undermine school attendance and involvement, impart few skills that will be useful in later life, and simultaneously skew the values of teen-agers" (paragraph 3). Berardinelli argues that *Avatar* succeeds because not only is the 3D experience "immersive," but even in 2D "the traditional film elements—story, character, editing, theme, emotional resonance, etc.—are . . . engrossing" (paragraph 2).

As you continue to analyze your subject and develop your argument, you may think of other reasons that would be convincing to your readers, given the generally accepted standards for evaluating this type of subject. Consider this list only a starting point. Continue to revise it as you learn more about your subject.

Finding Support for Your Reasons.   Make notes about how to support your most promising reasons. For support, most evaluations rely largely on details and examples from the subject itself. Therefore, you will have to reexamine the subject closely even if you know it quite well. Depending on the subject, evaluations may also make use of facts, quotations from experts, statistics, or the writer's personal experience.

Work back and forth between your list of reasons and notes for support. The reasons list will remind you of the support you need and help you discover which reasons have substance. The credibility of your argument will depend to a large extent on the amount of specific, relevant support you can bring to your argument.

Anticipating Readers' Alternative Judgments, Questions, and Objections.   List a few questions your particular readers would likely want to ask you or objections they might have to your argument. Write for a few minutes responding to at least two of these questions or objections. Now that you can begin to see how your argument might shape up, assume that some of your particular readers would judge your subject differently from the way you do. Remember that your responses—your counterargument—could simply acknowledge the disagreements, accommodate readers' views by conceding certain points, or refute readers' arguments as uninformed or mistaken.

Considering Visuals. Consider whether visuals—movie posters or screen shots, photographs, or drawings—would help you present your subject more effectively to readers or strengthen your evaluation of it. If you submit your essay electronically to other students and your instructor, or if you post it on a Web site, consider including snippets of film or sound as well as photographs or other memorabilia that might give readers a more vivid sense of your subject. Visual and audio materials are not at all a requirement of an effective evaluative argument, as you can tell from the readings in this chapter, but they could add a new dimension to your writing. If you want to use photographs or recordings of people, though, be sure to obtain their permission.

Considering Your Purpose.   Write for a few minutes exploring your purpose for writing an evaluative essay. The following questions may help you think about your purpose:

- What do I want my readers to believe or do after they read my essay?

- How can I connect to their experience with my subject (or subjects like it)? How can I interest them in a subject that is outside their experience?

- Can I assume that readers will share my standards for judging the subject, or must I explain and justify the standards?

- How can I offer a balanced evaluation that will enhance my credibility with readers?

Formulating a Working Thesis.   Draft a thesis statement. A working thesis—as opposed to a final, revised thesis—will help you begin drafting your essay purposefully. The thesis statement in an evaluative essay is simply a concise assertion of your overall judgment. Here are two examples from the readings:

- "McDonald's is bad for your kids." (Etzioni, paragraph 1)

- "While her logic *is* appropriate, believable, and consistent, her argument also has weaknesses. It seems incomplete because it neglects to anticipate parents' predictable questions and objections and because it fails to support certain parts fully." (Romano, paragraph 2)

Both of these thesis statements are clear and assertive. But whereas Etzioni's thesis is unmistakably negative in its overall judgment, Romano's is mixed. Another difference between these two thesis statements is that whereas Romano forecasts the reasons she will develop in the essay, Etzioni does not forecast his reasons. Forecasts are not required, but readers often find them helpful.

DRAFTING

The following guidelines will help you set goals for your draft, plan its organization, and think about a useful sentence strategy.

Setting Goals

Establishing goals for your draft before you begin writing will enable you to make decisions and work more confidently. Consider the following questions now, and keep them in mind as you draft. They will help you set goals for drafting as well as recall how the writers you have read in this chapter tried to achieve similar goals.

- *What is my primary purpose in writing this evaluation?* What do I want to accomplish with my evaluation? Is my primary purpose to make a recommendation, as Etzioni, Rosen, and Romano do? Do I want to celebrate my subject, as Berardinelli does; present a balanced evaluation, as Maurstad, Romano, and Ballesteros do; or expose its weaknesses, as Etzioni and Rosen do?

- *How can I present the subject so that I can inform and interest my readers in it?* How much experience evaluating a subject of this kind can I expect my readers to have? Can I assume familiarity, as Etzioni and Romano do? Will readers share my standards, as Berardinelli, Maurstad, and Ballesteros assume in their film reviews, or will I need to explain or defend some of my standards, as Etzioni and Rosen do?

- *How can I assert my judgment effectively?* How can I construct a clear, unambiguous thesis statement even if my judgment is mixed? Should I assert my judgment in the first paragraph and reassert it at the end of my evaluation, as Etzioni, Romano, and Ballesteros do? Or should I first describe my subject or provide a context for evaluating it, as the other writers do?

- *How can I give convincing reasons and adequate support for my reasons?* How can I ensure that the reasons I offer to justify my judgment will seem appropriate and convincing to my readers? Should I forecast my reasons, as Etzioni, Romano, and Ballesteros do? For my subject, will I offer a wide range of types of support, as Etzioni does? How can I gather an adequate amount of support for my reasons, as do all of the writers in this chapter? Should I rely on comparisons to support my reasoning, as all the writers do?

- *How can I anticipate readers' questions and alternative judgments?* Should I pointedly anticipate my readers' likely objections or alternative judgments, as Etzioni and Romano do?

Working with Sources

Using Summary to Support Your Evaluative Argument

Writers of evaluation often use summary to support their argument. As the following examples show, evaluations may summarize an expert source (as Etzioni and Rosen do in their evaluations of fast-food restaurant jobs and multitasking), the plot of a film or video game (as all of the film reviewers do to some extent), or an aspect of an essay or story (as Romano does in her evaluation of another essay in this book), to name just a few of the more common uses of summary. Here are examples of these various uses of summary:

> One study by researchers at the University of California at Irvine monitored interruptions among office workers; they found that workers took an average of twenty-five minutes to recover from interruptions such as phone calls or answering e-mail and return to their original task. (Rosen, paragraph 6)

> . . . contrast the harshness of reality with the eloquence and endurance of love. *Slumdog Millionaire* does just that. It is a simple, classical romance juxtaposed with the harsh reality of life in the slums of India. (Ballesteros, paragraph 1)

> In the anecdote, a seven-year-old makes himself vomit to avoid playing. (Romano, paragraph 5)

Now look at the following example from Romano's essay:

> For example, in paragraph 3, Statsky offers the reason that "overly competitive sports" may damage children's growing bodies and that contact sports, in particular, may be especially hazardous. She supports this reason by paraphrasing Koppett's statement that muscle strain or even lifelong injury may result when a twelve-year-old throws curve balls. She then quotes Tutko on the dangers of tackle football. (Romano, paragraph 3).

To understand how this summary works, it helps to compare Romano's summary to the original passage in Statsky's essay (paragraph 3):

> One readily understandable danger of overly competitive sports is that they entice children into physical actions that are bad for growing bodies. Although the official Little League Online Web site acknowledges that children do risk injury playing baseball, the league insists that "severe injuries . . . are infrequent,"—"far less than the risk of riding a skateboard, a bicycle, or even the school bus" ("What about My Child?"). Nevertheless, Leonard Koppett in *Sports Illusion, Sports Reality* claims that a twelve-year-old trying to throw a curve ball, for example, may put abnormal strain on developing arm and shoulder muscles, sometimes resulting in lifelong injuries (294). Contact sports like football can be even more hazardous. Thomas Tutko, a psychology professor at San Jose State

University and coauthor of the book *Winning Is Everything and Other American Myths*, writes:

> I am strongly opposed to young kids playing tackle football. It is not the right stage of development for them to be taught to crash into other kids. Kids under the age of fourteen are not by nature physical. Their main concern is self-preservation. They don't want to meet head on and slam into each other. But tackle football absolutely requires that they try to hit each other as hard as they can. And it is too traumatic for young kids. (qtd. in Tosches A1)

What is most significant about this summary is that Romano not only repeats Statsky's main ideas in a condensed form, but also describes Statsky's moves as a writer:

Statsky offers the reason. . . .

She supports this reason by paraphrasing Koppett's statement. . . .

She then quotes Tutko. . . .

This description of each step in Statsky's argument shows readers exactly how Statsky uses paraphrase and quotation to support her argument about the potential for "overly competitive sports" to endanger children. Note that in summarizing, Romano here refers directly to the writer (*Statsky, She*). By naming Statsky and describing what Statsky is doing in this passage (*offers, supports, quotes*), Romano does not focus on the content of the original passage (as she does in our previous example of her summarizing an anecdote in Statsky's essay). Instead, Romano focuses here on Statsky's argumentative strategy of providing support for her reasons. Not every summary needs to include this kind of play-by-play description of the writer's strategic moves, but when you are evaluating an argument, it does help readers see how the writer constructs the argument.

Notice also that in this summary, Romano puts quotation marks around only one of the phrases she borrows from Statsky ("overly competitive sports"). Perhaps the reason she uses quotation marks around this particular phrase "overly competitive" is that Statsky uses it twice in her essay (paragraphs 3 and 13). It is a key phrase for Statsky and captures the essence of her argument that organized sports may be too competitive for children. Romano may have decided not to use quotation marks around other borrowed phrases such as *contact sports* and *tackle football* because they are common expressions and not specific to Statsky. Readers of summaries expect to see some words from the original. If writers, like Romano, make it perfectly clear when they are representing a source's language and ideas and also include careful citations to indicate where in the original text the material comes from, there is little concern about plagiarizing. Remember, however, that putting quotation marks around quoted words and phrases would avoid any misunderstanding. If you are unsure about whether you need quotation marks, consult your instructor.

Organizing Your Draft

With goals in mind and invention notes at hand, you are ready to make a first outline of your draft. Review the list of reasons you have developed. Tentatively select from that list the reasons you think will most effectively convince your readers of the plausibility of your judgment. Then decide how you will sequence these reasons. Some writers prefer to save their most telling reason or reasons for the end, whereas others try to group the reasons in some other logical pattern (for example, discussing all the technical reasons in a movie review together). Still other writers like to begin with reasons based on standards of judgment familiar to their readers. Whatever sequence you decide on for your reasons, make sure it will not strike your readers as illogical or haphazard.

Considering a Useful Sentence Strategy

As you draft your evaluative essay, you may want to compare or contrast your subject with similar subjects to establish your authority with readers. In addition, you are likely to want to balance your evaluation by criticizing one or more aspects of the subject if you generally praise it or by praising one or more aspects of it if you generally criticize it. To do so, you will need to use sentences that express comparisons or contrasts, including ones that contrast criticism with praise and vice versa.

Use sentences comparing or contrasting your subject with similar subjects to help convince readers that you are knowledgeable about the kind of subject you are evaluating. These sentences often make use of key comparative terms, such as *more*, *less*, *most*, *least*, *as*, *than*, *like*, *unlike*, *similar*, and *dissimilar*, as the readings in this chapter illustrate.

As with *Dances with Wolves* and *The Last Samurai*, this is about a military man who finds himself transformed by the culture he adopts and ends up opposing his own people in an impossible battle. (Berardinelli, paragraph 6)

. . . this is **the most** technically amazing motion picture to have arrived on screens in many years—perhaps since Peter Jackson's *The Return of the King*. (Berardinelli, paragraph 1)

"Workers distracted by e-mail and phone calls suffer a fall in IQ **more than** twice that found in marijuana smokers." (Rosen [quoting a BBC report], paragraph 4)

"Even if you learn while multitasking, that learning is **less** flexible and **more** specialized, so you cannot retrieve the information as easily." (Rosen [quoting Russell Poldrack], paragraph 9)

The visual style of the film is emphasized through the abundant use of both warm and cool colors, **reminiscent** of films like *Traffic* and *Amores Perros*. (Ballesteros, paragraph 4).

Sometimes writers do not use comparative terms but simply put compared or contrasted information side by side, as in these examples:

Roy Rogers, Baskin Robbins, Kentucky Fried Chicken, et al. may at first seem nothing but a vast extension of the lemonade stand. (Etzioni, paragraph 5)

His narrative could almost be considered a science fiction version of *Dances with Wolves* (by way of *Surrogates*), and it works for many of the reasons *Dances* worked. (Berardinelli, paragraph 2)

You can also increase your authority with readers by using sentences expressing comparison or contrast to balance criticism and praise. In general, these sentences rely on words expressing contrast—*but*, *although*, *however*, *while*, and *yet*—to set up the shift between the two responses.

True, you still have to have the gumption to get yourself over to the hamburger stand, **but** once you don the prescribed uniform, your task is spelled out in minute detail. (Etzioni, paragraph 7)

While it is true that these places provide income, work, and even some training to such youngsters, they also tend to perpetuate their disadvantaged status. (Etzioni, paragraph 11)

The picture that emerges of these pubescent multitasking mavens is of a generation of great technical facility and intelligence **but** of extreme impatience, unsatisfied with slowness and uncomfortable with silence. . . . (Rosen, paragraph 11)

Various aspects of the film's production, including acting, directing, and editing, contribute to making *Slumdog Millionaire* a great movie; **although** other aspects of production—a less than stellar script, for example, and plot ambiguities—lessen the magnitude of its greatness. (Ballesteros, paragraph 1)

In addition to using sentences that make comparisons or contrasts with other subjects and sentences that balance criticism and praise, you can strengthen your evaluation with other kinds of sentences as well. You may want to look at the information about using appositives (pp. 275–76) and sentences that combine concession and refutation (pp. 402–04).

READING A DRAFT CRITICALLY

Getting a critical reading of your draft will help you see how to improve it. Your instructor may schedule class time for reading drafts, or you may want to ask a classmate or a tutor in the writing center to read your draft. Ask your reader to use the following guidelines and to write out a response for you to consult as you revise.

Read for a First Impression

1. **Read the draft without stopping, and then write two or three sentences giving your general impression.**

2. **Identify one aspect of the draft that seems especially effective.**

Read Again to Suggest Improvements

1. **Recommend ways to strengthen the presentation of the subject.**

   - Tell the writer if the subject is identified clearly, pointing out where there is not enough or too much information about it and whether any information seems unclear, inaccurate, or only partly true.

   - Suggest how the writer could clarify the kind of subject it is, either by identifying the category by name or giving examples of familiar subjects of the same type.

   - If you are surprised by the way the writer has presented the subject, briefly explain your expectations for reading evaluations about subjects of this kind.

   - If visuals are included in the draft, indicate what you think they add to it, if anything. If visuals are not included, indicate whether they would be helpful and, if so, where.

2. **Suggest ways to clarify the overall judgment.**

   - Find and underline the writer's overall judgment, the essay's thesis statement. Let the writer know if you can't find a clearly stated thesis statement, one that asserts the subject's good and/or bad qualities.

- If you find several restatements of the thesis, examine them closely for consistency. Look specifically at the value terms the writer uses to see whether they are unclear or waffling.

3. **Recommend ways to strengthen the reasons and support.**

   - Highlight the reasons given for the overall judgment and the support given for these reasons.

   - Point to any reasons that are not based on appropriate criteria or valid standards for judging this kind of subject, or that are unclear or unconvincing.

   - Indicate where more support is needed or where the support is not convincing or clearly related to the reason.

4. **Suggest ways to improve the essay's response to likely objections and alternative judgments.**

   - Locate passages where the writer anticipates readers' objections, and suggest how the counterargument to them could be strengthened. Let the writer know if you have other objections that the writer has not anticipated or responded to adequately.

   - If the writer does not acknowledge likely alternative judgments, offer advice on what these judgments are and how they could be counterargued.

5. **Suggest how the organizational plan might be improved.**

   - Look for a forecasting statement early in the essay to see how well it lays out the argument—reasons and support—as well as the counterarguments. If there is no forecast, let the writer know whether adding one would make the essay easier to follow. If the forecast is incorrect, point out what's wrong with it.

   - Let the writer know if you see ways to improve the essay by rearranging the order of material or by inserting new or better transitions.

   - Indicate if the conclusion seems abrupt or less than helpful.

REVISING

This section offers suggestions for revising your draft. Revising means reenvisioning your draft, trying to see it in a new way, given your purpose and readers, in order to develop a better-argued evaluation.

The biggest mistake you can make while revising is to focus initially on words or sentences. Instead, first try to see your draft as a whole to assess its likely impact on your readers. To improve readability and strengthen your argument, think imaginatively and boldly about cutting unconvincing material, adding new material, and moving material around. Your computer makes even drastic revisions physically easy, but you still need to make the mental effort and decisions that will improve your draft.

You may have received help with this challenge from a classmate or tutor who gave your draft a critical reading. If so, keep this feedback in mind as you decide which parts of your draft need revising and what specific changes you could make. The following suggestions will help you solve problems and strengthen your essay.

TROUBLESHOOTING YOUR DRAFT

To Present the Subject More Effectively

Problem	Suggestions for Revising
The subject is not identified clearly.	• Identify the subject by name—such as the title and author, or director and main characters. • Describe the subject—summarize what it's about, cite statistics that establish its importance, give examples to make it concrete. • Consider adding visuals—photographs, graphs, tables, or charts—to help clarify the subject.
There is too much detail about the subject.	• Eliminate detail that is not related to your criteria for evaluation.
It's not clear what kind of subject it is.	• Classify the subject into a genre or category. • Refer to other reviews or reviewers of subjects of this kind. • Compare your subject to other, better known subjects of the same kind.
A visual in the draft seems not to add anything to the evaluation.	• Refer to the visuals in your text, if possible. • Find a new visual that would better support your argument.

To Clarify the Overall Judgment

Problem	Suggestions for Revising
The overall judgment is not asserted in a clear thesis statement.	• State your thesis early in the essay. • Revise the language in your thesis statement either to eliminate ambiguity or to clarify that your overall judgment is mixed. • Qualify your thesis if it seems overstated or is not supported by your argument.

To Clarify the Overall Judgment

Problem	Suggestions for Revising
Your restatements of the judgment seem contradictory.	• Make sure that your judgment is consistent throughout. • If your judgment changes in the course of the argument, modify your thesis statement to accommodate your changed or mixed evaluation.

To Strengthen the Reasons and Support

Problem	Suggestions for Revising
A reason is not based on what readers consider appropriate criteria.	• Clarify the criteria you use and try to justify them—by citing authorities or other reviews of similar subjects, by making comparisons, by explaining why your criteria are appropriate and perhaps preferable to others readers may be more familiar with.
Support for a reason is not provided, not convincing, or not clearly related to the reason.	• Add support by citing respected experts or research studies, providing facts or statistics, or giving specific examples. • To make the support convincing, cite your sources and indicate why they can be depended on. • Explain how the support backs the reason.

To Improve the Counterargument

Problem	Suggestions for Revising
A likely objection has not been anticipated or responded to adequately.	• If the objection undermines your argument, try to refute it—showing it is not based on widely held or appropriate criteria, or that it misunderstands your argument or the subject. • If the objection cannot be refuted, acknowledge it but consider demonstrating that it is only a minor concern that does not make your evaluation invalid. Try using sentence openers like *I understand that . . . , What I think is,* and *It is true that . . . , but my point is. . . .*
A likely alternative judgment has not been anticipated or responded to adequately.	• Mention good or bad qualities of the subject that others emphasize, even if you disagree with them on the subject's overall value. • If an alternative judgment is based on criteria you do not consider appropriate, consider citing authorities or making comparisons with other subjects of the same kind.

To Make the Organizational Plan More Effective

Problem	Suggestions for Revising
There is no forecast or the forecast is inaccurate or unclear.	• Add or fix the forecasting statement. • Make sure the forecast is placed early in the essay. • Repeat the key terms from your forecasting statement in the topic sentences.
The essay seems disorganized or is hard to follow.	• Review the overall organization by outlining the essay. If necessary, move, add, or delete sections to strengthen coherence. Make sure your reasons follow a logical sequence. • Add appropriate transitions or improve the existing ones.
The conclusion seems abrupt or awkward.	• Add a transition to signal the conclusion. • Try restating your judgment or summarizing your argument. • Consider whether you can frame the essay by echoing something from the opening.

EDITING AND PROOFREADING

After you have revised your essay, be sure to spend some time checking for errors in usage, punctuation, and mechanics and considering matters of style. If you keep a list of errors you typically make, begin by checking your draft against this list. Ask someone else to proofread your essay before you print out a copy for your instructor or send it electronically.

From our research on student writing, we know that evaluative essays have frequent problems in sentences that set up comparisons. The comparisons can be incomplete, illogical, or unclear. Edit carefully any sentences that set up comparisons between your subject and others. Check a writer's handbook for help with making all comparisons complete, logical, and clear.

Reflecting on What You Have Learned

Evaluation

In this chapter, you have read critically several evaluative essays and have written one of your own. To better remember what you have learned, pause now to reflect on the reading and writing activities you completed in this chapter.

1. Write a page or so reflecting on what you have learned. Begin by describing what you are most pleased with in your essay. Then explain what you think contributed to your achievement. Be specific about this contribution.

   - If it was something you learned from the readings, indicate which readings and specifically what you learned from them.

   - If it came from your invention writing, point out the section or sections that helped you most.

   - If you got good advice from a critical reader, explain exactly how the person helped you—perhaps by helping you understand a particular problem in your draft or by helping you add a new dimension to your writing.

   - Try to write about your achievement in terms of what you have learned about the genre.

2. Reflect more generally on evaluative essays, a genre of writing that plays an important role in education and in many other areas of life and work in the United States. Consider some of the following questions: How confident do you feel about asserting a judgment and supporting it? How comfortable are you playing the role of judge and jury on the subject? How do your personal preferences and values influence your judgment? How might your gender, ethnicity, religious beliefs, age, or social class influence your ideas about the subject? What contribution might evaluative essays make to our society that other genres cannot make?

CHAPTER 7

Position Paper

Y ou may associate arguing with quarreling or with the in-your-face debating we often hear on radio and television talk shows. These ways of arguing may let us vent strong feelings, but they seldom lead us to consider seriously other points of view, let alone to look critically at our own thinking or learn anything new.

This chapter presents a more deliberative way of arguing that we call *reasoned argument* because it depends on giving reasons rather than raising voices. It demands that positions be supported rather than merely asserted. It also commands respect for the right of others to disagree with you as you may disagree with them. Reasoned argument requires more thought than quarreling but no less passion or commitment, as you will see when you read the position papers in this chapter.

Controversial issues are, by definition, issues about which people have strong feelings and sometimes disagree vehemently. The issue may involve a practice that has been accepted for some time, such as coeducational public schooling, or it may concern a newly proposed policy or recently controversial issue, such as whether the media is glorifying teen pregnancy and motherhood. People may agree about goals but disagree about the best way to achieve them, as in the perennial debate over how to guarantee adequate health care for all citizens. Or they may disagree about fundamental values and beliefs, as in the debate over affirmative action in college admissions.

As these examples suggest, position papers take on controversial issues that have no obvious "right" answer, no truth everyone accepts, no single authority everyone trusts. Consequently, simply gathering information—finding the facts or learning from experts—will not settle these disputes because ultimately they are matters of opinion and judgment.

Although it is not possible to prove that a position on a controversial issue is right or wrong, it is possible through argument to convince others to consider a particular position seriously or to accept or reject a position. To be convincing, a position paper must argue for its position by giving readers strong reasons and solid support. It also must anticipate opposing arguments.

As you read and discuss the selections in this chapter, you will discover why position papers play such an important role in college, the workplace, and civic life. You will also learn how position papers work. From the essays and from the ideas for writing that follow each selection, you will get many ideas for taking a position on an issue that you care about. As you read and write about the selections, keep in mind the following assignment, which sets out the goals for writing a position paper. To support your writing of this assignment, this chapter concludes with a Guide to Writing Position Papers.

THE WRITING ASSIGNMENT

Arguing a Position on an Issue

Choose an issue that you have strong feelings about, and write an essay arguing your position on this issue. Your purpose is to convince your readers to take your argument seriously. Therefore, you will need to acknowledge readers' opposing views as well as any objections or questions they might have.

WRITING SITUATIONS FOR POSITION PAPERS

Writing that takes a position on a controversial issue plays a significant role in college work and professional life, as the following examples indicate:

- A committee made up of business and community leaders investigates the issue of regulating urban growth. After reviewing the arguments for and against government regulation, committee members argue against it on the grounds that supply and demand alone will regulate development, that landowners should be permitted to sell their property to the highest bidder, and that developers are guided by the needs of the market and thus serve the people.

- For an economics class, a student writes a term paper on the controversies surrounding the rising cost of public education. She first learns about the subject from television news, but she knows that she needs more information to write a paper on the topic. Online and in the library, she finds several blogs, newspaper and magazine articles, and contemporary books that help her understand better the debate over the issues. In her paper, she presents the strongest arguments on the different sides but concludes that, to be economically viable, public education needs more financial support from various sectors, including business, government, and nonprofit organizations.

• For a political science class, a student is assigned to write an essay on public employees' right to strike. Having no well-defined position herself, she discusses the issue with her mother, a nurse in a county hospital, and her uncle, a firefighter. Her mother believes that public employees like hospital workers and teachers should have the right to strike but that police officers and firefighters should not because public safety would be endangered. The uncle disagrees, arguing that allowing hospital workers to strike would jeopardize public safety as much as allowing firefighters to strike. He insists that the central issue is not public safety but workers' rights. In her essay, the student supports the right of public employees to strike but argues that arbitration should be required whenever a strike might jeopardize public safety.

Thinking about Your Experience

Position Arguments

Before studying a type of writing, it is useful to spend some time thinking about what you already know on the subject. You may have discussed with friends or family your position on a controversial issue, and you may have written essays for classes examining the positions of experts in fields where controversial issues abound, such as in science, social science, business, education, and even your writing class. People in all fields, ranging from medicine and government to corporations and small businesses, deal with controversial issues every day and take positions based on their current knowledge.

Recall a time when you argued orally or in writing about a controversial issue that captured your interest. Then consider questions like these: What did you already know about the issue when you took your position? Who was your audience for your argument? What made you think it was significant?

Reflect also on the position arguments you have read, heard, or seen in the media. What made them interesting or convincing?

Write at least a page about your experiences with position arguments.

A GUIDE TO READING POSITION PAPERS

This guide introduces you to the basic features and strategies typical of essays that take a position on controversial issues by looking closely at a passionate essay in defense of science written by Brian Greene. Focus first on *reading for meaning*, seeking to understand and respond to Greene's argument as well as on the meanings you find in the essay—for example, your own feelings about science and the way it's taught. Then, to learn how Greene makes his essay thoughtful and fair, try *reading like a writer* by analyzing his writing strategies. These two activities—reading for meaning and reading like a writer—follow every reading in this chapter.

Brian Greene

Put a Little Science in Your Life

Brian Greene (b. 1963) earned his PhD from Oxford University as a Rhodes Scholar, and currently is professor of mathematics and physics at Columbia University, where he is also codirector of the Institute for Strings, Cosmology, and Astroparticle Physics (ISCAP). Greene is author of three books for a general audience about physics: The Elegant Universe: Super-strings, Hidden Dimensions, and the Quest for the Ultimate Theory *(1999);* The Fabric of the Cosmos: Space, Time, and the Texture of Reality *(2004); and* Icarus at the Edge of Time *(2008).* The Elegant Universe *was made into a PBS television special that won a 2003 Peabody Award.*

Greene, whose Web site can be found at http://www.iscap.columbia. edu, organized the annual World Science Festival in New York City in 2008, has made many media appearances, and helped actor John Lithgow with scientific dialogue for the television series 3rd Rock from the Sun. *He is a contributing editor for the* New York Times, *where the essay below was published in 2008. Greene believes science should be placed alongside music, art, and literature as fields that give life meaning. As you read, think about your own experiences with science, either in school or out of it.*

1   A couple of years ago I received a letter from an American soldier in Iraq. The letter began by saying that, as we've all become painfully aware, serving on the front lines is physically exhausting and emotionally debilitating. But the reason for his writing was to tell me that in that hostile and lonely environment, a book I'd written had become a kind of lifeline. As the book is about science—one that traces physicists' search for nature's deepest laws—the soldier's letter might strike you as, well, odd.

2   But it's not. Rather, it speaks to the powerful role science can play in giving life context and meaning. At the same time, the soldier's letter emphasized something I've increasingly come to believe: our educational system fails to teach science in a way that allows students to integrate it into their lives.

3   Allow me a moment to explain.

4   When we consider the ubiquity of cellphones, iPods, personal computers and the Internet, it's easy to see how science (and the technology to which it leads) is woven into the fabric of our day-to-day activities. When we benefit from CT scanners, M.R.I. devices, pacemakers and arterial stents,

we can immediately appreciate how science affects the quality of our lives. When we assess the state of the world, and identify looming challenges like climate change, global pandemics, security threats and diminishing resources, we don't hesitate in turning to science to gauge the problems and find solutions.

And when we look at the wealth of opportunities hovering on the horizon—stem cells, genomic sequencing, personalized medicine, longevity research, nanoscience, brain-machine interface, quantum computers, space technology—we realize how crucial it is to cultivate a general public that can engage with scientific issues; there's simply no other way that as a society we will be prepared to make informed decisions on a range of issues that will shape the future.

These are the standard—and enormously important—reasons many would give in explaining why science matters.

But here's the thing. The reason science really matters runs deeper still. Science is a way of life. Science is a perspective. Science is the process that takes us from confusion to understanding in a manner that's precise, predictive and reliable—a transformation, for those lucky enough to experience it, that is empowering and emotional. To be able to think through and grasp explanations—for everything from why the sky is blue to how life formed on earth—not because they are declared dogma but rather because they reveal patterns confirmed by experiment and observation, is one of the most precious of human experiences.

As a practicing scientist, I know this from my own work and study. But I also know that you don't have to be a scientist for science to be transformative. I've seen children's eyes light up as I've told them about black holes and the Big Bang. I've spoken with high school dropouts who've stumbled on popular science books about the human genome project, and then returned to school with newfound purpose. And in that letter from Iraq, the soldier told me how learning about relativity and quantum physics in the dusty and dangerous environs of greater Baghdad kept him going because it revealed a deeper reality of which we're all a part.

It's striking that science is still widely viewed as merely a subject one studies in the classroom or an isolated body of largely esoteric knowledge that sometimes shows up in the "real" world in the form of technological or medical advances. In reality, science is a language of hope and inspiration, providing discoveries that fire the imagination and instill a sense of connection to our lives and our world.

If science isn't your strong suit—and for many it's not—this side of science is something you may have rarely if ever experienced. I've spoken with so many people over the years whose encounters with science in school left them thinking of it as cold, distant and intimidating. They happily use the innovations that science makes possible, but feel that the science itself is just not relevant to their lives. What a shame.

11   Like a life without music, art or literature, a life without science is bereft of something that gives experience a rich and otherwise inaccessible dimension.

12   It's one thing to go outside on a crisp, clear night and marvel at a sky full of stars. It's another to marvel not only at the spectacle but to recognize that those stars are the result of exceedingly ordered conditions 13.7 billion years ago at the moment of the Big Bang. It's another still to understand how those stars act as nuclear furnaces that supply the universe with carbon, oxygen and nitrogen, the raw material of life as we know it.

13   And it's yet another level of experience to realize that those stars account for less than 4 percent of what's out there—the rest being of an unknown composition, so-called dark matter and energy, which researchers are now vigorously trying to divine.

14   As every parent knows, children begin life as uninhibited, unabashed explorers of the unknown. From the time we can walk and talk, we want to know what things are and how they work—we begin life as little scientists. But most of us quickly lose our intrinsic scientific passion. And it's a profound loss.

15   A great many studies have focused on this problem, identifying important opportunities for improving science education. Recommendations have ranged from increasing the level of training for science teachers to curriculum reforms.

16   But most of these studies (and their suggestions) avoid an overarching systemic issue: in teaching our students, we continually fail to activate rich opportunities for revealing the breathtaking vistas opened up by science, and instead focus on the need to gain competency with science's underlying technical details.

17   In fact, many students I've spoken to have little sense of the big questions those technical details collectively try to answer: Where did the universe come from? How did life originate? How does the brain give rise to consciousness? Like a music curriculum that requires its students to practice scales while rarely if ever inspiring them by playing the great masterpieces, this way of teaching science squanders the chance to make students sit up in their chairs and say, "Wow, that's science?"

18   In physics, just to give a sense of the raw material that's available to be leveraged, the most revolutionary of advances have happened in the last 100 years—special relativity, general relativity, quantum mechanics—a symphony of discoveries that changed our conception of reality. More recently, the last 10 years have witnessed an upheaval in our understanding of the universe's composition, yielding a wholly new prediction for what the cosmos will be like in the far future.

19   These are paradigm-shaking developments. But rare is the high school class, and rarer still is the middle school class, in which these breakthroughs

INSTRUCTOR'S MANUAL for

READING CRITICALLY
WRITING WELL

A Reader and Guide

NINTH EDITION

Rise B. Axelrod

*University of California,
Riverside*

Charles R. Cooper

*University of California,
San Diego*

Alison M. Warriner

*California State University,
East Bay*

Lawrence Barkley

Mt. San Jacinto College—Menifee

Gray Scott

*University of California,
Riverside*

Bedford/St. Martin's　　　　**Boston ◆ New York**

Manufactured in the United States of America.

5 4 3 2 1 0
f e d c b a

For information, write: Bedford/St. Martin's, 75 Arlington Street, Boston, MA 02116 (617-399-4000)

ISBN: 978-0-312-62799-7

CONTENTS

Part 5 TEACHING CHAPTER 1 _____ 28

Part 6 TEACHING CHAPTERS 2–9 _____ 30

Part 1 PURPOSE AND OVERVIEW OF THIS MANUAL

This *Instructor's Manual* supports teaching with *Reading Critically, Writing Well*, Ninth Edition. Beginning teachers will find comprehensive support for planning a course, presenting and discussing the readings, and giving and evaluating writing assignments. Experienced instructors will find resources to complement their teaching styles and to orient them quickly to the readings. Online teachers and teachers using course management systems such as Blackboard to enhance their on-campus classes will find examples of how to use the text in an online learning environment.

Part 2 of the manual offers a rationale for basic features of the text, and Part 3 outlines alternative course plans. Part 4 presents teaching activities to support your work with this text—activities like presenting and discussing readings, assigning journal work, organizing students to work collaboratively, organizing draft workshops, conferencing, evaluating students' work, and managing the workload. Instead of giving general advice, we share specific strategies and activities we have developed in our own programs. If you are a beginning instructor, you will find Part 4 particularly helpful. It will enable you to approach your course confidently and to get good work from your students right away. Part 5 discusses Chapter 1, which introduces students to the kinds of work they will be doing in each subsequent chapter.

Part 6, the longest part, discusses the genre chapters (Chapters 2–9) in general and then each chapter in turn, providing an orientation to the writing assignment, an overview of the readings, resources for teaching the Reading for Meaning and Reading like a Writer activities following the readings, and an outline of A Guide to Writing.

Part 2 RATIONALE FOR THE BASIC FEATURES OF THE TEXT

This part explains briefly why we wrote *Reading Critically, Writing Well* the way we did. Our discussion of the ideas behind the text takes up the following topics:

- the relation between reading and writing in a writing course;
- the rationale for teaching critical reading strategies for both texts and visuals and the way that practicing critical reading strategies contributes to writing development;
- the reasons students need a comprehensive framework of support as they draft and revise, with a focus on systematic invention;
- the text's chapter sequence and relations among the chapters; and
- the possibilities for library, Internet, and field research in a course using this text.

RELATING READING AND WRITING BY GENRE

Schemas—memory for text—guide our reading and writing. Novice writers must develop schemas for the genres they will read and write in college and on the job. These schemas are learned through reading many essays in a genre, by analyzing selected essays rhetorically and stylistically, and by writing and revising essays with genre criteria in mind. Genre schemas permit more confident, efficient reading and foster productive invention, planning, critical reading of drafts, and revising.

We understand a genre to be a social construct that has evolved over time to meet writers' needs in recurring and now familiar writing situations. Genres make communication possible within a particular culture or society. From a writer's point of view, genres are useful tools that enable and facilitate composing. While there can be a wide variety of form and strategy within a genre—as readings in this text illustrate—experienced readers and writers in a culture recognize paradigmatic instances. Though genres are stable over time—communication requires them to be—a particular genre may change or even disappear in response to a culture's changing rhetorical demands.

Current discourse theory and professional writers' experience confirm that each of the genres explored in Chapters 2 to 9—autobiography, observation, reflection, explaining concepts, evaluation, position paper, speculation about causes or effects, and proposal to solve a problem—requires of students a special way of thinking and composing. In each genre, students must solve unique rhetorical problems and use information, memories, or arguments in particular ways.

Unless they read widely and critically on their own or come from high schools with comprehensive writing programs where teachers understand the instructional implications of genre theory, students will need careful, focused instruction in the reading and writing of genres. This text provides the materials, activities, and assignments for such instruction.

Using this text, students write autobiography as they are reading it, or they write proposals to solve problems as they are reading problem-solution essays. The readings collected in each of the chapters (2–9) illustrate a wide range of strategies used by writers of that genre for different rhetorical purposes. Students observe many ways to begin, end, pattern, and develop a genre. They see writers solving predictable problems in different ways. This close matching of reading and writing by genre is the best way to realize fully the contribution reading can make to writing development in a composition course.

The text does more than simply match reading and writing by genre, however. An activity we call Reading like a Writer, which follows each reading, helps students understand the constraints and possibilities of a genre. They learn to read a genre—and they learn to read it the way a writer does.

CRITICAL READING

Reading critically, we believe, is a skill students can learn. We don't promise to make critical reading easy. In fact, we make reading harder and slower—but more productive. For every selection in the text, we invite students first to read for meaning and then to read like writers. And we ask them to read with pencil in hand, annotating the text from these two perspectives. Most important, we ask them to write about what they discover, using writing itself to explore ideas and to consolidate what they have learned. Writing becomes part of critical reading—an essential activity that provides a tentative record of meanings and insights students can then share with others and thereby further enlarge what they can learn from reading.

ADDITIONAL CRITICAL READING STRATEGIES In addition to these two critical reading strategies—Reading for Meaning and Reading like a Writer—we provide a Catalog of Critical Reading strategies in Appendix 1 in the text:

- Annotating
- Previewing
- Outlining
- Summarizing

- Paraphrasing
- Synthesizing
- Questioning to understand and remember
- Contextualizing
- Reflecting on challenges to your beliefs and values
- Exploring the significance of figurative language
- Looking for patterns of opposition
- Evaluating the logic of an argument
- Using a Toulmin analysis
- Recognizing logical fallacies
- Recognizing emotional manipulation
- Judging the writer's credibility
- Comparing and contrasting related readings

Each genre chapter includes reading activities that apply one or two of the listed methods to specific readings. You may assign those readings and reading activities in order to give students more exposure to the sorts of reading strategies just listed. Some of these strategies engage students in comparing and contrasting related readings as part of this edition's emphasis on linked readings. You may, of course, decide to have students use a strategy from this appendix with other readings.

The comprehensive, approachable, theory-based, and research-supported program of critical reading offered in the text provides no panacea, however. We know that what students get from a reading depends in part on what they bring to it. Consequently, when students read headnotes, we invite them to reflect on their knowledge of a reading's subject, and we offer them one purpose for reading. We also know that reading can be considerably enriched by discussion: textual meaning making at its best is in part a social activity. Consequently, we make it easy for you to help students share their writing in response to the Reading for Meaning and Reading like a Writer activities following every reading.

STRATEGIES FOR ANALYZING VISUALS Readers today must be skilled and savvy readers of visuals as well as of language, thanks to the Information Age's frequent marriage of text and visuals. For this reason, *Reading Critically, Writing Well* includes guidance for students on how to critically "read" images online, in film, or in other media. Instructors interested in having students practice or hone such skills may want to assign and discuss Appendix 3: Strategies for Analyzing Visuals, and follow up with any of the Analyzing Visuals activities in the genre chapters (2–9). The Analyzing Visuals activities for individual genre chapters are discussed in each of the associated sections of Part 6 in this manual.

WRITING INSTRUCTION

The pencil-in-hand critical reading strategies discussed above contribute directly to students' writing development. Though critical reading is necessary for developing writing skills in a genre, it is not sufficient. Students also need comprehensive support for invention, drafting, and revising an essay in a genre. This text provides such support through activities and guides.

READING LIKE A WRITER Students complete a full rhetorical analysis of each chapter's opening sample essay in A Guide to Reading. In addition, they analyze a key rhetorical strategy of each subsequent reading in a chapter. If they complete these activities for every reading, they learn about all the basic features and writing strategies of a genre.

What they learn greatly improves the chances for successful peer critique. (Part 4 discusses ways to organize peer critiques, or *draft workshops*, as we call them.)

CONSIDERING IDEAS FOR YOUR OWN WRITING Following each reading in Chapters 2 through 9 is a section titled Considering Ideas for Your Own Writing, which offers specific subjects and ways students can write in the genre they are learning to read critically. They can collect and focus promising subjects as they move from reading to reading, thereby getting a head start toward choosing a subject for an essay.

REVIEWING WHAT MAKES AN EFFECTIVE ESSAY This activity comes at the end of the readings and just before students begin working on the writing assignment. It asks students to review and consolidate everything they have learned about the rhetorical features and strategies of a genre.

GUIDES TO WRITING Each genre chapter (2–9) concludes with A Guide to Writing, which is concise but comprehensive. This guide leads (and encourages) students through the writing process: invention, drafting, reading a draft critically, revising, editing and proofreading, and reflecting on what they have learned. There now is solid evidence that guided, systematic invention enables students to write better. Therefore, each chapter provides genre-specific Invention and Research activities that are based on established heuristics like freewriting, answering questions, list making, outlining, and analyzing readers. Each activity requires only a few minutes (as few as one or two and rarely more than thirty). (See Part 4 of this manual for a discussion about assigning and encouraging invention.)

The Invention and Research activities, all of which involve some writing, enable students to find a subject, generate ideas about it, explore their writing situation fully, and even carry out any necessary research. These writings may record several days of a potentially rich invention process. Students who use the full resources for invention compose first drafts that are longer, more thoughtful, more interesting, and closer to their best work on a subject.

The guides also help students give and get critical readings of their drafts, set goals before and during drafting, and organize their essays prior to drafting. Each guide concludes with advice about revising to strengthen the essay and improve its readability, suggestions for editing and proofreading the revised essay, and an invitation to reflect on what has been learned.

These Guides to Writing complement the critical reading strategies. Together, they provide a comprehensive program in reading and writing. They bring reading and writing together in a way that gives every student a chance to become more literate.

CHAPTER SEQUENCE

Although the genre chapters can be presented in different sequences (see the discussion of various course plans in Part 3), we offer here a brief rationale for the text sequence. These are the chapters:

Chapter 2: Autobiography
Chapter 3: Observation
Chapter 4: Reflection
Chapter 5: Explaining Concepts
Chapter 6: Evaluation
Chapter 7: Position Paper

Chapter 8: Speculating about Causes or Effects
Chapter 9: Proposal to Solve a Problem

The sequence moves from experiential, observational, and explanatory writing (2–5) to persuasive or argumentative (6–9) writing. While an autobiographical essay is not necessarily easier to write than a position paper, there are certain advantages to our sequence. If students begin with autobiography, firsthand observation, and reflection, they need not struggle with library and Internet research. Instead, students work with familiar or immediately available material and learn to value their own memory and perception—developing a confident, assertive voice in their writing. Strategies of description and narration practiced in autobiography are central to observation and reflection. The anecdotes important to autobiography and reflection can emerge again very usefully in certain arguments.

Observation, reflection, and explanation offer opportunities for students to organize their material topically, use explicit topic sentences and cueing devices, and employ a variety of strategies (or modes) for developing their subjects and achieving their rhetorical purposes. Even autobiography that focuses on a remembered person typically is organized topically.

Chapter 6 begins an argument sequence that comprises half the genre chapters in the text. This sequence begins with evaluation and position papers to give students practice at expressing and defending judgments before they move on to more complicated genres of argument: speculating about causes and effects, and proposing solutions. The sequence closes with proposing solutions because this genre incorporates those that have gone before it. For example, when students write a proposal to solve a problem in Chapter 9, they may argue the causes or effects of the problem and evaluate alternative solutions.

The argument chapters emphasize strategies for devising plausible arguments for particular readers. The students' writing situation in each chapter can be viewed as follows:

- demonstrating the validity of a judgment (Chapter 6),
- defending a position on an issue (Chapter 7),
- conjecturing about possible causes or effects (Chapter 8),
- arguing the feasibility of a solution to a problem (Chapter 9).

This sequence provides a challenging introduction to the critical reading and writing of argumentation.

EMPHASIS ON LIBRARY, INTERNET, AND FIELD RESEARCH

Since research can strengthen student writing in Chapters 3 and 5 to 9, the text regularly invites library, Internet, or field research. In addition, Appendix 2 provides guidance with these three kinds of research. Although research can be emphasized toward the end of a course, students have so much to learn about finding and evaluating sources, integrating sources into their essays, and citing sources properly that we believe they should be doing some research early in the course. Hence, the text features field research in Chapter 3: Observation and library and Internet research in Chapter 5: Explaining Concepts. All subsequent chapters regularly invite students to do research. Such an emphasis on research provides a realistic introduction to writing in academic and professional situations. Many of the readings, including student readings, use and cite sources. Nevertheless, in a writing program that does not require students to use sources or does not take up sources until the second semester, students can easily skip the research steps in every chapter's Guide to Writing. They can instead support their arguments from personal experience and present knowledge.

5

Composition instructors typically organize their courses around writing assignments. Because *Reading Critically, Writing Well* covers eight genres and includes many ideas for writing in each genre chapter, it offers different possibilities for designing a course. This part describes a variety of course plans you can use as the basis of your own syllabus, beginning with a six-assignment plan. Then come plans for a two-semester program, a one-semester argument course, a quarter program, and a two-quarter program. Finally, we discuss the opportunities for research with the text, including an extended library and Internet research paper.

ONE-SEMESTER PLAN: SIX ASSIGNMENTS

This plan permits six essay assignments from Chapters 2 to 9. Though this plan does not include a formal, extended research paper, many assignments invite research. For example, beginning with Chapter 5, every chapter invites students to carry out library or Internet research.

From this plan, you could readily devise a syllabus for your course. All the suggested course plans in this section assume that you might be requiring frequent writing in a journal, making collaborative-learning assignments, arranging in-class workshops for peer critiques of drafts, or holding conferences over drafts. Part 4 offers advice on all these activities.

Here are the essay assignments, by chapter title, in this plan:

Autobiography (Chapter 2)
Observation (Chapter 3)
Reflection (Chapter 4)
Explaining Concepts (Chapter 5)
Evaluation (Chapter 6)
Proposal to Solve a Problem (Chapter 9)

This plan gives balanced attention to personal writing (Chapters 2, 4), explanatory writing (Chapters 3, 5), and argument (Chapters 6, 9). It uses all chapters except Chapter 7: Position Paper and Chapter 8: Speculating about Causes or Effects. Chapters 7 and 8 could be substituted for Chapters 6 and 9.

Keeping in mind that each of our assignment chapters offers many critical reading and writing activities, you might want to allow as much as three weeks for each assignment, especially if you ask students to revise their essays. Here's how one assignment sequence might play out over a three-week period in a class meeting three times weekly:

Week 1
M: Discuss the chapter opening and writing situations.
     Do in class the reflective activity, Thinking about Your Experience with [the Genre].
     Assign the introductory reading and Reading for Meaning activity.
W: Discuss Reading for Meaning writing.
     Do in class one of the Reading like a Writer activities.
     Assign the remaining Reading like a Writer activities.
F: Discuss Reading like a Writer activities.

Discuss possible essay subjects in Considering Ideas for Your Own Writing following each reading.

Assign the first Invention and Research activities in A Guide to Writing.

Assign the second and third readings and their Reading for Meaning and Reading like a Writer activities.

Week 2

M: Discuss the second and third readings and reading activities.
   Evaluate subjects for essays.
   Discuss Invention and Research activities.
   Assign the fourth and fifth readings and reading activities.
W: Discuss the fourth and fifth readings and reading activities.
   Do in class an Invention and Research activity from A Guide to Writing. Assign other Invention and Research activities.
   Do in class as a group activity Reviewing What Makes an Effective Essay.
   Discuss possible organizational plans.
F: Assign the remainder of Invention and Research activities.
   Assign the first draft.

Week 3

M: Hold a workshop on drafts.
W: Hold a further workshop on drafts or in-class work on revising drafts.
F: The revision is due.
   Conduct in-class editing and proofreading exercises.
   Do the Reflecting on What You Have Learned activity.

TWO-SEMESTER PLAN: TEN ASSIGNMENTS

Several colleges use *Reading Critically, Writing Well* as the basic text, usually along with a handbook or one or more trade books, for a two-semester writing program. A capacious two-semester plan like the following allows multiple resources in certain chapters to be used to the fullest. Here we list a possible essay sequence, assuming a pattern of course activities and assignments like that of the one-semester plan detailed above.

Assignment	Chapter
1	2, Autobiography: Narrating the Story
2	2, Autobiography: Describing People
3	3, Observation
4	4, Reflection
5	5, Explaining Concepts
6	6, Evaluation
7	7, Position Paper
8	8, Speculating about Causes or Effects (speculating about causes)
9	8, Speculating about Causes or Effects (speculating about effects)
10	9, Proposal to Solve a Problem

A variation on this plan is to do one autobiography assignment and then assign an observation, a reflection, or an evaluation essay centered on some part of the writing process. Students might reflect, in a formal graded essay, on their experiences writing a previous paper, or they might observe the writing process of a classmate or a team and write an observation paper about it, or they might write formal evaluations of essays written by classmates (as Christine Romano does in Chapter 6, where she evaluates Jessica Statsky's position paper from Chapter 7).

SEMESTER PLAN FOR AN ARGUMENT COURSE

The text includes enough material on argument to fill a one-semester course concerned solely with argument or persuasion:

Assignment	Chapter
1	6, Evaluation
2	7, Position Paper (without research)
3	7, Position Paper (with research)
4	8, Speculating about Causes or Effects (speculating about causes)
5	8, Speculating about Causes or Effects (speculating about effects)
6	9, Proposal to Solve a Problem

This plan could make good use of the critical reading strategies—such as Evaluating the Logic of an Argument, Using a Toulmin Analysis, Recognizing Emotional Manipulation, and Judging the Writer's Credibility—in Appendix 1. At the instructor's or student's discretion, some assignments might call for students to analyze visuals, using the strategies in Appendix 3. Assignments 1, 4, and 5 above are particularly well suited for visual analysis, as students could evaluate the effectiveness of a visual or craft arguments about the possible effects of the visual or the causes of particularly common visual elements.

QUARTER PLAN: FOUR ASSIGNMENTS

One-quarter courses can accommodate four of our assignments, though some courses that use our text give three or five assignments. Many programs at quarter-system campuses require students to complete two quarters of composition.

A one-quarter program faces hard choices. A sampling of personal, explanatory, and persuasive writing might look like this:

Assignment	Chapter
1	2, Autobiography
2	3, Observation
3	7, Position Paper
4	9, Proposal to Solve a Problem

TWO-QUARTER PLAN: EIGHT ASSIGNMENTS

A two-quarter program, with four assignments each quarter, might be organized as follows:

Assignment	Chapter
1	2, Autobiography
2	3, Observation
3	4, Reflection
4	5, Explaining Concepts
5	6, Evaluation
6	7, Position Paper

WHAT ABOUT THE RESEARCH PAPER?

Except for the Chapter 3 observational essay, which requires observing and interviewing, every essay arising from Chapters 2 to 9 can be completed without research. In fact, the ideas for writing following each reading and the choosing-a-subject section at the beginning of the Invention and Research sequence of each Guide to Writing are designed to suggest many possibilities for writing that allow students to rely on their own present knowledge, experience, and resources. At the same time, every chapter except Autobiography can engage students in research, if the instructor wishes. We expect at least limited research with nearly all the assignments in our own programs. Here we briefly outline the possibilities:

Chapter 3, Observation: Visiting a place, observing, interviewing, taking notes

Chapter 5, Explaining Concepts: Library research on the concepts that students explain

Chapter 6, Evaluation: Reseeing, revisiting, or rereading the subject being evaluated and taking notes

Chapter 7, Position Paper: Library research on an issue to define and describe it adequately and to assess others' positions

Chapter 8, Speculating about Causes or Effects: Library research on the event, trend, or phenomenon speculated about to describe it fully and to survey others' proposed causes or effects

Chapter 9, Proposal to Solve a Problem: Interviewing people to understand more fully a problem affecting them and to anticipate their preferred solutions; research on methods of implementing a proposed solution

Appendix 2: Strategies for Research and Documentation provides comprehensive support for field (observing and interviewing), library, and Internet research.

If your program requires an extended library-research paper, the most likely candidates in the text are Chapters 5 and 9—the one explanatory, the other argumentative. These chapters, along with Appendix 2, provide full support for an extended research essay. Any of our proposed plans, above, could be adjusted to allow time during the final three or four weeks of a course for a library-research paper.

Part 4 TEACHING ACTIVITIES FOR A COURSE USING THIS TEXT

This part outlines basic teaching activities to support your work with this text. These activities, we believe, are important to the success of any composition course, whatever the textbook or other materials.

If you are a beginning instructor, you will find this section particularly helpful. Along with a syllabus based on one of our course plans in Part 3, the activities outlined in this part permit you to organize a complete course from start to finish: schedule, assignments, classroom and homework activities, evaluation of student writing, and record keeping. Instead of offering general advice in this part, we share activities, assignments, and materials we have used in our own programs along with at least a hundred instructors who have worked with us over the years.

Note: This part presents proven teaching activities; the final two parts of this manual (Parts 5 and 6) provide specific support for teaching the introductory chapter and each genre chapter.

PRESENTING AND DISCUSSING READINGS

If students are to succeed with an essay assignment in one of our genre chapters, they should read—and critically reread—the selections in that chapter. They should compare and contrast readings to see the full range of possibilities for their own essay in a genre. Class discussions of readings should be focused, productive, and encouraging to students as writers. How might you ensure such critical reading and discussions? This section offers suggestions.

GIVING CLEAR AND COMPLETE ASSIGNMENTS Even in a casual, slow-moving course using *Reading Critically, Writing Well*, assignments will be frequent: both the writing and the reading call for almost daily student work. If you find our other recommendations in this section persuasive, you can pursue several complementary strands of work, engaging students in a variety of out-of-class assignments each week.

Probably the most effective way to give assignments is to prepare a once-a-week handout, or online announcement if your campus uses Blackboard or some other Internet-based course management system. Even though we give students a detailed course sylla-bus, we further detail assignments for each week. We put assignments in writing because students do not all hear the same thing, it seems, when we give assignments orally and also because we want to save class time by not dictating assignments or writing them on the board. The weekly assignment handout precludes giving hasty last-minute assignments orally as students gather up books and head for the door. Most important, we think, preparing the weekly assignment handout gives us an opportunity to think through carefully what we want to accomplish in a given week.

Except for drafting and revising full essays, assignments in a course using this text are relatively brief. For example, a single selection and its reading activities might take an hour. After a reading, exploring in one's journal an idea for writing might take ten or fifteen minutes. Each chapter's introductory reading and related activities might require two hours, time best divided into two or more working periods during one or two days, and some of these activities might even be conducted in class.

In A Guide to Writing in any genre chapter, invention work entails brief writings spread over two or three days. Such frequent writing—our goal for students is *daily* writing—lets the mind work on the readings, consolidate new rhetorical learning, and produce ideas for writing. Consequently, *frequency* and *variety* of writing are essential. Pacing work during the week and from week to week is crucial. Your weekly assignment handout can pace, sequence, and clarify this work. As a result, students can efficiently use their limited time to prepare for class.

We give weekly assignments at the beginning of the first class meeting of each week and take a few minutes to go over the assignments and answer any questions. Because we provide the handout, students who come late rarely take our time after class to discuss assignments. A student who must be absent can later pick up the assignment handout or download it.

Some instructors add to the assignment handout comments reiterating course goals, previewing an especially challenging assignment, forecasting a change of pace, praising or exhorting the class, summarizing progress and anticipating next developments, relating concepts and assignments to give students a larger view of the course, and so on.

PREVIEWING READINGS Most of the readings are preceded by "as you read" suggestions and questions. These questions are designed to help students activate prior knowledge of the subject and read more purposefully. These questions enrich readings, and they may also entice or invite students to read a reading. However, as you assign a reading, you can do still more to entice students to read it:

- Tell them some things you may know about the historical or cultural context of the reading.
- Tell them something about the author, or read a brief excerpt from one of the author's books. (For example, when you assign "An American Childhood" by Annie Dillard in Chapter 2, read aloud a few of Dillard's arresting, memorable aphorisms and analogies about writing from her best-selling book *The Writing Life*.)
- Show them the book or an issue of the magazine from which the reading was selected, and talk about the impact of the book, what you learned from it, or the purpose and readership of the magazine.
- Preview what they will learn as writers from the reading.
- Relate the reading to other readings in the chapter.

These enticements take only a few minutes, but they can increase students' willingness to begin a reading in the odd moments and places where homework gets done.

SETTING UP A READING JOURNAL A reading journal and collaborative reading/learning assignments (described later in this section) are essential features of our courses.

A reading journal differs from a personal journal, a writer's journal, or an exploratory dialogic (or double-entry) journal. It is concerned mainly or exclusively with using writing to learn about reading, through goal-focused journal tasks assigned by the instructor. For students keeping reading journals in a course using this text, the frequent journal writings assist them in learning from their reading what a *writer* needs to know. This is a special kind of rhetorical learning. It is based on critical reading (and especially on critical rereading). Its mode is analytic, and its outcome is conceptual.

One of us has completed research (with Susan McDonald) suggesting that in an assigned-readings course where a particular type of writing is to be the outcome, the reading journal we are proposing teaches students far more than an exploratory journal in which students initiate all the writing. (A dialogic or personal journal could be just the right choice for a different course.)

How do you set up a reading journal? After much trial and error over several years, we have discovered what works best for us and our instructors. Students buy a special loose-leaf three-ring binder and label it *Reading Journal*. (We recommend an inexpensive version with half-inch rings and a flexible cover; this size is more portable than heavy-duty binders.) Each journal entry begins on a separate piece of paper labeled with the student's name, the date, the source of the entry (e.g., Chapter 2, Dillard, Reading like a Writer), and any other information that will facilitate your record keeping.

Give reading journal assignments once a week as part of your weekly assignment handout. By going week by week, rather than planning journal assignments for a longer period, you have flexibility to speed or slow the pace, to insert assignments that arise from special problems or opportunities, and, most important, to match the assignments precisely to the week's sequence of reading and writing activities.

We collect loose-leaf journal entries every week or two and return them to students to reinsert in their binders at the next class meeting. The first time we collect journal entries, we spend more time reading and commenting than we do later: we want to be sure students know what we expect of their reading journals. If the entries are brief and thin, we insist on more writing in future journal entries. If the writing seems too serious, cautious, or planned, we encourage exploration, risk taking, digressions, even playfulness.

If you number your journal assignments sequentially from the beginning to the end of your course and ask students to do the same in their journals, then you always know where each student is in the sequence and whether at the midpoint or end of the course students have completed all assignments.

The reading journal also works well in a course management system such as Blackboard. Students post their weekly journal entries in the discussion thread section of the CMS. One advantage to this system is transparency: you can assign students to read each other's work, so you can easily reference emerging themes or other characteristics within a specific journal assignment. You can even identify samples of exemplary work online and direct students to read them as examples of good reading-journal entries. If you are giving the plus, check, or minus response, you can enter your responses into the CMS's grading system, which remains available only to the student being graded, unlike the journal posts, which are available to the class.

Consider weighting the reading journal as 20 percent or 25 percent of the course grade. We tell students that they must complete all journal assignments in a timely fashion to receive a C in the course. We do not actually grade the journal. Instead, we skim it quickly at the end of the course and decide whether it is exemplary, very good, acceptable, or complete but thin and perfunctory; we inform students of our judgment in a brief final note.

The goal is to spend as little time as possible reading journals while still encouraging students to sustain their work in the journal.

How should students approach reading-journal assignments? We outline various types of journal assignments below, each requiring a different approach. We can say in general, however, that journal writing is relatively informal. It is first-draft writing, not painstakingly planned, tight, or cautious. It is exploratory, discursive, digressive, and associational. A student may begin a journal entry with one idea and end it with quite a different one. In the reading journal, a student *writes to learn*, not merely to report what has been learned.

Handwritten journal entries may (and probably *should*) exhibit crossed-out (less time-consuming than erasing) phrases or sentences, marginal or interlinear additions, one or more parts added later to the end. While journal entries generated electronically will not show the same traces of revision, they will demonstrate the same benefits of reworking and developing ideas as do handwritten entries. They should not strike the reader as perfunctory. Instead, they should show evidence of commitment to learning through writing—of insight, discovery, confusion, and questioning.

What kinds of reading-journal assignments might you give? We recommend three basic kinds:

1. *Critical reading activities from the genre chapters* Keep in mind that our critical reading activities—Reading for Meaning and Reading like a Writer—require writing. The reading journal collects and organizes *all* critical reading activities—no small convenience for you when, in a semester plan, students may complete thirty to forty critical reading activities. The loose-leaf format enables students to exchange single entries, and you can evaluate one or more activities at a time, much in the same way the online journal allows you to selectively evaluate specific activities.

2. *Copy and comment* (as in the Commonplace Book, a staple of liberal arts education since the Middle Ages) Students occasionally copy a particularly striking sentence or brief passage from one of the readings and then comment, react, or analyze for a page or so. You could make a copy-and-comment assignment once with each genre chapter. In this way, the reading journal poses an activity prized by advocates of the dialogic journal.

3. *Reflections on learning and on the course* Recent research demonstrates that when students step back and review what they are learning, they remember it longer and put it to better use. In a course using this text, students learn how to read and write certain genres. To put it another way, they acquire rhetorical or textual knowledge.

Each genre chapter offers students three activities for reflecting:

- Thinking about Your Experience,
- Reviewing What Makes an Effective Essay, and
- Reflecting on What You Have Learned.

You can assign these activities as journal entries. The first activity appears just before A Guide to Reading in each chapter. It invites students to recall their prior experiences with the genre and reassures them that they already know something about it. The reviewing activity helps students make the transition from reading others' essays to writing their own essays in the same genre. This activity appears right after the last selection and before A Guide to Writing [the Genre]. The reflecting activity appears at the very end of the chapter, following A Guide to Writing [the Genre]. It gives students an opportunity to look back on their experiences reading and writing essays in the genre and to reflect on what they have learned.

These metacognitive activities focus on the kind of writing students are learning about in a particular chapter, but you can add a fourth reflecting activity that asks students to relate what they have learned from previous chapters to what they are learning in a current chapter. For example, students reflecting on what they have learned in Chapter 3: Observation can be asked which rhetorical concepts from Chapter 2: Autobiography informed their reading and writing of the observational essay, or students moving through the argument chapters (6–9) can be asked to compare and contrast the different types of argument.

Students might also be asked to comment on the course. With these tasks, you want to deflect personal evaluations of other students and of you and invite frank assessments of progress, problems with assignments or materials, misunderstandings, special insights, and frustrations. Questions like these, in various combinations, have worked very well for us:

- What has most surprised you so far about this course? Account for your surprise. (We ask this question and the next two early in a course.)
- What has most pleased you so far about this course? Most disappointed you? Account for your pleasure and disappointment.
- How is this course different from your high-school English courses, and how is it similar to them?
- How is this course influencing your reading and writing in your other courses? Give specific examples.
- How are your reading and writing changing as a result of this course? Give specific examples.
- We are now at the halfway point in the course. What are you most pleased with about your development as a reader and writer? What are your goals for the second half of the course?

- What one thing could I do to make the course more satisfying for you? What one thing could you do? Explain why these changes could be important for you.

We like to pose a journal task like this every two weeks or so. From students' writing, we learn a lot about the students and the course. You will readily think of other questions to ask as you get to know your students.

GIVING QUIZZES For many years, we resisted quizzing students to discover whether they had completed our reading assignments, assuming they had developed a mature understanding of the consequences of neglecting to do the reading. Now we collect or ask them to post in the class's course management system their Reading for Meaning activities — particularly, the Read to Comprehend activity — or give a quiz at the beginning of most class meetings or at the start of online sections for which readings have been assigned.

The reasons we changed our position are that (1) we came to recognize the competing demands on students' time and (2) we understand how important thoughtful critical reading is to students' development as writers. Therefore, we now provide every possible encouragement for students to complete reading assignments.

Giving clear reading assignments, previewing readings enticingly, and giving reading-journal assignments on the readings provide much of the encouragement. Quizzes provide the rest. Students rarely come to our reading-day discussions unprepared. And as a consequence, their essays are informed by rhetorical strategies from the assigned readings — and, therefore, stronger.

We rely on three basic quiz questions, which we give orally (we give only *one* on a quiz):

1. Summarize selection X. (based on the Read to Comprehend activity)
2. What can a writer learn from selection Y? (based on the Reading like a Writer activity)
3. How are selections X and Y alike and different? (based on the Special Reading Strategy: Comparing and Contrasting Related Readings)

Students write quickly for five or ten minutes. Students who are tardy or absent may not make up a missed quiz. We collect the quizzes and file them with other quizzes in a folder for each student. We do not grade or return them. Instead, we may periodically review these folders and write a note to (or chat with) a student whose quizzes are unsatisfactory. Most students write satisfactory quizzes. In one or two minutes, you can skim a quiz folder to tell any anxious student how well he or she is doing on the quizzes.

At the end of the course, you can just as quickly tell which students have consistently performed well on the quizzes. You can overlook one or two missing quizzes. To encourage students, you might weight quizzes 10 percent of the final grade.

Early in the course you can read aloud a few outstanding quizzes to give students an idea of what you expect. Be firm about the quizzes. Tell students why you give them: quizzes are only one small means toward a consequential end — better essays.

GIVING COLLABORATIVE-LEARNING ASSIGNMENTS We believe that collaborative-learning activities can contribute to students' understanding of what the readings offer them as critical readers and writers. We have students discuss readings in small groups to elaborate and consolidate their learning. Each student reads assigned selections and then meets with his or her collaborative-learning group to complete tasks we pose. These meetings are occasions primarily for rereading and talking, though some writing usually results as well. We sometimes talk about these groups as collaborative-reading groups.

Here are our two basic activities. We try to assign one or the other in each genre chapter, and both work well in online groups:

Group Report on a Reading

Carefully read the essay assigned to your group, and then meet with your group to work together on Read to Analyze Assumptions or the Reading like a Writer activity and to prepare a presentation for the rest of the class.

You will then share what you have learned. You should expect other members of the class to be familiar with the essay you will present. Needless to say, be sure that you are familiar with the essays assigned to the other groups. You must be prepared to participate in the discussion about the essays that the other groups present.

Group Evaluation of Two Readings

Your group has been assigned two readings. Carefully read the two assigned essays before you meet with your group. Decide on your own which reading you think is the better example of the genre.

Then meet with your group and discuss each person's choice of the better example. Prepare an oral report about your group's evaluation for the rest of the class.

In your report, you should explain your group's judgment and the reasons for making it. Be sure that you refer to the basic features of the genre. If one or two of your group cannot agree with the other members, give the class both minority and majority reports.

You should expect other members of the class to be familiar with these essays. Likewise, be sure that you are familiar with the essays assigned to the other groups. You must be able to participate in the other groups' presentations of their evaluations.

You will see many possible variations on these basic group activities. For example, you can use the Comparing and Contrasting Related Readings activity as a group activity to report on similarities and differences between the two readings rather than to argue that one is better. Or student teams might speculate about the possible causes or origins of genre features they identify in one or more readings.

Avoid assigning members to groups randomly or letting students assign themselves. Instead, as soon as possible, assign each student to a group of four. If students drop out during the term, you may need to combine reduced groups. In assigning members to groups, try to avoid homogeneous groupings. We recommend a mix of genders, cultural backgrounds, ages, or other factors that will ensure a heterogeneous group. You may also want to ensure a range of writing abilities in each group, because research shows that diversity in ability increases explanation in a group and improves learning.

If groups meet during class time, try to encourage full participation by all group members, possibly by listening in for a minute and then asking one of the quieter members a question. Research strongly suggests that the students who benefit most from group activities are the ones who spend group time explaining things. If group work requires more time than you can afford in class, you can ask students to schedule a regular time to meet outside class, or you can create group meeting spaces in a course management system.

Explain to students that the collaborative discussion of readings will contribute to their success in your course, and offer them general guidelines for collaboration. Their goal—at least in these two basic activities—is to prepare a brief report (five to eight minutes or a three- to four-page post in a course management system, depending on how many groups you have and how long your class meets) on what they learned about the readings. Tell them they must report as a *panel*, with each person contributing. Since the reports tend to sprawl, you will have to enforce time limits for in-class reports so that all groups may report but you will still have time for other activities.

FACILITATING CLASSROOM DISCUSSION OF READINGS The day arrives when students come to class to discuss the readings—a crucial moment in a course that helps students read critically and write well. This is potentially the *worst* moment in a writing course. Students look at the floor, or there is little activity in the course management system. No one volunteers to take your first question or post a first response. The first person you call on was not able to do the reading. The second person you call on thought the readings were assigned for the next class meeting. The third person you call on seems to have misread or only partially read the reading. The mood changes. You feel grim. The students feel embarrassed. What to do? Probably the only thing to do is to allow time for everyone to read a reading before you attempt to discuss it. As a result, only one of the readings you assigned receives any attention.

This nightmare scenario will likely never materialize in your course if in your planning and assignments you take the advice we suggest in earlier sections:

- reading assignments that you give on a weekly handout,
- enticing previews to motivate students to read,
- reading-journal assignments to complete the critical reading activities following assigned readings,
- a collaborative-learning assignment on the readings, and
- a quiz on the readings.

Here's the plan we find most productive for a class meeting about assigned readings:

- quiz
- reading aloud of journal entries, or Read to Comprehend and/or Read to Respond sections of the Reading for Meaning activity (two to four students)
- discussion of Read to Analyze Assumptions
- collaborative-learning reports on Read to Analyze Assumptions or the Reading like a Writer activity
- discussion
- your own close reading of a particular writing strategy exemplified in the reading or a brief explanation from you about the context of a reading, its author, its major ideas, and so on
- discussion of the rhetorical features in relation to the students' own invention writing

Notice that even though students have prepared carefully and must contribute to the presentation and discussion of readings, you still have a major role to play. Experienced teachers can arrange for students to say most of what needs to be said about readings, but they can rarely get them to say *all* that needs to be said. And so you say what they are not yet prepared to say. You make connections that will not be apparent to them as they are beginning to study a genre. They especially need your help in looking closely at features of a particular essay. As they observe you reading critically—reading rhetorically, reading like a writer—they learn to do it themselves.

It is important to begin each discussion by reminding students of the purpose for discussing the readings—to examine the basic features of and writers' strategies in a particular genre and to improve students' own writing as a result of this examination. As the discussion progresses, keep reminding students of the connections between the various readings and their own writing.

To complete the discussion of each reading, ask students to summarize the main things they have learned. You can then reiterate the main points of the discussion and help students to see the connections between the current reading and earlier ones. An in-class or online journal question can help students focus and reflect on what they have learned during the discussion.

Give up on discussions that do not seem to be going anywhere or that are not engaging most of the students. Do not stay on a single point (or a single essay) for too long.

Try to involve every student in every discussion so that a few students are not doing all the talking or posting. Many students are somewhat shy about speaking in class, so getting them to participate may take some special effort on your part. One way to elicit a spoken or posted response from even the shyest of students is to ask a simple, low-key question such as, What do you remember best about this selection? Most students should be able to answer this question on the spot, and they can then be encouraged to speculate about why a certain feature makes the selection memorable. If students have written responses to the Reading for Meaning and Reading like a Writer activities in class or as homework, you can ask them to read what they have written.

ORGANIZING DRAFT WORKSHOPS

The draft, or peer-critique workshop, brings class members together to read and respond to work in progress—usually, first or second drafts. In this section, we describe two workshop formats: (1) Two or three students bring copies of their drafts for the whole class and read their drafts aloud; then the whole class discusses the drafts. (2) Two students exchange drafts and write an analysis of each other's work; this format works well in a course management system. You could use one of these formats at one class meeting and the other at the next.

We recommend that you begin with whole-class discussion rather than with written analysis so that you can review the basic issues and requirements of the assignment. Even with the help of the chapter's Guide to Writing, there will still be students who have not quite brought the assignment into focus. By concentrating initially on one or two papers with the whole class, you can remind students of the basic issues of the kind of writing under discussion. At the end of the discussion, you can summarize these basic issues on the board and relate them to points in the chapter's Reading a Draft Critically. This flow should give students more confidence in helping each other and keep them focused on the central rhetorical issues of the assignment rather than the peripheral ones.

DISCUSSION FORMAT Arrange in advance for one or two students to post their essays in the course management system or to bring enough copies of their drafts for every two students to share. Alternatively, you can display the draft for the whole class to read, using a computer and projector or an overhead projector. The writer tells the class about any particular problems he or she has had in the draft and then reads it aloud while the rest of the class follows along on the copies, making marginal notes, or on the projected image. Class members will respond better if they hear and see the draft simultaneously.

At the end of the oral reading, the instructor chairs a discussion of the draft, appointing a scribe to record specific suggestions for revisions on behalf of the writer. The activities in Reading a Draft Critically can form the basis of this discussion. At the end of the discussion, the scribe gives the writer the discussion notes, and other students pass along their copies with marginal notes.

This whole-class discussion of one draft at a time simulates the traditional writers' workshop widely used in graduate programs. Many instructors using this workshop format ask that the writer not participate in the discussion. There are good reasons for this rule. At the draft stage, writers need to listen to the discussion and to reflect thoughtfully on what readers say, why they misunderstand, and what they have questions about. From listening to this sort of discussion of one's draft, a writer can know whether it struck readers as honest, engaging, authentic, informative, or convincing.

Working with the whole class on one draft allows you to guide the discussion and make observations that are relevant to the assignment and not just to the draft at hand. An alternative is to divide the class into small groups of four or five, with one member of each group bringing copies of his or her draft for the others in the group and reading it aloud to them. In a large class, this approach allows more students to receive group responses to their drafts and encourages the more reticent students to participate in the discussion. You can join one group or move among the groups. This format works best when students know what is expected and can work productively without your guidance.

WRITTEN-ANALYSIS FORMAT We typically begin by asking students to exchange drafts with another class member. Each student then spends the first twenty or twenty-five minutes reading the partner's draft silently and writing a critical response to it. Activities to guide this process can be found under Reading a Draft Critically in the chapter's Guide to Writing. As students first exchange drafts, they brief their partners on particular points they would like the partners to critique. The respondents write their responses on separate sheets of paper, labeled at the top to look like this:

Autobiographical Essay Draft
Workshop Response for John Smith by Yolanda Jenkins

During the first part of the workshop, while pairs of students are working silently on each other's drafts, you may choose to move among them to offer advice. Alternatively, you can arrange in advance for students to bring additional copies of their drafts for you to review during this time. When students have finished their written responses, each partner returns the draft and response to the other, and then they can discuss their responses.

To facilitate this critical exchange, you may want to pair students according to their writing abilities, changing the pairs so that each student receives responses from several others during the course.

In the online environment, we pair students according to their writing abilities. Paired students post their drafts in the discussion thread section of the course management system; their posts include notes on particular aspects on which they would like feedback. We offer comments as students post their work at varying intervals prior to the assignment due date.

Student writers tend to write their first workshop responses with some anxiety. A few will launch into devastatingly honest evaluations of a partner's draft, but most err on the side of conciliation. Influenced perhaps by the knowledge that their own drafts are undergoing similar scrutiny, they are usually eager to praise and offer little substantial criticism.

At the beginning of the course, they also lack the experience to make recommendations to the writer.

One way to address this problem in the first workshop is to take students through Reading a Draft Critically, modeling for them the kind of critique that lets the writer know what works, what needs work, and what to about weaknesses. A good response points to specific words in the draft, describes their effect on the reader tactfully but honestly, and suggests options the writer might consider. Questions to the writer beginning with "How about . . . ?" are often useful. To model such a critique, you can use copies of a class member's draft or copies of an anonymous draft written for a similar assignment in a previous course.

Student pairs could arrange to meet outside of class, exchange drafts, and complete a written analysis. Arriving in class with analyses in hand, they could review and discuss them and then move on to analyze still another student's draft in class or to discuss a draft with the whole class. As attractive as this alternative may seem—it can save class time for other matters—it has not worked well for us. Student pairs do not seem to finish their drafts very far in advance of the workshop class itself, or one student in a pair finishes in time for the scheduled exchange of drafts, and the other does not. All students seem to benefit from the same specific deadline: a draft must be completed by the time of the workshop class. (We accept partial drafts for workshops on the grounds that it is better for a student to get some advice on work in progress than no response at all, especially if he or she is struggling to understand the genre or to pull off a challenging rhetorical move, like integrating counterargument into an argument or interview notes into a profile.) In class, you can review with all students the criteria for an analysis and coach them in making a useful analysis.

PRACTICAL CONSIDERATIONS When a student comes to class late or without a draft, you have several options, depending on which workshop format the class is using:

- Have the student work on his or her own draft.
- Have the student join a pair and read a draft page by page as one partner finishes.
- Have the student wait for another late student to show up.
- Have the student respond to a copy of a draft that has been duplicated for the whole class.

In all these cases, the student must be reminded that he or she is responsible for obtaining another student's response to his or her own draft.

When the first and second drafts of the same assignment are read in subsequent workshops, some instructors ask students to choose a different partner to respond to the second draft. Other instructors allow students to use the same partners to read the second drafts so that the partners can comment on the progress made since the first drafts.

Some instructors find it useful to have students put their phone numbers or email addresses on their workshop responses so that writers can communicate with their workshop partners if they find they have questions as they revise their drafts. (If you are using Blackboard or another course management system, responding might be as simple as clicking "reply," but even if students are not engaging in online workshops, most CMS programs offer students the ability to email classmates. We find, however, that students are seldom aware of this feature, so it can be helpful to point it out or to have students write their email addresses on papers anyway.)

Some instructors ask all students to bring an extra copy of their drafts. During the pair workshop, while pairs are quietly writing their critiques of each other's drafts, the instructor quickly reviews all drafts, looking for the easy-to-spot problems.

HOLDING CONFERENCES

Conferences with students are time-consuming and difficult to schedule when classes are large, but we recommend them highly as a teaching practice, even if you can see students individually only once or twice during the course. Conferences allow you to develop a rapport with students, thus building the trust and self-confidence that many students need before they will take the risks in their writing that lead to real progress. For many students, these conferences are their only opportunities to work individually with a college instructor.

A conference may be scheduled at any time during the composing process. We find that the most useful time is after the first or second draft of an essay has been written, at a point when the student has spent some time thinking about the assignment, generating invention notes, and making at least one attempt to put the ideas into draft form but before the student has finished work on the essay. Ideally, the first draft is discussed in a conference and the second draft in a workshop with other students, or vice versa, before the student writes the final revision of the essay.

In the one-quarter courses we teach, we like to see each student in conference three times. The second of these, the midterm conference, allows us to review the student's progress and discuss the goals for the remainder of the course.

INDIVIDUAL DRAFT CONFERENCES We find that the best length for individual conferences is half an hour, although it is possible to make some progress in twenty minutes if the time is spent carefully.

The student comes to the conference with a draft in hand and may at first expect you to play the role of mechanic, making the necessary repairs on it while he or she waits in anxious silence. It is often tempting to take the draft from the student and go to work on it, but this defeats the objective of conferencing, which is to help students learn to work on their own drafts. To this end, we leave the draft in the student's hands for most of the conference and usually begin by asking the student either to read it aloud or talk about it. In the most successful conferences, the students do at least half the talking; our comments merely draw them out and let them make discoveries for themselves.

Because our questions at the beginning of the conference, or after the student has read the draft aloud, tend to be the same, we give them to students in advance on a handout, leaving space between questions for their notes. This means that students come to the conference prepared with a list of things to say and questions to ask, and we can begin work immediately. Following are general questions we might ask students:

1. What pleases you most about this draft? Which part seems most successful?
2. Which areas of the draft do you feel need work, and why? What would your toughest reader be likely to say about the draft?
3. Which were the hardest and easiest parts to write?
4. What did you notice when you read this draft aloud to a friend?
5. What have you learned from this assignment so far?
6. What changes are you considering for the next draft?
7. What new writing strategy were you trying to use in this draft?
8. What question would you like to ask me about this draft?

20

Here are questions we ask students about a draft of an essay analyzing the causes of a trend in response to the assignment in Chapter 8. You could readily write such questions for any genre assignment.

1. What trend are you analyzing?
2. Why is it a trend, as opposed to a fad or a phenomenon?
3. What causes are you presenting to explain this trend? Which causes seem to you to be the strongest? Weakest?
4. Do you have a strongest or most convincing cause? Why have you selected this one particular cause as likely to be most convincing for your readers?
5. What have you done thus far in this assignment that you feel confident about? It can be anything from your research to the ideas you've developed to explain the trend you're writing about.
6. What problems are you having with this essay? Do they have to do with library research, listing possible causes, or evaluating causes? Are you unsure as to whether you are talking about a trend or a fad? In what specific ways can I help you?

Questions like these provide a good starting point for discussion, and they encourage students to take responsibility for their writing and assume an active role in improving it.

SMALL-GROUP DRAFT CONFERENCES An alternative to the individual conference is the small-group conference. Instead of meeting with each student for half an hour, the instructor meets with three students for an hour, spending twenty minutes on each student's draft. In a typical group conference, each student brings copies of the draft for the other two students and the instructor. They each in turn read their drafts aloud while listeners make notes on their copies. At the end of each reading, the instructor and the writer talk about the draft. The other two students may quietly audit the discussion or contribute their views and suggestions. After twenty minutes, the writer collects the annotated copies, and attention turns to the next student's draft.

The group conference lacks the privacy of an individual conference, an important consideration for shy students. On the other hand, the group may generate ideas that would not emerge in a one-on-one conference. Some of the comments we make about the first student's draft usually apply to the other two as well, and students often decide to revise their own drafts in ways inspired by the discussion of another student's draft. Neither conference format is inherently better than the other; we recommend that you try both to decide which you prefer.

SCHEDULING CONFERENCES One way of scheduling conferences is to have students sign up for time slots in the class meeting before conference week, writing down their names and phone numbers on a sheet that you can then post on the door of your office or on an online course management system like Blackboard. If students find that they cannot keep the conference appointment, they go to the posted sheet and get the names and numbers of classmates who might change appointments with them. In this way, students are able to take care of rescheduling largely on their own, without having to call you.

One instructor finds it helpful to have students sign up for conference times *two* class meetings in advance—in pencil. She brings the list to the last meeting before the conference and circulates it once more so that students can double-check times and location and reschedule if necessary. Another keeps a running schedule on a course management system, using the discussion board format for students to request particular times, announce rescheduling needs, and check the schedule for their appointment times if they forget when to show up.

Students should be reminded to be on time for conference meetings, as even a few minutes can throw off your carefully planned schedule. If your office is difficult to locate, consider handing out a map or posting one online.

Of course, one could also simply hold conferences online, and skip the map altogether. Individual conferences on discussion boards do not require such detailed scheduling. We provide due dates and times for initial conference posts and subsequent responses so that students have enough time to consider offered feedback as they work on later drafts. The questions used in individual on-campus conferences also work well online, as do small-group conferences held in discussion threads. Finally, some course management systems have virtual-classroom or chat-room functions that enable instructors to meet with students online in real time, and some instructors teaching hybrid classes find these virtual meeting spaces effective.

EVALUATING STUDENT WRITING AND KEEPING RECORDS

Students completing an essay assignment will have generated a good deal of writing. We find it important to have a system of accounting for all the writing turned in and a method of reading and responding to it that allows us to give students helpful feedback while processing student work in a reasonable amount of time. Many instructors have students submit all their writing online, and they respond online as well. The suggestions in this section call for submission of writing the old-fashioned way, with hard copies.

At the beginning of the course, we give students a handout that specifies what they are to turn in for each writing assignment. Here is an example:

When you finish each assignment, you will turn in not only the final revision but *all* the writing you did for the assignment. Put this work in a flexible file folder with your name, your section, and the assignment written clearly on the outside. Each folder you turn in should contain the following five parts:

1. *Invention* Numerous pages of rough, unpolished invention based on A Guide to Writing [the Genre] for the assignment in *Reading Critically, Writing Well*.
2. *Drafting* Either one or two rough exploratory drafts, depending on the length of the assignment. They should be legible and labeled with your name, the assignment title, the draft number, and page numbers.
3. *Workshop response* The response written on one of your drafts by a classmate during the workshop. The classmate's name should be on the response.
4. *Revising* The final, revised version of the essay. This should be printed and proofread with any errors neatly corrected. Double-space, print on one side of the page only, and number each page. The title page should be labeled in the top right-hand corner like this:

    [Your name]
    [Chapter title for the assignment]
    Revision
    [Date]

5. *Reflecting on What You Have Learned* Follow the guidelines in the activity of this name at the end of each genre chapter.

This handout gives students a checklist of all the work they are to turn in. We find it reduces confusion, eases our management of the large amounts of writing, and speeds the reading and response process.

When we pull the handful of work from each student's folder, we skim to check that all the assigned writing is there and to see what the student has accomplished in the invention and drafts. The invention tends to be a good indicator of the depth and thoroughness of the revised essay, and problems in the revision can often be traced to deficiencies in the invention. We try to make this connection clear to students early in the course.

To keep track of the student's performance in the various stages of the composing process for each assignment, we use a record sheet. This sheet is for our own records, and the student does not see it.

The self-evaluation (Reflecting on What You Have Learned) asks the student to reflect critically on the composing process and to think about and take responsibility for the decisions he or she has made. At its worst, a self-evaluation will say no more than "Here it is. I like it. I hope you do too," as the student declines the invitation to take responsibility. At its best, however, it provides the student with an account of his or her composing process, and it provides you with a critical introduction to the essay. It can also clearly indicate the student's level of involvement with the assignment. We usually first skim the whole package and then read the self-evaluation carefully.

We then focus on the final revision. We make a few comments in the margins, noting both strong and weak points in the writing, and add a few sentences or a paragraph of comments at the end or on a separate piece of paper. You may want to keep a copy of these comments for your own records. We often use the computer to compose comments and save a file for each assignment. We try to find something in the essay to praise, and we find that critical comments work best when phrased in terms of what the student might have done in the essay or should try to do in the next one. Questions are useful, too, when they lead students to think about ways they might have addressed the problems in the paper. This approach casts the instructor in the role of expert adviser rather than hanging judge.

Our response to a student's essay is influenced by its location in the sequence of assignments. Our comments will be different in each of the following situations:

1. The student is to revise the essay one more time.
2. We plan to repeat the assignment.
3. The assignment will not be made again in the course, and we want to summarize the student's achievement.
4. The assignment is the first or last in a series of related writing assignments (for example, the assignments in Chapters 6 to 9 on argument).

When time is limited, we respond to features in the essay in order of priority. In an autobiographical essay, we begin by considering the larger rhetorical issues—the writer's goals in telling the story, its structure, the beginning and ending, and the pacing of the narrative. Next, we look at some particular feature of the genre—the quantity and vividness of descriptive details, the writer's recollection of feelings at the time of the event or toward the person, the use of dialogue, and the proportion of narration, description, and commentary in the story. Finally, we comment on the writer's style, diction, and sentence structure.

23

We do not comment on everything that could be improved in a paper. An inexperienced writer can be easily overwhelmed by too much criticism and become too discouraged to work on any of the problems. Rather, we try to focus on a few of the most important things that need attention, thereby giving the student achievable goals. We follow the same policy with mechanical errors and stylistic infelicities, assuming that if we mark every transgression in a weak writer's paper, the student will most likely attend to none of the problems. Instead, we mark every error in a particular section—a whole page or one or two paragraphs on a page—by placing a check mark in the margin next to the line where the error occurs. We put parentheses around long phrases or whole sentences that need to be revised. This conveys the message that the mechanics and style need serious attention, draws the student's attention to some particular examples, and saves us the bother of marking every mistake in the entire essay.

Then, most important, we ask students to identify and correct their mistakes. If you include the appropriate correction symbol from your handbook with each marginal check mark or set of parentheses, then students can go to the handbook for assistance in identifying the mistake and correcting it. We ask them to rewrite on the revision any sentence containing an error. If the error rate is high, a whole section may need to be rewritten. We check these rewrites as soon as possible, asking students to rewrite still again any errors that remain uncorrected. After two or three revisions have been marked and corrected in this way, we ask students to identify and analyze their own error patterns. They list and classify their errors, again using the handbook for assistance, and then write up briefly what they have learned. The result is that students begin to take responsibility for reducing the number of errors, syntactic garbles and awkwardness, and stylistic infelicities in their own writing—and they learn to use a handbook.

Finally, we do not hesitate to ask a student to revise still again an essay that fails to meet minimal requirements established by the chapter's readings and A Guide to Writing. This request sets standards more effectively than a low grade.

We usually do not grade individual essays but use a portfolio method of grading. We recognize, however, that students need some indication of their progress before the obligatory grades at the end of the course, so we fill out for all students midterm progress reports with grades that indicate what they can expect at the end of the course if they continue at their present levels of performance. This form shows students where they need to focus their attention in the remainder of the course. (An example appears on page 26.)

At the end of the course, we use a final course report to write a response to the final essay submitted and an evaluative summary of the student's performance in the whole course. (An example of this form appears on page 27.) This summary and the course grade are based on a quick review of a student's portfolio of revised essays. We ask that the portfolio be turned in along with the revision of the final essay.

We also review our records of a student's attendance, reading-journal entries, quizzes, workshop responses, and any other work we might have assigned. Then we give a final grade based on three criteria:

1. whether all the assigned work has been completed in a timely fashion;
2. whether the work has improved during the course; and
3. whether revised essays are fully realized rhetorically—that is, whether the student's revisions reveal substantial learning about the rhetorical and composing possibilities of the various genres assigned in the course.

Keep in mind that standards of success on the assignments in *Reading Critically, Writing Well* are comprehensively established by the readings in each chapter, the activities at the beginning of each chapter and following each reading, A Guide to Writing at the end of each chapter, and the peer-critique guide Reading a Draft Critically.

Here is an alternative:

1. Students put together a portfolio of their work to give you at the end of the course. The form of portfolio grading you might consider could include
   - all revisions,
   - all revisions, with one of them revised still further, and
   - a small selection of the best work that includes at least one revision, one workshop response, one complete writing process (invention, drafts, revision), and some small number of reading-journal entries. (You will no doubt think of other variations.)
2. Students write a reflective essay analyzing and evaluating their portfolio work. You will need to provide careful guidelines to engage students in thoughtful reflection on their learning in the whole course. The three reflective activities in each genre chapter can be helpful.
3. You review the portfolio and respond in writing.

The portfolio, especially if it includes further revised work, might be the culminating assignment in your course. Students could confer with each other and with you about portfolio selections and about further revision of one essay.

MIDTERM PROGRESS REPORT

Student _____   **Instructor** _____

Course _____   **Date** _____

Term _____   **Section** _____

QUANTITY OF WORK: Has the student completed all the assignments?

Invention _____

Drafts and revisions _____

Quizzes _____

Workshop responses _____

Critical reading activities _____

Self-evaluations _____

Attendance _____

QUALITY OF WORK: Has the student

used the guides to writing creatively? _____

revised drafts substantially? _____

given helpful workshop responses? _____

written perceptive self-evaluations? _____

edited and proofread carefully? _____

completed thoughtfully the critical reading activities? _____

participated in class discussions? _____

These areas need special attention in the remainder of the course:

_____

_____

_____

Midterm grade _____

FINAL COURSE REPORT

Student _____   Instructor _____

Course _____   Date _____

Term _____   Section _____

REMARKS ON FINAL ESSAY

_____
_____
_____
_____
_____
_____
_____
_____
_____
_____

REMARKS ON THE PORTFOLIO

_____
_____
_____
_____
_____
_____
_____
_____
_____
_____

Final grade _____

Chapter 1 is designed to catapult students quickly into the course. Through nine short, easy, interconnected activities, it introduces students to a variety of "academic habits of mind" expected of them in college settings—habits that can help them to achieve the two goals indicated in the book's title, reading critically and writing well. In the process, while the text walks the students along a single thread of inquiry on the subject of bullying, they briefly encounter such crucial concepts as the meaning of critical thinking, genre, styles of discourse, and writing as a generative activity, and to such essential moves as reading for meaning, reading like a writer, appreciating other viewpoints, forming hypotheses, reporting facts, synthesizing sources, and editing.

The chapter has five sections. The first two, the chapter introduction and Thinking Critically, acquaint students with college instructors' expectations for student thinking. The sections quickly introduce academic habits of mind, all connected to the common and approachable theme of *curiosity*. The two sections also introduce students to two reading strategies they will be asked to perform after each selection in the text: Reading for Meaning and Reading like a Writer. The last three sections of the chapter—Understanding Academic Discourse, Reading Critically, and Writing Well—help students begin to understand more specific ways in which they need to learn and apply academic habits of mind: in gaining an understanding of the distinctive discourse of the academy, using critical-thinking skills in their reading, and applying the knowledge and skills they have mastered in all these areas to the task of writing effectively.

INTRODUCTION Activity 1, which can be an effective in-class assignment for the first day of class, asks students to think about the habits of mind they may already possess by considering the ways they have previously familiarized themselves with a subject they were curious about. (They may revisit what they write for this exercise in Activity 9 at the end of the chapter, if you choose to use both activities.)

THINKING CRITICALLY In the Thinking Critically section, students are introduced to a quick clarification of what we mean by *critical thinking*. (It might be worthwhile to have someone read this part aloud in class, as misunderstandings of this term are common.) Then a series of short passages about the possible causes of bullying, by four authors, provides the class with a quick introduction to the idea of *genres*, along with a series of examples of one genre: speculating about causes and effects.

As they read, students are encouraged to imagine the curiosity-driven questions that the authors must have had when they were researching and writing. Activity 2, following the readings, asks students to arrive at their own questions. You might consider conducting Activity 2 in class, with students writing individually at first, then teaming up to create group lists of questions that can be presented to the class. By the end of the second activity, students will have identified being curious and asking provocative questions as two essential habits of mind, and they will have an idea of what is expected of them when they attempt the Reading for Meaning exercises in later chapters.

At this point, the section notes that readers can ask questions about the writing strategies that they see in addition to asking questions about the content, and this leads to Activity 3, in which students are asked to examine critically the way Michael Lemonick (the author of one of the excerpts about bullying) uses statistics and information in his article. This activity illustrates the sort of work students are expected to do when they attempt the Reading like a Writer activities in later chapters.

UNDERSTANDING ACADEMIC DISCOURSE The third section, Understanding Academic Discourse, points out something that astute readers will have already noticed: the four excerpts about bullying reflect a range of different styles, including two excerpts written for academic discourse communities. Activity 4, which you might ask students to complete as a take-home reading-journal entry, asks readers to analyze the four excerpts to determine which two are samples of academic discourse (readings 1 and 4) and which two are for general audiences (readings 2 and 3), an analysis that requires students to practice another academic habit of mind: reading with awareness of self and others, or critical reading. This sets up a natural transition to the next section.

READING CRITICALLY To prevent this concept from intimidating students, the section opens with examples of critical reading they may have already performed for other classes (discussing figurative language in literature, for instance). Activity 5 asks them to study two more excerpts on the subject of bullying and to make notes about ideas that challenge their own beliefs and the ways that the authors deal with opposing or alternative perspectives, an activity that introduces them to two new habits of mind: (1) experimenting with new ideas and challenging one's own beliefs; (2) seeing other points of view and showing respect for them.

Because this activity asks writers to frankly address their possible conflicts with the readings, it is probably better suited for individual journal entries than for group work, though you may want to open up the questions in Activity 5 for general discussion once everyone has written on them individually. (You might find it helps to get the discussion ball rolling if you start by identifying a piece of information or a position in the readings that was new or challenging to you.) In the first reading, the second sentence ("While a certain amount of conflict and harassment . . .") acknowledges a possible objection but deflects it by defining bullying as different from normal conflict. In the second piece, the second paragraph addresses people who think the problem is insignificant.

The section closes by asking students to engage in intellectual discussion and to generate hypotheses about the issue of bullying. Although this suggestion is not a numbered activity, it is a worthwhile exercise for class discussion: consider having some informal debates over the causes of and possible solutions for bullying. In so doing, you can introduce students to some of the argumentative or persuasive genres.

WRITING WELL This section emphasizes the oft-noted link between reading much and writing effectively, the recursive nature of writing, and the generative nature of writing. Activity 6, which is best conducted as an in-class writing exercise, gives students a chance to experience the generative nature of writing firsthand through *freewriting*. Again, students are asked to focus on the subject of bullying, and the activity provides a list of questions about experiences they may have had with bullies or bullying. The last step of the activity is critical: students are asked whether they surprised themselves with any of the material they created. You might consider having students share their answers to this final question with the class and listing some of the generated ideas, if students are willing to share them.

To get the best results with this initial freewrite, it is sometimes a good idea to let students know at the outset what the purpose of the activity is, perhaps by asking them how often they have found themselves coming up with new ideas while in the middle of writing a paper—ideas that maybe they wish they'd had before they started. (Many students have had this experience, often at about 4 a.m.) Mention that the goal of the exercise is to write until they come up with something promising that they hadn't originally thought of. Not all of them will reach that point, but some students should.

Because the questions in Activity 6 ask students for narratives, the freewrites can help you introduce another habit of mind: reporting facts and narrating events. To facilitate this move, the text follows up Activity 6 with a brief discussion of narrative and an example of an anecdote from Michael Lemonick's article on bullying. You might have a student read Lemonick's account aloud after one or more volunteers have shared their own from their freewriting. Then you might use this reading to discuss both the role of narration in expository writing and the use of summary: the final paragraph of Lemonick's excerpt boils down findings from some studies in order to put the previous anecdote into a larger context. This paragraph introduces writers to another habit of mind: summarizing ideas or information contained in a text.

As a follow-up to this discussion, Activity 7—which is suitable for group work—asks students to look back through the excerpts about bullying for other summarized information. (It might be worthwhile to point out that these summaries are not quoting the original sources—they are expressing ideas from those sources in the second author's own words. Students often assume that a citation means the same thing as quotation marks, and will imagine that the cited information in the academic articles represents quoted material, unless you clarify this.)

The discussion following Activity 7 introduces critical assessment of source materials and analysis of the ideas and arguments of others as two additional habits of mind worth cultivating. It notes that the authors of previous excerpts have surveyed a wide range of sources and woven them carefully into their own arguments. It also explains the nature of primary and peer-reviewed material, and points out that experienced writers often cite sources in order to criticize them or to point out shortcomings in their thinking or methodology.

Moreover, the section points out that each of the articles excerpted in this chapter *synthesizes* ideas and conclusions from multiple sources or studies, another effective habit of mind. To give students practice with this habit, Activity 8 asks them to draft a paragraph to the principals of their high schools in which they discuss bullying. The paragraph should synthesize the conclusions from the sources they have just read in this chapter.

Finally, Activity 9 asks students to revisit what they wrote in Activity 1 and what they have learned since. Students should write to a younger student, identifying habits of mind he or she ought to be practicing to prepare for college. This metacognitive activity, which could be written as a journal entry or discussion-board posting, prompts students to crystallize what they have learned so far and increases the likelihood they will make connections between this chapter and the rest of the book.

Part 6 TEACHING CHAPTERS 2–9

In Part 6, we begin with general suggestions for teaching the elements in Chapters 2 to 9. Then we discuss each of the chapters, providing specific suggestions for using the reading and writing activities following each essay as well as the chapter's Guide to Writing.

OVERVIEW OF CHAPTER STRUCTURE

Each chapter in the student book other than Chapter 1 follows the same pattern:

- brief introduction to the genre
- A Guide to Reading [the Genre]
- readings
- Reviewing What Makes an Effective Essay: [Genre]
- A Guide to Writing [the Genre]
- Reflecting on What You Have Learned

In the following paragraphs, we introduce these sections and discuss how you might teach them.

TEACHING THE CHAPTER INTRODUCTIONS

Each chapter introduction includes the following four features: a brief discussion of the genre's importance; the writing assignment; examples of writing situations in which the genre is used; and a reflective activity inviting students to think about their prior experience with the genre.

DISCUSSION OF THE GENRE'S IMPORTANCE The opening paragraphs usually describe the genre and discuss its importance for writers and readers. You will notice that the description previews the chapter's key terms and concepts. For example, in Chapter 2: Autobiography, the first paragraph focuses on telling stories and describing people, creating a vivid impression through sensory detail, and understanding the important concept of autobiographical significance.

The introduction also both contextualizes the genre and raises issues. For example, in Chapter 2: Autobiography, the issues of diversity and privacy are introduced. These are issues you may want to explore with your students as they read the autobiographical essays in the chapter and write their own. Similarly, the opening paragraphs of Chapter 7: Position Paper make a distinction between rhetorical situations in which people argue primarily to vent strong feelings and those in which people argue to reason and deliberate, examining their own as well as others' arguments with a critical eye.

You can have students read these introductory paragraphs on their own or go over them in class, where you can emphasize key terms and concepts and facilitate a discussion about the issues.

THE WRITING ASSIGNMENT We place the Writing Assignment right at the beginning of the chapter for two reasons: (1) so that students can begin thinking about specific subjects for their own essays and (2) so that students see the readings through the lens of that assignment. These writing assignments are presented in general terms, identifying the basic features and strategies of the genre and suggesting the purpose for writing in that genre for one's particular readers. In the Considering Ideas for Your Own Writing section that follows each reading (except the opening and closing ones), as well as in the chapter's Guide to Writing, we offer other specific subject suggestions. In addition, the chapter-specific pages in this manual discuss some of the problems students may have with each assignment, including problems with choosing a subject.

WRITING SITUATIONS FOR [THE GENRE] Each chapter opens with typical writing assignments from college courses across the disciplines and from professional life. These examples show diverse contexts in which students are likely to encounter the chapter's genre. We made up very few of the academic assignments: nearly all came from current academic texts or instructor's manuals. We did revise several of them to foreground aspects of the rhetorical situation or to make explicit what the student is expected to know and do. Unfortunately, not all academics consistently make clear to students what is required in answering essay-exam questions or in selecting subjects for papers. You might wish to discuss these issues with your students as they prepare for midterms or final exams in their other courses.

There is much you can do to involve students in analyzing the different contexts in which the genre may appear. Here are a few possibilities:

- You can analyze one situation as a demonstration, emphasizing its thinking and writing demands, and then have students analyze another (either in small groups or as a class).
- You can ask each student to find an assignment in another course that calls for the genre under study.
- You can ask students to bring in examples from other contexts in which the genre may work (such as family, social, or religious contexts).
- You can have students research the profession or graduate study they are interested in to discover which genres are commonly used. (You also might consider making this research part of their Observation essay for Chapter 3.)

THINKING ABOUT YOUR EXPERIENCE This is the first of three reflective, or metacognitive, activities in the chapter. This activity invites students to think about their prior experience with the genre. The second reflective activity, Reviewing What Makes an Effective Essay, follows the readings and precedes A Guide to Writing; the activity helps students make the transition from reading to writing. The third activity, Reflecting on What You Have Learned, comes at the end of A Guide to Writing and is designed to help students consolidate what they have learned—not only about the genre but also about reading critically and writing well. Taken as a set, these three activities empower students by making them aware that they have been learning from the reading selections, the reading apparatus, and their own writing.

You can use this first activity, Thinking about Your Experience with [the Genre], to spur class discussion when you are introducing the genre. This activity allows students to realize they have some familiarity, possibly more than they expected, with the genre, thereby reducing the anxiety that typically accompanies any new writing assignment.

Consider having students write for a few minutes and then, to launch the discussion, having a few read aloud what they have written. Notice that the questions prompt students to think about their oral *and* written experiences with the genre. Students are asked to think about the rhetorical situation in which they or someone else used the genre, considering the audience's expectations as well as the writer's purpose.

TEACHING THE GUIDES TO READING

A Guide to Reading [the Genre] in each chapter focuses on one selection. It introduces students to the two types of critical reading activities presented throughout the book: Reading for Meaning and Reading like a Writer. These critical reading activities provide students with a full introduction to the genre they will be reading and writing. The reading selection together with critical reading activities illustrates for students the work they will do with each reading selection in the chapter. In A Guide to Reading, we survey all the major features of the genre in four or five Reading like a Writer activities. In the readings that follow, each reading has just one Reading like a Writer activity, which singles out an important rhetorical feature of that reading. If you cannot use all the readings in a chapter, you may want to choose readings based on the rhetorical features you want to emphasize. The discussion of each chapter, which follows, identifies the Reading like a Writer topics in that chapter.

THE SAMPLE SELECTION The selection we have chosen to serve as the sample is fairly brief, and we find it interesting. But more important, the sample reading illustrates all the rhetorical features typical of the genre. Because it introduces students to the full array of Reading like a Writer activities they will study in the other chapter readings, instructors seldom skip this first exemplary reading.

READING FOR MEANING In A Guide to Reading, Reading for Meaning consists of three parts: Read to Comprehend, Read to Respond, and Read to Analyze Assumptions. These parts call for students to read and reread the selection for different purposes. Although the goal is for students eventually to read for all these purposes at the same time, we find that it helps students to practice reading for one purpose at a time. Of course, you may choose which parts your students do and the order in which they do them. Some instructors prefer to begin by having students respond to the reading, but instructors whose students have difficulty with basic comprehension may choose to focus on the first activity, even using it as the basis for a reading test. Read to Analyze Assumptions may be used as a reflective exercise after the reading has been discussed in class.

In our classes, we encourage students to annotate as they read. If you think annotating is as useful as we think it is, you may want to demonstrate—perhaps by means of an overhead projector—how students can layer their annotations as they reread for comprehension, response, and analysis. The section on annotating in Appendix 1: A Catalog of Critical Reading Strategies illustrates a number of ways to annotate. After demonstrating annotation techniques at the class level, we find it useful to have students practice annotating in small groups.

Following are general ideas for teaching Reading for Meaning. Again, the chapter-specific pages in this manual provide suggestions for teaching each reading.

Read to Comprehend
This activity usually begins by asking students to write a few sentences summarizing the reading or an important element of it. If you want to emphasize summarizing, you can extend this activity by using the section on summarizing in Appendix 1: A Catalog of Critical Reading Strategies, which provides suggestions on summarizing long passages or whole essays. Summarizing can be an in-class writing activity, whether students are writing just a few sentences or longer, more expanded summaries. Ask a few students to read their summaries aloud and to explain what they have chosen to emphasize and why. Sharing students' summaries on a regular basis will reinforce the importance of summarizing, give students a variety of strategies for summarizing, and ultimately make students more adept at summarizing. Summarizing, of course, is not simply a useful critical reading strategy but also a valuable writing strategy that can be used in all the kinds of writing covered in *Reading Critically, Writing Well*.

In addition to asking students to summarize, the Read to Comprehend activity invites students to focus on word choice and to identify unfamiliar words. Notice that although we encourage students to look up words in a college dictionary, we note that there are often multiple meanings from which to choose and that determining the meaning of a word requires paying close attention to the context in which the word is used. On a regular basis, you might select students to put on the board the words they did not know and the definitions they chose after considering the word's context. If several students choose different definitions for the same word, you may want to spend a few minutes exploring those choices. Making this activity a regular part of class reinforces the importance of word choice and encourages students to look up unknown words. Similarly, selected students can use a discussion thread in your campus's course-management system to create a weekly vocabulary list of unfamiliar words with definitions and links to audible pronunciations offered by free online dictionaries, such as Merriam-Webster's Online: http://www.m-w.com/.

The last part of the Read to Comprehend activity suggests that students use one of the critical reading strategies in Appendix 1. If you want to expose students to the array of strategies in Appendix 1, you can either focus on a different strategy for each reading or have students in groups use different strategies and report to the class what they have discovered.

Read to Respond

This activity acknowledges that reading for meaning involves, at least in part, actively responding to the text. A reader's mind is not a tabula rasa. Rather, the reader brings to the text a range of potential meanings based on his or her personal, cultural, and linguistic experiences. Consequently, readers need to analyze their own thoughts and feelings as they read, first by identifying what in the text seems salient or significant and then by trying to understand why they respond as they do.

This activity invites students to begin by focusing on anything in the text that stands out, resonates with their own experiences, or puzzles them. We offer several bulleted suggestions, but it is best if students relate to the text on their own terms. Students may feel self-conscious at first, but you can put them at ease by demonstrating that there really is no right or wrong answer. What counts is that students find a way to connect to something in the text and use that connection to explore the meanings created through their interaction with the text.

If you have students share their responses, they may discover that others in the class react in similar ways. They may also learn that still other students have very different responses based on the personal, cultural, and linguistic experiences that they bring to their reading. Seeing that readers find or make meaning in different ways will help students develop sensitivity as readers and will also make them more rhetorically aware writers.

You could discuss one or more of the bulleted items as a class. Most were chosen because they focus students' attention on significant or problematic aspects of the reading. The chapter-specific pages in this manual sometimes offer suggestions to supplement those in the text.

Read to Analyze Assumptions

This activity is the most challenging part of the Reading for Meaning sequence. It asks students to examine with a critical eye one or more of the assumptions, values, or beliefs underlying the reading. It also invites readers to think critically about their own assumptions. We open the activity with a paragraph or two modeling an analysis of one of the reading's assumptions. We also urge students to pay close attention to the writer's word choice and selection of examples, suggesting that these often signal underlying beliefs or values. The suggestions offered in the bulleted items focus on particular passages in the reading. In the chapter suggestions in this manual, we usually point to additional language in the reading you can use to stimulate further discussion in class.

We find that some students start out having difficulty with the concept of assumptions. They may skim the surface and even actively resist "reading too much into the text," as they sometimes say. Yet students usually catch on when you and other students in the class model reading for assumptions during class discussions and activities. Therefore, you might want to put off assigning this activity to students individually until you have spent considerable class time discussing some of the bulleted items and your students have worked in pairs or small groups on a passage they find interesting, exploring the possible underlying meanings together and then reporting to the rest of the class.

The critical reading strategies that we list in Appendix 1 may prove especially helpful for those students who initially struggle to analyze assumptions. You might want to have students practice one or more of these activities in small groups as well.

READING LIKE A WRITER A Guide to Reading in each chapter presents an array of Reading like a Writer activities. Taking the time to work through the entire set of activities as a class gives students an in-depth introduction to the rhetorical features and strategies typical of the genre. Each activity begins with a brief introduction, guides students through an analysis of a small part of the text, and concludes by asking students to write briefly about what they have learned, using specific examples from their textual analysis to support their conclusions. These analyses are designed to be easy for students to do. What is special about them is that they focus students' attention on the text. Perhaps for the first time, students look closely at the craft of writing. Seeing how a writer did what he or she did is one of the first steps students take as they expand their own repertoire of writing skills. You can help students make the connection between their reading and their writing by asking them to try out what they have learned as they plan and draft their essays.

As we recommend in Part 3 of this manual, you can easily devote two one-hour class meetings to these activities. We urge you not to rush through them. First-year students have very little experience with close textual analysis, and the skills they will learn from the close reading required by these activities will help them in many contexts, both within and beyond the academic world. You might do one or two activities as a class when you assign A Guide to Reading, just to get everyone started. Or you could give students time, in groups of two or three, to make notes toward an analysis they later write individually.

Students will need encouragement. At first, they may not go deep enough in their rhetorical analysis, but if you select and read aloud two or three strong examples, they will get the idea.

TEACHING THE OTHER READINGS

Each chapter usually has three additional professional publications and two student essays, with one essay often accompanied by an image and an Analyzing Visuals activity. If you cannot teach all the readings, you may want to choose readings either for their potential interest to your students or for the rhetorical features covered in the Reading like a Writer activities following the readings. This manual provides a brief description of each reading and a list of rhetorical features matched to each to help you decide. Notice also that the readings vary in length and difficulty.

Every reading is introduced by a headnote that tells about the writer and contextualizes the reading. The headnote concludes with prereading advice suggesting what students might look for as they read the selection for the first time.

All the readings except the final one in each chapter are followed by the same three-part apparatus: a complete Reading for Meaning activity; a Reading like a Writer activity, which focuses on a feature of the reading that is especially illustrative; and a section called Considering Ideas for Your Own Writing, which stimulates students' thinking about subjects for their own essays. The apparatus following the final reading includes guidance so that readers can devise their own Reading for Meaning and Reading like a Writer activities. It does not include a Considering Ideas for Your Own Writing section.

35

SPECIAL READING STRATEGY ACTIVITIES

Two additional activities appear in each chapter. One is a special critical reading strategy called Comparing and Contrasting Related Readings. This activity follows the first reading to compare with a later one. See, for example, page 32. The second activity addresses one of the other critical reading strategies from Appendix 1. See, for example, page 43. It works in concert with the Reading for Meaning activities. You might encourage students to draw from the catalog of strategies on a regular basis.

TEACHING THE REFLECTIVE ACTIVITY: REVIEWING WHAT MAKES AN ESSAY EFFECTIVE

This is the second reflective activity (see Thinking about Your Experience with [the Genre] on p. 32 of this manual). It helps students consolidate what they have learned from the readings about the genre and helps them transition from reading to writing. As we suggest in the text, this activity can be done individually or in small groups. You could even make it a kind of debate, with one group arguing the benefits of their favorite reading and another pointing out its shortcomings. If you are going to have students write evaluation essays, such a debate will help them rehearse. Finally, you might consider having students do oral presentations in which they discuss their findings for this activity and, if they have already picked their own essay topics or written drafts, how their understanding of one of the readings influenced their own work. You could spread out these oral presentations over an entire term so that several students present on each genre, rather than having everyone present on the same genre.

TEACHING THE GUIDES TO WRITING

Every assignment chapter concludes with A Guide to Writing, which leads students through a systematic composing process. A Guide to Writing is just that—a guide, not a set of inflexible orders. It is designed to help students ask themselves an array of questions and respond to those questions in writing, thereby generating drafts that are increasingly more complete and more coherent. Each guide is divided into five parts: Invention and Research, Drafting, Reading a Draft Critically, Revising, Editing and Proofreading, and Reflecting on What You Have Learned.

ENCOURAGING INVENTION AND RESEARCH Each Guide to Writing includes a sequence of Invention and Research activities designed to help students ask themselves questions and generate ideas and information useful for their essays. As teachers, we are especially careful to introduce our students to the Invention and Research activities because so few of them have ever participated in systematic invention. We ask our students to open their books to the Invention and Research section, and then we briefly explain the purpose of each activity. By having students turn the pages and skim the Invention and Research activities while you discuss them, you will be able to reduce students' apprehension about these unfamiliar activities and greatly increase the probability that they will successfully complete the Invention and Research section before beginning their drafts.

If, like us, you choose to emphasize these phases of the writing process, you might want to make them a routine part of every class. We either have students do invention writing in class or have them write out of class and then discuss their writing in class. You could do the first part of Invention, Choosing a Subject, as whole-class brainstorming or in small groups. When you model how to choose a subject, begin with the suggestions in the book (including those in the Considering Ideas for Your Own Writing section), and then move to choosing a subject and exploring it. Students can also do invention in small groups or share their work with their peers. For example, even though students are working on different subjects, we might first have them write individually and then talk with other students about their purpose or about the visuals they are thinking of using. We find that making Invention and Research activities a regular part of class, rather than simply out-of-class requirements, ensures that students do the work and also makes the activities more productive. Spreading the invention phase over several class sessions also tends to give ideas time to percolate. Once students become immersed in invention through regular class activities, student writers often find themselves thinking of details to add to their drafts or solutions to problems in their writing when they are otherwise engaged.

Research is comfortably included in our broad definition of invention—everything writers do before and during writing to produce ideas and evaluate them. Most of the writing assignments include the possibility for field research (interview and observation) and for library and Internet research, and subsections of Invention and Research suggest ways that students can use the Internet to find subjects for their essays or use the library to research subjects they have already chosen. You can decide how much library or Internet research your students should do or leave it to them to decide. We provide detailed guidance to help students find and cite sources in Appendix 2: Strategies for Research and Documentation.

MAKING DRAFTING PRODUCTIVE Invention may produce a number of complete paragraphs, several lists, a page of freewriting, an interview, or notes on library or Internet research—a plethora of material that must be organized before the student can write a draft. This much material poses a new problem for many students: What should they do with all of it?

A Guide to Writing in each chapter urges students to consider several alternative plans before settling on one. Often students are unaware of alternatives; we find it helpful to illustrate several, sometimes from the reading selections and sometimes from subjects suggested by students.

Each planning section reminds students, as they go on to draft, that what they have developed during the invention process is only a plan. In other words, it is expendable. The final test for the draft is not whether it follows the outline developed during invention but whether it works. The planning section, like many other parts of A Guide to Writing, requires that inexperienced writers sometimes try a new approach.

The box titled Working with Sources in each chapter offers students strategies for finding, evaluating, and integrating genre-specific sources into their writing. Students are often unfamiliar with the differences between genre-specific sources. At the start of the term, you might go over the Working with Sources boxes in class so that students learn to take genre-specific approaches to working with sources.

The drafting section called Considering a Useful Sentence Strategy (for example, p. 74) illustrates a sentence pattern that is commonly used in each genre. Here is a list of the strategies:

Chapter 2: Autobiography. Using participial phrases to show simultaneous action, to make an action or image more specific and vivid, or to relate what the writer or someone else was thinking or feeling at the time of an action.

Chapter 3: Observation. Using absolute phrases to show simultaneous parts of a complex action or to detail observations of a person or an object.

Chapter 4: Reflection. Using parallel grammatical structures to connect related ideas or examples.

Chapter 5: Explaining Concepts. Using appositives to identify people, introduce terms, and present details.

Chapter 6: Evaluation. Using sentences that express comparisons and contrasts, specifically ones that contrast criticism with praise and vice versa.

Chapter 7: Position Paper. Conceding the value of a likely criticism and then refuting it immediately, either in the same sentence or the next one.

Chapter 8: Speculating about Causes or Effects. Using clear topic sentences, especially ones that are grammatically parallel, to signal the stages of an argument.

Chapter 9: Proposal to Solve a Problem. Using rhetorical questions to engage and orient readers, to introduce and emphasize parts of an argument, to appeal to readers' emotions, and to provide transitions from problem to solution or among aspects of the proposal.

GIVING AND GETTING CRITICAL COMMENTS The box titled Reading a Draft Critically (for example, p. 75) poses a truly valuable critical reading task for students, especially for those who have experience only with simplified all-purpose peer-critique guidelines, which often appear in checklist form.

In *Reading Critically, Writing Well*, the peer reviewer's analysis is based on identifying and evaluating features of the genre that have been introduced and illustrated throughout the chapter. The goal is to have students read a draft closely in light of what they have learned about the genre and then write a response that describes the draft, evaluates it using criteria appropriate to the genre, and recommends possible revisions.

It is important to coach students to read a draft critically. Use modeling and explanation.

We recommend that you talk students through at least one step of the analysis the first time you assign them to do a critical reading of one another's drafts. When they complete their first critical reading, you can then select some expansive, helpful sections of analysis to share with them as examples of what you expect from all of them.

See Organizing Draft Workshops in Part 4 of this manual for more ways to use Reading a Draft Critically.

REVISING PRODUCTIVELY Research has shown that the more examples writers have seen of a genre, the larger the repertoire of strategies they can draw on to achieve their particular purpose. To help students make connections among their readings and the papers they are revising, the Troubleshooting Your Draft table included in each chapter (for example, p. 78) identifies common problems and strategies for dealing with them. If you go over the table with the class and highlight the ways these strategies connect back to the readings they have studied, they will be more likely to see the table as helpful and to focus on the sorts of global issues that are most critical at this stage, instead of only on sentence-level errors and infelicities.

Peer-critique draft workshops and student-teacher conferences are also invaluable in teaching students to revise. For information on class activities to support students' revising, see Organizing Draft Workshops and Holding Conferences in Part 4 of this manual.

TEACHING THE REFLECTIVE ACTIVITY: REFLECTING ON WHAT YOU HAVE LEARNED

A Guide to Writing in each chapter concludes with Reflecting on What You Have Learned. This activity has two parts. The first asks students to think about their composing process, including what they learned from reading examples of the genre and how their revision was influenced by readers of their drafts. The second part invites students to reflect on the role that the genre they just wrote plays in society, to consider its contributions, and to articulate the feelings, anxieties, or preferences they have when writing in the genre.

If students reflect in thoughtful detail on their own reading and writing processes, they can learn much about how they read and write. Students' responses to this activity can also help guide your comments on their papers. The student who has written a miserable paper and is miserable about it might get very different treatment from one who has done poorly but is uncritical. We believe that there is pedagogical value in responding directly to the student's reflections so that the teacher's comments are not self-contained but are part of a dialogue about the paper.

Chapter 2 AUTOBIOGRAPHY

Students usually find the readings in this chapter accessible and engaging, and they typically find it easy to recall significant events and people to write about. You will want to emphasize, as we do in the introduction and throughout the chapter, that good autobiographical writing should be both vivid and meaningful. It should enable readers to imagine what happened and what the people were like, but it also should convey to readers the significance of these subjects. The strategies of narrating a story and describing a person must serve the larger purpose of conveying to readers the event's or person's autobiographical significance. That is, the autobiographer's purpose is not just to present the event or person but also to help readers understand its importance in the writer's life.

This chapter can teach students to

- select personal experiences that represent themselves to others;
- practice strategies for narrating and describing;
- probe the significance of particular experiences and relationships;
- show significance through word choice, dramatic action, and vivid detail; and
- organize an essay narratively or topically.

You may want to emphasize the first item in the list above because the assignment to write something autobiographical can be misperceived by students as a requirement to make public something private. Students must be reminded that they are the ones who decide how they will represent themselves in their essays. They choose the person or event that lets them make this self-presentation. Students should not feel compelled to write about something they do not feel comfortable sharing. You could read aloud and discuss this passage from the third paragraph of the chapter introduction:

Whether you are reading or writing autobiography, it is important to remember that autobiography is public, not private. While it involves self-presentation and contributes to self-knowledge, it does not require writers to make unwanted self-disclosures. Autobiographers compose themselves for readers; they fashion a self in words, much as a novelist creates a character. As readers, we come to "know" the people we read about by the way they are portrayed. Consequently, when you write autobiography, you have to decide how to portray yourself. This decision depends on whom you expect to read your essay (your audience) and what you want to communicate to readers (your purpose).

WRITING ASSIGNMENT: Autobiography (p. 20)

Here is the writing assignment for Chapter 2 as it appears in the book:

Write an autobiographical essay about a significant event or person in your life. Choose the event or person with your readers in mind. The subject should be one that you feel comfortable presenting to others and that will lead readers to reflect on their own lives or on the differences between your personal experiences and their own. Present your experience dramatically and vividly so that readers can imagine what it was like for you. Through a careful choice of words and details, convey the meaning and importance in your life—what we call the *autobiographical significance*—of the event or person you've chosen to write about.

Problems Students May Have with This Assignment

We have noticed that students who try to write an autobiographical essay for the first time tend to have some predictable problems, especially with (1) developing a well-paced, dramatic narrative that also conveys the significance of the event or (2) putting together revealing anecdotes with interesting dialogue and vivid descriptions that show the relationship between the autobiographer and the remembered person. Students usually err by either telling without showing or showing without telling. Drawing on what they know of essayist conventions, students may frame the subject by opening with an introductory statement that announces the subject's general significance and ending with a pat and reductive moral. Students may also be so intent on making their story dramatic or description vivid that they forget to invest their narration and description with significance or to let readers know how the event or person affected them. If your students have either of these problems, direct them to the Invention and Research exercises (p. 67) or the Drafting ones (p. 72), which will help them rethink their approach.

A third common problem, more related to surface features than to substance, is the formatting conventions of dialogue; students may present entire conversations as single paragraphs, or turn speaker tags into separate sentences. Luis Rodriguez's "Always Running" provides an effective introduction to conventions of dialogue, and the Reconstructing Dialogue exercise in A Guide to Writing Autobiography also provides your class with an opportunity to teach these features: After students have practiced reconstructing dialogue, ask for some volunteers to share their material, and slowly work through it with the class, showing how the dialogue might be structured and formatted.

RESOURCES IN CHAPTER 2 FOR TEACHING AUTOBIOGRAPHY

FINDING SUBJECTS

Writing Situations for Autobiography (p. 20)

These three examples show both academic and nonacademic occasions for autobiographical writing. You might want to use these examples to point out the writers' different purposes and audiences and the different ways they achieve the self-disclosure and depth of insight appropriate to the particular rhetorical situation in which they are writing.

You may also emphasize the two basic features introduced in the first paragraph of the chapter—vivid impressions and autobiographical significance—by asking questions like, What sorts of details would be most important to the admissions essay about breakfast cereals? and What is the autobiographical significance of that event? The third example provides students with another illustration of the generative power of writing, an aspect you might draw attention to by asking whether the executive would have changed his management style if he had not written about his role model.

Considering Ideas for Your Own Writing

These activities follow each reading except the chapter-opening and closing ones. They are designed to help students think of subjects for their own essays by considering subjects related to the readings. Here is a list summarizing the subjects suggested after Chapter 2 readings by the following authors:

Shah   Events that you were looking forward to but that turned out differently than you expected (p. 38)

Rodriguez   Events that were traumatic, that turned out worse (or better) than you expected, or that showed a side of you that is usually hidden (p. 45)

Crapanzano People with whom you had complicated relationships or for whom you had conflicting feelings (p. 55)

Benioff   People like coaches, teachers, employers, and other mentors who have influenced your life, or people with whom you have disagreed (p. 61)

Because memories are readily accessible and require no trips to the library, and because writing quickly about similar subjects can help readers find new ways to connect to or respond to the texts they read, you might consider having students write out a response to at least one of the Considering Ideas for Your Own Writing shortly after they finish the associated reading. Then have students share rough drafts or brief anecdotes about their own, similarly themed, events and people as part of a class discussion.

Choosing a Subject (p. 67)

Choosing a Subject is the first activity under Invention and Research, the opening section of A Guide to Writing Autobiography. Students are offered bulleted lists of suggested subjects and are asked to make their own list of possible subjects. You might urge students from day one to begin compiling a list of possibilities. Ideas inspired by the suggestions in Considering Ideas for Your Own Writing could be part of this list.

Problems Students May Have Choosing a Subject

The writing assignment in this chapter gives students a wide choice of subjects. This choice, as students soon discover, presents problems as well as opportunities. When asked to choose a significant event or person, students frequently want to write about the first subject that comes to mind, often a recent experience or a traumatic one. An event that happened recently may appear to be important only because it is on the writer's mind. While writing about such an event will help the writer understand it, the event may turn out not to have much meaning after all. Traumatic events may also be problematic, not because they lack significance but because they are too significant. Writing about a traumatic event may involve more self-disclosure than seems appropriate given the writing situation. On the other hand, the student may decide that writing about a traumatic event such as the death of a loved one can be therapeutic.

Some students will also, understandably, want to write about major emotional landmarks such as high-school graduation, being selected for a team, surviving an accident, or failing a big test. Some of these peak experiences represent initiations or rites of passage. They are prominent in the minds of many students and, properly handled, can make excellent subjects. However, many such events lack conflict, an essential ingredient in effective narrative. Another problem is that they are common experiences, familiar to almost everyone. The challenge in writing about such events is to find a conflict to focus on and to avoid clichés by finding something unusual in the experience or by giving readers a new perspective on it. For these reasons, we encourage students to think twice before writing about their first thrilling experience on the ski slopes, the prom that was all it promised to be, or an event that would have embarrassed anyone. Experiences that exactly match expectations contain nothing surprising and no new insights about the writer or about human nature.

When students write about people, rather than events, they are sometimes most tempted to write about people for whom their feelings are clear and unalloyed, people for whom they feel nothing but adoration or nothing but contempt. However, the resulting essays can sound more like political ads than rich autobiography, and offer writers few opportunities to explore or express complicated ideas.

Students do best when they look beyond the obvious and consider the subtler experiences or relationships they have had—events that led to a discovery or realization, important changes within themselves or within people close to them, people with whom they had complicated relationships or about whom they had ambivalent feelings, or relationships that caused them to learn something new about themselves.

THINKING ABOUT YOUR EXPERIENCE WITH AUTOBIOGRAPHY (p. 21)

This activity allows students to realize they have a familiarity, possibly greater than they expected, with the genre, reducing the anxiety that typically accompanies composing an essay and making the remaining activities in this chapter easier.

CHOOSING READINGS

The reading selections in this chapter represent two major types of autobiographical subjects—remembered events and remembered people. Annie Dillard, Saira Shah, Luis J. Rodriguez, and Jean Brandt focus on events in their childhoods. Aleksandra Crapanzano and Brad Benioff present persons who played important roles in the writers' lives.

If you cannot teach all of the readings in this chapter, you will have to make some choices. There are at least two principles that may guide your selection—(1) the interest level of the reading and its usefulness in suggesting subjects for your students' essays and (2) the basic features covered in each of the Reading like a Writer activities.

INTEREST LEVELS OF THE READINGS

Here are brief descriptions from the table of contents to help you choose readings that might be of interest to your students:

Annie Dillard, **An American Childhood**. A celebrated essayist remembers, with strange affection, a childhood prank and its scary consequences. (p. 22)

Saira Shah, **Longing to Belong**. An award-winning journalist and documentary filmmaker recounts how events forced her to recognize the naïveté of her fairy-tale vision of her homeland. (p. 33)

Luis J. Rodriguez, **Always Running**. An ex-gang member and noted author describes a childhood game of night basketball and its deadly aftermath when the police arrive to stop the game. (p. 39)

Aleksandra Crapanzano, **Lobster Lessons**. A writer recalls what she taught her partner's elderly aunt about the pleasures of cooking and eating—and what she learned from the aunt's very different ideas on the subject. (p. 46)

Brad Benioff, **Rick**. A freshman composition student looks back at his complex relationship with a demanding, sometimes abusive, high-school coach. (p. 56)

Jean Brandt, **Calling Home**. A freshman composition student recalls a shoplifting incident during a Christmas holiday outing with her family when she was thirteen. (p. 62)

READING LIKE A WRITER ACTIVITIES

The first reading, Dillard's "An American Childhood," introduces all the basic features of autobiography through its Reading like a Writer activities. The final reading, Brandt's "Calling Home," does not specify Reading like a Writer activities but invites students to choose a feature of the readings they think is worth analyzing. Each of the other readings has one Reading like a Writer activity. Here is a list of these activities.

Conveying Autobiographical Significance: Saira Shah, "Longing to Belong" (p. 37)

A Special Reading Strategy: Contextualizing: Luis J. Rodriguez, "Always Running" (p. 32)

Presenting Places and People: Luis J. Rodriguez, "Always Running" (p. 43)

Presenting a Person through Anecdotes and Recurring Activities: Aleksandra Crapanzano, "Lobster Lessons" (p. 53)

Describing a Person through Visual Details: Brad Benioff, "Rick" (p. 60)

A GUIDE TO READING AUTOBIOGRAPHY (p. 22)

The essay that is the focus of A Guide to Reading Autobiography is Dillard's "An American Childhood."

READING FOR MEANING (p. 25)

Here are suggestions for teaching the Reading for Meaning activities following Dillard's reading.

Read to Comprehend (p. 25)
For the initial task in this section, you will want to keep your students from writing mere plot summaries. Direct your students to identify the meaning—for Dillard— of the experience she describes. You can then use their observations as a springboard to a discussion on the autobiographical significance of Dillard's essay. This discussion, in turn, will help prepare students to discover and convey the autobiographical significance of their own upcoming essays.

Other words students may need to define include *mazy* (paragraph 12), *impelled* (14), *labyrinths* (15), *cherishing* (16), and *prow* (16). Defining these words can lead naturally into a discussion of Dillard's use of metaphor.

Once the students have used one or more of the critical reading strategies to respond to "An American Childhood," you may wish to ask them to use the same strategy or strategies to explore the autobiographical event they plan to write about or in response to drafts by classmates during peer reviews. They could outline their own event's plot, summarize the autobiographical significance of a classmate's essay, paraphrase one of its scenes or some of its dialogue, or compose questions that will help them understand and remember it.

Read to Respond (p. 26)

Another passage you might ask students to respond to is Dillard's opening description of what she learned from the neighborhood boys about playing football:

> Best, you got to throw yourself mightily at someone's running legs. Either you brought him down or you hit the ground flat out on your chin, with your arms empty before you. It was all or nothing. If you hesitated in fear, you would miss and get hurt: you would take a hard fall while the kid got away, or you would get kicked in the face while the kid got away. But if you flung yourself wholeheartedly at the back of his knees—if you gathered and joined body and soul and pointed them diving fearlessly—then you likely wouldn't get hurt, and you'd stop the ball. Your fate, and your team's score, depended on your concentration and courage. Nothing girls did could compare with it. (paragraph 1)

You might ask your students about their own experiences—with sports or any other interest that they have pursued "body and soul." Try to get them to talk or write about what is involved in the total absorption and commitment that allow us to ignore what we might lose and think only about what we are trying to do. Many of us enjoy this focus in creative or intellectual activities such as writing, programming, or sewing.

Of course, students are likely to want to respond to Dillard's final comment, "Nothing girls did could compare with it." (Pointing out that the event she describes took place in 1952 might help students put the comment in context.) Discussing this comment provides a natural transition to the section Read to Analyze Assumptions, since the text of that section prompts students to think about the assumptions behind Dillard's remark.

Read to Analyze Assumptions (p. 26)

Before students engage with the assumptions categories, such as "assumptions about the value of rules and fair play," you might have a class discussion or a threaded discussion in a course management system (CMS) on how Dillard uses the ideas of *courage* and *heroism*. The discussion will prepare students for further identification and analysis of other assumptions in Dillard's essay, after which you might ask students to generate their own lists of assumptions they identify in Dillard's essay. As students work with the assumption categories, you might ask them to evaluate which assumptions on their lists fit into our three assumptions categories: "assumptions about the value of rules and fair play," "assumptions about the superiority of boys' play," and "assumptions about the desirability of committing yourself 'wholeheartedly.'"

The final activity in this section asks students to try out a critical reading strategy from Appendix 1—reflecting on challenges to your beliefs and values, exploring the significance of figurative language, or looking for patterns of opposition. Each of these strategies helps readers identify the assumptions and values of an author, and see how those sometimes hidden perspectives influenced the text, providing students with a natural transition to Reading like a Writer.

READING LIKE A WRITER (p. 28)

The four Reading like a Writer activities following Dillard's essay give students a thorough introduction to the craft of writing autobiography. You can have students do some or all of the activities here before going on to do selected Reading like a Writer activities for the subsequent readings. With the Dillard essay, students are introduced to major features of autobiographical writing—narrating the story, presenting people, describing places, and conveying the autobiographical significance. Each feature carries a reading and a writing activity that help students focus on Dillard's writing strategies.

Narrating the Story (p. 28)

After introducing students to such narrative concepts as *identification* and *surprise*, this section discusses the roles of verbs and verbals in describing the action. Many students naturally want to focus on adjectives and adverbs when they first attempt to write narratively, but ultimately stories are about actions, so the verbs they choose are crucial.

To illuminate this characteristic, the activity that follows this discussion asks students to consider how Dillard uses verbs and verbals to make her story dramatic. Before students begin analyzing the text on their own, you might quickly review these terms and help students locate the verbs and verbals in a brief passage (paragraph 16, perhaps). This review will give them confidence when they begin to analyze verb use in paragraphs 11 to 15 and in the essay as a whole for verbals. You might consider having them make their lists of verbs and verbals in class, and then go around the room, asking students to pick examples from their lists to put on the board for discussion.

Students will probably note that a high percentage of Dillard's verbs and verbals show action. They might also note that many of these words are simple ("ran," "chased") and that she repeats some of them. You might want to discuss why Dillard has not chosen more elaborate verbs and how the repetition speeds up the drama.

Have your students look at the last clauses of paragraph 13: "you have to fling yourself at what you're doing, you have to point yourself, forget yourself, aim, dive." Ask students if the verbs and verbals here are propelling the action or serving another function. They should see that these words are an important way that Dillard conveys her "immense discovery," the significance of this event for her at the time.

Presenting People (p. 29)

After completing this activity, students should see that experienced writers often use only a few well-chosen physical details rather than exhaustive lists to describe their characters. They should also note that presenting a character will involve a combination of strategies—physical description, characterization or evaluation, and dialogue.

Students should have marked only a few words and phrases in each paragraph they analyzed. You might ask them to speculate about how the essay would change if Dillard devoted an entire paragraph of description to the man who chased the kids. What would happen to the pace of her tale? You could also ask students to record in their own words their impressions of this man, then to go back to the essay to analyze what words and strategies gave them their impressions. Discuss the words Dillard uses to characterize the man: a "thin" man "in city clothes" (paragraph 10), with an "ordinary Pittsburgh accent" (20), but also "our hero" (16) and "sainted" (21). Ask students to consider how Dillard wants us to view this man and how her depiction of him allows us to begin to see the significance of the entire event.

Describing Places (p. 30)

Students may be familiar with the general concept of using details, but they might not understand the difference between *naming* and *detailing*. If they are struggling, you may want to offer examples: "tire chains" (naming) and "clanking from afar" (detailing) from paragraph 7, "door" (naming) and "wide black" (detailing) from paragraph 9, and "trees" (naming) and "messy winter" (detailing) from paragraph 16. After seeing more examples, they may more easily see that describing requires both naming objects and including details that allow a reader to experience that object the way the writer has intended.

45

Likewise, some students may not be trained to notice figurative language. You might have them report to the class whether the single comparison they chose to analyze is a simile or a metaphor so that they can be aware of that kind of comparison throughout Dillard's essay. Discuss which comparisons are particularly effective in helping them imagine the place. This discussion might lead into a more general discussion about the value of metaphor and simile and what description by comparison offers that literal description does not. You might follow up on the activity by having students brainstorm new comparisons as possible replacements for the ones used by Dillard and then evaluate them so that they develop some experience formulating and appraising new expressions.

Conveying the Autobiographical Significance (p. 31)

This activity helps students understand how a writer communicates autobiographical significance by describing remembered feelings and implying present perspectives. By analyzing specific words the author has chosen, students will discover how to infer the feelings of the writer at both the time of the event and the time of the writing. You might have students meet in small groups to list words and phrases in paragraphs 19 to 21 that reveal Dillard's childhood perception of the event as well as her changed perception of it as an adult. Then have the groups report while you make a master list on the board or with a projector. As a whole class, discuss how Dillard's word choice and view of the event change from childhood to adulthood.

To prepare students for their own autobiographical writing, you might ask them to start thinking about childhood experiences that impressed them in one way when they were children but that appear different now. Discuss some of their examples, and advise them to look for this dual perspective in other essays from this chapter.

A SPECIAL READING STRATEGY — COMPARING AND CONTRASTING RELATED READINGS: DILLARD'S "AN AMERICAN CHILDHOOD" AND RODRIGUEZ'S "ALWAYS RUNNING" (p. 32)

In this chapter, an additional reading activity follows the autobiography essay by Dillard. However, before having students complete this activity, you may wish to have them read and discuss the section on comparing and contrasting at the end of Appendix 1: A Catalog of Critical Reading Strategies. There students will find an explanation of comparing and contrasting and an annotated model comparing Lewis H. Van Dusen Jr.'s essay on civil disobedience with Martin Luther King Jr.'s "Letter from Birmingham Jail." It might also be useful to have the class move from the model presented in the appendix to a comparison of the same arguments point by point.

In order to get students to think about the similarities and differences between the Dillard and Rodriguez essays, we ask students to compare the two essays in terms of (1) their cultural and historical contexts and (2) the ways that Dillard and Rodriguez create a dramatic narrative. Because comparing and contrasting is such a fundamental way of thinking, learning, and writing, students should be introduced to it early.

READINGS

Saira Shah, "Longing to Belong" (p. 33)

READING FOR MEANING (p. 35)

Read to Comprehend (p. 35)

To be sure your students go beyond surface observation, you could ask the following questions: Why did Shah at first embrace the romantic, fairy-tale vision of becoming an Afghan bride? How was that vision (and her attitude) changed by her experience?

Other words that students may need to define are *visceral* (paragraph 2), *sanctum* (3), *demurely* (4), *piety* (5), *putative* (6), *chaff* (7), and *salvo* (7). The last two terms, once defined, might make students more aware of the ongoing warfare metaphor in that paragraph, as seen in the later "heaviest guns."

Read to Respond (p. 36)
Another dimension of the story to which you may wish to direct your students is Shah's portrayal of her female relatives' behavior. Shah writes that when her fiancé would walk into a room, a child would be placed in his arms and he would "pose with it, whiskers twitching, while the women cooed their admiration" (paragraph 3). What does Shah's choice of words reveal about her opinion of these staged moments?

Read to Analyze Assumptions (p. 36)
As a follow-up to the assumptions about the values underlying cultural differences, you might ask the class what assumptions Shah has made about the cultural backgrounds of her readers and their likely reactions to the details of her story, originally published in the *New York Times Magazine.* For the discussion of assumptions about the influence of fairy tales, you might expose students to some actual fairy tales from the Brothers Grimm tradition, which are considerably darker and less inviting than the "fairy tales" to which Shah obviously intends to allude. Finally, you might also direct students to her sudden recognition of her own assumptions, as she realizes that the teller of the stories she had in mind "was a man" (paragraph 5).

READING LIKE A WRITER: CONVEYING AUTOBIOGRAPHICAL SIGNIFICANCE (p. 37)

This Reading like a Writer activity helps students understand the two main ways an author conveys autobiographical significance—showing and telling. Students will probably be more confident in identifying where Shah tells than where she shows. To draw their attention to where Shah shows, ask students to look carefully at her description of the wedding reception for her uncle's son (paragraph 4) and to explain the meaning they infer from the description.

CONSIDERING IDEAS FOR YOUR OWN WRITING (p. 38)

This section lists several subjects, suggested by the reading, that may stimulate student writing. You may want to ask students what other ideas for subjects they get from the reading. We have found that routinely discussing possible subjects in class encourages students to try out new ideas. Remember that there is also an array of subject suggestions in the opening Invention and Research activities of A Guide to Writing Autobiography (p. 67).

Luis J. Rodriguez, "Always Running" (p. 39)

READING FOR MEANING (p. 41)

Read to Comprehend (p. 41)
To steer students away from a simple plot summary, you may wish to point out the storm references and imagery in the story and ask them how the storm works within the context of the narrative.

Other words students may need to define include *interspersed* (paragraph 15) and *scurried* (27).

Read to Respond (p. 41)

Students may also respond to

- Rodriguez's description of Mexicans—including himself—as "born with a hideous stain" (paragraph 26);
- Tino's cavalier attitude toward trespassing, response when the two sheriff's deputies appear, and Rodriguez's hesitation at both points.

Read to Analyze Assumptions (p. 42)

You might ask students to respond to the stereotypes identified here: Do they agree with Tino that he would have probably been beaten if caught by the police?

In addition, we learned as Tino and Rodriguez climb the fence that each boy is ten years old. What does Rodriguez seem to be saying about the two deputies who have drawn their guns while chasing two ten-year-olds on school grounds, and what assumptions drive that implied message? Does his emphasis on the age of the boys and on the school grounds as the setting suggest a larger assumption than the responsibilities of schools—perhaps, an assumption about the responsibilities of agencies of government such as the police?

A Special Reading Strategy: Contextualizing (p. 43)

An additional reading activity in this chapter follows the remembered-event essay by Rodriguez. Before students attempt this activity, you might have them look at the section on contextualizing in Appendix 1: A Catalog of Critical Reading Strategies. There students will find a demonstration of contextualizing. To consider the social and historical contexts of Rodriguez's essay, students are asked to identify the values and attitudes underlying Rodriguez's story and then to compare and contrast these values and attitudes with their own. You can expect students to have a spectrum of opinions about racism and its history in America. Teaching students to contextualize as they read will enable them to become aware of their own positionality—the fact that we all inevitably read through the screen of our own experiences, values, and attitudes. Students may be interested to discover that whereas their attitudes may seem unique to them as individuals, many of them are socially constructed and historically contingent.

Reading like a Writer: Presenting Places and People (p. 43)

This Reading like a Writer activity helps students understand how writers use naming, detailing, and comparing to introduce their readers to people and places. Ask students what impact the metaphors about flying, identified in the second task, have on the effectiveness of the story as a whole: do they make Tino's ultimate fate seem more shocking? After working through the examples, you may wish to ask students to look closely at paragraph 26 to identify Rodriguez's use of comparing or at paragraph 28 to identify his use of naming.

Considering Ideas for Your Own Writing (p. 45)

This section lists several subjects, suggested by the reading, that may stimulate student writing. You may want to ask students what other ideas for subjects they get from the reading. We have found that routinely discussing possible subjects in class encourages students to try out new ideas. Remember that there is also an array of subject suggestions in the opening Invention and Research activity of A Guide to Writing Autobiography.

Aleksandra Crapanzano, "Lobster Lessons" (p. 46)

READING FOR MEANING (p. 51)

Read to Comprehend (p. 51)

In addition to having students explain what they learned about Margaret, you may choose to have students illustrate their summaries by providing textual evidence.

Other words students may need to define include *spartan* (paragraph 3), *rationed* (8), *regimen* (10), *alchemy* (11), and *austerity* (13).

Read to Respond (p. 51)

Students may also respond to

- Crapanzano's campaign to change an older woman's traditional menu (paragraphs 10–13);
- the clashes of personality (15–19);
- John's final change of heart as he announces that salted tap water "wouldn't be the same" (19).

Read to Analyze Assumptions (p. 52)

As follow-up questions to the analytical work asked of students here, you might ask what assumptions Crapanzano is making about her audience's values as she describes which rituals she eventually honors and which she is determined to change. For instance, she clearly seems to assume they will understand why she insisted on butter rather than margarine, and that they will share her assumptions about eating and pleasure. (You might remind students answering this question that she originally wrote the article for no-longer-published *Gourmet* magazine.)

READING LIKE A WRITER: PRESENTING A PERSON THROUGH ANECDOTES AND RECURRING ACTIVITIES (p. 53)

Crapanzano's essay will probably be your students' first exposure to a remembered-person article in your class. Essays that follow this approach seldom have the option of following a single narrative thread. Instead, they weave together several threads. For this reason, it's important to emphasize the two narrative strategies discussed here: anecdotes and recurring activities. Most students will have little trouble spotting or spinning anecdotes, but the strategy of describing recurring activities may have previously been invisible to them. For this reason, you may need to emphasize the latter in class discussions. You might start with paragraph 2, which briefly summarizes recurring activities such as traveling and eating, and paragraph 3, which describes Margaret's "spartan daily regimen."

ANALYZING VISUALS (p. 54)

Students have a great deal of exposure to visuals but not a lot of practice in analyzing them for a class, so they may approach this task with anxiety or uncertainty, even though they may prove to have a lot to say on visuals once they get started. It might be a good idea, for this reason, to start small, with simple observations: Do the subjects in the photos look happy? What are they doing? Are the shots candid or posed? Who do they think took the photographs—someone at the scene or a photographer from the magazine? Who seems to be the focus of the two photographs, taken together? Build from there to the questions posed in the text, and break for a moment to let students work on their answers to them. Remind the students that there are no official, right answers to these questions and that they should feel free to speculate. Answers to the third bulleted question in the list, for instance, might range from a suggestion that the photographs focus on the people, rather than food, because the article is ultimately about people, to speculation that perhaps Margaret was unwilling to have a magazine publish pictures of her eating messy foods like lobster or print photos of the inside of her house.

CONSIDERING IDEAS FOR YOUR OWN WRITING (p. 55)

This section lists several subjects, suggested by the reading, that may stimulate student writing. You may want to ask students what other ideas for subjects they get from the reading. We have found that routinely discussing possible subjects in class encourages students to try out new ideas. Remember that there is also an array of subject suggestions in the opening Invention and Research activity of A Guide to Writing Autobiography (p. 67).

Brad Benioff, "Rick" (p. 56)

READING FOR MEANING (p. 58)

Read to Comprehend (p. 58)
Because readers' personal experiences will largely shape what they believe, encourage students to provide textual evidence to support their explanations so that they do not merely exchange their experiences with Benioff's.

Other words students may need to define include *maces* (paragraph 6) and *jovial* (6).

Read to Respond (p. 59)
Students may also respond to Benioff's mounting feelings of inadequacy as Rick silently evaluates him or to Benioff's epiphany in paragraph 25.

Read to Analyze Assumptions (p. 59)
Another assumption about masculinity your students may consider is the notion that anger, revenge, and hatred can drive a person to achieve greatness.

READING LIKE A WRITER: DESCRIBING A PERSON THROUGH VISUAL DETAILS (p. 60)

This Reading like a Writer activity asks students to focus specifically on the describing strategies Benioff uses in paragraph 6—detailing and comparing. Students should realize that Benioff's description is purposeful—to give readers an impression of Rick and an understanding of his significance.

CONSIDERING IDEAS FOR YOUR OWN WRITING (p. 61)

This section lists several subjects, suggested by the reading, that may stimulate student writing. You may want to ask students what other ideas for subjects they get from the reading. We have found that routinely discussing possible subjects in class encourages students to try out new ideas. Remember that there is also an array of subject suggestions in the opening Invention and Research activity of A Guide to Writing Autobiography (p. 67).

Jean Brandt, "Calling Home" (p. 62)

READING FOR MEANING (p. 65)

This Reading for Meaning activity invites students to apply to Brandt's essay what they have learned from the other readings in this chapter about reading to comprehend, reading to respond, and reading to analyze assumptions. You might want to have your class suggest words to define as well as brainstorm possibilities for response and analysis.

READING LIKE A WRITER (p. 65)

This Reading like a Writer activity offers students an opportunity to focus on one of the autobiographical-writing strategies covered in the other readings for this chapter— narrating the event or anecdotes, presenting people, presenting places, or conveying autobiographical significance.

REVIEWING WHAT MAKES AN EFFECTIVE ESSAY: AUTOBIOGRAPHY (p. 66)

This reflective activity makes a great transition from reading to writing. As the text suggests, this activity can be done individually or in small groups. As the introduction to Part 6 of this manual notes, you can also assign it as an oral presentation for a few students, with other students doing similar presentations on later genres at other points during the term.

A GUIDE TO WRITING AUTOBIOGRAPHY (p. 67)

To represent an event or person vividly, students will need to generate many concrete details. You may need to encourage students to complete the invention activities fully and thoughtfully, pointing out that although they are unlikely to use all the details they generate during invention it will be to their benefit to have a wealth of details from which to choose as they draft their essays. Additionally, you may want to take a few minutes of class time to allow your students to list the different resources they have available to them when writing autobiographical essays—such as memory, others' statements, and memorabilia (as explained in Working with Sources).

Whether they are writing about an event or a person, many students tend to opt for the simplest structure—a chronological organization—without stopping to consider alternatives. A chronological organization is acceptable, and many of the readings follow a chronological order. However, essays about remembered persons may be more effective if they follow topical organizations, and even students writing about events should realize that they need not begin their stories at the beginning and follow them all the way through to the end. A simple variation, for instance, is to begin the essay by engaging readers with some dialogue, action, or vivid description before filling in the context. And even if they do choose to follow a strict chronological sequence, students should remember that they can control the pace of the narrative, slowing down to present details about important parts and picking up the pace by summarizing less important parts. Students often spend too much time on less significant, preliminary incidents and not enough time on the most important moments.

Here is an outline of A Guide to Writing Autobiography:

Invention and Research
    Choosing a Subject
        Events
        People
    Developing Your Subject
        Recalling the Event or Person
        Presenting Important People
    Reflecting on Your Subject
        Recalling Your Feelings and Thoughts
        Exploring Your Present Perspective
        Considering Your Purpose
        Formulating a Tentative Thesis Statement

Drafting
    Setting Goals
    Organizing Your Draft
    Working with Sources: Using Memory and Memorabilia (box)
    Choosing Relevant Details
    Considering a Useful Sentence Strategy (Participial Phrases)
    Writing the Beginning

Reading a Draft Critically (box)
    Read for a First Impression
    Read Again to Suggest Improvements

Revising
    Troubleshooting Your Draft (table)
    To Make the Narrative More Dramatic and Telling
    To Present People Vividly
    To Describe Places Vividly
    To Convey the Autobiographical Significance
    To Make the Organizational Plan More Effective

Editing and Proofreading

Reflecting on What You Have Learned: Autobiography (box)

Chapter 3 OBSERVATION

Observation, the genre featured in this chapter, is closely related to the genres in the preceding chapter and in the two subsequent ones. The discussion of Chapter 5 in this manual covers some differences between observational, reflective, and explanatory writing. Here we point out the key difference between observational and autobiographical writing: Whereas autobiographical writing attempts to find personal meaning in experience and to transmit that meaning to readers through vivid storytelling, observational writing aims to present what writers have discovered about a subject foreign to them by observing it firsthand. Informing readers about the subject in a vivid, engaging way is the main purpose of observational writing.

This chapter can teach students to

- identify a place that may interest readers;
- interview people and integrate what they say into an essay;
- observe people closely and present them and their activities at a particular location vividly;
- practice strategies for describing, narrating, controlling the point of view, and creating a dominant impression; and
- organize an essay narratively or topically.

You may want to emphasize the firsthand research strategies of observing and interviewing. Appendix 2: Strategies for Research and Documentation devotes several pages to these field-research methods. Because research—particularly, field research like interviewing—can be time-consuming, students will have to plan and manage their time carefully. You might want to reassure them that if they choose a subject that truly interests them, the time they spend on research will be fascinating.

WRITING ASSIGNMENT: Observation (p. 82)

Here is the writing assignment that appears near the beginning of Chapter 3:

Write an observational essay about an intriguing place, person, or activity in your community. Your essay may be a brief profile of an individual based on one or two interviews; a description of a place or an activity observed once or twice; or a longer, more fully developed profile of a person, place, or activity based on observational visits and interviews conducted over several days. Observe your subject closely, and then present what you have learned in a way that both informs and engages readers.

Problems Students May Have with This Assignment

There are typically two problems students have with this assignment. The first has to do with focus of the essay and the other with scheduling.

The focusing problem comes from the overwhelming quantity of information that students usually gather. One of the best ways to focus an observational essay is to organize it around a dominant impression of the subject. By this we mean a unique or fresh perspective that reveals a new or unexpected insight into a given subject.

Writing up their notes from observations and exchanging these write-ups with others in the class can also help students focus their observations. The more they work with their material—analyzing it, writing about it, finding connections and patterns within it—the more cohesive their essays will be. As their drafts become more organized and cohesive, students will also be able to discover and develop the impressions they wish to convey.

The scheduling problem arises from the difficulty many students have in sustaining a long research project. In A Guide to Writing Observational Essays (p. 133), we recommend that students establish their own research schedules. But we also suggest that you set up deadlines for various stages of the project—writing notes on observational visits and interviews, preparing an outline, and writing the first draft—to help students keep on schedule. You could easily have students write their observations and interviews outside of class and then use class time for peer workshops on these write-ups.

RESOURCES IN CHAPTER 3 FOR TEACHING OBSERVATION

FINDING SUBJECTS

Writing Situations for Observational Essays (p. 82)

The situations that open this chapter suggest some of the possibilities for this kind of writing. Students can see right away that a profile may focus on an activity (mural painting), a person (scientist), or a place (urban renewal project). But they should also see that these categories overlap. Writing about a place involves presenting people and their activities; writing about a person involves describing the person's activities and the places in which they occur; writing about an activity involves the people who are doing the activity and the places in which it occurs. In addition, the third example, in which the student reads newspaper accounts of the urban renewal project, illustrates the ways that observational reporting can build on research. Finally, these situations show that observational writing may contrast the writer's expectations with the actual situation (visit with the scientist), uncover a controversy (the urban renewal project), or simply present something fascinating (mural painting).

Considering Ideas for Your Own Writing

These activities follow each reading except the chapter-opening and closing ones. They are designed to help students think of subjects for their own writing by considering subjects related to the readings. Here is a list summarizing the subjects suggested after Chapter 3 readings by the following authors:

Orlean   A person you find intriguing (p. 103)
Edge   Places that serve, produce, or sell something unusual (p. 110)
Orenstein A group of people who interact for a specific reason (p. 120)
Cable   Places or activities about which you have strong preconceptions (p. 127)

Choosing a Subject

Choosing a Subject is the first activity under Invention and Research, the opening section of A Guide to Writing Observational Essays (p. 133). Students are offered bulleted lists of suggested topics and are asked to make their own list of possible subjects. You might urge students from day one to begin compiling a list of possibilities. Ideas inspired by the suggestions in Considering Ideas for Your Own Writing could be part of this list.

Problems Students May Have Choosing a Subject

Choosing a suitable subject is particularly important for this assignment because students will invest a good deal of their time visiting the place or person, conducting interviews, and doing library or Internet research. Remind students of the subjects they thought about under Considering Ideas for Your Own Writing following each of the readings, and point out the suggestions under Choosing a Subject in A Guide to Writing Observational Essays.

For students who have just arrived at a university (or a new city), the observational essay offers an ideal chance for exploration. Students should be encouraged to seek out unusual activities, people, or places. Most campus Web pages have lists and directories of facilities, institutes, specialized libraries, exhibits, and activities located on campus, and students have written very good essays in the past about map libraries, other special collections, exhibits of old printing presses, and even the morning cleaning staff of their dormitories. The Yellow Pages provide a ready-made list of potential topics ranging from jewelry designers to printing companies. A map of the area or a local newspaper can also reveal interesting places to investigate.

When you give the assignment, urge students to avoid subjects with which they are overly familiar (for example, the summer job they have had for the last four years or their college dorm). If your students are writing a longer profile, they will need to pick a subject with plenty of activity, enough people for several interviews, and a circumscribed place that can be described specifically (profiles about "the beach" or "downtown" generally don't work, for instance).

Two other problems with selecting a subject are those of accessibility and security. Subjects that may sound exciting in theory may not be possible or appropriate in practice. A doctor or scientist may not be available for interviews; most elementary and high-school campuses have highly restricted access; legal considerations might prevent a student from profiling an emergency room; a military installation or a nuclear power plant may be inaccessible to the general public. Similarly, you may want to discourage students from exploring potentially dangerous subjects. It is natural, even commendable, for some people to want to do something a little daring, but it is not always a good idea. Students should think twice about profiling something like the county jail (which may be unavailable, anyway), a place in a neighborhood with a high incidence of crime, or an activity that presents a health or safety hazard. On the one hand, you do not want your students to select mundane or drab subjects; on the other hand, you should urge them to use discretion when picking a subject. All you really need to do is to encourage them to explore unfamiliar places or activities: the experience of discovery should be enough to yield a fresh and insightful angle. Part of the task, of course, is for students to get beneath the surface of whatever they are observing. You might suggest they think about people or places that once aroused curiosity in them but that they never had a chance to investigate. Students in our classes, for instance, have gone back to tiny desert towns where their cars have broken down to learn who lives there, or ventured off the freeway to investigate strange sights they had often wondered about during their regular commute

One way to help students gather rich feedback on their prospective subjects is to circulate subject sheets and have the students evaluate one another's ideas. You can easily do this in one of two ways. At the top of a sheet of paper, students write a tentative title for their essay. Then they describe in two or three sentences the person, place, or activity that will be the subject of their essay. In one sentence, they identify possible readers (class members, readers of a particular newspaper or magazine, or perhaps a special group of readers with a need to know what the writer will discover). These sheets then circulate around the class, with students writing questions or comments (and even commenting on other students' comments). Then you can invite each student to identify the subject he or she is eager to read about. Alternatively, you can accomplish the same objectives by having students post the same information in a course management system discussion board. Classmates can post questions and comments about students' initial posts and suggest relevant resource links that relate to students' subjects for the essay.

We encourage you to work closely with your students on this project, especially during this first stage of invention. Because students are unlikely to have previously undertaken a writing project like this, they need extra encouragement and scaffolding throughout the process.

THINKING ABOUT YOUR EXPERIENCE WITH OBSERVATION (p. 83)

This activity will allow students to realize they have a familiarity, possibly greater than they expected, with the genre, reducing the anxiety that typically accompanies composing an essay and making the remaining activities in this chapter easier. In particular, students often have great familiarity with observational reporting because they have watched such reporting on television or online. Television shows like *Dirty Jobs,* for which clips are available on YouTube, are particularly popular among teachers of observational reporting because they show students they have been watching observational reports of various sorts for most of their lives.

CHOOSING READINGS

If you cannot teach all the readings in this chapter, you will have to make some choices. There are at least three principles that may guide your selection: the type of observation, the interest level of the reading and its usefulness in suggesting subjects for your students' essays, and the basic features focused on in the Reading like a Writer activities.

TYPE OF OBSERVATION

The reading selections in this chapter, beginning with the sample *New Yorker* essay, "Soup," focus on one of three common observational subjects — people (or animals), places, and activities. "Soup" focuses on a person, the restaurant owner and chef Mr. Yeganeh. Susan Orlean's "Show Dog" focuses on a dog, rather than a person. Peggy Orenstein's essay observes many people in an eighth-grade math classroom. The student-authored selections by Brian Cable and Juan Diego Arellano profile a place and a person, respectively, and the essay by John T. Edge presents an activity.

INTEREST LEVELS OF THE READINGS

Here are brief descriptions from the table of contents to help you choose readings that might be of interest to your students:

The New Yorker, **Soup**. A magazine writer profiles a restaurateur — a temperamental master of the art of soup making — along with his tiny storefront establishment. (p. 84)

Susan Orlean, **Show Dog**. A novelist and essayist profiles Biff, a champion boxer, and the efforts that go into prepping him for the Westminster Kennel Club's show. (p. 93)

John T. Edge, **I'm Not Leaving until I Eat This Thing**. Daring himself to eat a food product that makes him queasy, an expert on Southern food observes a factory that processes and bottles pig lips. (p. 104)

Peggy Orenstein, **The Daily Grind: Lessons in the Hidden Curriculum**. An investigative reporter profiles an eighth-grade math class, revealing how gender affects students' interactions with one another and with their teacher. (p. 113)

Brian Cable, **The Last Stop**. A first-year composition student observes the unfamiliar world of a mortuary, ending up in the embalming room, which he leaves only after placing his finger on the firm, cold skin of a dead body. (p. 121)

Juan Diego Arellano, **A Trip to the Dentist**. A community-college student describes his visit to a pediatric dentistry office, which seemed pleasant enough until a five-year-old patient proved uncooperative. (p. 128)

READING LIKE A WRITER ACTIVITIES

The first reading, "Soup," introduces all the basic features of observation through its Reading like a Writer activities. The final reading, the essay by Arellano, does not specify

Reading like a Writer activities but invites students to choose a feature of the reading they think is worth analyzing. Each of the other readings has one Reading like a Writer activity. Below is a list of these activities.

Organizing Information from Various Sources: Susan Orlean, "Show Dog" (p. 102)

Choosing a Role and Organizing the Information: John T. Edge, "I'm Not Leaving until I Eat This Thing" (p. 109)

Describing People: Peggy Orenstein, "The Daily Grind: Lessons in the Hidden Curriculum" (p. 119)

Conveying a Dominant Impression of the Subject: Brian Cable, "The Last Stop" (p. 126)

A GUIDE TO READING OBSERVATIONAL ESSAYS (p. 83)

The essay that is the focus of A Guide to Reading Observational Essays is "Soup."

READING FOR MEANING (p. 86)

Here are suggestions for teaching the Reading for Meaning activities following "Soup."

Read to Comprehend (p. 86)

To help guide students, you may suggest they describe Yeganeh's attitude toward his customers as well as toward other restaurants.

Other words students may need to define include *alchemist* (paragraph 1), *concoctions* (1), and *bisque* (2).

Read to Respond (p. 87)

How do the students respond to Yeganeh's manner? Is his soup kitchen a place they would like to buy food? Some instructors bring in the DVD of the *Seinfeld* episode inspired by Yeganeh and his Soup Kitchen International and show it to students (who, in most classes, are likely to have been born after the episode aired). If you use the DVD, you may follow up by asking students to compare and contrast the characterization of Yeganeh and his storefront kitchen in the article with that in the episode.

Read to Analyze Assumptions (p. 87)

Students are familiar with bosses, coaches, teachers, and parents exercising power, and they also have a lot of experience with the restaurant industry, as customers if not as employees, so they should have a lot to say in response to the assumptions about power and the assumptions about customer service. Another assumption about customer service appears in the following sentence:

> The order of any well-behaved customer is accompanied by little waxpaper packets of bread, fresh vegetables (such as scallions and radishes), fresh fruit (such as cherries or an orange), a chocolate mint, and a plastic spoon. (paragraph 5)

The accompaniment seems to say something about Yeganeh's beliefs about human nature, reward, and punishment. You might ask students: How may these additional vegetables and fruit help condition Yeganeh's patrons to abide by the "strict rules for conduct in line" (1)? Is there a sense that Yeganeh treats and responds to his patrons as if they were children?

The four Reading like a Writer activities following "Soup" introduce students to the basic features and strategies of observational essays—describing people and places, organizing information from various sources, adopting an authorial role, and conveying a dominant impression of the subject. Each feature carries a reading and a writing activity that help students focus on the writing of the sample essay, "Soup."

Describing People and Places (p. 89)

This activity focuses on ways in which writers of observation vividly present their subjects. The introductory remarks connect what students learned in Chapter 2: Autobiography to what they learn in this chapter as they analyze observational essays like "Soup." In fact, like the activity in Chapter 2 following Brad Benioff's essay, "Rick," this activity asks students to survey the ways an author describes his or her subject. Unlike the Chapter 2 activity, however, this one encourages students initially to look at the way the author portrays Yeganeh mostly through his behavior, gestures, and speech rather than through visual description. As they write briefly about their analyses, students should be able to report that the behavioral details contribute to the readers' sense of who Yeganeh is. In the second task, students focus on the different senses that the article invokes in order to give readers a sense of the storefront as a location.

Organizing Information from Various Sources (p. 90)

This activity draws students' attention to the different ways in which observational writers gather and present information from field and background research. As students plan their observational essays, they will have to decide on the types of information to seek and how to organize their material. Students are introduced here to two of the basic methods of organizing observational essays—narrative and topical. As they plan and write their own observational essays, students will probably need to choose between these two methods or some combination of the two. The anonymous *New Yorker* author of "Soup" organizes observations topically, whereas Juan Diego Arellano, the author of a later essay in this chapter, organizes his essay narratively, while John Edge, the author of another essay in this chapter, uses a hybrid approach.

To analyze the organization of "Soup," students are asked to make a scratch outline identifying the topics in the first six paragraphs. Students tend to identify the same main topics, although they may use different words to name them and may identify different subtopics.

You might follow up by asking students to identify what the sources appear to be for each piece of information or quote in the section they studied. Identifying sources of information in the essay helps students see that to make their presentation coherent and interesting writers of observational essays must select details from the hodgepodge of information they initially collect.

Adopting an Authorial Role (p. 91)

This passage helps students think about how observational writers choose roles as spectator observers or participant observers. (Later in the chapter, John Edge in his essay "I'm Not Leaving until I Eat This Thing," combines roles.) Students are asked to explore the benefits and challenges of the two roles in preparation for the activity. We have found that most students are familiar with the spectator role, in which the writer reports about but is not a part of the activity. You may need to remind students who want to write as participant observers to include sufficient detail for readers unfamiliar with the subject. In this case, the author of "Soup" has adopted a spectator observer role, but you might find it worthwhile to have the class search the text for evidence to support this classification—doing so can help students cement what otherwise is a fairly abstract concept.

After reading this passage, consider having students share their responses to the analytical activity (or generate those responses): What would a participant-observer essay have looked like, and what might readers have learned from that perspective? Why do they think the author chose a spectator role?

Conveying a Dominant Impression of the Subject (p. 91)

This activity helps students think about how observational writers use details to convey what they find interesting about the subject. As we indicate in the text, the writer's angle on the subject may be stated directly or implied. Although students choose what they include in their observational essays, the main focus of the essay should, nevertheless, be descriptions of the subject and not students' evaluations or interpretations of the subject.

In analyzing "Soup," students are asked to mark places where the writer's attitudes and ideas come across. An additional activity for conveying a dominant impression of the subject follows Cable's essay later in the chapter.

Note that these activities build on what students who studied autobiography in Chapter 2 learned about conveying significance by showing and telling. You could take this opportunity to preview assignments in later chapters that require students to make explicit their point of view and argue for it.

READINGS

Susan Orlean, "Show Dog" (p. 93)

READING FOR MEANING (p. 100)

Read to Comprehend (p. 100)

To give students a reference point, you might ask them to think about or talk about other celebrity profiles they have read or seen on television. In what ways does Orlean's article imitate those profiles, and in what ways does it differ from them? What, generally, do your students think is the purpose of a celebrity profile? Do such articles have any common goals?

Other words students might need to define include *elemental* (paragraph 2), *percolate* (3), *ancillary* (4), and *zaftig* (11).

Also, if they don't home in on it themselves, you might have students take another look at the word *boxerabilia* (8), which they may not be able to find in dictionaries but can probably decipher quickly. (At the time of this writing, the only appearances of the word in a Google search were all quotes from Orlean's article.) Students often are surprised to learn that professional writers sometimes make up new words, and discovering this practice is acceptable sometimes inspires bursts of creativity in their writing. Discussing the ways this strategy can work (or not work) may be useful to them.

Read to Respond (p. 101)
Students may also respond to

- Orlean's tone as a dog enthusiast;
- the economics of owning a show dog;
- the amount of time Orlean seems to have spent interviewing the Truesdales and observing Biff.

Read to Analyze Assumptions (p. 101)

Most students will, as the text here hints for them to do, notice that Orlean anthropomorphizes Biff almost as frequently as the Truesdales do and, in fact, relies on this approach to hook the reader at the start of the article. After they have reviewed the anthropomorphizing at the beginning, and after they have discussed assumptions about the show dog business, have them look again at the very last paragraph of the article, in which Orlean describes Biff playing outside. Here, she appears to draw on another assumption, about the relationships among innocence, play, and work: she writes that "he acted as if it were the most fun he'd ever had" (paragraph 27). At this moment, Biff is no longer the humanlike figure of the introduction—he is a dog again, and acting like one. What do students make of this shift, and what point—if any—do they think the author might be making in these closing lines?

READING LIKE A WRITER: ORGANIZING INFORMATION FROM VARIOUS SOURCES (p. 102)

While Orlean's essay, like "Soup" (p. 84) is organized topically, it differs from other topically organized examples that students might have read. The difference is due to its use of jump cuts—omitted transitions between logically connected topics or scenes. Rather than relying on traditional transitions, Orlean relies on logical and linguistic connections to help readers along, and this activity helps students to spot the connections. It may be worth emphasizing to students that jump cuts are an advanced skill: Orlean isn't disorganized or ignoring structure. Her article is still logically planned, and she does use transitional phrases at points. After students have examined some of the jump cuts, you might have them practice identifying the logical and linguistic bridges at each jump cut so that they can see these hidden structures and begin to think about their possible uses.

CONSIDERING IDEAS FOR YOUR OWN WRITING (p. 103)

This section lists several subjects, suggested by the reading, that may stimulate student writing. You may want to ask students what other ideas for subjects they get from the reading. We have found that routinely discussing possible subjects in class encourages students to try out new ideas. Remember that there is also an array of subject suggestions in the opening Invention and Research activity of A Guide to Writing Observational Essays.

John T. Edge, "I'm Not Leaving until I Eat This Thing" (p. 104)

READING FOR MEANING (p. 107)

Read to Comprehend (p. 108)

In addition to having students explain how Farm Fresh Food Supplier obtains and packs pig lips, you may also have them briefly describe the essay's organization (the spectator segment of the essay is bracketed by segments involving the author's participation).

Other words students may need to define include *slurry* (paragraph 4), *carrion* (5), *viscera* (6), *cordovan* (8), *tinged* (11), *bravado* (11), *reverie* (14), and *flaccid* (18).

Read to Respond (p. 108)

Students also may respond to

- the mass slaughter of animals for consumption (factory farming);

- the fact that the selling of down-home merchandise ("Jason's Pickled Pig Lips") is still a rather competitive business ("We do our best to corner the market on lips" [paragraph 11]).

Read to Analyze Assumptions (p. 108)

In addition to the assumptions called out by the text, students might discuss Edge's assumption that he *ought* to try the pickled pig lip. Technically, nothing is forcing him to do so, but he seems to assume the obligation. Why? A further assumption you may wish to have your students explore is the perceived role of women and work. Point out to students that men now manage and will continue to manage Farm Fresh Food Supplier ("after he graduates from business school, Lionel's younger son, Matt, will take over operations at the plant" [paragraph 10]). Ask students to identify, in contrast, the roles of women in the essay, including Lionel Dufour's own daughter, Dana, "a button-cute college student who has won numerous beauty titles" (10).

READING LIKE A WRITER: CHOOSING A ROLE AND ORGANIZING THE INFORMATION (p. 109)

This Reading like a Writer activity focuses on Edge as a participant in the subject he is observing. Students are asked to review the introduction, paragraphs 1 and 2, to analyze how Edge sets up time and place in the essay. Students are also asked to evaluate how the sections in paragraphs 3 to 12 inform paragraphs 13 to 19, where Edge resumes his story about eating a pig lip. They should recognize that his discussion of the production of carrion products tells readers little about their appeal or taste, and that this discussion puts his attempt to eat a pig lip in context so that when he comes back to the bar in paragraph 13, we know what it is that he is trying to learn. You may also want to discuss how the essay would be different if the author were not a participant and what kinds of subjects benefit from author participation.

ANALYZING VISUALS (p. 110)

Students pursuing the questions listed under this activity might jump to the easy conclusion that Edge is reminding us that the pig was once an animal rather than food, and there is certainly nothing wrong with that interpretation. However, other valid answers are possible and might emerge if students are asked additional questions, like "Would many readers recognize pickled pig lips as pig lips if they were in a jar or on a plate?" As an additional exercise, you might ask students to search online for images they think could have been used with this article (or with another essay) and post them in a course-management system such as Blackboard. Then, in class, you and the students could look them over on an overhead projector, discussing the ways the different images might modify the message or impact of Edge's article.

CONSIDERING IDEAS FOR YOUR OWN WRITING (p. 111)

This section lists several subjects, suggested by the reading, that may stimulate student writing. You may want to ask students what other ideas for subjects they get from the reading. We have found that routinely discussing possible subjects in class encourages students to try out new ideas. Remember that there is also an array of subject suggestions in the opening Invention and Research activity of A Guide to Writing Observational Essays.

A Special Reading Strategy—Comparing and Contrasting Related Readings:
"Soup" and Edge's "I'm Not Leaving until I Eat This Thing" (p. 111)

In this chapter, a special reading strategy follows Edge's observational essay, comparing it with the earlier observational essay, "Soup." If your students have not read and discussed the section on comparing and contrasting related readings in Appendix 1: A Catalog of Critical Reading Strategies, you might want to take the time now to do so.

To get students to think about the similarities and differences between "Soup" and Edge's essay, we invite students to compare the two essays in terms of their cultural contexts, organization, and the roles taken by the writers. This is a lot of territory for students to cover. You might want to divide the class into groups, asking each group to address one of these topics and report their findings to the class as a whole.

Peggy Orenstein, "The Daily Grind: Lessons in the Hidden Curriculum" (p. 113)

READING FOR MEANING (p. 117)

Read to Comprehend (p. 117)
You may wish to indicate to students that while Orenstein's essay focuses primarily on a specific class, she uses detailed descriptions of the students' appearances and mannerisms to help differentiate the students from one another.

Other words students may need to define include *reigning* (paragraph 1), *gawky* (10), and *rebuke* (18).

Read to Respond (p. 117)
Students may also respond to

- how a teacher's attention shapes a student's learning;
- the idea of choosing to remain quiet in class;
- Orenstein's choosing to narrate Amy's answer as a mistake (paragraph 19).

Read to Analyze Assumptions (p. 118)
Students might also discuss whether Orenstein's description of Amy is based on an assumption that people tend to be consistent, or ought to be consistent, and whether they agree with such an assumption. Orenstein also appears to assume that Mrs. Richter's class is behaving the way it usually does—that it is not behaving differently because a strange observer (Orenstein) is there. What evidence can students find to defend or challenge such an assumption? If students conclude that Orenstein's presence is affecting behavior, what assumptions might they make (or retract) about Mrs. Richter's teaching performance?

READING LIKE A WRITER: DESCRIBING PEOPLE (p. 119)

The Reading like a Writer activity allows students to explain the different details Orenstein uses to describe people and invites students to consider how descriptions of people, including their dress, gestures, movements, and dialogue, contribute to observational essays and to our impressions of the people being described. You might, as a follow-up question, ask students to consider how emphasis of different details or alternative word choices might have changed readers' impressions of the people described in these sections.

This section lists several subjects, suggested by the reading, that may stimulate student writing. You may want to ask students what other ideas for subjects they get from the reading. We have found that routinely discussing possible subjects in class encourages students to try out new ideas. Remember that there is also an array of subject suggestions in the opening Invention and Research activity of A Guide to Writing Observational Essays.

Brian Cable, "The Last Stop" (p. 121)

Reading for Meaning (p. 124)

Read to Comprehend (p. 124)

Cable's essay is organized spatially. In his exploration of Goodbody Mortuaries, Cable moves from room to room. You may wish to have students use this organization to structure their summary of this selection. Students can describe the route Cable takes in his exploration, noting especially where he begins once inside and where he ends up before leaving. You may also wish to ask students how Cable's organizational strategy allows them, as readers, to better understand Cable's observations.

Other words students may need to define include *bereavement* (paragraph 10) and *hermetically* (21).

Read to Respond (p. 125)

Students may also respond to

- the epigraph (the Mark Twain quote) at the top of the essay;
- the cost of burying someone;
- the idea that one may study to become a mortician, "with courses in anatomy and embalming as well as in restorative art" (paragraph 25).

Read to Analyze Assumptions (p. 125)

You might start off a discussion of the assumptions (or a discussion of what students have written about assumptions) by asking students what assumptions of theirs were challenged by Cable's essay. Students might also explore the underlying cultural acceptance of humor in association with death and dying. One example appears in paragraph 25, in which Tim tells the author that becoming a mortician was "a profession I could live with." Twain's aforementioned quote, in the epigraph at the top of the essay, provides another such instance.

Reading like a Writer: Conveying a Dominant Impression of the Subject (p. 126)

This Reading like a Writer activity asks students to analyze the words and phrases Cable uses that suggest what he thinks or how he feels about his subject. We also ask that students evaluate how successful Cable is in conveying his impressions. Students may differ in their assessments, so an in-class discussion may be useful. During this discussion, ask students whether it is possible (or desirable) for a dominant impression to be ambivalent or complicated rather than simple and straightforward. Do they think Cable's essay falls into such a category or should?

CONSIDERING IDEAS FOR YOUR OWN WRITING (p. 127)

This section lists several subjects, suggested by the reading, that may stimulate student writing. You may want to ask students what other ideas for subjects they get from the reading. We have found that routinely discussing possible subjects in class encourages students to try out new ideas. Remember that there is also an array of subject suggestions in the opening Invention and Research activity of A Guide to Writing Observational Essays.

Juan Diego Arellano, "A Trip to the Dentist" (p. 128)

READING FOR MEANING (p. 131)

This Reading for Meaning activity invites students to apply to Arellano's essay what they have learned from the other readings in this chapter about reading to comprehend, reading to respond, and reading to analyze assumptions.

READING LIKE A WRITER (p. 131)

This Reading like a Writer activity offers students an opportunity to identify and evaluate one of Arellano's observational-writing strategies. Note that because Arellano specifically states what he is thinking at the end of the article, this reading can be used as an example of observational writing in which the author explicitly evaluates the subject in addition to providing a dominant impression.

REVIEWING WHAT MAKES OBSERVATIONAL ESSAYS EFFECTIVE (p. 132)

This reflective activity makes a great transition from reading to writing. As the text suggests, this activity can be done individually or in small groups.

A GUIDE TO WRITING OBSERVATIONAL ESSAYS (p. 133)

As students begin to investigate their subjects, you will want to stress the importance of field research in observational writing. Field research is an essential part of the work students will do for this assignment. Depending on their subjects, students are likely to use both observation and interviews. Few students will have much experience with either. In Appendix 2: Strategies for Research and Documentation, we give students a detailed overview of these types of research. We lead students through the observation and interview processes, and while some of this advice may seem like common sense (take a writing implement, prepare some questions in advance), most students find it useful. You might emphasize the importance of reflecting on their observations and interviews immediately after completing them, reviewing and adding to their notes while the memory of the experience is still fresh rather than after their memory of the event has faded.

Students often have difficulty deciding what impression they want to convey in their observational essays. You may want to devote some class time to discussing the Invention and Research questions under the heading Considering Your Purpose. At this stage in the composing process, the impressions students develop need only be provisional; reassure them that they can change impressions as they learn more about their subjects.

When planning their essays, students often organize information in the order in which they discovered it. Remind them that the writers they read organize their observational essays narratively or topically, or through a blend of both approaches. If students opt for a purely chronological organization, they should do so because that is the best way to present their information, not because it is the only option they have considered. Likewise, remind students of the variety of beginnings demonstrated by the selections in this chapter, and tell them that they need not wait for the ideal beginning before they start drafting.

We try to help our own students submit their revised and edited essays for publication and award extra credit to students whose work is published. You might suggest that students submit their finished pieces to a local newspaper or magazine that publishes observational articles, or you might let students identify the publication they would like to write for.

Here is an outline of A Guide to Writing Observational Essays:

Invention and Research
 Choosing a Subject
  People
  Places
  Activities
 Researching Your Subject
  Considering Your Own Role
  Making a Schedule
  Exploring Readers' and Your Own Preconceptions
  Visiting a Place
  Interviewing a Person
  Gathering Information
 Reflecting on Your Subject
  Considering Your Purpose
  Formulating a Tentative Thesis Statement
  Considering Visuals

Drafting
 Setting Goals
 Organizing Your Draft
 Working with Sources: Integrating Quotations from Interviews (box)
 Considering a Useful Sentence Strategy (Absolute Phrase)

Reading a Draft Critically (box)
 Read for a First Impression
 Read Again to Suggest Improvements

Revising
 Troubleshooting Your Draft (table)
  To Make Your Description of Places and People More Vivid
  To Make the Organization Clearer and More Effective
  To Make the Essay More Engaging and Informative
  To Strengthen the Essay's Dominant Impression

Editing and Proofreading

Reflecting on What You Have Learned: Observation (box)

Chapter 4 REFLECTION

What distinguishes the reflective essay is, to borrow Virginia Woolf's words, its "fierce attachment to an idea." In introducing reflection, you might help students make connections between this assignment and those in the two previous chapters. While autobiographers tell about significant events and people in their lives and writers of observation present what they have discovered about a subject firsthand, writers of reflection spin webs of ideas.

Reflective writing is a natural outgrowth of both autobiographical and observational writing. All three have their roots in personal experience, and all are concerned with the meaning or significance of that experience. But whereas autobiographers and observational writers need only present their experience vividly to show its significance, reflective writers must explore and elaborate on the meanings they find.

Autobiographers bring out personal significance; reflective writers (like writers of observation) look for general implications. Reflection stems from an observation or experience that raises a question or leads to an insight about the human condition. Reflective essayists write about the ways in which we live and interact, the goals toward which we strive, and the shortcomings that hobble us. The reflective essay is typically a public meditation on what makes us human. The reading and writing activities in this chapter should help students begin to appreciate the value of this genre.

This chapter can teach students to

- select personal experiences or observations that may have implications for social life;
- connect personal experiences and observations to larger social realities;
- practice strategies for narrating and describing; and
- organize an essay through thematic coherence.

Drawing out the implications of what one has seen or heard tends to be the greatest challenge of reflective writing, especially for young writers who lack confidence in their ideas or feel that teachers (or adults generally) are not interested in what they have to say. Success not only in this kind of writing but also in their other classes requires students to have confidence in their abilities to develop interesting ideas and to express them in engaging ways. Although challenging, this assignment can help students build their confidence.

WRITING ASSIGNMENT: Reflection (p. 148)

Here is the writing assignment for Chapter 4:

Write a reflective essay based on something you experienced or observed. Describe this occasion vividly so that readers can understand what happened and will care about what you have to say about it. In reflecting on the particular occasion, make some general statements exploring its possible meanings or cultural significance. Consider what the occasion might imply about how people in our society behave toward one another, what they value, and what assumptions or stereotypes they may hold consciously or unconsciously. Think of reflective writing as a stimulating conversation in which you seek to expose—and perhaps question—your readers' attitudes and beliefs as well as your own.

66

Problems Students May Have with This Assignment

In our experience, problems students have with this assignment fall into two fairly predictable categories—choosing workable subjects and developing reflections on them. In the latter area, students' difficulties have to do mainly with achieving some balance between particular material—in the form of occasions, examples, and illustrations—and general statements.

Exploratory drafts tend toward one extreme or the other. As our students begin writing, we often see first drafts that consist almost entirely of vague, abstract statements or that look very much like essays about events (especially if students have recently completed Chapter 2). A third type of problem draft comes from students who believe they need to reach a conclusion about their subject, perhaps anticipating upcoming argument assignments. All these problems can be minimized if you help students pay careful attention to both the general and the particular components of each reading selection as well as to both in their own developing essays.

Going over invention work early, in class, is particularly important with reflective writing. The discussion format of a draft workshop (see Part 4, Organizing Draft Workshops, p. 17) may also help students crystallize their understanding of the assignment's expectations and home in on reflection in their invention materials.

RESOURCES IN CHAPTER 4 FOR TEACHING REFLECTION

FINDING SUBJECTS

Writing Situations for Reflective Essays (p. 148)

These three examples show both academic and nonacademic occasions for reflective writing. You might want to use these examples to point out the writers' different purposes and audiences, the different subjects they consider worth thinking and writing about, and the different ways they sustain their reflections. For instance, how might the first writer present himself differently for his alumni magazine than he might for, say, a guest column on the sports page of the local newspaper?

Considering Ideas for Your Own Writing

These activities follow each reading except for the chapter-opening and closing ones. They are designed to help students think of subjects for their own essays by considering subjects related to the readings. Here is a list summarizing the subjects suggested after Chapter 4 readings by the following authors:

Jennings	Experiences involving your scars, tattoos, or surgeries (p. 169)
Doloff	Objects and what they symbolize (p. 173)
Dumas	Occasions that have led you to consider your heritage or change your name (p. 181)
Lee	Subjects related to ethnic or regional identity (p. 187)

Choosing a Subject

Finding a Particular Occasion and a General Subject is the first activity under Invention and Research, the opening section of A Guide to Writing Reflective Essays (p. 195). Here, students are shown how to make a chart that matches occasions and subjects they could consider writing about. As we suggested above, you could spend class time charting possible subjects on the board to help students see how general subjects for reflection can lead them to recall particular occasions they have observed and how particular occasions can lead to general reflections.

Because students often have difficulty choosing a suitable subject for reflection, it's advisable from day one to discuss possibilities with students. An easy way to do so is to ask students to keep a list of particular real-life occasions (such as overheard conversations or intriguing newspaper articles). Then you could lead the class in brainstorming general subjects suggested by these particular occasions. If you spend five to ten minutes of every class this way, your students will develop the habit of reflecting and begin to discover subjects they could develop into an essay. Similarly, during work in this chapter, you could have your students keep a daily journal in which they note things that happen to them or things they observe and the thoughts they have while dwelling on those experiences and observations. Sometimes the journal entries can become particular occasions or can remind students of occasions or subjects they might want to address.

Problems Students May Have Choosing a Subject

Although students will have discussed various subjects using the suggestions in the Considering Ideas for Your Own Writing sections following the readings, you may be surprised at the difficulty some students have in settling on an appropriate subject.

Students encounter two problems. Some try to write about abstract concepts (*love, truth, justice,* etc.) that they can't ground in concrete occasions, examples, and illustrations. Other students want to reflect on controversial issues, such as abortion or capital punishment, that lead them instead to take a position. Abstract concepts and controversial issues can lead to interesting reflective essays, but students tend to go astray unless instructors keep them focused on the basic features of reflective essays.

THINKING ABOUT YOUR EXPERIENCE WITH REFLECTION (p. 149)

This activity will allow students to realize they have a familiarity, possibly greater than they expected, with the genre, reducing the anxiety that typically accompanies composing an essay and making the remaining activities in this chapter easier.

CHOOSING READINGS

If you cannot teach all the readings in this chapter, you will have to make some choices. There are at least two principles that may guide your selection—(1) the interest level of the reading and its usefulness in suggesting topics for your students' essays, and (2) the basic features focused on in the Reading like a Writer activities.

INTEREST LEVELS OF THE READINGS

Here are brief descriptions from the table of contents to help you choose readings that might interest your students:

Brent Staples, **Black Men and Public Space**. A member of the *New York Times* editorial board notes how his presence on a city street triggers defensive reactions in white passersby and addresses the "alienation that comes of being ever the suspect." (p. 150)

Dana Jennings, **Our Scars Tell the Stories of Our Lives**. A newspaper columnist ponders the significance of his scars and the stories they tell. (p. 163)

Steven Doloff, **A Universe Lies on the Sidewalks of New York**. A professor contemplates the objects he has found on city sidewalks and what they might tell future generations about us. (p. 170)

Firoozeh Dumas, **The "F Word."** An Iranian-American writer reflects on the hilarious manglings of her "foreign" name by Americans unfamiliar with it, and her responses to their reactions. (p. 175)

Wendy Lee, **Peeling Bananas**. A Chinese-American high-school student contemplates the positive and negative aspects of growing up as "a hybrid of two cultures." (p. 182)

Katherine Haines, **Whose Body Is This?** A first-year composition student considers society's obsession with the perfect body—especially, the perfect female body—and the negative pressures this obsession creates. (p. 189)

READING LIKE A WRITER ACTIVITIES

The first reading, Staples's "Black Men and Public Space" (p. 150), introduces all the basic features of reflection through its Reading like a Writer activities. The final reading, Haines's "Whose Body Is This?" does not specify a Reading like a Writer activity but invites students to choose a feature of the reading they think is worth analyzing. Each of the other readings has one Reading like a Writer activity. Below is a list of these activities.

A Special Reading Strategy: Exploring the Significance of Figurative Language: Dana Jennings, "Our Scars Tell the Stories of Our Lives" (p. 167)

Presenting the Particular Occasion: Dana Jennings, "Our Scars Tell the Stories of Our Lives" (p. 168)

Engaging Readers: Steven Doloff, "A Universe Lies on the Sidewalks of New York" (p. 173)

Maintaining Topical Coherence: Firoozeh Dumas, "The 'F Word'" (p. 180)

Developing Reflections through Comparison and Contrast: Wendy Lee, "Peeling Bananas" (p. 186)

A Special Reading Strategy: Comparing and Contrasting Related Readings: Dumas's "The 'F Word'" and Lee's "Peeling Bananas" (p. 187)

A GUIDE TO READING REFLECTIVE ESSAYS (p. 150)

The essay that is the focus of A Guide to Reading Reflective Essays is Staples's "Black Men and Public Space."

READING FOR MEANING (p. 153)

Here are suggestions for teaching the Reading for Meaning activities following Staples's "Black Men and Public Space."

Read to Comprehend (p. 153)
After students have explained ways Staples tries to alleviate people's fear of him and commented on Staples's feelings about his encounters with fearful passersby, you may ask students to consider the following: The United States is a culture of violence, and many people consciously try to appear capable of violence to deter violence against themselves.

If Staples appears aggressive and antagonistic, why, in our culture of violence, does he wish to destroy that image?

Other words students may need to define include *uninflammatory* (paragraph 1), *warrenlike* (5), *solace* (5), *proprietor* (9), and *skittish* (11).

Read to Respond (p. 153)

Students may also respond to

- how they have reacted in the past, in situations similar to those of Staples's "victims";
- the measures Staples takes to make individuals and groups less anxious when he is present;
- Staples's belief that when he whistles melodies from classical composers people are less afraid of him.

Read to Analyze Assumptions (p. 154)

Students might also consider the set of cultural assumptions underlying why and how we respond to appearance. Using Staples's appearance and the reactions of people toward him as a starting point, you may ask students to explore and share their own experiences in responding to someone's appearance or receiving unwanted or unexpected responses because of their attire.

READING LIKE A WRITER (p. 156)

In these four Reading like a Writer activities, the focus shifts from the content and purpose of the essay to the specific strategies Staples uses to achieve his purpose. You can have students do some or all of the activities before doing the selected Reading like a Writer activities for the subsequent readings. In working on these four activities, students are introduced to the basic features of the reflective essay—presenting the particular occasion, developing the reflections, maintaining topical coherence, and engaging readers. Each feature carries a reading and a writing activity that help students examine Staples's writing strategies.

Presenting the Particular Occasion (p. 156)

This activity asks students to reread the opening paragraph of Staples's essay and to analyze the strategies he uses to present his occasion. By marking the names, details, and actions Staples uses to identify the participants in the scene, students should notice that Staples creates a contrast between "the victim" and himself, the "youngish black man." This contrast creates tension that engages readers, and it also sets up the reflection that will follow.

Developing the Reflections (p. 157)

This section requires students to look at the strategies Staples uses in general and the examples he uses in particular to develop his reflections. Students may differ on which instances of development are most effective; however, they should notice that Staples usually mentions an action or behavior in a general statement before making it vivid through an example.

Maintaining Topical Coherence (p. 157)

This activity will make students aware of how frequently Staples refers to time and place and how these markers keep a reader oriented. Some students may be anxious about providing order and structure in their own reflective writing. For that reason, this activity is important in showing how Staples achieves coherence and how they can as well. As a follow-up activity, you might have students note the way repeated wording helps maintain topical coherence. In addition to looking back at the activity's discussion of the "language of fear" and its associated words, students might look at the way Staples repeats words and themes related to race, darkness, or night.

Engaging Readers (p. 158)

This activity focuses on the ways Staples presents himself—his persona—as a means of engaging readers. Students should get the sense that Staples is reaching out to his readers. He wants them to view him as sensitive—"a softy who is scarcely able to take a knife to a raw chicken" (paragraph 2)—and reasonable—"I understand, of course, that the danger they perceive is not a hallucination" (5). This persona is attractive to readers, especially because it contrasts so starkly with the frightening persona that Staples unintentionally projects by his physical appearance.

Inexperienced writers often assume their reflections will automatically be of interest to readers. This activity will help students realize that they should make a conscious effort to engage readers.

A Special Reading Strategy—Comparing and Contrasting Related Readings: Brent Staples's "Black Men and Public Space" and an Excerpt from His Autobiography, *Parallel Time* (p. 159)

In this chapter, an additional reading activity follows the reflective essay by Staples. However, before having students complete this activity, you may wish to have them read and discuss the section on comparing and contrasting in Appendix 1: A Catalog of Critical Reading Strategies. There students will find an explanation of comparing and contrasting and an annotated model. For this special reading strategy, we ask students to compare Staples's two selections in terms of the way the particular occasion is described, the descriptions of "the language of fear," and the way in which Staples has remembered his thoughts and feelings.

READINGS

Dana Jennings, "Our Scars Tell the Stories of Our Lives" (p. 163)

Reading for Meaning (p. 166)

Read to Comprehend (p. 166)

The first step in this activity draws attention to the particular occasions that students will study later in the Reading like a Writer activity for this reading. Mapping out the occasions on the board may help students analyze the essay later.

Other words students might need to define include *parse* (paragraph 1), *motley* (1), *lunar* (4), *Superfund* (6), and *burnish* (11).

Read to Respond (p. 166)

Students may also respond to

- the mystery scars from Jennings's childhood;
- the incidents and events that Jennings describes;
- his question, "How do any of us get out of childhood alive?" (paragraph 3)

Read to Analyze Assumptions (p. 166)

Your class might also discuss these two apparently dueling, contradictory assumptions: (1) Jennings's scars are unusual enough to be interesting to others; (2) his degree of childhood damage is common enough that he wonders how "any of us" survive adolescence. Do students think these are irreconcilable notions, or can they see ways they possibly complement each other in this essay? Do they think either proposition is vulnerable to a challenge?

A SPECIAL READING STRATEGY: EXPLORING THE SIGNIFICANCE OF FIGURATIVE LANGUAGE (p. 167)

The special reading strategy for Jennings's essay invites students to look at the ways writers use metaphors, similes, and symbols in reflective writing. If your students have not read and discussed the section on exploring the significance of figurative language in Appendix 1: A Catalog of Critical Reading Strategies, you might take the time to do so now. The text shows that Jennings uses metaphors related to travel, but students are asked to identify other families of metaphors they find in his essay. Some of those metaphor groupings include *scars as text* (*footnotes* and *runes*, paragraph 1; *brand*, 6; *signposts*, 9; *signatures*, 12), and *scars as astronomical objects* (*starbursts*, 2; *lunar*, 4; *cratered*, 5).

READING LIKE A WRITER: PRESENTING THE PARTICULAR OCCASION (p. 168)

This Reading like a Writer activity asks students to consider how Jennings presents his occasion, which, in this essay, is not a specific event (as it was with Staples). Instead, it's a specific observation: He tells what he thinks as he looks over the scars on his body. The activity asks students to notice how Jennings structures his essay, starting with his overall point and the observations and memories that prompted it, and then moving onto a holistic reflection about the tour he has just conducted. As a follow-up activity, you could have students imitate these moves in a brief journal entry, giving a tour of what they are wearing or scars on their own body or what they see as they look around their dorm rooms, telling the stories behind the items they notice, and drawing some reflective conclusions. Conducting this sort of activity can help them spot the occasion in Jennings's essay, help them see the structure to his presentation of the occasion, and think (perhaps) of some occasions of their own, for their own essays.

CONSIDERING IDEAS FOR YOUR OWN WRITING (p. 169)

This section lists several subjects, suggested by the reading, that may stimulate student writing. You may want to ask students what other ideas for subjects they get from the reading. We have found that routinely discussing possible subjects in class encourages students to try out new ideas. Remember that there is also an array of subject suggestions in the opening Invention and Research activities of A Guide to Writing Reflective Essays.

ANALYZING VISUALS (p. 169)

As with other attempts to analyze visuals, the answers to these questions may vary, and students should be encouraged to debate the merits of their interpretations without fear of an official response that trumps theirs. It might be best, however, if they take the questions in the order presented, whether they're working in groups, as a class, or individually. The more concrete questions at the beginning, about the missing scars and the stitch marks, help pave the way for the more speculative questions later. As a possible variation on this exercise, you could have students make a list of the scars Jennings describes, and then draw (in groups or individually) what they think he looks like. When they're done, they could compare their "sketch artist" version to his self-portrait, note the differences, and speculate about the reasons for them.

READINGS

Steven Doloff, "A Universe Lies on the Sidewalks of New York" (p. 170)

READING FOR MEANING (p. 171)

Read to Comprehend (p. 171)
After students have written several sentences explaining what Doloff sees on the sidewalks of New York, you may ask students to discuss why they think he picked those particular items and not others—he does not, for instance, discuss candy wrappers, but it is probably safe to assume he has seen them. What do the details he *did* choose seem to say about his goals for the article?

Other words students may need to define include *snifter* (paragraph 1), *ordnance* (2), *bullish* (4), *futile* (6), and *untrammeled* (8).

Read to Respond (p. 171)
Students may also respond to

- Doloff's statement that "one could say that New York's sidewalks make up a kind of endless concrete newspaper from which we can read, in the minute flotsam and jetsam at our feet, news of the mass of people who walk them" (paragraph 3);
- his speculation about the ways that beings from another planet might react to the sidewalks of New York City.

Read to Analyze Assumptions (p. 172)
The assumptions suggested by the text (particularly the first one) can lead naturally to discussions about Doloff's confidence in making social projections based upon what he finds or, in the case of bullets, no longer finds on the sidewalks of New York. This sort of discussion offers you a useful transition to another critical reading strategy from Appendix 1: A Catalog of Critical Reading Strategies, specifically, Toulmin analysis. Each of Doloff's interpretations of the evidence involves an assumption, or *warrant*. Using a Toulmin analysis, students might unpack these assumptions and propose alternatives. Or since students often find the concept of *warrants* abstract and hard to comprehend, you could wait until a student has, in the course of discussion, suggested another interpretation for some of Doloff's discoveries. For instance, a student might argue that fewer crack vials and bullets could be evidence of better street-cleaning services rather than of less crime. Armed with such an observation, you could then show the class how it has just performed a kind of Toulmin analysis.

READING LIKE A WRITER: ENGAGING READERS (p. 173)

This Reading like a Writer activity helps students understand how reflective writers may establish a tone or project a voice that will engage the reader. It asks students to evaluate Doloff's ability to do so. You might wish to discuss with students how Doloff uses the personal pronouns *we* and *you*, as well as sights and experiences likely familiar to fellow New Yorkers, to engage his readers.

Considering Ideas for Your Own Writing (p. 173)

This section lists several subjects, suggested by the reading, that may stimulate student writing. You may want to ask students what other ideas for subjects they get from the reading. We have found that routinely discussing possible subjects in class encourages students to try out new ideas. Remember that there is also an array of subject suggestions in the opening Invention and Research activities of A Guide to Writing Reflective Essays.

Firoozeh Dumas, "The 'F Word'" (p. 175)

Reading for Meaning (p. 178)

Read to Comprehend (p. 178)
Students might follow up by discussing Dumas's decision to include parenthetical translations of names. How many students can identify the meanings of "American" names?

Other words students may need to define include *incites* (paragraph 1), *fraught* (2), *guttural* (2), and *clogs* (14).

Read to Respond (p. 178)
Students may also respond to

- what in the essay did not make them laugh but seemed like it was meant to do so;
- the challenges of unusual names or name changes (with which even students without obvious ethnic backgrounds often have some experience).

Read to Analyze Assumptions (p. 179)
The class might also discuss Dumas's apparent assumptions about the degree to which people in a culture should be alert and sensitive toward minority groups, or comfortable practicing someone's name in conversation until they get it right. Similarly, students might discuss the assumptions behind reactions to Dumas's name. Are the people she meets assuming that it's better (more polite?) to avoid Dumas than to get her name wrong? If so, what does the class think of such an assumption?

Reading like a Writer: Maintaining Topical Coherence (p. 180)

This Reading like a Writer activity focuses on how writers create coherence while covering new ground by repeating words in different contexts. Dumas maintains coherence through repetition of the word *name* as she moves from a discussion of names of relatives and friends to American "monosyllabic" names to sounds missing from those names to her decision to change her name to her off-the-record maiden name and then to a series of anecdotes about her switches from *Firoozeh* to *Julie* and back again. Another strategy for maintaining coherence that might be worth discussing with students is the way Dumas braids two cultural threads—references to American culture and references to her own culture—throughout the article.

Considering Ideas for Your Own Writing (p. 181)

This section lists several subjects, suggested by the reading, that may stimulate student writing. You may want to ask students what other ideas for subjects they get from the reading. We have found that routinely discussing possible subjects in class encourages students to try out new ideas. Remember that there is also an array of subject suggestions in the opening Invention and Research activities of A Guide to Writing Reflective Essays.

Wendy Lee, "Peeling Bananas" (p. 182)

READING FOR MEANING (p. 184)

Read to Comprehend (p. 184)
To further student comprehension, you may ask your students to identify (1) experiences by which Lee is made more aware of her American identity or (2) paragraphs in the essay where Lee uses comparison and contrast to explain the differences between American culture and Chinese culture. For the second option, require students to make a partial list of those differences.

Additional words that students may need to define are *epidermically* (paragraph 2), *calligraphy* (4), *tandem* (7), *plaintive* (7), and *pidgin* (8).

Read to Respond (p. 185)
Students may also respond to

- Lee's statement that for students at the Chinese School, heritage "probably doesn't play a big part in their futures" (paragraph 6);
- why the adult Chinese community described in Lee's essay strives so diligently to remind their children of their heritage.

Read to Analyze Assumptions (p. 185)
As the activity's prompt implies, Lee's assumption that the history of "American" culture is only as old as the United States itself might be worth discussing. What arguments can students think of to defend or refute her assumption?

Students might also explore

- the assumptions of the student who, when discovering Lee is Chinese, states, "Oh, I really like Chinese food" and Lee's own assumption about that student, as revealed by her mental rejoinder: "In the depths of her overfriendly eyes I saw fried egg-rolls and chow mein" (paragraph 3);
- the assumptions Lee makes when she concludes, based on the scenario she creates in paragraphs 7 and 8, that "as a hybrid of two cultures, I am unique, and perhaps that uniqueness should be preserved."

READING LIKE A WRITER: DEVELOPING REFLECTIONS THROUGH COMPARISON AND CONTRAST (p. 186)

This Reading like a Writer activity introduces a second basic strategy for extending ideas in a reflective essay: comparison and contrast. You can divide the class into three groups, each responsible for analyzing one of the instances of comparison and contrast and then reporting their findings to the class.

CONSIDERING IDEAS FOR YOUR OWN WRITING (p. 187)

This section lists several subjects, suggested by the reading, that may stimulate student writing. You may want to ask students what other ideas for subjects they get from the reading. We have found that routinely discussing possible subjects in class encourages students to try out new ideas. Remember that there is also an array of subject suggestions in the opening Invention and Research activities of A Guide to Writing Reflective Essays.

A SPECIAL READING STRATEGY: COMPARING AND CONTRASTING RELATED READINGS: DUMAS'S "THE 'F WORD'" AND LEE'S "PEELING BANANAS" (p. 187)

This special reading strategy following Wendy Lee's essay asks students to look at the ways Lee's and Dumas's ideas about identity compare as well as how the two writers use material to develop their reflections. If your students have not read and discussed the section on comparing and contrasting related readings in Appendix 1: A Catalog of Critical Reading Strategies, you might take the time to have them do so now. As a follow-up assignment or journal activity, you might ask students (1) to write about the multiple communities, groups, or cultures to which they belong and the ways they try to manage their identities in each, and (2) to compare their experiences with those of Dumas and Lee.

Katherine Haines, "Whose Body Is This?" (p. 189)

READING FOR MEANING (p. 192)

This Reading for Meaning activity invites students to apply to Haines's essay what they have learned from the other readings in this chapter about reading to comprehend, respond, and analyze assumptions. You might want to have your class suggest words to define, as well as brainstorm possibilities for response and analysis.

READING LIKE A WRITER (p. 192)

This Reading like a Writer activity offers students an opportunity to focus on one of the reflective-writing strategies covered in this chapter—presenting the particular occasion, developing the reflections, maintaining topical coherence, or engaging readers.

A SPECIAL READING STRATEGY—COMPARING AND CONTRASTING RELATED READINGS: HAINES'S "WHOSE BODY IS THIS?" AND KHELLA'S "THE ROUTE TO AMERICAN OBESITY" (p. 192)

Haines's reflection on the ways Americans obsess about bodies dovetails particularly well with the Chapter 8 speculation by Jeremy Khella about the causes of obesity. Both topics (unhealthful weight obsessions and the unhealthful rise in obesity) are popular among student writers, but seldom are students prompted to reconcile the two concerns. Once students do start comparing the two, they may initially see them as irreconcilable. If, after the initial comparisons, you encourage them to seek common ground between the two essays, you can help them discover more complicated and nuanced positions. Can the two concerns be combined in some way that makes them complementary?

One way to start might be to ask the class to examine the role of the media in both essays—do the authors' assumptions about the role of the media have anything in common? (Taken together, they blame the media for pushing images of perfect bodies while promoting quick, cheap junk food and labor-saving devices.) Answers to the two questions in the text, pursued with a focus on common ground, should help students notice that both essays are concerned with unhealthful eating habits (too little nutrition, too much junk) and that both think self-consciousness about weight can be destructive. (Khella's assumptions about self-consciousness and self-esteem may be hard for students to spot initially. See paragraph 10 of Khella for his assumption about self-esteem, which comes up only briefly.)

REVIEWING WHAT MAKES AN EFFECTIVE ESSAY: REFLECTION (p. 194)

This reflective activity makes a great transition from reading to writing. As the text suggests, this activity can be done individually or in small groups.

A GUIDE TO WRITING REFLECTIVE ESSAYS (p. 195)

Because this assignment is extremely challenging for many students, you may want to use class time helping students with Invention and Research, especially with Presenting the Particular Occasion and with Developing Your Reflections. You could have students work in small groups to read aloud to one another what they have written in their two-column charts and then discuss possibilities for expanding their ideas. Discussing their ideas with peers could encourage students who lack confidence in their ideas and spur thinking while helping confident students further refine their ideas.

Here is an outline of A Guide to Writing Reflective Essays:

Invention and Research
    Finding a Particular Occasion and a General Subject
    Testing Your Choices
    Presenting the Particular Occasion
        Narrating an Event
        Describing What You Observed
    Developing Your Reflections
        Generalizing
        Giving Examples
        Comparing and Contrasting
        Extending
        Analyzing
        Applying
        Considering Your Purpose
        Formulating a Tentative Thesis Statement
        Considering Visuals

Drafting
    Setting Goals
    Organizing Your Draft
    Working with Sources (box)
    Considering a Useful Sentence Strategy (Parallelism)

Reading a Draft Critically (box)
    Read for a First Impression
    Read Again to Suggest Improvements

Revising
    Troubleshooting Your Draft (table)
    To Present the Particular Occasion More Effectively
    To Develop the Reflections More Fully
    To Strengthen Topical Coherence
    To Better Engage Readers

Editing and Proofreading

Reflecting on What You Have Learned: Reflection (box)

Chapter 5 EXPLAINING CONCEPTS

If your students are going from Chapter 4 to Chapter 5, you might take time to discuss the similarities and differences between reflective and explanatory writing. Whereas the purpose of reflective writing is to try out ideas and help the reader see even the familiar in a new light, the purpose of explanatory writing is simply to explain something that is already well established. While explanatory writing may be every bit as entertaining and thought provoking as a reflective essay, it never loses sight of its primary goal—to inform the reader.

If your students are going directly from Chapter 3 to Chapter 5, you might want to point out some of the similarities and differences between observational and explanatory writing. Both present information in a way that readers find intelligible and interesting. Observational writing derives mainly from the writer's firsthand experiences and often relies on narrative and vivid description to communicate what the writer has learned about the subject. Although concept explanation may include the writer's personal experiences, it usually depends heavily on what the writer has learned from others. Writers of explanation synthesize, review, or summarize the work of others. They present information, draw connections, and discuss implications. They may also translate technical or specialized information into the language and contexts of readers outside the discipline.

In this chapter, we focus on one particular type of explanatory writing—writing to explain concepts. This focus enables students to work on the kind of explanation they are reading and writing in most of their courses. Throughout the disciplines, particularly in introductory courses, students are learning basic concepts. They learn by reading and writing. Understanding the rhetoric of explanatory discourse can help them become better learners as well as more effective explainers.

This chapter can teach students to

- identify a concept that may interest particular readers;
- narrow and research a concept;
- practice strategies of defining, illustrating, comparing or contrasting, classifying, narrating a process, or reporting causes or effects;
- organize an essay by classifying and dividing; and
- signal explicitly the move from one topic to the next.

The assignment to write essays explaining concepts can also be a good way to introduce students to library or Internet research. The student who knows little but is curious about a concept can gather information from the library, find information on the Internet, or talk with experts. Strategies for both firsthand and secondary-source research are covered in detail in Appendix 2: Strategies for Research and Documentation. You might want to refer students to this section early in the assignment.

WRITING ASSIGNMENT: Explaining Concepts (p. 208)

Here is the writing assignment that appears early in Chapter 5:

Choose a concept that interests you enough to study further. Write an essay explaining the concept. Consider carefully what your readers already know about the concept and how your essay can add to their knowledge.

Problems Students May Have with This Assignment

In our experience, the main problems students have with this assignment involve choice of subject and organization. Students may fail to do sufficient research, or instead they may allow their own writing to be eclipsed by their sources. Their essays then become dumping grounds for unprocessed (and sometimes plagiarized or patchwritten) information. The purpose of the assignment is twofold—to give students an opportunity to analyze and synthesize information and to have them organize the information and present it in a way that makes it understandable and interesting. The greatest challenge of this assignment may not be the gathering of information but the presentation of it. To succeed with this challenge, students will need to help readers understand unfamiliar terminology, build readers' knowledge incrementally, and provide cues to help readers to follow the organization.

You may need to help students focus on suitable concepts (some instructors even require subject proposals from students in order to identify students having difficulty understanding the task); to walk them through research options available at your library; and to give them in-class practice with summarizing, paraphrasing, and documenting sources. Following the tips below and in Part 4, above, can help you build on these approaches so that students can produce better written work.

RESOURCES IN CHAPTER 5 FOR TEACHING EXPLAINING CONCEPTS

FINDING SUBJECTS

Writing Situations for Essays Explaining Concepts (p. 208)

These three examples illustrate both academic and business occasions for writing that explains concepts. You might want to use these examples to point out some of the strategies writers use to present unfamiliar ideas. Note especially how often the writers in these examples use comparison and contrast to relate a new concept to another concept likely to be familiar. You might have students list questions they would have about these concepts, and have them decide which of the questions ought to be answered in a good explanation.

Considering Ideas for Your Own Writing

These activities follow each reading except the chapter-opening and closing ones. They are designed to help students think of subjects for their own essays by considering subjects related to the readings. Here is a list summarizing the subjects suggested after Chapter 5 readings by the following authors:

Tannen	Concepts in linguistics, gender studies, or sociology (p. 235)
Bailey	Concepts involving social values, behaviors, or attitudes (p. 247)
Bogle	Concepts involving on-campus issues or concepts from disciplines being studied (p. 254)
Ngo	A well-established human taboo or practice (p. 261)

Choosing a Concept (p. 268)

Choosing a Concept is the first activity under Invention and Research, the opening section of A Guide to Writing Essays Explaining Concepts. Students are shown concepts grouped by fields of study. They are then asked to make a list of concepts they would consider writing about. You might urge students from day one to begin compiling a list of possibilities. Ideas inspired by the suggestions in Considering Ideas for Your Own Writing could be part of this list.

Problems Students May Have Choosing a Subject

One solution to the problem of subject choice is to encourage students to write about subjects introduced in their other courses. In the Invention and Research section, many concepts from academic subjects are suggested. If students lack confidence in writing about a concept from one of their academic subjects, you might allow them to write about concepts drawn from their extracurricular interests.

Students will need your help in finding a focus for their essays. Because many concepts are too big—too much is known about them—for most writing situations, students need to focus their essays and write about one aspect of the concept. Notice how the Invention and Research activities are set up to lead students first to a broad overview of the concept and then to focus on one aspect of it. When we teach this assignment, we require students to describe both the concept and the aspect of it they will focus on, either to us or to the whole class during a subject discussion session.

THINKING ABOUT YOUR EXPERIENCE EXPLAINING CONCEPTS (p. 209)

This activity will allow students to realize they have a familiarity, possibly greater than they expected, with the genre, reducing the anxiety that typically accompanies composing an essay and making the remaining activities in this chapter easier.

CHOOSING READINGS

If you cannot teach all the readings in this chapter, you will have to make some choices. There are two main principles that may guide your selection—(1) the interest level of the reading and its usefulness in suggesting subjects for your students' essays and (2) the basic features covered in each of the Reading like a Writer activities.

The reading selections in this chapter, beginning with the sample essay by Chris Anderson, represent a variety of concepts and ways of explaining them. Nevertheless, all the concepts presented here refer to cultural or social phenomena: Anderson on the online marketplace, Tannen on marked forms, Bailey on dating, Bogle on remembering, Ngo on cannibalism, and Ton on hip-hop. However, articles and books on astronomy, biology, chemistry, and physics also lend considerable time to explaining concepts of natural science, and might be used as supplemental examples.

INTEREST LEVELS OF THE READINGS

Here are brief descriptions from the table of contents to help you choose readings that might be of interest to your students:

Chris Anderson, **The Long Tail**. The editor-in-chief of *Wired* magazine explains the concept of the "long tail," a marketing term that defines how online availability of products—music, books, and movies—shapes the tastes and purchasing choices of consumers. (p. 210)

Deborah Tannen, **Marked Women**. A linguist explains the linguistic concept of marked forms: "Each of the women at the conference had to make decisions about hair, clothing, makeup and accessories, and each decision carried meaning. Every style available to us was marked." (p. 227)

Beth L. Bailey, **Dating**. A sociologist explains the concept of dating and shows how courtship rituals have changed over the years—to the disadvantage of poor men and strong-minded women. (p. 236)

Kathleen A. Bogle, **"Hooking Up": What Educators Need to Know**. A professor of sociology and criminal justice explains a social behavior that she believes college administrators and instructors need to understand in order to better serve their students. (p. 248)

Linh Kieu Ngo, **Cannibalism: It Still Exists**. A first-year composition student explains the anthropological concept of cannibalism, delineating the three functional categories of survival, dietary, and ritual cannibalism. (p. 255)

Justin Ton, **Hip-Hop You Don't Stop**. A college student explains the origins and "four pillars" of hip-hop music, detailing its evolution and arguing that it turns young people away from violence and toward positive expression. (p. 262)

READING LIKE A WRITER ACTIVITIES

The first reading, Anderson's "The Long Tail," introduces all the basic features of the essay explaining a concept through its Reading like a Writer activities. The final reading, Ton's "Hip Hop You Don't Stop," does not specify a Reading like a Writer activity but invites students to choose a feature of the reading they think is worth analyzing. Each of the other readings has one Reading like a Writer activity. Below is a list of these activities.

Engaging Readers' Interest: Deborah Tannen, "Marked Women" (p. 235)

Explaining through Comparison/Contrast: Beth L. Bailey, "Dating" (p. 246)

Devising a Readable Plan: Kathleen Bogle, "'Hooking Up': What Educators Need to Know" (p. 253)

Integrating Sources Smoothly: Linh Kieu Ngo, "Cannibalism: It Still Exists" (p. 260)

A GUIDE TO READING ESSAYS EXPLAINING CONCEPTS (p. 209)

Here are suggestions for teaching the Reading for Meaning activities following Anderson's "The Long Tail."

READING FOR MEANING (p. 219)

Read to Comprehend (p. 219)
If students have trouble explaining the economics of Anderson's model, you may wish to have them start by explaining why it is called "the long tail."

Other words that students may need to define include *harrowing* (paragraph 1), *rhapsodic* (3), and *profligacy* (20).

Read to Respond (p. 220)
Students may also respond to

- Anderson's economic calculations about the decision to download songs;
- Anderson's suggestion to price items by demand.

Read to Analyze Assumptions (p. 220)
Students may also want to consider the assumption by online sellers that customers need or want recommendations about items in the long tail, or Anderson's assumption that examples of a few notable failures are sufficient evidence to support his conclusion that a seller needs both mainstream hits and long-tail merchandise to be successful.

The four Reading like a Writer activities following Anderson's essay give students a comprehensive introduction to the rhetorical features and writing strategies of essays explaining concepts. You can have students do some or all of the activities here before going on to do selected Reading like a Writer activities for the subsequent readings. With the Anderson essay, students are introduced to major features of concept explanation—devising a readable plan, using appropriate explanatory strategies, integrating sources smoothly, and engaging readers' interest. Each feature carries a reading and a writing activity that help students focus on Anderson's writing strategies.

Devising a Readable Plan (p. 222)

This activity calls students' attention to the cueing strategies Anderson uses to make his points clear and easy to follow. Students are asked to identify forecasting statements, topic sentences, transitions, and summaries. Although these devices will be familiar to many students, you might find it useful to walk the class through part (or all) of Anderson's essay, making sure students can identify where and how he uses each strategy. Here are some examples that might be worth highlighting after students have attempted to find the cues on their own:

- "What happened?" in paragraph 3 employs a rhetorical question as a transition.
- The first sentence of paragraph 5 transitions from his opening example to the concept itself.
- Paragraph 19 forecasts the "three big lessons" of the new economic model, which Anderson then describes.
- The penultimate paragraph, the conclusion, summarizes the most important lessons of the article.

Your students may be reluctant to use these sorts of road signs in their own writing for fear of being too blunt. The failure to be explicit plagues the explanatory essays of many inexperienced writers. You could discuss the issue and try to discover why some students shy away from stating their points directly.

Using Appropriate Explanatory Strategies (p. 222)

This section offers students a brief catalog of the most useful rhetorical strategies for writers in this genre. The strategies discussed here not only are central to essays explaining concepts but also figure prominently in position papers, which students are exposed to in Chapter 7. Although this section introduces students to six specific strategies, it asks them to select only one to focus on. You might ask the class to form groups based on the strategy they choose, discuss their findings, and report to the class. Your students should be familiar with these strategies, but they may need extra help in identifying precisely where Anderson uses each strategy. The activity specifies paragraph numbers to help students get started.

Integrating Sources Smoothly (p. 223)

This task asks students to consider Anderson's decision in paragraph 16 to quote directly, focusing on his use of a signal phrase to introduce Kevin Laws and his quoted material. This is a good time to clarify the rules on colon usage, and to highlight the independent nature of the clause preceding the colon in this case. The activity also asks students to study Anderson's use of statistics without quotation, and it might be worthwhile for the class to discuss how Anderson came up with that information, and to study the ways he has paraphrased it. You might also wish to have students look at the different method Anderson uses to integrate a quote from Steve Jobs in paragraph 39.

If your students research their concepts, they also will have to decide how to present source material and integrate it smoothly into their writing. You may wish to point out to students how other writers in the chapter use sources. Tannen summarizes another linguist's ideas and quotes his exact words in paragraphs 24 to 28, while Bailey and Ngo use outside sources throughout their essays. The Reading like a Writer activity after Ngo's essay (p. 260) follows up on this activity by focusing on integration of sources and on parenthetical citations.

Engaging Readers' Interest (p. 224)

This activity invites students to consider the strategies that writers of potentially dry subjects use to attract and sustain interest in their concept explanations. Anderson starts with references to two popular best-sellers about an exciting subject: mountain climbing. He also tells, essentially, an underdog story about a little-read book that emerged from obscurity—the sort of tale that tends to resonate with readers. Most students are likely to note that Anderson's first five paragraphs engage readers' curiosity even before he defines the concept—and well before he names that concept, finally, in paragraph 12.

Another engaging strategy you might want to discuss with students is Anderson's use of anecdotes, which also help bring to life what might otherwise be a dry, market-oriented discussion. Students might consider the effectiveness of the opening anecdote about Simpson's book; the story about the Netflix CEO who got the rights to a documentary (22); Rhapsody's experiment in elastic demand (38); and the story about MP3.com (42).

ANALYZING VISUALS (p. 225)

This activity asks students to analyze two images: 5.1, "The Anatomy of the Long Tail" (p. 212) and 5.2, "The Real Cost of Music" (p. 215). Before students conduct this activity, you might want to have them review (or read for the first time) Appendix 3: Strategies for Analyzing Visuals. The first visual focuses on three companies, each one representing a different entertainment industry—music, books, and movie rentals. The second, a pie chart, attempts to show why Anderson believes the pricing model for music will change. Students might additionally speculate as to why Anderson presents new economy statistics in yellow in the first image, while he shows old economy elements in a hatched red pattern that nearly blends into the overall red background. They might start by thinking about the traditional meaning of red in discussions of business statistics, accounting, and finance.

READINGS

Deborah Tannen, "Marked Women" (p. 227)

READING FOR MEANING (p. 233)

Read to Comprehend (p. 233)

You might also ask students to describe Tannen's emotional response to the concept of "marking."

Other words that students may need to define include *frivolousness* (paragraph 11), *parthenogenesis* (26), and *apologist* (33).

Read to Respond (p. 233)

Students may also respond to

- the fact that Tannen's conclusions are based primarily on her observations of three women and eight men at a conference;
- Tannen's assertion that when a woman takes her husband's surname, she announces that she has traditional values;
- an unaddressed question—if women are marked, who did the marking?

Read to Analyze Assumptions (p. 234)

You might also ask students to write about the cultural assumptions, values, and beliefs underlying Tannen's statement that women do not have the freedom to be unmarked, or her assumption that the men at her conference—despite their beards, differences in clothing, and other traits—were unmarked because she didn't recognize what they wore as symbolizing anything.

READING LIKE A WRITER: ENGAGING READERS' INTEREST (p. 235)

This Reading like a Writer activity focuses on Tannen's efforts to engage her readers. Students should recognize that Tannen's use of an informal, conversational tone and of the first-person pronoun I allows them greater accessibility than if she had used a formal, scholarly tone and more objective third-person pronouns. This exercise may be especially useful for students who have difficulty imagining an audience and who consequently assume that their subjects are engaging simply because they are writing about them.

CONSIDERING IDEAS FOR YOUR OWN WRITING (p. 235)

This section lists several subjects, suggested by the reading, that may stimulate student writing. You may want to ask students what other ideas for subjects they get from the reading. We have found that routinely discussing possible subjects in class encourages students to try out new ideas. Remember that there is also an array of subject suggestions in the opening Invention and Research activity of A Guide to Writing Essays Explaining Concepts (p. 268).

Beth L. Bailey, "Dating" (p. 236)

READING FOR MEANING (p. 244)

Read to Comprehend (p. 244)

In addition to having students list the differences between calling and dating, you may wish to have students restate Bailey's thesis to help them better understand why Bailey is providing readers a brief history of dating.

Other words that students may need to define include *waxed* (paragraph 3), *tantamount* (3), *myriad* (5), and *apocryphal* (20).

Read to Respond (p. 244)

Students may also respond to

- the link between dating and prostitution;
- the idea that the advent of dating eventually further marginalized women, forcing "women to act as men's dependents" (paragraph 28);

- the fact that, as women have started to take more initiative in dating, they have not returned to the "calling" model of courtship.

Read to Analyze Assumptions (p. 245)

Another possibility includes considering the assumptions and values that at the turn of the twentieth century dictated the need for chaperones—or at least some type of supervision— for respectable middle- and upper-class young women on dates. Students might also analyze the assumptions of the historical men and women described by Bailey, such as the men who assumed they were not getting a fair deal out of the dating regime, or even the young man in the opening anecdote who assumed he could ask to call on the woman, and assumed he understood what her answer meant. What might his assumptions imply about the 1920s, when the joke was told, and what do those assumptions seem to imply to Bailey?

READING LIKE A WRITER: EXPLAINING THROUGH COMPARISON/CONTRAST (p. 246)

This Reading like a Writer activity calls attention to the strategy of explaining something new by comparing or contrasting it with something known. We point out that Bailey reverses the typical strategy by explaining something known, dating, by relating it to something unknown, calling. You might ask students to find more typical examples of comparing or contrasting in the other essays that explain concepts. Anderson, for instance, compares the economics of online retailers with those of conventional brick-and-mortar stores, while Tannen explains the marked nature of women by drawing parallels with marked language, which may be more obvious to readers. Ngo compares and contrasts several categories of cannibalism.

CONSIDERING IDEAS FOR YOUR OWN WRITING (p. 247)

This section lists several subjects, suggested by the reading, that may stimulate student writing. You may want to ask students what other ideas for subjects they get from the reading. We have found that routinely discussing possible subjects in class encourages students to try out new ideas. Remember that there is also an array of subject suggestions in the opening Invention and Research activity of A Guide to Writing Essays Explaining Concepts (p. 268).

Kathleen A. Bogle, "'Hooking Up': What Educators Need to Know" (p. 248)

READING FOR MEANING (p. 251)

Read to Comprehend (p. 251)

In addition to explaining Bogle's concept of "hooking up," students might find it useful to identify the two reasons she thinks campus officials should know about the phenomenon.

Other words that students may need to define include *lamentations* (paragraph 1), in loco parentis (2), *unfettered* (3), and *allay* (8).

Read to Respond (p. 251)

Students might also respond to

- Bogle's definitions and descriptions of "hooking up," if their own understanding differs from hers;
- Bogle's assertion that hooking up isn't new.

Read to Analyze Assumptions (p. 252)

If students agree with Bogle's assumption that hooking up is common, you might ask them to consider Bogle's speculation in paragraph 11 that college students might assume it's more common than it really is, or that their friends are going further than they really are. In what ways and to what extent does that suggestion undermine or complicate her own assumption about hooking up being common? Students might also analyze the assumptions that other students make about the practice, about its novelty, and about its extent.

READING LIKE A WRITER: DEVISING A READABLE PLAN (p. 253)

This Reading like a Writer activity highlights the importance of transitions, which students are asked to outline—a feat that may be easier for them if you tell them before they read to annotate the essay with its structure and transitions in mind. A partial outline of Bogle's transitions might look like this:

¶ 1 (first sentence): She opens with a reference to a 2001 report on hooking up and lists some reactions to it.

¶ 1 (last sentence): She explains that college officials need to understand the issue because of its links to alcohol abuse and sexual assaults involving students (forecasting statement).

¶ 2 (first sentence): She explains that hooking up is not new—a statement set up in the earlier paragraph by her use of scare quotes in the phrase "their concern over students' 'new,' morally questionable sexual activity."

¶ 2: She uses *in fact* to transition to the origins of the practice.

¶ 3: After having discussed one pattern of changes initiated in the 1960s, she indicates she is going to discuss another, signaling the addition with the word *also*.

¶ 3: She ends with a statement summarizing her main points from paragraphs 2 and 3, indicating the transition to this summary with the word *so*.

CONSIDERING IDEAS FOR YOUR OWN WRITING (p. 254)

This section lists several subjects, suggested by the reading, that may stimulate student writing. You may want to ask students what other ideas for subjects they get from the reading. We have found that routinely discussing possible subjects in class encourages students to try out new ideas. Remember that there is also an array of subject suggestions in the opening Invention and Research activity of A Guide to Writing Essays Explaining Concepts (p. 268).

A SPECIAL READING STRATEGY—COMPARING AND CONTRASTING RELATED READINGS: BAILEY'S "DATING" AND BOGLE'S "'HOOKING UP'" (p. 254)

As noted in the text, both Bailey and Bogle explain concepts related to courtship and sexual relations. Because the concepts are very similar, students might be more aware at first of the commonalities. If they remain focused on the instructions of the prompt, however (or if you redirect them to those instructions), once they begin looking at explanatory strategies, they will note differences. For instance, although both authors place a heavy emphasis on the causes of these social practices and their effects, and on process narration to describe how the customs work, Bailey frequently illustrates her explanation with specific examples, often providing evidence from the time period she's describing in the form of quotes from magazines. Bogle provides an illustration of a typical encounter but avoids specific instances.

Moreover, their purposes differ in important ways that affect their strategies: Bailey aims to illuminate the past, whereas Bogle uses the past briefly as a torch to illuminate the present. Bailey's focus is on rich understanding, but Bogle's is on current policy. Bailey can afford to spend more time explaining the causes of the change to dating practices than does Bogle, who spends most of her time trying to clarify or define exactly what hooking up is and what its current consequences are.

Linh Kieu Ngo, "Cannibalism: It Still Exists" (p. 255)

READING FOR MEANING (p. 259)

Read to Comprehend (p. 259)
After asking students to explain the differences between the several types of cannibalism, you may also wish to ask them to clarify the cultural significance of each type.

Other words that students may need to define include *marsupials* (paragraph 9) and *avenged* (12).

Read to Respond (p. 259)
Students may also respond to

- the theory Ngo suggests to explain why the Miyanmin society practices cannibalism (paragraph 9);
- the Bimin-Kuskusmin accounts involving the eating of parts of raw genitals to ensure fertility (13);
- the arrangement of Ngo's essay, especially the introductory anecdote meant to engage the reader and the closing proposition.

Read to Analyze Assumptions (p. 259)
You might also ask students to consider (1) the underlying values that explain why Vietnamese refugees "did not kill people to get human flesh for nourishment, but instead waited until the people had died" (paragraph 7) or (2) the assumptions that Ngo makes about the reliability of his sources' descriptions of tribal practices in distant parts of the world—descriptions that might not have been fact-checked.

READING LIKE A WRITER: INTEGRATING SOURCES SMOOTHLY (p. 260)

This Reading like a Writer activity follows up on the Integrating Sources Smoothly activity (p. 223) for the Anderson essay. Students will be exposed to various options for integrating sources into their essays. A class discussion of these options can be useful because many students integrate quotations awkwardly or may not be confident about when and how to summarize or paraphrase.

Indeed, many students misunderstand what a citation means and assume that any cited material is a quotation, even if it does not appear within quotation marks. Believing the citations and quotation marks to be largely redundant, they may leave out one or the other at times without ever realizing they are plagiarizing by doing so. Going over Ngo's material and even slowing down to point out how the author has paraphrased a source or explaining what the citations for unquoted material mean can help students dispel some of this confusion.

CONSIDERING IDEAS FOR YOUR OWN WRITING (p. 261)

This section lists several subjects, suggested by the reading, that may stimulate student writing. Other possibilities include rituals, customs, or practices that students have heard of and that they think of as bizarre or exotic. You may want to ask students what other ideas for subjects they get from the reading. We have found that routinely discussing possible subjects in class encourages students to try out new ideas. Remember that there is also an array of subject suggestions in the opening Invention and Research activity of A Guide to Writing Essays Explaining Concepts (p. 268).

A SPECIAL READING STRATEGY: SUMMARIZING (p. 261)

This activity invites students to apply the critical reading strategy of summarizing to Ngo's essay. A summary of Ngo's essay might look something like this:

> After telling the story of fifty-five Vietnamese refugees who resorted to cannibalism when they were lost at sea, Ngo defines and gives a brief social history of cannibalism. Ngo then divides cannibalism into its two main categories: exocannibalism—eating foreigners—and endocannibalism—eating members of one's own group. Within these two main categories that Ngo describes, there are several types of functional cannibalism, the three most common being survival cannibalism, dietary cannibalism, and religious or ritual cannibalism. Humans resort to survival cannibalism when faced with the choice to die or to eat others. Humans practicing dietary cannibalism eat others for nourishment, as part of their culture's traditional food practices. Humans practicing religious or ritual cannibalism eat others as part of traditional ceremonies, not for nourishment. Ngo concludes by noting that though developed societies do not practice cannibalism—with the exception of survival cannibalism when the only alternative is starvation—our distant ancestors were possibly cannibals.

Justin Ton, "Hip-Hop You Don't Stop" (p. 262)

READING FOR MEANING (p. 265)

This Reading for Meaning activity invites students to apply to Ton's essay what they have learned from the other readings in this chapter about reading to comprehend, reading to respond, and reading to analyze assumptions.

READING LIKE A WRITER (p. 266)

This Reading like a Writer activity offers students an opportunity to focus on one of the writing strategies covered in this chapter on explaining concepts—devising a readable plan, using appropriate explanatory strategies, integrating sources smoothly, or engaging readers' interest.

REVIEWING WHAT MAKES AN EFFECTIVE ESSAY: EXPLAINING CONCEPTS (p. 267)

This reflective activity makes a great transition from reading to writing. As the text suggests, this activity can be done individually or in small groups.

A GUIDE TO WRITING ESSAYS EXPLAINING CONCEPTS (p. 268)

The biggest challenge for writers of explanatory essays is selecting and arranging the material in a way that will be clear and interesting to readers. Three steps in the composing process address this problem—analyzing your readers (p. 269), focusing your explanation (p. 270), and organizing your draft (p. 272)—and students should give them special attention. Thinking carefully about these three steps—and then following through with rich, exploratory invention writing—can help prevent students from submitting undigested reports of information.

Here is an outline of A Guide to Writing Essays Explaining Concepts:

Invention and Research
> Choosing a Concept
> Analyzing Your Readers
> Researching the Concept
>> Exploring What You Already Know about the Concept
>> Finding More Information
>> Consulting Experts
>> Focusing Your Explanation
>> Confirming Your Focus
>> Formulating a Working Thesis
>> Considering Visuals

Drafting
> Setting Goals
> Organizing Your Draft
> Working with Sources: Introducing Sources Carefully and Precisely (box)
> Considering a Useful Sentence Strategy (Appositives)

Reading a Draft Critically (box)
> Read for a First Impression
> Read Again to Suggest Improvements

Revising
> Troubleshooting Your Draft
>> To Make the Concept Clearer and More Focused
>> To Improve the Organization
>> To Strengthen the Explanatory Strategies
>> To Integrate Quotations Smoothly and Acknowledge Sources Properly

Editing and Proofreading

Reflecting on What You Have Learned: Explaining Concepts (box)

Chapter 6 EVALUATION

This is a pivotal chapter in the book because it is the first that deals with argument. The preceding chapters introduce types of personal and explanatory essays. In this chapter, students encounter essays that make and defend value judgments. Evaluation is one of the basic elements of argumentative writing, and students need to recognize the role that evaluation plays in the other types of argument that are treated in the remaining chapters of *Reading Critically, Writing Well*—Position Paper (Chapter 7), Speculating about Causes or Effects (Chapter 8), and Proposal to Solve a Problem (Chapter 9). Essays speculating about causes or effects, for example, judge the relative value of alternative explanations or predictions. Similarly, proposals assess alternative solutions, and position papers gauge opposing positions.

This chapter begins with a discussion of the evaluations that students make every day and suggests academic and other occasions for evaluative writing. The purpose here is to remind students that they already know something about evaluative discourse—that is, they know when, why, by whom, and for whom evaluations are written. This chapter builds on and refines what most students already know.

The introduction also draws a distinction between evaluations and expressions of taste. Students could explore this distinction by defining terms such as *taste, preference*, and *judgment* and by conjecturing about the different purposes of expressing, explaining, justifying, and convincing. The main point is to help students classify the evaluative essay they will write as an argument because it requires that the writer's judgment—the thesis—be backed with reasons and support.

Students can learn a great deal from this challenging assignment, including how to

- choose an appropriate subject to evaluate;
- present a subject to readers;
- assert a clear, authoritative judgment, qualifying it as necessary;
- give reasons for a judgment, based on recognized standards;
- support reasons by providing evidence and by comparing or contrasting a subject to similar subjects;
- organize an essay through logically related reasons; and
- signal explicitly the stages of an evaluative argument.

WRITING ASSIGNMENT: Evaluation (p. 283)

Here is the writing assignment that appears near the beginning of Chapter 6:

Choose a subject that you can both evaluate and make a confident judgment about. Write an essay evaluating this subject. State your judgment clearly, and back it up with reasons and support. Describe the subject for readers unfamiliar with it, and give them a context for understanding it. Your purpose is to convince readers that your judgment is informed and based on generally accepted standards for judging this kind of subject.

Problems Students May Have with This Assignment

This seems like a straightforward assignment—say whether you like or dislike something, and then say why—but it can go wrong in many ways the first time students try it. Students may not be willing to assert firm judgments, or they may not understand—even after the readings and Reading like a Writer activities in the text—that they are to make and defend their own judgments with reasons and support. In addition, because they are unaccustomed to being held to the rhetorical requirements of a specific writing situation, student writers may overlook the requirement to describe the subject for readers unfamiliar with it. They may also unwittingly merge or blur their reasons because they lack confidence in them. Students also may not fully understand which standards for evaluating apply to their subjects, or they may assume mistakenly that their readers share the same standards. You might ask your class to brainstorm standards for several similar but different subjects (horror films and dramas, perhaps, or roadside cafes and five-star restaurants) to help students see that readers will expect them to use standards appropriate for their specialized subjects.

These problems suggest that before you ask students to analyze each other's drafts, you may want to model a critical reading of several students' drafts. This way you can emphasize the rhetorical requirements of the assignment. Furthermore, the challenging nature of evaluation makes it a good choice for assigning twice. You could first have everyone in the class evaluate the same subject—perhaps a short story or a movie you show in class. Many short films are now available online. Then students could do a second essay evaluating a subject of their own choice. (You need not *grade* both papers. The first attempt could be a practice run; you might even have students do the practice run in groups, and then use a projector to evaluate each group's evaluation.)

Another way to deal with the common instinct to simply express a verdict without supporting it is to encourage or require students to evaluate by comparing their subject with another appropriate subject in the same category: they might compare two Vietnamese restaurants near campus to determine which is the better deal for students, or compare two summer movies to determine which offers the better thrills. (See the third scenario in Writing Situations for Evaluations, p. 283, for another example.) Students are used to breaking subjects down into points or subtopics for comparisons, and, for this reason, often find it easier to think of ways to back up their opinions in this format.

Perhaps the biggest problem that you need to anticipate arises when students risk doing this assignment from memory. A subject to be evaluated needs to be analyzed closely during invention and possibly reexamined during drafting and revising. Students should not evaluate a movie, for example, unless they can see it two or three times; nor should they evaluate a novel unless they have time to review it very carefully. Similarly, they should not evaluate a consumer product unless they are currently using it and are knowledgeable—or can quickly become knowledgeable—about the general type of product.

RESOURCES IN CHAPTER 6 FOR TEACHING EVALUATION

FINDING SUBJECTS

Writing Situations for Evaluations (p. 283)
These three writing situations illustrate a wide range of evaluations, academic and otherwise. Each product demonstrates the characteristics mentioned in the writing assignment by presenting a definitive judgment and backing it up with sound reasons and support. The third situation, in which a college student evaluates colleges for his younger brother, does not highlight judgment quite as prominently as the first two writing situations do. In this situation, the writer offers his brother criteria by which he can make his own judgment. This example might be useful in introducing the central role that the strategy of comparison and contrast often plays in evaluative writing.

Considering Ideas for Your Own Writing
These activities follow each reading except the chapter-opening and closing ones. They are designed to help students think of subjects for their own essays by considering subjects related to the readings. Here is a list summarizing the subjects suggested after Chapter 6 readings by the following authors:

Berardinelli A film, a television show or series, or another visual or media event (p. 302)
Maurstad New innovations in film, television, automobiles, or other fields (p. 307)
Rosen A hobby, leisure activity, or profession (p. 315)
Romano An essay, an article from a print or online magazine, a book, or a Web site (p. 324)

Choosing a Subject

Choosing a Subject is the first activity under Invention and Research, the opening section in A Guide to Writing Evaluations (p. 330). Students are shown a bulleted list of suggested subjects and are asked to make their own list of possible subjects. You might want to brainstorm with your students additional categories with which they are familiar.

Problems Students May Have Choosing a Subject

Our experience has shown that the most successful essays are those that draw heavily on an individual student's interest or expertise. Students who express an avid interest in skateboarding often write fine essays on skateboard magazines, skateboard parks, or skateboarding equipment. Not only are they familiar with the standards that are usually applied to that field of interest, but also they are able to make pertinent comparisons and contrasts. Even if they do not seem academic, subjects like these can be quite ambitious and demanding when students are enthusiastic and take them seriously. Students may even be able to publish authoritative evaluations of such topics in magazines or on the Web.

By and large, students have the least difficulty evaluating consumer products. Standards are fairly easy to establish, the essays themselves are not difficult to organize, and comparisons can be found easily. Still, there are some dangers in permitting students to write such essays. All too often, students slip into a kind of Madison Avenue prose, uncritically touting the virtues of their chosen product and making claims of comfort or style unsupported by any kind of evidence. Often, they frame details the same ways they have seen them framed in ads, press releases, and company Web sites, or even borrow language from these sources, without recognizing the impact such moves have on their credibility. Trivial criteria or judgments based on personal taste instead of on generally established standards are often applied to consumer-product evaluations, and students should be warned in advance about such potential problems.

Evaluations of people are likely to be successful only when students are careful to establish clear and reasonable standards that others share. Teachers are a popular choice but lend themselves to simplistic judgments ("He was a friend to his students as well as a teacher") that are supported only by personal experience.

We are also wary of attempts to evaluate abstract concepts such as friendship or greed. Though it is theoretically possible to write such evaluations, it is difficult to decide on appropriate standards. Even more difficult is determining the kind of support that might be brought to bear on such a topic. Our students have occasionally written credible essays evaluating capitalism or democracy, but the key to their success seems to lie in the fact that these concepts can be illustrated with specific examples. Evaluations of philosophical abstractions almost always lead to more problems than rewards.

Easily the most promising subjects are discrete, tangible objects or events that can be closely and repeatedly analyzed—a story or novel, movie, musical recording, concert, play performance, essay (perhaps in this book), magazine article, restaurant, computer program, or Web site. Before drafting, students can examine the subject, taking careful notes. They can revisit it once again before revising, keeping the subject present throughout the writing process. Such an immediate presence of subjects makes it easier for students to amass the supporting examples required in a strong evaluation essay.

THINKING ABOUT YOUR EXPERIENCE WITH EVALUATIONS (p. 284)

This activity will allow students to realize they have a familiarity, possibly greater than they expected, with the genre, reducing the anxiety that typically accompanies composing an essay and making the remaining activities in this chapter easier.

CHOOSING READINGS

The reading selections in this chapter, beginning with the sample essay by Amitai Etzioni, represent an array of subjects for evaluation. If you cannot assign all the readings in this chapter, you will have to make some choices. There are two main principles that may guide your selection—(1) the interest level of the reading and its usefulness in suggesting subjects for your students' essays and (2) the basic features covered in each of the Reading like a Writer activities.

INTEREST LEVELS OF THE READINGS

Here are brief descriptions from the table of contents to help you choose readings that would be of interest to your students:

Amitai Etzioni, **Working at McDonald's**. A respected sociologist argues that after-school jobs at fast-food restaurants are bad for teenagers. (p. 284)

James Berardinelli, ***Avatar***. A leading online film critic praises what he calls not only "the most technically amazing motion picture to have arrived on screens in many years" but also "entertainment of the highest order." (p. 294)

Tom Maurstad, ***Avatar***. A writer for the *Dallas Morning News* finds *Avatar* "an unconditionally innovative achievement" but "a clumsy and cliché-filled drama" that would have worked better as a video game. (p. 303)

Christine Rosen, **The Myth of Multitasking**. A prominent writer and commentator on such subjects as bioethics, fundamentalism, feminism, and technology warns that "when people do their work . . . with crumbs of attention rationed out among many competing tasks, their culture may gain in information, but it will surely weaken in wisdom." (p. 308)

Christine Romano, **Jessica Statsky's "Children Need to Play, Not Compete": An Evaluation**. A first-year college student applies critical reading skills to another student's essay and comes up with an assertive but carefully balanced evaluation. (p. 317)

Larry Ballesteros, **A Winning Formula? A Review of *Slumdog Millionaire***. A college student argues that the Oscar-winning film succeeds as a classical love story, despite a few flaws of plot and camerawork. (p. 325)

READING LIKE A WRITER ACTIVITIES

The first reading, Etzioni's "Working at McDonald's," introduces all the basic features of evaluation through its Reading like a Writer activities. The last essay, Ballesteros's review of *Slumdog Millionaire*, does not specify a Reading like a Writer activity but invites students to choose a feature of the reading they think is worth analyzing. Each of the other readings has one Reading like a Writer activity. Here is a list showing the activities following these readings.

Presenting the Subject: James Berardinelli, *"Avatar"* (p. 301)
Asserting an Overall Judgment: Tom Maurstad, *"Avatar"* (p. 306)

Giving Reasons and Support: Christine Rosen, "The Myth of Multitasking" (p. 315)
Anticipating Objections and Alternative Judgments: Christine Romano, "Jessica Statsky's 'Children Need to Play, Not Compete': An Evaluation" (p. 323)

A GUIDE TO READING EVALUATIONS (p. 284)

The essay that is the focus of A Guide to Reading Evaluations is Etzioni's "Working at McDonald's."

READING FOR MEANING (p. 288)

Here are suggestions for teaching the Reading for Meaning activities following Etzioni's "Working at McDonald's."

Read to Comprehend (p. 288)
You may also ask students to reread the several places in the essay (paragraphs 8–9, 10, and 14) where Etzioni refers to studies, and then have students briefly summarize each study's argument and Etzioni's rebuttal to it.

You might also point out to students that the essay's opening sentence includes the use of the second-person possessive, *your*, and in this context suggests that Etzioni's audience is parents. However, the audience shifts in the concluding sentence to the teens about whom Etzioni has been writing. Point out that this sentence uses the second person: "Go back to school" (22), with *you* being the understood subject. You might ask students why Etzioni would make a direct address to teens at the end of an essay primarily directed at parents. Note that the essay was originally published as an opinion piece in a newspaper. You might suggest that Etzioni includes teens as part of his audience from the beginning.

Other words students may need to define include *gumption* (7), *don* (7), *affluent* (13), and *intrinsic* (19).

Read to Respond (p. 288)
Students may also respond to

- Etzioni's brusque and at times harsh tone (for example, the essay's opening sentence, "McDonald's is bad for your kids");
- Etzioni's observations on the use and what he considers the general abuse (paragraphs 18-20) of the money the teens earn.

Read to Analyze Assumptions (p. 289)
You might also ask students to consider teens' underlying values and assumptions that would allow them to feel "they were entitled to $50 severance 'pay' on their last day on the job" (16), or the assumption that Etzioni himself is challenging—the assumption that part-time jobs might be a good experience for a teenager.

READING LIKE A WRITER ACTIVITIES (p. 290)

This section helps students shift their focus from the content to how the writer presents his evaluation. Students are introduced here to four major elements of evaluative writing—presenting the subject, asserting an overall judgment, giving reasons and support, and anticipating objections and alternative judgments. Each feature carries a reading and a writing activity that help students focus on Etzioni's strategies.

Presenting the Subject (p. 291)

This activity asks students to reread and analyze specific paragraphs that present factual details describing the employees at fast-food restaurants and their work. In addition to locating the information in the essay, students are urged to speculate on how Etzioni gathered this information. They are also asked to evaluate the information and to imagine what he may have left out. Imagining what the writer omitted is a valuable critical reading activity, and it underscores a writer's need to make choices about what to include and what to leave out.

Asserting an Overall Judgment (p. 291)

This task addresses the way that writers of evaluation assert their judgments. Students should note that Etzioni states his judgment emphatically at the beginning of the essay and in slightly different forms throughout the selection. For instance, in paragraph 11, he aims his thesis specifically toward minority youngsters. Students are asked to consider whether Etzioni modifies his judgment at any point. You might discuss with students the strategy of acknowledging both a subject's good and bad qualities instead of treating only one or the other.

Giving Reasons and Support (p. 292)

This section invites students to analyze and evaluate one of Etzioni's reasons, along with the support he offers. Students are asked to consider the reason's appropriateness to Etzioni's overall argument and then to judge the reliability of the support. Some students may find that the three reasons—that fast-food jobs are too routinized, that these jobs interfere with education, and that on-the-job supervision is inadequate or inappropriate—seem calculated to appeal not to student workers but to parents. Students may also be critical of Etzioni's evidence to support these reasons. While the evidence of long hours and late closing times seems plausible in support of the second reason, the evidence in support of Etzioni's claims about routinization and supervision may strike some students as exaggerated, condescending, or both.

Anticipating Objections and Alternative Judgments (p. 293)

This activity leads students to notice how Etzioni deals with readers' likely objections or alternative judgments. You could divide the class into groups to focus on different counterarguments and then report their findings to the rest of the class. In small groups, students may feel more comfortable arguing with one another about a counterargument's strengths and weaknesses.

READINGS

James Berardinelli, *"Avatar"* (p. 294)

READING FOR MEANING (p. 299)

Read to Comprehend (p. 299)

You may also wish to have students discuss Berardinelli's possible reasons for his implied and stated judgments of other films or practices (3D, other effects-driven movies, other directors).

Other words your students may need to define include *pervasive* (paragraph 5), *menagerie* (6), *dungeon master's* (6), and *ephemeral* (10).

Read to Respond (p. 299)
Students may also respond to

- Berardinelli's judgments of other films like *2012* and *Transformers 2*;
- Berardinelli's complicated take on the character of Colonel Quaritch.

Read to Analyze Assumptions (p. 300)
Students might also discuss Berardinelli's opinion that *Avatar*'s borrowing of familiar tropes from Cameron's other films as well as from *Dances with Wolves* and *The Last Samurai* is artistically acceptable rather than (as Tom Maurstad argues in a later article) reliance on weary clichés, an opinion that seems to be informed by different assumptions about what is acceptable in screenwriting.

Reading like a Writer: Presenting the Subject (p. 301)

This Reading like a Writer activity focuses on Berardinelli's choice of words in paragraph 2 to describe the genre, or genres, of the film: *science fiction, space/military culture, cross-cultural romance, love story, alien world, epic clash*. Along the way, as the text notes, he compares the film with other films in similar genres, including former Best Picture winners *Dances with Wolves* and *Titanic*. The second question asks students to think about the criteria used to judge films in these genres. This second question raises a subject that may make for a fruitful in-class discussion, given its complexity: Berardinelli has identified the film as a science-fiction, space/military, culture-clash romance, which implies a wide range of possible criteria, some of which his review might not address to reader or student satisfaction.

Considering Ideas for Your Own Writing (p. 302)

This section lists several subjects, suggested by the reading, that may stimulate student writing. You may want to ask students what other ideas for subjects they get from the reading. We have found that routinely discussing possible subjects in class encourages students to try out new ideas. Remember that there is also an array of subject suggestions in the opening Invention and Research activities of A Guide to Writing Evaluations (p. 330).

Analyzing Visuals (p. 302)

Before assigning this activity, you may want to have students familiarize themselves with Appendix 3: Strategies for Analyzing Visuals. One area that students might focus on in the poster (p. 295) accompanying Berardinelli's review is the area bounded on the left by the crescentlike outline of a moon in the distant background, and focused on the faces of the two leads. The moonlit area is nearly heart-shaped, and though the faces are placed at different distances from the viewer, the lips of Neytiri and Jake are close enough to each other to appear on the verge of kissing. If students struggle with analyzing the poster, you might draw the class's attention to each element, and ask what students make of the details, taken together.

Tom Maurstad, *"Avatar"* (p. 303)

READING FOR MEANING (p. 304)

Read to Comprehend (p. 304)
You may also wish to have students compare Maurstad's reasons and criteria with those of Berardinelli.

Other words your students may need to define include *indeterminate* (paragraph 5), *MacGuffin* (5), and *cantankerous* (6). You might also have students look up some of the cultural references, like *Jane Goodall* (7).

Read to Respond (p. 305)
Students may also respond to

- Maurstad's decision to treat *Avatar* almost as though it were two movies;
- Maurstad's unfavorable comparison of the film to a video game.

Read to Analyze Assumptions (p. 305)
Another possibility to consider, when debating Maurstad's assumptions about originality, is that Maurstad may be indicting the film on the grounds that it is *too obviously* similar to previous, familiar storylines, a recycler of tropes rather than a subtle or creative weaver of themes capable of making them seem new again. Or students might debate the film's apparent assumption that the Na'vi needed an outsider to save them, and that Scully would be able to achieve things they themselves could not. Finally, students might consider Cameron's and Maurstad's shared assumption that the Na'vi—with their warrior culture, dangerous rites of passage, and rigid chain of command—are substantially, culturally different from the invading humans.

READING LIKE A WRITER: ASSERTING AN OVERALL JUDGMENT (p. 306)

This Reading like a Writer activity asks students to identify where Maurstad makes his overall opinion clear. Students should have little difficulty finding the spot, since Maurstad uses letter grades. You might ask whether, given that his opinion is complicated, Maurstad's use of letter grades helps make his opinion more clear than it might otherwise have been, particularly given the imbalance noted in item 2. Maurstad spends considerably more time discussing the problems he sees with the story than he does praising the film's technical achievements. Interpretations of the imbalance might vary a bit. Students might see it as a sign that he mostly hated the film and that the *C* average he gives it is dishonest. Others might see the disproportionate amount of text dedicated to the film's problems as a necessary side effect of anticipating objections by readers over the more controversial part of his opinion.

CONSIDERING IDEAS FOR YOUR OWN WRITING (p. 307)

This section lists several subjects, suggested by the reading, that may stimulate student writing. You may want to ask students what other ideas for subjects they get from the reading. We have found that routinely discussing possible subjects in class encourages students to try out new ideas. Remember that there is also an array of subject suggestions in the opening Invention and Research activity of A Guide to Writing Evaluations (p. 330).

One of the benefits of using movie reviews to teach evaluation is the ease of comparing multiple reviews of the same film. This activity asks students to compare the ways that Berardinelli and Maurstad describe *Avatar*'s story, the ways they categorize the film, and how they apply criteria based on those classifications (or not). It may be helpful if you use a class-discussion format for this activity or, as a follow-up, list genres and criteria on the board as students identify them, so that you can then chart the similarities and differences.

Christine Rosen, "The Myth of Multitasking" (p. 308)

Reading for Meaning (p. 313)

Read to Comprehend (p. 313)
In addition to asking students to explain why Rosen criticizes multitasking, you might also ask students to list reasons other people think of multitasking as good.

Other words students may need to define include *parallel processing* (paragraph 2), *perennial* (4), and *extols* (5).

Read to Respond (p. 313)
Students may also respond to

- the assertion in the title and in the Hallowell quote that multitasking is "mythical" (paragraph 5);
- the study that concluded workers lost twenty-five minutes after each interruption of concentration (paragraph 6).

Read to Analyze Assumptions (p. 314)
If students do not tackle the text's questions about the causes of unfocused attention, you might want to dedicate some time in class to them—not only will doing so give students good practice at identifying a shift in assumptions, it will also give them practice at speculating about causes, another genre of argument supported in Chapter 8. Another assumption that students might want to explore is the implied assumption by Rosen that because the term *multitasking* is a relatively recent invention, the phenomenon must also be new, or dramatically on the rise, rather than an old habit now backed by technology. Does Lord Chesterfield's quote undermine such an assumption at all? In reading his advice to his son, should we assume the behavior he praises is common, or rare?

Reading like a Writer: Giving Reasons and Support (p. 315)

This Reading like a Writer activity asks students to analyze Rosen's use of authorities—often university research studies—as support for her points. Students might discuss whether they find such studies persuasive. Would their opinions change if she had, instead, claimed support from articles in the *Los Angeles Times*, from *ABC News* polls, or from About.com? As a research exercise, you might also have students try to find one of the studies mentioned by Rosen and analyze it to see what information she left out. Do they think she represented the source material accurately and fairly? Did she leave out any information that they think might have made her argument stronger?

CONSIDERING IDEAS FOR YOUR OWN WRITING (p. 315)

This section lists several subjects, suggested by the reading, that may stimulate student writing. You may want to ask students what other ideas for subjects they get from the reading. We have found that routinely discussing possible subjects in class encourages students to try out new ideas. Remember that there is also an array of subject suggestions in the opening Invention and Research activity of A Guide to Writing Evaluations (p. 330).

A SPECIAL READING STRATEGY: LOOKING FOR PATTERNS OF OPPOSITION (p. 316)

This special reading strategy invites students to look into the ways that Rosen frames (or reframes) *multitasking* and *focused attention* through word choices. Many students will find this task difficult and mystifying unless they use the two-column chart recommended in the instructions or have done this sort of thing before. You might find it helpful to have the students complete the first step on their own, then set up a chart on the board or project one and fill in the first couple of binary patterns from Chesterfield to get them started:

Focused Attention	Multitasking
"Steady and undissipated attention" *	"Hurry, bustle, and agitation"
"mark of a superior genius" *	"symptoms of a weak and frivolous mind"

After students have the idea, you might set them loose to work individually or in teams on the rest of the activity.

Christine Romano, "Jessica Statsky's 'Children Need to Play, Not Compete': An Evaluation" (p. 317)

READING FOR MEANING (p. 321)

Read to Comprehend (p. 321)
Before having students explain the strengths and weaknesses of Statsky's arguments according to Romano, you may wish to have your students review scratch outlines, discussed in Outlining in Appendix 1: A Catalog of Critical Reading Strategies. After students have reviewed Appendix 1, they can create scratch outlines of Romano's essay. Here's one possibility:

¶ 1 Overview of Statsky's essay
¶ 2 Thesis paragraph
¶ 3–6 Strengths in Statsky's essay according to Romano
¶ 7–9 Weaknesses in Statsky's essay according to Romano
¶ 10 Conclusion

You may wish to have students further detail paragraphs 3–6 and 7–9, but even a scratch outline will clarify for students the structure of Romano's essay.

Another word students may need to define is *derived* (paragraph 9). In addition, because the four words form the basis for Romano's evaluation, you might have students agree on definitions for *appropriate*, *believable*, *consistent*, and *complete*. For instance, how much information on a subject does an essay have to include to be complete, and does the evaluator have to agree with or be persuaded by the argument before calling it "believable"?

Read to Respond (p. 321)

Students may also respond to

- the fact that Romano does not explain the logical fallacy "of failing to accept the burden of proof" (paragraph 7), which she accuses Statsky of committing;
- Romano's gross generalization that "most parents know that big cities receive special federal funding for evening, weekend, and summer recreation" (7).

Read to Analyze Assumptions (p. 322)

Students may further consider the assumptions underlying Romano's criticism of Statsky for not addressing an audience who believes that competitive sports "create a sense of community with a shared purpose," "build character through self-sacrifice and commitment to the group," and "teach children to face their fears early" (paragraph 8).

READING LIKE A WRITER: ANTICIPATING OBJECTIONS AND ALTERNATIVE JUDGMENTS (p. 323)

This Reading like a Writer activity asks students to identify Romano's anticipations of objections that parents and other supporters of competitive sports might raise against Statsky's argument, and also to evaluate Romano's accommodation or refutation of each point. Because counterarguing is a fundamental skill for all argumentative or persuasive writing tasks, you might want to devote some class time to discussing Romano's objections (both her phrasing and her positioning of objections within her paragraphs) and her kinds of support. Students should notice that in both paragraphs 7 and 8 Romano acknowledges positive qualities in Statsky's argument, even though her overall point in each paragraph is critical. Because students learning to write argument for the first time often think such positive remarks might make their arguments seem inconsistent or weak, you might discuss these aspects of her argument with the class at length.

CONSIDERING IDEAS FOR YOUR OWN WRITING (p. 324)

This section lists several subjects, suggested by the reading, that may stimulate student writing: leisure activities, hobbies, and professions with which students are familiar. A related option is for students to explore and evaluate activities they find interesting but do not participate in regularly themselves.

As a final option, you may want to ask students what other ideas for subjects they get from the reading. We have found that routinely discussing possible subjects in class encourages students to try out new ideas. Remember that there is also an array of subject suggestions in the opening Invention and Research activities of A Guide to Writing Evaluations.

Larry Ballesteros, "A Winning Formula? A Review of *Slumdog Millionaire*" (p. 325)

READING FOR MEANING (p. 328)

This Reading for Meaning activity invites students to apply to Ballesteros's essay what they have learned from the other readings in this chapter about reading to comprehend, reading to respond, and reading to analyze assumptions. You might want to have your class suggest words to define as well as brainstorm possibilities for student response and analysis.

READING LIKE A WRITER (p. 328)

This Reading like a Writer activity offers students an opportunity to focus on one of the evaluation-writing strategies covered in this chapter—presenting the subject, asserting an overall judgment, giving reasons and support, or anticipating objections and alternative judgments.

REVIEWING WHAT MAKES AN EFFECTIVE ESSAY: EVALUATIONS (p. 329)

This reflective activity makes a great transition from reading to writing. As the text suggests, this activity can be done individually or in small groups.

A GUIDE TO WRITING EVALUATIONS (p. 330)

Probably the most challenging Invention and Research activity is Developing Your Argument (p. 331). Students tend to have two kinds of difficulty—identifying standards they and their readers are likely to share and marshaling specific support for their judgments.

You can address the first problem by having students in small groups discuss why they think readers will or will not find the writer's reasons appropriate. The second problem—finding support—requires students to have ready access to the subject that is being evaluated and take careful notes so that they can, for example, quote or paraphrase bits of dialogue from a movie.

Here is an outline of A Guide to Writing Evaluations:

Invention and Research
> Choosing a Subject
> Developing Your Argument
>> Exploring Your Subject
>> Analyzing Your Readers
>> Considering Your Judgment
>> Testing Your Choice
>> Listing Reasons
>> Finding Support for Your Reasons
>> Anticipating Readers' Alternative Judgments, Questions, and Objections
>> Considering Visuals
>> Considering Your Purpose
>> Formulating a Working Thesis

Drafting
> Setting Goals
> Working with Sources: Using Summary to Support Your Evaluative Argument (box)
> Organizing Your Draft
> Considering a Useful Sentence Strategy (Comparative Terms)

Reading a Draft Critically (box)
> Read for a First Impression
> Read Again to Suggest Improvements

Revising

Editing and Proofreading

Reflecting on What You Have Learned: Evaluation (box)

Chapter 7 POSITION PAPER

This is the second of four chapters that deal with important types of argument: Evaluation (Chapter 6), Position Paper (Chapter 7), Speculating about Causes or Effects (Chapter 8), and Proposal to Solve a Problem (Chapter 9). The introduction to this chapter contrasts the position paper with the proposal—pointing out that proposals have a specific, practical purpose, whereas position papers tend to be more general and philosophical. The position paper relates to the proposal in rather the same way that the reflective essay relates to the autobiographical essay. Just as reflective writing differs from autobiographical writing in its "fierce attachment to an idea," so the position paper differs from the proposal in its central concern for principles. The crux of a proposal is often a pragmatic issue—whether a particular solution will solve the problem at hand. At the heart of a position paper, there are nearly always ethical questions— questions of right and wrong —that can seldom be resolved by facts alone.

When students take a position on a controversial issue, they discover not only that people differ but also that they may have good reasons for their different views. Students learn to respect the complexity of the issues they read and write about as well as the subtlety of others' reasoning. This chapter's emphasis on the rhetorical aspects of argumentation helps students avoid polemics. Students learn to develop an argument that is responsive to their readers' concerns and that builds a bridge of shared values.

The writing assignment requires that students examine the issue critically as they write instead of framing an argument to support an already formed opinion. We encourage students to use the entire composing process to help them analyze and evaluate the issue and the different points of view on it. We urge them to examine their own underlying assumptions as critically as they would those of others. We want them to recognize the value of thinking through the issue and of basing their positions on solid reasoning and sound supporting evidence.

Students writing position papers can learn to

- choose an arguable issue and define it carefully;
- assert a position on an issue;
- give reasons that readers should take a position seriously;
- support each reason with examples, facts, analogies, statistics, anecdotes, or quotes from authorities;
- anticipate readers' questions and positions on an issue, counterarguing as needed;
- organize an essay through logically ordered reasons; and
- explicitly signal the stages in an argument taking a position.

WRITING ASSIGNMENT: Position Paper (p. 346)

Here is the writing assignment that appears near the beginning of Chapter 7:

Choose an issue that you have strong feelings about, and write an essay arguing your position on this issue. Your purpose is to convince your readers to take your argument seriously. Therefore, you will need to acknowledge readers' opposing views as well as any objections or questions they might have.

Problems Students May Have with This Assignment

Probably the greatest problem students encounter when they begin writing position papers is mistaking assertion for argumentation. This problem manifests itself in sweeping generalizations unsupported by reasons and evidence. Students with little experience developing an argument usually assume that all they need do is state what they think. They do not realize that they have to give reasons for their position and evidence to support it. Nor do they recognize how important it is to anticipate readers' objections and questions and then either to modify their own positions by acknowledging reasonable objections or to defend them by refuting unreasonable ones.

For some students, the essential problem is lack of experience in reasoning. Some students simply may be unused to setting out their reasons in a way that others can follow. For them, reading a diversity of arguments will provide instructive models. If, however, the problem stems from a lack of thoughtfulness—from the habit of relying on unexamined assumptions and biases—then the solution is more difficult. These students need first to accept the value of introspection and logical reasoning. They must recognize that the aim of argumentation is not merely to voice their own opinion but to examine it critically. The root of the problem for some students might be cognitive as well as emotional. Some students have little experience in self-analysis, let alone audience analysis. They may be able to assert their own opinions forcefully but tend to have difficulty looking critically at their own assumptions or describing carefully their own train of thought. In our experience, students with this kind of problem respond well when argumentative writing is presented as an act of communication rather than one of aggression. When the emphasis is on creating common ground instead of squashing opponents, students feel less defensive and more open to alternative ways of seeing.

RESOURCES IN CHAPTER 7 FOR TEACHING POSITION PAPERS

FINDING SUBJECTS

Writing Situations for Position Papers (p. 346)

The three brief writing situations presented early in the chapter demonstrate that writers argue for positions on controversial issues in both academic and nonacademic settings. The situations also suggest some of the many issues debated in position papers—the regulation of urban development, the cost of public education, and the right of public employees to strike. You might ask your students to brainstorm a list of other issues even before reading further in the chapter, or you might refer to these writing situations just before asking students to list subjects on which they might consider writing. During discussion of these scenarios, you might draw attention to the research described in the second and third examples. The example of the economics student describes a range of sources, but you might ask students to think of others she might have tried. The example of the political science student describes interviews of family members, both of them public employees. You might ask students to debate the advantages and disadvantages of the student's choice of sources.

Considering Ideas for Your Own Writing
These activities follow each reading except the chapter-opening and closing ones. They are designed to help students think of subjects for their own essays by considering subjects related to the readings. Here is a list summarizing the subjects suggested after Chapter 7 readings by the following authors:

Stabiner	Issues in contemporary culture, such as gender or education (p. 365)
Page	Trends that appear to pose dangers to society (p. 371)
Kirp	Issues related to university admissions policies (p. 379)
Hsu	A controversial marketing issue (p. 385)

Choosing an Issue (p. 396)
Choosing an Issue is the first activity under Invention and Research, the opening section of A Guide to Writing Position Papers. Students are urged to list possible issues in the form of *should* questions and are shown a few examples. Then they are asked to choose an arguable issue—that is, an issue "that people disagree about but that cannot be resolved simply with facts or by authorities."

Problems Students May Have Choosing an Issue
We have found no simple rule for prejudging the promise of issues for position papers. The key is for students to do the work necessary to become informed about the different points of view that people take on the issue. If they are interested only in supporting their own positions and not in learning about other points of view, then their arguments are likely to be taken seriously only by those who already agree with them.

Without making the assignment a full-blown research project, you might encourage students to discuss the issue with others and to do some reading about it. Exploring opposing views should be a required part of the invention process. Sometimes, however, students make their research one sided. It is good to seek reasons and evidence to support a position, but writers also need to be able to anticipate objections and to appeal to values and concerns they might share with others. If you choose to make this assignment a substantial research project, you might require that your students explore a minimum of two sources presenting positions that oppose their initial positions.

In A Guide to Writing Position Papers, we offer a list of possibilities to get students thinking about issues they could write about. Many of the issues we suggest are ones we think students will know and care about. Caring about the issue is essential for good writing, particularly for argumentative writing. This requirement comes as a surprise to some students—and may even be threatening to them. We have been amazed at the number of students reluctant to express an opinion. Many have been taught that it is inappropriate for them to do so. Some have been made to feel that they know too little to have an opinion worth sharing. Others believe that they are in school to consume ideas and opinions, not to produce them. For these students, we emphasize the process over the product. We explain that taking a position teaches them to analyze issues critically and to evaluate arguments. With experience, students gain confidence in their reasoning abilities and come to enjoy developing a thoughtful, well-supported argument.

104

THINKING ABOUT YOUR EXPERIENCE WITH POSITION ARGUMENTS (p. 347)

This activity will allow students to realize they have a familiarity, possibly more than they expected, with the genre, reducing the anxiety that typically accompanies the composing of any essay and making easier the remaining activities in this chapter.

CHOOSING READINGS

If you cannot teach all of the readings in this chapter, you will have to make some choices. There are at least two principles that may guide your selection: first, the interest level of the reading and its usefulness in suggesting topics for your students' essays; second, the basic features focused on in the Reading like a Writer activities.

INTEREST LEVELS OF THE READINGS

The reading selections in this chapter, beginning with the sample essay by Brian Greene, present a variety of different issues and ways of arguing. Here are brief descriptions from the table of contents to help you choose readings that might be of interest to your students:

Brian Greene, **Put a Little Science in Your Life**. A scientist argues that science is "a way of life" and that to practice and understand it is to undergo a "transformation . . . that is empowering and emotional . . . and one of the most precious of human experiences." (p. 348)

Karen Stabiner, **Boys Here, Girls There: Sure, If Equality's the Goal**. A journalist defends the position that single-sex schools benefit girls, especially those in low-income families. (p. 358)

Cristina Page, **A Mom before the Prom**. Arguing that lately the media have glamorized teenage pregnancy, an author and reproductive-rights activist points out several sobering realities about teen parenthood. (p. 367)

David L. Kirp, **Diversity Hypocrisy: The Myriad, and Often Perverse, Implications of Admissions Policies**. A professor and nationally syndicated columnist argues that the current policies to achieve diversity in admission to top colleges and universities not only fail to do so but also privilege applicants who already enjoy favoritism. (p. 372)

Tan-Li Hsu, **High on Caffeine: Regulating Energy Drinks**. Alarmed at the level of caffeine in popular energy drinks, a college student argues that the drinks put young people at risk and urges marketers to label cans and issue warnings accordingly. (p. 380)

Jessica Statsky, **Children Need to Play, Not Compete**. Documenting the excesses and dangers of competitive sports for children under the age of thirteen, a first-year college student argues for eliminating such programs in favor of programs "emphasizing fitness, cooperation, sportsmanship, and individual performance." (p. 388)

READING LIKE A WRITER ACTIVITIES

The first reading, Greene's "Put a Little Science in Your Life," introduces all the basic features of position papers through its Reading like a Writer activities. The final reading, Statsky's "Children Need to Play, Not Compete," does not specify a Reading like a Writer activity but invites students to choose a feature of the reading they think is worth analyzing.

Each of the other readings has one Reading like a Writer activity. Here is a list of these activities.

> **Counterarguing Objections and Opposing Positions:** Karen Stabiner, "Boys Here, Girls There: Sure, If Equality's the Goal" (p. 364)

> **Arguing Directly for the Position:** Cristina Page, "A Mom before the Prom" (p. 371)

> **Presenting the Issue:** David L. Kirp, "Diversity Hypocrisy: The Myriad, and Often Perverse, Implications of Admissions Policies" (p. 377)

> **Asserting a Clear, Unequivocal Position:** Tan-Li Hsu, "High on Caffeine: Regulating Energy Drinks" (p. 384)

A GUIDE TO READING POSITION PAPERS (p. 347)

The essay that is the focus of A Guide to Reading Position Papers is Greene's "Put a Little Science in Your Life."

READING FOR MEANING (p. 351)

Here are suggestions for teaching the Reading for Meaning activities following the Greene essay.

Read to Comprehend (p. 351)
To help students better understand Greene's purpose, have the class discuss the differences between the easy argument that Greene summarizes in paragraphs 4 and 5, and the more significant one he starts to make in paragraph 7.

Other words students may need to define include *ubiquity* (paragraph 4), *predictive* (7), *relativity* (8), *esoteric* (9), and *paradigm* (19).

Read to Respond (p. 351)
Students may also respond to

- Greene's occasional assertion that we enjoy the technological fruits of science even if we think science is "cold, distant and intimidating" (paragraph 10);
- the "big questions" he lists (17).

Read to Analyze Assumptions (p. 352)
Students might also debate Greene's assumptions that, in today's educational environment, science needs better public relations, and that comparing science to the humanities is to science's advantage. A related assumption that might be discussed is Greene's clear implication that art, music, and literature hold value as practices that give life meaning—an assumption not always shared by those who shape the curriculum.

READING LIKE A WRITER (p. 353)

This section helps students move from examining the content and purpose of essays to analyzing the strategies used by writers to accomplish their purposes. The five Reading like a Writer activities following Greene's essay give students a comprehensive introduction to the basic features of essays arguing a position—presenting the issue; asserting a clear, unequivocal position; arguing directly for the position; counterarguing objections and opposing positions; and establishing credibility. Each feature carries a critical reading and a writing activity that help students focus on Greene's writing strategies.

Presenting the Issue (p. 354)

This activity highlights the need for writers of position papers to inform their readers about the issue and to convince them that the issue is worth taking a position on. The activity focuses on the way Greene sets up the issue in his opening paragraphs, particularly in paragraphs 4 and 5. Students may be surprised that, in an argument about why science is important, he shows why people already believe it to be important. His position is that most people cite the wrong reasons, not that their conclusions are wrong. Students may find it productive to discuss the value of such arguments. Is it worthwhile to try to improve on an existing argument, as Greene is attempting?

Asserting a Clear, Unequivocal Position (p. 354)

This section reminds students that although informing readers about the issue is certainly part of a writer's task in taking a position, a writer must also assert a definitive position on the issue. The idea that position papers need to be assertive may lead some students to think that complicated or nuanced theses are unacceptable, so you might want to take time to discuss with students the way this section of the text qualifies its death-penalty example, emphasizing that a clear position need not be simple or monolithic. Before having students move on to the tasks in this activity, you should make sure most of them are able to reconcile qualifying with assertively stating the thesis.

The activity asks students to notice where Greene states and restates his position and to examine the context of each restatement. Some students, especially those uncomfortable with the explicitness of most position papers, may think he is being unnecessarily repetitive. The challenge is getting them to consider why he chooses to repeat his thesis —what his rhetorical purpose might be for this particular move.

Arguing Directly for the Position (p. 355)

This section lists various kinds of support that writers of position papers typically use. Students are then asked to analyze one of Greene's claims—that big questions are an important aspect of science—and the examples in paragraphs 17 and 18 that he uses to support the claim. Paragraph 17 presents examples of big questions that science poses. Paragraph 18 gives examples of theories that have recently emerged as possible answers in the field of physics. Finally, students are asked to assess the likely persuasiveness of this kind of support. As the text notes, examples are not proof (nor are they claimed by Greene to be), but they can persuade through emotions. The questions in paragraph 17, then, might be deemed effective if they awaken in readers a primal sense of awe or wonder. The list of theories in paragraph 18, however, includes no explanations or descriptions of those theories and thus might be persuasive only to readers already familiar with them. Then again, if Greene succeeds in generating a sense of mystery in paragraph 17, and readers are then surprised to hear there are possible answers to such questions in the theories he later names, they might look up those theories.

Counterarguing Objections and Opposing Positions (p. 356)

Effective arguments also address alternative and opposing viewpoints, sometimes acknowledging them, sometimes accommodating, sometimes refuting. Arguments in this chapter as well as essays in the other argumentative chapters indeed address other viewpoints. In the paragraphs students are asked to analyze for this activity, Greene both accommodates and refutes opposing viewpoints. There are, essentially, two viewpoints that he addresses: first, that science is cold and impersonal; second, that science instruction should emphasize mastery of the technicalities. He sees the first as a "shame" (paragraph 10), but understandable in light of the second viewpoint, which he believes makes science seem so cold. In dealing with each argument, he concedes some ground—science is often presented as dull, technical facts, and these facts are indeed important to a scientific education—but he also counters that science education would engage students more if teachers addressed the big questions at the heart of scientific inquiry. By taking this approach, Greene shows himself to be understanding and sympathetic to those who might oppose him rather than deliberately confrontational, and as a result, his counterargument may seem to readers to be more an extension of some shared common ground than an attack. Students may be unfamiliar and uncomfortable with this kind of "yes, but" approach; they should be encouraged to try it and practice it. One way to do so might be to have students turn, at this point, to Considering a Useful Sentence Strategy (pp. 402–04), to study and practice sentences that concede in part but follow up with immediate refutations.

Establishing Credibility (p. 357)

This activity invites students to examine their own responses as readers and, through this self-examination, to grasp more firmly the slippery concept of tone and its rhetorical effects on readers. Students are asked first to locate passages that seem credible as well as those that are problematic. Then they are urged to try to describe the tone of each passage they have marked and to follow up with a close analysis of the passage to see what triggered their responses. After they have explored their own responses and tried to identify what in the text they are reacting to, students should be ready to compare their responses with those of their classmates. This activity works well in a classroom and a course management system.

READINGS

Karen Stabiner, "Boys Here, Girls There: Sure, If Equality's the Goal" (p. 358)

READING FOR MEANING (p. 363)

Read to Comprehend (p. 363)

In addition to asking your students to explain why Stabiner favors single-sex schools for girls, you might also ask them to list the opposing arguments Stabiner identifies and responds to.

Other words that your students may need to define include *parochial* (paragraph 5), *stark* (7), *bipartisan* (9), *grudgingly* (15), and *handmaidens* (17).

Read to Respond (p. 363)

Students might also respond to

- any of Stabiner's points in light of experiences they have had with coeducation;
- Stabiner's suggestion that "the political debate about vouchers and school choice" (paragraph 19) may be shaping the discussion about single-sex schools;
- Stabiner's argument that "single-sex public schools and classes, as odd as it may sound, are about inclusion; any school district that wants one can have one and everyone can learn from the experience" (20).

Read to Analyze Assumptions (p. 363)

You might also ask students to explore

- the assumptions behind Stabiner's use of the word *handmaiden* in her sentence "Will there be a group of educational handmaidens, girls who are consigned to coed schools to keep the boys from acting out?" (paragraph 17);
- the assumptions suggested by the comment after the dash in the following sentence: "The new educational reform law is called the No Child Left Behind Act, an irresistible sentiment with a chilling edge to it—did we ever actually intend to leave certain children behind?" (21).

READING LIKE A WRITER: COUNTERING OBJECTIONS AND OPPOSING POSITIONS (p. 364)

This Reading like a Writer activity focuses on Stabiner's strategy for counterarguing and how she structures her argument in relation to likely objections from her readers. Students are asked to identify where Stabiner acknowledges, refutes, and concedes the objections. You might have a class discussion or use a course management system to have a discussion about how convincingly she frames the issue of same-sex schools when she addresses her opposition.

CONSIDERING IDEAS FOR YOUR OWN WRITING (p. 365)

This section lists several subjects, suggested by the reading, that may stimulate student writing. You may want to ask students what other ideas for subjects they get from the reading. We have found that routinely discussing possible subjects in class encourages students to try out new ideas. Remember that there is also an array of subject suggestions in the opening Invention and Research activities of A Guide to Writing Position Papers (p. 396).

A SPECIAL READING STRATEGY—COMPARING AND CONTRASTING RELATED READINGS: ORENSTEIN'S "THE DAILY GRIND: LESSONS IN THE HIDDEN CURRICULUM" AND STABINER'S "BOYS HERE, GIRLS THERE: SURE, IF EQUALITY'S THE GOAL" (p. 366)

Orenstein's observational essay in Chapter 3 and Stabiner's position paper in Chapter 7 harmonize well, since both concern the ways that a mix of boys and girls in a classroom can complicate education. It may be tempting for students who read both essays to answer the first part of the activity with a simple, "Yes, Stabiner's single-sex classes would make Orenstein and her subject Amy Wilkinson happier," but the question also asks what girls like Wilkinson might lose in the switch to all-girl classrooms. There is no right or wrong answer to this question, but students should consider or even debate this part of the question before moving onto the second part of the activity. The second part gives students another opportunity to think about differences between the two essays, by considering their differing purposes and genres. Another way to express this question, if students seem stumped, is to ask, "What strategic advantages might Orenstein's observational essay have that Stabiner's does not? What advantages might an overt position paper like Stabiner's have over an observational essay?"

Cristina Page, "A Mom before the Prom" (p. 367)

Read to Comprehend (p. 369)
Students might also explain the position that Page assigns to teen girls watching *Juno* and Bristol Palin, the position that Page is opposing.

Other words students might need to define include *lavish* (paragraph 5) and *foisted* (7).

Read to Respond (p. 369)
Students might also respond to

- Page's decision to include a fictitious character who many saw as a positive role model (*Juno*) among her targets;
- the notion of pregnancy pacts;
- the relative inattention that is paid, in such discussions, to the teen fathers.

Read to Analyze Assumptions (p. 369)
Other assumptions that students might discuss include

- the assumption that Bristol Palin's child would receive a Secret Service detail;
- the assumption that three famous Caucasian girls from middle- or upper-class families would have much influence on the many American teens who do not belong to their ethnic group or social classes;
- Page's assumption that issues highly correlated with teen pregnancy are caused by teen pregnancy.

READING LIKE A WRITER: ARGUING DIRECTLY FOR THE POSITION (p. 371)

This Reading like a Writer activity asks students to choose two of the strategies Page uses to support her position and to analyze and evaluate them. This activity is an excellent opportunity for students to work in small groups in class or in a course management system. Each group can report to the class or post its findings on one strategy, offering an assessment of how convincing Page is, with examples from the essay.

CONSIDERING IDEAS FOR YOUR OWN WRITING (p. 371)

This section lists several subjects, suggested by the reading, that may stimulate student writing. You may want to ask students what other ideas for subjects they get from the reading. We have found that routinely discussing possible subjects in class encourages students to try out new ideas. Remember that there is also an array of subject suggestions in the opening Invention and Research activity of A Guide to Writing Position Papers (p. 396).

David L. Kirp, "Diversity Hypocrisy: The Myriad, and Often Perverse, Implications of Admissions Policies" (p. 372)

Read to Comprehend (p. 375)
Kirp clearly expects that many readers might be shocked or even offended by his argument. Students might want to take some time to describe the beliefs that Kirp seems

to believe his readers hold. Students might also want to identify what sort of change Kirp favors.

Other words students may need to define include *mantra* (paragraph 1), *retrograde* (1), *quota* (2), *trolls* (8), *double-speak* (9), *wonted* (10), *boon* (13), and *cachet* (14).

Read to Respond (p. 376)
Students might also respond to Kirp's argument that Asian students are "the new Jews" or to the described plight of male athletes.

Read to Analyze Assumptions (p. 376)
Students may find Kirp's argument difficult to follow, partly because he uses difficult words at a higher rate than some other authors in the book but also because his thesis isn't as explicitly stated as students might be used to. If they have had trouble summarizing his argument in Read to Comprehend (above), you might want to spend time walking them through the second part of Read to Analyze Assumptions, "assumptions about what admissions policies *should* be" (p. 377). That section focuses their attention on what Kirp wants to see happen and on the places in his essay where his idea is most clear.

Students might also discuss Kirp's assumption that the goal of admitting more poor, minority students remains valid, even if he thinks the policies enacted to pursue that goal don't work. Another idea students might explore is the common assumption (implied in Kirp's argument) that the right admissions policy will fix large-scale social imbalances, even if current preparation levels and on-campus support systems remain the same.

READING LIKE A WRITER: PRESENTING THE ISSUE (p. 377)

This Reading like a Writer activity focuses on Kirp's strategy of redefining an issue. Students are asked to identify key words connected to *diversity* as they skim the first few paragraphs to see how Kirp develops his argument about admissions policies. After students have written about how Kirp redefines or reframes the history of diversity-oriented admissions policies to argue that they have been hypocritical, you might have a discussion online or in class about how persuasive his reframing is.

A SPECIAL READING STRATEGY: EVALUATING THE LOGIC OF AN ARGUMENT (p. 378)

Here students are directed to review the guidelines (in Appendix 1: A Catalog of Critical Reading Strategies) for evaluating the logic of an argument and apply them to Kirp's essay. You might divide up the essay and assign chunks to different student teams; they might start by highlighting, identifying, or listing the support Kirp offers in his essay and noting which claims each piece of evidence backs. Until the students have a list of the claims and supporting evidence used in the essay, analyzing for appropriateness, believability, consistency, and completeness will be challenging. As additional preparation for this activity, students might read or review Christine Romano's essay in Chapter 6 (p. 317) evaluating Jessica Statsky's essay in this chapter (p. 388), since it applies the same test of logic at length.

CONSIDERING IDEAS FOR YOUR OWN WRITING (p. 379)

This section lists several subjects, suggested by the reading, that may stimulate student writing. You may want to ask students what other ideas for subjects they get from the reading. We have found that routinely discussing possible subjects in class encourages students to try out new ideas. Remember that there is also an array of subject suggestions in the opening Invention and Research activity of A Guide to Writing Position Papers (p. 396).

Tan-Li Hsu, "High on Caffeine: Regulating Energy Drinks" (p. 380)

READING FOR MEANING (p. 383)

Read to Comprehend (p. 383)

In addition to summarizing Hsu's position on energy drinks, students might list or review his characterizations of the positions of others, such as advocates for the beverage industry.

Other terms students may need to define include *stimulant* (paragraph 1) and *vicious cycle* (8).

Read to Respond (p. 383)

Students may also respond to

- the dangers of caffeine intoxication (which might be news to readers);
- the vicious cycle described in paragraph 8;
- Hsu's characterization of energy-drink manufacturers.

Read to Analyze Assumptions (p. 383)

In a case of nested assumptions, Hsu assumes that the beverage industry assumes it will lose sales if it puts warnings on its cans. Either of these assumptions (Hsu's or the imagined beverage industry assumption) could be worthwhile to discuss or debate. Later, Hsu assumes marketers "fail to realize the consequences" (paragraph 6) of their marketing strategies, but others might assume they realize the consequences but do not care. Both Hsu's assumption and the alternative one presented here could be subjects for an engaging discussion.

READING LIKE A WRITER: ASSERTING A CLEAR, UNEQUIVOCAL POSITION (p. 384)

This Reading like a Writer activity focuses on how Hsu states, restates, and qualifies his position. Students are directed to specific paragraphs and are asked to notice whether Hsu's position statements are clear and unequivocal. In class discussion or in a discussion thread of a course management system, students could first address the overall effectiveness of Hsu's position statements and then consider whether or not his statements appear consistent. (Students who read too quickly might think Hsu contradicts himself because in some paragraphs, like paragraph 4, he is anticipating manufacturer objections at the same time that he's restating his position, which some students might interpret as self-refutation. Having them read more slowly, or aloud, may help dispel this confusion.) Ask students if Hsu's position statements are equally effective for all readers — or if a certain audience may respond more favorably.

CONSIDERING IDEAS FOR YOUR OWN WRITING (p. 385)

This section lists several subjects, suggested by the reading, that may stimulate student writing. You may want to ask students what other ideas for subjects they get from the reading. We have found that routinely discussing possible subjects in class encourages students to try out new ideas. Remember that there is also an array of subject suggestions in the opening Invention and Research activity of A Guide to Writing Position Papers (p. 396).

A SPECIAL READING STRATEGY: USING A TOULMIN ANALYSIS (p. 386)

The special reading strategy following Hsu's essay asks students to perform a Toulmin analysis as presented in Appendix 1: A Catalog of Critical Reading Strategies. If your students have not read and discussed the section on using a Toulmin analysis, you should have them do so now. Although we walk students through the first example of how to analyze the claim, reasons, and grounds, students are likely to find applying Toulmin to the second and third examples a challenging task. They may need your guidance and some practice. Perhaps the most valuable part of Toulmin's approach to argumentation is the focus on the writer's language and the emotional associations of word choices. You may need to spend some time helping students unpack the connotations.

Jessica Statsky, "Children Need to Play, Not Compete" (p. 388)

ANALYZING VISUALS (p. 393)

Students may be inspired by Statsky's inclusion of a relevant cartoon to include cartoons or other art with their work as well. For this reason, discussing its connections to the text and what it adds to the argument may be worthwhile even if you are not regularly using the Analyzing Visuals features. The questions listed in the activity prompt are particularly well suited for exploring the connections between argument and cartoon, ending with an invitation to imagine another illustration, a move that can give students some practice in thinking about ways to illustrate an argument. (Some may decide that selecting an illustration is harder than it looks.)

The cartoon itself might also be analyzed more closely. For instance, you might ask students how they interpret these details:

- Mrs. Enright is already at the plate and ready to swing the bat;
- the coach is taking no actions, other than to speak to her politely;
- Tommy appears to be looking up (toward whom? with what sort of expression?);
- the catcher is ready to play, even with Mrs. Enright at bat, and most of the other characters in the background seem to be carrying on with business as usual.

READING FOR MEANING (p. 394)

This Reading for Meaning activity invites students to apply to Statsky's essay what they have learned from the other readings in this chapter about reading to comprehend, reading to respond, and reading to analyze assumptions. You might want to have your class suggest words to define as well as brainstorm possibilities for response and analysis.

READING LIKE A WRITER (p. 394)

This Reading like a Writer activity offers students an opportunity to focus on one of the strategies for writing position papers covered in this chapter—presenting the issue, asserting a clear and unequivocal position, arguing directly for a position, counterarguing objections and opposing positions, or establishing credibility.

REVIEWING WHAT MAKES AN EFFECTIVE ESSAY: POSITION PAPERS (p. 395)

This reflective activity makes a great transition from reading to writing. As the text suggests, this activity can be done individually or in small groups.

A GUIDE TO WRITING POSITION PAPERS (p. 396)

Throughout the guide, we encourage students to consider their purpose and audience, and we also emphasize the deliberative aspects of argumentation, asking students to explore their own perspectives as well as other points of view. When advising students on how to address readers, you might want to discuss with them how likely it is that they will change their readers' minds. This is an important point because students often believe that the objective of a position paper is to prove the opposition wrong. In fact, many position papers have much more modest goals, such as merely to convince an entrenched opposition that the writer's position is reasonable and deserves serious consideration and respect. Readers may disagree with the writer, but a position paper serves a valuable purpose if readers gain a better understanding of the writer's view and a more tolerant attitude toward it.

Here is an outline of A Guide to Writing Position Papers:

Invention and Research
    Choosing an Issue
    Developing Your Argument
        Defining the Issue
        Considering Your Own Position and Reasons for It
        Researching the Issue
        Analyzing Your Readers
        Rehearsing the Argument for Your Position
        Rehearsing Your Counterargument
        Testing Your Choice
        Considering Visuals
        Considering Your Purpose
        Formulating a Working Thesis

Drafting
    Setting Goals
    Organizing Your Draft
    Working with Sources: Quoting and Paraphrasing (box)
    Considering a Useful Sentence Strategy (Concession and Immediate Refutation)

Reading a Draft Critically (box)
    Read for a First Impression
    Read Again to Suggest Improvements

Revising
    Troubleshooting Your Draft (table)
        To Present the Issue More Effectively
        To Assert the Position More Clearly and Unequivocally
        To Strengthen the Argument Directly for the Position
        To Improve the Counterargument

Chapter 8 SPECULATING ABOUT CAUSES OR EFFECTS

This is the third in a series of four chapters dealing with important types of argument: Evaluation (Chapter 6), Position Paper (Chapter 7), Speculating about Causes or Effects (Chapter 8), and Proposal to Solve a Problem (Chapter 9). In this chapter, students learn about causal argument—argument about the influence of one thing on another, when the nature of this influence cannot be proved. Since this kind of argumentation concerns explanation and prediction, it is a crucial mode of inquiry and writing in the sciences and social sciences. Arguments about causes or effects, in turn, become important elements in proposals as writers use these arguments to explain what has caused a problem, what its effects will be if no solution is found, and what effects each possible solution is likely to have.

In discussing the introduction to this chapter, you should help students see that the focus is on analysis and argument about possible causes or effects of events, trends, or phenomena. The selections do not simply summarize others' proposed causes or effects but argue inventively for the writers' own beliefs about causes or effects for a subject that cannot presently (or perhaps ever) be explained definitively. Students' essays should also present speculative arguments. Students may very well research proposed causes or effects that they do not report in their essay. During research, they will weigh and evaluate each cause or effect in light of their understanding of the subject and their chosen argument. They should then argue for their preferred causes or effects, whether they discovered them on their own or turned them up in their research.

In the process of reading and writing essays that speculate on causes or effects, students learn a great deal. This chapter can teach students to

- choose an event, trend, or phenomenon that remains open to speculation about its possible causes or effects;
- present a subject to be speculated about;
- propose likely causes or effects;
- support proposed causes or effects with facts, examples, statistics, cases, quotes from authorities, or anecdotes;
- anticipate readers' questions and preferred causes or effects, counterarguing as needed;
- organize an essay through a logical sequence of causes or effects; and
- signal explicitly the stages of cause or effect reasoning.

You could emphasize that this assignment builds on what students have learned writing other genres in *Reading Critically, Writing Well*. Students may recall thinking and writing about causes or effects when writing autobiography (Chapter 2), observation (Chapter 3), reflection (Chapter 4), or explaining concepts (Chapter 5). When evaluating causes and effects proposed by others, students may need to remember what they learned when writing evaluations (Chapter 6). In previous chapters, students also gain considerable experience supporting assertions with facts, examples, anecdotes, and quotes from authorities. In addition, they have read and written essays that are organized logically by topic and cued explicitly. All this experience should increase students' confidence as they approach this challenging new assignment.

WRITING ASSIGNMENT: Speculating about Causes or Effects (p. 411)

Here is the writing assignment that appears near the beginning of Chapter 8:

Choose a subject—an event, a phenomenon, or a trend—that invites you to speculate about its causes or effects: why it may have happened or what its effects may be. Write an essay arguing for your proposed causes or effects. Essays about causes look to the past to ponder why something happened, whereas essays about effects guess what is likely to happen in the future. Whether you choose to write about causes or effects, you need to do two things: (1) establish the existence and significance of the subject, and (2) convince readers that the causes or effects you propose are plausible.

Problems Students May Have with This Assignment

Speculating about causes or effects really requires making a double argument. The writer must first establish the existence of the event, phenomenon, or trend and then argue for possible causes or effects of it. Both parts are important, but students sometimes neglect one or the other. Students who choose a trend have the added burden of demonstrating that the rate of something actually is increasing over a specified time period. Students may need special encouragement and help to make sure that they do justice to both parts of the assignment.

Another common problem students may encounter involves presenting only predictable or obvious causes or effects, leading the reader to ask, So what? This particular problem is most likely to occur when students choose a widely recognized trend, event, or phenomenon. They rely on the obvious instead of coming up with more inventive or probing explanations. Students also go amiss when they mention alternative causes or effects but do not refute or give reasons for accepting them. An even more fundamental problem occurs when students fail to consider alternative causes or effects, merely presenting those they think are likely and ignoring other possibilities.

A Guide to Writing Essays Speculating about Causes or Effects (p. 469) has been devised to forestall problems like these, but your students may need extra coaching—especially, if you want them to write about causes, which tend to be more challenging than effects. Consider spending some class time on one or two students' subjects. List obvious causes or effects and then develop them with background causes or long-term effects. You might also consider having students do this assignment twice: in small groups with your active support and then by themselves. The first time around you could supply a rather circumscribed subject, possibly one that does not require research or for which you might provide research material.

RESOURCES IN CHAPTER 8 FOR TEACHING ESSAYS SPECULATING ABOUT CAUSES OR EFFECTS

Finding Subjects

Writing Situations for Essays Speculating about Causes or Effects (p. 412)

These three brief writing situations demonstrate that writers analyze and explain the causes or effects of events, phenomena, and trends in both academic and nonacademic settings. The three situations also illustrate two important decisions students will make as they begin to consider writing their own essays: whether to write about causes or effects and whether to write about events, phenomena, or trends. The first writing situation examines the causes of a phenomenon (which students may note might also have been treated as a trend), the second speculates about causes of a trend, and the third analyzes the effects of a subject that could be treated as either a phenomenon or trend. Discuss the situations with the class, emphasizing both the particular decisions the writers had to make and the unique features of this kind of writing. While discussing these scenarios, consider asking students to speculate about alternative causes or effects for each of the three situations, and ask which alternatives probably ought to be addressed by each of the three authors.

Considering Ideas for Your Own Writing

These activities follow each reading except the chapter-opening, online, and closing ones. They are designed to help students think of subjects for their own essays by considering subjects related to the readings. Here is a list summarizing the subjects suggested after Chapter 8 readings by the following authors:

Wallis	Phenomena or trends caused by changes in technology (p. 435)
Sunstein	The causes of a significant social problem (p. 443)
Carr	The effects of trends or phenomena related to new technologies (p. 455)
Khella	Phenomena or trends related to health, exercise, or body-consciousness (p. 463)

Choosing a Subject (p. 469)

Choosing a Subject is the first activity under Invention and Research, the opening section of A Guide to Writing Essays Speculating about Causes or Effects. Students are shown possible subjects, grouped under the categories *trends*, *events*, and *phenomena*. You might urge students from day one to begin compiling a list of possibilities. You might spend a few minutes at the beginning of each class discussing their ideas.

Problems Students May Have Choosing a Subject

We have found that most of our students need careful guidance in choosing subjects for this assignment. You may need to steer them away from events with a single obvious cause or effect. For students who want to write about a phenomenon, you will probably need to remind them that they must demonstrate that their subjects involve established patterns of behavior and are not merely one-time events or trends. For those writing about a trend, you will almost certainly need to help them establish that the pattern really is a significant trend, involving long-term changes in behavior rather than short-term, faddish shifts.

The following types of topics pose particular challenges for students:

- Causes or effects of historical events, phenomena, or past trends (for instance, an explanation of the increase in brain size during early human evolution). These subjects involve students in a different kind of research than that required by more current topics. These essays tend to read like research reports of others' observations. One way to help students stay on task is to encourage them to look for areas of dispute in the literature so that, at the very least, they are taking sides in a debate about causes and effects.
- Causes or effects of phenomena observed in personal life (competitiveness, procrastination, popularity, laziness). Students writing about these subjects may

tend to rely exclusively on anecdotal information from their own experience rather than generalize from their own experiences to larger conclusions about the phenomenon.

- Causes of trends relating to technology (increasing use of scanners and digital cameras, declining cost of televisions). Students sometimes choose to write about these subjects because it is easy to document the existence of the trend itself; however, students often have difficulty going beyond the obvious explanation of technological advances in analyzing the causes of such trends.

- Subjects that could be approached as either phenomena or trends (teenage suicide, popular activities like windsurfing or snowboarding). Students will need to decide whether to treat the topic as a trend or as a phenomenon.

Since subject choice is so important and problematic, you might try this in-class activity. After discussing the readings, list several possible events, phenomena, or trends on the board. Ask small groups of students to choose a subject and prepare a defense of it for the class. They must argue that the subject is actually an event, a phenomenon, or a trend; that it is a researchable subject; and that its causes or effects are not already settled—that is, that they still require speculation.

THINKING ABOUT YOUR EXPERIENCE: SPECULATING ABOUT CAUSES AND EFFECTS (p. 412)

This activity will allow students to realize they have a familiarity, possibly greater than they expected, with the genre, reducing the anxiety that typically accompanies composing any essay and making the remaining activities in this chapter easier.

CHOOSING READINGS

If you cannot teach all the readings in this chapter, you will have to make some choices. There are at least three principles that may guide your selection: (1) the type of speculative essay; (2) the interest level of the reading and its usefulness in suggesting subjects for your students' essays; (3) the basic features focused on in the Reading like a Writer activities.

TYPES OF SPECULATIVE ESSAYS

The reading selections in this chapter, beginning with the sample essay by Stephen King, represent different types of speculative essays. Four explain causes (King, Sunstein, Khella, and Slick), and two explain effects (Wallis and Carr). Two treat established phenomena (King and Sunstein), and four treat ongoing trends (Wallis, Carr, Khella, and Slick). There are no examples of essays speculating on the causes or effects of a one-time event.

INTEREST LEVELS OF THE READINGS

Here are brief descriptions from the table of contents to help you choose readings that might be of interest to your students:

Stephen King, **Why We Crave Horror Movies**. America's best-known writer of horror novels and film scripts speculates about why we continue "daring the nightmare" in order to watch horror movies. (p. 413)

READING LIKE A WRITER ACTIVITIES

The first reading, King's "Why We Crave Horror Movies," introduces all of the basic features of speculating about causes or effects through the Reading like a Writer activities. The final reading, Slick's "Not Just for Nerds Anymore," does not specify a Reading like a Writer activity but invites students to choose a feature of the reading they think is worth analyzing. Each of the other readings has one Reading like a Writer activity. Here is a list of these activities.

Presenting the Subject: Claudia Wallis, "The Multitasking Generation" (p. 434)

Supporting Proposed Effects: Cass Sunstein, "To Become an Extremist, Hang Around with People You Agree With" (p. 443)

Counterarguing: Nicholas Carr, "Is Google Making Us Stupid?" (p. 454)

Establishing Credibility: Jeremy Khella, "The Route to American Obesity" (p. 462)

A GUIDE TO READING ESSAYS SPECULATING ABOUT CAUSES OR EFFECTS (p. 413)

The essay that is the focus of A Guide to Reading Essays Speculating about Causes or Effects is King's "Why We Crave Horror Movies."

READING FOR MEANING (p. 416)

Read to Comprehend (p. 416)
To better enable students to understand King's essay, you may wish to have them, individually or in groups, identify the movies (you may wish for them to check The Internet Movie Database, http://www.imdb.com) and the people King references: Freda Jackson (paragraph 4); *Die, Monster, Die!* (4); Robert Redford (4); Diana Ross (4); Cleveland Torso Murderer (8); Jack the Ripper (8); Leonard Nimoy (9); *Dawn of the Dead* (12); and Lennon and McCartney (13).

Other words students may need to define include *reactionary* (4), *status quo* (9), and *morbidity* (12).

Read to Respond (p. 416)
Students may also respond to

- King's informal, conversational style, or the voice (a little insane at times) King uses in composing the essay;
- King's contention that horror films are "innately conservative, even reactionary" (paragraph 4);
- the simile (paragraphs 12 and 13) in which King compares the human subconscious to a subterranean river infested with alligators.

Read to Analyze Assumptions (p. 416)
Students may also consider the assumptions underlying King's claim that "the potential lyncher is in almost all of us" (paragraph 9) and his comparison of our emotions and fears to a body needing exercise (9).

READING LIKE A WRITER ACTIVITIES

The four Reading like a Writer activities following King's essay give students a thorough introduction to writing essays speculating about causes. This section introduces students to the major elements of writing about causes or effects—presenting the subject; making a logical, step-by-step cause-and-effect argument; counterarguing; and establishing credibility. Each feature carries a reading and a writing activity that help students focus on King's writing strategies.

Presenting the Subject (p. 418)
This activity leads students to look at the way King uses examples to present the subject and establish its importance. Students will notice that King presents his subject as a phenomenon rather than as a one-time event or a trend. Students should also note that King seems to assume that he doesn't have to prove that some people crave horror movies because the phenomenon is common knowledge.

Making a Logical, Step-by-Step Cause-and-Effect Argument (p. 419)
This activity focuses on King's use of analogy, a special kind of comparison he uses to support his argument. We urge students to identify and test King's analogies. Because he is such an engaging, persuasive writer, you might need to spend some time getting students to think critically about King's use of analogy. Students need to be alert to the potential pitfalls of supporting an argument with analogy as well as other possible fallacies common to cause-and-effect argument, such as confusing correlation with cause or assuming that simply because one thing precedes another, the first causes the second.

Counterarguing (p. 419)
This section highlights the importance of anticipating objections readers might have to the argument. Students are asked specifically to consider the effectiveness of King's ventriloquizing the objection "Why bother?" (paragraph 13). This activity could generate some lively argument, depending to a large extent on students' own attitudes toward horror movies.

Establishing Credibility (p. 420)

This activity asks students to think about the ways King gains readers' confidence. Since King is a well-known writer of horror novels, several of which have been made into movies, the reader is clearly expected to consider him an authoritative source.

Students may or may not find this authority convincing on its own (or may not even recognize it, if they are unfamiliar with his work, as many students today may be). Some students may ask why King's argument makes no reference to the large body of psychological and social science research on this subject, while others may defend King's strategy, arguing that such a reference is neither necessary nor appropriate, given his original audience of *Playboy* magazine readers.

You could also point out that King attempts to bond with readers by linking his observations about human behavior to actions most people have experienced or witnessed: "We've all known people who talk to themselves" (paragraph 2); we've all heard "sick" jokes (paragraph 11); most of us have experienced emotions that might be called "uncivilized." King's recognition that these experiences are shared, which is reflected in his use of the first-person plural pronouns *we* and *us*, helps readers accept his argument.

READINGS

Claudia Wallis, "The Multitasking Generation" (p. 422)

READING FOR MEANING (p. 432)

Read to Comprehend (p. 433)

After having students explain Wallis's argument about the effects of multitasking, you might have them also identify the trend she describes (increasing multitasking) and the causes she credits for it.

Other words students may need to define include *space-time* (paragraph 2), *MacArthur "genius" grant* (10), *perfunctory* (11), *quaint* (13), *prowess* (15), and *toggling* (19).

Read to Respond (p. 433)

Students may also respond to

- Wallis's evidence that humans can't really multitask as they think they do;
- the idea that young people try on identities;
- Wallis's argument that human minds need breaks, or downtime.

Read to Analyze Assumptions (p. 433)

Students may also explore

- Wallis's apparent assumption that some of the tasks multitasked by Generation M cannot become "highly practiced" like slicing an onion;
- the assumption that there's a significant difference between "multitasking" and "sequential processing";
- the assumption that perceived lower tolerance for ambiguity (paragraph 28) is connected to multitasking.

121

READING LIKE A WRITER: PRESENTING THE SUBJECT (p. 434)

This Reading like a Writer activity draws students' attention to the examples, statistics, and authorities Wallis uses in paragraphs 1–9 and 11 to present her subject, multitasking, and to show some of its impacts on family life. The final question asks students to find evidence of these effects repeated throughout the essay (say, in paragraph 34), but some students might skip or overlook the question. For this reason, you might wish to have students list the effects they've found and then, as a class, look through the essay for repeated themes and effects.

CONSIDERING IDEAS FOR YOUR OWN WRITING (p. 435)

This section lists several subjects, suggested by the reading, that may stimulate student writing. You may want to ask students what other ideas for subjects they get from the reading. We have found that routinely discussing possible subjects in class encourages students to try out new ideas. Remember that there is also an array of subject suggestions in the opening Invention and Research activity of A Guide to Writing Essays Speculating about Causes or Effects (p. 469).

A SPECIAL READING STRATEGY — COMPARING AND CONTRASTING RELATED READINGS: WALLIS'S "THE MULTITASKING GENERATION" AND ROSEN'S "THE MYTH OF MULTITASKING" (p. 436)

This special reading strategy following Wallis's essay provides an opportunity for students to see how writers use different genres to discuss the same subject. If your students have not read and discussed the section on comparing and contrasting related readings in Appendix 1: A Catalog of Critical Reading Strategies, you might have them take the time to do so now. We ask students to explore the authors' definitions of *multitasking* and their approaches to the subject. If you find such activities productive, you might have students compare these two essays with Nicholas Carr's "Is Google Making Us Stupid?," later in this chapter. Carr's essay, like Wallis's, expresses alarm at the declining ability of people to focus deeply and also seems to link that decline to use of the Internet.

Cass Sunstein, "To Become an Extremist, Hang Around with People You Agree With" (p. 437)

READING FOR MEANING (p. 441)

Read to Comprehend (p. 441)

You may also ask students to explain briefly how Sunstein applies the theory of group polarization to specific incidents, or to summarize his complicated opinion of extremism (see paragraph 16).

Other words students may need to define include *fascism* (paragraph 1), *group dynamics* (3), *tentative* (11), and *corroboration* (11).

Read to Respond (p. 441)

Students may also respond to

- Sunstein's specific examples, some of which might seem to readers to be good, worthwhile movements;

- the utility or applicability of Sunstein's argument, possibly by applying it to examples he did not discuss himself.

Read to Analyze Assumptions (p. 442)

Students may very well be able to think of group experiences in which the group changed its mind, emerged fairly moderate, or arrived at a conclusion the members themselves did not support. If they seem to assume these examples falsify Sunstein's argument, you might ask them how many different opinions they heard in such instances—do their examples verify Sunstein's corollary that mixed groups may be better inoculated against polarization? You might also ask students to consider the assumptions that people with minority viewpoints make when the groups around them seem to agree on a different direction. Do they tend to assume there will be negative consequences if they speak up to disagree? Is such an assumption always warranted?

READING LIKE A WRITER: SUPPORTING PROPOSED EFFECTS (p. 443)

This Reading like a Writer section asks students to explain how Sunstein supports his proposed effect and to evaluate how successfully he does so. His strategy in the designated paragraphs is to argue from examples, and he chooses many of them from a wide range of scenarios, perhaps in the hopes that readers will be familiar with at least one of the subjects and recognize the sort of behavior he's alluding to. In this case, the examples don't seem to be intended to address pathos or awaken emotions; instead, they seem calculated to persuade by raising the likelihood that readers will recognize that they have already seen the phenomenon of group polarization but maybe did not understand the mechanism that drove it. This sort of move—attempting to connect with truths already accepted by readers—is often a useful strategy and thus worth highlighting.

CONSIDERING IDEAS FOR YOUR OWN WRITING (p. 443)

This section lists several subjects, suggested by the reading, that may stimulate student writing. You may want to ask students what other ideas for subjects they get from the reading. We have found that routinely discussing possible subjects in class encourages students to try out new ideas. Remember that there is also an array of subject suggestions in the opening Invention and Research activity of A Guide to Writing Essays Speculating about Causes or Effects (p. 469).

Nicholas Carr, "Is Google Making Us Stupid?" (p. 445)

READING FOR MEANING (p. 452)

Read to Comprehend (p. 452)

In addition to having students summarize Carr's concerns, you might have them discuss the point Carr is trying to make with his allusions to *2001: A Space Odyssey*. (It might be helpful to find the scene online or bring in a DVD to play the scene in question.)

Other words students may need to define include *staccato* (paragraph 6), *cognition* (7), *consortium* (7), *sea change* (7), *plastic* (10)—note that here it is used in a way that might be unfamiliar to students), *clockwork* (11), *gewgaws* (13), *ethic* (15), *Luddites* (22), and *stoked* (22).

Read to Respond (p. 452)

Students may also respond to

- their previous experiences with deep reading—not only of novels but of substantive nonfiction;
- the ambitions of Google's founders to augment our minds with artificial intelligence;
- the idea that the mind, even in adulthood, remains "plastic" (paragraph 10).

Read to Analyze Assumptions (p. 452)

You might also ask students to consider

- the assumption by both Carr and Wallis (p. 422) that ambiguity is a good thing that's not fully appreciated anymore;
- Carr's assumption about who his readers are, given his references to *2001*, the length of his article, and his frequent quoting of fellow writers who have made similar observations;
- the assumptions by Google's founders that we would be better off with much of our thinking handled or augmented by artificial intelligence.

READING LIKE A WRITER: COUNTERARGUING (p. 454)

This Reading like a Writer activity asks students to evaluate Carr's counterarguments and their support, an exploration that is useful training not only for this genre of writing but for the other argumentative genres as well. You might divide students into teams and have each team analyze and evaluate a counterargument from a different paragraph.

Paragraph 7 is particularly interesting because in it Carr anticipates an objection to his *evidence* rather than to a specific point he has made ("Anecdotes alone don't prove much. . . ."). However, astute students may notice that he's using the anecdotes more for clarity and for ethos than for proof: His anecdotes all center on professional writers who once could read deeply but now struggle to do so rather than on young people who supposedly no longer read books. His choice of examples clarifies his concern—he's not saying that Johnny can't read but that he himself no longer can. This move changes the character of his argument from one about a supposed fault of others to a concern about a personal loss, which makes it harder to question or criticize and has the potential to disarm knee-jerk dismissals that might arise if he were simply to talk about "today's students" while not one himself.

As a follow-up to this activity, the class might look at the original article online, where they can read Carr's historical anecdotes about Plato reacting to the written word and Squarciafico responding to the invention of the printing press—a section that does not appear in our version. (Note: Wallis also alludes to the Plato example.) In this section, Carr acknowledges that each major invention in information technology raises concerns that are valid—but that also bring unforeseen benefits. He grants that the Internet may be no different. Students might find it worthwhile to discuss the ways in which this argument is a concession, and the ways in which it acts as a refutation. A good discussion should pick up on the fact that although the section appears to be mostly a concession, it also slides in evidence that critics of such technologies have historically been right in their indictments, implying that perhaps Carr, like them, is being prescient.

The full, online article can be found at http://www.theatlantic.com/magazine/archive/2008/07/is-google-making-us-stupid/6868/.

The image that accompanies Carr's essay (a cartoon by Guy Billout) depicts a pedestrian with a book, who has presumably been pulled over for moving too slowly: The sign posts a minimum speed limit that, although not entirely legible, appears to approximate or even exceed the speed of light, depending on whether the last set of characters is "mps" and on whether that stands for "meters per second" or "miles per second." Perhaps the most useful detail for any discussion is the fact that the man with the book is a pedestrian, without a car. The only car belongs to the ticketing officer. To figure out what Billout means by the image, students will need to decide what the Internet patrol car symbolizes and what, perhaps, to make of the book. An additional detail that students might find interesting to discuss is the posture of the man with the book, compared with the posture of the ticketing officer.

CONSIDERING IDEAS FOR YOUR OWN WRITING (p. 455)

This section lists several subjects, suggested by the reading, that may stimulate student writing. You may want to ask students what other ideas for subjects they get from the reading. We have found that routinely discussing possible subjects in class encourages students to try out new ideas. Remember that there is also an array of subject suggestions in the opening Invention and Research activity of A Guide to Writing Essays Speculating about Causes or Effects (p. 469).

Jeremy Khella, "The Route to American Obesity" (p. 456)

READING FOR MEANING (p. 460)

Read to Comprehend (p. 460)
You might also have students discuss whether the essay has added to their previous understanding of the subject, and if so, in what ways.

Other terms students may need to define include *saturated fat* (paragraph 3) and *foster* (6).

Read to Respond (p. 460)
Students might also write about

- Khella's explanation of the causes for the fast-food craze—obesity essays are common in college classes, but Khella's goes a step further than most by trying to explain how the fast-food environment developed the way it has;
- the speculated role of high-fructose corn syrup in fast food and weight gain.

Read to Analyze Assumptions (p. 461)
Students might also consider

- the assumption by Khella and others citing obesity statistics that those numbers are based on valid, unproblematic definitions of *overweight* and *obese*, or that the obesity trend reflects changes in waistlines rather than changes in data gathering;
- the assumption that greed—rather than a desire to remain competitive enough to stay in business, to continue employing workers, or to provide customers with the prices and speed they desire—drives the fast-food industry's behavior;
- Khella's assumption that a solution must require government action;

- the assumption by consumers, described by Khella, that a trip to McDonald's is faster and cheaper than making food at home.

Reading like a Writer: Establishing Credibility (p. 462)

This Reading like a Writer activity engages readers in an extensive analysis and evaluation of the credibility of Khella's essay. Students are asked to examine credibility by assessing the writer on four elements—knowledge of the subject, representation of its complexity, use of explicit counterarguments, and implied attitudes and assumptions about readers. Working in groups on this activity might help students read closely. You could have each group find one example of each element in the text. Or you could divide the class into four groups and have each group examine one of four elements more extensively, finding several examples to support its judgment.

Along the way, students considering the first question are asked to evaluate Khella's sources and how he uses them. Students pursuing this thread may remark on

- the large number and diversity of sources he draws on (books, corporate Web pages, scholarly articles, Web pages of people identified in the essay as nutrition professors);
- his inclusion of an additional "works consulted" (which will probably be novel to many students);
- the frequency with which he paraphrases his information instead of quoting it; what this pattern suggests to them about his understanding of the subject;
- his organization of source material, weaving sources together by topic instead of talking first about one source and then about another (see paragraph 3, about high-fructose corn syrup, which cites four sources).

You may find that discussing Khella's use of sources before students tackle the exercise opens the door to a better analysis of his overall approach to credibility in student responses to the other three questions. Addressing the topic may also let you deal with some common unvoiced concerns that students have about sourcing—such as the popular assumption among writers-in-training that a student who cites sources "too frequently" looks to professors and graders like he or she is lazy and has not written an original paper. (This assumption drives many students not to cite sources as frequently as they ought to.) Focusing on Khella's unique arrangement and analysis of source material, his paraphrasing of that material, and the places in the text in which his own ideas shape the argument may help alleviate some of these anxieties about sourced work.

A Special Reading Strategy: Evaluating the Logic of an Argument (p. 463)

This activity asks students to apply the Evaluating the Logic of an Argument tests from Appendix 1: A Catalog of Critical Reading Strategies to Khella's text. If your class has not yet used this analytical tool, you may want to work through the Martin Luther King Jr. example in the appendix before assigning students this section on Khella. However, resist the temptation to have students work in teams for this activity. If you do, the instinctive approach for most students will be to divide up the duties among team members, with each student taking one question—and students who divide to conquer often miss out on logical connections among the points (Another option to consider may be to have students read Christine Romano's essay in Chapter 6, since it uses this test as its primary analytical tool.)

CONSIDERING IDEAS FOR YOUR OWN WRITING (p. 463)

This section lists several subjects, suggested by the reading, that may stimulate student writing. You may want to ask students what other ideas for subjects they get from the reading. We have found that routinely discussing possible subjects in class encourages students to try out new ideas. Remember that there is also an array of subject suggestions in the opening Invention and Research activity of A Guide to Writing Essays Speculating about Causes or Effects (p. 469).

Joshua Slick, "Not Just for Nerds Anymore" (p. 464)

READING FOR MEANING (p. 466)

This Reading for Meaning activity invites students to apply to Slick's essay what they have learned from the other readings in this chapter about reading to comprehend, reading to respond, and reading to analyze assumptions. You might want to have your class suggest words to define, as well as to brainstorm possibilities for response and analysis.

READING LIKE A WRITER (p. 466)

This Reading like a Writer activity offers students an opportunity to analyze one of the main strategies for writing essays that speculate about causes or effects—presenting the subject; making a logical, step-by-step cause-and-effect argument; supporting or arguing for each cause or effect; handling readers' likely objections to the proposed causes or effects; evaluating readers' alternative or preferred causes or effects; and establishing credibility.

REVIEWING WHAT MAKES AN EFFECTIVE ESSAY: SPECULATING ABOUT CAUSES OR EFFECTS (p. 468)

This reflective activity makes a great transition from reading to writing. As the text suggests, this activity can be done individually or in small groups.

A GUIDE TO WRITING ESSAYS SPECULATING ABOUT CAUSES OR EFFECTS (p. 469)

Some students have trouble understanding the terms *trend* and *phenomenon*. Perhaps the simplest way to define and distinguish these terms would be to say that a trend is a changing pattern of human behavior, while a phenomenon is a pattern that remains constant.

Perennial traditions and persistent problems are phenomena; shifts in the pattern of human behavior and problems that are improving or deteriorating are trends. If your students find this distinction too subtle, illustrate it by discussing the difference between the causes of a long-standing local problem and the causes of a sudden worsening of this problem. Different reasons are needed to explain the changing situation.

Some students also have difficulty distinguishing between a trend and a fad. A trend has some momentum and staying power and reflects significant changes in behavior or circumstances. Fads may be widespread, but they tend to be short-lived and whimsical: Changes in fashion, for instance, are often caused simply by the desire for novelty.

When students start considering causes or effects, they may need some guidance to distinguish causes from effects and to distinguish various kinds of causes and effects from one another. Background causes precede and prepare indirectly for an event or a trend, immediate causes trigger it, and perpetuating causes sustain a trend or phenomenon.

If students are writing an analysis of effects, they should consider immediate, long-term, and indirect effects of their event, trend, or phenomenon. If it has been around for some time, they may also be able to consider past effects.

Ask students to work out the relationships among their causes or effects. For instance, are any of the causes connected? Are there chains of causes to be traced? Which are the most influential causes? These sorts of questions are particularly useful for students—and there will be many of them—who find evidence of multiple causes and are tempted to conclude simply that the answer is a combination of all of them. Instead of identifying a single cause, such students might consider trying to rank the multiple causes in order of significance (giving reasons for the rankings) or show how they are related. These kinds of moves can help students steer away from easy answers toward more intellectually rewarding analytical work.

Here is an outline of A Guide to Writing Essays Speculating about Causes or Effects:

Invention and Research
    Choosing a Subject
        Trends
        Events
        Phenomena
    Developing Your Subject
        Exploring Your Subject
        Considering Causes or Effects
        Researching Your Subject
        Analyzing Your Readers
        Rehearsing Part of Your Argument
        Testing Your Choice
        Considering Visuals
        Considering Your Purpose
        Formulating a Working Thesis

Drafting
    Setting Goals
    Organizing Your Draft
    Working with Sources: Citing a Variety of Sources (box)
    Considering a Useful Sentence Strategy (Grammatically Parallel Topic Sentences)

Reading a Draft Critically (box)
    Read for a First Impression
    Read Again to Suggest Improvements

Revising
    Troubleshooting Your Draft (table)
        To Present the Subject More Effectively
        To Strengthen the Cause-and-Effect Argument
        To Strengthen the Counterargument
        To Enhance Credibility
        To Make the Organization More Effective

Editing and Proofreading

Reflecting on What You Have Learned: Speculating about Causes or Effects (box)

Chapter 9 PROPOSAL TO SOLVE A PROBLEM

This is the last in a series of four chapters dealing with important types of argument: Evaluation (Chapter 6), Position Paper (Chapter 7), Speculating about Causes or Effects (Chapter 8), and Proposal to Solve a Problem (Chapter 9). Proposals are one of the most complex kinds of argument because they can incorporate so many other kinds of writing—in fact, most of the genres presented in this book. Proposal writers often use their own experiences or observations of other people to present a problem and establish its seriousness. They explain concepts needed to understand the problem. They both evaluate the problem to demonstrate that it is serious enough to require a solution and evaluate alternative solutions to show that the proposed solution is the best one. Finally, writers analyze the problem's causes and effects to argue that the proposed solution will remove the causes and have positive, not negative, effects.

Proposals are an important and common type of writing, and many students can expect to write proposals during their postcollege careers. Jobs in government, business, science, and technology often depend on proposal writing. Although students do not ordinarily read or write many proposals in school, they may write proposals for term papers, research projects, or student-government activities. Studying proposal writing helps students learn to reconceive situations in terms of problems and solutions. The educational system teaches students to think in terms of good and bad (appropriate to writing evaluations), cause and effect (appropriate to speculation about causes or effects), and right and wrong (appropriate to position papers) but not as often in terms of problem and solution (appropriate to proposals). Nevertheless, problem solving is basic to creativity and an invaluable guide to acting in the world.

This is an especially promising assignment for a course with a service-learning component. You could first assign an observation essay (Chapter 3) in which students visit and interview people at a local site—such as a literacy program at a library, an AIDS prevention hotline, a voter-registration and information group such as the League of Women Voters—to identify problems people at the site are trying to solve. These problems would then become the subjects of students' proposals.

Students writing proposals can learn to

- choose a problem that needs solving and come up with a feasible solution;
- describe a problem and solution;
- give readers reasons that they should support a solution;
- support each reason with examples, facts, analogies, cases, scenarios, statistics, quotes from authorities, or anecdotes;
- anticipate readers' questions and preferred solutions, counterarguing as needed;
- organize an essay through logically ordered reasons; and
- signal explicitly the stages in an argument to support a solution.

You might want to reassure students that they have already practiced giving reasons and support, anticipating readers' objections and counterarguing, organizing essays logically, and giving explicit cues. The complexity of proposal writing makes it challenging, but students who have worked through the other chapters in *Reading Critically, Writing Well* should be well prepared.

WRITING ASSIGNMENT: Proposal to Solve a Problem (p. 484)

Here is the writing assignment that appears near the beginning of Chapter 9:

Write an essay proposing a solution to a problem affecting a community or group to which you belong. Your tasks are to analyze the problem and establish that it is serious enough to need solving, to offer a solution that will remedy the problem or at least help solve it, and to lay out the particulars by which your proposed solution would be put into effect. Address your proposal to one or more members of the group or to outsiders who could help solve the problem, being sure to take into account readers' likely objections to your proposed solution as well as any alternative solutions they might prefer.

Problems Students May Have with This Assignment

Difficulties students sometimes encounter as they write proposals involve the choice of subject and the need to establish the problem's existence and seriousness. Even though students are asked to write about a problem faced by a group to which they belong, they sometimes take on problems too abstract or complicated for them to research fully and handle effectively in a short time. It is understandable that students should want to solve the major problems our society faces—such as violence in schools, the widening gulf between rich and poor, or the general lack of civility. As much as we want to encourage students to explore these problems and try to help solve them, we also want students to have every chance of succeeding in their first effort at writing an effective proposal. Therefore, we encourage our students to choose problems that they can address at a local level and can write about in specific, rather than general, terms.

A good proposal needs to both argue for a solution and define and establish the problem. We have found that even the student who argues effectively for a solution may sometimes fail to establish the problem's existence and seriousness. This student might assume that the reader agrees there is a problem or that all readers will understand the problem in the same way. Defining the problem requires careful assessment of the rhetorical situation. Writers must gauge their readers' current understanding of the problem and construct an argument to convince readers that the problem needs and deserves their attention.

RESOURCES IN CHAPTER 9 FOR TEACHING PROPOSALS

Finding Subjects

Writing Situations for Proposals (p. 484)

The chapter opens with three brief writing situations that suggest a range of occasions for writing proposals—writing for a business situation (one of the most common domains for proposal writing), for a college political science course, and for an economics course. You might want to use these situations in a discussion of possible subjects by pointing out the different purposes and audiences, the different kinds of problems, and the different ways writers support their arguments. You may also wish to have students identify the two parts to a proposal—the establishment of the problem and the proposed course of action—in each example. Students might also benefit from discussing the method of inquiry that the managers at the pharmaceutical company used to arrive at their solution, and from estimating the amount of work involved in creating the proposal.

Finally, it might be worth stressing to students that two of the examples showcase situations in which the authors did not start out with fully crystallized ideas of how they would solve their problems. Many students are uncomfortable picking subjects or problems for which they cannot think of obvious solutions. As a result, they sometimes gravitate toward topics that have already been heavily addressed by national public-awareness campaigns designed to change the habits of readers or viewers. Students uncomfortable with problems lacking obvious solutions also tend to propose raising awareness as a first-draft solution, essentially turning their papers (or the reading of them) into their solutions. A good first step toward making students more comfortable with uncertainty in their quest for a solution is to show them that other people have made that same journey.

Considering Ideas for Your Own Writing

These activities follow each reading except the chapter-opening and closing ones. They are designed to help students think of subjects for their own essays by considering subjects related to the readings. Here is a list summarizing subjects suggested after Chapter 9 readings by the following authors:

Shughart II	A popular sport that could be improved (p. 508)
Beck	Improving the living or working conditions of a particular group of people (p. 515)
Kornbluh	A problem that seems to be national but might be solvable on a local scale (p. 524)
O'Malley	Established practices in high school and college that could be improved or refined (p. 532)

Choosing a Problem (p. 538)

Choosing a Problem is the first activity under Invention and Research, the opening section of A Guide to Writing Proposals. Students are urged to list groups or organizations to which they belong and then think of problems faced by these institutions. We encourage students to choose problems plaguing communities in which they are actively involved—such as their neighborhood, dorm, or sports team—both to motivate them and to provide a real-world context for their writing.

Problems Students May Have Choosing a Subject

Choosing an appropriate subject is probably the hardest part of proposal writing. Some students know immediately what they want to write about, while others struggle to find something appropriate. Perhaps the greatest stumbling block is abstraction. The more distant the problem is from personal experience, the harder it is to write about. That is why we urge students to choose a problem affecting a group to which they belong. Even the most abstract problems can be treated in a local context. Those concerned with broad educational problems, for example, might find evidence of the problem in their own high school or college. Those concerned with social and economic problems like homelessness and unemployment might look in their communities.

Writing about a problem of a group to which they belong will also help students with the crucial task of analyzing their readers. They can more easily anticipate possible objections to their solutions and alternative solutions readers might prefer. They can also draw on common values and experience to establish the seriousness of the problem and argue for the feasibility of the proposed solution.

THINKING ABOUT YOUR EXPERIENCE WITH PROPOSALS (p. 485)

This activity will allow students to realize they have a familiarity, possibly greater than they expected, with the genre, reducing the anxiety that typically accompanies composing an essay and making the remaining activities in this chapter easier.

CHOOSING READINGS

The reading selections in this chapter, beginning with the sample essay by Steven Hill, present a variety of different issues and ways of arguing. If you cannot teach all the readings in this chapter, you will have to make some choices. There are at least two principles that may guide your selection: (1) the interest level of the readings and their usefulness in suggesting subjects for your students' essays; (2) the basic features focused on in the Reading like a Writer activities.

INTEREST LEVELS OF THE READINGS

Here are brief descriptions from the table of contents to help you choose readings that might be of interest to your students:

Steven Hill, **Instant Runoff Voting**. An election system based on having voters rank the candidates on a ballot rather than vote for just one of them would help revitalize American democracy by reducing polarized partisan politics, argues a leading proponent of the change. (p. 486)

William F. Shughart II, **Why Not a Football Degree?** Impatient with what he calls "half-measures" that have been adopted or proposed to try to reform college sports, an economics professor recommends a three-pronged solution that treats the issue as a business proposition. (p. 501)

Gary Beck, **Not Your Everyday Homeless Proposal.** A writer and theater director proposes an urban-rural partnership solution to the problem of homelessness. (p. 509)

Karen Kornbluh, **Win-Win Flexibility**. An economist and political activist proposes a solution to a problem faced by the new "juggler family," in which parents have trouble balancing their time between working and caring for their children and elderly parents. (p. 516)

Patrick O'Malley, **More Testing, More Learning**. In a strongly reasoned message to professors on his campus, a first-year college student advocates an increase in testing throughout the academic term. (p. 525)

Jeff Varley, **High-School Starting Time**. A first-year college student, remembering the difficulty of having to attend early-morning classes in high school, proposes a simple solution: changing the starting time. (p. 533)

READING LIKE A WRITER ACTIVITIES

The first reading, Hill's "Instant Runoff Voting," introduces all the basic features of proposals through its Reading like a Writer activities. The final reading, Varley's "High-

School Starting Time," does not specify a Reading like a Writer activity but invites students to choose a feature of the reading they think is worth analyzing. Each of the other readings has one Reading like a Writer activity. Here is a list of these activities.

Introducing the Problem: William F. Shughart II, "Why Not a Football Degree?" (p. 507)

Presenting the Proposed Solution: Gary Beck, "Not Your Everyday Homeless Proposal" (p. 514)

Counterarguing Readers' Objections and Alternative Solutions: Karen Kornbluh, "Win-Win Flexibility" (p. 523)

Arguing Directly for the Proposed Solution: Patrick O'Malley, "More Testing, More Learning" (p. 531)

A GUIDE TO READING PROPOSALS (p. 486)

The essay that is the focus of A Guide to Reading Proposals is Hill's "Instant Runoff Voting."

READING FOR MEANING (p. 494)

Here are suggestions for teaching the Reading for Meaning activities following "Instant Runoff Voting."

Read to Comprehend (p. 494)

Before students read the whole essay, you might also have them, as a class, define each of these words from paragraph 4: *runoff*, *House*, *Senate*, *inaugurate*, *bipartisan*, *pragmatic*, *partisan*, *primary*, and *nomination*. Once the class has defined these terms in their proper context, consider discussing the meaning of paragraph 4 as a whole. Young students in particular, being new to voting and with civics classes a distant memory, often quietly suffer from confusion when they read paragraphs that assume basic literacy with national politics. Some students may have a vague or inaccurate idea of what the House and Senate do, may not realize those are two houses of Congress, and may be unfamiliar with the election process. Since paragraph 4 assumes familiarity with all of these and needs to be understood to make much sense of the rest of the article, spending time on these terms and the paragraph's meaning as a whole may pay dividends in comprehension of the whole piece.

Students might also need to define *electorate* in paragraph 2, since that term might be taken to mean quite its opposite, and they may also benefit from a clarification of the term *spoiler candidate*.

After students have explained the benefits of Hill's proposal, you might have them identify the problem he is proposing to solve (dissatisfaction with government) as well as the cause of that problem (the current voting system).

Read to Respond (p. 495)
Students may also respond to

- Hill's predictions of who would have won previous races under his preferred system;
- Hill's enthusiasm for "empowering the political center";
- the countries and communities we would be emulating by following his proposal.

Read to Analyze Assumptions (p. 495)

Students might also be interested in discussing the following assumptions:

- Hill's assumption that having majority winners is a good thing;
- his assumption that spoiler candidates are bad, or serve little purpose;
- his assumption that more political debate, with more ideas under discussion, would be an improvement.

READING LIKE A WRITER ACTIVITIES (p. 496)

The four Reading like a Writer activities following Hill's proposal give students a comprehensive introduction to proposals to solve problems and help students move from examining the content and purpose of essays to analyzing the strategies used by writers to accomplish their purposes. You can have students do some or all of these activities before doing selected Reading like a Writer activities for subsequent readings. Students are introduced to the basic features and strategies of proposal writing: introducing the problem; presenting the proposed solution; arguing directly for the proposed solution; and counterarguing readers' objections and alternative solutions. The tasks in this section directly anticipate the thinking that students will do as they read the other chapter selections and begin their own essays.

Introducing the Problem (p. 497)

This Reading like a Writer activity focuses students' attention on Hill's efforts to show readers that the causes of our political problems may be structural or systemic, and that changing that system might alleviate some of the problems. It may be that some of the problems students are considering writing about would also benefit from looking at what might be the root causes of the problems and how addressing those causes might improve the outcome. As the first question hints at, however, Hill must also establish for the reader that elections with more than two candidates are common enough that his proposal would make sense.

Presenting the Proposed Solution (p. 498)

Hill first introduces his solution in paragraph 3 but describes the mechanics of it briefly and vaguely, spending half of that paragraph summarizing its benefits. However, after Hill has introduced the problem and established that elections with more than two candidates are common enough for his proposal to be feasible, he repeats his solution and embellishes the procedural aspects of it—aspects he had skipped over in his initial description. A class discussion might focus on the advantages and disadvantages of this approach. Such a discussion might start by imagining what effect the article might have had on an undecided reader if Hill had included all the steps of the instant-runoff process at the outset.

Arguing Directly for the Proposed Solution (p. 498)

This section underscores how important it is for authors to explain their solutions clearly and show how they will solve (or help solve) the problem. Students are asked to analyze a series of paragraphs in which Hill touts the benefits of his solution: that IRV would give voters more choice, encourage candidates to build coalitions, "empower the political center" (paragraph 4) while disempowering extremists, reduce partisan "bickering" (4), eliminate spoilers, increase majority rule, improve political debate, and discourage mudslinging.

The key step in student analysis for this activity, however, is to compare those benefits with the problems Hill describes. For instance, he opens up by talking about an "unresponsive government" and "ethical scandals" (paragraph 1). Do student readers think his solution adequately (or clearly) addresses these issues? After students have worked on this activity alone and have written their paragraphs, consider discussing their findings in class. You might organize this discussion by drawing a chart on the board: list the problems Hill identifies and the benefits he gives for his proposal, and have students determine how (or whether) the benefits apply to the solutions.

Counterarguing Readers' Objections and Alternative Solutions (p. 499)
This section reminds students of three ways in which writers counterargue: acknowledgement, accommodation, and refutation. It then asks students to consider the final section of Hill's essay, "IRV Is Gaining Momentum," and to study the way he anticipates and counterargues the potential objection that his approach would favor a particular point of view. Students will notice that he relies primarily upon refutation, firing off a diverse list of examples of people, groups, and communities that have embraced the idea despite their differing perspectives. The implication of the list is that instant runoff voting can't be said to benefit a particular party or viewpoint, or else there would seem to be more polarization within the list of supporters and adopters. You might ask students to consider whether they can think of any point of view that is favored by instant runoff voting—or a point of view that stands to lose if the plan is implemented. (Astute readers might notice that Hill himself has identified winners and losers in another part of his article: moderates and centrists stand to gain, while those with extreme positions presently represented well by the two-party system stand to lose.)

ANALYZING VISUALS (p. 500)

This analytical activity introduces students to a purpose of visuals not explored much in previous chapters' Analyzing Visuals sections: to clarify or illustrate a complicated idea. Effectively designed diagrams, maps, and flowcharts can often bring clarity to an explanation, and properly prepared tables or charts can make statistical discussions clearer. Hill's article includes two visuals: a sample ballot (accompanied by another explanation) and a flowchart to illustrate how the votes would be processed. Visuals such as these can often improve clarity when readers have to follow many steps or many elements. After discussing whether the images included by Hill are effective, students might try their hand at redesigning them or devising their own illustrations of Hill's concepts—or of another concept from a different reading.

READINGS

William F. Shughart II, "Why Not a Football Degree?" (p. 501)

READING FOR MEANING (p. 505)

Read to Comprehend (p. 505)
Since Shughart starts by pointing to the many rule violations of the NCAA, you may wish to have students research, before they come to class to discuss this essay, whether such violations have increased in the past ten years.

Other words students may need to define include *revelations* (paragraph 2), *extracurricular* (7), and *inducements* (11).

Read to Respond (p. 506)

Students may also respond to

- Shughart's belief that "a college education is no more necessary for success in the art world than it is in the world of sports" (paragraph 5);
- Shughart's assertion that students pursuing a stage career spend less time in the classroom than do PE majors (5).

Read to Analyze Assumptions (p. 506)

You may also wish to ask students to examine the beliefs underlying Shughart's observation that "and notwithstanding the high moral principles and concern for players usually expressed by debaters on all sides of the issue, the interests of the athlete are in fact often the last to be considered" (paragraph 15).

READING LIKE A WRITER: INTRODUCING THE PROBLEM (p. 507)

This Reading like a Writer activity focuses on how Shughart introduces the problem to his readers. You could make this a small-group activity, with each group responsible for identifying words Shughart uses to introduce the problem, and for explaining what those words, within the context of the text, convey to readers.

CONSIDERING IDEAS FOR YOUR OWN WRITING (p. 508)

This section lists several subjects, suggested by the reading, that may stimulate student writing. You may want to ask students what other ideas for subjects they get from the reading. We have found that routinely discussing possible subjects in class encourages students to try out new ideas. Remember that there is also an array of subject suggestions in the opening Invention and Research activity of A Guide to Writing Proposals (p. 538).

Gary Beck, "Not Your Everyday Homeless Proposal" (p. 509)

READING FOR MEANING (p. 512)

Read to Comprehend (p. 512)

In addition to having students explain Beck's proposed solution, you may ask them to identify what urban area Beck is focusing on (New York City) and what the small towns and the families moving into them under the "small town pioneering" program would gain from participating.

Other words students may need to define include *curricula* (paragraph 2), *infrastructure* (5), *replicable* (9), and *amelioration* (10).

Read to Respond (p. 513)

Students may also respond to

- Beck's assertion that homeless people could be moved to "economically depressed communities, using upstate New York as an example" as a means of revitalizing the communities (paragraph 4);
- how families participating in such a program might feel about being introduced "to the local residents: shopkeepers, teachers, town officials, neighbors, etc." (8).

Read to Analyze Assumptions (p. 513)

You may wish to ask students to examine Beck's assumption that "renovation of the properties would stimulate local employment and generate earnings for businesses that sell construction materials and supplies" (paragraph 5), considering that the pilot plan calls for "one- or two-family homes" (8) to house ten families (7).

READING LIKE A WRITER: PRESENTING THE PROPOSED SOLUTION (p. 514)

This Reading like a Writer activity directs students to paragraphs 4 to 9, where Beck presents his solution. You could ask students to work in pairs or small groups to summarize the point in each paragraph in a phrase or brief sentence. Record their responses on the board to create a scratch outline of the solution. This approach will provide a chance to discuss and evaluate each part of Beck's solution.

CONSIDERING IDEAS FOR YOUR OWN WRITING (p. 515)

This section lists several subjects, suggested by the reading, that may stimulate student writing. You may want to ask students what other ideas for subjects they get from the reading. We have found that routinely discussing possible subjects in class encourages students to try out new ideas. Remember that there is also an array of subject suggestions in the opening Invention and Research activity of A Guide to Writing Proposals (p. 538).

Karen Kornbluh, "Win-Win Flexibility" (p. 516)

READING FOR MEANING (p. 521)

Read to Comprehend (p. 521)

After having students explain the proposed solution, you may also have them identify why Kornbluh proposes beginning with a "'soft-touch' at first" (paragraph 16).

Other words your students may need to define include *sector* (paragraph 11) and *mediocre* (13).

Read to Respond (p. 521)

Students may also respond to

- Kornbluh's use of statistics to support her proposed solution;
- Kornbluh's representation of life for employees without flexible work schedules.

Read to Analyze Assumptions (p. 522)

You might also ask students to examine

- Kornbluh's assumption that all workers would have the knowledge to "make a written application providing details on the change in work, the effect on the employer, and solutions to any problems caused to the employer" (paragraph 18);
- Kornbluh's statement that "to be decent parents, caregivers, and members of their communities, workers now need greater flexibility than they once did" (2).

137

This Reading like a Writer activity focuses on Kornbluh's ability to counterargue by showing why existing alternative solutions aren't working and (though it may not initially be obvious this is what she is doing) by anticipating the objection that some employees might cheat. You could easily make this task a small-group activity, with each group responsible for identifying and evaluating the effectiveness of one or more of Kornbluh's counterarguments.

CONSIDERING IDEAS FOR YOUR OWN WRITING (p. 524)

For an example of a local solution to a problem that seems national, students might take a look at the article by Beck (p. 509), which focuses on the homelessness issue in New York City.

As with other Considering Ideas for Your Own Writing activities, you may want to ask students what other ideas for subjects they get from the reading. We have found that routinely discussing possible subjects in class encourages students to try out new ideas. Remember that there is also an array of subject suggestions in the opening Invention and Research activity of A Guide to Writing Proposals (p. 538).

A SPECIAL READING STRATEGY — RECOGNIZING EMOTIONAL MANIPULATION (p. 524)

This special reading strategy following Karen Kornbluh's proposal asks students to think about the role of emotion, or pathos, in argumentation. Before assigning this section, you might want to have your students read and discuss the section on recognizing emotional manipulation in Appendix 1: A Catalog of Critical Reading Strategies. A key question for students to address is the fine line between appropriate use of emotional content and manipulation. As readers, do students find that they start to resist an argument if they recognize emotional manipulation? As writers, what principles can they think of for using pathos so that their arguments are more, rather than less, likely to persuade?

Patrick O'Malley, "More Testing, More Learning" (p. 525)

READING FOR MEANING (p. 529)

Read to Comprehend (p. 529)
After having students explain the problem O'Malley identifies, the solution he proposes, and the alternative solutions he recognizes, you may wish to have them summarize the counterarguments O'Malley provides to refute the alternative solutions.

Another word that students may need to define is *panacea* (paragraph 12).

Read to Respond (p. 529)
Students may also respond to

- the alternative solutions O'Malley recognizes and his counterarguments to them;
- O'Malley's use of personal experience as evidence.

Read to Analyze Assumptions (p. 530)
You might also ask students to explore the underlying values and assumed student behaviors revealed by this statement: "If students had frequent exams in all their courses,

they would have to schedule study time each week and gradually would develop a habit of frequent study" (5).

READING LIKE A WRITER: ARGUING DIRECTLY FOR THE PROPOSED SOLUTION (p. 531)

This Reading like a Writer activity asks students to analyze several paragraphs where O'Malley argues for his solution, to categorize the kinds of support he provides, and to decide which of his reasons is most convincing. You could also ask students to compare the kinds of support O'Malley provides with that provided by another author in this chapter.

CONSIDERING IDEAS FOR YOUR OWN WRITING (p. 532)

This section lists several subjects, suggested by the reading, that may stimulate student writing. You may want to ask students what other ideas for subjects they get from the reading. We have found that routinely discussing possible subjects in class encourages students to try out new ideas. Remember that there is also an array of subject suggestions in the opening Invention and Research activity of A Guide to Writing Proposals (p. 538).

A SPECIAL READING STRATEGY: COMPARING AND CONTRASTING RELATED READINGS: O'MALLEY'S AND VARLEY'S PROPOSALS TO IMPROVE EDUCATION (p. 532)

This special reading strategy following O'Malley's essay invites students to see how writers construct proposals on similar subjects. If your students have not read and discussed the section on comparing and contrasting related readings in Appendix 1: A Catalog of Critical Reading Strategies, you might have them take the time to do so now. This activity focuses on how the two student writers present the problem and argue for their solutions. Comparing the two essays is an excellent way for students to consolidate their learning about proposal writing. You might ask different groups to analyze and evaluate the way the two writers present their problems and argue for their solutions.

Jeff Varley, "High-School Starting Time" (p. 533)

READING FOR MEANING (p. 536)

This Reading for Meaning activity invites students to apply to Varley's essay what they have learned from the other readings in this chapter about reading to comprehend, respond, and analyze assumptions. You might want to have your class suggest words to define as well as brainstorm possibilities for response and analysis.

READING LIKE A WRITER (p. 536)

This Reading like a Writer activity offers students an opportunity to analyze one of the main strategies for writing essays that propose a solution—introducing the problem, presenting the solution, arguing directly for the proposed solution, and counterarguing readers' objections and alternative solutions.

REVIEWING WHAT MAKES AN EFFECTIVE ESSAY: PROPOSALS (p. 537)

This reflective activity makes a great transition from reading to writing. As the text suggests, this activity can be done individually or in small groups.

A GUIDE TO WRITING PROPOSALS (p. 538)

Since we argue that proposal writing requires a strong sense of audience, peer critique can be especially useful. We encourage students in a draft workshop—see Reading a Draft Critically (p. 546)—to pretend they are the readers addressed in the proposal. Role-playing like this can be informative and fun. Having two or three students listen as the writer reads the draft aloud parallels the way proposals are often presented. The discussion that follows the reading could help the writer see how readers are likely to respond.

Here is an outline of A Guide to Writing Proposals:

Invention and Research
    Choosing a Problem
    Developing Your Proposal
        Analyzing the Problem
        Considering Your Readers
        Finding a Tentative Solution
        Supporting Your Solution
        Anticipating Readers' Objections
        Counterarguing Alternative Solutions
        Researching Your Proposal
        Formulating a Working Thesis
        Considering Visuals

Drafting
    Setting Goals
    Organizing Your Draft
    Working with Sources: Citing Statistics to Establish the Problem's Existence and
        Seriousness (box)
    Considering a Useful Sentence Strategy (Rhetorical Questions)

Reading a Draft Critically
    Read for a First Impression
    Read Again to Suggest Improvements

Revising
    Troubleshooting Your Draft (table)
        To Introduce the Problem More Effectively
        To Present the Solution More Effectively
        To Strengthen the Argument for the Proposed Solution
        To Improve the Counterargument
        To Make the Organizational Plan More Effective

Editing and Proofreading

Reflecting on What You Have Learned: Proposal to Solve a Problem (box) are introduced. It's much the same story in classes for biology, chemistry and mathematics.

At the root of this pedagogical approach is a firm belief in the verti-   20 cal nature of science: you must master *A* before moving on to *B*. When *A* happened a few hundred years ago, it's a long climb to the modern era. Certainly, when it comes to teaching the technicalities—solving this equation, balancing that reaction, grasping the discrete parts of the cell—the verticality of science is unassailable.

But science is so much more than its technical details. And with care-   21 ful attention to presentation, cutting-edge insights and discoveries can be clearly and faithfully communicated to students independent of those details; in fact, those insights and discoveries are precisely the ones that can drive a young student to want to learn the details. We rob science education of life when we focus solely on results and seek to train students to solve problems and recite facts without a commensurate emphasis on transporting them out beyond the stars.

Science is the greatest of all adventure stories, one that's been unfold-   22 ing for thousands of years as we have sought to understand ourselves and our surroundings. Science needs to be taught to the young and communicated to the mature in a manner that captures this drama. We must embark on a cultural shift that places science in its rightful place alongside music, art and literature as an indispensable part of what makes life worth living.

It's the birthright of every child, it's a necessity for every adult, to look   23 out on the world, as the soldier in Iraq did, and see that the wonder of the cosmos transcends everything that divides us.

READING FOR MEANING

This section presents three activities that will help you think about the meanings in Greene's position argument.

Read to Comprehend

Write a few sentences briefly explaining what Greene is arguing for.

Identify any words with meanings you are unsure of—such as *bereft* (paragraph 11) and *intrinsic* (14)—and find the dictionary definition for each word that makes the best sense in the context.

To help you understand the essay better, also consider trying one of these critical reading strategies, explained in Appendix 1: *outlining, paraphrasing,* or *questioning to understand and remember.*

Read to Respond

Write a paragraph or two exploring your initial thoughts and feelings about Greene's position argument. Focus on anything that stands out for you, perhaps because it resonates with your own experience or because you find a statement puzzling. For example, consider writing about one of the following:

- your response to Greene's assertion that "in teaching our students, we continually fail to activate rich opportunities for revealing the breathtaking vistas opened up by science, and instead focus on the need to gain competency with science's underlying technical details" (paragraph 16), perhaps in reference to your own science education;

- the idea that "Science is the greatest of all adventure stories" (22);

- why you think Greene chooses to begin his essay with a letter from a soldier in Iraq (1).

To help develop your response, also consider trying one of these critical reading strategies, explained in Appendix 1: *contextualizing*, *recognizing emotional manipulation*, or *judging the writer's credibility*.

Read to Analyze Assumptions

All writing contains *assumptions*—ideas and attitudes that are taken for granted as commonly accepted truths. Personal or individual assumptions also tend to reflect the values and beliefs of a particular community, which help shape the way those in the group think, act, and understand the world. All writing reflects assumptions held by the writer, but assumptions held by others, such as readers or sources cited by the writer, may also be present. Sometimes assumptions are stated explicitly, but often they are only implied, so you may have to search for underlying assumptions in the word choices and examples.

Why go to the effort to analyze assumptions in a reading? Assumptions have powerful effects. They influence our opinions and judgments by leading us to value some things and devalue others. These effects are even more powerful because they are taken for granted, often accepted without question by those who hold them. To understand a reading on a deep level, then, it is necessary to bring its assumptions to the surface and to question them. To think critically about assumptions, here are some kinds of questions you could ask: Who holds this assumption (the writer, readers, and/or others cited in the essay)? What are the effects of the assumption in the context of the essay specifically or in society more generally? What do you think about the assumption, and is there anything in the essay that raises doubts about it? How does the assumption reinforce or critique commonly held views, and are there any alternative ideas, beliefs, or values that would challenge this assumption?

Write a paragraph or two analyzing an assumption in Greene's essay. You might choose an assumption from the list below, using the questions accompanying it in addition to the ones above to help you get started. Or you can choose another assumption in the essay to explore.

- **assumptions about the intrinsic excitement and pleasure of discovery.** In almost every paragraph, Greene asserts the idea not only that science matters, but that it creates a "transformation . . . that is empowering and emotional" (paragraph 7) and is "a language of hope and inspiration, providing discoveries that fire the imagination and instill a sense of connection to our lives and our world" (9).

   To think critically about the assumptions in this essay related to the excitement and pleasure of discovery, ask yourself questions like these: What kinds of discoveries does Greene mention, and what do they mean to you? Does discovery play a part in your own existence? Are your discoveries (if you have made them) scientific, or are they in other fields? How do you feel when you've made a discovery? How do you think others feel?

- **assumptions about the transforming role of education.** Greene believes that science should be taught in schools "alongside music, art, and literature as an indispensable part of what makes life worth living" (paragraph 22), and he uses language like "transformation" (7) and "transporting them out beyond the stars" (21) to describe the effect he thinks it should have on children. He points out that children "begin life as little scientists" (14) but that they lose their "intrinsic scientific passion" (14) because schools "fail to activate rich opportunities for revealing the breathtaking vistas opened up by science, and instead focus on the need to gain competency with science's underlying technical details" (16).

   To think critically about the assumptions in this essay related to the transforming role of education, ask yourself questions like these: Why does Greene liken science to music, art, and literature? What view of education is held by those who teach science as a "vertical" (20) subject? Do you think Greene's view of science as "the greatest of all adventure stories" (22) is held by most people? Is it the duty of education to be transforming—"to make students sit up in their chairs and say, 'Wow . . .'" (17) or to make them recognize "the wonder of the cosmos" (23)? If so, what is the best way to go about it?

To help you analyze assumptions in Greene's essay, also consider trying one of these critical reading strategies, explained in Appendix 1: *looking for patterns of opposition* or *evaluating the logic of an argument.*

READING LIKE A WRITER

This section leads you through an analysis of Greene's argumentative writing strategies: *presenting the issue; asserting a clear, unequivocal position; arguing directly for the position; counterarguing objections and opposing positions;* and *establishing credibility.* For each strategy, you will be asked to reread and annotate part of Greene's essay to see how he uses the strategy to accomplish his particular purpose.

When you study the selections later in this chapter, you will see how different writers of position papers use the same strategies for different purposes. The Guide to Writing Position Papers near the end of this chapter suggests ways you can use these strategies in your own writing.

Presenting the Issue

For position papers published during an ongoing public debate, writers may need only to mention the issue. In most cases, however, writers need to identify the issue as well as explain it to readers. To present the issue, writers may provide several kinds of information. They may, for example, place the issue in its historical or cultural context, cite specific instances to make the issue seem less abstract, show their personal interest in the debate, or establish or redefine the terms of the debate.

Analyze

1. Reread paragraphs 2 to 7, where Greene introduces the issue, and make notes about the approach he takes.

2. Then reread paragraphs 4 and 5, where Greene provides context for the issue. Look closely at his lists of everything connected to science that we use or see every day, and underline any words that might lead readers to take his argument seriously.

Write

Write several sentences describing how Greene presents the issue. How does he introduce the issue and connect it to his readers' experiences and interests? Then add a few sentences evaluating how successfully Greene presents the issue and prepares readers for his argument.

Asserting a Clear, Unequivocal Position

Writers of position papers always take sides. Their primary purposes are to assert a position of their own and to influence readers' thinking. The assertion is the main point of the essay—its thesis. Writers try to state the thesis simply and directly, although they may limit the scope of it. For example, a thesis in favor of the death penalty might limit capital punishment to certain kinds of crimes. The thesis statement often forecasts the stages of the argument as well, identifying the main reason or reasons that will be developed and supported in the essay.

Where the thesis is placed depends on various factors. Most likely, you will want to place the thesis early in the essay to let readers know right away where you stand. But when you need to spend more time presenting the issue or defining the terms of the debate, you might postpone introducing your own position. Restating the thesis at various points in the body of the essay and at the end can also help keep readers oriented.

Analyze

1. Find the first place where Greene explicitly asserts his position (at the end of paragraph 2), and underline the sentence that states the thesis.

2. Skim paragraphs 7, 8, 9, 11, 14, 16, 17, 19, 21, and 22, and put brackets around the sentences in these paragraphs that restate the thesis.

3. Examine the context for each of these restatements. Look closely at the language Greene uses to see whether he repeats key words, uses synonyms for them, or adds new phrasing.

Write

Write a few sentences explaining what you have learned about how Greene states and restates his position. Describe the different contexts in which he restates the thesis and how the wording changes. Cite examples from the reading. Then add a few sentences speculating about the possible reasons for reasserting a thesis so often in a brief essay like this one.

Arguing Directly for the Position

Not only do writers of position papers explicitly assert their positions, but they also give reasons for them. Moreover, they usually support their reasons with facts, statistics, examples, anecdotes, quotes from authorities, and analogies:

- *Facts* are statements that can be proven objectively to be true, but readers may need to be reassured that the facts come from trustworthy sources.

- Although *statistics* may be mistaken for facts, they often are only interpretations or correlations of numerical data. Their reliability depends on how and by whom the information was collected and interpreted.

- *Examples* and *anecdotes* are not usually claimed to be proof of the writer's position or to be evidence that the position applies in every case. Instead, they present particular stories and vivid images that work by appealing to readers' emotions.

- Also useful for support are *expert opinions* and *analogies*. Readers must decide whether to regard quotations from experts as credible and authoritative. They must also decide how much weight to give analogies—comparisons that encourage readers to assume that what is true about one thing is also true about something to which it is compared.

Analyze

1. Reread paragraphs 7, 17, and 18 where Greene develops his reason that the study of science should include the big questions as well as the technical details, and put brackets around the sentence or sentences in each paragraph that state this part of his argument.

2. Look closely at paragraphs 17 and 18 where Greene supports this reason with appropriate questions to ask and the scientific theories developed in the last one hundred years. Underline these questions and theories throughout both paragraphs, and then compare them to each other.

3. Consider how persuasive his examples are in paragraphs 17 and 18.

Write

Write several sentences briefly describing Greene's strategy of argument by examples. Cite these examples. Then add a few sentences speculating about the persuasiveness of his strategy. Do you think that some readers would find the argument in this part of the essay compelling and other readers would not? If so, why?

Counterarguing Objections and Opposing Positions

Writers of position papers often try to anticipate the likely objections, questions, and opposing positions that readers might raise. Writers may concede points with which they agree and may even modify a thesis to accommodate valid objections. But when they think that the criticism is groundless or opposing arguments are flawed, writers counterargue aggressively. They refute the challenges to their argument by poking holes in their opponents' reasoning and support.

Analyze

1. Reread paragraphs 9, 10, 15, and 16, where Greene introduces opposing arguments to his position. Underline the sentence in each paragraph that best states an opposing position.

2. Examine these paragraphs to see how Greene counterargues these opposing arguments. For example, notice that he both concedes and refutes, and consider why he would attempt to do both. What seems to be his attitude toward those who disagree with him or who object to parts of his argument?

3. Consider how the information about the verticality of science in paragraph 20 connects to readers' common views of science education.

Write

Write several sentences briefly explaining Greene's counterarguments. Then add a few sentences evaluating the probable success of these strategies with his readers.

Establishing Credibility

Readers judge the credibility of a position paper about a controversial issue by the way it presents the issue, argues for the position, and counterargues objections and opposing positions. Critical readers expect writers to advocate forcefully for their position, but at the same time they expect writers to avoid misrepresenting other points of view, attacking opponents personally, or manipulating readers' emotions. To establish credibility, writers thus aim instead to support their position responsibly with the help of authoritative sources and a well-reasoned, well-supported argument.

Another factor that can influence readers' judgment of an argument's credibility is whether the writer seems to share at least some of their values, beliefs, attitudes, and ideals. Readers often are more willing to trust a writer who expresses concerns that they also have about an issue. Many readers respect arguments based on strong values even if they do not share those particular values or hold to them as strictly. Yet readers also tend to dislike moralizing and resent a condescending or belittling tone as much as a shrill or lecturing one. Instead, readers usually appreciate a tone that acknowledges legitimate differences of opinion, while seeking to establish common ground where possible.

Analyze

1. Quickly reread Greene's entire essay. As you read, put a question mark in the margin next to any passages where you doubt Greene's credibility, and put a check mark next to any passages where he seems especially trustworthy.

2. Review the passages you marked. Where possible, note in the margin a word or phrase that describes the dominant tone of each marked passage.

3. Then consider what language, information, or other element in the marked passages contributes to your judgment of Greene's credibility.

Write

Write several sentences describing your impression of Greene's credibility. Cite examples from the reading to support your view.

READINGS

Karen Stabiner

Boys Here, Girls There: Sure, If Equality's the Goal

Karen Stabiner is a journalist who is a regular contributor to the Huffington Post *and the* Los Angeles Times Opinion *section, a contributing editor for* Mother Jones, *a columnist for* New West, *and an adjunct professor at the Columbia University School of Journalism. Stabiner has written several books on relationships and single-sex education. Her most recent are* My Girl: Adventures with a Teen in Training *(2005) and* The Empty Nest: Thirty-one Parents Tell the Truth about Relationships, Love, and Freedom after the Kids Fly the Coop *(2007). In her novel,* Getting In *(2010), Stabiner writes about the challenge of getting a child into the perfect college.*

"Boys Here, Girls There: Sure, If Equality's the Goal" was first published in the Washington Post Sunday Outlook *section in 2002. The occasion was the George W. Bush administration's endorsement of single-sex schools as part of the No Child Left Behind Act. Before you read, think about the role that gender played in your high-school education. Do you feel that boys and girls were treated differently, and if so, how? If they were treated the same, do you think it would have been better had they been treated differently? Why? As you read, pay special attention to Stabiner's strategies for responding to those who disagree with her.*

Many parents may be wondering what the fuss was about this past week, when the Bush administration endorsed single-sex public schools and classes. Separating the sexes was something we did in the days of auto shop and home ec, before Betty Friedan, Gloria Steinem and Title IX.[1] How, then, did an apparent return to the Fifties come to symbolize educational reform? 1

Why does Stabiner list these "parallel" possibilities for what matters at school?

Here's how: By creating an alternate, parallel universe where smart matters more than anything, good looks hold little currency and a strong sense of self trumps a date on Saturday night—a place where "class clown" is a label that young boys dread and "math whiz" is a term of endearment for young girls. 2

[1] Betty Friedan (1921–2006) and Gloria Steinem (b. 1934) were pioneers in the Second Wave feminist movement that began in the 1960s. Title IX of the Education Amendments of 1972 is the federal legislation that bans sexual discrimination in public schools, whether in academics or athletics.

3   I have just spent three years working on a book about two all-girls schools, the private Marlborough School in Los Angeles, and The Young Women's Leadership School of East Harlem (TYWLS), a six-year-old public school in New York City. I went to class, I went home with the girls, I went to dances and basketball games and faculty meetings, and what I learned is this: Single-sex education matters, and it matters most to the students who historically have been denied access to it.

How does this paragraph enhance Stabiner's credibility?

4   Having said that, I do not intend to proselytize. Single-sex education is not the answer to everyone's prayers. Some children want no part of it and some parents question its relevance. The rest of us should not stop wondering what to do with our coeducational public schools just because of this one new option.

Why would Stabiner mention how single-sex education might not "matter" to some people?

5   But single-sex education can be a valuable tool—if we target those students who stand to benefit most. For years, in the name of upholding gender equity, we have practiced a kind of harsh economic discrimination. Sociologist Cornelius Riordan says that poor students, minorities and girls stand to profit most from a single-sex environment. Until now, though, the only students who could attend a single-sex school were the wealthy ones who could afford private tuition, the relatively few lucky students who received financial aid or those in less-expensive parochial schools. We denied access to the almost 90 percent of American students who attend public schools.

What is the effect of Stabiner's bringing in another source and statistics to buttress her contention that gender equity in schools has resulted in economic discrimination? Why does she include herself (see highlighted "we") among those she blames for this situation?

6   For the fortunate ones—like the girls at Marlborough—the difference is one of attitude, more than any quantifiable measure; their grades and scores may be similar to the graduates of coed prep schools, but they perceive themselves as more competent, more willing to pursue advanced work in fields such as math and science.

7   At TYWLS, though, the difference is more profound. Students there are predominantly Latina and African American, survivors of a hostile public system. Half of New York's high school students fail to graduate on time, and almost a third never graduate. Throughout the nation, one in six Latina and one in five African American teens become pregnant every year. But most of the members of TYWLS's two graduating classes have gone

on to four-year colleges, often the first members of their families to do so, and pregnancy is the stark exception.

There are now 11 single-sex public schools in the United States, all of which serve urban students, many of them in lower-income neighborhoods. Most are side-by-side schools that offer comparable programs for boys and girls in the same facility. The stand-alone girls' schools say that they are compensating for years of gender discrimination; several attempts at similar schools for boys have failed, however, casualties of legal challenges. 8

Compare this paragraph to paragraph 1. How have the intervening paragraphs educated you about single-sex schools?

Now, thanks to a bipartisan amendment to President Bush's education reform bill, sponsored by Sens. Kay Bailey Hutchison (R-Tex.) and Hillary Rodham Clinton (D-N.Y.), the administration is about to revise the way it enforces Title IX, to allow for single-sex schools and classes. 9

The first objections last week came from the National Organization for Women and the New York Civil Liberties Union, both of which opposed the opening of TYWLS in the fall of 1996. The two groups continue to insist—as though it were 1896 and they were arguing *Plessy v. Ferguson*[2]—that separate can never be equal. I appreciate NOW's wariness of the Bush administration's endorsement of single-sex public schools, since I am of the generation that still considers the label "feminist" to be a compliment—and many feminists still fear that any public acknowledgment of differences between the sexes will hinder their fight for equality. 10

Why does Stabiner mention her appreciation of NOW's wariness and of feminism?

Why does Stabiner make the point that boys and girls develop differently?

But brain research has shown us that girls and boys develop and process information in different ways; they do not even use the same region of the brain to do their math homework. We cannot pretend that such information does not exist just because it conflicts with our ideology. If we hang on to old, quantifiable measurements of equality, we will fail our children. If we take what we learn and use it, we have the chance to do better. 11

---

[2]In *Plessy v. Ferguson* (1896), the U.S. Supreme Court upheld racial segregation by stating that separate facilities for blacks and whites in public accommodations were constitutional as long as they were equal. The ruling was reversed by the Supreme Court in *Brown v. Board of Education* (1954).

12   Educators at single-sex schools already get it: Equality is the goal, not the process. There may be more than one path to the destination—but it is the arrival, not the itinerary, that counts.

Why does Stabiner make this paragraph so short?

13   Some researchers complain that we lack definitive evidence that single-sex education works. There are so many intertwined variables; the students at TYWLS might do well because of smaller class size, passionate teachers and an aggressively supportive atmosphere. Given that, the absence of boys might be beside the point.

Again Stabiner introduces the arguments her opponents might use; how does she follow up on these?

14   The American Association of University Women called for more research even after publishing a 1998 report that showed some girls continued to suffer in the coed classroom. But it is probably impossible to design a study that would retire the question permanently, and, as TYWLS's first principal, Celenia Chevere, liked to say, "What am I supposed to do with these girls in the meantime?"

15   What is this misplaced reverence for the coed school? Do not think that it was designed with the best interests of all children at heart. As education professors David and Myra Sadker explained in their 1994 book, *Failing at Fairness: How America's Schools Cheat Girls*, our schools were originally created to educate boys. In the late 1700s, girls went to class early in the morning and late in the day—and unlike the boys, they had to pay for the privilege. When families demanded that the public schools do more for their girls, school districts grudgingly allowed the girls into existing classrooms—not because it was the best way to teach children but because no one had the money to build new schools just for girls. Coed classrooms are not necessarily better. They just are.

Does giving the history of girls' attendance in public schools seem a surprising way for Stabiner to present her issue? What difference could this information make to her argument?

16   For those who like hard data, here is a number: 1,200 girls on the waiting list for a handful of spaces in the ninth grade at TYWLS. There is a growing desire for public school alternatives, for an answer more meaningful than a vague if optimistic call for system-wide reform. The demand for single-sex education exists—and now the Bush administration must figure out how to supply it.

17   Implementation will not be easy. Girls may learn better without boys, but research and experience show that some boys seem to need the socializing influence

How do these questions that Stabiner poses add to her argument?

of girls: Will there be a group of educational handmaidens, girls who are consigned to coed schools to keep the boys from acting out? Who will select the chosen few who get to go to single-sex schools, and how will they make that choice? Will they take students who already show promise or those who most need help? Or perhaps the philosophy of a new pair of boys' and girls' schools in Albany, N.Y., provides the answer: Take the poorest kids first.

Whatever the approach, no one is calling for a 18 wholesale shift to segregation by gender, and that means someone will be left out. Single-sex public schools perpetuate the kind of two-tiered system that used to be based solely on family income, even if they widen the net. But that has always been true of innovative public schools, and it is no reason to hesitate.

The most troubling question about single-sex public 19 education—Why now?—has nothing to do with school. When support comes so readily from opposite ends of the political spectrum, it is reasonable to ask why everyone is so excited, particularly given the political debate about vouchers and school choice.

If single-sex schools could benefit coed schools, who might still object to single-sex education?

If the intention is to strengthen the public school 20 system by responding to new information about how our children learn, then these classes can serve as a model of innovative teaching techniques, some of which can be transported back into existing coed classrooms. Single-sex public schools and classes, as odd as it may sound, are about inclusion; any school district that wants one can have one and everyone can learn from the experience.

In this final paragraph, Stabiner calls into question the motivation of those who support single-sex schools for the best and brightest. Why would she end her essay on this note?

But if this is about siphoning off the best and poten- 21 tially brightest, and ignoring the rest, then it is a cruel joke, a warm and fuzzy set-up for measures like vouchers. If single-sex becomes a satisfying distraction from existing schools that desperately need help, then it only serves to further erode the system. The new educational reform law is called the No Child Left Behind Act, an irresistible sentiment with a chilling edge to it—did we ever actually intend to leave certain children behind? The challenge, in developing these new schools and programs, is to make them part of a dynamic, ongoing reform, and not an escape hatch from a troubled system.

READING FOR MEANING

This section presents three activities that will help you think about the meanings in Stabiner's position argument.

Read to Comprehend

Write a few sentences briefly explaining why Stabiner favors single-sex public schools for girls.

Identify any words with meanings you are unsure of—such as *proselytize* (paragraph 4), *implementation* (17), and *perpetuate* (18)—and find the dictionary definition for each word that makes the best sense in the context.

To help you understand the essay better, also consider trying one of these critical reading strategies, explained in Appendix 1: *previewing* or *contextualizing*.

Read to Respond

Write several paragraphs exploring your initial thoughts and feelings about Stabiner's position argument. Focus on anything that stands out for you, perhaps because it resonates with your own experience or because you find a statement puzzling. For example, consider writing about one of the following:

- any experience you have had with single-sex schools;

- your response to Stabiner's assertion that "[f]or years, in the name of upholding gender equity, we have practiced a kind of harsh economic discrimination" (paragraph 5); or

- whether you think a difference in *attitude* (6) can make the kind of difference Stabiner explores in her essay.

To help develop your response, also consider trying one of these critical reading strategies, explained in Appendix 1: *looking for patterns of opposition* or *reflecting on challenges to your beliefs and values*.

Read to Analyze Assumptions

Write a paragraph or two analyzing an assumption in Stabiner's essay. To think critically about assumptions, here are some kinds of questions you could ask: Who holds this assumption (the writer, readers, and/or others cited in the essay)? What are the effects of the assumption in the context of the essay specifically or in society more generally? What do you think about the assumption, and is there anything in the essay that raises doubts about it? How does the assumption reinforce or critique commonly held views, and are there any alternative ideas, beliefs, or values that would challenge this assumption?

You might choose an assumption from the list below, using the questions accompanying it in addition to the ones above to help you get started. Or you can choose another assumption in the essay to explore.

- **assumptions about the effects of innovations in education.** In paragraph 20, speaking about single-sex classrooms, Stabiner notes that "[i]f the intention is to strengthen the public school system by responding to new information about how our children learn, then these classes can serve as a model of innovative teaching." What kinds of innovative teaching might Stabiner mean?

  To think critically about the assumptions in this essay related to the effects of innovations in education, ask yourself questions like these: What is your response to the principal of TYWLS, who asks, referring to the American Association of University Women's call for more research on coed versus single-sex schools, "What am I supposed to do with these girls in the meantime?" (14). What would happen to schools if innovations were encouraged (rather than being seen as a threat to the status quo) or if students—both boys and girls—were treated as "experiments" to see how they would turn out under single-sex circumstances? What kinds of circumstances could lead to disastrous innovations? To wondrous innovations? Would teaching innovations for girls necessarily be transferable to boys?

- **assumptions about how poverty affects learning.** In paragraph 17, Stabiner asks a series of questions about how girls would be chosen for single-sex schools, and at the end of the paragraph she opts for an answer given by single-sex schools in Albany: "Take the poorest kids first." Earlier, she asserts that "Single-sex education . . . matters most to the students who historically have been denied access to it" (3), by whom she means "poor students, minorities and girls" (5).

  To think critically about the assumptions in this essay related to poverty and learning, ask yourself questions like these: What would be the consequences if single-sex public schools took "poorest kids first"? Why does a difference in "attitude" (6) among students in single-sex schools lead them to pursue advanced degrees? How are attitude and economics linked?

To help you analyze assumptions in Stabiner's essay, also consider trying one of these critical reading strategies, explained in Appendix 1: *evaluating the logic of an argument* or *recognizing logical fallacies* (pp. 579–82, 587–93).

READING LIKE A WRITER

COUNTERARGUING OBJECTIONS AND OPPOSING POSITIONS

One of the challenges—and pleasures—of writing position papers is that in nearly every writing situation writers recognize that some or all of their readers will hold opposing positions or will at least question or object to some part of the argument. Therefore, one of the special challenges of the position paper is to counterargue readers' positions or objections. To do so convincingly, writers must succeed with two basic moves—(1) demonstrating that they understand these criticisms of their argument and (2) conceding or refuting the criticisms without exasperating or insulting readers. To *concede* is to admit the usefulness or wisdom of opposing views, at least to some extent. To *refute* is to argue that such views are too limited or simply wrong. (For more on counterarguing, turn to the Reading like a Writer section on p. 356, and to Considering a Useful Sentence Strategy on p. 402.)

Stabiner counterargues extensively. In fact, she organizes her argument around particular objections she anticipates her readers will raise.

Analyze

1. In paragraph 4, underline the last three sentences, which acknowledge the objections that single-sex schools cannot solve all of the problems of education and that many parents and students don't find them an answer.

2. Reread paragraphs 10 and 13 and the first sentences of 15 and 21, where Stabiner acknowledges objections to single-sex schools. Then reread paragraphs 11, 12, and 14 and the rest of 15 and 21. Make notes in the margins about what strategies Stabiner uses, noticing where she refutes, where she concedes, and what her attitude seems to be toward those who oppose single-sex schools.

Write

Write several sentences explaining what you have learned about how Stabiner counterargues. Give examples from the reading. Then add a few sentences evaluating how convincingly Stabiner counterargues. What do you find most and least convincing in her counterargument—and why?

CONSIDERING IDEAS FOR YOUR OWN WRITING

Consider the many issues in contemporary culture that involve gender. Many issues concern reproductive rights, such as abortion and fetal selection (where parents choose to abort a fetus because it has genetic disorders or, in some cultures, is female) and requirements for parental notification if a teenager seeks advice for birth control. The subject of education also yields many issues: Is the current structure of high schools best for educating teenagers? Are college admissions fair? Is more testing a solution to our national educational crisis? Is there a national educational crisis? Should we change our notion of the right of every citizen to a public education? Does the profession of teaching need to change, and if so, how? Should everyone have a right to a college education? Since you have already reached college, you may want to take a position on one of these topics.

A Special Reading Strategy

Comparing and Contrasting Related Readings: Orenstein's "The Daily Grind: Lessons in the Hidden Curriculum" and Stabiner's "Boys Here, Girls There: Sure, If Equality's the Goal"

Comparing and contrasting related readings is a critical reading strategy useful both in reading for meaning and in reading like a writer. This strategy is particularly applicable when writers present similar subjects, as in the observational essay in Chapter 3 by Peggy Orenstein (p. 113) and the position paper in this chapter by Karen Stabiner (p. 358). Both essays focus on gender in the classroom. To compare and contrast these two essays, think about issues such as these:

- Compare these essays in terms of their cultural contexts. How do you think Orenstein or her subject Amy Wilkinson would react to Stabiner's argument in favor of single-sex education? If Wilkinson's school were single sex instead of coed, what do you think she would gain and/or lose?

- Compare these essays in terms of their purpose and genre. Orenstein's essay describing her observations of a coed classroom may lead readers to question coed education, but she does not argue, at least not directly, either for or against it. Stabiner, on the other hand, makes an explicit argument in favor of giving public-school students the opportunity to attend single-sex schools. Compare the way these two essays try to influence readers.

See Appendix 1 (pp. 596–601) for detailed guidelines on comparing and contrasting related readings.

Cristina Page

A Mom before the Prom

*Cristina Page is a prominent reproductive rights activist and a consul-
tant for several national pro-choice groups, including the Adoption Access
Network and the National Institute for Reproductive Health. She moderates an online forum <http://www.rhrealitycheck.org/commonground>
that seeks "to highlight ideas and foster dialogue among individuals and
organizations involved in the search for common ground" on abortion.
Page's first book was* The Smart Girl's Guide to College: A Serious Book
Written by Women in College to Help You Make the Perfect College
Choice *(1999), and her most recent book is* How the Pro-Choice Movement Saved America: Freedom, Politics and the War on Sex *(2006). Her
commentary has appeared in the* New York Times, *the* Guardian UK, *the*
Chicago Sun Times, *and* Newsday. *She is a regularly featured contributor
to the* Huffington Post.*

The essay below was published in the Huffington Post *in October
2008, in response to a series of celebrity teen pregnancies, among them the
pregnancy of Bristol Palin, daughter of the Republican candidate for vice
president in the 2008 election. As you read, think about your own attitude
toward teenage pregnancy and how it was shaped.*

Now that the national attention on Bristol Palin's pregnancy is fading   1
(for the time being) it seems the only discussion it inspired was about John
McCain's vetting process and, by extension, his decision-making abilities.
But there is another far more important subject raised by the 17-year-old's
pregnancy. For decades, teen pregnancy has been viewed as a problem, a
danger to the children of young mothers and a hurdle to the success of the
adolescent mothers.

But recent public displays of contraceptive failure by girls of visibility   2
and means give the misleading appearance that teen motherhood might
be a lifestyle upgrade. Clearly one of the exacerbating factors is that someone like Bristol Palin is part of what feels like a growing trend: the normalizing of teen pregnancy and teen motherhood in the United States.
Bristol is not alone in suggesting that to be a 17-year-old mother is not
only acceptable, but exciting. Last year Jamie Lynn Spears, Britney's then
16-year-old sister, had her baby. (The Spears, it's worth noting, were proponents of abstinence-only too.) Last year also featured the movie *Juno, in*
which star Ellen Page played a 16-year-old whose quick wit and sarcasm
made her unwanted pregnancy seem as challenging as a bad case of acne.
The attention garnered by each of these girls stripped away layers of what
had for years been cautions against this very fate.

None of these occasions has prompted examination of the risks and   3
damage caused by teen pregnancy and teen motherhood. And, it should

be noted, recent data show that the rate of teen pregnancy in the U.S., which is already the highest in the developed world, is on the rise. The last year witnessed a dramatic 3 percent spike in the number of pubescent parents.

4   Of course, Bristol, Juno and Jamie Lynn don't exemplify the average American girl confronting unintended pregnancy. And the problem is the average American teen doesn't really know that. Take it from school officials in Gloucester, Massachusetts who witnessed a fourfold increase in teen pregnancies last year. The principal even suspected the spike was a coordinated effort charging that the 18 girls planned a "pact" to all get pregnant. It's clear that girls today are getting a glamorized message about teen pregnancy. The choice the fictional character Juno made, adoption, is almost a fiction these days too. Approximately 1 percent of pregnant teens opt to give a child up for adoption. And then Jamie Lynn Spears is a teen millionaire. Her pregnancy only enhanced her fortune. The first photos of her baby fetched a million dollars. The spotlight on Bristol Palin offers false comfort too. Bristol has resources available to her that none of her pregnant teen counterparts does—like the Secret Service, the ultimate nanny.

5   The average teen girl would be led to believe that teen pregnancy doesn't ruin adolescence, but instead brings lavish amounts of attention, an adoring and adorable teen father, and an endless supply of parental support. The reality for most teen moms could not be more different. According to the National Campaign to Prevent Teen and Unplanned Pregnancy, eight in 10 teen fathers do not marry the mother of their first child. Kids without involved fathers are twice as likely to drop out of school, twice as likely to abuse alcohol or drugs, twice as likely to end up in jail, and two to three times more likely to need help for emotional or behavioral problems. Children who live apart from their fathers are also five times more likely to be poor than children with both parents at home.

6   Teen mothers, typically left to go it alone, are less likely to complete the education necessary to qualify for a well-paying job—in fact, parenthood is the leading cause of school drop out among teen girls. College then becomes the remotest of possibilities. Less than two percent of mothers who have children before age 18 complete college by the age of 30.

7   Too often heartbreaking sacrifices are also foisted on the child of a teenage mom. The children of teen mothers are more likely to be born prematurely at low birthweight compared to children of older mothers, which raises the probability of infant death and disease, mental retardation, and mental illness. Children of teen mothers are 50 percent more likely to repeat a grade and are less likely to complete high school. The children of teen parents also suffer higher rates of abuse and neglect (two times higher).

8   Teen girls and their children are not the only ones paying dearly. Teen childbearing in the United States costs taxpayers (federal, state, and local)

approximately $9.1 billion each year. Most of the costs are associated with services to address the negative consequences detailed above.

Teen pregnancy needs to be discussed honestly whenever the next   9
Juno, Jamie Lynn or Bristol takes her baby bump primetime. Otherwise, "pregnancy pact" is a term we can all start getting used to.

READING FOR MEANING

This section presents three activities that will help you think about the meanings in Page's position argument.

Read to Comprehend

Write a few sentences briefly explaining the position Page takes regarding teen pregnancy and motherhood.

Identify any words with meanings you are unsure of—such as *exacerbating* (paragraph 2), *garnered* (2), and *pubescent* (3)—and find the dictionary definition for each word that makes the best sense in the context.

To help you understand the essay better, also consider trying one of these critical reading strategies, explained in Appendix 1: *previewing* or *outlining*.

Read to Respond

Write several paragraphs exploring your initial thoughts and feelings about Page's position argument. Focus on anything that stands out for you, perhaps because it resonates with your own experience or because you find a statement puzzling. For example, consider writing about one of the following:

- your own feelings about teenage pregnancy;

- whether you think your views of the subject have been affected by the media (like *Juno*) or public figures (like Bristol Palin or Jamie Lynn Spears) and if so, how;

- your response to the facts and statistics Page presents about the negative effects of teenage pregnancy.

To help develop your response, also consider trying one of these critical reading strategies, explained in Appendix 1: *contextualizing* or *using a Toulmin analysis*.

Read to Analyze Assumptions

Write a paragraph or two analyzing an assumption in Page's essay. To think critically about assumptions, here are some kinds of questions you could ask: Who holds this assumption (the writer, readers, and/or others cited in the essay)? What are the effects of the assumption in the context of the essay specifically or in society more generally? What do you think about the assumption, and is there anything in the essay that raises doubts about it? How does the assumption reinforce or critique commonly held views, and are there any alternative ideas, beliefs, or values that would challenge this assumption?

You might choose an assumption from the list below, using the questions accompanying it in addition to the ones above to help you get started. Or you can choose another assumption in the essay to explore.

- **assumptions about what influences teenagers**. Page begins her second paragraph with the lament that "recent public displays of contraceptive failure by girls of visibility and means give the misleading appearance that teen motherhood might be a lifestyle upgrade." Citing widespread attention to the pregnancies of Bristol Palin and Jamie Lynn Spears and the attitude of the pregnant teenager in *Juno*, Page claims that "girls today are getting a glamorized message about teen pregnancy" (paragraph 4), and that "[t]he average teen girl would be led to believe that teen pregnancy doesn't ruin adolescence. . . ." (5).

  To think critically about the assumptions in this essay about what influences teenagers, and particularly teenage girls' attitudes toward pregnancy, ask yourself questions like these: What or whom does Page seem to be blaming for "the normalizing of teen pregnancy and teen motherhood in the United States" (2)? The news media, for publicizing pregnancies like those of Palin and Spears? The parents, political consultants, or public-relations people who are involved? The entertainment media, for presenting teen pregnancy in too lighthearted a way? To what extent are you influenced by the media? In what ways? Are teenagers more vulnerable than adults to media messages? If so, why? Do celebrities or public figures have more influence over teens' attitudes to things like teen pregnancy than their families and friends do?

- **the assumption that people avoid behavior with terrible consequences.** Page lists many of the terrible consequences of teenage pregnancy to the mothers and their children, especially in paragraphs 5 to 8. In paragraph 9, she says that "[t]een pregnancy needs to be discussed honestly," implying that if the media or authority figures informed teens about these consequences, they would change their behavior.

  To think critically about the assumptions in this essay regarding whether or how people change behavior that may result in terrible consequences, ask yourself questions like these: Does knowledge of presumed consequences change the behavior of most people? In what circumstances? Are teenage girls likely to change their behavior once they learn some of the statistics Page sets forth? Of the information Page gives in her essay, which parts do you think would most likely make them change their behavior? Why?

To help you analyze assumptions in Page's essay, also consider trying one of these critical reading strategies, explained in Appendix 1: *evaluating the logic of an argument* or *judging a writer's credibility*.

READING LIKE A WRITER

ARGUING DIRECTLY FOR THE POSITION

Central to creating a successful position paper is the development of a strong argument in support of the writer's position on the issue. The writer may effectively counterargue readers' or opponents' objections and opposing positions, but doing so does not complete the argument. Readers also want to know in positive terms why the writer holds his or her particular position and what sort of reasoned argument the writer can devise. In brief, they expect reasons and support.

Page's essay shows how writers of position papers make use of several strategies to support their reasons.

Analyze

1. Reread the following paragraphs, looking for examples of the strategies Page uses to support her reasons: reporting on or speculating about results (every paragraph), citing statistics (paragraphs 2 through 8), citing authorities (4, 5), giving examples (2 through 8), setting up comparisons or contrasts (2 through 6), and creating analogies (2, 4).

2. Select two of these strategies to analyze and evaluate, and look closely at the relevant paragraphs to see how Page uses each strategy.

3. Make notes in the margin about how she develops the strategy. What kinds of details does she include, and what sorts of sentences does she rely on?

4. Evaluate how effectively Page uses each strategy to support her reasons. What is most and least convincing about the support? What does it contribute to the overall argument?

Write

Write several sentences explaining Page's use of the two strategies you analyzed. Support your explanation with details from the paragraphs. Then add a few sentences evaluating how successfully Page uses the strategies.

CONSIDERING IDEAS FOR YOUR OWN WRITING

Consider imitating Page's approach by taking a position on a trend that you see becoming increasingly damaging to society, for example, the decline in reading, the rise in gambling, or the increase in political anger and polarization. You could also write on issues that concern teens, such as bullying in middle or high schools, the trials and triumphs of getting into college, social or curricular adjustments to college, or an issue related to sexuality, gangs, fashion, or other teenage interests. Or, you could consider any social issues about which you have a strong opinion.

David L. Kirp

Diversity Hypocrisy: The Myriad, and Often Perverse, Implications of Admissions Policies

David L. Kirp is a professor at the Goldman School of Public Policy at the University of California, Berkeley. Previously, he taught at the Harvard Graduate School of Education and was the founding director of the Harvard Center on Law and Education, which sponsors legal efforts to ensure equal opportunity to education.

Kirp's research has explored a wide range of social policy areas, including primary and higher education, race and gender equality, affordable housing, and the AIDS crisis. His published work includes some fifteen books, among them Shakespeare, Einstein, and the Bottom Line: The Marketing of Higher Education *(2003), as well as many articles in leading social science journals and law reviews. His latest book is* The Sandbox Investment: The Preschool Movement and Kids-First Politics *(2007). A former newspaper editor and syndicated columnist, Kirp continues to contribute to leading national print media, including the* New York Times, *the* Atlantic Monthly, *the* American Prospect *and the* Nation, *and appears as a policy expert on radio and television programs.*

The selection below was published in National CrossTalk, *a publication of the National Center for Public Policy and Higher Education, in 2007. In it, Kirp addresses the issue of achieving "diversity" in college admissions. As you read, think about your own experiences with college admissions; have you seen evidence of the scenarios he paints below?*

1   In the continuing debates over who ought to be admitted to America's top colleges, "diversity" has been both a mantra and a moral trump card. In academe, to question it risks being labeled as hopelessly retrograde. I'll take that risk. Contrary to the conventional wisdom, many of the winners in the diversity sweepstakes aren't poor or minority students, and many of the losers have powerful justice-based claims.

2   From the start, the incantation of diversity has been an act of hypocrisy. In the 1978 Bakke case, Supreme Court Justice Lewis Powell declared that promoting diversity justified the use of race as one among multiple factors in admitting students. Powell may have envisioned an admissions committee constructing a class composed of would-be Einsteins, Warhols, kids from Appalachia, point guards and minorities, but insiders appreciated that the opinion legitimated quotas. To pass muster the "diversity" formula had to be built backwards. Rather than starting out with a straightforward quota—admit *X* percentage of minorities—the university simply had to calculate how heavily to weight race in order to admit the desired number.

The 2003 University of Michigan cases enshrined this hypocrisy. 3
An explicitly race-based formula, which the university used to admit
undergraduates, was found to be unconstitutional. But it was okay to consider an applicant's race in the context of a tailored, "holistic" review, as
the law school did. That's a distinction without a difference since, no matter
how nuanced, the process can be rigged to generate the desired racial outcome; the law school's own data indicated as much.

THE WINNERS

Minorities win and whites lose—that's how the diversity issue is pub- 4
licly framed, but the facts are otherwise. Most of the applicants who
receive favored treatment are not minorities. Many are the offspring of
alumni—"legacies," a quaint term suggestive of feudal entitlement. In an
article called "Ivy League Confidential," *Forbes Magazine* advised parents
that "the first thing to determine is whether your child will count as a
legacy." That's smart counsel, since being a legacy, observed *Wall Street
Journal* reporter Daniel Golden in his 2006 book, *The Price of Admission*,
can be as valuable as 300 or more points on the SAT.

Children of the famous are similarly pampered, most notoriously at 5
Brown, where the arrival of John F. Kennedy Jr., "John John," helped to put
the habitual doormat of the Ivy League on the map. A host of celebrities'
kids followed in his wake. They have been courted with a Don Juan-esque
avidity, for the university has figured out that while star power doesn't
translate directly into dollars, it does generate invaluable buzz.

The scions of the super-rich also receive special treatment. They are 6
referred to as "development cases," a term of art that calls to mind
deals made with a third-world country. The transaction isn't made
crassly explicit—a couple of million dollars will buy a place in the
freshman class for your son or daughter—because everyone understands the rules.

It's not just the elite private universities that play this game. The same 7
formula that the University of Michigan used in order to favor disadvantaged minorities also explicitly favored children of alumni and potential
donors. In the 150-point "Selection Index" the university constructed, the
admissions committee could give 20 points to such applicants—but only
if they were white or Asian. Although youngsters from "underrepresented"
minorities qualified for an automatic 20 points, they could not be awarded
these discretionary points.

What killed the university, constitutionally speaking, wasn't its pursuit 8
of the wealthy but the paper trail. In 2006 Michigan's voters barred the use
of race as an admissions criterion, but there's little doubt that the university still trolls for the rich. At Ann Arbor, more undergraduates come from
families with incomes greater than a quarter of a million dollars than from
families earning less than $40,000.

9   Diversity makes for wonderful double-speak. When challenged to explain how her university could admit applicants whose only virtue was having been born rich, Nannerl Keohane, then president of Duke, responded with an homage to diversity. "We are committed to ethnic, racial, cultural, socio-economic and geographic diversity, to becoming more international, giving particular support to students from North and South Carolina (by reason of our founding indenture and our commitment to our region), admitting students with a range of probable academic commitments (engineers, pre-meds, classicists, historians, etc.), succeeding in athletics, making sure that our drama and music and arts programs have students who will continue and enjoy their traditions, and more." Only at the end of that 76-word sentence did Keohane acknowledge that "alumni and development concerns" (not students, tellingly, but "concerns") were "part of the mix."

10   Professors are equally good at gussying up their own self-interest. Even as they may decry the dumbing down of their classes because of legacies and athletes, at many schools their own children benefit greatly from preferential treatment. It is a remarkable perk, for not only do they get the same kind of admissions breaks received by other preferred groups, they also receive generous scholarships. Faculty members insist that this favored handling is vital to the institutional culture. And as Tufts president Lawrence Bacow learned to his sorrow, tightening admissions standards for faculty brats risks revolt. Even as Tufts turned down 193 applicants solely because it didn't have enough financial aid, one professor got his daughter admitted with a full scholarship by threatening that, otherwise, he couldn't "go about [his] work with [his] wonted energy and enthusiasm."

THE LOSERS

11   Who loses out? Contrary to popular belief, it isn't suburban middle class white youngsters like the plaintiffs in the University of Michigan case, beaten out by less well-qualified minorities.

12   Surprisingly, Asian Americans are among those who fare worst—"the new Jews," as they are called in *The Price of Admission*. They don't count as an underrepresented minority, and they are seldom legacies or celebrities' kids. They're also all too easy to stereotype. When asked why a Korean applicant named Henry Park, who had a spectacular record at Groton, was turned down, MIT's admissions director Marilee Jones rationalized that "it's possible that [he] looked like a thousand other Korean kids with the exact same profile of grades and activities . . . yet another textureless math grind." Imagine the brouhaha if Jones had been talking about someone who was, say, Latino or Jewish.

13   Another surprise is that working-class male athletes also fare badly. When the topic of athletics comes up, most people think of football and basketball, two sports at which disadvantaged kids excel. But universities, obliged

by the Title IX requirement to pay equal attention to women's and men's sports, have built up programs in areas like women's golf, field hockey, rowing, tennis and swimming. Those sports are the near-exclusive preserve of girls from well-to-do families, who receive the kind of gold-plated scholarships once reserved for quarterbacks. Meanwhile, wrestling and gymnastics, sports that poor boys do play in high school, are being curtailed in the name of gender equality. Giving athletes favored treatment, often justified in terms of diversity, has become a boon to the well-off.

The biggest losers, of course, are children from poor families. They 14 have neither the cachet of the rich or famous nor the cosseting that raises grades and test scores. A widely reported study of the 146 most selective colleges by the Century Foundation showed that 74 percent of students came from families in the upper quartile of the income bracket; just three percent came from the bottom quartile.

This issue has attracted lots of attention during the past few years. 15 Most colleges claim to favor "strivers" over more advantaged youngsters with similar academic records, but the facts are otherwise. Poor students actually fare worse than they would under a system of admissions based entirely on grades and test scores.

In the late 1990s, the *Chronicle of Higher Education* reported recently, 16 the Educational Testing Service halted research designed to help admissions committees identify such strivers with greater statistical precision. While this tool could have increased economic as well as racial diversity, ETS apparently feared it could be used in arguing against explicitly race-based affirmative action. "It seems that higher education would prefer to see race-based preferences be shot down state by state rather than introduce selection processes that would aid poor Americans of all backgrounds," wrote Thomas Benton, commenting on the news story in a *Chronicle* column.

Thomas Benton turns out not to be the author's real name. It's the 17 pseudonym for an English professor at a liberal arts college. The fact that "Benton" feels he can't show his face when writing on this topic speaks volumes about how hard it is to talk about the myriad, and often perverse, implications of diversity.

READING FOR MEANING

This section presents three activities that will help you think about the meanings in Kirp's position argument.

Read to Comprehend

Write a few sentences briefly explaining what you think is the main idea Kirp wants his readers to take away from his essay.

Identify any words with meanings you are unsure of—such as *incantation* (paragraph 2) and *scions* (6)—and find the dictionary definition for each word that makes the best sense in the context.

To help you understand the essay better, also consider trying one of these critical reading strategies, explained in Appendix 1: *previewing* or *outlining*.

Read to Respond

Write several paragraphs exploring your initial thoughts and feelings about Kirp's position argument. Focus on anything that stands out for you, perhaps because it resonates with your own experience or because you find a statement puzzling. For example, consider writing about one of the following:

- your own experience with the college admissions process;

- the idea that children of alumni and potential donors get preference in admissions even at public universities;

- your response to the statement by Thomas Benton (the man who uses a pseudonym) that "[i]t seems that higher education would prefer to see race-based preferences be shot down state by state rather than introduce selection processes that would aid poor Americans of all backgrounds" (paragraph 16).

To help develop your response, also consider trying one of these critical reading strategies, explained in Appendix 1: *contextualizing* or *reflecting on challenges to your beliefs and values*.

Read to Analyze Assumptions

Write a paragraph or two analyzing an assumption in Kirp's essay. To think critically about assumptions, here are some kinds of questions you could ask: Who holds this assumption (the writer, readers, and/or others cited in the essay)? What are the effects of the assumption in the context of the essay specifically or in society more generally? What do you think about the assumption, and is there anything in the essay that raises doubts about it? How does the assumption reinforce or critique commonly held views, and are there any alternative ideas, beliefs, or values that would challenge this assumption?

You might choose an assumption from the list below, using the questions accompanying it in addition to the ones above to help you get started. Or you can choose another assumption in the essay to explore.

- **assumptions about who is helped or hurt by diversity policies.** Kirp asserts that his argument is "contrary to the conventional wisdom" (paragraph 1), because the public assumes that poor and minority applicants are the main beneficiaries of admissions policies seeking "diversity" at "America's top colleges" (1) and that "suburban middle class white youngsters" (11) are the main losers from such policies. "Minorities win and whites lose—that's how the diversity issue is publicly framed," he argues, "but the facts are otherwise" (4). He presents evidence that "many of the winners in the diversity sweepstakes" (1) are actually children of alumni (4), of the famous and "super-rich" (5–9), and of professors (10), along with athletic girls from wealthy families (13). As for "Who loses out?" (11), he cites Asian Americans (12) and "working-class male athletes" (13), and then asserts that "[t]he biggest losers . . . are children from poor families" (14).

To think critically about the assumptions in this essay related to who is helped or hurt by diversity policies, ask yourself questions like these: What kind of applicants do you think the public assumes such policies favor? Do you share these assumptions? Did Kirp's argument change any of your assumptions about this issue? If so, how? Could admissions policies be altered to satisfy both the public and Kirp? If so, how, and if not, why not? From a broader perspective, how does variety in students' backgrounds and talents benefit—or not—students as a group and the university and society in general?

- **assumptions about what admissions policies *should* be.** After Kirp demonstrates that diversity policies at elite colleges do not favor those students that the public thinks get preferential treatment, he asserts what he has found: "Poor students actually fare worse than they would under a system of admissions based entirely on grades and test scores" (paragraph 15). He cites a column from the *Chronicle of Higher Education* claiming that although affirmative action admission programs based explicitly on race are no longer legally acceptable, "higher education would prefer to see race-based preferences be shot down state by state rather than introduce selection processes that would aid poor Americans of all backgrounds" (16).

To think critically about the assumptions in this essay related to what university admissions policies should be, ask yourself questions like these: Where else do you see evidence that Kirp feels economics would be a fairer basis for seeking diversity in admissions? What is the link, if any, between ethnic diversity and economic diversity? How does one determine what admissions policy is "fair"? Should "diversity" be taken into consideration at all? Should grades and test scores be the only criteria for admission?

To help you analyze assumptions in Kirp's essay, also consider trying one of these critical reading strategies, explained in Appendix 1: *recognizing logical fallacies* or *judging the writer's credibility*.

READING LIKE A WRITER

PRESENTING THE ISSUE

Every position paper begins with an issue. Consequently, in planning and drafting a position paper, one of the first questions that a writer must answer is how much readers know about the issue. If readers are familiar with the issue, the writer may need to tell them very little about it. If they are unfamiliar with it, however, the writer may need to present it in great detail. Whether they are familiar or unfamiliar with it, readers may benefit from knowing about its history. They may also appreciate the writer's speculations about the larger social significance of the issue and even its likely immediate personal importance to themselves. Writers generally should not assume that readers will find an issue immediately engaging and worth their reading time. Therefore, they will often want to open a position paper with an interesting anecdote, arresting quotation, troubling fact, doomsday scenario, rhetorical question, or something else that is likely to engage readers' interest.

In addition, writers must address another important question—how to define the issue. Often, writers seek to redefine an issue to convince readers to look at it in a new way. If they succeed, then they can argue about the issue in their own terms, as they have redefined it. Kirp offers an example of this strategy. He begins his essay with two landmark examples that shaped the issue of affirmative action in college admissions, the 1978 Bakke case and the 2003 University of Michigan cases. He claims that "[f]rom the start, the incantation of diversity has been an act of hypocrisy" (2).

Analyze

1. Reread paragraphs 1 through 3, and underline key words connected to diversity and every instance of the word "diversity."

2. Then skim the essay, noting ways Kirp develops the argument that university claims of aiming for diversity are hypocritical.

Write

Write several sentences describing how Kirp demonstrates the national hypocrisy about diversity. Then add a few sentences explaining what you think he might prefer as a standard for admissions to elite colleges.

A Special Reading Strategy

Evaluating the Logic of an Argument

To evaluate the logic of an argument, apply the ABC test by asking yourself three basic questions:

A. How *appropriate* is the support for each reason offered?

B. How *believable* is the support?

C. How *consistent and complete* is the overall argument?

Such an evaluation requires a comprehensive and thoughtful critical reading, but your efforts will help you understand more fully what makes a position paper successful. To evaluate the logic of Kirp's argument, follow the guidelines in Appendix 1. There you will find definitions and explanations (pp. 579–82) as well as an illustration based on an excerpt from a famous essay by Martin Luther King Jr. (pp. 553–57).

CONSIDERING IDEAS FOR YOUR OWN WRITING

Consider writing about an issue related to Kirp's concern about university admissions policies. Should athletes receive preferential treatment? Should testing criteria be changed? Should tests themselves be changed? Should students be admitted only if they are college-ready, with no need for remedial classes? Or you could expand your questions to other national issues that are controversial: Should marijuana be legalized? Should the Social Security system be changed? Or you could write on a more general topic that has local resonance: Should community growth be limited? Should height and design restrictions be placed on new commercial buildings? Should there be a review board to handle complaints against the police? Should skateboarding be banned from all sidewalks? Should parents be held responsible legally and financially for crimes committed by their children under age eighteen? One major advantage of writing a position paper on a local civic issue is that you can gather information by researching the issue in local newspapers and talking with community leaders and residents.

Tan-Li Hsu

High on Caffeine: Regulating Energy Drinks

Tan-Li Hsu wrote "High on Caffeine: Regulating Energy Drinks" for one of his college classes. Addressing the issue of the high caffeine content in energy drinks that are targeted at teenagers, and arguing for labeling and warnings on the cans, Hsu takes a clear position and documents his paper in MLA style, an appropriate citation format for much academic writing.

Think about your own experience with energy drinks or with any marketed substances that have clear warnings on the labels. Did the warnings change your behavior? As you read, think about the strategies for position papers that you have been studying, and annotate the text when you spot these strategies.

1   The market for energy drinks is continually expanding, which is not surprising given that the demand has grown immensely since 1997 when Red Bull was introduced in the United States. Roland Griffiths, a professor of psychiatry and neuroscience at Johns Hopkins University School of Medicine and author of a study published in the journal *Drug and Alcohol Dependence,* estimates that the market now totals at least $5.4 billion a year (Doheny). These popular drinks are packed with caffeine, a stimulant that is able to freely diffuse into the brain and temporarily increase alertness. Although the Food and Drug Administration places a limit on how much caffeine food products can contain—71 milligrams for each 12-ounce can—energy drinks are considered to be dietary supplements and not food products, therefore allowing caffeine content in these drinks to remain unregulated (Roan).

2   As a result, hundreds of brands of energy drinks with ridiculous amounts of caffeine not specified on labels flourish in the market. Furthermore, marketers intentionally target teenagers who are more susceptible to drinking multiple cans because they tend to live active lifestyles that leave them sleep deprived. It's no wonder that "[t]hirty-one percent of U.S. teenagers say they drink energy drinks," according to Simmons Research. "That represents 7.6 million teens" ("Teens"). With the increase in the usage of energy drinks and the failure to post caffeine content and warning labels on cans, emergency room doctors and poison control centers are reporting more cases of caffeine intoxication. I agree with Dr. Griffiths and the other authors of the Johns Hopkins study that energy drink manufacturers should clearly indicate the amount of caffeine on labels and shift marketing efforts away from teenagers.

3   All energy drinks list caffeine as an ingredient on labels, but many don't specify how many milligrams of caffeine are present. The truth is some brands like "Wired" and "Fixx" have 500 mg of caffeine per 20-oz

serving, about 10 times the caffeine found in cans of soda. In addition, another ingredient called guarana is a source of a similar substance that adds to the danger of the high caffeine content. According to Nancy Shute, in her article "Over the Limit?," unsuspecting teens who crave a buzz by drinking several cans of energy drinks are putting themselves at risk for the irregular heartbeat and nausea associated with caffeine intoxication. In rare cases, as shown by 19-year-old James Stone, who took "two dozen caffeine pills for putting in long hours on a job search" (Shute), intoxication may even lead to death by cardiac arrest.

It is possible to promote responsible consumption of energy drinks by 4 including possible health hazards along with caffeine content on can labels that encourage drinking in moderation. The reason such warning labels don't already exist could be because marketers are more concerned with money than with the health of consumers. "Vying for the dollars of teenagers with promises of weight loss, increased endurance and legal high . . . top-sellers Red Bull, Monster and Rockstar . . . make up a \$3.4 billion-a-year industry that grew by 80 percent last year" ("Teens"). By warning about the possible health hazards of drinking too much caffeine, manufacturers of energy drinks risk a decrease in purchases. Maureen Storey, a spokeswoman for the American Beverage Association, argues that "most mainstream energy drinks contain the same amount of caffeine, or even less, than you'd get in a cup of brewed coffee. If labels listing caffeine content are required on energy drinks, they should also be required on coffeehouse coffee" (Doheny). This argument has some validity, but it fails to include ingredients in energy drinks such as guarana that function as a hidden source of caffeine. Guarana is a berry that grows in Venezuela and contains a high amount of guaranine, a substance that has the same properties as caffeine. Assuming that energy drinks and coffee have the same amount of caffeine, the risk of caffeine intoxication from energy drinks is much higher because of the guaranine.

It is obvious that marketers are taking advantage of teens and encour- 5 aging them to drink more with attractive brand names such as Rockstar, Monster, and Cocaine Energy Drink that promise to enhance performance. One reason marketers target teenagers instead of a more mature age group may be that teens are more easily tricked by claims that energy drinks will increase endurance and mental awareness. Also, teens are often out partying late at night, as compared to an adult who recognizes the importance of a good night's sleep. It's no surprise that marketers are targeting exhausted teenagers who are more likely to purchase these drinks than an adult who makes sure he is in bed by 10 p.m.

However, marketers fail to realize the consequences of such market- 6 ing techniques. A study led by Dr. Danielle McCarthy of Northwestern University showed "a surprising number of caffeine overdose reports to a Chicago poison control center" ("Teens"). "Although adults of all ages are known to use caffeine, it is mainly abused by young adults who want to stay awake or even get high," McCarthy said ("Study").

7   Preteens are getting hooked on caffeine as well: "A 2003 study of Columbus, Ohio, middle schoolers found some taking in 800 milligrams of caffeine a day—more than twice the recommended maximum for adults of 300 milligrams" (Shute). The problem for preteens is especially dire because " 'their body weight is low,' says Wahida Karmally, the director of nutrition for the Irving Center for Clinical Research at Columbia University Medical Center" (qtd. in Shute). Researchers do not know how such high levels of caffeine consumption affect the child's developing body.

8   Manufacturers argue that marketing to teenagers and preteens is perfectly fine because energy drinks can be part of a balanced lifestyle when consumed sensibly. While convincing, this argument does not demonstrate a clear understanding of the scope of the problem. If a student drinks an energy drink while studying at night and can't sleep because of it, he might drink another in the morning to help wake up. According to Richard Levine, a professor of pediatrics and psychiatry at Penn State University College of Medicine and chief of the division of adolescent medicine and eating disorders at Penn State Milton S. Hershey Medical Center, "too much caffeine can make it harder to nod off, even when you're tired. Then you risk falling into a vicious cycle of insomnia caused by energy drinks followed by more caffeine to wake up" (Seltzer). Those who fall into this cycle become addicted to energy drinks and this addiction threatens the very idea of sensible consumption. For example, 15-year-old Eric Williams explained that he "used to drink two to four energy drinks a day, and sometimes used them to stay awake to finish a big homework project." The headaches he got when he didn't drink them convinced him to quit "although it took him two weeks" to break the habit (Seltzer). Teens shouldn't rely on energy boosters to achieve a balanced lifestyle; they should learn time management and get into the habit of a good night's sleep every day.

9   It should now be clear that energy drink manufacturers are intentionally targeting a younger audience. Brand names, appealing promises of enhanced performance, and failure to post clear warning labels have allowed the energy drink market to grow into a billion-dollar industry. Although manufacturers are enjoying profits, consumers are placing themselves at risk for serious health problems associated with caffeine intoxication. The most susceptible to intoxication are teenagers who either drink to delay exhaustion or to get a buzz. Caffeine content and overdose warnings must be placed on cans in order to make teens aware of the potential dangers of drinking too much.

Works Cited

Doheny, Kathleen. "Energy Drinks: Hazardous to Your Health?" *Health & Cooking. WebMD.* 24 Sept. 2008. Web. 22 Mar. 2010.

Roan, Shari. "Energy Drinks Can Cause Caffeine Intoxication." *Los Angeles Times.* Los Angeles Times, 28 Sept. 2008. Web. 22 Mar. 2010.

Seltzer, Rick. "Heavy Use of Energy Drinks Can Threaten Teens' Health." *Atlanta Journal-Constitution.* Atlanta Journal-Constitution, 27 Aug. 2008. Web. 16 Jan. 2009.

Shute, Nancy. "Over the Limit?" *U.S. News & World Report.* U.S. News & World Report, 15 Apr. 2007. Web. 16 Jan. 2009.

"Study: More People Abusing, Getting 'High' on Caffeine." *FoxNews.* Fox News, 24 Feb. 2009. Web. 24 Feb. 2009.

"Teens Abusing Energy Boosting Drinks, Doctors Fear." *FoxNews.* Fox News, 31 Oct. 2006. Web. 16 Feb. 2009.

READING FOR MEANING

This section presents three activities that will help you think about the meanings in Hsu's position paper.

Read to Comprehend

Write a few sentences briefly explaining Hsu's position on energy drinks.

Identify any words with meanings you are unsure of—such as *susceptible* (paragraph 2) and *dire* (7)—and find the dictionary definition for each word that makes the best sense in the context.

To help you understand the essay better, also consider trying one of these critical reading strategies, explained in Appendix 1: *outlining* or *paraphrasing.*

Read to Respond

Write a paragraph or two exploring your initial thoughts and feelings about Hsu's position argument. Focus on anything that stands out for you, perhaps because it resonates with your own experience or because you find a statement puzzling. For example, consider writing about one of the following:

- any experience you might have had with caffeine-based drinks, whether energy drinks, coffee, colas, or any other substances that alter your energy level.

- your response to Hsu's assertion that marketers should include "possible health hazards along with caffeine content on can labels that encourage drinking in moderation" (paragraph 4).

To help develop your response, also consider trying one of these critical reading strategies, explained in Appendix 1: *recognizing emotional manipulation* or *judging the writer's credibility.*

Read to Analyze Assumptions

Write a paragraph or two analyzing an assumption in Hsu's essay. To think critically about assumptions, here are some kinds of questions you could ask:

Who holds this assumption (the writer, readers, and/or others cited in the essay)? What are the effects of the assumption in the context of the essay specifically or in society more generally? What do you think about the assumption, and is there anything in the essay that raises doubts about it? How does the assumption reinforce or critique commonly held views, and are there any alternative ideas, beliefs, or values that would challenge this assumption?

You might choose an assumption from the list below, using the questions accompanying it in addition to the ones above to help you get started. Or you can choose another assumption in the essay to explore.

- **assumptions about the responsibilities of companies toward consumers.** Hsu notes that "marketers intentionally target teenagers" (paragraph 2), that "marketers are more concerned with money than with the health of consumers" (4), and that "energy drink manufacturers are intentionally targeting a younger audience" (9).

  To think critically about assumptions regarding the responsibilities of companies toward consumers, ask yourself questions like these: Do you believe manufacturers have a responsibility to protect consumers from misusing or abusing their products? Do you think warning labels and posted caffeine contents would alleviate the problem of teen overdosing? Can you think of other instances where companies have had to curtail their marketing for similar reasons? Can you think of any other ways to solve this problem?

- **assumptions about the benefits of a "balanced lifestyle."** Hsu reports that energy drinks can be part of a "balanced lifestyle when consumed sensibly" (paragraph 8). At the end of that paragraph he says: "Teens shouldn't rely on energy boosters to achieve a balanced lifestyle; they should learn time management and get into the habit of a good night's sleep every day" (8).

  To think critically about assumptions regarding the benefits of a balanced lifestyle, ask yourself questions like these: Where else in the essay does Hsu assume that "balance" is more important than temporary wakefulness or extra energy? Why would it be important for teenagers in particular to learn how to achieve balance? What kinds of benefits do you think a balanced lifestyle confers? What factors besides sleep and energy might be involved in it? Are there times when balance could be undesirable?

READING LIKE A WRITER

ASSERTING A CLEAR, UNEQUIVOCAL POSITION

The writer's statement of position is the sun that lights up a position paper. Like moons and planets, the other sentences reflect the light of this position statement. Without it, the essay might explain the debate on an issue but would not argue for a position on it.

Writers usually (but not always) assert their positions early in an essay. To keep readers in focus, they may reassert the position later in the essay and nearly always do so in the conclusion. Because readers must be able to understand the writer's position readily, it should be stated clearly and without waffling. However, the position should be carefully qualified if necessary. Key terms must be precisely defined unless there is little likelihood that readers will differ over what they mean.

Analyze

1. Underline Hsu's statement, restatements, and qualifications of his position (you will find these sentences at the end of paragraph 2, the beginnings of paragraphs 3, 4, and 9, the middle of paragraph 4, and the end of paragraph 9).

2. Consider whether the writer's position statements are clear and unequivocal. Think about where they are located in relation to the other parts of his argument.

Write

Write several sentences reporting what you have learned about how Hsu asserts his position on the issue of labeling the caffeine content in energy drinks. Point to places where he restates or qualifies his position. What does each statement add to the others? Then add a few sentences evaluating how effectively Hsu asserts his position for his particular readers. Write down your judgments about the clarity of the statements.

CONSIDERING IDEAS FOR YOUR OWN WRITING

Consider writing a position paper on a controversial marketing issue, such as the following: Should all advertisements for liquor be banned? Should all advertisements for cigarettes? Can you think of issues that involve limiting marketing strategies, such as Hsu advocates? Or, since marketing is an economically motivated form of "education," you could consider education as a broad area full of controversial issues: Should there be exit exams in schools? Should there be reforms in the way classes are conducted, such as lengthening the time of classes but holding them less often or taking the classroom into the field so that students get more hands-on learning? Should subjects such as art, music, physical education, and similar nonacademic topics be reinstated in schools that have discontinued them to save money? (You could also argue the opposite.) Are there subjects currently not taught in schools that you think should be the schools' responsibility? Should school be mandatory year-round? Should after-school programs be expanded? Should there be general education classes in college? (Or the reverse: Should we abolish general education in colleges and universities?) Should we expand our notion of what constitutes a "major" in college?

A Special Reading Strategy

Using a Toulmin Analysis

To analyze the logic of Hsu's essay, perform a Toulmin analysis on it. Identify his claim and the reasons and evidence he gives to support it. Then try to discover the beliefs, values, and assumptions that connect his reasons and evidence to his claim—that is, the underlying ideas that lead him to use these reasons and this evidence to justify this claim. (Stephen Toulmin, who developed this system of analysis, called evidence "grounds," and assumptions "warrants.")

A useful approach is to list the claim and reasons using a sentence with a "because" clause.

Claim: energy drink manufacturers should clearly indicate the amount of caffeine on labels and shift marketing efforts away from teenagers (paragraph 2).

Reason 1: because energy drinks contain so much caffeine that "unsuspecting teens . . . are putting themselves at risk for the irregular heartbeat and nausea associated with caffeine intoxication" (3).

Reason 2: because teenagers "are more easily tricked" than adults "by claims that energy drinks will increase endurance and mental awareness" and less likely to realize "the importance of . . . sleep"(5).

Reason 3: because "[p]reteens are getting hooked on caffeine as well" (7).

Singling out the reasons enables you to examine the logic behind each one. First, list the evidence—or grounds—provided to support Reason 1: "because unsuspecting teens . . . are putting themselves at risk for the irregular heartbeat and nausea associated with caffeine intoxication." Use as much of the writer's own wording as possible, because doing so will help you identify his assumptions and beliefs.

Grounds

1. The authority, Simmons Research, says that "[t]hirty-one percent of U.S. teenagers say they drink energy drinks. . . . That represents 7.6 million teens" (2).

2. Emergency room doctors and poison control centers are reporting more cases of caffeine intoxication (2).

3. Authors of a Johns Hopkins study say that "energy drink manufacturers should clearly indicate the amount of caffeine on labels and shift marketing efforts away from teenagers" (2).

Now consider the denotations and connotations—the basic meanings and the emotional associations—of key words and phrases used by the writer in the reason and grounds. For example, consider his reference to "a professor of psychiatry and neuroscience at Johns Hopkins University School of Medicine and author of a study published in the journal *Drug and Alcohol Dependence*" in paragraph 1, who gives the evidence for Ground 3. (Hsu mentions several other doctors in his essay.) Consider also his phrases "teens . . . are putting themselves at risk" and "caffeine intoxication" (3). Why does Hsu use this language, or any other particular language you note? What comes to *your* mind when you hear these words and phrases?

For example, you can tell that Hsu values the opinions of Simmons Research and of medical and scientific authorities, such as Johns Hopkins School of Medicine, and that he expects his readers to share this belief. He also seems to value—and to expect that his readers value—the idea that teens need protection from unfamiliar dangers. Once you have stated in your own words what the key terms tell you about Hsu's values, speculate about what alternative assumptions or different values some readers might find in the connotations of these terms. For example, many people do not believe that marketers of manufactured products are responsible for the behavior of people who use these products. Others believe that teens should be protected or regulated by their parents, not by marketers. Still other people believe that teens need to learn life's lessons on their own, and if they get intoxicated on caffeine, they will learn not to do it again.

Finally, compare your own values and beliefs with Hsu's. Do you share the same views, or do you find some differences? What are they?

Once you have completed this analysis for Hsu's first reason, try doing the same kind of analysis for Reasons 2 and 3.

Appendix 1 (pp. 583–86) provides detailed guidelines on using a Toulmin analysis.

Jessica Statsky

Children Need to Play, Not Compete

Jessica Statsky was a college student when she wrote this position paper, in which she argues that organized sports are not good for children between the ages of six and twelve. Recall your own experiences as an elementary school student playing competitive sports, either in or out of school. If you were not actively involved yourself, did you know anyone who was? Was winning emphasized? What about having a good time? Getting along with others? Developing athletic skills and confidence? As you read, notice how Statsky supports the reasons for her position and how she handles readers' likely objections to her argument. Also note the visible cues that Statsky provides to guide you through her argument step by step. Annotate the text, paying special attention to the features of a position paper—presenting the issue, asserting a clear, unequivocal position, arguing directly for the position, counterarguing objections and opposing positions, and establishing credibility.

The other readings in this chapter are followed by reading and writing activities. Following this reading, however, you are on your own to decide how to read for meaning and read like a writer.

1   Over the past several decades, according to the National Center for Sports Safety, participation in organized sports for children has become higher in the United States than ever before (Ellis). And though many adults regard Little League Baseball and Peewee Football as a basic part of childhood, the games are not always joyous ones. When overzealous parents and coaches impose adult standards on children's sports, the result can be activities that are neither satisfying nor beneficial to children.

2   I am concerned about all organized sports activities for children between the ages of six and twelve. The damage I see results from non-contact as well as contact sports, from sports organized locally to those organized nationally. Highly organized competitive sports such as Pee-wee Football and Little League Baseball are too often played to adult standards, which are developmentally inappropriate for children and can be both physically and psychologically harmful. Furthermore, because they eliminate many children from organized sports before they are ready to compete, they are actually counterproductive for developing either future players or fans. Finally, because they emphasize competition and winning, they unfortunately provide occasions for some parents and coaches to place their own fantasies and needs ahead of children's welfare.

3   One readily understandable danger of overly competitive sports is that they entice children into physical actions that are bad for growing bodies. Although the official Little League Online Web site acknowledges that children do risk injury playing baseball, the league insists that "severe injuries . . . are infrequent"—"far less than the risk of riding a skateboard, a bicycle,

or even the school bus" ("What about My Child?"). Nevertheless, Leonard Koppett in *Sports Illusion, Sports Reality* claims that a twelve-year-old trying to throw a curve ball, for example, may put abnormal strain on developing arm and shoulder muscles, sometimes resulting in lifelong injuries (294). Contact sports like football can be even more hazardous. Thomas Tutko, a psychology professor at San Jose State University and coauthor of the book *Winning Is Everything and Other American Myths*, writes:

> I am strongly opposed to young kids playing tackle football. It is not the right stage of development for them to be taught to crash into other kids. Kids under the age of fourteen are not by nature physical. Their main concern is self preservation. They don't want to meet head on and slam into each other. But tackle football absolutely requires that they try to hit each other as hard as they can. And it is too traumatic for young kids. (qtd. in Tosches A1)

As Tutko indicates, even when children are not injured, fear of being   4 hurt detracts from their enjoyment of the sport. Little League Online ranks fear of injury as the seventh of seven reasons children quit ("What about My Child?"). One mother of an eight-year-old Peewee Football player explained, "The kids get so scared. They get hit once and they don't want anything to do with football anymore. They'll sit on the bench and pretend their leg hurts" (qtd. in Tosches A1). Some children are driven to even more desperate measures. For example, in one Peewee Football game, a reporter watched the following scene as a player took himself out of the game:

> "Coach, my tummy hurts. I can't play," he said. The coach told the player to get back onto the field. "There's nothing wrong with your stomach," he said. When the coach turned his head, the seven-year-old stuck a finger down his throat and made himself vomit. When the coach turned back, the boy pointed to the ground and told him, "Yes there is, coach. See?" (Tosches A33)

Despite such extreme reactions, parents often introduce their children   5 to organized sports because of their concerns for their children's health (Ellis), and, with childhood obesity an epidemic in our country, it is important for children to be active. But, as Dr. Russell Ellis points out on the Web site of the National Center for Sports Safety, "even if the child can understand what is being taught, he or she may not have the strength or coordination to perform the task. An important point to remember is that kids will not acquire certain skills faster just because they start trying to learn them earlier in life." Ellis also cites studies that have suggested that "participating in only one sport at an early age may cause more injuries and lead to cessation of that sport at an earlier age."

6   Besides physical hazards and anxieties, competitive sports pose psychological dangers for children. Martin Rablovsky, a former sports editor for the *New York Times,* says that in all his years of watching young children play organized sports, he has noticed very few of them smiling. "I've seen children enjoying a spontaneous pre-practice scrimmage become somber and serious when the coach's whistle blows," Rablovsky says. "The spirit of play suddenly disappears, and sport becomes joblike" (qtd. in Coakley 94). The primary goal of a professional athlete—winning—is not appropriate for children. Their goals should be having fun, learning, and being with friends. Although winning does add to the fun, too many adults lose sight of what matters and make winning the most important goal. Several studies have shown that when children are asked whether they would rather be warming the bench on a winning team or playing regularly on a losing team, about 90 percent choose the latter (Smith, Smith, and Smoll 11).

7   On their Web site in January 2010, the American Academy of Pediatrics warns parents that "all children are unique individuals. They grow and mature at different rates. Age, weight, and size shouldn't be the only measures used to decide if your child is ready to play a sport. Emotional development is also important. Children shouldn't be pushed into a sport or be placed in a competition they are not physically or emotionally ready to handle."

8   Winning and losing may be an inevitable part of adult life, but they should not be part of childhood. Too much competition too early in life can affect a child's development. Children are easily influenced, and when they sense that their competence and worth are based on their ability to live up to their parents' and coaches' high expectations—and on their ability to win—they can become discouraged and depressed. Little League advises parents to "keep winning in perspective" (*Little League Online,* "Your Role"), noting that the most common reasons children give for quitting, aside from change in interest, are lack of playing time, failure and fear of failure, disapproval by significant others, and psychological stress (*Little League Online,* "What about My Child?"). According to Dr. Glyn C. Roberts, a professor of kinesiology at the Institute of Child Behavior and Development at the University of Illinois, 80 to 90 percent of children who play competitive sports at a young age drop out by sixteen (Kutner C8).

9   This statistic illustrates another reason I oppose competitive sports for children: because they are so highly selective, very few children get to participate. Far too soon, a few children are singled out for their athletic promise, while many others who may be on the verge of developing the necessary strength and ability are screened out and discouraged from trying out again. Like adults, children fear failure, and so even those with good physical skills may stay away because they lack self-confidence. Consequently, teams lose many promising players who with some encouragement and experience might have become stars. The problem is that many parent-sponsored, out-of-school programs give more importance to having a winning team than

to developing children's physical skills and self-esteem. As "Tom C." writes in his article "Sport Safety for Children" on the *Gather* blog, "[t]he competitive nature of sport is driven by the desire for victory, and unfortunately, the desire is presented in a win at all costs mentality in sport society."

Indeed, it is no secret that too often scorekeeping, league standings, and 10 the drive to win bring out the worst in adults who are more absorbed in living out their own fantasies (as shown in fig. 1) than in enhancing the quality of the experience for children (Smith, Smith, and Smoll 9). The news provides plenty of horror stories. *Los Angeles Times* reporter Rich Tosches, for example, tells the story of a brawl among seventy-five parents that began following a Peewee Football game when a parent from one team confronted a player from the other team (A33). Another example is provided by an *L.A. Times* editorial about a Little League manager who intimidated the opposing team by setting fire to one of its jerseys on the pitching mound before the game began. As the editorial writer commented, the manager showed his young team that "intimidation could substitute for playing well" ("The Bad News" B6). In addition, a report by Bill Topp on the Web site of the National Association of Sports Officials lists an appalling number of incidences of attacks on referees and field supervisors, including Thomas Juntas's fatal beating of a Massachusetts man who had been supervising a pick-up hockey game in which Juntas's son was playing.

"Please, Mrs. Enright, if I let you pinch-hit for Tommy, all the mothers will want to pinch-hit."

FIG. 1. Too many parents use their children's sports programs as a way to live out their own fantasies, as shown in this cartoon by James Mulligan from the *New Yorker*.

11   Ellis addresses this problem in his article "Sports Participation in Children: When to Begin?" where he argues that: "Coaches and parents generally do not possess the skills to effectively teach the very young. This deficiency is not because of lack of training and experience in the sport, but because of a lack of experience formally educating children and a relatively poor knowledge of child development." The seriousness of the problem is illustrated by the fact that Adelphi University in Garden City, New York, offers a sports psychology workshop for Little League coaches that is designed to balance their "animal instincts" with "educational theory" in hopes of reducing the "screaming and hollering," in the words of Harold Weisman, manager of sixteen Little Leagues in New York City (Schmitt B2). In a three-and-one-half-hour Sunday morning workshop, coaches learn how to make practices more fun, treat injuries, deal with irate parents, and be "more sensitive to their young players' fears, emotional frailties, and need for recognition." Little League is to be credited with recognizing the need for such workshops.

12   Some parents would no doubt argue that children cannot start too soon preparing to live in a competitive free-market economy. After all, secondary schools and colleges require students to compete for grades, and college admission is extremely competitive. And it is obvious how important competitive skills are in finding a job. Yet the ability to cooperate is also important for success in life. Before children are psychologically ready for competition, maybe we should emphasize cooperation and individual performance in team sports rather than winning.

13   Many people are ready for such an emphasis. One New York Little League official who had attended the Adelphi workshop tried to ban scoring from six- to eight-year-olds' games—but parents wouldn't support him (Schmitt B2). An innovative children's sports program in New York City, City Sports for Kids, emphasizes fitness, self-esteem, and sportsmanship. In this program's basketball games, every member on a team plays at least two of six eight-minute periods. The basket is seven feet from the floor rather than ten feet, and a player can score a point just by hitting the rim (Bloch C12). I believe this kind of local program should replace overly competitive programs like Peewee Football and Little League Baseball. For example, childhood-fitness expert Stephen Virgilio of Adelphi University recommends "positive competition," which encourages children to strive to do their best without comparing themselves to an opponent. Virgilio also suggests that improvements can come from a few simple rule changes, such as rotating players to different positions several times during each game to show that "you're more interested in skill development than just trying to win a game" (qtd. in Rosenstock).

14   Authorities have clearly documented the excesses and dangers of many competitive sports programs for children. It would seem that few children benefit from these programs and that those who do would benefit even more from programs emphasizing fitness, cooperation, sportsmanship, and

individual performance. Thirteen- and fourteen-year-olds may be eager for competition, but few younger children are. These younger children deserve sports programs designed specifically for their needs and abilities.

Works Cited

American Academy of Pediatrics. "Preventing Injury in Children's Sports." *Healthy Children*. 5 Jan. 2010. Web. 19 Mar. 2010.

"The Bad News Pyromaniacs?" Editorial. *Los Angeles Times*. Los Angeles Times, 16 June 1990: B6. Web. 16 May 2008.

Bloch, Gordon B. "Thrill of Victory Is Secondary to Fun." *New York Times*. New York Times, 2 Apr. 1990, late ed.: C12. Web. 14 May 2008.

C., Tom. "Sport Safety for Children." *Gather*. n.d. Web. 19 Mar. 2010.

Coakley, Jay J. *Sport in Society: Issues and Controversies*. St. Louis: Mosby, 1982. Print.

Ellis, Russell. "Sports Participation in Children: When to Begin?" *National Center for Sports Safety*. 2010. Web. 19 Mar. 2010.

Frank, L. "Contributions from Parents and Coaches." *CYB Message Board*. N.p., 8 July 1997. Web. 14 May 2008.

Koppett, Leonard. *Sports Illusion, Sports Reality*. Boston: Houghton, 1981. Print.

Kutner, Lawrence. "Athletics, through a Child's Eyes." *New York Times*. New York Times, 23 Mar. 1989, late ed.: C8. Web. 15 May 2008.

Mulligan, James. Cartoon. *New Yorker* 7 May 1979. *The Cartoon Bank*. Condé Nast Publications. n. d. Web. 19 Mar. 2010.

Rosenstock, Bonnie."Competitive Sports for Kids: When Winning Becomes Cumbersome Instead of Fun." *Parentsknow.com Database*. Web. 29 June 2004.

Schmitt, Eric. "Psychologists Take Seat on Little League Bench." *New York Times*. New York Times, 14 Mar. 1988, late ed.: B2. Web. 14 May 2008.

Smith, Nathan, Ronald Smith, and Frank Smoll. *Kidsports: A Survival Guide for Parents*. Reading: Addison, 1983. Print.

Topp, Bill. "Poor Sporting Behavior Reported to NASO." *National Association of Sports Officials*. Feb. 2004. Web. 29 June 2004.

Tosches, Rich. "Peewee Football: Is It Time to Blow the Whistle?" *Los Angeles Times*. Los Angeles Times, 3 Dec. 1988: A1+. Web. 22 May 2008.

"What about My Child?" *Little League Online*. Little League Baseball, Incorporated, 1999. Web. 30 May 2008.

"Your Role as a Little League Parent." *Little League Online*. Little League Baseball, Incorporated, 1999. Web. 30 May 2008.

READING FOR MEANING

Reading for meaning involves three activities:

- reading to comprehend,

- reading to respond, and

- reading to analyze assumptions.

Write a page or so explaining your understanding of Statsky's essay, a personal response you have to it, and one of its assumptions.

READING LIKE A WRITER

Writers of position papers

- present the issue,

- assert a clear, unequivocal position,

- argue directly for the position,

- counterargue objections and opposing positions, and

- establish credibility.

Choose one of these strategies in Statsky's essay, and analyze it carefully through close rereading and annotating. Then write several sentences explaining what you have learned, giving specific examples from the reading to support your explanation. Add a few sentences evaluating how successfully Statsky uses the strategy to argue convincingly for her position.

ANALYZING VISUALS

Write a paragraph analyzing the cartoon included in Statsky's position paper (Fig.1) and explaining what it contributes to the essay. To do the analysis, you can use the criteria chart for the Analysis of Visuals in Appendix 3 on pp. 670–72. Don't feel you have to answer all of the questions on the chart: focus on those that seem most productive in helping you write a paragraph-length analysis. To help you get started, consider adding these questions that specifically refer to Statsky's visual:

- How does this cartoon illustrate Statsky's concerns about parents' involvement in their children's competitive sports?

- What does the caption—what the coach is saying to Mrs. Enright— say about parents as role models for their children?

- Two schools of thought about how to raise children are (1) to show them what to do and (2) to allow them to learn on their own, including making mistakes. Clearly this cartoon illustrates the first school, taken to an extreme. How might you illustrate the second school?

Reviewing What Makes an Effective Essay

Position Papers

Analyze

Choose one reading from this chapter that seems to you especially effective. Before rereading the selection, jot down one or two reasons you remember it as an example of a good position argument.

Reread your chosen selection, adding further notes about what makes it a particularly successful example. Consider the selection's purpose and how well it achieves that purpose for its intended readers. (You can make an informed guess about the intended readers and their expectations by noting the publication source of the essay.) Then assess how well the essay uses the writing strategies of presenting the issue, asserting a clear, unequivocal position, arguing directly for the position, counterarguing, and establishing credibility.

Write

Write at least a page supporting your choice of this reading as an example of an effective position argument. Refer to details and specific parts of the essay as you explain how it works as a position essay and as you justify your evaluation of its effectiveness. You need not argue that it is the best reading in the chapter or that it is flawless, only that it is, in your view, a strong example of the genre.

A GUIDE TO WRITING POSITION PAPERS

The readings in this chapter have helped you learn a great deal about position papers. Now that you have seen how writers construct arguments supporting their position on issues for their particular readers, you can approach this type of writing confidently. The readings will remain an important resource for you as you develop your own position paper. Use them to review how other writers solved the types of problems you will encounter in your writing.

This Guide to Writing is designed to assist you in writing your position paper. Here you will find activities to help you choose an issue and discover what to say about it, organize your ideas and draft the essay, read the draft critically, revise the draft to strengthen your argument, and edit and proofread the essay to improve readability.

INVENTION AND RESEARCH

The following activities will help you choose an issue to write about and to develop an argument to support your position on the issue. Completing these activities will produce enough information to write a detailed and convincing first draft.

Choosing an Issue

List the most promising issues you can think of, beginning with any you listed for the Considering Ideas for Your Own Writing activities following the readings in this chapter. Rather than limiting yourself to the first subject that comes to mind, take a few minutes to consider your options and list as many issues as you can.

List the issues in the form of questions like these:

- Should local school boards have the power to ban such books as *The Adventures of Huckleberry Finn* and *Of Mice and Men* from school libraries?

- Should teenagers be required to get their parents' permission to obtain birth-control information and contraceptives?

- Should businesses remain loyal to their communities, or should they move to wherever labor costs, taxes, and other conditions are more favorable?

After you have completed your list, choose an arguable issue, one that people disagree about but that cannot be resolved simply with facts or by authorities. If your instructor does not specify whether your essay must include outside sources, decide whether your issue requires research and, if so, whether you have time for it. Issues that have been written about extensively—such as whether weapons searches should be conducted on high-school campuses or affirmative action should be continued in college admissions—make excellent topics for extended research. Other issues—such as whether students should be required to perform community service or be discouraged from taking part-time jobs that interfere with their studies—may be confidently based on personal experience.

Developing Your Argument

The writing and research activities that follow will enable you to test your choice of an issue and discover good ways to argue for your position on the issue.

Defining the Issue.   To see how you can define the issue, write nonstop about it for a few minutes. This brief but intensive writing will help stimulate your memory, letting you see what you already know about the issue and whether you will need to do research to discover more about it.

Considering Your Own Position and Reasons for It.   Briefly state your current position on the issue and give a few reasons you take this position. You may change your position as you develop your ideas and learn more about the issue, but for now say as directly as you can where you stand and why.

Researching the Issue.   If your instructor requires you to research the issue, or if you decide your essay would benefit from research, consult Appendix 2, Strategies for Research and Documentation, for guidelines on finding library and Internet sources. Research can help you look critically at your own thinking and help you anticipate your readers' arguments and possible objections to your argument.

Analyzing Your Readers.   Write for a few minutes identifying who your readers are, what they know about the issue, and how they can be convinced that your position may be plausible. Describe your readers briefly. Mention anything you know about them as a group that might influence the way they would read your position paper. Speculate about how they will respond to your argument.

Rehearsing the Argument for Your Position.   Consider the reasons you could give for your position, and then write for a few minutes about the one reason you think would be most convincing to your readers. Which reason do you think is the strongest? Which is most likely to appeal to your readers? As you write, try to show your readers why they should take this reason seriously.

Rehearsing Your Counterargument.   List what will likely be the one or two strongest opposing arguments or objections to your argument, and then write for a few minutes either conceding or refuting each one. Try to think of arguments or objections your readers will expect you to know about and respond to, especially any criticism that could seriously undermine your argument.

Testing Your Choice.   Pause now to decide whether you have chosen an issue about which you will be able to make a convincing argument. If your interest in the issue is growing and you are gaining confidence in the argument you want to make, you have probably made a good choice. However, if your interest in the issue is waning or you have been unable to come up with at least two or three plausible reasons why you take the position you do, you might want to choose another issue. If your issue does not seem promising, return to your list of possible subjects to select another.

Considering Visuals.   Consider whether visuals—drawings, photographs, tables, or graphs—would strengthen your argument. You could construct your own visuals, scan materials from books and magazines, or download them from the Internet. If you submit your essay electronically to other students and your instructor or if you post it on a Web site, consider including snippets of film or sound as well as photographs. Visual and auditory materials are not at all a requirement of a successful position paper, as you can tell from the readings in this chapter, but they could add a new dimension to your writing. If you want to use photographs or recordings of people, though, be sure to obtain their permission.

Considering Your Purpose.   Write for several minutes about your purpose for writing this position paper. The following questions will help you think about your purpose:

- What do I hope to accomplish with my readers? How do I want to influence their thinking? What one big idea do I want them to grasp and remember?

- How much resistance to my argument should I expect from my readers? Will they be largely receptive? Skeptical but convincible? Resistant and perhaps even antagonistic?

- How can I interest my readers in the issue? How can I help my readers see its significance—both to society at large and to them personally?

Formulating a Working Thesis.   Draft a thesis or position statement. A working thesis—as opposed to a final or revised thesis—will help you bring your invention writing into focus and begin your draft with a clear purpose. As you draft and revise your essay, you may decide to modify your position and reformulate your thesis. Remember that the thesis for a position paper should assert your position on the issue and may qualify that position. In addition, the thesis usually forecasts the parts of your argument; it might also forecast your counterargument. The thesis and forecasting statements, therefore, may occupy several sentences. Here are four examples from the readings:

- ". . . our educational system fails to teach science in a way that allows students to integrate it into their lives." (Greene, paragraph 2)

- "Contrary to the conventional wisdom, many of the winners in the diversity sweepstakes aren't poor or minority students, and many of the losers have powerful justice-based claims." (Kirp, paragraph 1)

- ". . . energy drink manufacturers should clearly indicate the amount of caffeine on labels and shift marketing efforts away from teenagers." (Hsu, paragraph 2)

- "When overzealous parents and coaches impose adult standards on children's sports, the result can be activities that are neither satisfying nor beneficial to children.

  "I am concerned about all organized sports activities for children between the ages of six and twelve. The damage I see results from noncontact as well as contact sports, from sports organized locally to those organized nationally. Highly organized competitive sports such as Peewee Football and Little League Baseball are too often played to adult standards, which are developmentally inappropriate for children and can be both physically and psychologically harmful. Furthermore, because they eliminate many children from organized sports before they are ready to compete, they are actually counterproductive for developing either future players or fans. Finally, because they emphasize competition and winning, they unfortunately provide occasions for some parents and coaches to place their own fantasies and needs ahead of children's welfare." (Statsky, paragraphs 1 and 2)

DRAFTING

The following guidelines will help you set goals for your draft, plan its organization, and consider a useful sentence strategy.

Setting Goals

Establishing goals for your draft before you begin writing will enable you to make decisions and work more confidently. Consider the following questions now, and keep them in mind as you draft. They will help you set goals for drafting as well as recall how the writers you have read in this chapter tried to achieve similar goals.

- *How can I present the issue in a way that will interest my readers?* Should I open with an anecdote as Greene does, a response to a debate under way as Kirp does, or a connection to my personal experience as Greene and Stabiner do? Do I need to define the issue explicitly, as Kirp, Hsu, and Statsky do? Should I present the issue in a historical context, as Stabiner, Page, Kirp, and Statsky do? Or should I start with alarming statistics, as Hsu does?

- *How can I support my argument in a way that will win the respect of my readers?* Should I quote authorities or offer statistics from research studies, as Stabiner, Page, Kirp, and Statsky do? Should I argue that my position is based on shared values, as all the writers in this chapter do? Should I create analogies, as Greene and Page do? Should I provide examples or speculate about consequences, like all the writers? Should I support my argument with personal experience, as Greene and Stabiner do?

- *How can I counterargue effectively?* Should I introduce my argument by reviewing readers' opposing positions and likely objections, as Kirp does? Should I attempt to refute such views, as all the writers do? Should I concede the wisdom of some of these views, as Greene, Stabiner, and Statsky do?

- *How can I establish my authority and credibility on the issue?* Should I support my argument through research, as all the writers in this chapter do? Should I risk bringing in my personal experience, as Greene does? How can I refute opposing views without attacking readers, as Stabiner manages to do? Should I make an appeal to possible shared moral values with readers, as Stabiner, Page, Kirp, and Hsu do?

Organizing Your Draft

With goals in mind and invention notes in hand, you are ready to make a tentative outline of your draft. First, list the reasons you plan to use as support for your argument. Decide how you will sequence these reasons. Writers of position papers often end with the strongest reasons because this organization gives the best reasons the greatest emphasis. Then add to your outline the opposing positions or objections that you plan to counterargue.

Working with Sources

Quoting and Paraphrasing

How you represent the views of those who disagree with your position is especially important because it affects your credibility with readers. If you do not represent your opponents' views fairly and accurately, readers very likely will—and probably should—question your honesty. One useful strategy is to insert quoted words and phrases into your summary of the source.

But how do you decide which elements to quote and which to put in your own words? The following sentences from Jessica Statsky's essay illustrate how you might make this decision. Compare the sentence below from paragraph 3 of Statsky's essay to the passage from her source, the Little League Online Web site. The words Statsky quotes are highlighted:

> **Statsky:** Although the official Little League Online Web site acknowledges that children do risk injury playing baseball, the league insists that "severe injuries . . . are infrequent"—"far less than the risk of riding a skateboard, a bicycle, or even the school bus" ("What about My Child?").

> **Little League Online:** We know that injuries constitute one of parents' foremost concerns, and rightly so. Injuries seem to be inevitable in any rigorous activity, especially if players are new to the sport and unfamiliar with its demands. But because of the safety precautions taken in Little League, severe injuries such as bone fractures are infrequent. Most injuries are sprains and strains, abrasions and cuts and bruises. The risk of serious injury in Little League Baseball is far less than the risk of riding a skateboard, a bicycle, or even the school bus.

Statsky summarizes Little League's acknowledgment that playing competitive sports can be harmful by condensing the second sentence ("Injuries seem to be inevitable in any rigorous activity, especially if players are new to the sport and unfamiliar with its demands") into one simple clause ("children do risk injury playing baseball"). Note what her summary leaves out—Little League's explanation that injuries are "inevitable in any rigorous activity," its emphasis on the increased likelihood of injury when the sport is "new" and "unfamiliar," and the claim that Little League takes "safety precautions" to prevent serious injury. Statsky omitted these statements because they try to explain away the basic fact she wants to emphasize—that "children do risk injury playing baseball." Demonstrating that Little League— renowned as the first and probably the most famous provider of organized sports for children—agrees with her about this basic fact lends credibility to Statsky's argument.

But when you omit language and ideas from your summary, you must take care not to misrepresent your source. Statsky makes clear in the second part of her sentence that although Little League agrees with her on the risk of injury, it disagrees about the seriousness of that risk. By quoting ("the league insists that 'severe injuries . . . are infrequent'—'far less than the risk of riding a skateboard, a bicycle, or even the school bus'"), she assures readers she has not distorted Little League's position.

Using Ellipsis Marks in Quotations to Avoid Plagiarism

In an earlier draft, Statsky omitted the quotation marks around the phrase "severe injuries . . . are infrequent"—either because she did not know how to make the language from the original fit smoothly into her sentence or because she did not realize she could have multiple separate quotations from the same source in one sentence. Below is part of her original sentence, followed by the source with the quoted words highlighted.

> **Statsky:** the league insists that severe injuries are infrequent— "far less than the risk of riding a skateboard, a bicycle, or even the school bus" ("What about My Child?").

> **Little League Online:** severe injuries such as bone fractures are infrequent. Most injuries are sprains and strains, abrasions and cuts and bruises. The risk of serious injury in Little League Baseball is far less than the risk of riding a skateboard, a bicycle, or even the school bus.

Even though Statsky cites the source, this failure to use quotation marks around language that is borrowed amounts to plagiarism. A simple way to avoid plagiarizing is to use ellipsis marks (. . .) to indicate that words have been omitted: "severe injuries . . . are infrequent." When you cite sources in a position paper, use quotation marks whenever you use phrases from your source, *and* indicate your source. Doing one or the other is not enough; you must do both. For more information on quoting and using ellipses to integrate language from sources into your own sentences, see pages 635–43 in Appendix 2, Strategies for Research and Documentation.

Considering a Useful Sentence Strategy

As you draft your essay, you will need to move back and forth smoothly between direct arguments for your position and counterarguments to your readers' likely objections and opposing positions. One useful strategy for making this move is to concede some value in a likely criticism but then immediately refute the idea that it weakens your larger point. The refutation may appear either in the same sentence or in the next one. Here are two examples from Statsky's essay that illustrate ways to use concessions (shown in italics) and refutations (shown in bold):

The primary goal of a professional athlete—winning—is not appropriate for children. Their goals should be having fun, learning, and being with friends. *Although winning does add to the fun,* **too many adults lose sight of what matters and make winning the most important goal.** (paragraph 6)

And it is obvious how important competitive skills are in finding a job. **Yet the ability to cooperate is also important for success in life.** (12)

In these examples from different stages in her argument, Statsky concedes the importance or value of some of her readers' likely objections, but then firmly refutes them. (Because these illustrations are woven into an extended argument, you may better appreciate them if you look at them in context by turning to the paragraphs where they appear.)

Here are two examples from other readings in the chapter:

These are the standard—and enormously important—reasons many would give in explaining why science matters.

But here's the thing. The reason science really matters runs deeper still. Science is a way of life. Science is a perspective. Science is the process that takes us from confusion to understanding in a manner that's precise, predictive and reliable—a transformation, for those lucky enough to experience it, that is empowering and emotional. (Greene, paragraphs 6 and 7)

Educators at single-sex schools already get it: Equality is the goal, not the process. *There may be more than one path to the destination—***but it is the arrival, not the itinerary, that counts.** (Stabiner, paragraph 12)

This important counterargument strategy sometimes begins not with concession but with acknowledgment; that is, the writer simply restates part of an opponent's argument without conceding the wisdom of it. Here are some examples:

It's striking that science is still widely viewed as merely a subject one studies in the classroom or an isolated body of largely esoteric knowledge that sometimes shows up in the "real" world in the form of technological or medical advances. **In reality, science is a language of hope and inspiration, providing discoveries that fire the imagination and instill a sense of connection to our lives and our world.** (Greene, paragraph 9)

What is this misplaced reverence for the coed school? **Do not think that it was designed with the best interests of all children at heart.** (Stabiner, paragraph 15)

The average teen girl would be led to believe that teen pregnancy doesn't ruin adolescence, but instead brings lavish amounts of attention, an adoring and adorable teen father, and an endless supply of parental support. **The reality for most teen moms could not be more different.** (Page, paragraph 5)

But it was okay to consider an applicant's race in the context of a tailored, "holistic" review, as the law school did. **That's a distinction without a difference since, no matter how nuanced, the process can be rigged to generate the desired racial outcomes; the law school's own data indicated as much.** (Kirp, paragraph 3)

The concession-refutation move, sometimes called the "yes-but" strategy, is important in most arguments. Following is a list of some of the other language this chapter's authors rely on to introduce their concession-refutation moves:

Introducing the Concession	*Introducing the Refutation That Follows*
But it's not . . .	Rather, it speaks to . . .
When we look at . . .	We realize . . .
As a practicing scientist, I know . . .	But . . . you don't have to be a scientist . . .
It's one thing . . .	It's another . . .
A great many studies have focused . . .	But most of these studies . . . avoid . . .
Having said that . . .	I do not intend to proselytize . . .
The two groups continue to insist . . .	But brain research has shown . . .
Some researchers complain . . .	But it is probably impossible to design . . .
But if this is about . . .	then it is a cruel joke . . .
When challenged to explain . . .	Only at the end . . .
Contrary to popular belief . . .	Surprisingly, . . .
While convincing . . .	this argument does not demonstrate

In addition to using concession and refutation, you can strengthen your position paper with other rhetorical strategies. You may want to review the section on using appositives to identify or establish the authority of a source in Chapter 5 (pp. 275–76).

READING A DRAFT CRITICALLY

Getting a critical reading of your draft will help you see how to improve it. Your instructor may schedule class time for reading drafts, or you may want to ask a classmate or a tutor in the writing center to read your draft. Ask your reader to use the following guidelines and to write out a response for you to consult during revision.

Read for a First Impression

1. **Read the draft without stopping, and then write a few sentences giving your general impression.**

2. **Identify one aspect of the draft that seems particularly effective.**

Read Again to Suggest Improvements

1. **Suggest ways of presenting the issue more effectively.**

   - Read the paragraphs that present the issue, and tell the writer if you have trouble understanding what it is or what the controversy about it is.

   - Point to any key terms used to present the issue that seem surprising, confusing, or antagonizing to readers who disagree with the writer's position.

   - If you think a visual such as a photograph or chart would help readers understand the issue better, tell the writer so.

2. **Recommend ways of asserting the position more clearly and unequivocally.**

   - Find the writer's thesis, or position statement, and underline it. If you cannot find a clear thesis, let the writer know.

   - If you find several restatements of the thesis, examine them closely for consistency.

   - If the position seems extreme or overstated, suggest how it might be qualified and made more reasonable.

3. **Help the writer strengthen the argument directly for the position.**

   - Look at the reasons the writer gives for the position. Indicate any that seem unconvincing, and explain briefly why you think so.

   - Look at the support the writer provides for each reason. If you find any of it ineffective, explain why you think so and how it could be strengthened. If no support for a reason is provided, suggest what kinds (facts, statistics, quotations, anecdotes, examples, analogies, visuals) the writer might consider adding—and why.

4. **Suggest ways of improving the counterargument.**

   - If a likely objection or opposing position has not been addressed, tell the writer what it is. If possible, suggest how and where it could be addressed.

- If any refutation seems weak, suggest what the writer could add or change.

- If only the weakest criticisms have been addressed, remind the writer of stronger ones that should be taken into account.

5. **Suggest how credibility can be enhanced.**

- Tell the writer whether the intended readers are likely to find the essay authoritative and trustworthy. Point to places where the argument seems most and least trustworthy.

- Identify places where the writer seeks to establish a common ground of shared values, beliefs, and attitudes with readers. Suggest other ways the writer might do so.

6. **Suggest ways of improving readability.**

- Consider whether the beginning adequately engages readers' interest and sets the stage for the argument, perhaps by establishing the tone or forecasting the argument.

- If the organization does not seem to follow a logical plan, suggest how it might be rearranged or where transitions could be inserted to clarify logical connections.

- Note whether the ending gives the argument a satisfactory sense of closure.

REVISING

This section offers suggestions for revising your draft. Revising means reenvisioning your draft, trying to see it in a new way, given your purpose and readers, to develop a well-argued position paper.

The biggest mistake you can make while revising is to focus initially on words or sentences. Instead, first try to see your draft as a whole to assess its likely impact on your readers. Think imaginatively and boldly about cutting unconvincing material, adding new material, and moving material around. Your computer makes even drastic revisions physically easy, but you still need to make the mental effort and decisions that will improve your draft.

You may have received help with this challenge from a classmate or tutor who gave your draft a critical reading. If so, keep this feedback in mind as you decide which parts of your draft need revising and what specific changes you could make. The following suggestions will help you solve problems and strengthen your essay.

TROUBLESHOOTING YOUR DRAFT

To Present the Issue More Effectively

Problem	Suggestions for Revising
Readers don't understand what is at stake with the issue.	• Add anecdotes, examples, facts, or visuals to make the issue more specific and vivid. • Explain systematically, following the suggestions in "drafting," why you see the issue as you do.
Your terms are surprising or are antagonistic to readers who disagree with your position.	• Use more familiar or neutral terms. • Use the sentence strategies of concession and refutation or acknowledgment and refutation.

To Assert the Position More Clearly and Unequivocally

Problem	Suggestions for Revising
Your position on the issue is unclear.	• Reformulate it or spell it out in more detail.
The thesis statement is hard to find.	• State it more directly or position it more boldly.
The thesis is not qualified to account for valid opposing arguments or objections.	• Limit the scope of your thesis.

To Strengthen the Argument Directly for the Position

Problem	Suggestions for Revising
A reason given for the position seems unconvincing.	• Clarify its relevance to the argument. • Add support for your reasoning.
The support for a reason is inadequate.	• Review invention notes or do more research to find facts, statistics, quotations, examples, or other types of support to add.

To Improve the Counterargument

Problem	Suggestions for Revising
Your argument ignores a strong opposing position or reasonable objection.	• Address the criticism directly, perhaps using the sentence strategy of concession and refutation. • If necessary, modify your position to accommodate the criticism.
Your refutation of a criticism is unconvincing or attacks opponents on a personal level.	• Provide more or better support (such as facts and statistics from reputable sources). • Revise to eliminate personal attacks.

To Enhance Credibility

Problem	Suggestions for Revising
Readers consider some of your sources questionable.	• Establish the sources' credibility by providing background information about them. • Choose more reputable sources.
You ignored likely objections or opposing arguments.	• Demonstrate to readers that you know and understand, even if you do not accept, these criticisms. • Use the sentence strategy of concession and refutation or acknowledgment and refutation.
Your tone is harsh or offensive.	• Look for ways to show respect for and establish common ground with readers. • Revise your essay to create a more respectful tone. • Again, consider the concession-refutation strategy.

To Improve Readability

Problem	Suggestions for Revising
The beginning is dull or unfocused.	• Rewrite it, perhaps by adding a surprising or vivid anecdote.
Your argument is disorganized or hard to follow.	• Add a brief forecast of your main points at the beginning of the essay. • Reorder your points in a logical arrangement, such as least to most important. • Announce each reason more explicitly. • Add transitions to make the connections between points clearer.
The end is weak or trails off.	• Search your invention and research notes for a memorable quotation or a vivid example to end with. • Explain the consequences if your position is adopted.

EDITING AND PROOFREADING

After you have revised your essay, be sure to spend some time checking for errors in usage, punctuation, and mechanics and considering matters of style. If you keep a list of errors you typically make, begin by checking your draft against this list. Ask someone else to proofread your essay before you print out a copy for your instructor or send it electronically.

From our research on student writing, we know that essays arguing positions have a high percentage of sentence fragment errors involving subordinating conjunctions as well as punctuation errors involving conjunctive adverbs. Because arguing a position often requires you to use subordinating conjunctions (such as *because, although,* and *since*) and conjunctive adverbs (such as *therefore, however,* and *thus*), you want to be sure you know the conventions for punctuating sentences that include these types of words. Check a writer's handbook for help with avoiding sentence fragments and using punctuation correctly in sentences with subordinating conjunctions and conjunctive adverbs.

Reflecting on What You Have Learned

Position Papers

In this chapter, you have read critically several position arguments and have written one of your own. To better remember what you have learned, pause now to reflect on the reading and writing activities you completed in this chapter.

1. Write a page or so reflecting on what you have learned. Begin by describing what you are most pleased with in your essay. Then explain what you think contributed to your achievement. Be specific about this contribution.

   - If it was something you learned from the readings, indicate which readings and specifically what you learned from them.

   - If it came from your invention writing, point out the section or sections that helped you most.

   - If you got good advice from a critical reader, explain exactly how the person helped you—perhaps by helping you understand a particular problem in your draft or by helping you add a new dimension to your writing.

   - Try to write about your achievement in terms of what you have learned about the genre.

2. Reflect more generally on position papers, a genre of writing that plays an important role in our society. Consider some of the following questions: How important are reasons and supporting evidence? When people argue positions on television, on radio talk shows, and in online discussion forums like blogs, do they tend to emphasize reasons and support? If not, what do they emphasize? How does their purpose differ from the purpose of the writers you read in this chapter and from your own purpose in writing a position paper? What contribution might position papers make to our society that other genres of writing cannot make?

CHAPTER 8

Speculating about Causes or Effects

W hen a surprising event occurs, we automatically look to the past and ask, "Why did that happen?" Whether we want to understand the event, prevent its recurrence, or make it happen again, we need to speculate about what *caused* it.

Sometimes our focus may shift from "Why did that happen?" to "What is going to happen?" Anticipating the possible *effects* of an event can be useful in planning and decision making.

In many cases, questions about causes and effects are relatively easy to answer. Through personal experience or scientific experimentation, we know what causes some things to happen and what the effects will be. For example, scientists have discovered that the HIV virus causes AIDS, and we all know its potential deadly effects. We cannot be completely certain, however, what causes the virus to develop into AIDS in particular individuals or what long-term effects AIDS will have on society. In these situations, the best we can do is to *speculate*—to make educated guesses. In this chapter, you will read and write speculative essays about causes and effects that cannot be known for certain.

This kind of speculative cause-and-effect writing is published every day. A political analyst conjectures about the cause of the outcome of the most recent presidential election. An economist suggests some likely effects of a particular war on the U.S. economy. A sportswriter speculates about why the Pacific Ten nearly always defeats the Big Ten in the Rose Bowl.

Speculation about causes or effects also plays an important role in government, business, and education. To give credit where it is due, a mayor asks the police commission to report on why complaints by African Americans and Latinos against the police have decreased recently. A salesperson writes a memo to the district sales manager explaining why a local advertising campaign may have failed to increase sales of "green" cars. Before proposing changes in the math curriculum, a school principal appoints a committee to investigate the causes of falling math test scores at the school.

Cause-and-effect speculation is equally important in college study. For example, you might read a history essay in which a noted scholar first evaluates other scholars' proposed causes of the Civil War and then argues for a never-before-considered cause. (If the essay merely summarizes other scholars' proposed causes, the historian would be reporting established information, not speculating about new possibilities.) Or you might encounter a sociological report conjecturing about a recent increase in marriages among the elderly. The writer may not know for certain why this trend exists but could conjecture about its possible causes—and then argue with relevant facts, statistics, or anecdotes to support the conjectures.

Writing an essay in which you speculate about causes or effects involves some of the most challenging problem-solving and decision-making situations a writer can experience. You will test your powers of reasoning and creativity as you search out hidden, underlying causes or speculate about effects that are surprising yet plausible. You will continue to develop a sensitivity to your readers' knowledge and attitudes, anticipating their objections and discovering ways to convince them to take your speculations seriously.

The readings in this chapter will help you see what makes arguments about causes or effects convincing. From the readings and from the ideas for writing that follow each reading, you will get ideas for your own essay speculating about causes or effects. As you read and write about the selections, keep in mind the following assignment, which sets out the goals for writing an essay speculating about causes or effects. To support your writing of this assignment, the chapter concludes with a Guide to Writing Essays Speculating about Causes or Effects.

THE WRITING ASSIGNMENT

Speculating about Causes or Effects

Choose a subject—an event, a phenomenon, or a trend—that invites you to speculate about its causes or effects: why it may have happened or what its effects may be. Write an essay arguing for your proposed causes or effects. Essays about causes look to the past to ponder why something happened, whereas essays about effects guess what is likely to happen in the future. Whether you choose to write about causes or effects, you need to do two things: (1) establish the existence and significance of the subject, and (2) convince readers that the causes or effects you propose are plausible.

WRITING SITUATIONS FOR ESSAYS SPECULATING ABOUT CAUSES OR EFFECTS

The following examples suggest further the kinds of causal arguments writers typically make:

- A science writer notes that relatively few women get advanced degrees in science and speculates that social conditioning may be the major cause. To support her causal argument, she cites research on the way boys and girls are treated differently in early childhood. She also gives examples to attempt to show that the social pressure to conform to female role expectations may discourage middle-school girls from doing well in math and science. She acknowledges that other as-yet-unrecognized causes may contribute as well.

- A student writes in the school newspaper about the rising number of pregnancies among local high-school students. Interviews with pregnant students lead her to speculate that the chief cause of the trend is a new requirement that parents must give written consent for minors to get birth-control devices at the local clinic. She explains that many students fail to get birth-control information, let alone devices, because of this regulation. She reports that her interviews do not support alternative explanations—that young women have babies to give meaning to their lives, gain status among their peers, or live on their own supported by public assistance.

- A psychology student writes about the effects—positive and negative—of extensive video-game playing among preteens. Based on his own experience and observation, he suggests that video games may improve children's hand-eye coordination, as well as their ability to concentrate on a single task. He speculates that, on the negative side, some children may spend too much time playing video games, and their grades may suffer as a result.

> ### Thinking about Your Experience
> ## Speculating about Causes or Effects
>
> Before studying a type of writing, it is useful to spend some time thinking about what you already know about it. You may have discussed with friends or family members why a certain phenomenon, event, or trend occurred, in which case you were trying to figure out the causes. Or you may have discussed what a phenomenon, event, or trend might lead to or result in, in which case you were speculating about effects. In school, you may have written essays examining the causes, say, of a

scientific phenomenon such as the extinction of the dinosaurs or the effects of a social trend such as an increase in interracial marriage.

- Recall times when you were arguing — orally or in writing — for the reasons you think something happened or the effects that would result *from* some event, phenomenon, or trend, and then consider questions like these: What triggered your speculations? What did you want your audience to learn? What made you think the issue was significant? Did you address the causes, the effects, or both?

- Reflect also on the cause or effect arguments that have been told to you or that you have read or seen in films or on television. How did the author make the argument convincing?

- Write at least a page about your experience with cause or effect arguments.

A GUIDE TO READING ESSAYS SPECULATING ABOUT CAUSES OR EFFECTS

This guide introduces you to the basic features and strategies typical of cause-and-effect writing by looking closely at a brief but powerful causal argument by novelist and screenwriter Stephen King, who speculates about why we like horror movies. Focus first on *reading for meaning*, seeking to grasp the phenomenon's significance as well as the meanings you find. Then, to learn about how King makes his argument convincing, try *reading like a writer* by analyzing his writing strategies. These two activities—reading for meaning and reading like a writer—follow every reading in this chapter.

Stephen King

Why We Crave Horror Movies

Stephen King (b. 1947) is internationally known for his best-selling horror novels, such as Carrie *(1974),* The Shining *(1977),* Misery *(1987),* Bag of Bones *(1998),* Cell *(2006),* Lisey's Story *(2006),* Duma Key *(2008), and* Under the Dome *(2009). He also has published a number of short-story collections, including* Just after Sunset *(2009), which won several short-story awards; the serial novels* The Green Mile *(1996–2000) and* The Dark

Tower *(1982–2004); and the nonfiction book* On Writing: A Memoir of the Craft *(2001). Many of his novels have been made into movies, and some of his works have been dramatized on television* (Salem's Lot, Riding the Bullet). *He has received numerous awards, among them the Lifetime Achievement Award from the Horror Writers Association (2003), the Medal for Distinguished Contribution to American Letters (2003), and the Grand Masters Award from Mystery Writers of America (2007).*

The following selection originally appeared in Playboy *magazine in 1981. As King's title indicates, the essay attempts to explain the causes for a common phenomenon: most people's liking—even craving—for horror movies. Think about the horror movie that you remember best and consider why it appeals to you. As you read, test King's argument about the appeal of horror movies against your own experience. On first reading, how convincing do you find his causal speculations?*

1   I think that we're all mentally ill; those of us outside the asylums only hide it a little better—and maybe not all that much better, after all. We've all known people who talk to themselves, people who sometimes squinch their faces into horrible grimaces when they believe no one is watching, people who have some hysterical fear—of snakes, the dark, the tight place, the long drop . . . and, of course, those final worms and grubs that are waiting so patiently underground.

2   When we pay our four or five bucks and seat ourselves at tenth-row center in a theater showing a horror movie, we are daring the nightmare.

3   Why? Some of the reasons are simple and obvious. To show that we can, that we are not afraid, that we can ride this roller coaster. Which is not to say that a really good horror movie may not surprise a scream out of us at some point, the way we may scream when the roller coaster twists through a complete 360 or plows through a lake at the bottom of the drop. And horror movies, like roller coasters, have always been the special province of the young; by the time one turns 40 or 50, one's appetite for double twists or 360-degree loops may be considerably depleted.

4   We also go to re-establish our feelings of essential normality; the horror movie is innately conservative, even reactionary. Freda Jackson as the horrible melting woman in *Die, Monster, Die!* confirms for us that no matter how far we may be removed from the beauty of a Robert Redford or a Diana Ross, we are still light-years from true ugliness.

5   And we go to have fun.

6   Ah, but this is where the ground starts to slope away, isn't it? Because this is a very peculiar sort of fun, indeed. The fun comes from seeing others menaced—sometimes killed. One critic has suggested that if pro football has become the voyeur's version of combat, then the horror film has become the modern version of the public lynching.

7   It is true that the mythic, "fairy tale" horror film intends to take away the shades of gray. . . . It urges us to put away our more civilized and adult penchant for analysis and to become children again, seeing things in pure

blacks and whites. It may be that horror movies provide psychic relief on this level because this invitation to lapse into simplicity, irrationality, and even outright madness is extended so rarely. We are told we may allow our emotions a free rein . . . or no rein at all.

If we are all insane, then sanity becomes a matter of degree. If your 8 insanity leads you to carve up women like Jack the Ripper or the Cleveland Torso Murderer, we clap you away in the funny farm (but neither of those two amateur-night surgeons was ever caught, heh-heh-heh); if, on the other hand, your insanity leads you only to talk to yourself when you're under stress or to pick your nose on your morning bus, then you are left alone to go about your business . . . though it is doubtful that you will ever be invited to the best parties.

The potential lyncher is in almost all of us (excluding saints, past and pres- 9 ent; but then, most saints have been crazy in their own ways), and every now and then, he has to be let loose to scream and roll around in the grass. Our emotions and our fears form their own body, and we recognize that it demands its own exercise to maintain proper muscle tone. Certain of these emotional muscles are accepted—even exalted—in civilized society; they are, of course, the emotions that tend to maintain the status quo of civilization itself. Love, friendship, loyalty, kindness—these are all the emotions that we applaud, emotions that have been immortalized in the couplets of Hallmark cards and in the verses (I don't dare call it poetry) of Leonard Nimoy.

When we exhibit these emotions, society showers us with positive 10 reinforcement; we learn this even before we get out of diapers. When, as children, we hug our rotten little puke of a sister and give her a kiss, all the aunts and uncles smile and twit and cry, "Isn't he the sweetest little thing?" Such coveted treats as chocolate-covered graham crackers often follow. But if we deliberately slam the rotten little puke of a sister's fingers in the door, sanctions follow—angry remonstrance from parents, aunts, and uncles; instead of a chocolate-covered graham cracker, a spanking.

But anticivilization emotions don't go away, and they demand periodic 11 exercise. We have such "sick" jokes as "What's the difference between a truckload of bowling balls and a truckload of dead babies?" (You can't unload a truckload of bowling balls with a pitchfork . . . a joke, by the way, that I heard originally from a ten-year-old.) Such a joke may surprise a laugh or a grin out of us even as we recoil, a possibility that confirms the thesis: If we share a brotherhood of man, then we also share an insanity of man. None of which is intended as a defense of either the sick joke or insanity but merely as an explanation of why the best horror films, like the best fairy tales, manage to be reactionary, anarchistic, and revolutionary all at the same time.

The mythic horror movie, like the sick joke, has a dirty job to do. It 12 deliberately appeals to all that is worst in us. It is morbidity unchained, our most base instincts let free, our nastiest fantasies realized . . . and it all happens, fittingly enough, in the dark. For those reasons, good liberals often shy away from horror films. For myself, I like to see the most aggressive of them—*Dawn of the Dead*, for instance—as lifting a trap door in the civilized forebrain and throwing a basket of raw meat to the hungry alligators swimming around in that subterranean river beneath.

13   Why bother? Because it keeps them from getting out, man. It keeps them down there and me up here. It was Lennon and McCartney who said that all you need is love, and I would agree with that.

14   As long as you keep the gators fed.

READING FOR MEANING

This section presents three activities that will help you think about the meanings in King's causal argument.

Read to Comprehend

Write a few sentences briefly explaining why King thinks we watch horror movies. Identify any words with meanings you are unsure of—such as *innately* (paragraph 4) and *anarchistic* (11)—and find the dictionary definition for each word that makes the best sense in the context.

To help you understand the essay better, also consider trying one of these critical reading strategies, explained in Appendix 1: *outlining, paraphrasing,* or *questioning to understand and remember.*

Read to Respond

Write a paragraph or two exploring your initial thoughts and feelings about King's causal argument. Focus on anything that stands out for you, perhaps because it resonates with your own experience or because you find a statement puzzling. For example, consider writing about one of the following:

- the reasons that King writes "[i]f we are all insane, then sanity becomes a matter of degree" (paragraph 8)

- the difference between procivilization and "anticivilization" emotions as King presents them in paragraphs 10 to 13, indicating what you think about his distinction between these two kinds of emotions

To help develop your response, also consider trying one of these critical reading strategies, explained in Appendix 1: *contextualizing, recognizing emotional manipulation,* or *judging the writer's credibility.*

Read to Analyze Assumptions

All writing contains *assumptions*—ideas and attitudes that are taken for granted as commonly accepted truths. Personal or individual assumptions also tend to reflect the values and beliefs of a particular community, which help shape the way those in the group think, act, and understand the world. All writing reflects assumptions held by the writer, but assumptions held by others, such as readers or sources cited by the writer, may also be present. Sometimes assumptions are stated explicitly, but often they are only implied, so you may have to search for underlying assumptions in the word choices and examples.

Why go to the effort to analyze assumptions in a reading? Assumptions have powerful effects. They influence our opinions and judgments by leading us to value some things and devalue others. These effects are even more powerful because they are taken for granted, often accepted without question by those who hold them. To understand a reading on a deep level, then, it is necessary to bring its assumptions to the surface and to question them. To think critically about assumptions, here are some kinds of questions you could ask: Who holds this assumption (the writer, readers, and/or others cited in the essay)? What are the effects of the assumption in the context of the essay specifically or in society more generally? What do you think about the assumption, and is there anything in the essay that raises doubts about it? How does the assumption reinforce or critique commonly held views, and are there any alternative ideas, beliefs, or values that would challenge this assumption?

Write a paragraph or two analyzing an assumption in King's essay. You might choose an assumption from the list below, using the questions accompanying it in addition to the ones above to help you get started. Or you can choose another assumption in the essay to explore.

- **assumptions about the universality and range of human emotions.** King asserts that "[t]he mythic horror movie . . . has a dirty job to do. It deliberately appeals to all that is worst in us" (paragraph 12). He adds that "[i]t is morbidity unchained, our most base instincts let free, our nastiest fantasies realized" (12).

  To think critically about the assumptions in this essay related to human emotions, ask yourself: What if we don't watch horror movies, don't like them, or don't believe they represent our "nastiest fantasies"? If you don't share King's assumption about universal human nastiness, how do you respond to his essay? What alternatives to his thinking occur to you? In a culture that has a different view of the human mind, what other causes of horror movies' popularity might be just as believable?

- **assumptions about differences between younger and older people.** King asserts that "horror movies . . . have always been the special province of the young" (3) and that we go to see them "to put away our more civilized and adult penchant for analysis and to become children again" (7).

  To think critically about assumptions in this essay related to the differences between people of different ages, ask yourself: What viewpoints do children have that adults do not have or have outgrown? What does King assume distinguishes them in, say, their attitude toward scary situations (3) or complex ones (7)? Why would adults want to become children again?

  To help you analyze assumptions in King's essay, also consider trying one of these critical reading strategies, explained in Appendix 1: *reflecting on challenges to your beliefs and values* or *exploring the significance of figurative language.*

READING LIKE A WRITER

This section leads you through an analysis of King's argumentative strategies: *presenting the subject*, *making a logical, step-by-step cause-and-effect argument*, *counterarguing*, and *establishing credibility*. For each strategy, you will be asked to reread and annotate part of King's essay to see how he uses the strategy to accomplish his particular purpose.

When you study the selections later in this chapter, you will see how different writers use the same strategies to make causal arguments or speculate about effects. The Guide to Writing Essays Speculating about Causes or Effects near the end of the chapter suggests ways you can use these strategies in your own writing.

Presenting the Subject

In presenting the subject of an essay speculating about causes or effects, the writer must be sure that readers will recognize and understand the subject. In some writing situations, the writer can safely assume that readers will already know a great deal about a familiar subject. In this case, the writer can simply identify the subject and immediately begin the speculations about its causes or effects. In many other cases, however, writers must present an unfamiliar subject in enough detail for readers to understand it fully. On occasion, writers may even need to convince readers that their subject is important and worth speculating about.

When writers decide they need to prove that the trend or phenomenon they are writing about exists, they may describe it in detail, give examples, offer factual evidence, cite statistics, or quote statements by authorities. To establish the importance of the trend or phenomenon, writers may show that it involves a large number of people or has great importance to certain people.

Analyze

1. How does King present horror movies as a particular movie genre? Skim the essay to see which horror movies he mentions by title. Are the few examples he cites sufficient? Do you think readers need to have seen the movies he mentions to get the point? What does King seem to assume about his readers' experiences with horror films?

2. Consider how King establishes the importance of his subject. Underline one or two comments King makes about the subject that are likely to increase his readers' curiosity about why people crave horror movies.

Write

Write several sentences explaining how King presents his subject.

Making a Logical, Step-by-Step Cause-and-Effect Argument

At the heart of an essay speculating about causes or effects is an argument. The argument is made up of at least two parts—(1) the description of the proposed causes or effects and (2) the reasoning and support for each cause or effect. In addition, the writer may anticipate readers' objections or questions, a strategy we take up in the next section on counterargument. In analyzing King's argument, we will look at some of the causes he proposes and how he supports them.

Writers speculating about causes or effects rarely consider only one possibility. They know that most puzzling phenomena (like people's attraction to horror movies) have multiple possible causes. However, they also know that it would be foolish to try to identify every possible cause. Writers must therefore be selective if they hope to make a convincing argument. The best arguments avoid the obvious. They offer new and imaginative ways of thinking—either proposing causes or effects that will surprise readers or arguing for familiar causes or effects in new ways.

Writers support their arguments with various kinds of evidence—facts, statistical correlations, personal anecdotes, testimony of authorities, examples, and analogies. In this activity, we focus on King's use of analogies.

Analyze

1. Reread paragraphs 3 and 12, and identify the analogy in each paragraph. An analogy is a special form of comparison in which one part of the comparison is used to explain the other. In arguing by analogy, the writer reasons that if two situations are alike, their causes will also be similar.

2. Think about how well the comparisons in paragraphs 3 and 12 hold up. For example, you may be able to use your personal experience to test whether watching a horror movie is much like riding a roller coaster. Ask yourself in what ways the two are alike—and different. Are they more alike than different? Also consider how you are or are not like a hungry alligator when you watch a horror movie.

Write

Describe and evaluate King's support by analogy in paragraphs 3 and 12. Explain the parts of each analogy—the two separate things being compared. Evaluate how well each analogy works logically. In what ways are the two things being compared actually alike? Also evaluate what the two analogies contribute to King's causal argument. How is the essay strengthened by them?

Counterarguing

When causes or effects cannot be known for certain, there is bound to be disagreement. Consequently, writers try to anticipate possible objections and alternative causes or effects readers might put forward. Writers bring these objections and alternatives directly into their essays and then either refute (argue against) them or find a way to accommodate them in the argument.

Analyze

1. King anticipates a possible objection from readers when he poses the question "Why bother?" in paragraph 13. Reread paragraphs 11 and 12 to understand the context in which King anticipates the need to pose that question. Notice his direct answer to the question in paragraph 13.

2. Think about the effectiveness of King's counterargument. Consider whether it satisfactorily answers the objection.

Write

Write a few sentences explaining why you think King asks the question at this point in his argument. Consider whether some of King's readers would ask themselves this question. Evaluate how satisfied they would be with King's response.

Establishing Credibility

Because cause-and-effect writing is highly speculative, its effectiveness depends in large part on whether readers trust the writer. Readers sometimes use information about the writer's professional and personal accomplishments in forming their judgments about the writer's credibility. The most important information, however, comes from the writing itself, specifically how writers argue for their own proposed causes or effects, as well as how they handle readers' objections.

Writers seek to establish their credibility with readers by making their reasoning clear and logical, their evidence relevant and trustworthy, and their handling of objections fair and balanced. They try to be authoritative (knowledgeable) without appearing authoritarian (opinionated and dogmatic).

Analyze

1. Reread the headnote that precedes King's essay, and reflect on what his *Playboy* readers might have already known about him. King is more widely known now than he was when "Why We Crave Horror Movies" was published in 1981, but his readers at that time would likely have heard of him.

2. With King's readers in mind, skim the essay to decide whether the reasoning is clear and logical and the examples and analogies relevant and trustworthy. Notice that King's reasoning is psychological. He argues that mental and

emotional needs explain why some people crave horror films. Therefore, you, along with King's intended readers, can evaluate King's credibility in light of your own personal experience—your understanding of the role horror novels and films play in your own life. On the basis of your own experience and your evaluation of the logic and consistency of King's argument, decide whether you think most readers would consider him a credible writer on the subject of horror films.

Write

Write several sentences describing the impression readers might get of King from reading both the headnote and his essay on horror films. What might make them trust or distrust what he says about his subject?

READINGS

Claudia Wallis

The Multitasking Generation

Claudia Wallis is editor-at-large at Time Magazine, *where as both a writer and an editor she has specialized in stories about science and health, medicine, education, family, and social issues. Wallis has written more than forty cover stories for* Time. *Her writing has won citations from the National Mental Health Association, the Newspaper Guild of New York, and the Susan G. Komen Breast Cancer Foundation, among other organizations. Her most recent work is on autism, for which she maintains a Web site: http://claudiawallis.com/autism/. Wallis was the founding editor of* Time for Kids, *which debuted in 1995 and now has a circulation of over 4 million. She is also a conference speaker and panel leader.*

"The Multitasking Generation" was published by online Time/CNN in 2006. In it, Wallis describes the relationship between multitasking and Generation "M," and she questions the notion that multitaskers get more done. As you read, add your own notes to the annotations, especially where Wallis surprises you or supports her causal argument with evidence—facts, statistics, personal anecdotes, testimony of authorities, examples, or analogies. Consider also how plausible you find Wallis's argument about the effects of multitasking.

1   It's 9:30 p.m., and Stephen and Georgina Cox know exactly where their children are. Well, their bodies, at least. Piers, 14, is holed up in his bedroom—eyes fixed on his computer screen—where he has been logged onto a MySpace chat room and AOL Instant Messenger (IM) for the past three hours. His twin sister Bronte is planted in the living room, having commandeered her dad's iMac—as usual. She, too, is busily IMing, while chatting on her cell phone and chipping away at homework.

2   By all standard space-time calculations, the four members of the family occupy the same three-bedroom home in Van Nuys, Calif., but psychologically each exists in his or her own little universe. Georgina, 51, who works for a display-cabinet maker, is tidying up the living room as Bronte works, not that her daughter notices. Stephen, 49, who juggles jobs as a squash coach, fitness trainer, event planner and head of a cancer charity he founded, has wolfed down his dinner alone in the kitchen, having missed supper with the kids. He, too, typically spends the evening on his cell phone

Why do you think Wallis introduces her essay with 9 paragraphs of anecdote, followed by two paragraphs about academic research? What is the effect on you?

and returning e-mails—when he can nudge Bronte off the computer. "One gets obsessed with one's gadgets," he concedes.

3   Zooming in on Piers' screen gives a pretty good indication of what's on his hyperkinetic mind. O.K., there's a Google Images window open, where he's chasing down pictures of Keira Knightley. Good ones get added to a snazzy Windows Media Player slide show that serves as his personal e-shrine to the actress. Several IM windows are also open, revealing such penetrating conversations as this one with a MySpace pal:

4   MySpacer: suuuuuup!!! (Translation: What's up?)
5   Piers: wat up dude
6   MySpacer: nmu (Not much. You?)
7   Piers: same

8   Naturally, iTunes is open, and Piers is blasting a mix of Queen, AC/DC, classic rock and hip-hop. Somewhere on the screen there's a Word file, in which Piers is writing an essay for English class. "I usually finish my homework at school," he explains to a visitor, "but if not, I pop a book open on my lap in my room, and while the computer is loading, I'll do a problem or write a sentence. Then, while mail is loading, I do more. I get it done a little bit at a time."

9   Bronte has the same strategy. "You just multitask," she explains. "My parents always tell me I can't do homework while listening to music, but they don't understand that it helps me concentrate." The twins also multitask when hanging with friends, which has its own etiquette. "When I talk to my best friend Eloy," says Piers, "he'll have one earpiece [of his iPod] in and one out." Says Bronte: "If a friend thinks she's not getting my full attention, I just make it very clear that she is, even though I'm also listening to music."

10   The Coxes are one of 32 families in the Los Angeles area participating in an intensive, four-year study of modern family life, led by anthropologist Elinor Ochs, director of UCLA's Center on Everyday Lives of Families. While the impact of multitasking gadgets was not her original focus, Ochs found it to be one of the most dramatic areas of change since she conducted a similar study 20 years ago. "I'm not certain how the children can monitor all those things at the same time, but I think it is pretty

When a researcher shifts focus because of her findings (highlighted), does it add to or detract from her credibility?

consequential for the structure of the family relationship," says Ochs, whose work on language, interaction and culture earned her a MacArthur "genius" grant.

One of the things Ochs' team of observers looks at 11 is what happens at the end of the workday when parents and kids reunite—and what doesn't happen, as in the case of the Coxes. "We saw that when the working parent comes through the door, the other spouse and the kids are so absorbed by what they're doing that they don't give the arriving parent the time of day," says Ochs. The returning parent, generally the father, was greeted only about a third of the time, usually with a perfunctory "Hi." "About half the time the kids ignored him or didn't stop what they were doing, multitasking and monitoring their various electronic gadgets," she says. "We also saw how difficult it was for parents to penetrate the child's universe. We have so many videotapes of parents actually backing away, retreating from kids who are absorbed by whatever they're doing."

Human beings have always had a capacity to attend 12 to several things at once. Mothers have done it since the hunter-gatherer era—picking berries while suckling an infant, stirring the pot with one eye on the toddler. Nor is electronic multitasking entirely new: we've been driving while listening to car radios since they became popular in the 1930s. But there is no doubt that the phenomenon has reached a kind of warp speed in the era of Web-enabled computers, when it has become routine to conduct six IM conversations, watch American Idol on TV and Google the names of last season's finalists all at once.

That level of multiprocessing and interpersonal con- 13 nectivity is now so commonplace that it's easy to forget how quickly it came about. Fifteen years ago, most home computers weren't even linked to the Internet. In 1990 the majority of adolescents responding to a survey done by Donald Roberts, a professor of communication at Stanford, said the one medium they couldn't live without was a radio/CD player. How quaint. In a 2004 follow-up, the computer won hands down.

Today 82% of kids are online by the seventh grade, 14 according to the Pew Internet and American Life Project. And what they love about the computer, of course, is that it offers the radio/CD thing and so much more—games, movies, e-mail, IM, Google, MySpace. The big finding of

Is this homecoming scenario familiar to you? Does it happen in your own household?

a 2005 survey of Americans ages 8 to 18 by the Kaiser Family Foundation, co-authored by Roberts, is not that kids were spending a larger chunk of time using electronic media—that was holding steady at 6.5 hours a day (could it possibly get any bigger?)—but that they were packing more media exposure into that time: 8.5 hours' worth, thanks to "media multitasking"—listening to iTunes, watching a DVD and IMing friends all at the same time. Increasingly, the media-hungry members of Generation M, as Kaiser dubbed them, don't just sit down to watch a TV show with their friends or family. From a quarter to a third of them, according to the survey, say they simultaneously absorb some other medium "most of the time" while watching TV, listening to music, using the computer or even while reading.

How does this brief history of "media multitasking," along with current statistics from authorities, help you understand the issue Wallis is addressing?

15   Parents have watched this phenomenon unfold with a mixture of awe and concern. The Coxes, for instance, are bowled over by their children's technical prowess. Piers repairs the family computers and DVD player. Bronte uses digital technology to compose elaborate photo collages and create a documentary of her father's ongoing treatment for cancer. And, says Georgina, "they both make these fancy PowerPoint presentations about what they want for Christmas." But both parents worry about the ways that kids' compulsive screen time is affecting their schoolwork and squeezing out family life. "We rarely have dinner together anymore," frets Stephen. "Everyone is in their own little world, and we don't get out together to have a social life."

How does Wallis shift here from presenting the subject to making her effects argument?

16   Every generation of adults sees new technology—and the social changes it stirs—as a threat to the rightful order of things: Plato warned (correctly) that reading would be the downfall of oral tradition and memory. And every generation of teenagers embraces the freedoms and possibilities wrought by technology in ways that shock the elders: just think about what the automobile did for dating.

How does this paragraph on the history of new technologies help to put the effects of multitasking in perspective?

17   As for multitasking devices, social scientists and educators are just beginning to assess their impact, but the researchers already have some strong opinions. The mental habit of dividing one's attention into many small slices has significant implications for the way young people learn, reason, socialize, do creative work and understand the world. Although such habits may prepare kids for today's frenzied workplace, many cognitive

What is the effect on you of Wallis's acknowledgment of the counterargument that multitasking may prepare kids for work? How do you respond to her assertion that many cognitive scientists find the trend alarming?

scientists are positively alarmed by the trend. "Kids that are instant messaging while doing homework, playing games online and watching TV, I predict, aren't going to do well in the long run," says Jordan Grafman, chief of the cognitive neuroscience section at the National Institute of Neurological Disorders and Stroke (NINDS). Decades of research (not to mention common sense) indicate that the quality of one's output and depth of thought deteriorate as one attends to ever more tasks. Some are concerned about the disappearance of mental downtime to relax and reflect. Roberts notes Stanford students "can't go the few minutes between their 10 o'clock and 11 o'clock classes without talking on their cell phones. It seems to me that there's almost a discomfort with not being stimulated—a kind of 'I can't stand the silence.'"

Gen M's multitasking habits have social and psychological implications as well. If you're IMing four friends while watching *That '70s Show*, it's not the same as sitting on the couch with your buddies or your sisters and watching the show together. Or sharing a family meal across a table. Thousands of years of evolution created human physical communication—facial expressions, body language—that puts broadband to shame in its ability to convey meaning and create bonds. What happens, wonders UCLA's Ochs, as we replace side-by-side and eye-to-eye human connections with quick, disembodied e-exchanges? Those are critical issues not just for social scientists but for parents and teachers trying to understand—and do right by—Generation M.

Look at the highlighted words. What do you think Wallis is trying to communicate in this paragraph? What might be lost by multitasking?

18

YOUR BRAIN WHEN IT MULTITASKS

Although many aspects of the networked life remain scientifically uncharted, there's substantial literature on how the brain handles multitasking. And basically, it doesn't. It may seem that a teenage girl is writing an instant message, burning a CD and telling her mother that she's doing homework—all at the same time—but what's really going on is a rapid toggling among tasks rather than simultaneous processing. "You're doing more than one thing, but you're ordering them and deciding which one to do at any one time," explains neuroscientist Grafman.

Wallis continues to present her effects argument, this time in several paragraphs on the physical processes the brain undergoes while multitasking. Why do you suppose she chooses to include the brain in her presentation?

19

20   Then why can we so easily walk down the street while engrossed in a deep conversation? Why can we chop onions while watching *Jeopardy*? "We, along with quite a few others, have been focused on exactly this question," says Hal Pashler, psychology professor at the University of California at San Diego. It turns out that very automatic actions or what researchers call "highly practiced skills," like walking or chopping an onion, can be easily done while thinking about other things, although the decision to add an extra onion to a recipe or change the direction in which you're walking is another matter. "It seems that action planning—figuring out what I want to say in response to a person's question or which way I want to steer the car—is usually, perhaps invariably, performed sequentially" or one task at a time, says Pashler. On the other hand, producing the actions you've decided on—moving your hand on the steering wheel, speaking the words you've formulated—can be performed "in parallel with planning some other action." Similarly, many aspects of perception—looking, listening, touching—can be performed in parallel with action planning and with movement.

21   The switching of attention from one task to another, the toggling action, occurs in a region right behind the forehead called Brodmann's Area 10 in the brain's anterior prefrontal cortex, according to a functional magnetic resonance imaging (fMRI) study by Grafman's team. Brodmann's Area 10 is part of the frontal lobes, which "are important for maintaining long-term goals and achieving them," Grafman explains. "The most anterior part allows you to leave something when it's incomplete and return to the same place and continue from there." This gives us a "form of multitasking," he says, though it's actually sequential processing. Because the prefrontal cortex is one of the last regions of the brain to mature and one of the first to decline with aging, young children do not multitask well, and neither do most adults over 60. New fMRI studies at Toronto's Rotman Research Institute suggest that as we get older, we have more trouble "turning down background thoughts when turning to a new task," says Rotman senior scientist and assistant director Cheryl Grady. "Younger adults are better at tuning out stuff when they want to," says Grady. "I'm in my 50s, and I know that I can't work and listen to music with lyrics; it was easier when I was younger."

But the ability to multiprocess has its limits, even 22
among young adults. When people try to perform two or
more related tasks either at the same time or alternating
rapidly between them, errors go way up, and it takes far
longer—often double the time or more—to get the jobs
done than if they were done sequentially, says David E.
Meyer, director of the Brain, Cognition and Action Laboratory at the University of Michigan: "The toll in terms
of slowdown is extremely large—amazingly so." Meyer
frequently tests Gen M students in his lab, and he sees
no exception for them, despite their "mystique" as master
multitaskers. "The bottom line is that you can't simultaneously be thinking about your tax return and reading an
essay, just as you can't talk to yourself about two things at
once," he says. "If a teenager is trying to have a conversation on an e-mail chat line while doing algebra, she'll
suffer a decrease in efficiency, compared to if she just
thought about algebra until she was done. People may
think otherwise, but it's a myth. With such complicated
tasks [you] will never, ever be able to overcome the inherent limitations in the brain for processing information during multitasking. It just can't be, any more than the best of
all humans will ever be able to run a one-minute mile."

Here Wallis focuses on the counterargument that a little stimulation can be good. How does she respond?

Other research shows the relationship between 23
stimulation and performance forms a bell curve: a
little stimulation—whether it's coffee or a blaring
soundtrack—can boost performance, but too much
is stressful and causes a fall-off. In addition, the brain
needs rest and recovery time to consolidate thoughts
and memories. Teenagers who fill every quiet moment
with a phone call or some kind of e-stimulation may not
be getting that needed reprieve. Habitual multitasking
may condition their brain to an overexcited state, making it difficult to focus even when they want to. "People
lose the skill and the will to maintain concentration, and
they get mental antsyness," says Meyer.

Why do you suppose Wallis uses headings throughout her essay?

IS THIS ANY WAY TO LEARN?

Longtime professors at universities around the U.S. 24
have noticed that Gen M kids arrive on campus with a different set of cognitive skills and habits than past generations. In lecture halls with wireless Internet access—now
more than 40% of college classrooms, according to the

Campus Computing Project—the compulsion to multi-task can get out of hand. "People are going to lectures by some of the greatest minds, and they are doing their mail," says Sherry Turkle, professor of the social studies of science and technology at M.I.T. In her class, says Turkle, "I tell them this is not a place for e-mail, it's not a place to do online searches and not a place to set up IRC [Internet relay chat] channels in which to comment on the class. It's not going to help if there are parallel discussions about how boring it is. You've got to get people to participate in the world as it is."

Wallis shifts back to personal anecdotes to present her effects argument. Why does she use university professors to make her case?

25   Such concerns have, in fact, led a number of schools, including the M.B.A. programs at UCLA and the University of Virginia, to look into blocking Internet access during lectures. "I tell my students not to treat me like TV," says University of Wisconsin professor Aaron Brower, who has been teaching social work for 20 years. "They have to think of me like a real person talking. I want to have them thinking about things we're talking about."

26   On the positive side, Gen M students tend to be extraordinarily good at finding and manipulating information. And presumably because modern childhood tilts toward visual rather than print media, they are especially skilled at analyzing visual data and images, observes Claudia Koonz, professor of history at Duke University. A growing number of college professors are using film, audio clips and PowerPoint presentations to play to their students' strengths and capture their evanescent attention. It's a powerful way to teach history, says Koonz. "I love bringing media into the classroom, to be able to go to the website for Edward R. Murrow and hear his voice as he walked with the liberators of Buchenwald." Another adjustment to teaching Generation M: professors are assigning fewer full-length books and more excerpts and articles. (Koonz, however, was stunned when a student matter-of-factly informed her, "We don't read whole books anymore," after Koonz had assigned a 350-page volume. "And this is Duke!" she says.)

What do these two paragraphs on the "positive side" (26 and 27) add to Wallis's argument?

27   Many students make brilliant use of media in their work, embedding audio files and video clips in their presentations, but the habit of grazing among many data streams leaves telltale signs in their writing, according to some educators. "The breadth of their knowledge and

their ability to find answers has just burgeoned," says Roberts of his students at Stanford, "but my impression is that their ability to write clear, focused and extended narratives has eroded somewhat." Says Koonz: "What I find is paragraphs that make sense internally, but don't necessarily follow a line of argument."

Wallis returns to the dangers of multitasking, keeping her argument consistent. Upon what assumptions do you think this paragraph rests?

Koonz and Turkle believe that today's students are less 28 tolerant of ambiguity than the students they taught in the past. "They demand clarity," says Koonz. They want identifiable good guys and bad guys, which she finds problematic in teaching complex topics like Hutu-Tutsi history in Rwanda. She also thinks there are political implications: "Their belief in the simple answer, put together in a visual way, is, I think, dangerous." Koonz thinks this aversion to complexity is directly related to multitasking: "It's as if they have too many windows open on their hard drive. In order to have a taste for sifting through different layers of truth, you have to stay with a topic and pursue it deeply, rather than go across the surface with your toolbar." She tries to encourage her students to find a quiet spot on campus to just think, cell phone off, laptop packed away.

GOT 2 GO. TXT ME L8ER

Paragraphs 29–33 set out both benefits and dangers to adolescents from multitasking. How does Wallis enhance her credibility in these paragraphs?

But turning down the noise isn't easy. By the time 29 many kids get to college, their devices have become extensions of themselves, indispensable social accessories. "The minute the bell rings at most big public high schools, the first thing most kids do is reach into their bag and pick up their cell phone," observes Denise Clark Pope, lecturer at the Stanford School of Education, "never mind that the person [they're contacting] could be right down the hall."

Parents are mystified by this obsession with 30 e-communication—particularly among younger adolescents who often can't wait to share the most mundane details of life. Dominique Jones, 12, of Los Angeles, likes to IM her friends before school to find out what they plan to wear. "You'll get IMs back that say things like 'Oh, my God, I'm wearing the same shoes!' After school we talk about what happened that day, what outfits we want to wear the next day."

Turkle, author of the recently reissued *The Second Self:* 31 *Computers and the Human Spirit*, has an explanation for this breathless exchange of inanities. "There's an extraordinary fit between the medium and the moment, a heady, giddy fit in terms of social needs." The online environment, she points out, "is less risky if you are lonely and afraid of intimacy, which is almost a definition of adolescence. Things get too hot, you log off, while in real time and space, you have consequences." Teen venues like MySpace, Xanga and Facebook—and the ways kids can personalize their IM personas—meet another teen need: the desire to experiment with identity. By changing their picture, their "away" message, their icon or list of favorite bands, kids can cycle through different personalities. "Online life is like an identity workshop," says Turkle, "and that's the job of adolescents—to experiment with identity."

32   All that is probably healthy, provided that parents set limits on where their kids can venture online, teach them to exercise caution and regulate how much time they can spend with electronics in general. The problem is that most parents don't. According to the Kaiser survey, only 23% of seventh- to 12th-graders say their family has rules about computer activity; just 17% say they have restrictions on video-game time.

33   In the absence of rules, it's all too easy for kids to wander into unwholesome neighborhoods on the Net and get caught up in the compulsive behavior that psychiatrist Edward Hallowell dubs "screen-sucking" in his new book, *CrazyBusy*. Patricia Wallace, a technopsychologist who directs the Johns Hopkins Center for Talented Youth program, believes part of the allure of e-mail—for adults as well as teens—is similar to that of a slot machine. "You have intermittent, variable reinforcement," she explains. "You are not sure you are going to get a reward every time or how often you will, so you keep pulling that handle. Why else do people get up in the middle of the night to check their e-mail?"

GETTING THEM TO LOG OFF

34   Many educators and psychologists say parents need to actively ensure that their teenagers break free of compulsive engagement with screens and spend time in the physical company of human beings—a growing challenge not just because technology offers such a handy alternative

but because so many kids lead highly scheduled lives that leave little time for old-fashioned socializing and family meals. Indeed, many teenagers and college students say overcommitted schedules drive much of their multitasking.

Just as important is for parents and educators to teach kids, preferably by example, that it's valuable, even essential, to occasionally slow down, unplug and take time to think about something for a while. David Levy, a professor at the University of Washington Information School, has found, to his surprise, that his most technophilic undergraduates—those majoring in "informatics"—are genuinely concerned about getting lost in the multitasking blur. In an informal poll of 60 students last semester, he says, the majority expressed concerns about how plugged-in they were and "the way it takes them away from other activities, including exercise, meals and sleep." Levy's students talked about difficulties concentrating and their efforts to break away, get into the outdoors and inside their head. "Although it wasn't a scientific survey," he says, "it was the first evidence I had that people in this age group are reflecting on these questions." 35

Why do you think Wallis chooses to conclude her essay with a passage from Hallowell about what you are not *doing when you are multitasking?*

For all the handwringing about Generation M, technology is not really the problem. "The problem," says Hallowell, "is what you are not doing if the electronic moment grows too large"—too large for the teenager and too large for those parents who are equally tethered to their gadgets. In that case, says Hallowell, "you are not having family dinner, you are not having conversations, you are not debating whether to go out with a boy who wants to have sex on the first date, you are not going on a family ski trip or taking time just to veg. It's not so much that the video game is going to rot your brain, it's what you are not doing that's going to rot your life." 36

Generation M has a lot to teach parents and teachers about what new technology can do. But it's up to grownups to show them what it can't do, and that there's life beyond the screen. 37

READING FOR MEANING

This section presents three activities that will help you think about the meanings in Wallis's effects argument.

Read to Comprehend

Write a few sentences briefly explaining the argument Wallis is making about the effects on youth of multitasking.

Identify any words with meanings you are unsure of—such as *implications* (paragraph 17), *reprieve* (23), and *evanescent* (26)—and find the dictionary definition for each word that makes the best sense in the context.

To help you understand the essay better, also consider trying one of these critical reading strategies, explained in Appendix 1: *outlining* or *summarizing*.

Read to Respond

Write a paragraph or two exploring your initial thoughts and feelings about Wallis's effects argument. Focus on anything that stands out for you, perhaps because it resonates with your own experience or because you find a statement puzzling. For example, consider writing about one of the following:

- researchers' findings that "students are less tolerant of ambiguity" today than in the past and have an "aversion to complexity" (paragraph 28).

- researchers' findings that people in Gen M tend to feel "almost a discomfort with not being stimulated" (17) or to "get mental antsyness" (23)

- the effect on you of Wallis's use of many different kinds of authorities, such as the recipient of a MacArthur grant, several professors, authors of books, heads of foundations, and members of families.

- your own experiences with multitasking, and your own view of its effects.

To help develop your response, also consider trying one of these critical reading strategies, explained in Appendix 1: *looking for patterns of opposition* or *judging the writer's credibility*.

Read to Analyze Assumptions

Write a paragraph or two analyzing an assumption in Wallis's essay. To think critically about assumptions, here are some kinds of questions you could ask: Who holds this assumption (the writer, readers, and/or others cited in the essay)? What are the effects of the assumption in the context of the essay specifically or in society more generally? What do you think about the assumption, and is there anything in the essay that raises doubts about it? How does the assumption reinforce or critique commonly held views, and are there any alternative ideas, beliefs, or values that would challenge this assumption?

You might choose an assumption from the list below, using the questions accompanying it in addition to the ones above to help you get started. Or you can choose another assumption in the essay to explore.

- **assumptions about the value of thinking deeply.** Wallis notes that "the quality of one's output and depth of thought deteriorate as one attends to ever more tasks" (paragraph 17) and quotes Claudia Koonz, a professor of history, who says "In order to have a taste for sifting through different layers of truth, you have to stay with a topic and pursue it deeply, rather than go across the surface with your toolbar" (28). Wallis urges parents and educators to teach kids to "slow down, unplug and take time to think about something for a while" (35).

To think critically about the assumptions in this essay related to the value of thinking deeply, ask yourself questions like these: What evidence does Wallis provide that thinking deeply is a value her audience shares with her? What are the effects on society of its members' thinking deeply? How would you define "deep thinking" in your own words? What happens if you don't think deeply?

- **assumptions about the value of face-to-face socializing.** Wallis quotes Stephen Cox's complaint that his family members "'rarely have dinner together anymore.' . . . 'Everyone is in their own little world, and we don't get out together to have a social life'" (paragraph 15). "What happens," asks researcher Elinor Ochs, "as we replace side-by-side and eye-to-eye human connections with quick, disembodied e-exchanges?" (18). Wallis asks parents to help teens "spend time in the physical company of human beings" (34), and she concludes her essay with a quotation from Edward Hallowell about social occasions teens are *not* engaging in when they are multitasking—family dinners, conversations, family ski trips—"it's what you are not doing that's going to rot your life" (36).

  To think critically about the assumptions in this essay related to the value of face-to-face socializing, ask yourself questions like these: How is the socializing over e-mail or Facebook or other online platforms different from face-to-face? What advantages does face-to-face socializing have over technological socializing? What are its disadvantages? Do you share Wallis's view that it is superior to the alternative? Why or why not?

To help you analyze assumptions in Wallis's argument, also consider trying one of these critical reading strategies, explained in Appendix 1: *evaluating the logic of an argument* or *using a Toulmin analysis*.

READING LIKE A WRITER

PRESENTING THE SUBJECT

When writers speculate about the effects of a trend, they must define or describe the trend for readers. Readers must be assured that the trend actually exists. Furthermore, readers are more likely to be engaged by the speculations if they can recognize or be convinced that the trend is important to them personally or has a larger significance. In some writing situations, writers may safely assume that readers are thoroughly familiar with the trend and therefore need little more than a mention of it. In most situations, however, writers know that readers will require a relatively full presentation of the subject. Wallis knows that her readers are aware of the prevalence of technological devices, but they may not know just how much young people are using them, what is being sacrificed in favor of them, and what the consequences of using many of them at once—multitasking—might be. She therefore presents her subject through anecdotes, gives many examples, cites statistics, and quotes authorities, all to help the reader to see the negative effects of multitasking. Below you will explore just one of her approaches.

Analyze

1. Reread paragraphs 1 to 9. Underline all of the tasks mentioned.

2. Now reread paragraph 11. Think about the consequences all of these tasks have on the family.

Write

Write several sentences explaining how Wallis presents her subject in the first several paragraphs. Then add a few more sentences evaluating how successfully she does so. Do these paragraphs serve as a good introduction to her subject? What effects does she mention? Do you see these effects reappear in the rest of her essay?

CONSIDERING IDEAS FOR YOUR OWN WRITING

Think about other phenomena or trends that have occurred as a result of the technological revolution. Have attitudes toward research changed? How about attitudes toward privacy? Toward intellectual property (ownership of ideas, words, music, etc.)? Do communication devices such as cell phones or storage devices such as Blackberries or Palm Pilots make a significant difference to society or components of it? How has education changed—in positive or negative ways—as a result of technology? How are classes taught differently, and are the changes for better or worse?

Wallis and other researchers seem to believe that social life is changing as a result of technology. Can you think of other phenomena or trends—or even an event—that also has changed social life? You would then be looking at causes, rather than effects. Select one group whose behavior is changing, and consider how you would convince readers that the behavior is in fact changing. What kind of evidence would you need to gather in the library or on the Internet to corroborate your personal impressions? As a writer speculating about a behavioral change, consider how you would come up with some possible causes for the trend.

A Special Reading Strategy

Comparing and Contrasting Related Readings: Claudia Wallis's "The Multitasking Generation" and Christine Rosen's "The Myth of Multitasking".

Comparing and contrasting related readings is a critical reading strategy useful both in reading for meaning and in reading like a writer. This strategy is particularly applicable when writers present similar subjects, as is the case in the essays by Wallis (p. 422) and Rosen (p. 308), both of whom write about multitasking. To compare and contrast these two essays, think about issues such as these:

- Compare how the two writers define multitasking. Are the definitions similar or different? Is one preferable to the other? If so, why?

- Compare the approach of each author to multitasking. Do they have the same sense of alarm about it, or are their attitudes different? Do they provide a similar history of it? How similar are their examples?

See Appendix 1 (pp. 596–601) for detailed guidelines on comparing and contrasting related readings.

Cass Sunstein

To Become an Extremist, Hang Around with People You Agree With

Cass R. Sunstein (b. 1954) is Felix Frankfurter Professor of Law at Harvard Law School. He previously taught for many years at the University of Chicago, in both law and political science. An adviser to President Obama, Sunstein is the author of dozens of books, among them Risk and Reason *(2002),* Why Societies Need Dissent *(2003),* The Second Bill of Rights: Franklin Delano Roosevelt's Unfinished Revolution and Why We Need It More Than Ever *(2004), (with Richard H. Thaler),* Nudge: Improving Decisions about Health, Wealth, and Happiness *(2008),* Going to Extremes: How Like Minds Unite and Divide *(2009),* On Rumors: How Falsehoods Spread, Why We Believe Them, What Can Be Done *(2009), and* Law and Happiness *(2010).*

Sunstein's 2001 book, Republic.com, *argued that the Internet may weaken democracy because it allows citizens to isolate themselves within groups that share their own views and experiences; thus, they cut themselves off from any information that might challenge their beliefs, a phenomenon known as* cyber balkanization. *In the article below, an edited extract from* Going to Extremes *that was published in the British magazine* Spectator *(note the British spelling of certain words), Sunstein unveils his new theory of "group polarization," and explains why, when like-minded people spend time with each other, their views become not only more confident but more extreme. As you read, think about your own experiences with groups, and measure whether you agree or disagree with Sunstein's argument, and why.*

To see more about Sunstein, visit his Web site: http://www.law.harvard .edu/faculty/directory/index.html?id=552.

What explains the rise of fascism in the 1930s? The emergence of student radicalism in the 1960s? The growth of Islamic terrorism in the 1990s? The Rwandan genocide of 1994? Ethnic conflict in the former Yugoslavia and in Iraq? Acts of torture and humiliation by American soldiers at Abu Ghraib prison? The American financial crisis of 2008? The widespread belief, in some parts of the world, that Israel or the United States was responsible for the attacks of September 11, 2001? And what, if anything, do these questions have to do with one another? 1

Here is a clue. Some years ago, a number of citizens of France were assembled into small groups to exchange views about their president and about the intentions of the United States with respect to foreign aid. Before they started to talk, the participants tended to like their president and to distrust the intentions of the United States. After they talked, some strange things happened. Those who began by liking their president ended up 2 liking their president significantly more. And those who expressed mild distrust toward the United States moved in the direction of far greater distrust. The small groups of French citizens became more extreme. As a result of their discussions, they were more enthusiastic about their leader, and far more sceptical of the United States, than similar people in France who had not been brought together to speak with one another.

3   This tale reveals a general fact of social life: much of the time groups of people end up thinking and doing things that group members would never think or do on their own. This is true for groups of teenagers, who are willing to run risks that individuals would avoid. It is certainly true for those prone to violence, including terrorists and those who commit genocide. It is true for investors and corporate executives. It is true for government officials, neighbourhood groups, social reformers, political protestors, police officers, student organisations, labour unions and juries. Some of the best and worst developments in social life are a product of group dynamics, in which members of organisations, both small and large, move one another in new directions.

4   Of course, the best explanations of fascism are not adequate to explain student rebellions, and even if we understand both of these, we will not be able to explain ethnic conflict in Iraq, the Rwandan genocide, abuse and brutality at Abu Ghraib, conspiracy theories involving Israel, or the subprime crisis. For particular events, general explanations can uncover only parts of the picture. But there are striking similarities among a wide range of social phenomena. The unifying theme is simple: when people find themselves in groups of like-minded types, they are especially likely to move to extremes. And when such groups include authorities who tell group members what to do, or who put them into certain social roles, very bad things can happen.

5   In exploring why this is so, I hope to see what might be done about unjustified extremism, which is a threat to security, to peace, to economic development and to sensible decisions in all sorts of domains. My emphasis throughout is on the phenomenon of group polarisation. This phenomenon offers important lessons about the behaviour of the market, religious organisations, political parties, liberation movements, executive agencies, legislatures, racists, judicial panels, those who make peace, those who make war, and even nations as a whole.

6   Political extremism is often a product of group polarisation and social segregation is a useful tool for producing polarisation. In fact, a good way to create an extremist group, or a cult of any kind, is to separate members from the rest of society. The separation can occur physically or psychologically, by creating a sense of suspicion about non-members. With such separation, the information and views of those outside the group can be discredited, and hence nothing will disturb the process of polarisation as group members continue to talk. Deliberating enclaves of like-minded

people are often a breeding ground for extreme movements. Terrorists are made, not born, and terrorist networks often operate in just this way. As a result, they can move otherwise ordinary people to violent acts. But the point goes well beyond such domains. Group polarisation occurs in our daily lives; it involves our economic decisions, our evaluations of our neighbours, even our decisions about what to eat, what to drink and where to live.

So why do like-minded people go to extremes? The most important   7
reason for group polarisation, which is key to extremism in all its forms, involves the exchange of new information. Group polarisation often occurs because people are telling one another what they know, and what they know is skewed in a predictable direction. When they listen to each other, they move.

Suppose that you are in a group of people whose members tend to think   8
that Israel is the real aggressor in the Middle East conflict, that eating beef is unhealthy, or that same-sex unions are a good idea. In such a group, you will hear many arguments to that effect. Because of the initial distribution of views, you will hear relatively fewer opposing views. It is highly likely that you will have heard some, but not all, of the arguments that emerge from the discussion. After you have heard all of what is said, you will probably shift further in the direction of thinking that Israel is the real aggressor, opposing eating beef, and favouring civil unions. And even if you do not shift—even if you are impervious to what others think—most group members will probably be affected.

When groups move, they do so in large part because of the impact   9
of information. People tend to respond to the arguments made by other people—and the pool of arguments, in a group with a predisposition in a particular direction, will inevitably be skewed in the direction of the original predisposition. Certainly this can happen in a group whose members tend to support aggressive government regulation to combat climate change. Group members will hear a number of arguments in favour of aggressive government regulation and fewer arguments the other way. If people are listening, they will have a stronger conviction, in the same direction from which they began, as a result of deliberation. If people are worried about climate change, the arguments they offer will incline them toward greater worry. If people start with the belief that climate change is a hoax and a myth, their discussions will amplify and intensify that belief. And indeed, a form of "environmental tribalism" is an important part of modern political life. Some groups are indifferent to environmental problems that greatly concern and even terrify others. The key reason is the information to which group members are exposed. If you hear that genetically modified food poses serious risks, and if that view is widespread in your community, you might end up frightened. If you hear nothing about the risks associated with genetically modified food, except perhaps that

some zealots are frightened, you will probably ridicule their fear. And when groups move in dangerous directions—toward killing and destruction—it is usually because the flow of information supports that movement.

10   Those who lack confidence and who are unsure what they should think tend to moderate their views. Suppose that you are asked what you think about some question on which you lack information. You are likely to avoid extremes. It is for this reason that cautious people, not knowing what to do, tend to choose some midpoint between the extremes. But if other people seem to share their views, people become more confident that they are correct.

11   As a result, they will probably move in a more extreme direction. What is especially noteworthy is that this process of increased confidence and increased extremism is often occurring simultaneously for all participants. Suppose that a group of four people is inclined to distrust the intentions of the United States with respect to foreign aid. Seeing their tentative view confirmed by three others, each member is likely to feel vindicated, to hold their view more confidently, and to move in a more extreme direction. At the same time, the very same internal movements are also occurring in other people (from corroboration to more confidence, and from more confidence to more extremism).

12   But those movements will not be highly visible to each participant. It will simply appear as if others "really" hold their views without hesitation. As a result, our little group might conclude, after a day's discussion, that the intentions of the United States, with respect to foreign aid, cannot be trusted at all. We have a clue here about the great importance of social networks, on the Internet and in ordinary life, in creating movements of various sorts. Social networks can operate as polarisation machines because they help to confirm and thus amplify people's antecedent views. Those who are inclined to support a cause or a candidate may become quite excited if support is widespread on their social network.

13   In 2008 Barack Obama greatly benefited from this process, in a way that created extreme enthusiasm for his candidacy. Some of this was planned; his campaign self-consciously promoted social networks that spread favourable information. But some of this was spontaneous. Obama supporters, especially young people, worked hard on their own to take advantage of existing networks and create new ones that would turn curiosity and tentative support into intense enthusiasm and active involvement.

14   A very different example is provided by Islamic terrorism, which is also fuelled by spontaneous social networks, in which like-minded people discuss grievances with potentially violent results. The terrorism specialist Marc Sageman explains that at certain stages, "the interactivity among a 'bunch of guys' acted as an echo chamber, which progressively radicalised them collectively to the point where they were ready to collectively join a terrorist organisation. Now the same process is taking place online." The

major force here is not websites, which people read passively; it consists of Listservs (which enable group emails), blogs and discussion forums, which are crucial in the process of radicalisation. Islamic terrorism is a product, in significant part, of group polarisation.

In the private sector, economic disasters, for individuals and large groups, 15 are often a product of conversations among like-minded people, in which some investment or project seems to be a sure winner. The economic crisis that began in 2008 was a product, in significant part, of a form of group polarisation, in which sceptics about the real estate bubble, armed with statistical evidence, did not receive a fair hearing or were in a sense silenced. The best companies, and the best investors, benefit from internal checks and balances.

Of course, not all extreme movements are bad. Some extreme move- 16 ments may be desirable even when they result from mechanisms of the sort traced here. And even when they are not desirable, extreme positions can do a great deal of good. Nothing said here is meant to deny these claims. But if extreme movements are to occur, it should be because they are sensible and right and not because of the predictable effects of interactions among the like-minded.

READING FOR MEANING

This section presents three activities that will help you think about the meanings in Sunstein's effect argument.

Read to Comprehend

Write a few sentences briefly explaining what phenomenon happens when group polarization occurs.

Identify any words with meanings you are unsure of—such as *enclaves* (paragraph 6) and *antecedent* (12)—and find the dictionary definition for each word that makes the best sense in the context.

To help you understand the essay better, also consider trying one of these critical reading strategies, explained in Appendix 1: *outlining* or *synthesizing*.

Read to Respond

Write a paragraph or two exploring your initial thoughts and feelings about Sunstein's effects argument. Focus on anything that stands out for you, perhaps because it resonates with your own experience or because you find a statement puzzling. For example, consider writing about one of the following:

- whether you have ever been influenced by a group, and whether the influence of the group led to any action on your part or the group's part.

- why you think Sunstein presents extensive lists of examples to support his thesis (paragraphs 1, 3, and 4)

To help develop your response, also consider trying one of these critical reading strategies, explained in Appendix 1: *contextualizing* or *judging the writer's credibility*.

Read to Analyze Assumptions

Write a paragraph or two analyzing an assumption in Sunstein's essay. To think critically about assumptions, here are some kinds of questions you could ask: Who holds this assumption (the writer, readers, and/or others cited in the essay)? What are the effects of the assumption in the context of the essay specifically or in society more generally? What do you think about the assumption, and is there anything in the essay that raises doubts about it? How does the assumption reinforce or critique commonly held views, and are there any alternative ideas, beliefs, or values that would challenge this assumption?

You might choose an assumption from the list below, using the questions accompanying it in addition to the ones above to help you get started. Or you can choose another assumption in the essay to explore.

- **assumptions about the universality of group behavior.** To explain how extremism grows out of group behavior, Sunstein asserts "a general fact of social life: much of the time groups of people end up thinking and doing things that group members would never think or do on their own" (paragraph 3). He adds: "when people find themselves in groups of like-minded types, they are especially likely to move to extremes" (4). And again: "Social networks can operate as polarisation machines because they help to confirm and thus amplify people's antecedent views" (12).

  To think critically about the assumptions in this essay related to the universality of group behavior, ask yourself questions like these: Do you believe that most or all groups behave in the same way? Have you seen any examples of groups in which opinion about a topic became less rather than more extreme over time or the balance of opinion shifted from one side to the other? Do you believe that having groups made up of people with a mixture of opinions offsets the polarizing nature of group dynamics, as Sunstein implies when he says "[t]he best companies, and the best investors, benefit from internal checks and balances" (15)?

- **assumptions about the subjective nature of information.** Sunstein says that when members of like-minded groups shift their collective opinion, "they do so in large part because of the impact of information" (paragraph 9): the "pool of arguments" expressed within the group "will inevitably be skewed" to reflect the group's "predisposition in a particular direction," and therefore increasing exposure to those arguments will tend to move opinion in that direction (9).

  To think critically about the assumptions in this essay related to the subjective nature of information, ask yourself questions like these: Do most groups start out as a group of like-minded people? Is "factual" information subject to being skewed? If so, how? If not, how could it be skewed? What about simple omissions of information—could that lead to skewed information?

To help you analyze assumptions in Sunstein's essay, also consider trying one of these critical reading strategies, explained in Appendix 1: *using a Toulmin analysis* or *recognizing logical fallacies.*

READING LIKE A WRITER

SUPPORTING PROPOSED EFFECTS

Sunstein proposes that the effect of socializing in groups can be extremism. To convince readers to take this effect seriously, Sunstein must argue for—or support—it in ways that enhance its plausibility. All writers speculating about effects have many resources available to them to support their proposed effects—examples, statistics, quotations from authorities, personal anecdotes, analogies, scenarios, quotes from interviews, and more. As a writer speculating about causes or effects, you will need to support your speculations in these ways to make them plausible. You can learn more about supporting speculations by analyzing how Sunstein does so.

Analyze

1. Reread paragraphs 8 and 9. Underline all the *examples* and *scenarios* Sunstein presents to support his contention that group polarization occurs because of the exchange of new information (paragraph 7).

2. Examine this support carefully. Do the examples and scenarios seem logical to you? Do they seem believable? Evaluate the support in light of your own experiences or beliefs. Does it seem appropriate for the proposed effect? Does it seem believable and trustworthy?

Write

Write several sentences explaining how Sunstein supports the effect of group polarization from the exchange of new information. Also evaluate the plausibility of the support he offers. Give details from the paragraphs you have analyzed. As one of Sunstein's intended readers, explain how convincing you find the support.

CONSIDERING IDEAS FOR YOUR OWN WRITING

Consider speculating, as Sunstein does, about the effects of a significant social problem. List several major social problems (local or national) that concern you. Your list might include, for example, the high pregnancy rate among unmarried teenagers, high-school dropout rates, high costs of a college education, unsafe working conditions at your job, shortages of adequate day-care facilities for working parents, or uncontrolled development in your community. Choose one problem, and consider how you can speculate about its effects. What effects can you argue for? As a writer, how could you convince readers that your proposed effects are plausible? Will you need to research the problem to write about it authoritatively? Remember, your purpose is not to propose a solution to the problem but to speculate about its possible effects.

Alternatively, you could recall a recent controversial decision by college or community leaders that concerns you, such as a decision about campus life (safety, recreation, tutoring, or other special services) or about the future of your community (growth, transportation, safety). List several such decisions, and then choose one you would like to write about. Consider how you would write a letter to your college or community newspaper speculating about the effects or consequences of the decision. What short-term and long-term consequences would you propose? How would you convince readers to take your ideas seriously?

Nicholas Carr

Is Google Making Us Stupid?

Nicholas Carr (b. 1959) writes on the social, economic, and business implications of technology. Early in his career, he was executive editor of the Harvard Business Review *and a principal at Mercer Management Consulting. He is the author of* Does IT Matter? *(2004), on the economics of information technology;* The Big Switch: Rewiring the World, from Edison to Google *(2008), on cloud computing; and* The Shallows: What the Internet Is Doing to Our Brains *(2010). Carr has also written for many periodicals, including the* Atlantic Monthly, *the* New York Times Magazine, Wired, *the* Financial Times, *the* Futurist, *and* Advertising Age, *and has been a columnist for the* Guardian *and the* Industry Standard. *Carr has also been a speaker at many academic, corporate, governmental, and professional events throughout the world. He is a member of the Encyclopaedia Britannica's editorial board of advisers and is on the steering board of the World Economic Forum's cloud computing project. You can learn more about Carr at his Web site, http://www.nicholasgcarr.com, and you can visit his blog,* Rough Type, *at http://www.roughtype.com.*

The essay below was the cover story of the Atlantic Monthly's *Ideas issue in 2008. In it, Carr argues that the Internet is having a disturbing effect on our cognitive activities—the work of our brains. As you read, think about your own habits of concentration and focus, considering whether you are able to focus deeply for long periods of time or whether you move from one idea to another fairly swiftly. Also think about whether concentration has to be sacrificed for the sake of acquiring more information.*

"Dave, stop. Stop, will you? Stop, Dave. Will you stop, Dave?" So the   1
supercomputer HAL pleads with the implacable astronaut Dave Bowman in a famous and weirdly poignant scene toward the end of Stanley Kubrick's *2001: A Space Odyssey.* Bowman, having nearly been sent to a deep-space death by the malfunctioning machine, is calmly, coldly disconnecting the memory circuits that control its artificial "brain." "Dave, my mind is going," HAL says, forlornly. "I can feel it. I can feel it."

I can feel it, too. Over the past few years I've had an uncomfortable   2
sense that someone, or something, has been tinkering with my brain, remapping the neural circuitry, reprogramming the memory. My mind isn't going—so far as I can tell—but it's changing. I'm not thinking the way I used to think. I can feel it most strongly when I'm reading. Immersing myself in a book or a lengthy article used to be easy. My mind would get caught up in the narrative or the turns of the argument, and I'd spend hours strolling through long stretches of prose. That's rarely the case anymore. Now my concentration often starts to drift after two or three pages. I get fidgety, lose the thread, begin looking for something else to do. I feel as if I'm always dragging my wayward brain back to the text. The deep reading that used to come naturally has become a struggle.

3   I think I know what's going on. For more than a decade now, I've been spending a lot of time online, searching and surfing and sometimes adding to the great databases of the Internet. The Web has been a godsend to me as a writer. Research that once required days in the stacks or periodical rooms of libraries can now be done in minutes. A few Google searches, some quick clicks on hyperlinks, and I've got the telltale fact or pithy quote I was after. Even when I'm not working, I'm as likely as not to be foraging in the Web's info-thickets, reading and writing e-mails, scanning headlines and blog posts, watching videos and listening to podcasts, or just tripping from link to link to link. (Unlike footnotes, to which they're sometimes likened, hyperlinks don't merely point to related works; they propel you toward them.)

4   For me, as for others, the Net is becoming a universal medium, the conduit for most of the information that flows through my eyes and ears and into my mind. The advantages of having immediate access to such an incredibly rich store of information are many, and they've been widely described and duly applauded. "The perfect recall of silicon memory," *Wired*'s Clive Thompson has written, "can be an enormous boon to thinking." But that boon comes at a price. As the media theorist Marshall McLuhan pointed out in the 1960s, media are not just passive channels of information. They supply the stuff of thought, but they also shape the process of thought. And what the Net seems to be doing is chipping away my capacity for concentration and contemplation. My mind now expects to take in information the way the Net distributes it: in a swiftly moving stream of particles. Once I was a scuba diver in the sea of words. Now I zip along the surface like a guy on a Jet Ski.

I'm not the only one. When I mention my troubles with reading to   5
friends and acquaintances—literary types, most of them—many say
they're having similar experiences. The more they use the Web, the more
they have to fight to stay focused on long pieces of writing. Some of the
bloggers I follow have also begun mentioning the phenomenon. Scott
Karp, who writes a blog about online media, recently confessed that he
has stopped reading books altogether. "I was a lit major in college, and
used to be [a] voracious book reader," he wrote. "What happened?" He
speculates on the answer: "What if I do all my reading on the web not so
much because the way I read has changed, i.e. I'm just seeking convenience, but because the way I THINK has changed?"

Bruce Friedman, who blogs regularly about the use of computers in   6
medicine, also has described how the Internet has altered his mental
habits. "I now have almost totally lost the ability to read and absorb a longish article on the web or in print," he wrote earlier this year. A pathologist
who has long been on the faculty of the University of Michigan Medical
School, Friedman elaborated on his comment in a telephone conversation
with me. His thinking, he said, has taken on a "staccato" quality, reflecting
the way he quickly scans short passages of text from many sources online.
"I can't read *War and Peace* anymore," he admitted. "I've lost the ability
to do that. Even a blog post of more than three or four paragraphs is too
much to absorb. I skim it."

Anecdotes alone don't prove much. And we still await the long-term   7
neurological and psychological experiments that will provide a definitive picture of how Internet use affects cognition. But a recently published
study of online research habits, conducted by scholars from University
College London, suggests that we may well be in the midst of a sea change
in the way we read and think. As part of the five-year research program,
the scholars examined computer logs documenting the behavior of visitors
to two popular research sites, one operated by the British Library and one
by a U.K. educational consortium, that provide access to journal articles,
e-books, and other sources of written information. They found that people
using the sites exhibited "a form of skimming activity," hopping from one
source to another and rarely returning to any source they'd already visited.
They typically read no more than one or two pages of an article or book
before they would "bounce" out to another site. Sometimes they'd save a
long article, but there's no evidence that they ever went back and actually
read it. The authors of the study report:

> It is clear that users are not reading online in the traditional sense;
> indeed there are signs that new forms of "reading" are emerg-
> ing as users "power browse" horizontally through titles, contents
> pages and abstracts going for quick wins. It almost seems that
> they go online to avoid reading in the traditional sense.

8   Thanks to the ubiquity of text on the Internet, not to mention the popularity of text-messaging on cell phones, we may well be reading more today than we did in the 1970s or 1980s, when television was our medium of choice. But it's a different kind of reading, and behind it lies a different kind of thinking—perhaps even a new sense of the self. "We are not only *what* we read," says Maryanne Wolf, a developmental psychologist at Tufts University and the author of *Proust and the Squid: The Story and Science of the Reading Brain*. "We are *how* we read." Wolf worries that the style of reading promoted by the Net, a style that puts "efficiency" and "immediacy" above all else, may be weakening our capacity for the kind of deep reading that emerged when an earlier technology, the printing press, made long and complex works of prose commonplace. When we read online, she says, we tend to become "mere decoders of information." Our ability to interpret text, to make the rich mental connections that form when we read deeply and without distraction, remains largely disengaged.

9   Reading, explains Wolf, is not an instinctive skill for human beings. It's not etched into our genes the way speech is. We have to teach our minds how to translate the symbolic characters we see into the language we understand. And the media or other technologies we use in learning and practicing the craft of reading play an important part in shaping the neural circuits inside our brains. Experiments demonstrate that readers of ideograms, such as the Chinese, develop a mental circuitry for reading that is very different from the circuitry found in those of us whose written language employs an alphabet. The variations extend across many regions of the brain, including those that govern such essential cognitive functions as memory and the interpretation of visual and auditory stimuli. We can expect as well that the circuits woven by our use of the Net will be different from those woven by our reading of books and other printed works. . . .

10   The human brain is almost infinitely malleable. People used to think that our mental meshwork, the dense connections formed among the 100 billion or so neurons inside our skulls, was largely fixed by the time we reached adulthood. But brain researchers have discovered that that's not the case. James Olds, a professor of neuroscience who directs the Krasnow Institute for Advanced Study at George Mason University, says that even the adult mind "is very plastic." Nerve cells routinely break old connections and form new ones. "The brain," according to Olds, "has the ability to reprogram itself on the fly, altering the way it functions." . . .

11   The process of adapting to new intellectual technologies is reflected in the changing metaphors we use to explain ourselves to ourselves. When the mechanical clock arrived, people began thinking of their brains as operating "like clockwork." Today, in the age of software, we have come to think of them as operating "like computers." But the changes, neuroscience tells us, go much deeper than metaphor. Thanks to our brain's plasticity, the adaptation occurs also at a biological level.

The Internet promises to have particularly far-reaching effects on cogni-   12
tion. In a paper published in 1936, the British mathematician Alan Turing
proved that a digital computer, which at the time existed only as a theoretical machine, could be programmed to perform the function of any
other information-processing device. And that's what we're seeing today.
The Internet, an immeasurably powerful computing system, is subsuming
most of our other intellectual technologies. It's becoming our map and our
clock, our printing press and our typewriter, our calculator and our telephone, and our radio and TV.

When the Net absorbs a medium, that medium is re-created in the   13
Net's image. It injects the medium's content with hyperlinks, blinking ads,
and other digital gewgaws, and it surrounds the content with the content
of all the other media it has absorbed. A new e-mail message, for instance,
may announce its arrival as we're glancing over the latest headlines at
a newspaper's site. The result is to scatter our attention and diffuse our
concentration.

The Net's influence doesn't end at the edges of a computer screen,   14
either. As people's minds become attuned to the crazy quilt of Internet
media, traditional media have to adapt to the audience's new expectations. Television programs add text crawls and pop-up ads, and magazines
and newspapers shorten their articles, introduce capsule summaries, and
crowd their pages with easy-to-browse info-snippets. When, in March of
this year, *The New York Times* decided to devote the second and third
pages of every edition to article abstracts, its design director, Tom Bodkin,
explained that the "shortcuts" would give harried readers a quick "taste" of
the day's news, sparing them the "less efficient" method of actually turning
the pages and reading the articles. Old media have little choice but to play
by the new-media rules.

Never has a communications system played so many roles in our   15
lives—or exerted such broad influence over our thoughts—as the Internet
does today. Yet, for all that's been written about the Net, there's been little
consideration of how, exactly, it's reprogramming us. The Net's intellectual ethic remains obscure. . . .

Google's headquarters, in Mountain View, California—the Googleplex—   16
is the Internet's high church. . . . Google, says its chief executive, Eric
Schmidt, is "a company that's founded around the science of measure-
ment," and it is striving to "systematize everything" it does. Drawing on
the terabytes of behavioral data it collects through its search engine and
other sites, it carries out thousands of experiments a day, according to
the *Harvard Business Review*, and it uses the results to refine the algo-
rithms that increasingly control how people find information and extract
meaning from it. . . .

The company has declared that its mission is "to organize the world's   17
information and make it universally accessible and useful." It seeks to

develop "the perfect search engine," which it defines as something that "understands exactly what you mean and gives you back exactly what you want." In Google's view, information is a kind of commodity, a utilitarian resource that can be mined and processed with industrial efficiency. The more pieces of information we can "access" and the faster we can extract their gist, the more productive we become as thinkers.

18   Where does it end? Sergey Brin and Larry Page, the gifted young men who founded Google while pursuing doctoral degrees in computer science at Stanford, speak frequently of their desire to turn their search engine into an artificial intelligence, a HAL-like machine that might be connected directly to our brains. "The ultimate search engine is something as smart as people—or smarter," Page said in a speech a few years back. "For us, working on search is a way to work on artificial intelligence." In a 2004 interview with *Newsweek*, Brin said, "Certainly if you had all the world's information directly attached to your brain, or an artificial brain that was smarter than your brain, you'd be better off." Last year, Page told a convention of scientists that Google is "really trying to build artificial intelligence and to do it on a large scale."

19   Such an ambition is a natural one, even an admirable one, for a pair of math whizzes with vast quantities of cash at their disposal and a small army of computer scientists in their employ. A fundamentally scientific enterprise, Google is motivated by a desire to use technology, in Eric Schmidt's words, "to solve problems that have never been solved before," and artificial intelligence is the hardest problem out there. Why wouldn't Brin and Page want to be the ones to crack it?

20   Still, their easy assumption that we'd all "be better off" if our brains were supplemented, or even replaced, by an artificial intelligence is unsettling. It suggests a belief that intelligence is the output of a mechanical process, a series of discrete steps that can be isolated, measured, and optimized. In Google's world, the world we enter when we go online, there's little place for the fuzziness of contemplation. Ambiguity is not an opening for insight but a bug to be fixed. The human brain is just an outdated computer that needs a faster processor and a bigger hard drive.

21   The idea that our minds should operate as high-speed data-processing machines is not only built into the workings of the Internet, it is the network's reigning business model as well. The faster we surf across the Web—the more links we click and pages we view—the more opportunities Google and other companies gain to collect information about us and to feed us advertisements. Most of the proprietors of the commercial Internet have a financial stake in collecting the crumbs of data we leave behind as we flit from link to link—the more crumbs, the better. The last thing these companies want is to encourage leisurely reading or slow, concentrated thought. It's in their economic interest to drive us to distraction.

Maybe I'm just a worrywart. Just as there's a tendency to glorify tech-   22
nological progress, there's a countertendency to expect the worst of every
new tool or machine. . . . Perhaps those who dismiss critics of the Internet
as Luddites or nostalgists will be proved correct, and from our hyperactive,
data-stoked minds will spring a golden age of intellectual discovery and
universal wisdom. Then again, the Net isn't the alphabet, and although it
may replace the printing press, it produces something altogether different.
The kind of deep reading that a sequence of printed pages promotes is valuable not just for the knowledge we acquire from the author's words but for
the intellectual vibrations those words set off within our own minds. In the
quiet spaces opened up by the sustained, undistracted reading of a book,
or by any other act of contemplation, for that matter, we make our own
associations, draw our own inferences and analogies, foster our own ideas.
Deep reading, as Maryanne Wolf argues, is indistinguishable from deep
thinking. If we lose those quiet spaces, or fill them up with "content," we
will sacrifice something important not only in our selves but in our culture.
In a recent essay, the playwright Richard Foreman eloquently described
what's at stake:

> I come from a tradition of Western culture, in which the ideal (my
> ideal) was the complex, dense and "cathedral-like" structure of the
> highly educated and articulate personality—a man or woman who
> carried inside themselves a personally constructed and unique
> version of the entire heritage of the West. [But now] I see within
> us all (myself included) the replacement of complex inner density
> with a new kind of self—evolving under the pressure of infor-
> mation overload and the technology of the "instantly available."

As we are drained of our "inner repertory of dense cultural inheritance,"   23
Foreman concluded, we risk turning into "'pancake people'—spread wide
and thin as we connect with that vast network of information accessed by
the mere touch of a button."

I'm haunted by that scene in *2001*. What makes it so poignant, and   24
so weird, is the computer's emotional response to the disassembly of its
mind: its despair as one circuit after another goes dark, its childlike plead-
ing with the astronaut—"I can feel it. I can feel it. I'm afraid"—and its
final reversion to what can only be called a state of innocence. HAL's out-
pouring of feeling contrasts with the emotionlessness that characterizes
the human figures in the film, who go about their business with an almost
robotic efficiency. Their thoughts and actions feel scripted, as if they're
following the steps of an algorithm. In the world of *2001*, people have
become so machinelike that the most human character turns out to be a
machine. That's the essence of Kubrick's dark prophecy: as we come to
rely on computers to mediate our understanding of the world, it is our own
intelligence that flattens into artificial intelligence.

READING FOR MEANING

This section presents three activities that will help you think about the meanings in Carr's effects argument.

Read to Comprehend

Write a few sentences briefly explaining what is worrying Nicholas Carr.

Identify any words with meanings you are unsure of—such as *ubiquity* (paragraph 8) and *ideograms* (9)—and find the dictionary definition for each word that makes the best sense in the context.

To help you understand the essay better, also consider trying one of these critical reading strategies, explained in Appendix 1: *contextualizing* or *reflecting on challenges to your beliefs and values.*

Read to Respond

Write a paragraph or two exploring your initial thoughts and feelings about Carr's effects argument. Focus on anything that stands out for you, perhaps because it resonates with your own experience or because you find a statement puzzling. For example, consider writing about one of the following:

- the effect on you of Carr's anecdotes in the first six paragraphs. Did they draw you into the essay? Help you identify with the writer? Make you think he'd better give some hard evidence if you were to believe him?

- your own experience with reading on the Internet, and whether you share Carr's concern that the kind of reading fostered there is undermining "deep reading" (paragraph 2).

- your response to the title, "Is Google Making Us Stupid?"

To help develop your response, also consider trying one of these critical reading strategies, explained in Appendix 1: *recognizing emotional manipulation* or *judging the writer's credibility.*

Read to Analyze Assumptions

Write a paragraph or two analyzing an assumption in Carr's essay. To think critically about assumptions, here are some kinds of questions you could ask: Who holds this assumption (the writer, readers, and/or others cited in the essay)? What are the effects of the assumption in the context of the essay specifically or in society more generally? What do you think about the assumption, and is there anything in the essay that raises doubts about it? How does the assumption reinforce or critique commonly held views, and are there any alternative ideas, beliefs, or values that would challenge this assumption?

You might choose an assumption from the list below, using the questions accompanying it in addition to the ones above to help you get started. Or you can choose another assumption in the essay to explore.

- **assumptions about the value of sustained concentration.** Carr returns again and again to ways the Net is reducing our ability to sustain concentration and focus for an extended period of time. He reports that he and his friends "have to fight to stay focused on long pieces of writing" (paragraph 5), cites a study that finds "there are signs that new forms of 'reading' are emerging as users [of research sites] 'power browse' . . . going for quick wins" (7), and worries that "the last thing these companies [Google and others] want is to encourage leisurely reading or slow, concentrated thought" (21). Finally, he summarizes the ideas of developmental psychologist Maryanne Wolf, stating that "Deep reading . . . is indistinguishable from deep thinking. If we lose those quiet spaces, or fill them up with 'content,' we will sacrifice something important not only in our selves but in our culture" (22).

  To think critically about the assumptions in this essay related to the value of sustained concentration, ask yourself questions like these: What difference does it make to our minds to engage in the intellectual activity of sustained concentration versus the activity of acquiring many bits of information? How does Carr support his contention that we lose something valuable if we lose sustained concentration? Is there a compromise—a way to have both sustained concentration and all the knowledge we need?

- **assumptions about the value of the human over the machine.** Carr seems to be concerned that machines will take over humans or that we will become like machines, losing something important to our humanity. He says that "Google's world" sees the human brain as "just an outdated computer that needs a faster processor and a bigger hard drive (paragraph 20), and that "[t]he idea that our minds should operate as high-speed data-processing machines is . . . built into the workings of the Internet. . . ." (21). In Carr's view, expanded knowledge from online "content" is not enough; we also need the "intellectual vibrations . . . words set off within our own minds" (22). In his conclusion, he laments that in the movie *2001*, "people have become so machinelike that the most human character turns out to be a machine" (24).

  To think critically about the assumptions in this essay related to the value of the human over the machine, ask yourself questions like these: How would you define "human" in the context of Carr's essay? What kind of threat is the "machine" to the "humans"? What do you think of Carr's concerns about the danger machines pose to humans, especially machines that mimic the human mind? What could be the long-lasting consequences of *not* prizing the human?

To help you analyze assumptions in Carr's essay, also consider trying one of these critical reading strategies, explained in Appendix 1: *recognizing emotional manipulation* or *judging the writer's credibility.*

READING LIKE A WRITER

COUNTERARGUING

Writers speculating about causes must work imaginatively and persistently to support their proposed causes, using all the relevant resources available to them—quoting authorities, citing statistics and research findings, comparing and contrasting, posing rhetorical questions, offering literary allusions, and crafting metaphors, among other strategies. (Carr uses all of the resources in this list.) In addition to supporting their proposed causes, they usually do more. Because they aim to convince particular readers of the plausibility of their causal argument, writers try to be keenly aware that at every point in the argument their readers will have questions, objections, and other causes in mind. Anticipating and responding to these questions, objections, and alternative causes is known as *counterarguing*.

As readers work their way through a causal argument, nearly all of them will think of questions they would like to ask the writer. They also might resist or object to certain aspects of the support, such as the way the writer uses facts or statistics, relies on an authority, sets up an analogy, or presents an example or personal experience. Readers may doubt whether the support is appropriate, believable, or consistent with the other support provided by the writer. They may come to believe that the writer relies too much on emotional appeals and too little on reason. Readers may also resist or reject the writer's proposed causes, or they may believe that other causes better explain the trend or phenomenon. Experienced writers anticipate all of these predictable concerns. Just as imaginatively as they argue for their proposed causes, they attempt to answer readers' questions, react to their objections, and evaluate their preferred causes. When you write your essay about causes or effects, anticipating and responding to your readers' concerns will be one of the most challenging and interesting parts of constructing your argument.

Analyze

1. Carr counterargues in several places in his causal argument—paragraphs 4, 7, 8, 10, 17, 18, 19, and 22. Reread these paragraphs, and identify and underline the main objections that Carr anticipates his readers will have to his argument. For example, in paragraph 4, he anticipates readers' likely objection that having access to so much information is a terrific advantage.

2. Examine closely how Carr counterargues readers' objections and questions. For at least three of the objections or questions you identified in the paragraphs you read, notice the kinds of support he relies on to argue against each objection. Decide whether the support is similar or different among the three cases.

Write

Write several sentences reporting what you have learned about how Carr anticipates his readers' objections. Specifically, in each case, how does he support his counterargument? How appropriate do you, as one of his intended readers, find his support? How believable do you find it?

ANALYZING VISUALS

Write a paragraph analyzing the cartoon included in Carr's essay and explaining what it contributes to the essay. To do the analysis, you can use the criteria chart for the Analysis of Visuals in Appendix 3 on pp. 670–72. Don't feel you have to answer all of the questions on the chart: focus on those that seem most productive in helping you write a paragraph-length analysis. To help you get started, consider adding these questions that specifically refer to Carr's visual:

- Why do you suppose the Internet is portrayed as the policing agent, while the man with the book is portrayed as getting a ticket?

- The sign says, "Minimum Speed," followed by a group of numbers and letters. What kinds of meanings could be read into this message?

CONSIDERING IDEAS FOR YOUR OWN WRITING

Technology is certainly blossoming in the twenty-first century. Following Carr's lead, you could speculate about the causes of a trend or phenomenon in technology that you have noticed or that has been pointed out to you and you want to investigate. Some examples include the rise of the e-book (including iPads and similar devices), computers in automobiles, technology in the classroom, and technology in movies.

Jeremy Khella

The Route to American Obesity

Jeremy Khella wrote the essay below for an assignment when he was a student at Chaffey College in California. In it he speculates about the causes of the obesity epidemic in the United States. Khella is also interested in helping Americans put a stop to this phenomenon, as evidenced throughout his essay when he mentions or implies alternatives to existing policies, and especially in his last two paragraphs, where he offers a specific proposal and asserts that we need to make healthy eating and regular exercise easier choices.

As you read, think about whether the reasons Khella presents for the rise in obesity are plausible, and whether he includes enough of them to establish his credibility.

1   Over the past couple of decades, the United States has become known as one of the fattest nations on Earth. According to a national survey of health behaviors and nutrition, sixty-six percent of American adults are considered overweight or obese, with a whopping seventy-two million people categorized as obese. Some researchers predict that at our current rates, "seventy-five percent of adults will be overweight or obese, and forty-one percent will be obese" by the year 2015 (Wang and Beydoun)—a staggering statistic that could increase already inflated U.S. health care costs. Obesity is one of the top underlying preventable causes of death in the United States (Datz). Furthermore, it is affecting children and adolescents at an alarming rate, to the point that one out of every three kids is considered overweight or obese (Gavin). In spite of all the obesity-related laws that have recently been passed, the increasing attention of the media to the issue, and mass educational campaigns about the benefits of physical activity and a healthier lifestyle, the prevalence of obesity in the United States continues to grow. Tally the relatively few Americans who actually practice a healthy lifestyle compared to the many others who practice the art of "super-sizing," and it will be no surprise why this phenomenon has occurred.

2   The obesity epidemic did not happen overnight; Americans did not suddenly become a country of overly hungry people eating everything in sight. One of the many culprits is none other than the fast-food industry. In reality, many people do not know what fast-food restaurants are actually putting into their food; many do not even want to know. Too many unhealthy and fatty foods are being sold to the public in restaurants and supermarkets in misleading manners. But it's the convenience of the fast food that perpetuates its popularity.

3   The obesity rate has gradually grown since around the 1980s, when fast-food restaurants started to become popular ("Statistics") and their

menus began to reflect some significant changes. In the 1970s two new food products—high-fructose corn syrup and palm oil—were approved for use in the United States. Combined, they would decrease costs of ingredients for the food industry, an especially appealing factor during the severe recession and high inflation of the 1970s. High-fructose corn syrup (HFCS) reduced the amount of more-expensive sugar needed in soft drinks, sweet foods, and prepackaged meals. This ingredient quickly found its way into many popular American foods and beverages: Huwerl Thornton Jr., a health nutrition professor at Yale, points out that "[a]ccording to the USDA, in 2001, the average person consumed almost 63 pounds of high-fructose corn syrup." The problem with HFCS is that "as a result of the manufacturing process . . . the fructose molecules in the sweetener are free and unbound, ready for absorption and utilization"; therefore the fructose in HFCS is more quickly and easily absorbed by the body than sugar and more easily "metabolized to produce fat" (Parker). Likewise, palm oil is cheaper than the soybean oil it replaced in many products, but it contains more saturated fat—even more than hog lard (Critser 15).

These cheaper ingredients allowed restaurants to sell larger portions   4
for lower prices, eventually leading to "super-sized" meals. A normal McDonald's meal that used to be only 590 calories is now a massive 1550 calories, nearly the total daily recommended calorie intake for an average person (Critser 28). What used to be a standard twelve-ounce bottle of Coca Cola has now become a sixty-four ounce Big Gulp jug. A normal sandwich has turned into a foot long sub sandwich, or longer. Over time, Americans became accustomed to these super-sized proportions, and are now eating, on average, an extra 300 calories each day (Levi et al. 23). America is the land of overconsumption.

Many Americans lead busy lives consumed by work, school, a social   5
life, and a family, all of which can drain a person to the point of exhaustion. As a way to free up some time, too many people cut home cooking out of their lives. As they see it, there is no reason to waste hours cooking when they can go down the street and purchase an affordable, tasty meal in less than a couple of minutes. Fast-food restaurants just so happen to fit conveniently into most people's lives. Even though their products are usually loaded with calories—not to mention fats, cholesterol, and sodium—people who are hungry and do not have much time to spare usually choose immediate gratification over health and nutrition. In the process of doing so, they increase their risk for obesity.

In addition to the fast-food industry, a lack of physical activity is also   6
to blame for making Americans plumper and unhealthier. Although there are many advertisements for sports equipment, and the popularity of athletes may give the impression that Americans love a good workout, the facts are not so positive. As Rebecca J. Donatelle states in her book *Access to Health*, "Data from the National Health Interview

Survey shows that as many as twenty-five percent of adults in the United States never engage in any exercise, sports, or physically active hobbies in their leisure time" (294). Many elements of America's twenty-first century convenience are to blame for this lack of exercise. More and more automobiles, remote controls, office jobs and Internet use all affect how much—or how little—Americans move. Many residential communities are now designed to foster driving, not biking or walking, and often any sidewalks provided are poorly maintained. Walking areas are often unsafe and inconvenient. The production of video technology encourages kids to surf the Internet rather than ride their bicycles after school and on weekends. Nowadays, instead of going for a walk after dinner, their parents sit on their couch watching their favorite television shows, with their handy remote control eliminating the need to exercise anything but their thumbs. And during the commercials, they are bombarded with food advertisements. The lack of physical activity essentially makes Americans lazy. New technologies have created a culture that has urged people not only to move less, but also to eat more.

7   Schools might seem to be an exception, since they provide physical education and nutritious meals, but unfortunately they are another main source of the increase in obesity. Schools have reduced the amount of physical education, recess, and recreation time allowed, and they now provide a variety of food and beverage options that are conveniently available in vending machines and school cafeterias throughout the school day, including soda, fast food, and fruit drinks that contain more sugar than actual juice. Not only do they provide more sweets and treats, but they often do not devote enough time to teaching students healthy eating and exercise habits.

8   Many schools do not have much time or money to spare to fit in more productive activities and lectures on health. But as little as an extra hour a day can resolve that issue. In that extra hour of school, a student can be informed about the dangers of obesity and familiarized with healthy habits, and can shed a couple pounds through exercise. This will help children become accustomed to a healthy lifestyle. According to the Centers for Disease Control and Prevention, "while kids are packing on the pounds now, the problem gets worse with age . . . overweight teens have an 80% chance of becoming overweight adults" (Morgan). People are more likely to continue their healthy habits if they begin them at a young age. In theory, these students will pass down their knowledge to their own kids. Therefore, future American generations will be educated about obesity and will adapt to a healthy lifestyle.

9   Even if this solution were adopted, one more problem still lies within the schools. If students have easy access to soda and sweets, via a vending machine, then there is nothing stopping their temptation to indulge in those gratifying treats. Instead of allowing vending machines filled with

treats supersaturated with fats, sugars, and salt, schools should only allow fruits and vegetables in vending machines.

In order to help combat obesity in America on a larger scale, the gov-   10
ernment should become more involved by providing information about how to make healthy lifestyle choices and by providing an environment that allows individuals to do so. If the government were to set up free gyms that were accessible only to overweight Americans, it would give many Americans an opportunity to live a healthy lifestyle. It would also provide an environment where those exercising are all in the same condition and where no one would be judged.

In earlier times, people were more active in the normal course of their   11
daily lives. However, with technological advances people have become lazier and now expend fewer calories in daily activities. Many Americans have also developed poor eating habits owing to marketing, social, and economic influences, as well as personal choice. Most people are aware that they should be active and consume more fruit and vegetables, but they continue to live among advertisements that seduce them into eating processed foods; settle for a quick, easy meal instead of a healthy, home-cooked one; and spend hours sitting in front of their television or computer. In order to affect behavior and reverse the obesity epidemic, the healthy choice needs to become an easier choice.

Works Cited

Critser, Greg. *Fat Land: How Americans Became the Fattest People in the World*. New York: Mariner, 2004. Print.

Datz, Todd. "Smoking, High Blood Pressure and Being Overweight Top Three Preventable Causes of Death in the U.S." *Harvard Science*. President and Fellows of Harvard College, 26 Apr. 2009. Web. 3 Nov. 2009.

Donatelle, Rebecca J. *Access to Health*. 11th ed. San Francisco: Benjamin Cummings, 2010. Print.

Gavin, Mary L. "Overweight and Obesity." *KidsHealth*. KidsHealth, Feb. 2009. Web. 2 Nov. 2009.

Levi, Jeffery, Serena Vinter, Liz Richardson, Rebecca Laurent, and Laura Segal. "F as in Fat: How Obesity Policies Are Failing in America 2009." *Trust for America's Health*. Robert Wood Johnson Foundation, 30 July 2009. Web. 3 Nov. 2009.

"McDonald's USA Nutrition Facts for Popular Menu Items." *McDonald's*. McDonald's, n.d. Web. 3 Nov. 2009.

Morgan, John, and Stephen A. Shoop, "Jared Takes Steps to Help Kids Fight Fat." *USA Today*. 15 July 2004. Web. 31 Mar. 2010.

Parker, Hilary. "A Sweet Problem: Princeton Researchers Find That High-Fructose Corn Syrup Prompts Considerably More Weight Gain." *News at Princeton*. The Trustees of Princeton University, 22 Mar. 2010. Web. 31 Mar. 2010.

"Statistics Related to Overweight and Obesity." *WIN - Weight-control Information Network*. NIDDK, n.d. Web. 30 Nov. 2009.

Thornton, Huwerl, Jr. "Childhood Obesity and High Fructose Corn Syrup. What Is It Good For? Absolutely Nothing!" *Yale National Initiative.* Yale University, n.d. Web. 3 Nov. 2009.

Wang, Youfa, and May A. Beydoun. "The Obesity Epidemic in the United States—Gender, Age, Socioeconomic, Racial/Ethnic, and Geographic Characteristics: A Systematic Review and Meta-Regression Analysis." *Epidemiologic Reviews.* 29 (2007): n. pag. Web. 2 Nov. 2009.

Work Consulted

Davis, Brennan, and Christopher Carpenter. "Proximity of Fast-Food Restaurants to Schools and Adolescent Obesity." *American Journal of Public Health* 99.3 (2009): 505–510. *Academic Search Premier.* Web. 3 Nov. 2009.

READING FOR MEANING

This section presents three activities that will help you think about the meanings in Khella's causal argument.

Read to Comprehend

Write a few sentences briefly explaining Khella's argument about the causes of obesity in the United States.

Identify any words with meanings you are unsure of—such as, *perpetuates* (paragraph 2) and *gratification* (5)—and find the dictionary definition for each word that makes the best sense in the context.

To help you understand the essay better, also consider trying one of these critical reading strategies, explained in Appendix 1: *previewing* or *paraphrasing*.

Read to Respond

Write a paragraph or two exploring your initial thoughts and feelings about Khella's causal argument. Focus on anything that stands out for you, perhaps because it resonates with your own experience or because you find a statement puzzling. For example, consider writing about one of the following:

- how you respond to the last sentence of the essay: "the healthy choice needs to become an easier choice" (paragraph 11).

- Khella's argument that technology has contributed to the rise in obesity.

- experiences you may have had with health issues related to dieting or to exercise.

To help develop your response, also consider trying one of these critical reading strategies, explained in Appendix 1: *summarizing* or *synthesizing*.

Read to Analyze Assumptions

Write a paragraph or two analyzing an assumption in Khella's essay. To think critically about assumptions, here are some kinds of questions you could ask: Who holds this assumption (the writer, readers, and/or others cited in the essay)? What are the effects of the assumption in the context of the essay specifically or in society more generally? What do you think about the assumption, and is there anything in the essay that raises doubts about it? How does the assumption reinforce or critique commonly held views, and are there any alternative ideas, beliefs, or values that would challenge this assumption?

You might choose an assumption from the list below, using the questions accompanying it in addition to the ones above to help you get started. Or you can choose another assumption in the essay to explore.

- **assumptions about the responsibility of schools for health.** Almost everyone in America attends or has attended school, the majority in public schools. Khella seems to think that schools bear a major responsibility for the health of U.S. citizens, and that lately they have not been living up to that responsibility: "Not only do they [schools] provide more sweets and treats, but they often do not devote enough time to teaching students healthy eating and exercise habits" (paragraph 7).

  To think critically about the assumptions in the essay related to the responsibility of schools for our health, ask yourself questions like these: Can or should schools play a significant role in fighting obesity? Would parents or taxpayers support such a role for schools? What if they have a limited budget and healthy food is more expensive? What if they must cut activities that keep students exercising? How could schools educate students better about healthy eating and appropriate exercise for healthy weight?

- **the assumption that Americans lack the willpower to resist temptations to obesity.** Khella concludes that although Americans know "they should be active and consume more fruit and vegetables, . . . they continue to live among advertisements that seduce them into eating processed foods; settle for a quick, easy meal instead of a healthy, home-cooked one; and spend hours sitting in front of their television or computer." He writes that to change behavior, "the healthy choice needs to become an easier choice" (paragraph 11).

  To think critically about the assumptions in this essay related to Americans' willpower, ask yourself questions like these: Do you share Khella's assumption that it is just too hard to resist the temptation to eat fattening foods and to engage in activities that preclude exercise? Can you think of reasons other than those Khella provides to explain the rise in obesity? Can you think of plausible ways Americans might be able to reverse the rise in obesity?

To help you analyze assumptions in Khella's essay, also consider trying one of these critical reading strategies, explained in Appendix 1: *using a Toulmin analysis* or *evaluating the logic of an argument.*

READING LIKE A WRITER

ESTABLISHING CREDIBILITY

To be credible is to be believable. When you write an essay speculating about the causes or effects of something, readers will tend to find your argument believable when you are able to show the various complexities of your subject. Therefore, you will establish your credibility with readers if you do not oversimplify, trivialize, or stereotype your subject; if you do not overlook possible objections or alternative causes or effects that will occur to readers; and if you convey more than casual knowledge of your subject and show that you have thought about it deeply and seriously.

Consider how Khella establishes his credibility to speculate about the reasons for the rise in American obesity.

Analyze

1. Reread this essay, and annotate it for evidence of credibility or lack of it. (Because you cannot know Khella personally, you must look closely at the text of his essay to decide whether he constructs a credible argument.) Examine closely how knowledgeable he seems about the subject. Where does his knowledge assure or even impress you as one of his intended readers? Where does it seem thin? Consider especially how he presents the subject and phenomenon (paragraph 1). Assess also the sources he relies on and how effectively he uses them.

2. Look for evidence that Khella has not trivialized a complex subject. Keeping in mind that he appropriately limits himself to speculating about possible causes, note how his argument reflects the complexity of his subject or fails to do so.

3. Consider how Khella's counterargument (paragraphs 2, 5, 6, 8, and 9) influences your judgment of his credibility.

4. Examine his approach to readers. What assumptions does he make about their knowledge and beliefs? What attitude does he have toward his readers? Note evidence of his assumptions and attitude.

Write

Write several sentences presenting evidence of Khella's attempts to establish his credibility. Then add a few more sentences evaluating how credible his essay is to you as one of his intended readers. To explain your judgment, point to parts of the essay, and comment on the influence of your own attitudes about and knowledge of the causes of obesity.

A Special Reading Strategy ――――――――――――――――――

Evaluating the Logic of an Argument

To evaluate the logic of an argument speculating about causes, ask yourself three basic questions:

- How appropriate is the support for each cause being speculated about?

- How believable is the support?

- How consistent and complete is the overall argument?

Such an evaluation requires a comprehensive and thoughtful critical reading, but your efforts will help you understand more fully what makes a causal argument successful. To evaluate the logic of Khella's argument, follow the guidelines in Appendix 1 (pp. 579–82). There you will find definitions and explanations as well as an illustration based on an excerpt from a famous essay by Martin Luther King Jr. (the excerpt appears on pp. 553–57).

CONSIDERING IDEAS FOR YOUR OWN WRITING

Consider writing about a health issue that you might be interested in, perhaps on nutrition, as Khella did, or on the increase (or decrease) in exercise or meditation or other forms of body-consciousness or care. You might consider the increase in laser eye surgeries or surgeries for cosmetic purposes, or another kind of "body" trend, such as piercings or tattoos. You could examine how the war in Iraq has changed the phenomenon of "field hospitals," or how those changes led to different kinds of health care during natural catastrophes, such as the earthquakes of 2010 in Haiti and in Chile. The field of medicine is changing rapidly and offers many opportunities for studying causes or effects.

Joshua Slick

Not Just for Nerds Anymore

Joshua Slick was a student at Hawkeye Community College in Iowa when he wrote this essay speculating about the causes of the increase in online dating. Like Jeremy Khella, Slick relies in large part on speculations from a wide range of published research to put together his argument. He is in control of the argument because he selects certain speculations (and not others) and weaves them into his own design.

As you read, notice how Slick discusses his causes in the same order as he presents them in his first paragraph and that he intersperses his speculations with references to reasons that people object to online dating, addressing those concerns as he writes.

The other readings in this chapter are followed by reading and writing activities. Following this reading, however, you are on your own to decide how to read for meaning and read like a writer.

1   It's Friday night, and instead of going out to a bar to look for Mr. or Ms. Right, you are sitting at home in front of your computer, talking in a chatroom with a couple dozen other people your age or perusing a list of people in your area. Some would call you lazy or antisocial, but that number is dwindling. Online dating is becoming more mainstream. The increase in the use of the Internet as a dating tool in the last ten years is due to the increase in homes with computers, the increase in Web sites and chatrooms whose purpose it is to bring people together, and the ease with which daters can now research potential mates.

2   According to a U.S. Census Bureau report from September 2001, the number of homes with computers dramatically increased from 1993 to 2000: "In August 2000, 54 million households, or 51 percent, had one or more computers," up from 22.8 percent in 1993 (U.S. Department of Commerce, 2001, p. 1). Internet use has also increased: "In 1997, less than half of households with computers had someone using the Internet. In 2000, more than 4 in 5 households with a computer had at least one member using the Internet at home" (U.S. Department of Commerce, 2001, p. 2). These changes are due largely to the increased power and decreased cost of computers. David D. Thornburg (2005) makes this comparison:

> A 1980 model Cray supercomputer was the fastest machine of its day. It cost $12 million, weighed 10,000 pounds, consumed 150 kilowatts of electricity—and had only 8 megabytes of RAM and operated at a speed of 80 MHz. You can't find personal computers that poorly equipped on the market now. A typical personal computer today has about twice the raw power of that $12 million Cray and can be purchased for $2,500.

Even these figures—from 1998—are laughably out of date. My computer has a gigabyte of RAM and runs at 1.9 gigahertz, and it cost me less than a thousand dollars. More and more people have access to the Internet in their homes; it's only logical that they would use it to find other people to converse with and date.

The online dating industry has also grown by leaps and bounds in the last few years. *CNNMoney* staff writer Shaheen Pasha writes that although the growth of the industry has slowed, it is still growing: by 77 percent in 2003 and 19 percent in 2004. There are currently nearly a thousand dating Web sites, and one in a hundred Internet users visits such sites (Pasha, 2005). Chatrooms are also plentiful, and singles visit them to interact with other singles. The newest kind of chatroom is the niche site, which focuses on some specific quality, belief, or interest such as religion or ethnicity (Pasha). Another development is the introduction of social networking sites such as MySpace and Friendster, which don't try to match singles but rather link users with friends of friends. Of course, socializing—whether online or off—often leads to dating (Pasha, 2005).

The inherent danger of dealing with strangers is one of the major reasons that online dating has been looked down on. That is all changing, however. Michael Bazeley (2005) mentions the online ratings and review systems that have been around since the Internet got started; eBay's user feedback system is a perfect example. Bazeley refers to these as "reputation-management systems." This model has been applied to the Internet dating scene on sites like TrueDater, which let users give feedback on others to warn and inform. Sites like Opinity also allow users to list their user names from other sites, making it easier to track them down (Bazeley, 2005). Because the Web can now be used to research everything from pictures to credit reports, Rebecca Heslin (2005) of Gannett News Services states in a USA Today.com article that "technology has made anonymity largely a thing of the past." With online background check sites, Google, and specific Web sites for singles doing searches such as TrueDater, you can find out virtually anything about anyone without ever leaving your home. By increasing knowledge of the person on the other computer, these tools have led to more comfort about potentially dating him or her.

The world of conventional dating isn't going to go away. Technological advancements have just given singles another option to explore the possibilities and find meaningful relationships. At some point, there must be some real-life interaction, and only then will daters be able to judge the effectiveness of the online arena. Even so, more and more people are finding that online dating is just as viable for meeting people as going to church or bars. In a recent study released by the University of Bath, England, Dr. Jeff Gavin and associates found that Internet dating can be just as successful as more traditional dating. Of those surveyed, 94 percent who had established a significant relationship online and then met their "e-partner" face to face went on to see him or her more than once. Of those relationships, 18 percent continued for more than a year ("Internet Dating," 2005). With the combination of increased ownership and usage of home computers, the saturation of Web sites that cater to singles, and the ready availability of tools to research people and ensure safety, online dating has definitely shaken off its stigma to become a mainstream tool to help singles meet their potential partners.

References

Bazeley, M. (2005). Web of anonymity. *San Jose Mercury News*. Retrieved September 23, 2005, from http:// infoweb.newsbank.com

Heslin, R. (2005, August 21). With the Internet, the blind date is vanishing. *USA Today.com*. Retrieved from http://www.usatoday.com

Internet dating is much more successful than previously thought, study shows. (2005, February 14). *University of Bath News*. Retrieved from http://www.bath.ac.uk/pr/ releases/internet-dating.htm

Pasha, S. (2005, August 18). Online dating feeling less attractive. *CNNMoney*. Retrieved from http://money.cnn.com/2005/08/18/technology/online_dating/index.htm

Thornburg, D. (1998). Reading the future: Here's what's on hand for technology and education. *Electronic School*. Retrieved from http://www.electronicschool.com/ 0698f1.html

U.S. Department of Commerce, Economics and Statistics Administration. (2001). *Home computers and Internet use in the United States: August 2000*. U.S. Census Bureau, Washington, DC. Retrieved from http:// www.census.gov/ prod/2001pubs/p23-207.pdf

READING FOR MEANING

Reading for meaning involves three activities:

- reading to comprehend,

- reading to respond, and

- reading to analyze assumptions.

Write a page or so explaining your understanding of the basic meaning or main point of Slick's essay, a personal response you have to it, and one of its assumptions.

READING LIKE A WRITER

Writers of essays speculating about causes or effects

- present the subject,

- make a logical, step-by-step cause-and-effect argument,

- take into account readers' likely objections to the proposed causes or effects as well as readers' alternative or preferred causes or effects, and

- establish their credibility.

Choose one of these strategies in Slick's essay, and analyze it carefully through close rereading and annotating. Then write several sentences explaining what you have learned, giving specific examples from the reading to support your explanation. Add a few sentences evaluating how successfully Slick uses the strategy to argue convincingly for what has caused the increase in online dating.

Reviewing What Makes an Effective Essay

Speculating about Causes or Effects

Analyze

Choose one reading from this chapter that seems to you especially effective. Before rereading the selection, jot down one or two reasons you remember it as an example of good cause or effect writing.

Reread your chosen selection and add further notes about what makes it a particularly successful example. Consider the selection's purpose and how well it achieves that purpose for its intended readers. (You can make an informed guess about the intended readers and their expectations by noting the publication source of the essay.) Then assess how well the essay uses the writing strategies of presenting the subject; making a logical, step-by-step cause-and-effect argument; supporting each cause or effect; counterarguing; and establishing credibility.

Write

Write at least a page supporting your choice of this reading as an example of effective cause or effect writing. Refer to details and specific parts of the essay as you explain how it works as a cause or effect argument and as you justify your evaluation of its effectiveness. You need not argue that it is the best reading in the chapter or that it is flawless, only that it is, in your view, a strong example of the genre.

A GUIDE TO WRITING ESSAYS SPECULATING ABOUT CAUSES OR EFFECTS

This Guide to Writing is designed to assist you in writing your essay. Here you will find activities to help you identify a subject and discover what to say about it, organize your ideas and draft the essay, read the draft critically, revise the draft to strengthen your argument, and edit and proofread the essay to improve its readability.

INVENTION AND RESEARCH

The following activities will help you find a subject and begin developing your argument. Completing these activities will produce a detailed and convincing first draft.

Choosing a Subject

List the most promising subjects you can think of, beginning with any you listed for the Considering Ideas for Your Own Writing activities following the readings in this chapter. Rather than limiting yourself to the first subject that comes to mind, take a few minutes to consider your options and list as many subjects as you can. Try to list specific subjects, and make separate lists for trends, events, and phenomena. Here are some additional ideas to consider:

Trends

- Increasing reliance on the Internet for research, entertainment, shopping, and conversation

- Changes in men's or women's roles and opportunities in marriage, education, or work

- Changing patterns in leisure, entertainment, lifestyle, religious life, health, or technology

- Completed artistic or historical trends (art movements or historical changes)

- Long-term changes in economic conditions or political behavior or attitudes

Events

- A recent national or international event that is surrounded by confusion or controversy

- A recent surprising or controversial event at your college, such as the closing of a tutorial or health service, the cancellation of popular classes, a change in library hours or dormitory regulations, the loss of a game by a favored team, or some hateful or violent act by one student against another

- A recent puzzling or controversial event in your community, such as the abrupt resignation of a public official, a public protest by an activist group, a change in traffic laws, a zoning decision, or the banning of a book from school libraries

- A historical event about which there is still some dispute as to its causes or effects

Phenomena

- A social problem, such as discrimination, homelessness, child abuse, illiteracy, high-school dropout rates, youth suicides, or teenage pregnancy

- One or more aspects of college life, such as libraries too noisy to study in, large classes, lack of financial aid, difficulties in scheduling classes, shortcomings in student health services, or insufficient availability of housing (in this essay you would not need to propose solutions to the problems, only to speculate about their causes or effects)

- A human trait, such as anxiety, selfishness, fear of success or failure, leadership, jealousy, insecurity, envy, opportunism, curiosity, or restlessness

After you have completed your lists, reflect on the possible topics you have compiled. Because an authoritative essay analyzing causes or effects requires sustained thinking, drafting, revising, and possibly even research, you will want to choose a subject to which you can commit yourself enthusiastically for a week or two. Above all, choose a topic that interests you, even if you feel uncertain about how to approach it.

Then consider carefully whether you are more interested in the causes or the effects of the event, trend, or phenomenon. Consider, as well, whether the subject in which you are interested invites speculation about its causes or effects or perhaps even precludes speculation about one or the other. For example, you could speculate about the causes for increasing membership in your church, whereas the effects of the increase might for now be so uncertain as to discourage plausible speculation. Some subjects invite speculation about both their causes and their effects. For this assignment, however, you need not do both.

Developing Your Subject

The writing and research activities that follow will enable you to test your subject choice and to discover what you have to say about it.

Exploring Your Subject. You may discover that you know more about your subject than you suspect if you write about it for a few minutes without stopping.

This brief sustained writing will stimulate your memory, help you probe your interest in the subject, and enable you to test your subject choice. As you write, consider the following questions:

- What about this subject interests me? What about it will interest my readers?

- What do I already know about the subject?

- Why does the trend, event, or phenomenon not already have an accepted explanation for its causes or effects? What causes or effects have others already suggested for it?

- How can I learn more about the subject?

Considering Causes or Effects.   Before you research your subject (should you need to), you want to discover which causes or effects you can already imagine. Make a list of possible causes or effects. For *causes* consider underlying or background causes as well as immediate or instigating causes. For example, say you have noticed that the number of students in your classes has increased sharply in the past year.

- An underlying cause could be that years ago the voters in your state passed a bill that sharply reduced income for public colleges, and now the effects are beginning to show;

- An immediate cause could be that the college has had to lay off one-third of its faculty.

For *effects*, consider both short-term and long-term consequences, as well as how one effect may lead to another in a kind of chain reaction. Try to think of obvious causes or effects and also of those that are likely to be overlooked in a superficial analysis of your subject.

Identify the most convincing causes or effects in your list. Do you have enough to make a strong argument? Imagine how you might convince readers of the plausibility of some of these causes or effects.

Researching Your Subject.   When developing an essay speculating about causes or effects, you can often help yourself by researching your subject. (See Appendix 2, Strategies for Research and Documentation.) Research can give you a greater understanding of the event, trend, or phenomenon and may suggest to you plausible causes or effects you have overlooked. You may also find support for your own counterarguments to readers' objections or to others' proposed causes or effects.

If you are speculating about the causes or effects of a trend, you will also need to do some research to confirm that it actually is a trend and not just a short-term fluctuation or a fad. To do so, you will need to find examples and probably statistics that show an increase or a decrease in the phenomenon over time and that indicate the date when this change began. (For example, recall that

Claudia Wallis cites authorities and statistics to demonstrate that multitasking has increased). If you are unable to find evidence to confirm that a trend exists, you will have to choose a different subject for your essay.

Analyzing Your Readers.   Write for a few minutes, identifying who your readers are, what they know about your subject, and how they can be convinced by your proposed causes or effects. Describe your readers briefly. Mention anything you know about them as a group that might influence the way they would read your essay. Estimate how much they know about your subject, in how much detail you will have to present it to them, and what is required to demonstrate to them the importance of the subject. Speculate about how they will respond to your argument.

Rehearsing Part of Your Argument.   Select one of your causes or effects and write several sentences about it, trying out an argument for your readers. The heart of your essay will be the argument you make for the plausibility of your proposed causes or effects. Like a ballet dancer or baseball pitcher warming up for a performance, you can prepare for your first draft by rehearsing part of the argument you will make. How will you convince readers to take this cause or effect seriously? This writing activity will focus your thinking and encourage you to keep discovering new arguments until you start drafting. It may also lead you to search for additional support for your speculations.

Testing Your Choice.   Pause now to decide whether you have chosen a subject about which you will be able to make a convincing argument. At this point you have probed your subject in several ways and have some insights into how you would attempt to present and argue for it with particular readers. If your interest in the subject is growing and you are gaining confidence in the argument you want to make, you have probably made a good choice. However, if your interest in the subject is waning or you have been unable to come up with several plausible causes or effects beyond the simply obvious ones, you may want to consider choosing another subject. If your subject does not seem promising, return to your list of possible subjects to select another.

Considering Visuals.   Think about whether visuals—drawings, photographs, tables, or graphs—would strengthen your argument. You could construct your own visuals, scan materials from books and magazines, or download them from the Internet. If you submit your essay electronically to other students and your instructor, or if you post it on a Web site, consider including snippets of film or sound as well as photographs. Visual and audio materials are not a requirement of an effective causal essay, as you can tell from the readings in this chapter, but they could add a new dimension to your writing. If you want to use photographs or recordings of people, though, be sure to obtain their permission. If you want to post a visual on the Web, ask permission from the source. Also, be sure to document the sources of visuals just as you would for written texts.

Considering Your Purpose.   Write for several minutes about your purpose for writing this essay. The following questions will help you think about your purpose:

- What do I hope to accomplish with my readers? What one big idea do I want them to grasp and remember?

- How can I interest them in my subject? How can I help them see its importance or significance? How can I convince them to take my speculations seriously?

- How much resistance should I expect from readers to each of the causes or effects I propose? Will my readers be largely receptive? Skeptical but convinceable? Resistant and perhaps even antagonistic?

Formulating a Working Thesis.   Draft a thesis statement. A *working*—as opposed to final—*thesis* enables you to bring your invention work into focus and begin your draft with a clearer purpose. At some point during the drafting of your essay, you will likely decide to revise your working thesis or even try out a new one. A thesis for an essay speculating about causes or effects nearly always announces the subject; it may also mention the proposed causes or effects and suggest the direction the argument will take. Here are two sample thesis statements from the readings in this chapter:

- "But there are striking similarities among a wide range of social phenomena. The unifying theme is simple: when people find themselves in groups of like-minded types, they are especially likely to move to extremes" (Sunstein, paragraph 4).

- "Online dating is becoming more mainstream. The increase in the use of the Internet as a dating tool in the last ten years is due to the increase in homes with computers, the increase in Web sites and chatrooms whose purpose it is to bring people together, and the ease with which daters can now research potential mates" (Slick, paragraph 1).

Notice, for instance, that Slick's thesis clearly announces his subject—an increase in online dating—as well as how he will approach the subject: by speculating about the causes of the increase in online dating. His thesis also forecasts his speculations, identifying the causes and the order in which he will argue for them in the essay.

DRAFTING

The following guidelines will help you set goals for your draft, plan its organization, and think about a useful sentence strategy.

Setting Goals

Establishing goals for your draft before you begin writing will enable you to make decisions and work more confidently. Consider the following questions now, and keep them in mind as you draft.

- *How can I convince my readers that my proposed causes or effects are plausible?* Should I give many examples, as Wallis, Sunstein, and Carr do, or quote authorities and published research, as Wallis, Sunstein, Carr, Khella, and Slick all do? Can I, like Carr, include personal anecdotes and cases or, like King and Wallis, introduce analogies?

- *How should I anticipate readers' objections to my argument?* What should I do about alternative causes or effects? Should I anticipate readers' objections and questions, as Carr does, or answer readers' likely questions, like Slick? Can I refute alternative causes, as Wallis does? How can I find common ground—shared attitudes, values, and beliefs—with my readers, even with those whose objections or alternative causes I must refute?

- *How much do my readers need to know about my subject?* Do I need to describe my subject in some detail, in the way that Wallis describes multitasking or Khella describes the rise in obesity? Or can I assume that my readers have personal experience with my subject, as King seems to assume? If my subject is a trend, how can I demonstrate that the trend exists?

- *How can I begin engagingly and end conclusively?* Should I begin, as Khella does, by emphasizing the importance or timeliness of my subject? Might I begin with an anecdote like Wallis, Carr, and Slick, or with an unusual statement like King's? Can I conclude by returning to an idea in the opening paragraph (as Carr does), or restating the urgency of the problem (Sunstein and Khella)?

- *How can I establish my authority and credibility about my subject?* Can I do this by showing a comprehensive understanding of the likely effects of the phenomenon, as Wallis, Sunstein, and Carr do, or by showing a willingness to consider a wide range of causes, like Khella? Or can I do this by displaying my research (Khella and Slick), by counterarguing responsibly (Carr), or by relying on what I have learned through research and interviews (Wallis and Khella)?

Organizing Your Draft

With goals in mind and invention notes at hand, you are ready to make a tentative outline of your draft. The sequence of proposed causes or effects will be at the center of your outline, but you may also want to plan where you will consider alternatives or counterargue objections. Notice that some writers speculating about causes consider alternative causes—evaluating and refuting them—before they present their own. Much of an essay analyzing causes may be devoted to considering alternatives. Writers also usually address readers' possible objections to the proposed causes or effects. If you must provide readers with a great deal of information about your subject as context for your argument, you may want to outline this information carefully. Your plan should make the information readily accessible to your readers. This outline is tentative; you may decide to change it after you start drafting.

Working with Sources
Citing a Variety of Sources

To establish that the causes or effects they offer are plausible, writers often rely on evidence from experts or others who have researched and thought about the topic. But using too few sources or using sources that are too narrow in scope can undercut the effectiveness of the argument because readers may feel they are being provided with only a limited vision of the evidence. Consequently, offering information from a number of sources and from sources that reflect a variety of areas of expertise can be useful.

Look, for example, at the sources that Joshua Slick refers to in speculating about the causes for the growing trend of Internet dating in his essay "Not Just for Nerds Anymore," which appears on pp. 464–66. He cites the U.S. Census Bureau and the U.S. Department of Commerce to report how the number of homes with computers has risen and how Internet use also has increased (paragraph 2). He then cites David D. Thornburg, a writer for a technology magazine for K–12 educators, *Electronic School*, which is published as a supplement to *American School Board Journal* in cooperation with a program of the National School Boards Association (2). All of these sources carry a great deal of weight.

To indicate how the online dating industry has grown, in paragraph 3 Slick uses a less scholarly source, *CNNMoney*, a popular special-interest magazine. As he gets deeper into his essay, Slick adds to his own credibility by using varied sources, such as the newspapers *San Jose Mercury News* and *USA Today* (4), to support his argument that potential dates can be evaluated through online ratings and reviews. He makes his final point—that online dating is as viable an option for social contacts as bars or churches—by citing a study released by the University of Bath (5). Altogether, the number of expert and popular sources he cites is impressive, and the variety of his sources adds to his credibility.

In his essay "The Route to American Obesity" (pp. 456–60), Jeremy Khella also cites a variety of sources, including some he quotes directly and others he paraphrases. They include extremely reputable scientific sources such as *Harvard Science*, the *Yale National Initiative*, and *Epidemiologic Reviews* and represent a combination of books, journals, and Web sites, one of which is the McDonald's site, from which he obtains nutrition information on McDonald's meals. Another site he uses is *KidsHealth*, which identifies itself as sponsored by the Nemours Foundation's Center for Children's Health and says it "provides families with perspective, advice, and comfort about a wide range of physical, emotional, and behavioral issues that affect children and teens."

This site is careful to list its awards and other validations of its authority to speak to medical issues. Because Khella is writing about a current issue, he is careful to use up-to-date sources.

As you determine how many and what kinds of sources to cite in your essay, keep in mind that readers of essays speculating about causes or effects are more likely to be persuaded if the sources you rely on are neither too few nor too narrowly focused. When you begin to draft, if you find that your research seems skimpy, you may need to return to your source and to new sources to cast a wider net.

Considering a Useful Sentence Strategy

As you draft your essay, you will want to help your readers recognize the stages of your argument and the support you offer for each proposed cause or effect. One effective way to do so is to use clear topic sentences, especially ones that are grammatically parallel.

Topic sentences usually open the paragraph or are placed early in the paragraph. They can announce a new cause or effect, introduce counterargument (the writer's response to readers' likely objections or alternative causes or effects), or identify different parts of the support for a cause, an effect, or a counterargument. Topic sentences may also include key terms that the writer introduced in a thesis statement at the beginning of the essay, and they may take identical or similar sentence forms so that readers can recognize them more easily. The following topic sentences from King's essay identify what King believes to be the three main causes for many moviegoers' attraction to horror movies:

> To show that we can, that we are not afraid, that we can ride this roller coaster. (paragraph 3)
>
> We also go to re-establish our feelings of essential normality. (4)
>
> And we go to have fun. (5)

King assists readers in identifying each new stage of his argument by introducing the grammatical subject *we* in the first topic sentence and then repeating it to signal the next two stages: "we can," "We also go," "And we go."

While King relies on topic sentences within paragraphs to signal the stages in his argument, as do all the writers in this chapter, Carr uses them also to signal a change from citing his own personal experience as evidence to citing the experience of others. After his initial paragraph about HAL, the computer that is

being dismantled in *2001*, Carr introduces each of the next four paragraphs with
a reference to himself:

> I can feel it, too. (paragraph 2)
>
> I think I know what's going on. (3)
>
> For me, as for others, the Net is becoming a universal medium, the
> conduit for most of the information that flows through my eyes and ears
> and into my mind. (4)
>
> I'm not the only one. (5)

Like King's, these topic sentences are not strictly parallel grammatically, but
three of them create a parallel effect because they are all very short and begin with
I. In the last two, Carr begins to refer to the experiences of others as well as himself. After that his essay proceeds with little reference to himself and a great deal
of support—as well as counterarguments—from third parties.

In addition to using topic sentences that help readers follow the stages of
your argument and using parallel grammatical form to present related examples,
you can strengthen your causal argument by using other sentence strategies as
well. You may want to look at the information about using appositives (pp. 275–76)
and sentences that combine concession and refutation (pp. 402–04).

READING A DRAFT CRITICALLY

Getting a critical reading of your draft will help you see how to improve it.
Your instructor may schedule class time for reading drafts, or you may want to
ask a classmate or a tutor in the writing center to read your draft. Ask your reader
to use the following guidelines and to write out a response for you to consult during your revision.

Read for a First Impression

1. **Read the draft without stopping, and then write a few sentences giving
   your general impression.**

2. **Identify one aspect of the draft that seems especially effective.**

Read Again to Suggest Improvements

1. **Recommend ways to make the presentation of the subject more effective.**

   - Read the opening paragraphs that present the subject to be speculated
     about, and then tell the writer what you find most interesting and useful
     there.

- Point out one or two places where a reader unfamiliar with the subject might need more information.

- Suggest ways the writer could make the subject seem more interesting or significant.

- If the subject is a trend, explain what you understand to be the increase or decrease and let the writer know whether you think further evidence is required to demonstrate conclusively that the subject is indeed a trend.

- If the beginning seems unlikely to engage readers, suggest at least one other way of beginning.

2. **Suggest ways to strengthen the cause or effect argument.**

- List the causes or effects. Tell the writer whether there seem to be too many, too few, or just about the right number. Identify any cause or effect that seems especially imaginative or surprising and any that seems too obvious. Make suggestions for dropping or adding causes or effects.

- Evaluate the support for each cause or effect separately. To help the writer make every cause or effect plausible to the intended readers, point out where the support seems thin or inadequate. Point to any support that seems irrelevant to the argument, hard to believe, or inconsistent with other support. Consider whether the writer has overlooked important resources of support: anecdotes, examples, statistics, analogies, or quotations from publications or interviews.

3. **Suggest ways to strengthen the counterargument.**

- Locate every instance of counterargument—places where the writer anticipates and refutes readers' objections to their preferred alternative causes or effects. Mark these in the margin of the draft. Review these as a set, and then suggest objections and alternative causes or effects the writer seems to have overlooked.

- Identify counterarguments that seem weakly supported, and suggest ways the writer might strengthen the support.

- If any of the refutations attack or ridicule readers, suggest ways the writer could refute without insulting or unduly irritating readers.

4. **Suggest how credibility can be enhanced.**

- Tell the writer whether the intended readers are likely to find the essay knowledgeable and authoritative. Point to places where it seems most and least authoritative.

- Identify places where the writer seeks common ground—shared values, beliefs, and attitudes—with readers. Try to identify other places where the writer might do so.

5. **Suggest how the organizational plan could be improved.**

- Consider the overall plan, perhaps by making a scratch outline (see Appendix 1). Analyze closely the progression of the proposed causes or effects, and decide whether they follow a logical sequence. If not, suggest ways they might be more logically sequenced, such as by putting them in chronological order or the order of their importance.

- Review the places where counterarguments appear and consider whether they are smoothly woven into the argument. If not, suggest where to move them.

- Indicate where new or better transitions might more clearly cue the steps in the argument and keep readers on track.

6. **Evaluate the effectiveness of visuals.**

- Look at any visuals in the essay, and tell the writer what they contribute to your understanding of the writer's speculations.

- If any visuals do not seem relevant or if there are too many visuals, identify the ones that the writer could consider dropping, explaining your thinking.

- If a visual does not seem appropriately placed, suggest a better place for it.

REVISING

This section offers suggestions for revising your draft. Revising means reenvisioning your draft, trying to see it in a new way, given your purpose and readers, to strengthen your cause or effect argument.

The biggest mistake you can make while revising is to focus initially on words or sentences. Instead, first try to see your draft as a whole to assess its likely impact on your readers. Think imaginatively and boldly about cutting unconvincing material, adding new material, and moving material around. Your computer makes even drastic revisions physically easy, but you still need to make the mental effort and decisions that will improve your draft.

You may have received help with this challenge from a classmate or tutor who gave your draft a critical reading. If so, keep this feedback in mind as you decide which parts of your draft need revising and what specific changes you could make. The following suggestions will help you solve problems and strengthen your essay.

TROUBLESHOOTING YOUR DRAFT

To Present the Subject More Effectively

Problem	Suggestions for Revising
Readers unfamiliar with the subject don't understand it readily.	• Provide more introductory information about the subject.
The significance of the subject is not clear.	• Dramatize its significance with an anecdote. • Highlight its social or cultural implications.
The subject is a trend, but its existence is not established.	• Show evidence of a significant increase or decrease over time.

To Strengthen the Cause-or-Effect Argument

Problem	Suggestions for Revising
There are too many proposed causes or effects.	• Clarify the role of each one and the way it is related to others. • Drop one or more that seem too obvious, obscure, or minor.
A cause or effect lacks adequate support.	• Provide further examples, anecdotes, statistics, or quotations from authorities. • Drop it if you cannot find more support.

To Strengthen the Counterargument

Problem	Suggestions for Revising
A likely question or objection readers will have is not addressed.	• Add information to answer the question. • Accommodate the objection by conceding the point and making it part of your own argument. • Refute the objection, arguing that it need not be taken seriously.
An alternative cause or effect readers would propose is not addressed.	• Concede or refute it.
Readers are attacked or ridiculed in a refutation.	• Refute their ideas decisively while showing respect for them as people. • Use the sentence strategy of concession and refutation (p. 402–04)

To Enhance Credibility

Problem	Suggestions for Revising
The essay does not establish common ground with readers.	• Figure out what you might have in common with your audience—some shared values, attitudes, or beliefs—and include them in your argument.
Readers question your credibility.	• Learn more about your subject, and use what you learn to support your argument more fully. • Address more of readers' likely questions, objections, and alternatives. • Talk with others who can help you think more imaginatively about your speculations.

To Make the Organization More Effective

Problem	Suggestions for Revising
The causes or effects are not presented in a logical sequence.	• Change the sequence into some kind of logical order, such as chronological or spatial. You may find that you need to add or drop certain causes or effects.
Connections between ideas are not clear.	• Provide clearer transitions from one step in the argument to the next. • Use clear topic sentences to signal the stages of your argument and the support you provide for each cause or effect.
Your counterarguments are introduced awkwardly or unexpectedly.	• Move them around or add transitions to integrate them more smoothly.

EDITING AND PROOFREADING

After you have revised your essay, be sure to spend some time checking for errors in usage, punctuation, and mechanics and considering matters of style. If you keep a list of errors you typically make, begin by checking your draft against this list. Ask someone else to proofread your essay before you print out a copy for your instructor or send it electronically.

From our research on student writing, we know that essays speculating about causes or effects have a high percentage of errors in the use of numbers and "reason is because" sentences. Because you must usually rely on numbers to present statistics when you support your argument or demonstrate the existence of a trend, you will need to learn and follow the conventions for presenting different kinds of numbers. Because you are usually drawn into "reason is because" sentences when you make a causal argument, you will need to know options for revising such sentences. Check a writer's handbook for help with these potential problems.

Reflecting on What You Have Learned

Speculating about Causes or Effects

In this chapter, you have read critically several essays that speculate about causes or effects and have written one of your own. To better remember what you have learned, pause now to reflect on the reading and writing activities you completed in this chapter.

1. Write a page or so reflecting on what you have learned. Begin by describing what you are most pleased with in your essay. Then explain what you think contributed to your achievement. Be specific about this contribution.

    - If it was something you learned from the readings, indicate which readings and specifically what you learned from them.

    - If it came from your invention writing, point out the section or sections that helped you most.

    - If you got good advice from a critical reader, explain exactly how the person helped you—perhaps by helping you understand a particular problem in your draft or by helping you add a new dimension to your writing.

    - Try to write about your achievement in terms of what you have learned about the genre.

2. Reflect more generally on speculating about causes or effects, a genre of writing that plays an important role in social life and public policy in the United States. Consider some of the following questions: Do you tend to adopt a tentative or an assertive stance when making such speculations about public issues? Why? How might your personal preferences and values influence your speculations about, for example, the causes of health-care cost inflation or the effects of same-sex marriage? How about your gender, ethnicity, religious beliefs, age, or social class? What contribution might writing that speculates about causes or effects make to our society that other genres cannot make?

Proposal to Solve a Problem

Proposals are vital to democratic institutions. By reading and writing them, citizens and colleagues learn about problems affecting their well-being and explore possible actions that could be taken to remedy these problems. People read and write proposals every day in government, business, education, and other professions.

Many proposals address social problems and attempt to influence the direction of public policy. For example, a student activist group writes a proposal advocating that all campus food services be restricted from using genetically manufactured foods until the potential health hazards of such foods have been fully researched. A special United Nations task force recommends ways to eliminate acid rain worldwide. The College Entrance Examination Board commissions a report proposing strategies for reversing the decline in Scholastic Assessment Test (SAT) scores. A specialist in children's television writes a book suggesting that the federal government fund the development of new educational programming for preschool and elementary school students.

Proposals are also a basic ingredient of the world's work. A team of engineers and technical writers in a transportation firm, for example, might write a proposal to compete for a contract to build a new subway system. The manager of a fashion outlet might write a memo to a company executive proposing an upgrading of the computer system to include networking within the chain of stores. Seeking funding to support her research on a new cancer treatment, a university professor might write a proposal to the National Institutes of Health.

Still other proposals are written by individuals who want to solve problems involving groups or communities to which they belong. A college student irritated by long waits to see a nurse at the campus health clinic writes to the clinic director, proposing a more efficient way to schedule and accommodate students. After funding for dance classes has been cut by their school board, students and parents interested in dance write a proposal to the school principal, asking her help in arranging after-school classes taught by a popular high-school teacher who would be paid with community funds. The board of directors of a historical society in a small ranching community proposes to the county board of supervisors that it donate an unused county building to the society so it can display historical records, photographs, and artifacts.

Proposal writing requires a critical questioning attitude—wondering about alternative approaches to bringing about change, puzzling over how a goal might be achieved, questioning why a process unfolds in a particular way, posing challenges to the status quo. In addition, it demands imagination and creativity. To solve a problem, you need to see it anew, to look at it from new perspectives and in new contexts.

In addition, proposal writers must be especially sensitive to readers' needs and different perspectives. Readers need to know details of the problem and the solution and to be convinced that the problem is a serious one and that the solution will correct it and can be implemented. If readers initially favor a different solution, knowing why the writer rejects it will help them decide whether to support or reject the writer's proposed solution. Readers may be wary of costs, demands on their time, superficial changes, and grand schemes. Knowing what your readers know, what their assumptions and biases are, and what kinds of arguments appeal to them is crucial to proposal writing, as it is to all good argumentative writing.

Reading the proposal essays in this chapter will help you discover why the genre is so important and how it works. From the readings and from the suggestions for writing that follow each reading, you will get ideas for your own proposal essay. As you read and write about the selections, keep in mind the following assignment, which sets out the goals for writing a proposal. To support your writing of this assignment, the chapter concludes with a Guide to Writing Proposals.

THE WRITING ASSIGNMENT

Write an essay proposing a solution to a problem affecting a community or group to which you belong. Your tasks are to analyze the problem and establish that it is serious enough to need solving, to offer a solution that will remedy the problem or at least help solve it, and to lay out the particulars by which your proposed solution would be put into effect. Address your proposal to one or more members of the group or to outsiders who could help solve the problem, being sure to take into account readers' likely objections to your proposed solution as well as any alternative solutions they might prefer.

WRITING SITUATIONS FOR PROPOSALS

Writing that proposes solutions to problems plays a significant role in college and professional life, as the following examples indicate:

- Frustrated by what they see as the failure of high schools to prepare students for the workplace, managers of a pharmaceuticals company decide to develop a proposal to move vocational and technical training out of an ill-equipped high-school system and onto the plant's floor. Seven divisional managers plus the firm's technical writers meet weekly to plan the proposal. They read about other on-the-job training programs and interview selected high-school teachers and current employees who attended the high-school program they want to replace. After several weeks' research, they present to the company CEO and to the school board a proposal that includes a time-table for implementing their solution and a detailed budget.

- For a political science class, a college student analyzes the question of presidential term limits. Citing examples from recent history, she argues that U.S. presidents spend the first year of each term getting organized and the fourth year either running for reelection or weakened by their status as a lame duck. Consequently, they are fully productive for only half of their four-year terms. She proposes limiting presidents to one six-year term, claiming that this change would remedy the problem by giving presidents four or five years to put their programs into effect. She acknowledges that it could make presidents less responsive to the public will but insists that the system of legislative checks and balances would make that problem unlikely.

- For an economics class, a student looks into the many problems arising from maquiladoras—industries in Mexico near the border with the United States that provide foreign exchange for the Mexican government, low-paying jobs for Mexican workers, and profits for American manufacturers. Among the problems are inadequate housing and health care for workers, frequent injuries on the job, and environmental damage. His instructor encourages him to select one of the problems, research it more thoroughly, and propose a solution. Taking injuries on the job as the problem most immediately within the control of American manufacturers, he proposes that they observe standards established by the U.S. Occupational Safety and Health Administration.

Thinking about Your Experience

Proposals

Before studying a type of writing, it is useful to spend some time thinking about what you already know about it. You may have discussed with friends an idea of yours or theirs that you hoped would solve a problem or make changes for the better. You might have written essays for classes examining the proposals of experts in a field such as sociology or political science, or you might have written a proposal of your own to solve a social or political problem. Mathematicians, astronomers, anthropologists, physicists, philosophers—people in these and other disciplines are called upon to make proposals to solve problems in their fields.

- Recall a time when you argued—orally or in writing—for a plan or an action that interested or concerned you. What did you hope to achieve with your proposal? Did you need to explain the problem that prompted your solution, or did your audience already understand it? Did you show how your proposal would solve the problem? Argue that it was feasible—not too expensive or time consuming—and better than the alternatives?

- Reflect on the proposal arguments you have read or heard. If you recall someone else's argument in detail, try to identify what made it interesting to you. Was it the problem itself, or did the author's solution seem uniquely imaginative or practical to you? How did the author make the argument for the proposal convincing?

- Write at least a page about your experience with proposals to solve problems.

A GUIDE TO READING PROPOSALS

This guide introduces you to the basic features and strategies typical of proposal writing by looking closely at a proposal by Steven Hill to change the way we vote for our elected officials. Focus first on *reading for meaning* to grasp Hill's argument and then try *reading like a writer* to learn how he constructed the argument to make it convincing for his readers. These two activities—reading for meaning and reading like a writer—follow every reading in this chapter.

Steven Hill

Instant Runoff Voting

Steven Hill is the director of the Political Reform Program of the New America Foundation, a group trying to build a broad-based coalition to seek reforms in the way elections are conducted in the United States. His articles and commentaries have appeared in many important journals in the United States, including the New York Times, Washington Post, Chicago Tribune, *and* Salon.com, *and throughout the world, including the*

Guardian *(England)*, Le Monde Diplomatique *(France), and the* Taiwan News. *His books include* Fixing Elections: The Failure of America's Winner Take All Politics *(2003), and* 10 Steps to Repair American Democracy *(2006), and* Europe's Promise: Why the European Way Is the Best Hope for an Insecure Age *(2010). This proposal first appeared in April 2008 in the* New York Times *"The Way We Live Now" column. As you read, think about how Hill tries to convince readers that a fairly simple change in the way we vote can actually make a big difference in revitalizing our democracy.*

The U.S. political system has been shaken in recent years by increasing   1
partisan polarization, unresponsive government, and ethical scandals—all
of which have resulted in a crisis of confidence in our elected officials.
Opinion polls routinely reveal the public's disdain for Congress and both
major political parties, and grave concern about the direction of the country. Despite the high stakes in the 2006 elections over which party would
control Congress, a mere 40 percent of eligible voters bothered to vote.
Americans need a broadly representative and responsive government that
can build a political consensus capable of addressing the nation's challenges, yet our political system is founded on antiquated practices that
produce this polarized, paralyzed politics.

Our outdated electoral methods and institutions are greatly responsible   2
for the widening chasm between the electorate and those who hold office.
Plurality-wins-all elections allow "spoiler" candidates and "lesser of two
evil" dilemmas to bedevil voters. Party primaries empower the political
extremes in each party and discourage moderates, creating legislatures
that are unable to reach compromise and are subject to gridlock. A
plurality-wins-all system also discourages competition from independent
and third-party candidates.

It's time to bring our electoral system into the 21st century by adopt-   3
ing modern electoral methods, including instant runoff voting (IRV), which
will result in leaders who better represent the broad range of Americans.
IRV produces winners with majority support in a single election by allowing voters to rank first, second, and third choices on their ballots. If a voter's first choice cannot win and is eliminated from the runoff, his or her
vote goes to the candidate he or she ranked second; this is the voter's
runoff choice. Instant runoff voting liberates citizens to vote for the candidates they really like instead of the lesser of two evils. And IRV encourages
candidates to campaign by building coalitions rather than tearing down
opponents. If used in party primaries, IRV would empower the political
center because candidates would need to win with a majority of votes,
and politically moderate candidates would thus have a greater chance of
advancing to the general election.

Using instant runoff voting to elect members of the U.S. House and   4
Senate will expand voter choice, inaugurate a new era of bipartisan

cooperation in Congress, and encourage pragmatic problem solving over partisan bickering on countless issues. Using IRV for congressional primary elections would loosen the stranglehold party extremists have on the nomination process.

THE PROBLEM

5   When asked whether they would prefer to have more political choices on Election Day, including independent and third-party candidates, a clear majority of Americans say yes. Yet our 18th-century electoral methods perpetuate the two-party system and restrict voters' choices. That's because under our current electoral system, three's a crowd. Our plurality election process, in which the candidate with the most votes wins—even if that candidate receives less than a popular majority—can produce skewed results when more than two candidates run for the same office. For example, in a three-way race, a candidate with only 37 percent of the vote can win, even though 63 percent of the voters wanted a different candidate.

6   This is not merely a theoretical consideration. In three of our last four presidential elections, the winning candidate in a multi-candidate field did not have a majority of the national popular vote. Since 2000, the governors of 20 states have won without a majority of the popular vote, five governors in 2006. From 1994 through 2004, there were 247 plurality wins in U.S. House primaries and 35 in U.S. Senate primaries (with 77 more House plurality winners and 14 more Senate plurality winners avoided by the use of second-round runoff elections).

7   Our plurality-wins-all electoral system leads to the following problems:

- **Nonmajority winners**. We can send a man to the moon, we can map the human genome, yet we use an electoral method that cannot guarantee that the candidate with the most support will win. This undermines majority rule, one of the cornerstones of our democracy.

- **Spoiler candidacies**. Plurality-wins-all elections are vulnerable to spoiler candidacies. In such cases, the votes of like-minded voters are split between candidates with similar positions, resulting in their least favorite candidate winning. Independent and less popular candidates thus feel pressure not to run or, even worse, their candidacy helps elect someone whom a majority of voters oppose. This dynamic tends to suppress new candidates and their ideas, which in turn suppresses political debate. This alienates voters who get tired of voting for the lesser of two evils instead of for candidates they really like.

- **Partisan primaries and loss of moderates.** Primary elections are typically restricted to registered party voters (though specific rules differ from state to state) and usually have very low turnout. In our plurality-wins-all system, candidates can win their party's nomination with low percentages of the vote, relying on a narrow core of voters. As a result, the extremes in each party have an influence over national politics that is far out of proportion to their actual numbers in the electorate. Candidates with politically moderate views have a much more difficult time winning primary elections and advancing to the general election. Yet since moderate politicians play a crucial role as legislative bridge builders, their absence leads to a polarized government in which representatives have great difficulty working together.

- **Mudslinging campaigns.** Plurality-wins-all elections encourage negative campaigns, where often the winning strategy consists of driving voters away from an opponent by mudslinging rather than attracting voters by building coalitions and consensus. The head-to-head combat of plurality-wins-all elections inevitably leads to bruising, attack-style campaigns that alienate voters, lower public trust in government, and damage the eventual officeholder. The winner of a divisive election is likely to have to work much harder to gain the public trust that is essential to strong leadership.

THE SOLUTION: INSTANT RUNOFF VOTING

Instant runoff voting is a reliable and tested solution to our broken plurality-wins-all politics. It produces winners with majority support in a single election. You rank candidates in order of preference: a first ranking for your favorite candidate, a second ranking for your next favorite, and so on. If a candidate wins a majority of first-choice rankings, he or she wins the election. If not, the "instant runoff" begins.

The candidate with the fewest first-choice rankings is eliminated, and voters for the eliminated candidate have their ballots counted immediately for their second-ranked candidate—i.e., the candidate they would have supported if forced to come back to the polls for a traditional two-round runoff. All ballots are recounted, and if a candidate has a majority, that candidate is the winner. If not, the process is repeated until one candidate has majority support. In other words, voters are ranking their runoff choices at the same time as they are indicating their first choice, and these runoff rankings are used to determine instantly which candidate has support from a popular majority in a single election.

With IRV, voters are liberated to vote for the candidates they really like instead of the lesser of two evils, and they don't have to worry about

8

9

10

HOW INSTANT RUNOFF VOTING WORKS

You vote for your favorite candidate, just like you do now. But you also RANK your runoff choices at the same time – 1, 2, 3, on your ballot. If a candidate has a majority of first rankings, he or she wins. If not, the second and third rankings are used to determine the majority winner – **instantly** – in a single November election.

Y. Kim	2
J. Smith	3
S. Lopez	1

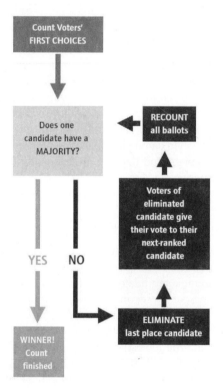

Count Voters' **FIRST CHOICES**

Does one candidate have a **MAJORITY?**

RECOUNT all ballots

Voters of eliminated candidate give their vote to their next-ranked candidate

YES NO

ELIMINATE last place candidate

WINNER! Count finished

spoiler candidates splitting the vote. IRV would help moderate candidates break the stranglehold that partisan voters now have on the congressional primary process. Instead of congressional elections being dominated by the most partisan Democratic and Republican nominees, more centrist candidates would have a chance of making it through the primary gauntlet and ending up on the November ballot.

11   In effect, instant runoff voting asks the voters to reveal more of their political thinking. Okay, you're a moderate Republican, but what about

this moderate Democratic candidate? Might that candidate be acceptable as your second or third choice? Or maybe you are a Libertarian Party or a Green Party supporter—which would be your second or third choice if your Libertarian or Green candidate can't win? Voters can think more about which candidates they like regardless of partisan labels. This in turn fires the synapses of voters and liberates them to send a message with their first rankings in ways that the current system can never do. The nation receives a much better snapshot of where the electorate really stands.

This is not some academic exercise. Instant runoff voting can change outcomes and produce fairer results. If IRVhad been in place for the 1992 presidential election, President George H. W. Bush might have won enough second-choice rankings from Ross Perot supporters to have beaten Bill Clinton, who won the presidency with only 43 percent of the popular vote. And if, in 2000, the nearly 100,000 Ralph Nader voters in Florida had had the option of ranking a second choice, probably thousands of them would have turned to Al Gore, who would have been the recipient of all their runoff rankings, most likely winning Florida and the presidency.

THE BENEFITS OF INSTANT RUNOFF VOTING

There are many good reasons for using instant runoff voting, but the following are especially important.

- **Majority winners.** With IRV, a number of candidates can run and not worry about the split votes that lead to nonmajority winners, and majority winners are elected in a single race.

- **No more spoiler dilemmas.** With IRV, voters are liberated to vote for the candidates they really like without worrying about spoilers wasting their vote. If your first choice can't win, your vote moves to your second choice, so you aren't forced to vote for the lesser of two evils. Election results will more accurately reflect the level of support for all candidates. Like-minded candidates can form coalitions without splitting the vote and knocking each other off. This in turn will attract a higher caliber of alternative candidates, giving voters a broader range of choices.

- **Increased political debate.** The spoiler dynamic suppresses new candidates and their ideas, which in turn suppresses political debate. Third parties and independent candidates have often played an important role in the American political system as "laboratories for new ideas." Third parties and independents first proposed the abolition of slavery (Free Soil Party), prohibition (Prohibition Party), the income tax (Populist Party), the New Deal coalition (Progressive Party), balanced budgets (Reform Party), women's suffrage, the 40-hour workweek, food and drug safety laws, public libraries, direct election of U.S. senators, and government regulation of monopolies.

Third parties and independent candidates not only introduce new ideas and issues but also a new type of candidate who speaks directly to various constituencies and mobilizes them with a personal touch that only an authentic voice can provide. Ross Perot, during his two candidacies in 1992 and 1996, gave expression to the frustrations of a Middle America fed up with budget deficits and an indifferent two-party tango, and wanting to "toss the bums out." IRV would open up the electoral system and empower voters to support such candidates—and their ideas—without the unintended consequences of spoiling. And that would encourage more political debate, which would be good for America.

- **Less mudslinging.** IRV would also cut down on the negative campaigning that has become a fixture of American political campaigns. That's because currently in our winner-take-all elections, candidates win as easily by driving voters away from their opponents as by attracting them to their own candidacy. The last candidate standing wins, so the optimal campaign strategy becomes attacking your opponent and taking as few stands on issues as possible to avoid alienating a potential bloc of voters. This strategy is greatly augmented by the use of polling and focus groups to figure out what sound bites will work most effectively against an opponent, as well as what the least risky positions are on the most pressing issues. Unsurprisingly, our elections are sorely lacking in substance, and alienating to many.

  Instant runoff voting discourages this sort of negative campaigning. In order to win under this system, a candidate may need to attract the second or third rankings from the supporters of rival candidates, so candidates will have to be more careful about what they say about each other. IRV will result in a major shift in campaign strategy because finding common ground and building coalitions with other candidates, rather than tearing them down, will pay dividends at the polls. In San Francisco, where instant runoff voting is used to elect local officeholders, some races have seen candidates endorsing their opponents, sharing slate mailers, and cosponsoring fundraisers. One *New York Times* headline read: "New Runoff System in San Francisco Has the Rival Candidates Cooperating." Such coalition building in the midst of a campaign is certain to benefit the eventual winner in governing. For those tired of polarized politics and mudslinging campaigns, IRV has much to offer.

- **Empowering the political center.** Instant runoff voting provides a solution to the problem of partisan primaries. With IRV, candidates who can build coalitions by attracting support beyond their core supporters are more likely to be successful. In party primaries, candidates would need to win with a majority of votes, so politically moderate candidates would have a greater chance of advancing to the general election in November.

An even better idea would be to get rid of partisan congressional primary elections entirely and hold a single election in November with instant runoff voting. This structure would mimic a blanket primary (sometimes known as an open primary), which was very popular with voters in several states but was eliminated following an adverse U.S. Supreme Court ruling. The blanket primary, which allowed voters to choose from all candidates regardless of party affiliation, gives voters more choices. Getting rid of the low-turnout primary elections would save the tens of millions of tax dollars currently spent to administer them. Since the Supreme Court has ruled that a political party's primary is a private affair and that a state cannot force parties to open their primaries to all voters, why should taxpayers foot the bill? Let the parties pay for a primary or a caucus themselves, and nominate as many or as few candidates as they wish for each race in November. And then instant runoff voting can be used to elect the majority winners in a single election.

Eliminating primaries will also spare candidates the burden of raising money for a second election. Having to raise money for two elections instead of one gives the advantage to incumbents and other well-connected candidates who can raise more money, undermining the good that comes from campaign finance reform. Eliminating party primaries and electing congressional representatives using instant runoff voting would transform our politics. Together, these reforms would significantly boost voter choice, reduce mudslinging, improve political debate, inaugurate a new era of bipartisan cooperation, and save the taxpayers money.

IRV IS GAINING MOMENTUM

Instant runoff voting favors neither the left nor the right; it is a nonpartisan reform measure that seeks simply to make our electoral process more democratic and efficient. It has been used for decades to elect the president of Ireland and Australia's House of Representatives. It is also used to elect the mayor of London and the presidents of Malta and Sri Lanka. India uses IRV to indirectly elect its president. And it has been used to good effect in divided societies: ranked ballots have been instrumental in facilitating cross-ethnic or cross-tribal coalitions in troubled nations like Bosnia, Fiji, and Papua New Guinea. . . .

16   The movement toward use of instant runoff voting in government elections is gaining momentum throughout the United States because it answers a real need. In the November 2006 elections, IRV was passed by voters in four different locations: Oakland, California, with 67 percent of the vote, Minneapolis with 65 percent, Davis, California, with 55 percent and Pierce County, Washington, with 53 percent. What is interesting about the four victories is that they occurred in quite different locations. Oakland is a very diverse, working-class city; Minneapolis is a Midwestern values city; Pierce County is mostly a rural county with large numbers of independent voters that replaced a partisan primary with a single November election using IRV; and Davis is a smaller university town. Yet in every place instant runoff voting provided a unique solution to problems with representative government and democracy. . . .

17   IRV has broad, bipartisan support and has been endorsed by Sen. John McCain as well as by Democratic National Committee Chairman Howard Dean; Alaska's Republican Party and California's Democratic Party have both endorsed it. It also has support from good government and advocacy groups like Common Cause, the League of Women Voters, California PIRG, the Greenlining Institute, the Asian Law Caucus, the National Latino Congress, and Southwest Voter. . . . To date, bills for IRV have been introduced in the legislatures of 22 states.

18   Our current plurality-wins-all voting system is a horse and buggy relic of the 18th century. It does not meet the most basic requirements for fair and efficient elections in the 21st century. Instant runoff voting is an idea whose time has come. It will produce a more robust political debate, and it will give voters more choices and a greater voice in the American political process.

READING FOR MEANING

This section presents three activities that will help you think about the meanings in Hill's essay proposing a solution to a problem.

Read to Comprehend

Write a few sentences briefly summarizing Hill's argument about the benefits of instant runoff voting.

Identify any words with meanings you are unsure of—such as *disdain* (paragraph 1) and *gridlock* (2)—and find the dictionary definition for each word that makes the best sense in the context.

To help you understand the essay better, also consider trying one of these critical reading strategies, explained in Appendix 1: *outlining* or *questioning to understand and remember.*

Read to Respond

Write a paragraph or two exploring your initial thoughts and feelings about Hill's proposal. Focus on anything that stands out for you, perhaps because it resonates with your own experience or because you find a statement puzzling. For example, consider writing about one of the following:

- Hill's argument that instant runoff voting would discourage attack ads and negative campaigning ("The Problem," bulleted list item 3, and "The Benefits . . . ," bulleted list item 4);

- the support Hill offers for his assertion that instant runoff voting "is not some academic exercise," but can really "change outcomes and produce fairer results" (12); or

- your own experience with choosing between candidates in an election.

To help develop your response, also consider trying one of these critical reading strategies, explained in Appendix 1: *contextualizing* or *judging the writer's credibility.*

Read to Analyze Assumptions

All writing contains *assumptions*—ideas and attitudes that are taken for granted as commonly accepted truths. Personal or individual assumptions also tend to reflect the values and beliefs of a particular community, which help shape the way those in the group think, act, and understand the world. All writing reflects assumptions held by the writer, but assumptions held by others, such as readers or sources cited by the writer, may also be present. Sometimes assumptions are stated explicitly, but often they are only implied, so you may have to search for underlying assumptions in the word choices and examples.

Why go to the effort to analyze assumptions in a reading? Assumptions have powerful effects. They influence our opinions and judgments by leading us to value some things and devalue others. These effects are even more powerful because they are taken for granted, often accepted without question by those who hold them. To understand a reading on a deep level, then, it is necessary to bring its assumptions to the surface and to question them. To think critically about assumptions, here are some kinds of questions you could ask: Who holds this assumption (the writer, readers, and/or others cited in the essay)? What are the effects of the assumption in the context of the essay specifically or in society more generally? What do you think about the assumption, and is there anything in the essay that raises doubts about it? How does the assumption reinforce or critique commonly held views, and are there any alternative ideas, beliefs, or values that would challenge this assumption?

Write a paragraph or two analyzing an assumption in Hill's essay. You might choose an assumption from the list below, using the questions accompanying it in addition to the ones above to help you get started. Or you can choose another assumption in the essay to explore.

- **assumptions about the importance of consensus building**. In his opening paragraph, Hill claims that Americans need to replace our current "polarized, paralyzed" political system with "a broadly representative and responsive government that can build a political consensus capable of addressing the nation's challenges."

  To think critically about the assumptions in this essay regarding the importance of consensus building, ask yourself questions like these: To form a consensus, people with different political views have to come to an agreement on problems facing the nation and how they should be addressed. Hill seems to assume that consensus building requires that people moderate their views—in other words, that they take less extreme positions in order to find common ground with their political opponents. Why do you think Hill thinks building coalitions is a good goal for politicians? Why might others think moderation or compromise is not beneficial?

- **assumptions about the destructiveness of negative campaigning**. Hill argues that our current system rewards negative campaigning because "candidates win as easily by driving voters away from their opponents as by attracting them to their own candidacy" ("The Benefits," bulleted list item 4). In other words, candidates do not have to offer voters a reason to vote for them. They just have to give them a reason not to vote for their opponents.

  To think critically about the assumptions in this essay regarding the destructiveness of negative campaigning, ask yourself questions like these: Why do you think Hill believes that negative campaigning is a bad thing for American politics and for America in general? Many voters complain about negative ads, but the fact remains that the ads usually work: they turn voters against the candidates who are being attacked. It is often assumed that negative ads also hurt the candidates who run them, but apparently they hurt their opponents—the target of their ads—more. Why do you think negative ads work?

To help you analyze assumptions in Hill's essay, also consider trying one of these critical reading strategies, explained in Appendix 1: *reflecting on challenges to your beliefs and values, exploring the significance of figurative language,* or *looking for patterns of opposition.*

READING LIKE A WRITER

This section leads you through an analysis of Hill's writing strategies: *introducing the problem; presenting the proposed solution; arguing directly for the proposed solution;* and *counterarguing readers' objections, questions, and alternative solutions.*

For each strategy, you will be asked to reread and annotate part of Hill's essay to see how he uses the strategy to accomplish his particular purpose.

When you study the selections later in this chapter, you will see how different proposal writers use these same strategies for different purposes. The Guide to Writing Proposals near the end of the chapter suggests ways you can use these strategies in your own essay proposing a solution to a problem.

Introducing the Problem

Every proposal begins with a problem. What writers say about the problem and how much space they devote to it depend on what they assume their readers know and think about the problem. Some problems require more explanation than others. Obviously, if readers are already immersed in discussing the problem and possible solutions, then the writer may not have to say much to introduce the problem. Nevertheless, savvy proposal writers try to present even familiar problems in a way that alerts readers to the problem's seriousness and prepares them for the writer's preferred solution.

For example, Hill reminds readers there is "a crisis of confidence" in the U.S. political system, supporting his claim by referring to opinion polls and voter turnout in a major election (paragraph 1). He then uses a cause-effect analysis to place blame primarily (note that he uses the hedging phrase "greatly responsible") on the "outdated" system of "plurality-wins-all" elections (paragraph 2). Introducing the problem by identifying its causes is a common move for proposal writers and a useful one because it sets up the argument for a solution that eliminates at least one of the main causes of the problem. But before writers can argue for the solution, they have to convince readers that the problem is important enough to require change. In addition to the two introductory paragraphs that identify the problem, Hill devotes the next section, headed "The Problem," to laying out the problem's detrimental effects.

Analyze

1. Reread paragraphs 5–6 to see how Hill uses statistics to further support his claim that plurality elections occur fairly often. Why is it important for his proposal to establish this fact?

2. Review paragraph 7, where Hill lists four reasons plurality-wins-all elections have led to the "crisis of confidence" he identified in paragraph 1. Why do you think his handling of the first bullet point is especially brief? What else could he have said? Choose one of the other bullet points, and examine how he supports it.

Write

Write several sentences explaining what you have learned about Hill's strategies for introducing the problem. Add another sentence or two assessing how convincing you find this part of his argument.

Presenting the Proposed Solution

For proposed solutions that already exist, the writer may need only to give the solution a name and perhaps also to identify where it is being applied successfully. The proposal writer's primary purposes are to convince readers of the wisdom of the proposed solution and to convince them to take action on its implementation. To achieve these purposes, the writer must ensure that readers understand what is being proposed and can imagine how the solution could be implemented.

Analyze

1. Reread paragraph 3 where Hill introduces his preferred solution, which is also the title of his proposal essay. Put brackets around his brief explanation of instant runoff voting.

2. Then reread paragraphs 8 and 9 to see what he adds to his earlier explanation of the process involved in instant runoff voting. (The Analyzing Visuals activity on page 500 invites you also to examine how the two visuals help make this written explanation even clearer.)

Write

Write a sentence or two describing how Hill explains instant runoff voting. Add another couple of sentences assessing the effectiveness of Hill's explanation.

Arguing Directly for the Proposed Solution

In arguing for solutions, writers rely on two interrelated strategies: arguing directly for the proposed solution and counterarguing readers' likely objections and alternative solutions. (We take up the second strategy, counterargument, in the next section.)

Whatever else proposal writers do, they must argue energetically, imaginatively, and sensitively for their proposed solutions. A proposal may describe a problem well, complain with great feeling about it, and explain the solution clearly and enthusiastically; if it goes no further, however, it is not a proposal likely to succeed. The writer must also try to convince readers that the solution presented will actually help to solve the problem, even if it does not eliminate it altogether. In this essay, after establishing that plurality-wins-all elections have caused "polarized, paralyzed politics" (1), Hill needs to convince readers that his solution of instant runoff elections can eliminate or reduce the polarization and paralysis.

Writers sometimes use arguments based on supporting evidence such as examples, statistics, hypothetical scenarios, and quotations from authorities. For example, in paragraph 11, Hill uses a hypothetical scenario to demonstrate how making a second or third choice "liberates" voters and provides "a much better snapshot of where the electorate really stands." Similarly, in paragraph 12, he gives historical examples to show how instant runoff voting could have affected the presidential elections in 1992 and 2000.

Analyze

1. Reread paragraphs 3 and 4 where Hill lists the benefits of instant runoff voting. Highlight each benefit in these paragraphs. Also note where each benefit is repeated in paragraphs 10 through 13, including the bullet points that follow 13.

2. Choose one of the benefits that you think would be especially helpful in solving the problem, and analyze Hill's argument for it, paying particular attention to the kinds of support he uses.

Write

Write a few sentences summarizing the benefit you analyzed. In particular, explain how this benefit would help solve the problem Hill identified. Add another sentence or two assessing the effectiveness of this part of his argument.

Counterarguing Readers' Objections and Alternative Solutions

As they present the problem and then present and argue for the solution, writers need to anticipate readers' possible objections to these various parts of the argument as well as alternative solutions readers may prefer. In counterarguing, writers have several options. They may acknowledge that an objection or alternative solution has some value and *accommodate* it by modifying the proposal. Alternatively, writers may *refute* an objection by demonstrating that it is mistaken or refute an alternative solution by showing that it is inferior to the one being proposed. Ignoring likely objections or alternative solutions is not a wise strategy because it gives the impression that the writer either does not fully understand the issue or can't counter criticism.

Analyze

Reread paragraphs 15 to 18, where Hill anticipates the most likely objection—namely, that instant runoff voting favors one particular point of view or political party. Examine these paragraphs to see how Hill counterargues—by accommodating or refuting the objection—and the strategies he uses to do so.

Write

Write a few sentences explaining how Hill counterargues, giving examples of how he handles the objection. Add another sentence or two evaluating his counterargument.

ANALYZING VISUALS

Write a paragraph analyzing the two visuals included in Hill's proposal and explaining what they contribute to the essay. To do the analysis, you can use the criteria chart for the Analysis of Visuals in Appendix 3. Don't feel you have to answer all of the questions in the chart; focus on those that seem most productive in helping you write a paragraph-length analysis. To help you get started, consider adding these questions that specifically refer to Hill's visuals:

- Compare the first visual, showing how to rank your runoff choices, to paragraph 8, where Hill explains the same process. What does the visual add to the paragraph's explanation? How does the text in the visual help make clear what the visual is designed to illustrate?

- Compare the second visual—the flow chart—to paragraph 9, where Hill explains how instant runoff voting works. What additional information, if any, do readers learn from the flow chart? How does the flow chart help to clarify the written explanation in paragraph 9?

READINGS

William F. Shughart II

Why Not a Football Degree?

William F. Shughart II (b. 1947) is the Frederick A. P. Barnard distinguished professor of economics at the University of Mississippi. A senior fellow at the Independent Institute, Shughart serves as the editor in chief of the scholarly journal Public Choice *and the associate editor of the* Southern Economic Journal. *His honors include the University of Mississippi Outstanding Researcher Award, the Sir Anthony Fisher International Memorial Award, and the* Business Week *Award. Shughart has written many books, including* Policy Challenges and Political Responses: Public Choice Perspectives on the Post–9/11 World *(2005) and* The Economics of Budget Deficits *(2002). He also publishes in popular newspapers such as the* Wall Street Journal, Chicago Tribune, *and* Los Angeles Times.

This essay originally appeared in the Wall Street Journal *in 1990 and was updated by Shughart in 2007. As you read his proposal, notice that Shughart dismisses as "half-measures" (paragraph 3) the efforts by the National Collegiate Athletic Association (NCAA) to solve the problem of "loss of amateurism in college sports" (2). In their place, he offers a three-pronged solution designed to help student athletes succeed in their academic studies as well as in their collegiate sports careers and also to eliminate what he calls "illegal financial inducements" (11) while at the same time removing the "built-in advantages" (14) of the most successful college sports programs. Consider how well Shughart's "three suggestions" (3) would work together to offer a complete solution to the problem.*

1   The college football career of 2006's Heisman Trophy winner, Ohio State University quarterback Troy Smith, nearly was cut short at the end of his sophomore year following allegations that he had accepted $500 from a Buckeye booster. He was barred from playing in the 2005 Alamo Bowl and the next season's opener against Miami (Ohio). Quarterback Rhett Bomar was dismissed from the University of Oklahoma's football team after it was disclosed that he had earned substantially more than justified by the number of hours worked during the summer of 2006 at a job arranged for him by a patron of OU athletics. As a result of charges that, from 1993 to 1998, Coach Clem Haskins paid to have more than 400 term papers ghost-written for 18 of his players, the post-season tournament victories credited to the University of Minnesota's basketball team were erased from the

How does knowing that this is a proposal essay affect your understanding of the title and opening paragraph?

NCAA's record books and the program was placed on a four-year probation from which it has not yet recovered. In recent years, gambling and point-shaving scandals have rocked the basketball programs at Arizona State, Northwestern, and Florida; player suspensions and other penalties have been handed out for illegal betting on games by members of the Boston University, Florida State, and University of Maryland football teams.

Each of these events, which are only the latest revela-   2
tions in a long series of NCAA rule violations, has generated the usual hand-wringing about the apparent loss of amateurism in college sports. Nostalgia for supposedly simpler times when love of the game and not money was the driving force in intercollegiate athletics has led to all sorts of reform proposals. The NCAA's decision in the late 1980s to require its member institutions to make public athletes' graduation rates is perhaps the least controversial example. Proposition 48's mandate that freshman athletes must meet more stringent test score and grade point requirements to participate in NCAA-sanctioned contests than is demanded of entering non-student-athletes has been criticized as a naked attempt to discriminate against disadvantaged (and mostly minority) high-school graduates who see college sports as a way out of poverty.

Why does Shughart mention these two earlier reforms before he explains his own proposed solution?

But whether or not one supports any particular   3
reform proposal, there seems to be a general consensus that something must be done. If so, why stop at half-measures? I hereby offer three suggestions for solving the crisis in college athletics.

1. *Create four-year degree programs in football and*   4
basketball. Many colleges and universities grant bachelors' degrees in vocational subjects. Art, drama, and music are a few examples, but there are others. Undergraduates who major in these areas typically are required to spend only about one of their four years in introductory English, math, history and science courses; the remainder of their time is spent in the studio, the theater or the practice hall honing the creative talents they will later sell as professionals.

Although a college education is no more necessary for   5
success in the art world than it is in the world of sports, no similar option is available for students whose talents lie on the athletic field or in the gym. Majoring in physical education is a possibility, of course, but while PE is

hardly a rigorous, demanding discipline, undergraduates pursuing a degree in that major normally must spend many more hours in the classroom than their counterparts who are preparing for careers on the stage. While the music major is receiving academic credit for practice sessions and recitals, the PE major is studying and taking exams in kinesiology, exercise physiology and nutrition. Why should academic credit be given for practicing the violin, but not for practicing a three-point shot?

How convincing is this argument based on an analogy between the arts and sports?

6   2. *Extend the time limit on athletic scholarships by two years.* In addition to practicing and playing during the regular football or basketball season, college athletes must continue to work to improve their skills and keep in shape during the off-season. For football players, these off-season activities include several weeks of organized spring practice as well as year-round exercise programs in the weight room and on the running track. Basketball players participate in summer leagues and practice with their teams during the fall. In effect, college athletes are required to work at their sports for as much as 10 months a year.

7   These time-consuming extracurricular activities make it extremely difficult for college athletes to devote more than minimal effort to the studies required for maintaining their academic eligibility. They miss lectures and exams when their teams travel, and the extra tutoring they receive at athletic department expense often fails to make up the difference.

8   If the NCAA and its member schools are truly concerned about the academic side of the college athletic experience, let them put their money where their collective mouth is. The period of an athlete's eligibility to participate in intercollegiate sports would remain at four years, but the two additional years of scholarship support could be exercised at any time during the athlete's lifetime. Athletes who use up their college eligibility and do not choose careers in professional sports would be guaranteed financial backing to remain in school and finish their undergraduate degrees. Athletes who have the talent to turn pro could complete their degrees when their playing days are over.

This suggestion is likely to be controversial. How well do you think Shughart supports it?

9   3. *Allow a competitive marketplace to determine the compensation of college athletes.* Football and basketball players at the top NCAA institutions produce millions of dollars in benefits for their respective schools.

Successful college athletic programs draw more fans to the football stadium and to the basketball arena. They generate revenues for the school from regular season television appearances and from invitations to participate in postseason play. There is evidence that schools attract greater financial support from public and private sources—both for their athletic and academic programs—if their teams achieve national ranking. There even is evidence that the quality of students who apply for admission to institutions of higher learning improves following a successful football or basketball season.

How convincing is Shughart's strategy of referring to "evidence" here?

Despite the considerable contributions made to the wealth and welfare of his or her school, however, the compensation payable to a college athlete is limited by the NCAA to a scholarship that includes tuition, books, room and board, and a nominal expense allowance. Any payment above and beyond this amount subjects the offending athletic program to NCAA sanctions. In-kind payments to players and recruits in the form of free tickets to athletic contests, T-shirts, transportation and accommodations likewise are limited. These restrictions apply to alumni and fans as well as to the institutions themselves. The NCAA also limits the amount of money athletes can earn outside of school by curtailing the use of summer jobs as a means by which coaches and boosters can pay athletes more than authorized. 10

The illegal financial inducements reported to be widespread in collegiate football and basketball supply conclusive evidence that many college athletes are now underpaid. The relevant question is whether the current system of compensation ought to remain in place. Allowing it to do so will preserve the illusion of amateurism in college sports and permit coaches, athletic departments and college administrators to continue to benefit financially at the expense of the players. On the other hand, shifting to a market-based system of compensation would transfer some of the wealth created by big time athletic programs to the individuals whose talents are key ingredients in the success of those programs. 11

Why do you think Shughart calls amateurism in college sports an "illusion"?

It would also cause a sea change in the distribution of power among the top NCAA institutions. Under the present NCAA rules, some of the major college athletic programs, such as Southern Cal, LSU and Florida in football, and Duke, North Carolina and Florida in basketball, 12 have developed such strong winning traditions over the years that they can maintain their dominant positions without cheating.

13   These schools are able to attract superior high-school athletes season after season by offering packages of non-monetary benefits (well-equipped training facilities, quality coaching staffs, talented teammates, national exposure and so on) that increases the present value of an amateur athlete's future professional income relative to the value added by historically weaker athletic programs. Given this factor, along with NCAA rules that mandate uniform compensation across the board, the top institutions have a built-in competitive advantage in recruiting the best and brightest athletes.

14   It follows that under the current system, the weaker programs are virtually compelled to offer illegal financial inducements to players and recruits if they wish to compete successfully with the traditional powers. It also follows that shifting to a market-based system of compensation would remove some of the built-in advantages now enjoyed by the top college athletic programs. It is surely this effect, along with the reductions in the incomes of coaches and the "fat" in athletic department budgets to be expected once a competitive marketplace is permitted to work, that is the cause of the objection to paying student-athletes a market-determined wage, not the rhetoric about the repugnance of professionalism.

Shughart's phrase *It . . . follows* suggests that his conclusion is logical, perhaps even inevitable. How convincing do you find it?

15   It is a fight over the distribution of the college sports revenue pie that lies at the bottom of the debate about reforming NCAA rules. And notwithstanding the high moral principles and concern for players usually expressed by debaters on all sides of the issue, the interests of the athlete are in fact often the last to be considered.

Why do you think Shughart ends his essay this way? How effective is this ending?

READING FOR MEANING

This section presents three activities that will help you think about the meanings in Shughart's proposal essay.

Read to Comprehend

Write a few sentences briefly summarizing the solution Shughart is proposing.

Identify any words with meanings you are unsure of—such as *point-shaving* (paragraph 1) and *sanctions* (10)—and find the dictionary definition for each word that makes the best sense in the context.

To help you understand the essay better, also consider trying one of these critical reading strategies, explained in Appendix 1: *outlining* or *questioning to understand and remember.*

Read to Respond

Write several paragraphs exploring your initial thoughts and feelings about Shughart's proposal. Focus on anything that stands out for you, perhaps because it resonates with your own experiences or because you find a statement puzzling. For example, consider writing about one of the following:

- the rule violations that Shughart lists in the first paragraph, perhaps adding other, more recent violations with which you are familiar;

- Shughart's idea that academic credit should be given to "practicing a three-point shot" (paragraph 5); or

- Shughart's observation that playing and practicing sports "make it extremely difficult for college athletes to devote more than minimal effort" to their studies (7), perhaps in relation to your own experience as an athlete in college or high school.

To help develop your response, also consider trying one of these critical reading strategies, explained in Appendix 1: *reflecting on challenges to your beliefs and values* or *judging the writer's credibility.*

Read to Analyze Assumptions

Write a paragraph or two analyzing an assumption in Shughart's essay. To think critically about assumptions, here are some kinds of questions you could ask: Who holds this assumption (the writer, readers, and/or others cited in the essay)? What are the effects of the assumption in the context of the essay specifically or in society more generally? What do you think about the assumption, and is there anything in the essay that raises doubts about it? How does the assumption reinforce or critique commonly held views, and are there any alternative ideas, beliefs, or values that would challenge this assumption?

You might choose an assumption from the list below, using the questions accompanying it in addition to the ones above to help you get started. Or you can choose another assumption in the essay to explore.

- **assumptions about the benefits of amateurism.** NCAA rules require that to play college sports, athletes must retain amateur status, meaning that they cannot be paid by recruiters and that their scholarships can cover only such things as tuition and housing. Shughart argues, however, that amateurism in college sports is an "illusion" (paragraph 11).

To think critically about the assumptions in this essay related to amateurism, ask yourself questions like these: Who, according to Shughart, benefits from keeping college athletes amateurs, and who would benefit if they were allowed to become professionals? If the NCAA assumes that amateur status protects college athletes and perhaps also college sports, what is it supposed to protect them from and how effective has it been? What values are associated with the terms *amateur* and *professional*?

- **assumptions about the purpose of college.** Shughart compares football to "vocational subjects" such as art, drama, and music (paragraph 4). He argues that football should be a major in its own right, like music where students receive "academic credit for practice sessions and recitals" (5).

  To think critically about the assumptions in this essay related to the purpose of college, ask yourself questions like these: Traditionally, an undergraduate degree (or at least the first two years of college) has sought to give students a broad or what is often called a liberal education and to leave vocational training to specialized upper-division majors or graduate programs. What do you and other students at your college assume that the purpose of college should be—Vocational training? A liberal education? Something else? What does Shughart seem to assume it should be?

To help you analyze assumptions in Shughart's essay, also consider trying one of these critical reading strategies, explained in Appendix 1: *reflecting on challenges to your beliefs and values* or *looking for patterns of opposition*.

READING LIKE A WRITER

INTRODUCING THE PROBLEM

Before they can tell readers how they think a problem could be solved, proposal writers need to introduce the problem. Depending on their purpose and what they expect readers to know and think about the problem, writers must decide whether they also need to establish that the problem exists and is serious. For problems most readers are unfamiliar with or that seem distant from their personal experience, writers often give examples or anecdotes.

This activity will help you analyze Shughart's method of introducing the problem to his readers.

Analyze

1. Reread paragraphs 1 and 2, where Shughart introduces the problem by citing examples of it. Underline the specific details he provides about each example—such as dates, names, schools, and violations. Consider how the sheer number of examples plus the details about each example contribute to establishing that the problem exists and is serious.

2. Notice also Shughart's word choices. For example, why do you think Shughart describes the problem at the beginning of paragraph 2 as "the apparent loss of amateurism in college sports"? And why does he use the expression "[n]ostalgia for supposedly simpler times"? Consider what words like *apparent* and *supposedly* are intended to convey to readers in this context.

Write

Write several sentences describing how Shughart uses examples to introduce the problem and emphasize its importance in paragraphs 1 and 2. Add another sentence or two about Shughart's word choices and how they affect the tone of his proposal in the opening paragraphs.

CONSIDERING IDEAS FOR YOUR OWN WRITING

Consider proposing a way to improve a popular sport. Your idea need not revolutionize the sport, though it might. It could offer only a small refinement such as changing a rule or adding a feature to the game. (Developments such as the designated hitter in baseball and instant replays to resolve disputed official calls in football were originally subjects of proposals.) Your proposal could seek to improve the safety of the game for participants, the way records are kept, the way athletes are recruited into the sport, the way athletes are treated, or the entertainment value of the game to spectators. You could focus on either a professional or amateur sport, a team sport or individual competition, high school or college teams. You could address your proposal to players, officials, fans, or the general public.

Gary Beck

Not Your Everyday Homeless Proposal

Gary Beck has spent most of his adult life as a theater director and worked as an art dealer when he couldn't earn a living in the theater. He has also been a tennis pro, a ditchdigger, and a salvage diver. His own plays and translations of Molière, Aristophanes, and Sophocles have been produced off Broadway and toured colleges. Expectations, Beck's collection of poems, was published in 2010.

This essay, "Not Your Everyday Homeless Proposal," was first published in 2006 in Outcry Magazine, *an online publication that describes itself as "the voice of the voiceless." Beck acknowledges that there are "no simple solutions" to the problem of homelessness and cites a pressing need for "innovative" solutions (paragraph 4). As you read, consider how innovative Beck's proposed solution is and how practical it would be to implement.*

Homelessness has become a persistent problem in urban environments   1
and multiplies rapidly in the periods of economic downturn that follow cycles of prosperity. In New York City, for example, recognized by some as the homeless capital of the world, the dim economic forecast through at least the year 2007 makes it exceedingly improbable that there will be additional funds to alleviate the resurgent homeless situation. Families with children are entering the homeless system in record numbers that have surpassed even the dreadful surge of homelessness during the Koch administration in the 1980s.[1] Regardless of the reasons that homeless families enter the shelter system, they should be accorded the highest priority of attention, because children are the group most vulnerable to the pernicious effects of homelessness. There is a moral and constitutional duty to insure that homeless children, who are the victims rather than the cause of their family's plight, will have a chance for education, happiness and an opportunity to obtain a piece of the mythical American dream.

Too often in New York City there is an ongoing struggle between not-   2
for-profit advocacy groups and the Department of Homeless Services, regarding issues related to intake, shelter and services for the homeless. Without the efforts of the non-government organizations the shelter system would be in even more dismal shape. Not every city has a staunch defender of the rights of the homeless like Justice Helen E. Freedman of the New York State Supreme Court. She has played a major role in shaping the city's policies for the homeless, with particular concern for the treatment of families with children. Despite all efforts by government and the private sector, the situation of the homeless remains perilous. Successive

[1]Edward Koch was the mayor of New York City from 1978 to 1989.

New York City administrations have continued to house homeless families in deteriorated and dangerous welfare hotels and motels, rife with drugs, prostitution and violence, that are the children's learning curricula in these unchartered crime academies.

3   Since it is an acknowledged fact that cities cannot afford to build a sufficiency of low-income housing with concomitant support services for the homeless, other options should be explored. A New York City proposal to house the homeless in an abandoned prison showed a typical government insensitivity to this population group. . . . it appeared that the government was going to put the homeless in jail. When the homeless problem became a major embarrassment to the Koch administration in the mid-eighties, homeless families were placed in decrepit midtown Manhattan hotels, where no tourists in their right minds would have conceived of spending even one night. These hotels could not previously rent rooms for $29.00 per night. Suddenly they were billing the city $100.00 per night. . . . The Bloomberg administration continues to house the homeless in tawdry hotels and motels at the cost of $3,500.00 to $4,500.00 per month, for rooms that most people would deem uninhabitable.[2] . . . It was beyond the capacity of the Giuliani administration to address the needs of the working poor.[3] Therefore, a convoluted mechanism to avoid the issue was contrived: emergency funds for temporary housing only, however extravagant the cost of the rentals. We are confronted with a peculiar dysfunction when the government pays upper-middle-class rental rates for accommodations below slum standards.

4   There are no simple solutions for this desperate situation that devours the futures of hundreds of youth annually. The real problem is society's lack of will to urgently address an issue that should have been resolved in the 19th century: cooperation between the government and the private sector to provide solutions for the problems of the needy. There is an overwhelming need to develop innovative plans that will concentrate efforts on alleviating the burdens of homelessness on the most fragile group, families with children. One possible plan would target economically depressed communities, using upstate New York as an example, that are struggling to remain solvent and functional. This could be a model for other areas of the country. Depressed communities face a grim future, with little hope of the arrival of new industries that will replace lost blue collar and farm jobs. Certain qualifying communities could be offered a partnership with select pioneer homeless families, in a venture that could benefit both groups.

5   Appropriate towns that have an infrastructure of schools, transportation, medical services, grocery stores, laundromats and most important, a civic system capable of problem solving would be identified. They would

[2]Michael Bloomberg became mayor in 2002.

[3]Rudolph Giuliani was mayor from 1994 to 2001.

be approached by designated personnel who would present a proposal that would demonstrate the economic benefits to the towns for providing residential sites and a supportive environment for designated homeless families. Abandoned property would be leased, reactivating the tax base for the towns. Renovation of the properties would stimulate local employment and generate earnings for businesses that sell construction materials and supplies. Support services for the families would develop new jobs that would infuse cash in the towns. Some jobs, after negotiations with the towns, would be reserved for the new residents. Living expenses of the families would directly contribute cash to the local economies.

Suitable families would be recruited for "small town pioneering" after a careful selection and preparation process. The first requirement would be functionality. The mentally ill homeless would not be an appropriate target group. But at least 25% to 30% of homeless families are functional, many having fallen into the system because of economic disaster like loss of job, or a fire that destroyed home or apartment, etc. The benefits of small town life would be presented as a positive alternative to the stress of urban shelters and poverty communities. The families would have to be prepared to adapt to a new and unaccustomed environment. The towns would also need preparation to receive a new population group as welcome neighbors. Job development for both town residents and the newcomer families would be a priority.

The small town pioneering program would start as a pilot project. Appropriate personnel would be assigned to contact potentially qualified towns. Ten towns would be chosen to house ten families each, for a total of one hundred families. Questionnaires should be developed in cooperation with NGOs[4] and the Departments of Homeless Services to identify qualified families, willing to undergo a major change in their way of life. Funds required for the initial phase of the project, outreach to the designated towns and families, are minimal. If funds are not available from the Department of Homeless Services, or other concerned government agencies, they would be solicited from private foundations. Once towns and families have been selected, project activities would commence simultaneously in the towns and the homeless shelters.

The towns should identify suitable residential space, preferably one- or two-family homes that have been underutilized or abandoned, that would then be renovated for habitation. Assisted living services would be identified and organized. Social workers, one per town, each to manage a caseload of ten families, would be recruited, with incentives offered to induce them to live in the community. Budgets for living expenses would be prepared. Training for the families in small town living skills would be followed by orientation tours of the intended communities. There would be

[4]NGOs are nongovernmental organizations, or private nonprofit groups.

introductions to the local residents: shopkeepers, teachers, town officials, neighbors, etc. The families and towns respectively should be prepared to fulfill their obligations to each other. The nearest colleges should be invited to participate in the project and provide educational services, as well as job or career training.

9   Funding for this demonstration program would be requested from the New York State legislature, various federal agencies, the New York City Department of Homeless Services, the office of the Mayor of New York City, private foundations and corporations. Small town pioneering should be developed as a model program that would be replicable, after an appropriate demonstration period. The relatively low start-up cost per family, as well as proportionately low operating costs, would be far less than the cost of housing a family in a temporary shelter. This would make it possible to run the program for far less than the cost to maintain a family in a shelter, which is approximately $45,000 annually for a family of three. The savings to the taxpayer would be considerable and the benefits to both towns and families would be immense.

10   Concerned officials, agencies and NGOs should consider this program as a possible amelioration to the problem of homelessness for a substantial number of families capable of rebuilding their future. This proposal is presented as only one possible solution to a major problem for which many new initiatives are needed. Other programs that could be explored might include: the development of co-operative apartment houses; an urban pioneering initiative utilizing abandoned buildings in poverty neighborhoods, for reclamation as housing stock; perhaps a more daring venture in commune/kibbutz experiments. Hopefully, these suggestions will stimulate consideration by those concerned with the future well-being of neglected members of our society, of the urgent need for new, practical solutions for the problems of homeless families with children.

READING FOR MEANING

This section presents three activities that will help you think about the meanings in Beck's proposal essay.

Read to Comprehend

Write a few sentences briefly summarizing Beck's proposed solution.

Identify any words with meanings you are unsure of—such as *resurgent* (paragraph 1) and *concomitant* (3)—and find the dictionary definition for each word that makes the best sense in the context.

To help you understand this reading better, also consider trying one of these critical reading strategies, explained in Appendix 1: *outlining* or *questioning to understand and remember.*

Read to Respond

Write a paragraph or two exploring your initial thoughts and feelings about Beck's proposal. Focus on anything that stands out for you, perhaps because it resonates with your own experience or because you find a statement puzzling. For example, consider writing about one of the following:

- the fact that New York City has paid to "house the homeless in tawdry hotels and motels at the cost of $3,500.00 to $4,500.00 per month, for rooms that most people would deem uninhabitable" (paragraph 3);

- the ways that the "pioneer homeless families" and residents of small towns might react to Beck's proposed solution or the ways that you might react if you were in their place (4); or

- your feelings, as a college student, about Beck's suggestion that local colleges "provide," presumably free of charge, "educational services, as well as job or career training" to the pioneer homeless families (8).

To help develop your response, also consider trying one of these critical reading strategies, explained in Appendix 1: *contextualizing* or *reflecting on challenges to your beliefs and values*.

Read to Analyze Assumptions

Write a paragraph or two analyzing an assumption in Beck's essay. To think critically about assumptions, here are some kinds of questions you could ask: Who holds this assumption (the writer, readers, and/or others cited in the essay)? What are the effects of the assumption in the context of the essay specifically or in society more generally? What do you think about the assumption, and is there anything in the essay that raises doubts about it? How does the assumption reinforce or critique commonly held views, and are there any alternative ideas, beliefs, or values that would challenge this assumption?

You might choose an assumption from the list below, using the questions accompanying it in addition to the ones above to help you get started. Or you can choose another assumption in the essay to explore.

- **assumptions about society's responsibility to children.** In paragraph 1, Beck asserts that our society has "a moral and constitutional duty to insure that homeless children . . . will have a chance for education, happiness and an opportunity to obtain a piece of the mythical American dream."

   To think critically about the assumptions in this essay related to society's responsibility to children, homeless or not, ask yourself questions like these: In referring to "a moral and constitutional duty," what does Beck assume is the basis for society's responsibility? Do you think that most Americans, and do you individually, agree that we share a *moral* as well as a *constitutional* responsibility to help the homeless? Why do you think Beck assumes the American dream is *mythical*?

- **assumptions about causes of homelessness.** In defining the problem of homelessness, Beck suggests that it is part of a larger issue: "the needs of the working poor" (3) and "the problems of the needy" (4). He also makes a distinction between "mentally ill" and "functional" homeless people (6) and points out that "at least 25% to 30% of homeless families are functional, many having fallen into the system because of economic disaster like loss of job, or a fire that destroyed home or apartment" (6).

    To think critically about the assumptions in this essay related to the causes of homelessness, ask yourself questions like these: Why do you think Beck makes this distinction and puts homelessness in a broader economic context? What does he seem to assume about the reasons people become homeless, and whom does he hold responsible? How does the knowledge that some homeless people have jobs affect Beck's—and possibly your own—attitude toward the homeless?

To help you analyze assumptions in Beck's essay, also consider trying one of these critical reading strategies, explained in Appendix 1: *evaluating the logic of an argument* or *judging the writer's credibility*.

READING LIKE A WRITER

PRESENTING THE PROPOSED SOLUTION

In some cases, the solution can simply be named and briefly described. However, Beck cannot point to an example of his solution that has already been put into practice. Therefore, he calls his proposed solution "innovative" (paragraph 4) and sets out a detailed plan to show how it could be implemented. Explaining how the solution could be put into effect not only introduces the solution but also serves as part of the argument for it because if readers are not convinced that the solution is feasible and can be put into effect, they are unlikely even to consider it. The need to show how it could be implemented is especially crucial in Beck's case because his proposal is unusual and would require the enthusiastic cooperation of the homeless families who would be relocated, the government officials who would administer the program, the voters who would have to fund it, and the small-town residents and officials who would have to accommodate strangers into their communities.

Analyze

1. Reread paragraphs 4 to 9, where Beck provides many details about how his "small town pioneering program" could be implemented. Note in the margin each element of his implementation plan as it is brought up.

2. Choose one element of the implementation to analyze closely. Consider who, in particular, he's addressing, what concerns he anticipates they

have, and how he tries to convince them that this part of his plan is indeed workable.

Write

Write several sentences identifying the main elements of Beck's implementation plan and then focus on the part of the plan you analyzed, explaining how Beck tries to convince readers that this part of his plan is workable.

CONSIDERING IDEAS FOR YOUR OWN WRITING

Beck's topic suggests a type of proposal that you might want to consider for your essay—a proposal to improve the living or working conditions of one or more groups of people. You could focus on a particular category of people and a problem they face. For example, you might think of ways to help elderly and infirm people in your community who need transportation, or you might want to help elementary school kids who have no after-school music or sports programs. If you were to write about developing a job-training and referral program for your campus to help college students find work to pay for their education, you could begin by finding out what resources are already available on your campus and check the Internet to discover if other campuses provide any services that might be useful. You might also interview students as well as employers in the community to see whether a new campus job-referral service could be developed or an existing one could be improved.

Karen Kornbluh

Win-Win Flexibility

Karen Kornbluh worked in the private sector as an economist and management consultant and in the public sector as director of the office of legislative and intergovernmental affairs at the Federal Communications Commission before becoming the deputy chief of staff at the Treasury Department in the Clinton administration. She has been a senior adviser to President Barack Obama and served as the ambassador to the Organization for Economic Co-operation and Development.

As director of the Work and Family Program at the New America Foundation, a nonprofit, nonpartisan institute that sponsors research and conferences on public policy issues, Kornbluh led an effort to change the American workplace to accommodate what she calls the new "juggler family," in which parents have to juggle their time for parenting and work. Her book Running Harder to Stay in Place: The Growth of Family Work Hours and Incomes *was published in 2005 by the New America Foundation, and Kornbluh's articles have appeared in such venues as the* New York Times, *the* Washington Post, *and the* Atlantic Monthly. *The following proposal was published in 2005 by the Work and Family Program.*

As you read, think about your own experiences as a child or a parent and the ways that they affect your response to Kornbluh's proposal. Have you or your parents had to juggle time for parenting and work—and if so, how did you or they manage it?

INTRODUCTION

1   Today fully 70 percent of families with children are headed by two working parents or by an unmarried working parent. The "traditional family" of the breadwinner and homemaker has been replaced by the "juggler family," in which no one is home full-time. Two-parent families are working 10 more hours a week than in 1979 (Bernstein and Kornbluh).

2   To be decent parents, caregivers, and members of their communities, workers now need greater flexibility than they once did. Yet good part-time or flex-time jobs remain rare. Whereas companies have embraced flexibility in virtually every other aspect of their businesses (inventory control, production schedules, financing), full-time workers' schedules remain largely inflexible. Employers often demand workers be available around the clock. Moreover, many employees have no right to a minimum number of sick or vacation days; almost two-thirds of all workers—and an even larger percentage of low-income parents—lack the ability to take a day off to care for a family member (Lovell). The Family and Medical Leave Act (FMLA) of 1993 finally guaranteed that workers at large companies could take a leave of absence for the birth or adoption of a baby, or for the illness of a family member. Yet that guaranteed leave is unpaid.

Many businesses are finding ways to give their most valued employees flexibility but, all too often, workers who need flexibility find themselves shunted into part-time, temporary, on-call, or contract jobs with reduced wages and career opportunities—and, often, no benefits. A full quarter of American workers are in these jobs. Only 15 percent of women and 12 percent of men in such jobs receive health insurance from their employers (Wenger). A number of European countries provide workers the right to a part-time schedule and all have enacted legislation to implement a European Union directive to prohibit discrimination against part-time workers. 3

In America, employers are required to accommodate the needs of employees with disabilities—even if that means providing a part-time or flexible schedule. Employers may also provide religious accommodations for employees by offering a part-time or flexible schedule. At the same time, employers have no obligation to allow parents or employees caring for sick relatives to work part-time or flexible schedules, even if the cost to the employer would be inconsequential. 4

In the twenty-first-century global economy, America needs a new approach that allows businesses to gain flexibility in staffing without sacrificing their competitiveness and enables workers to gain control over their work lives without sacrificing their economic security. This win-win flexibility arrangement will not be the same in every company, nor even for each employee working within the same organization. Each case will be different. But flexibility will not come for all employees without some education, prodding, and leadership. So employers and employees must be required to come to the table to work out a solution that benefits everyone. American businesses must be educated on strategies for giving employees flexibility without sacrificing productivity or morale. And businesses should be recognized and rewarded when they do so. 5

America is a nation that continually rises to the occasion. At the dawn of a new century, we face many challenges. One of these is helping families to raise our next generation in an increasingly demanding global economy. This is a challenge America must meet with imagination and determination. 6

BACKGROUND: THE NEED FOR WORKPLACE FLEXIBILITY

Between 1970 and 2000, the percentage of mothers in the workforce rose from 38 to 67 percent (Smolensky and Gootman). Moreover, the number of hours worked by dual-income families has increased dramatically. Couples with children worked a full 60 hours a week in 1979. By 2000 they were working 70 hours a week (Bernstein and Kornbluh). And more parents than ever are working long hours. In 2000, nearly 1 out of every 8 couples with children was putting in 100 hours a week or more on the job, compared to only 1 out of 12 families in 1970 (Jacobs and Gerson). 7

8   In addition to working parents, there are over 44.4 million Americans who provide care to another adult, often an older relative. Fifty-nine percent of these caregivers either work or have worked while providing care ("Caregiving").

9   In a 2002 report by the Families and Work Institute, 45 percent of employees reported that work and family responsibilities interfered with each other "a lot" or "some" and 67 percent of employed parents report that they do not have enough time with their children (Galinksy, Bond, and Hill).

10   Over half of workers today have no control over scheduling alternative start and end times at work (Galinksy, Bond, and Hill). According to a recent study by the Institute for Women's Policy Research, 49 percent of workers—over 59 million Americans—lack basic paid sick days for themselves. And almost two-thirds of all workers—and an even larger percentage of low-income parents—lack the ability to take a day off to care for a family member (Lovell). Thirteen percent of non-poor workers with caregiving responsibilities lack paid vacation leave, while 28 percent of poor caregivers lack any paid vacation time (Heymann). Research has shown that flexible arrangements and benefits tend to be more accessible in larger and more profitable firms, and then to the most valued professional and managerial workers in those firms (Golden). Parents with young children and working welfare recipients—the workers who need access to paid leave the most—are the least likely to have these benefits, according to research from the Urban Institute (Ross Phillips).

11   In the U.S., only 5 percent of workers have access to a job that provides paid parental leave. The Family and Medical Leave Act grants the right to 12 weeks of unpaid leave for the birth or adoption of a child or for the serious illness of the worker or a worker's family member. But the law does not apply to employees who work in companies with fewer than 50 people, employees who have worked for less than a year at their place of employment, or employees who work fewer than 1,250 hours a year. Consequently, only 45 percent of parents working in the private sector are eligible to take even this unpaid time off (Smolensky and Gootman).

12   Workers often buy flexibility by sacrificing job security, benefits, and pay. Part-time workers are less likely to have employer-provided health insurance or pensions and their hourly wages are lower. One study in 2002 found that 43 percent of employed parents said that using flexibility would jeopardize their advancement (Galinksy, Bond, and Hill).

13   Children, in particular, pay a heavy price for workplace inflexibility (Waters Boots 2004). Almost 60 percent of child care arrangements are of poor or mediocre quality (Smolensky and Gootman). Children in low-income families are even less likely to be in good or excellent care settings. Full-day child care easily costs $4,000 to $10,000 per year—approaching the price of college tuition at a public university. As

a result of the unaffordable and low-quality nature of child care in this country, a disturbing number of today's children are left home alone: Over 3.3 million children age 6–12 are home alone after school each day (Vandivere et al.).

Many enlightened businesses are showing the way forward to a twenty- 14 first-century flexible workplace. Currently, however, businesses have little incentive to provide families with the flexibility they need. We need to level the playing field and remove the competitive disadvantages for all businesses that do provide workplace flexibility.

This should be a popular priority. A recent poll found that 77 percent 15 of likely voters feel that it is difficult for families to earn enough and still have time to be with their families. Eighty-four percent of voters agree that children are being short-changed when their parents have to work long hours. . . .

PROPOSAL: WIN-WIN FLEXIBILITY

A win-win approach in the U.S. to flexibility . . . might function as fol- 16 lows. It would be "soft touch" at first—requiring a process and giving business an out if it would be costly to implement—with a high-profile public education campaign on the importance of workplace flexibility to American business, American families, and American society. A survey at the end of the second year would determine whether a stricter approach is needed.

Employees would have the right to make a formal request to their 17 employers for flexibility in the number of hours worked, the times worked, and/or the ability to work from home. Examples of such flexibility would include part-time, annualized hours,[1] compressed hours,[2] flex-time,[3] job-sharing, shift working, staggered hours, and telecommuting.

The employee would be required to make a written application provid- 18 ing details on the change in work, the effect on the employer, and solutions to any problems caused to the employer. The employer would be required to meet with the employee and give the employee a decision on the request within two weeks, as well as provide an opportunity for an internal appeal within one month from the initial request.

The employee request would be granted unless the employer demon- 19 strated it would require significant difficulty or expense entailing more than ordinary costs, decreased job efficiency, impairment of worker safety,

---

[1]*Annualized hours* means working different numbers of hours a week but a fixed annual total.

[2]*Compressed hours* means working more hours a day in exchange for working fewer days a week.

[3]*Flex-time* means working on an adjustable daily schedule.

infringement of other employees' rights, or conflict with another law or regulation.

20 The employer would be required to provide an employee working a flexible schedule with the same hourly pay and proportionate health, pension, vacation, holiday, and FMLA benefits that the employee received before working flexibly and would be required thereafter to advance the employee at the same rate as full-time employees.

21 *Who would be covered:* Parents (including parents, legal guardians, foster parents) and other caregivers at first. Eventually all workers should be eligible in our flexible, 24 × 7 economy. During the initial period, it will be necessary to define non-parental "caregivers." One proposal is to define them as immediate relatives or other caregivers of "certified care recipients" (defined as those whom a doctor certifies as having three or more limitations that impede daily functioning—using diagnostic criteria such as Activities of Daily Living (ADL)/Instrumental Activities of Daily Living (IADL)—for at least 180 consecutive days). . . .

22 *Public Education:* Critical to the success of the proposal will be public education along the lines of the education that the government and business schools conducted in the 1980s about the need for American business to adopt higher quality standards to compete against Japanese business. A Malcolm Baldridge–like award[4] should be created for companies that make flexibility win-win. A public education campaign conducted by the Department of Labor should encourage small businesses to adopt best practices of win-win flexibility. Tax credits could be used in the first year to reward early adopters.

Works Cited

Bernstein, Jared, and Karen Kornbluh. "Running Harder to Stay in Place: The Growth of Family Work Hours and Incomes." *New America Foundation*. The New America Foundation, n.d. Web. 1 June 2005.

"Caregiving in the U.S." *The National Alliance for Caregiving* and *AARP*. Met Life Foundation, n.d. Web. 6 June 2005.

Galinksy, Ellen, James Bond, and Jeffrey E. Hill. "Workplace Flexibility: What Is It? Who Has It? Who Wants It? Does It Make a Difference?" *Families and Work Institute*. Families and Work Institute and IBM, n.d. Web. 1 June 2005.

Golden, Lonnie. "The Time Bandit: What U.S. Workers Surrender to Get Greater Flexibility in Work Schedules." *Economic Policy Institute*. Economic Policy Institute, n.d. Web. 1 June 2005.

Heymann, Jody. *The Widening Gap: Why America's Working Families Are in Jeopardy—and What Can Be Done about It*. New York: Basic, 2000. Print.

[4]The Malcolm Baldridge National Quality Award is given by the U.S. president to outstanding businesses.

Jacobs, Jerry, and Kathleen Gerson. *The Time Divide: Work, Family and Gender Inequality*. Cambridge: Harvard UP, 2004. Print.

Lovell, Vicky. "No Time to Be Sick: Why Everyone Suffers When Workers Don't Have Paid Sick Leave." *Institute for Women's Policy Research*. Institute for Women's Policy Research, n.d. Web. 3 June 2005.

Phillips, Katherin Ross. "Getting Time Off: Access to Leave among Working Parents." *Urban Institute*. Urban Institute, n.d. Web. 3 June 2005.

Smolensky, Eugene, and Jennifer A. Gootman, eds. *Working Families and Growing Kids: Caring for Children and Adolescents*. Washington, DC: National Academies P, 2003. Print.

Vandivere, Sharon, et al. "Unsupervised Time: Family and Child Factors Associated with Self-Care." *Urban Institute*. Urban Institute, n.d. Web. 1 June 2005.

Waters Boots, Shelley. "The Way We Work: How Children and Their Families Fare in a Twenty-first-Century Workplace." *New America Foundation*. New America Foundation, n.d. Web. 3 June 2005.

Wenger, Jeffrey. "Share of Workers in 'Nonstandard' Jobs Declines." *Economic Policy Institute*. Economic Policy Institute, n.d. Web. 1 June 2005.

READING FOR MEANING

This section presents three activities that will help you think about the meanings in Kornbluh's essay.

Read to Comprehend

Write a few sentences briefly summarizing Kornbluh's proposed solution.

Identify any words with meanings you are unsure of—such as *shunted* (paragraph 3) and *inconsequential* (4)—and find the dictionary definition for each word that makes the best sense in the context.

To help you understand the essay better, also consider trying one of these critical reading strategies, explained in Appendix 1: *summarizing* or *questioning to understand and remember*.

Read to Respond

Write several paragraphs exploring your initial thoughts and feelings about Kornbluh's proposal. Focus on anything that stands out for you, perhaps because it resonates with your own experience or because you find a statement puzzling. You might consider writing about the following:

- Kornbluh's assertion that the "traditional family of the breadwinner and homemaker has been replaced by the 'juggler family,' in which no one is home full-time" (paragraph 1);

- the fact that "[p]arents with young children and working welfare recipients—the workers who need access to paid leave the most—are the least likely to have" flexible arrangements at work (10);

- the idea that "[c]hildren, in particular, pay a heavy price for workplace inflexibility" (13), perhaps related to your own experience as a child or a parent.

To help develop your response, also consider trying one of these critical reading strategies, explained in Appendix 1: *contextualizing* or *reflecting on challenges to your beliefs and values*.

Read to Analyze Assumptions

Write a paragraph or two analyzing an assumption in Kornbluh's essay. To think critically about assumptions, here are some kinds of questions you could ask: Who holds this assumption (the writer, readers, and/or others cited in the essay)? What are the effects of the assumption in the context of the essay specifically or in society more generally? What do you think about the assumption, and is there anything in the essay that raises doubts about it? How does the assumption reinforce or critique commonly held views, and are there any alternative ideas, beliefs, or values that would challenge this assumption?

You might choose an assumption from the list below, using the questions accompanying it in addition to the ones above to help you get started. Or you can choose another assumption in the essay to explore.

- **assumptions about the poor quality of U.S. child-care arrangements.** In paragraph 13, Kornbluh cites research that finds that "[a]lmost 60 percent of child care arrangements are of poor or mediocre quality." She concludes that "[a]s a result of the unaffordable and low-quality nature of child care in this country, a disturbing number of today's children are left home alone: Over 3.3 million children age 6–12 are home alone after school each day (Vandivere et al.)." Note that she seems to assume that readers will accept the research she cites and yet she gives us no information about the standards used to evaluate different child-care arrangements.

  To think critically about assumptions in this essay related to child care, ask yourself questions like these: What criteria would you apply? What assumptions do you make about the quality of different child-care arrangements—such as a relative's or a teenager's babysitting or various kinds of private or public day-care facilities? Kornbluh also assumes that being "home alone after school" is bad for children age six to twelve. At what age do you think that it is safe to leave children home alone? What age do other people you know (including, perhaps, your parents) consider appropriate?

- **assumptions about motivating American business.** Kornbluh asserts that companies have been "largely inflexible" regarding "full-time workers' schedules" (paragraph 2). But she seems to assume that if business were educated and prodded as well as "rewarded," companies would give "employees flexibility without sacrificing productivity or morale" (5).

To think critically about the assumptions in this essay related to American business, ask yourself questions like these: Why do you think Kornbluh assumes companies would respond to government leadership, including education and prodding? Also, why would business need to be recognized and rewarded for doing something that does not sacrifice worker productivity or morale but actually might improve them?

To help you analyze assumptions in Kornbluh's essay, also consider trying one of these critical reading strategies, explained in Appendix 1: *looking for patterns of opposition* or *judging the writer's credibility*.

READING LIKE A WRITER

COUNTERARGUING READERS' OBJECTIONS AND ALTERNATIVE SOLUTIONS

Because proposal writers want their readers to accept their proposed solution and even to take action to help implement it, they must make an effort to anticipate objections to their argument as well as alternative solutions with which readers may be familiar. This task is a major part of what is known as counterargument. Kornbluh knows she faces tough opposition because changing the way businesses treat workers with family obligations calls for a significant change in thinking. Her proposal also involves money, and employers don't usually like to spend money on benefits for workers if they do not see how doing so would benefit their business. Kornbluh therefore devotes part of her proposal to counterargument. The following activity will guide you in analyzing her approach. It will also prepare you to anticipate and effectively counterargue readers' likely objections and popular alternative solutions in your own proposal.

Analyze

1. Reread paragraphs 2 to 3 and 10 to 12, noting where Kornbluh refers to alternative solutions readers could claim are already in place to solve the problem of the "juggler family." Look closely at the way Kornbluh presents these alternatives and consider whether she is able to demonstrate that they are not solving the problem.

2. Reread paragraph 21 where Kornbluh anticipates an objection to her proposal—that people (other than parents) could cheat by claiming to be caregivers. Notice how she handles this objection and consider whether her counterargument is likely to allay readers' concerns.

Write

Write several sentences explaining how Kornbluh anticipates and counter-argues alternative solutions and objections. Add a few sentences evaluating her counterarguments.

CONSIDERING IDEAS FOR YOUR OWN WRITING

Consider writing about a problem that seems to be national but might be solvable on a local scale for your community or college. For example, you might have your own ideas to add to Kornbluh's about how to solve the problem of getting adequate local child care for working parents. Or you might want to investigate whether local companies have policies about flex time for working parents. Other national problems are binge drinking and hazing in college fraternities or other social groups that sometimes lead to serious injury or even death. Perhaps you could propose a solution for groups in your college that are experiencing problems. "Suburban sprawl" is another national issue that might be affecting your area; do some research on planned growth to see if you could make a proposal to solve this or a similar problem.

A Special Reading Strategy

Recognizing Emotional Manipulation

Proposals sometimes try to arouse emotion in readers to fuel their desire to solve the problem or to urge readers to take a particular action. Following the guidelines for recognizing emotional manipulation in Appendix 1 (pp. 593–94), analyze Kornbluh's use of emotion in this proposal, and write a few sentences exploring what you have learned.

Patrick O'Malley

More Testing, More Learning

Patrick O'Malley wrote the following proposal while he was a first-year college student. He proposes that college professors give students frequent brief examinations in addition to the usual midterm and final exams. After discussing his unusual rhetorical situation—a student advising teachers on how to plan their courses—with his instructor, O'Malley decided to revise the essay into the form of an open letter to professors on his campus, a letter that might appear in the campus newspaper.

O'Malley's essay may strike you as unusually authoritative. This air of authority is due in large part to what O'Malley learned from interviewing two professors (his writing instructor and the writing program director) and several students in his classes. As you read, notice particularly how O'Malley responds to the objections to his proposal that he expects many professors to raise as well as their preferred solutions to the problem he identifies.

It's late at night. The final's tomorrow. You got a C on the midterm, so   1
this one will make or break you. Will it be like the midterm? Did you study
enough? Did you study the right things? It's too late to drop the course. So
what happens if you fail? No time to worry about that now—you've got a
ton of notes to go over.

Although this last-minute anxiety about midterm and final exams is   2
only too familiar to most college students, many professors may not realize how such major, infrequent, high-stakes exams work against the best
interests of students both psychologically and intellectually. They cause
unnecessary amounts of stress, placing too much importance on one or
two days in the students' entire term, judging ability on a single or dual
performance. They don't encourage frequent study, and they fail to inspire
students' best performance. If professors gave additional brief exams at
frequent intervals, students would be spurred to learn more, study more
regularly, worry less, and perform better on midterms, finals, and other
papers and projects.

Ideally, a professor would give an in-class test or quiz after each unit,   3
chapter, or focus of study, depending on the type of class and course material. A physics class might require a test on concepts after every chapter
covered, while a history class could necessitate quizzes covering certain
time periods or major events. These exams should be given weekly or at
least twice monthly. Whenever possible, they should consist of two or
three essay questions rather than many multiple-choice or short-answer
questions. To preserve class time for lecture and discussion, exams should
take no more than 15 or 20 minutes.

The main reason professors should give frequent exams is that when   4
they do and when they provide feedback to students on how well they

are doing, students learn more in the course and perform better on major exams, projects, and papers. It makes sense that in a challenging course containing a great deal of material, students will learn more of it and put it to better use if they have to apply or "practice" it frequently on exams, which also helps them find out how much they are learning and what they need to go over again. A 2006 study reported in *Psychological Science* journal concluded that "taking repeated tests on material leads to better long-term retention than repeated studying," according to the study's coauthors, Henry L. Roediger and Jeff Karpicke. When asked what the impact of this breakthrough research would be, they responded: "We hope that this research may be picked up in educational circles as a way to improve educational practices, both for students in the classroom and as a study strategy outside of class" (ScienceWatch.com, 2008). "Incorporating more frequent classroom testing into a course," the study concludes, "may improve students' learning and promote retention of material long after a course has ended" (qtd. in Science Blog, 2006). Many students already recognize the value of frequent testing, but their reason is that they need the professor's feedback. A Harvard study notes students' "strong preference for frequent evaluation in a course." Harvard students feel they learn least in courses that have "only a midterm and a final exam, with no other personal evaluation." They believe they learn most in courses with "many opportunities to see how they are doing" (Light, 1990, p. 32). In a review of a number of studies of student learning, Frederiksen (1984) reports that students who take weekly quizzes achieve higher scores on final exams than students who take only a midterm exam and that testing increases retention of material tested.

5   Another, closely related argument in favor of multiple exams is that they encourage students to improve their study habits. Greater frequency in test taking means greater frequency in studying for tests. Students prone to cramming will be required—or at least strongly motivated—to open their textbooks and notebooks more often, making them less likely to resort to long, kamikaze nights of studying for major exams. Since there is so much to be learned in the typical course, it makes sense that frequent, careful study and review are highly beneficial. But students need motivation to study regularly, and nothing works like an exam. If students had frequent exams in all their courses, they would have to schedule study time each week and gradually would develop a habit of frequent study. It might be argued that students are adults who have to learn how to manage their own lives, but learning history or physics is more complicated than learning to drive a car or balance a checkbook. Students need coaching and practice in learning. The right way to learn new material needs to become a habit, and I believe that frequent exams are key to developing good habits of study and learning. The Harvard study concludes that "tying regular evaluation

to good course organization enables students to plan their work more than a few days in advance. If quizzes and homework are scheduled on specific days, students plan their work to capitalize on them" (Light, 1990, p. 33).

By encouraging regular study habits, frequent exams would also   6 decrease anxiety by reducing the procrastination that produces anxiety. Students would benefit psychologically if they were not subjected to the emotional ups and downs caused by major exams, when after being virtually worry-free for weeks they are suddenly ready to check into the psychiatric ward. Researchers at the University of Vermont found a strong relationship among procrastination, anxiety, and achievement. Students who regularly put off studying for exams had continuing high anxiety and lower grades than students who procrastinated less. The researchers found that even "low" procrastinators did not study regularly and recommended that professors give frequent assignments and exams to reduce procrastination and increase achievement (Rothblum, Solomon, & Murakami, 1986, pp. 393, 394).

Research supports my proposed solution to the problems I have described.   7 Common sense as well as my experience and that of many of my friends support it. Why, then, do so few professors give frequent brief exams?

Some believe that such exams take up too much of the limited class   8 time available to cover the material in the course. Most courses meet 150 minutes a week—three times a week for 50 minutes each time. A 20-minute weekly exam might take 30 minutes to administer, and that is one-fifth of each week's class time. From the student's perspective, however, this time is well spent. Better learning and greater confidence about the course seem a good trade-off for another 30 minutes of lecture. Moreover, time lost to lecturing or discussion could easily be made up in students' learning on their own through careful regular study for the weekly exams. If weekly exams still seem too time consuming to some professors, their frequency could be reduced to every other week or their length to 5 or 10 minutes. In courses where multiple-choice exams are appropriate, several questions could be designed to take only a few minutes to answer.

Another objection professors have to frequent exams is that they take too   9 much time to read and grade. In a 20-minute essay exam, a well-prepared student can easily write two pages. A relatively small class of 30 students might then produce 60 pages, no small amount of material to read each week. A large class of 100 or more students would produce an insurmountable pile of material. There are a number of responses to this objection. Again, professors could give exams every other week or make them very short. Instead of reading them closely they could skim them quickly to see whether students understand an idea or can apply it to an unfamiliar problem; and instead of numerical or letter grades they could give a plus, check, or minus. Exams could be collected and responded to only every third or fourth week. Professors who have readers or teaching assistants could rely on them to grade or check exams. And the Scantron machine is always available for instant grading of multiple-choice exams. Finally, frequent exams could be given *in place of* a midterm exam or out-of-class essay assignment.

10   Since frequent exams seem to some professors to create too many problems, however, it is reasonable to consider alternative ways to achieve the same goals. One alternative solution is to implement a program that would improve study skills. While such a program might teach students how to study for exams, it cannot prevent procrastination or reduce "large test anxiety" by a substantial amount. One research team studying anxiety and test performance found that study skills training was not effective in reducing anxiety or improving performance (Dendato & Diener, 1986, p. 134). This team, which also reviewed other research that reached the same conclusion, did find that a combination of "cognitive/relaxation therapy" and study skills training was effective. This possible solution seems complicated, however, not to mention time consuming and expensive. It seems much easier and more effective to change the cause of the bad habit rather than treat the habit itself. That is, it would make more sense to solve the problem at its root: the method of learning and evaluation.

11   Still another solution might be to provide frequent study questions for students to answer. These would no doubt be helpful in focusing students' time studying, but students would probably not actually write out the answers unless they were required to. To get students to complete the questions in a timely way, professors would have to collect and check the answers. In that case, however, they might as well devote the time to grading an exam. Even if it asks the same questions, a scheduled exam is preferable to a set of study questions because it takes far less time to write in class, compared to the time students would devote to responding to questions at home. In-class exams also ensure that each student produces his or her own work.

12   Another possible solution would be to help students prepare for midterm and final exams by providing sets of questions from which the exam questions will be selected or announcing possible exam topics at the beginning of the course. This solution would have the advantage of reducing students' anxiety about learning every fact in the textbook, and it would clarify the course goals, but it would not motivate students to study carefully each new unit, concept, or text chapter in the course. I see this as a way of complementing frequent exams, not as substituting for them.

13   From the evidence and from my talks with professors and students, I see frequent, brief in-class exams as the only way to improve students' study habits and learning, reduce their anxiety and procrastination, and increase their satisfaction with college. These exams are not a panacea, but only more parking spaces and a winning football team would do as much to improve college life. Professors can't do much about parking or football, but they can give more frequent exams. Campus administrators should get

behind this effort, and professors should get together to consider giving exams more frequently. It would make a difference.

References

Dendato, K. M., & Diener, D. (1986). Effectiveness of cognitive/relaxation therapy and study skills training in reducing self-reported anxiety and improving the academic performance of test-anxious students. *Journal of Counseling Psychology, 33,* 131–135.

Frederiksen, N. (1984). The real test bias: Influences of testing on teaching and learning. *American Psychologist, 39,* 193–202.

Light, R. J. (1990). *Explorations with students and faculty about teaching, learning, and student life.* Cambridge, MA: Harvard University Graduate School of Education and Kennedy School of Government.

Rothblum, E. D., Solomon, L., & Murakami, J. (1986). Affective, cognitive, and behavioral differences between high and low procrastinators. *Journal of Counseling Psychology, 33,* 387–394.

ScienceBlog. (2006, March 7). To learn something, testing beats studying. [Web log message.]. Retrieved from http://www.scienceblog.com/cms/to_learn_something_testing_beats_studying_10161.html

ScienceWatch.com. (2008, February). Fast Breaking Papers - 2008. [Interview with authors H. L. Roediger & J. Karpicke about journal article Test-enhanced learning: Taking memory tests improves long-term retention]. Retrieved from http://sciencewatch.com/dr/fbp/2008/08febfbp/08febfbpRoedigerETAL/

READING FOR MEANING

This section presents three activities that will help you think about the meanings in O'Malley's proposal.

Read to Comprehend

Write a few sentences briefly explaining the problem O'Malley is trying to solve. Identify any words with meanings you are unsure of—such as *retention* (paragraph 4) and *kamikaze* (5)—and find the dictionary definition for each word that makes the best sense in the context.

To help you understand the essay better, also consider trying one of these critical reading strategies, explained in Appendix 1: *annotating* or *contextualizing*.

Read to Respond

Write several paragraphs exploring your initial thoughts and feelings about "More Testing, More Learning." Focus on anything that stands out for you, perhaps because it resonates with your own experience or because you find a statement puzzling. You might consider writing about the following:

- whether O'Malley's proposal, if it were adopted by professors, would make a difference in your own study habits or address any problems that you have with studying;

- the relation O'Malley attempts to establish between high-pressure exams and poor performance (paragraph 2), testing it against your own experience; or

- kinds of classes, in your experience, that are and are not suited to frequent brief exams.

To help develop your response, also consider trying one of these critical reading strategies, explained in Appendix 1: *looking for patterns of opposition* or *judging the writer's credibility.*

Read to Analyze Assumptions

Write a paragraph or two analyzing an assumption in O'Malley's essay. To think critically about assumptions, here are some kinds of questions you could ask: Who holds this assumption (the writer, readers, and/or others cited in the essay)? What are the effects of the assumption in the context of the essay specifically or in society more generally? What do you think about the assumption, and is there anything in the essay that raises doubts about it? How does the assumption reinforce or critique commonly held views, and are there any alternative ideas, beliefs, or values that would challenge this assumption?

You might choose an assumption from the list below, using the questions accompanying it in addition to the ones above to help you get started. Or you can choose another assumption in the essay to explore.

- **assumptions about the relationship between motivation and procrastination.** In paragraph 5, O'Malley argues that college students would be "strongly motivated . . . to open their textbooks and notebooks more often" if they had to take exams frequently. He explains that the assumption underlying this argument is that "students need motivation to study regularly." In the next paragraph, however, he reviews research on procrastination that "found that even 'low' procrastinators did not study regularly" (6).

   To think critically about the assumptions in this essay related to motivation and procrastination, ask yourself questions like these: What seems to be the relationship, if any, between motivation and procrastination? If even students categorized as "low" procrastinators "did not study regularly," does it make sense to assume, as O'Malley does, that frequent tests would motivate most students to do so? Given your own experiences and observations of other students, what would be likely to motivate most students and overcome their tendency to procrastinate?

- **assumptions about the "right way to learn."** O'Malley claims, "Students need coaching and practice in learning. The right way to learn new material needs to become a habit" (paragraph 5). He seems to assume that studying regularly is the "right way to learn" and that cramming the night before the exam is the wrong way.

To think critically about the assumptions in this essay related to the "right way to learn," ask yourself questions like these: Why does O'Malley assume that cramming is inferior to studying regularly? In your experience and observations of other students, to what extent, if any, does cramming result in poorer performance on exams? If students studied regularly, wouldn't they need to cram the night before the exam anyway to remind themselves of what they had studied days and weeks earlier? Do you think there is a single "right way"—or at least, a best way—for students to study? If so, what is it?

To help you analyze assumptions in O'Malley's essay, also consider trying one of these critical reading strategies, explained in Appendix 1: *reflecting on challenges to your beliefs and values* or *using a Toulmin analysis*.

READING LIKE A WRITER

ARGUING DIRECTLY FOR THE PROPOSED SOLUTION

Writers argue directly for a proposed solution by giving reasons and support. The reasons usually include the argument that the proposed solution would indeed solve the problem, and writers often also argue that it is feasible—in other words, could realistically be implemented in a practical way. But reasons alone will not convince critical readers. They need supporting evidence from authoritative sources—for example, testimony from experts who have experience with similar problems and solutions. To make readers see how the proposed solution is logically connected to the problem and convince them that it will work, writers may, for example, argue and provide evidence that the solution is likely to eliminate an important cause of the problem or that a similar solution has worked before in a comparable context.

Analyze

1. Skim paragraphs 4 to 6 of O'Malley's essay. In each paragraph, underline the sentence that announces the reason for the solution.

2. Note in the margin the kinds of support O'Malley relies on in these paragraphs.

3. Evaluate how effectively O'Malley argues to support his solution. Do the reasons seem plausible? Is one reason more convincing to you than the others? How convincing do you think O'Malley's intended readers—professors—would find the evidence he offers?

Write

Write a sentence or two describing how O'Malley supports his reasons. Add several sentences indicating which parts of the argument you find most and least convincing, and why.

CONSIDERING IDEAS FOR YOUR OWN WRITING

Much of what happens in high school and college is predictable and conventional. Examples of conventional practices that have changed very little over the years are exams, classroom lectures, graduation ceremonies, required courses, and lower admission requirements for athletes. Think of additional examples of established practices in high school or college. Then select one that you believe needs to be improved or refined in some way. What changes would you propose? What individual or group might be convinced to take action on your proposal for improvement? What questions or objections should you anticipate? How could you discover whether others have previously proposed improvements in the practice you are concerned with? Whom might you interview to learn more about the practice and the likelihood of changing it?

A Special Reading Strategy

Comparing and Contrasting Related Readings: O'Malley's and Varley's Proposals to Improve Education

Comparing and contrasting related readings is a critical reading strategy useful both in reading for meaning and in reading like a writer. This strategy is particularly applicable when writers present similar subjects, as is the case in the proposals by Patrick O'Malley (p. 525) and Jeff Varley (p. 533). These writers have identified problems that affect the quality of education at the high-school and college levels. To compare and contrast these two proposals, think about issues such as these:

- Compare how the two writers describe the problems they are trying to solve. Highlight the places in each essay where the problem is presented. What strategies—such as narrating an anecdote, presenting a scenario, citing statistics, and quoting authorities—does each of the writers use to help readers understand the problem and appreciate its significance?

- Compare how the two writers support their proposed solutions and how they counterargue objections or questions that readers might raise as well as alternative solutions that readers might prefer. How effectively do you think each writer addresses readers' likely concerns?

See Appendix 1 (pp. 596–601) for detailed guidelines on comparing and contrasting related readings.

Jeff Varley

High-School Starting Time

Jeff Varley wrote this essay for a first-year college composition course. As you read, think about your own experiences waking up early to attend class. How well do you think that Varley supports his proposed solution?

The other readings in this chapter are followed by reading and writing activities. Following this reading, however, you are on your own to decide how to read for meaning and read like a writer.

Ah, sweet memories of high school: waking up at 6:30 in the morning, stumbling into the bathroom to get ready for the day, dressing while still half asleep, munching a piece of toast while listening to our parents tell us that if we just went to bed earlier we wouldn't be so sleepy in the morning (or worse, listening to our parents call us lazy), catching the bus as the sun began to top the trees, and wandering into our first period classes merely to lay our head down on our desks to doze off for the next fifty-five minutes.

We never could seem to catch up on our sleep, especially during the week. And even if we followed our parents' advice and tried going to bed earlier, the earlier bed time did not make much, if any, difference in how awake we were the next morning. In fact, for those of us who tried going to bed earlier, we generally just lay there until 10:30 or 11:00 before finally going to sleep. The next school morning we were still as tired as when we had gone to bed later.

But recent studies have provided evidence that the sleep patterns for adolescents are significantly different from those of both young children and adults. Studies by Mary Carskadon, a professor of psychiatry and human behavior at the Brown University School of Medicine and Director of Sleep and Chronobiology Research at E. P. Bradley Hospital in East Providence, Rhode Island, on sleep patterns in people revealed that adolescents, as opposed to younger children or adults, actually function better when they go to bed later and awake later. Professor Carskadon's research demonstrates that most adolescents' biological clocks are naturally set to a different pattern than the clocks of most children and adults.

The timing of the need for sleep also shows biological changes as children reach puberty. Melatonin, a hormone produced in the pineal gland, is an indicator for the biological clock that influences wake/sleep cycles. Carefully controlled studies found that "more mature adolescents had a later timing of the termination of melatonin secretion" (Carskadon 351). This indicates that postpubescent teens have a biological need to sleep later in the morning. The impact of forcing people to try to be alert when every nerve in their body is begging for more sleep can only be negative.

This discovery has a major impact on high-school students who are required to awaken early in order to arrive at school early, for asking teens to learn a complex subject, such as math, science, or English, before the brain is awake is futile.

5   Tardiness, poor grades, depression, automobile accidents, after-school-on-the-job accidents, and general lethargy have all been identified as the consequences of insufficient sleep among high-school students. Yet school districts persist in retaining high-school starting times that begin early in the morning, usually around 7:30 a.m. But such an early starting time does not benefit the students for whom the educational system is supposedly structured. How do we resolve the conflict of early high-school starting times versus sleepy students?

6   One obvious solution would be to start high-school classes later in the morning. A later starting time for high schools can be a controversial proposal if all of the affected parties are not consulted and kept informed. Kyla Wahlstrom of the Center for Applied Research and Educational Improvement at the University of Minnesota points out that "changing a school's starting time provokes the same kind of emotional reaction from stakeholders as closing a school or changing a school's attendance area" (Wahlstrom 346). Presumably, if parents and other interested parties knew about Carskadon's research, they would be more willing to consider changing the start time for high school.

7   Some schools have recognized the benefits of later starting time and have implemented a new schedule. One such school is located in eastern Minnesota. In 1996 the Edina School District pushed back the start time for 1,400 high-school students from 7:25 to 8:30 a.m. Edina Public School District Superintendent Kenneth Dragseth reported that the later schedule has led to better grades, fewer behavioral problems, and a better-rested student body (Dragseth). Dragseth's anecdotal evidence that better-rested students perform better is supported by research performed by psychologists at the College of the Holy Cross in Worcester, Massachusetts. Working with Carskadon, the psychologists "surveyed more than 3,120 Providence [Rhode Island] area high-school students and found students who got A's and B's averaged about 35 minutes more sleep on both weeknights and weekends than students who received D's and F's" (Bettelheim 557).

8   In addition to better grades, other positive effects cited by researchers include better attendance, fewer tardies, far fewer students falling asleep at their desks, more alert students more engaged in the learning process, less depression, fewer problems at home and among friends, enhanced school atmosphere, and fewer illnesses (Lawton; Wahlstrom and Taylor). With so many benefits to starting high-school classes later, why haven't more districts done so?

9   One of the most common concerns comes from participants in extra-curricular activities. If practices currently often run until 8 or 9 p.m. with

a school day that begins at 7:30 a.m., what will happen if school starts an hour later? This is a legitimate concern that would need to be addressed on a team-by-team or group-by-group basis. Some practice sessions could be held immediately after class in the early afternoon. Some activities could convene after a short dinner break. If these activities began earlier in the evening, they could be finished sooner in the evening. The one factor every coach or sponsor would have to consider is how important any extracurricular activity is in relation to the primary mission of the school, which, of course, is learning and education, not sports or clubs.

Availability of buses is another concern for many school districts when   10
any discussion of changing schedules begins. School officials in Montgomery County, Maryland, estimate it would cost $31 million to buy enough buses to accommodate later start times for high school without inconveniencing elementary and middle-school students (Bettelheim 557). Minneapolis, which buses 90 percent of the 50,000 students in the school district, solved the transportation problems caused by starting high-school classes later by starting the grade school classes earlier (Lawton). This has the added benefits of bringing younger children to school at a time when many of them are most alert and decreasing the need for before-school child care for these students (Reiss; Lawton). With careful planning and scheduling, the transportation tribulations can be addressed in cost-effective ways.

As the world we live in becomes ever more complex, education   11
becomes ever more important. It is important that the time spent on education be spent as effectively as possible. It is time to look at school schedules that provide the best education at times that are most appropriate to the students. James Maas, a psychologist at Cornell University, points out that "people are beginning to realize it doesn't make sense to pay heavy school taxes when the audience you're teaching is asleep" (qtd. in Bettelheim 556).

Works Cited

Bettelheim, Adriel. "Sleep Deprivation." *CQ Researcher* 8 (1998): 555–62. Print.

Carskadon, Mary A. "When Worlds Collide: Adolescent Need for Sleep versus Societal Demands." *Phi Delta Kappan* 80 (1999): 348–53. Print.

Dragseth, Kenneth A. "A Minneapolis Suburb Reaps Early Benefits from a Late Start." *American Association of School Administrators.* AASA, n.d. Web. 22 Mar. 2003.

Lawton, Millicent. "For Whom the Bell Tolls." *American Association of School Administrators.* AASA, n.d. Web. 22 Mar. 2003.

Reiss, Tammy. "Wake-up Call on Kids' Biological Clocks." *NEA Today* 6.6 (1998): 19. Print.

Wahlstrom, Kyla L. "The Prickly Politics of School Starting Times." *Phi Delta Kappan* 80 (1999): 345–47. Print.

Wahlstrom, Kyla L., and John S. Taylor. "Sleep Research Warns: Don't Start High School without the Kids." *Education Digest* 66 (2000): 15–20. *MasterFILE Premier*. Web. 22 Mar. 2003.

READING FOR MEANING

Reading for meaning involves three activities:

- reading to comprehend,
- reading to respond, and
- reading to analyze assumptions.

Write a page or so explaining your understanding of the meaning of Varley's essay, a personal response you have to it, and one of its assumptions.

READING LIKE A WRITER

Writers of proposals

- introduce the problem,
- present the solution,
- argue directly for the proposed solution, and
- counterargue readers' objections and alternative solutions.

Choose one of these strategies in Varley's essay, and analyze it carefully through close rereading and annotating. Then write several sentences explaining what you have learned, giving examples from the reading to support your explanation. Add a few sentences evaluating how successfully Varley uses the strategy to construct a persuasive argument.

Reviewing What Makes an Effective Essay

Proposals

Analyze

Choose *one* reading from this chapter that seems to you especially effective. Before rereading the selection, jot down one or two reasons you remember it as an example of good proposal writing.

Reread your chosen selection and add further notes about what makes it a particularly successful example. Consider the selection's purpose and how well it achieves that purpose for its intended readers. (You can make an informed guess about the intended readers and their expectations by noting the publication source of the essay.) Then assess how well the essay uses the writing strategies of introducing the problem, presenting the solution, arguing directly for the proposed solution, and counterarguing readers' objections and alternative solutions.

Write

Write at least a page supporting your choice of this reading as an example of effective proposal writing. Refer to details and specific parts of the essay as you explain how it works as a proposal and as you justify your evaluation of its effectiveness. You need not argue that it is the best reading in the chapter or that it is flawless, only that it is, in your view, a strong example of the genre.

A GUIDE TO WRITING PROPOSALS

This Guide to Writing is designed to assist you in writing your essay. Here you will find activities to help you identify a subject and discover what to say about it, organize your ideas and draft the essay, read the draft critically, revise the draft to strengthen your argument, and edit and proofread the essay to improve readability.

INVENTION AND RESEARCH

The following activities will help you choose a problem for study, analyze the problem and identify a solution, consider your readers, develop an argument for your proposed solution, and research your proposal.

Choosing a Problem

List the most promising subjects you can think of, beginning with any you listed for the Considering Ideas for Your Own Writing activities following the readings in this chapter. Rather than limiting yourself to the first subject that comes to mind, take a few minutes to consider your options and list as many subjects as you can. Below are some criteria that can help you choose a promising subject.

Criteria for Choosing a Subject

The problem should be

- important to you and of concern to others;
- solvable, at least in part;
- one that you know a good deal about and/or can research in the time you have.

A good choice for a problem is one facing a group to which you belong or have access, so that you can interview people affected by the problem and know who might be in a position to take action to solve it. Consider making a list of communities you are a part of (for example, your residence hall, hometown neighborhood, or religious community), groups you have joined (for example, a sports team, multiplayer online game site, or garage band), and places you have worked (for example, college radio station, community pool, or fast-food restaurant). Then, try to think of problems plaguing some of the places or groups you listed. For example, if you work as a tutor in the learning center, you might have noticed problems having to do with scheduling or with training and supervision. Your residence hall may have problems with noise, food, or parking space.

DEVELOPING YOUR PROPOSAL

The writing and research activities that follow will enable you to test your problem and develop an argument supporting your proposed solution.

Analyzing the Problem.   Write a few sentences in response to each of these questions:

- Does the problem really exist? How can you tell?

- What caused this problem? Consider immediate and deeper causes.

- What is the history of the problem?

- What might be the long-term consequences of the problem?

- Who in the community or group is affected by the problem?

- Does anyone benefit from the existence of the problem?

Considering Your Readers.   With your understanding of the problem in mind, write for a few minutes about your intended readers. Will you be writing to all members of your group or to only some of them? To an outside committee that might supervise or evaluate the group or to an individual in a position of authority inside or outside the group? Briefly justify your choice of readers. Then gauge how much they already know about the problem and what solutions they might prefer. Consider the problem's direct or indirect impact on them. Comment on what values and attitudes you share with your readers and how they have responded to similar problems in the past.

Finding a Tentative Solution.   List at least three possible solutions to the problem. Think about solutions that have already been tried as well as solutions that have been proposed for related problems. Find, if you can, solutions that eliminate causes of the problem. Also consider solutions that reduce the symptoms of the problem. If the problem seems too complex to be solved all at once, list solutions for one or more parts of it. Maybe a series of solutions is required and a key solution should be proposed first. From your list, choose the solution that seems to you most timely and practicable and write two or three sentences describing it.

Supporting Your Solution.   Write down every plausible reason why your solution should be heard or tried. Then review your list and highlight the strongest reasons, the ones most likely to persuade your readers. Write for a few minutes about the single most convincing reason. Support this reason in any way you can. You want to build an argument that readers will take seriously.

Anticipating Readers' Objections.   Write a few sentences defending your solution against each of the following predictable objections. For your proposal to succeed, readers must be convinced to take the solution seriously. Try to imagine how your prospective readers will respond.

- It won't really solve the problem.

- I'm comfortable with things as they are.

- We can't afford it.

- It will take too long.

- People won't do it.

- Too few people will benefit.

- It's already been tried, with unsatisfactory results.

- You're making this proposal because it will benefit you personally.

Counterarguing Alternative Solutions. Identify two or three other solutions that your readers may prefer to your own. Choose the one that poses the most likely or serious challenge to your proposed solution. Then write a few sentences comparing your solution with the alternative one, weighing the strengths and weaknesses of each. Explain how you might demonstrate to readers that your solution has more advantages and fewer disadvantages than the alternative.

Researching Your Proposal. In exploring the problem, considering possible solutions, and trying to develop your argument and counterargument, you may have identified questions you need to research. Make notes about the kinds of support that might help you establish the seriousness of the problem and convince readers that your proposed solution is preferable to other solutions they might prefer. Doing research with your questions and notes in mind will help you work efficiently. But recognize that you might also find contradictory evidence that leads you to rethink your ideas.

If you are proposing a solution to a problem about which others have written, you will want to do library and Internet research to find out how they have defined the problem and what solutions they have proposed, as well as any that have already been tried. If the problem is in a group to which you belong or have access, consider conducting interviews to see how people in the group are affected by the problem, what they know about its history, what solutions they prefer, and how they react to your proposed solution.

Formulating a Working Thesis. Draft a working thesis statement. A working thesis helps you begin drafting your essay purposefully. The thesis statement in a proposal is simply a statement of the solution you propose. Keep in mind that you may need to revise your working thesis as you learn more about your subject and as you draft your essay.

Review the readings in this chapter to see how other writers construct their thesis statements. For example, recall that Patrick O'Malley states his thesis in paragraph 2:

> If professors gave additional brief exams at frequent intervals, students would be spurred to learn more, study more regularly, worry less, and perform better on midterms, finals, and other papers and projects.

O'Malley's thesis announces his solution—brief, frequent exams—to the problems that students experience in courses where testing is limited to anxiety-producing, high-stakes midterms and finals. The thesis lists the reasons that students will benefit from the solution in the order in which the benefits appear in the essay. A forecast is not a requirement of a thesis statement, but it does enable readers to predict the stages of the argument and thereby increases their understanding.

As you draft your own thesis statement, pay attention to the language you use. It should be clear and unambiguous, emphatic but appropriately qualified. Although you will probably refine your thesis statement as you draft and revise your essay, trying now to articulate it will help give your planning and drafting direction and impetus.

Considering Visuals.   Think about whether visuals—drawings, photographs, tables, or graphs—would strengthen your proposal. You could construct your own visuals, scan materials from books and magazines, or download them from the Internet. If you submit your essay electronically to other students and your instructor or if you post it on a Web site, consider including snippets of film or sound as well as photographs. Visual and auditory materials are not a requirement of a successful proposal, as you can tell from the readings in this chapter, but they could add a new dimension to your writing. If you want to use photographs or recordings of people, though, be sure to obtain their permission.

DRAFTING

The following guidelines will help you set goals for your draft, plan its organization, and consider a useful sentence strategy for it.

Setting Goals

Establishing goals for your draft before you begin writing will enable you to make decisions and work more confidently. Consider the following questions now, and keep them in mind as you draft. They will help you set goals for drafting as well as recall how the writers you have read in this chapter tried to achieve similar goals.

- *How can I introduce the problem in a way that interests my readers and convinces them that it needs to be solved?* Do I have to convince my readers that there really is a problem, as Kornbluh does? Can I demonstrate that the problem exists with examples, as Shughart, O'Malley, and Varley do, or with statistics, as Hill and Kornbluh do? Should I cite research to stress the problem's importance, as Kornbluh, O'Malley, and Varley do?

- *How should I present my proposed solution?* Should I describe in detail how the solution might be implemented, as do Hill, Kornbluh, and Beck? Or need I describe the solution only briefly, as the other writers do, letting other interested parties work out the details and take action?

- *How can I argue convincingly for my proposed solution?* Should I give examples of my solution that have proved successful, as Hill does? Describe the benefits of my solution, as Beck, O'Malley, and Varley do? Offer statistics, like Kornbluh, or refer to research, like Kornbluh, O'Malley, and Varley?

- *How should I counterargue readers' objections?* Should I refute readers' likely objections to the argument for my solution, as Hill and O'Malley do? Should I attempt to answer readers' concerns, as Varley does? Should I accommodate objections by modifying my proposal, as O'Malley does?

- *How should I counterargue alternative solutions?* Can I argue that they are too expensive and time consuming, as O'Malley does; that they will not really solve the problem, as Kornbluh does; or that they make the problem worse? In rejecting these other solutions, should I criticize their proponents, as Beck does; simply provide my reasons, as O'Malley does; or marshal statistics, as Kornbluh does?

Organizing Your Draft

With goals in mind and invention notes at hand, you are ready to make a first outline of your draft. The basic parts are quite simple—the problem, the solution, and the reasons in support of the solution. This simple plan is nearly always complicated by other factors, however. In outlining your material, you must take into consideration many other details, such as whether readers already recognize the problem, how much agreement exists on the need to solve the problem, how much attention should be given to alternative solutions, and how many objections and questions by readers should be expected.

Your outline should reflect your own writing situation. You should not hesitate to change this outline after you start drafting. For example, you might discover a more convincing way to order the reasons for adopting your proposal, or you might realize that counterargument must play a larger role than you first imagined. The purpose of an outline is to identify the basic features of your proposal, not to lock you in to a particular structure.

Working with Sources

Citing Statistics to Establish the Problem's Existence and Seriousness

Statistics can be helpful in establishing that the problem exists and is serious. For example, Patrick O'Malley cites research to support his assertion that students prefer frequent exams to fewer high-stakes exams: "A Harvard study notes students' 'strong preference for frequent evaluation in a course'" (paragraph 4). But his argument would have been stronger and possibly more convincing if he had cited statistics to support the study's conclusion. Karen Kornbluh, in contrast, bombards readers with statistics. Let us look at some of the ways that Kornbluh uses statistics to define the problem.

The success of Kornbluh's proposal depends on her ability to persuade readers that the problem really exists and that it is serious and widespread enough to require a solution. Therefore, she cites statistics to demonstrate that the "juggler family," as she calls it, has taken the place of the "traditional family" that had a homemaker capable of taking care of children and dependent parents:

> Today fully 70 percent of families with children are headed by two working parents or by an unmarried working parent. The "traditional family" of the breadwinner and homemaker has been replaced by the "juggler family," in which no one is home full-time. (paragraph 1)

Kornbluh begins with an impressive statistic: "fully 70 percent of families with children." But how many people is this? She does not answer this question with a number, but at other points in the essay Kornbluh does provide the raw numbers along with the statistics. Here are a couple of examples:

> In addition to working parents, there are over 44.4 million Americans who provide care to another adult, often an older relative. Fifty-nine percent of these caregivers either work or have worked while providing care ("Caregiving"). (8)

> Over half of workers today have no control over scheduling alternative start and end times at work (Galinksy, Bond, and Hill). According to a recent study by the Institute for Women's Policy Research, 49 percent of workers—over 59 million Americans—lack basic paid sick days for themselves. (10)

Because of the raw numbers, readers can see at a glance that the percentages that Kornbluh cites are truly significant: 59 percent of 44.4 million people have worked while providing care to another adult, and 59 million people lack paid sick leave. Her use of statistics here is especially convincing because of the large numbers of people affected by the problem. Note that Kornbluh spells out some of the numbers she provides and uses numerals for others, depending on whether the number begins a sentence.

Kornbluh also compares different time periods to show that the problem has worsened over the last thirty years. Here are several examples from paragraph 7. Note that Kornbluh represents statistics in three different ways—percentages, numbers, and proportions:

> Between 1970 and 2000, the percentage of mothers in the workforce rose from 38 to 67 percent (Smolensky and Gootman). Moreover, the number of hours worked by dual-income families has increased dramatically. Couples with children worked a full 60 hours a week in 1979. By 2000 they were working 70 hours a week (Bernstein and Kornbluh). And more parents than ever are working long hours. In 2000, nearly 1 out of every 8 couples with children was putting in 100 hours a week or more on the job, compared to only 1 out of 12 families in 1970 (Jacobs and Gerson).

To establish that there is a widespread perception among working parents that the problem is serious, Kornbluh cites survey results in paragraph 9:

> In a 2002 report by the Families and Work Institute, 45 percent of employees reported that work and family responsibilities interfered with each other "a lot" or "some" and 67 percent of employed parents report that they do not have enough time with their children (Galinksy, Bond, and Hill).

This example shows that a large percentage, nearly half of all employees surveyed, are aware of interference between work and family responsibilities. The actual amount of interference is vague, however, because "some" and "a lot" may mean different things to different survey respondents. Nevertheless, the readers that Kornbluh is addressing—employers—are likely to find this statistic important because it suggests that their employees are spending work time worrying about family instead of focusing on work.

For statistics to be considered credible, they must be from sources that readers consider reliable. Readers need to know who did the study so they can determine whether its researchers can be trusted. Researchers' trustworthiness depends, in turn, on their credentials as experts in the field they are investigating and also on the degree to which they are disinterested, or free from bias.

> Kornbluh provides a works-cited list, identifying her sources so that readers can check to determine whether the sources are indeed reliable. Some of Kornbluh's sources are books published by major publishers (Harvard University Press and Basic Books, for example), which helps establish their credibility. Other sources she cites are research institutes (such as New America Foundation, Economic Policy Institute, and Families and Work Institute) that readers can easily check on the Internet. Another factor that adds at least to the appearance of reliability is that Kornbluh cites statistics from a range of sources instead of relying on only one or two sources. Moreover, the statistics are current and clearly relevant to her argument.

Considering a Useful Sentence Strategy

As you draft your essay proposing a solution to a problem, you will want to connect with your readers. You will also want readers to become concerned with the seriousness of the problem and thoughtful about the challenge of solving it. Sentences that take the form of rhetorical questions can help you achieve these goals.

A *rhetorical question* is conventionally defined as a sentence posing a question that the writer does not expect the reader to answer. (In most cases, a reader could not possibly answer it.) In proposals, however, rhetorical questions do important rhetorical work—that is, they assist writers in realizing a particular purpose and they influence readers in certain ways. In particular, you can use rhetorical questions to engage and orient your readers and to introduce and emphasize parts of your argument.

Shughart uses a question as the title of his essay: "Why Not a Football Degree?" Similarly, O'Malley begins his proposal with a series of rhetorical questions designed to engage readers:

> Will it be like the midterm? Did you study enough? Did you study the right things? It's too late to drop the course. So what happens if you fail? (O'Malley, paragraph 1)

O'Malley uses these rhetorical questions to dramatize the plight of students studying for a high-risk exam to put his primary readers—professors who are capable of implementing his solution—in a receptive frame of mind.

Other writers in this chapter use different kinds of rhetorical questions for various purposes:

- to make a transition from establishing the problem to presenting the solution:

  If so, why stop at half-measures? (Shughart, paragraph 3)

  How do we resolve the conflict of early high-school starting times versus sleepy students? (Varley, paragraph 5)

- to provide transitions to other aspects of the proposal:

Who would be covered (Kornbluh, paragraph 21)

Why, then, do so few professors give frequent brief exams? (O'Malley, paragraph 7)

With so many benefits to starting high-school classes later, why haven't more districts done so? (Varley, paragraph 8)

If practices currently often run until 8 or 9 p.m. with a school day that begins at 7:30 a.m., what will happen if school starts an hour later? (Varley, paragraph 9)

Kornbluh puts her question in italics but she replaces the question mark with a colon to indicate that what follows is the answer. Thus, her rhetorical question functions as a heading introducing an important part of the argument: who would be affected by the solution? O'Malley and Varley use their rhetorical questions as transitions to counterarguing readers' likely concerns about and objections to their proposed solutions.

- to emphasize particular points in the argument:

Okay, you're a moderate Republican, but what about this moderate Democratic candidate? Might that candidate be acceptable as your second or third choice? Or maybe you are a Libertarian Party or a Green Party supporter— which would be your second or third choice if your Libertarian or Green candidate can't win? Voters can think more about which candidates they like regardless of partisan labels. (Hill, paragraph 11)

Since the Supreme Court has ruled that a political party's primary is a private affair and that a state cannot force parties to open all their primaries to all voters, why should taxpayers foot the bill? (Hill, "Benefits" bulleted list item 5)

Why should academic credit be given for practicing the violin, but not for practicing a three-point shot? (Shughart, paragraph 5)

Because rhetorical questions appeal directly to readers, they tend to be used sparingly in academic writing. Even though they are useful, they are not a requirement for a successful proposal and should be used only for a specific purpose. They should not be overused because readers may find them annoying and unnecessary.

READING A DRAFT CRITICALLY

Getting a critical reading of your draft will help you see how to improve it. Your instructor may schedule class time for reading drafts, or you may want to ask a classmate or a tutor in the writing center to read your draft. Ask your reader to use the following guidelines and to write out a response for you to consult during your revision.

Read for a First Impression

1. **Read the draft without stopping, and then write a few sentences giving your general impression.**

2. **Identify one aspect of the draft that seems particularly effective.**

Read Again to Suggest Improvements

1. **Recommend ways to present the problem more effectively.**

   - Locate places in the draft where the problem is defined and described. Point to any places where you believe the intended readers will need more explanation or where the presentation seems unclear or confusing.

   - Consider whether the writer does enough to establish the seriousness of the problem, creating a sense of urgency to gain readers' support and to excite their curiosity about solutions. If not, suggest ways to do so.

2. **Suggest ways to present the solution more effectively.**

   - Find the solution, and decide whether it is immediately clear. If not, point to places where it should be made clearer, and suggest how if possible.

   - If the draft does not lay out steps for implementation, advise the writer whether doing so would help.

3. **Recommend ways to strengthen the argument for the solution.**

   - List the reasons the writer gives for adopting the solution or considering it seriously. Point out the reasons most and least likely to be convincing. Let the writer know if there are too many or too few reasons. If the reasons are not in a logical order, suggest a new order.

   - Evaluate the support for each reason. Point out any passages where the support seems insufficient, and recommend further kinds of support. If necessary, tell the writer how to make the solution seem more practical, workable, and cost-effective.

4. **Suggest ways to extend and improve the counterargument.**

   - Locate places where the writer anticipates readers' likely objections to the proposal. Evaluate how successfully the writer accommodates or refutes each objection, and, if necessary, recommend ways to make the response to particular objections more convincing.

   - Suggest any likely objections and questions the writer has overlooked.

   - Identify any alternative solutions the writer mentions. If necessary, give advice on how the writer could present them more clearly and responsibly and could accommodate or refute them more convincingly.

5. **Suggest how the organization might be improved.**

- Consider the overall plan, perhaps by making a scratch outline. Decide whether the reasons and counterarguments follow a logical sequence. Suggest a more logical sequence, if necessary.

- Indicate where new or better transitions might help identify steps in the argument and keep readers on track.

6. **Evaluate the effectiveness of visuals.**

- Look at any visuals in the essay, and tell the writer what they contribute to your understanding of the argument.

- If any visual does not seem useful, or if adding a visual would strengthen the argument, explain your thinking.

REVISING

This section offers suggestions for revising your draft. Revising means reenvisioning your draft, trying to see it in a new way, given your purpose and readers, in order to develop a more convincing proposal.

You may have received help with this challenge from a classmate or tutor who gave your draft a critical reading. If so, keep this feedback in mind as you decide which parts of your draft need revising and what specific changes you could make. The following suggestions will help you solve problems and strengthen your essay.

TROUBLESHOOTING YOUR DRAFT

To Introduce the Problem More Effectively	
Problem	**Suggestions for Revising**
Readers doubt that the problem exists or that it is very serious.	• Discuss its history. • Add statistics, examples, anecdotes, or visuals.

To Present the Solution More Effectively	
Problem	**Suggestions for Revising**
The solution being proposed is not clear.	• Describe the solution in more detail. • Outline the steps of its implementation. • Add a visual illustrating the solution.

To Strengthen the Argument for the Proposed Solution

Problem	Suggestions for Revising
Readers are not convinced that the proposed solution would solve the problem.	• Explain how the solution addresses specific aspects of the problem. • Point out where else the solution has worked. • Cite experts.

To Improve the Counterargument

Problem	Suggestions for Revising
Likely objections to the solution have not been adequately addressed.	• Acknowledge valid objections and modify your solution to accommodate them. • Refute invalid objections by presenting reasons and supporting evidence.
Alternative solutions preferred by readers have not been adequately addressed.	• Address alternative solutions directly, acknowledging their strengths as well as their weaknesses. • Try to show why your solution is preferable—for example, it is easier to implement, costs less, takes less time, has fewer negative side effects, would garner more support.

To Make the Organizational Plan More Effective

Problem	Suggestions for Revising
The essay is hard to follow.	• Mark each stage in the argument more clearly with explicit topic sentences and transitions. • Add a forecasting statement. • Consider adding headings. • Decide whether the reasons or other sections need to be reorganized.

EDITING AND PROOFREADING

After you have revised the essay, be sure to spend some time checking for errors in usage, punctuation, and mechanics and considering matters of style. If you keep a list of errors you typically make, begin by checking your draft against this list. Ask someone else to proofread your essay before you print out a copy for your instructor or send it electronically.

From our research on student writing, we know that proposal writers tend to refer to the problem or solution by using the pronoun *this* or *that* ambiguously.

Edit carefully any sentences with *this* or *that* to ensure that a noun immediately follows the pronoun to make the reference clear. Check a writer's handbook for help with avoiding ambiguous pronoun reference.

Reflecting on What You Have Learned

Proposal to Solve a Problem

In this chapter, you have read critically several proposals and have written one of your own. To better remember what you have learned, pause now to reflect on the reading and writing activities you completed in this chapter.

1. Write a page or so reflecting on what you have learned. Begin by describing what you are most pleased with in your essay. Then explain what you think contributed to your achievement. Be specific about this contribution.

   - If it was something you learned from the readings, indicate which readings and specifically what you learned from them.

   - If it came from your invention writing, point out the section or sections that helped you most.

   - If you got good advice from a critical reader, explain exactly how the person helped you—perhaps by helping you understand a particular problem in your draft or by helping you add a new dimension to your writing.

   - Try to write about your achievement in terms of what you have learned about the genre.

2. Reflect more generally on proposals, a genre of writing that plays an important role in our society. Consider some of the following questions: How confident do you feel about making a proposal that might lead to improvements in the functioning of an entire group or community? Does your proposal attempt fundamental or minor change in the group? How necessary is your proposed change in the scheme of things? Whose interest would be served by the solution you propose? Who else might be affected? In what ways does your proposal challenge the status quo in the group? What contribution might essays proposing solutions to problems make to our society that other genres of writing cannot make?

A Catalog of Critical Reading Strategies

Serious study of a text requires a pencil in hand—
how much pride that pencil carries.
—Irving Howe

Here we present seventeen specific strategies for reading critically, strategies that you can learn readily and then apply to the selections in this book as well as to your other college reading. Mastering these strategies will make reading much more satisfying and productive for you and help you handle difficult material with confidence:

- *Annotating:* recording your reactions to and questions about a text directly on the page

- *Previewing:* learning about a text before reading it closely

- *Outlining:* listing the main idea of each paragraph to see the organization of a text

- *Summarizing:* briefly presenting the main ideas of a text

- *Paraphrasing:* restating and clarifying the meaning of a few sentences from a text

- *Synthesizing:* combining ideas and information selected from different texts

- *Questioning to understand and remember:* inquiring about the content

- *Contextualizing:* placing a text within an appropriate historical and cultural framework

- *Reflecting on challenges to your beliefs and values:* examining your responses to reveal your own unexamined assumptions and attitudes

- *Exploring the significance of figurative language:* seeing how metaphors, similes, and symbols enhance meaning

- *Looking for patterns of opposition:* discovering what a text values by analyzing its system of binaries or contrasts

- *Evaluating the logic of an argument:* testing the argument of a text to see whether it makes sense

- *Using a Toulmin analysis:* evaluating the underlying assumptions of an argument

- *Recognizing logical fallacies:* looking for errors in reasoning

- *Recognizing emotional manipulation:* looking for false or exaggerated appeals

- *Judging the writer's credibility:* determining whether a text can be trusted

- *Comparing and contrasting related readings:* exploring likenesses and differences between texts to understand them better

ANNOTATING

For each of these strategies, annotating directly on the page is fundamental. *Annotating* means underlining key words, phrases, or sentences; writing comments or questions in the margins; bracketing important sections of the text; connecting ideas with lines or arrows; numbering related points in sequence; and making note of anything that strikes you as interesting, important, or questionable. (If writing on the text itself is impossible or undesirable, you can annotate a photocopy.)

Most readers annotate in layers, adding further annotations on second and third readings. Annotations can be light or heavy, depending on a reader's purpose and the difficulty of the material.

For several of the strategies in this appendix, you will need to build on and extend annotating by *taking inventory*: analyzing and classifying your annotations, searching systematically for patterns in the text, and interpreting their significance. An inventory is basically a list. When you take inventory, you make various kinds of lists in order to find meaning in a text. As you inventory your annotations on a particular reading, you may discover that the language and ideas cluster in various ways.

Inventorying annotations is a three-step process:

1. Examine your annotations for patterns or repetitions of any kind, such as recurring images or stylistic features, related words and phrases, similar examples, or reliance on authorities.

2. Try out different ways of grouping the items.

3. Consider what the patterns you have found suggest about the writer's meaning or rhetorical choices.

The patterns you discover will depend on the kind of reading you are analyzing and on the purpose of your analysis. (See Exploring the Significance of Figurative Language, p. 573, and Looking for Patterns of Opposition, p. 575, for examples of inventorying annotations.) These patterns can help you reach a deeper understanding of the text.

The following selection has been annotated to demonstrate the processes required by the critical reading strategies we describe in the remainder of Appendix 1. As you read about each strategy, you will refer back to this annotated example.

Martin Luther King Jr.

An Annotated Sample from "Letter from Birmingham Jail"

Martin Luther King Jr. (1929–1968), a Baptist minister, first came to national notice in 1955, when he led a successful one-year bus boycott in Montgomery, Alabama, against state and city laws requiring racial segregation on public buses. He subsequently formed a national organization, the Southern Christian Leadership Conference, that brought people of all races from across the country to the South to fight nonviolently for racial integration. In 1963, King led demonstrations that protested segregation in Birmingham's downtown stores and restaurants. He was arrested in April and spent eight days in jail. Some of the peaceful demonstrations were met with violence: in September, members of the Ku Klux Klan bombed a black church, killing four little girls. While King was in jail, he wrote this famous "Letter from Birmingham Jail" to answer local clergy's criticism. King begins by discussing his disappointment with the lack of support he received from white moderates, such as the group of clergymen who published their criticism in the local newspaper (the complete text of the clergymen's published criticism appears at the end of this appendix).

The following brief excerpt from King's "Letter" is annotated to illustrate some of the ways you can annotate as you read. Since annotating is the first step for all critical reading strategies in this catalog, these annotations are referred to throughout this appendix. As you read, add your own annotations in the right-hand margin.

1   . . . I must confess that over the past few years I have been gravely disappointed with the <u>white moderate</u>. I have almost reached the regrettable conclusion that the Negro's [great stumbling block in his stride toward freedom] is not the White Citizen's Counciler or the Ku Klux Klanner, but the white moderate, who is more devoted to <u>"order"</u> than to <u>justice</u>; who prefers a <u>negative peace</u> which is the <u>absence of tension</u> to a <u>positive peace</u> which is the <u>presence of justice</u>; who constantly says: "I agree with you in the <u>goal</u> you seek, but I cannot agree with your <u>methods</u> of direct

¶1 *White moderates block progress*

Order vs. justice
Negative vs. positive

Ends vs. means

Treating others like children

action"; who (paternalistically) believes he can set the timetable for another man's freedom; who lives by a mythical concept of time and who constantly advises the Negro to wait for a "more convenient season." <u>Shallow understanding from people of good will</u> is more frustrating than <u>absolute misunderstanding from people of ill will</u>. [Lukewarm acceptance is much more bewildering than outright rejection.]

¶2 Tension necessary for progress

I had hoped that the white moderate would understand that <u>law and order exist for the purpose of establishing justice</u> and that when they fail in this purpose they become the [dangerously structured <u>dams</u> that block the flow of social progress.] I had hoped that the white moderate would understand that the <u>present tension</u> in the South is a <u>necessary phase of the transition</u> from an [obnoxious <u>negative peace</u>,] in which the Negro passively accepted his unjust plight, to a [substantive and positive peace,] in which all men will respect the dignity and worth of human personality. Actually, <u>we who engage</u> in

Tension already exists

<u>nonviolent direct action are not the creators of tension. We merely bring to the surface the hidden tension</u> that is already alive. We bring it out in the open, where it can be seen and dealt with. [<u>Like a boil</u> that can never be cured so long as it is covered up but must be opened with all its ugliness to the natural medicines of air and light, injustice must be exposed, with all the tension its exposure creates, to the <u>light of human conscience and the air of national opinion before it can be cured.</u>]

Simile: hidden tension is "like a boil"

True?

¶3 Questions clergymen's logic of blaming the victim

In your statement you assert that <u>our actions</u>, even though peaceful, must be <u>condemned</u> because they precipitate violence. But is this a logical assertion? <u>Isn't this like condemning</u> [a robbed man] because his possession of money precipitated the evil act of robbery? <u>Isn't this like condemning</u> [Socrates] because his unswerving commitment to truth and his philosophical inquiries precipitated the act by the misguided populace in which they made him drink hemlock? Isn't this like condemning [Jesus] because his unique God-consciousness and never-ceasing devotion to God's will precipitated the evil act of crucifixion? We must come to see that, as the federal courts have consistently affirmed, it is wrong to urge an individual to cease his efforts to gain his <u>basic constitutional rights</u> because the question may precipitate violence. [Society must protect the robbed and punish the robber.]

Yes!

¶4 Justifies urgency

I had also hoped that the white moderate would reject the <u>myth concerning time</u> in relation to the struggle for freedom. I have just received a letter from a white brother in Texas. He writes: "All Christians know that the colored people will receive equal rights eventually, but it is possible that you are in too great a religious hurry. It has taken Christianity almost two thousand years to accomplish what it has. The teachings of Christ take time to come to earth." Such an attitude stems from a tragic misconception of time, from the strangely irrational notion that there is something in the very flow of time that will inevitably cure all ills. [Actually, time itself is neutral; it can be used either destructively or constructively.] More and more I feel that the people of ill will have used time much more effectively than have the people of good will. We will have to repent in this generation not merely for the [hateful words and actions of the bad people] but for the [appalling silence of the good people.] Human progress never rolls in on [wheels of inevitability;] it comes through the tireless efforts of men willing to be co-workers with God, and without this hard work, time itself becomes an ally of the forces of social (stagnation.) [We must use time creatively, in the knowledge that the time is always ripe to do right.] Now is the time to make real the promise of democracy and transform our pending [national elegy] into a creative (psalm) of brotherhood.] Now is the time to lift our national policy from the [quicksand of racial injustice] to the [solid rock of human dignity.]

5   You speak of our activity in Birmingham as extreme. At first I was rather disappointed that fellow clergymen would see my nonviolent efforts as those of an extremist. I began thinking about the fact that I stand in the middle of two opposing forces in the Negro community. One is a [force of complacency,] made up in part of Negroes who, as a result of long years of oppression, are so drained of self-respect and a sense of "somebodiness" that they have adjusted to segregation; and in part of a few middle-class Negroes, who because of a degree of academic and economic security and because in some ways they profit by segregation, have become insensitive to the problems of the masses. The other [force is one of bitterness and hatred,] and it comes perilously close to advocating violence. It is expressed in the various black nationalist [groups that are springing up] across the nation, the largest and best-known being Elijah Muhammad's Muslim movement. Nourished by the Negro's frustration over the continued existence of racial discrimination, this movement is made up of people who have lost faith in America, who have absolutely repudiated Christianity, and who have concluded that the white man is an incorrigible "devil."

Quotes white moderate as example

Critiques assumptions

Silence is as bad as hateful words and actions

Not moving

Elegy = mourning; psalm = celebration Metaphors: quicksand, rock

¶5 Refutes criticism that he's an extremist

Complacency vs, hatred

Malcolm X?

¶16 *Claims to offer better choice*

I have tried to stand between these two forces, saying that we need emulate neither the "do-nothingism" of the complacent nor the hatred and despair of the black nationalist. For there is the more excellent way of love and nonviolent protest. I am grateful to God that, through the influence of the Negro church, the way of nonviolence became an integral part of our struggle.   6

¶17 *Claims his movement prevents racial violence*

if...then... Veiled threat?

If this philosophy had not emerged, by now many streets of the South would, I am convinced, be flowing with blood. And I am further convinced that if our white brothers dismiss as "rabble-rousers" and "outside agitators" those of us who employ nonviolent direct action, and if they refuse to support our nonviolent efforts, millions of Negroes will, out of frustration and despair, seek solace and security in black-nationalist ideologies—a development that would inevitably lead to a frightening racial nightmare.   7

¶18 *Change inevitable: evolution or revolution?*

Spirit of the times

Worldwide uprising against injustice

Why "he," not "I"? Repeats "let him"

Not a threat?

"I" channel discontent

[Oppressed people cannot remain oppressed forever.] The yearning for freedom eventually manifests itself, and that is what has happened to the American Negro. Something within has reminded him of his birthright of freedom, and something without has reminded him that it can be gained. Consciously or unconsciously, he has been caught up by the *Zeitgeist,* and with his black brothers of Africa and his brown and yellow brothers of Asia, South America and the Caribbean, the United States Negro is moving with a sense of great urgency toward the [promised land of racial justice.] If one recognizes this [vital urge that has engulfed the Negro community,] one should readily understand why public demonstrations are taking place. The Negro has many [pent-up resentments] and latent frustrations, and he must release them. So let him march; let him make prayer pilgrimages to the city hall; let him go on freedom rides—and try to understand why he must do so. If his repressed emotions are not released in nonviolent ways, they will seek expression through violence; this is not a threat but a fact of history. So I have not said to my people: "Get rid of your discontent." Rather, I have tried to say that this normal and healthy discontent can be [channeled into the creative outlet of nonviolent direct action.] And now this approach is being termed extremist.   8

¶19 *Justifies extremism for righteous ends*

But though I was initially disappointed at being categorized as an extremist, as I continued to think about the matter I gradually gained a measure of satisfaction from the label. Was not Jesus an extremist for love: "Love your enemies, bless them that curse you, do good to them that hate you, and pray for   9 them which despitefully use you, and persecute you." Was not Amos an extremist for justice: "Let justice roll down like waters and righteousness like an ever-flowing stream." Was not Paul an extremist for the Christian gospel: "I bear in my body the marks of the Lord Jesus." Was not Martin Luther an extremist: "Here I stand; I cannot do otherwise, so help me God." And John Bunyan: "I will stay in jail to the end of my days before I make a butchery of my conscience." And Abraham Lincoln: "This nation cannot survive half slave and half free." And Thomas Jefferson: "We hold these truths to be self-evident, that all men are created equal. . . ." [So the question is not whether we will be extremists, but what kind of extremists we will be.] Will we be extremists for hate or for love? Will we be extremists for the preservation of injustice or for the extension of justice? In that dramatic scene on Calvary's hill three men were crucified. We must never forget that all three were crucified for the same crime—the crime of extremism. Two were extremists for immorality, and thus fell below their environment. The other, Jesus Christ, was an extremist for love, truth and goodness, and thereby rose above his environment. Perhaps the South, [the nation and the world are in dire need of creative extremists.]

Hebrew prophet

Apostle

Founded Protestantism

English preacher

Freed slaves

Wrote Declaration of Independence

No choice but to be extremists, but what kind?

10   I had hoped that the white moderate would see this need. Perhaps I was too optimistic; perhaps I expected too much. I suppose I should have realized that few members of the oppressor race can understand the deep groans and passionate yearnings of the oppressed race, and still fewer have the vision to see that [injustice must be rooted out] by strong, persistent and determined action. I am thankful, however, that some of our white brothers in the South have grasped the meaning of this social revolution and committed themselves to it. They are still all too few in quantity, but they are big in quality. Some—such as Ralph McGill, Lillian Smith, Harry Golden, James McBride Dabbs, Ann Braden and Sarah Patton Boyle—have written about our struggle in eloquent and prophetic terms. Others have marched with us down nameless streets of the South. They have languished in filthy, roach-infested jails, suffering the abuse and brutality of policemen who view them as "dirty nigger-lovers." Unlike so many of their moderate brothers and sisters, they have recognized the urgency of the movement and sensed the need for powerful ["action" antidotes] to combat the [disease of segregation.]

¶10 Disappointed in white moderate critics; thanks supporters

Who are they?

Been left in distress

Framing—recalls boil simile

CHECKLIST

Annotating

To annotate a reading,

1. Mark the text using notations.
    - Circle words to be defined in the margin.
    - Underline key words and phrases.
    - Bracket important sentences and passages.
    - Use lines or arrows to connect ideas or words.
    - Use question marks to note any confusion or disagreement.

2. Write marginal comments.
    - Number each paragraph for future reference.
    - State the main idea of each paragraph.
    - Define unfamiliar words.
    - Note responses and questions.
    - Identify interesting writing strategies.
    - Point out patterns.

3. Layer additional markings on the text and comments in the margins as you reread for different purposes.

PREVIEWING

Previewing enables you to get a sense of what the text is about and how it is organized before reading it closely. This simple critical reading strategy includes seeing what you can learn from headnotes, biographical notes about the author, or other introductory material; skimming to get an overview of the content and organization; and identifying the genre and rhetorical situation.

Learning from Headnotes

Many texts provide some introductory material to orient readers. Books often have brief blurbs on the cover describing the content and author, as well as a preface, an introduction, and a table of contents. Articles in professional and academic journals usually provide some background information. Scientific articles, for example, typically begin with an abstract summarizing the main points. In this book, as in many textbooks, headnotes introducing the author and identifying the circumstances under which the selection was originally published precede the reading selections.

Because Martin Luther King Jr. is a well-known figure, the headnote might not tell you anything you do not already know. If you know something else about the author that could help you better understand the selection, you might want to make a note of it. As a critical reader, you should think about whether the writer has authority and credibility on the subject. Information about the writer's education, professional experience, and other publications can help. If you need to know more about a particular author, search Google, Wikipedia, or biographical sites on the Web, such as Lives, the Biography Resource: http://amillionlives.com. In the library or using your library's Web site as a portal, you could also consult a biographical dictionary or encyclopedia such as *Who's Who*, *Biography Index*, *Current Biography*, *American National Biography*, or *Contemporary Authors*.

Skimming for an Overview

When you *skim* a text, you give it a quick, selective, superficial reading. For most explanations and arguments, a good strategy is to read the opening and closing paragraphs. The first usually introduces the subject and may forecast the main points, while the last typically summarizes what is most important in the essay. You should also glance at the first sentence of every internal paragraph because it may serve as a topic sentence, introducing the point discussed in the paragraph. Because narrative writing is usually organized chronologically rather than logically, often you can get a sense of the progression by skimming for time markers such as *then*, *after*, and *later*. Heads and subheads, figures, charts, and the like also provide clues for skimming.

To illustrate, turn back to the King excerpt, and skim it. Notice that the opening paragraph establishes the subject: the white moderate's criticism of King's efforts. It also forecasts many of the main points that are taken up in subsequent paragraphs—for example, the moderate's greater devotion to order than to justice (paragraph 2), the moderate's criticism that King's methods, though nonviolent, precipitate violence (3), and the moderate's "paternalistic" timetable (1).

Identifying the Genre and Rhetorical Situation

Reading an unfamiliar text is like traveling in unknown territory: you can use a map to check what you see against what you expect to find. In much the same way, previewing for genre equips you with a set of expectations to guide your reading. *Genre,* meaning "kind" or "type," is generally used to classify pieces of writing according to their particular social function. Nonfiction prose genres include autobiography, observation, reflection, explanations of concepts, and various forms of argument, such as evaluation, position papers on controversial issues, analysis of causes or effects, and proposals to solve a problem. These genres are illustrated in Chapters 2 through 9 with guidelines to help you analyze and evaluate their effectiveness. After working through these chapters, you will be able to identify the genre of most unfamiliar pieces of writing you encounter.

You can make a tentative decision about the genre of a text by first looking at why the piece was written and to whom it was addressed. These two elements—purpose and audience—constitute the rhetorical or writing situation. Consider the writing of "Letter from Birmingham Jail." The title explicitly identifies this particular selection as a letter. We know that letters are usually written with a particular reader in mind but can also be written for the reading public (as in a letter to the editor of a magazine), that they may be part of an ongoing correspondence, and that they may be informal or formal.

Read the clergymen's statement at the end of this appendix (pp. 601–02) to gain some insights into the situation in which King wrote his letter and some understanding of his specific purpose for writing. As a public letter written in response to a public statement, "Letter from Birmingham Jail" may be classified as a position paper—one that argues for a particular point of view on a controversial issue.

Even without reading the clergymen's statement, you can get a sense of the rhetorical situation from the opening paragraph of the King excerpt. You would not be able to identify the "white moderate" with the clergymen who criticized King, but you would see clearly that he is referring to people he had hoped would support his cause but who, instead, have become an obstacle. King's feelings about the white moderate's lack of support are evident in the first paragraph, where he uses such words as "gravely disappointed," "regrettable conclusion," "frustrating," and "bewildering." The opening paragraph, as noted earlier, also identifies the white moderate's specific objections to King's methods. Therefore, you learn quickly the essay's genre (position paper), the points of disagreement between the two sides, and the writer's attitude toward those with whom he disagrees.

Knowing that this is an excerpt from a position paper allows you to appreciate the controversiality of the subject King is writing about and the sensitivity of the rhetorical situation. You can see how he asserts his own position at the same time that he tries to bridge the gap separating him from his critics. You can then evaluate the kinds of points King makes and the persuasiveness of his argument.

Previewing

To orient yourself before reading closely,

1. See what you can learn from headnotes or other introductory material.

2. Skim the text to get an overview of the content and organization.

3. Identify the genre and rhetorical situation.

OUTLINING

Outlining is an especially helpful critical reading strategy for understanding the content and structure of a reading. Outlining, which identifies and organizes the text's main ideas, may be done as part of the annotating process, or it may be done separately. Writing an outline in the margins of the text as you read and annotate makes it easier to find information later. Writing an outline on a separate piece of paper or on a computer screen gives you more space to work with and thus usually includes more detail.

The key to effective outlining is distinguishing between the main ideas and the supporting material, such as examples, factual evidence, and explanations. The main ideas form the backbone that holds the various parts of the text together. Outlining the main ideas helps you uncover this structure, but you must exercise judgment in deciding which are the most important ideas.

You may make either a *formal, multileveled outline* with roman (I, II) and arabic (1, 2) numerals together with capital and lowercase letters, or an *informal, scratch outline* that lists the main idea of each paragraph. A formal outline is harder and more time-consuming to create than a scratch outline. You might choose to make a formal outline of a reading about which you are writing an in-depth analysis or evaluation. For example, on the next two pages is a formal outline that a student wrote for a paper evaluating the logic of the King excerpt. Notice the student's use of roman numerals for the main ideas or claims, capital letters for the reasons, and arabic numerals for supporting evidence and explanation.

Making a scratch outline takes less time than creating a formal outline but still requires careful reading. A scratch outline records less information than a formal outline, but it is sufficient for most critical reading purposes. To make a scratch outline, you need to locate the topic of each paragraph. The topic is usually stated in a word or phrase, and it may be repeated or referred to throughout the paragraph. For example, the opening paragraph of the King excerpt (pp. 553–54) makes clear that its topic is the white moderate.

After you have found the topic of the paragraph, figure out what is being said about it. To return to our example: If the white moderate is the topic of the opening paragraph, then what King says about the topic can be found in the second sentence, where he announces the conclusion he has come to—namely, that the white moderate is "the Negro's great stumbling block in his stride toward freedom." The rest of the paragraph specifies the ways the white moderate blocks progress.

When you make an outline, you can use the writer's words, your own words, or a combination of the two. A paragraph-by-paragraph outline appears in the margins of the selection, with numbers for each paragraph (see pp. 553–57). Here is the same outline as it might appear on a separate piece of paper, slightly expanded and reworded:

Paragraph Scratch Outline

¶1 White moderates block progress in the struggle for racial justice.

¶2 Tension is necessary for progress.

¶3 The clergymen's criticism is not logical.

¶4 King justifies an urgent use of time.

¶5 Clergymen accuse King of being extreme, but he claims to stand between two extreme forces in the black community.

¶6 King offers a better choice.

¶7 King's movement has prevented racial violence by blacks.

¶8 Discontent is normal and healthy but must be channeled creatively rather than destructively.

¶9 Creative extremists are needed.

¶10 Some whites have supported King.

CHECKLIST

Outlining

To make a scratch outline of a text,

1. Reread each paragraph systematically, identifying the topic and what is being said about it. Do not include examples, specific details, quotations, or other explanatory and supporting material.

2. List the main ideas in the margin of the text or on a separate piece of paper.

Formal Outline

I. The Negro's great stumbling block in his stride toward freedom is . . . the white moderate
   A. *Because* the white moderate is more devoted to "order" than to justice (paragraph 2)
      1. Law and order should exist to establish justice
      2. Law and order compare to dangerously structured dams that block the flow of social progress
   B. *Because* the white moderate prefers a negative peace (absence of tension) to a positive peace (justice) (paragraph 2)
      1. The tension already exists
      2. It is not created by nonviolent direct action
      3. Society that does not eliminate injustice compares to a boil that hides its infections. Both can be cured only by exposure (boil simile)
   C. *Because* even though the white moderates agree with the goals, they do not support the means to achieve them (paragraph 3)
      1. The argument that the means—nonviolent direct action—are wrong because they precipitate violence is flawed
      2. Analogy of the robbed man condemned because he had money
      3. Comparison with Socrates and Jesus
   D. *Because* the white moderates paternalistically believe they can set a time-table for another man's freedom (paragraph 4)
      1. Rebuts the white moderate's argument that Christianity will cure man's ills and man must wait patiently for that to happen
      2. Argues that time is neutral and that man must use time creatively for constructive rather than destructive ends

II. Creative extremism is preferable to moderation
   A. Classifies himself as a moderate (paragraphs 5–8)
      1. I stand between two forces: the white moderate's complacency and the black Muslim's rage
      2. If nonviolent direct action were stopped, more violence, not less, would result
      3. "[M]illions of Negroes will, out of frustration and despair, seek solace and security in black-nationalist ideologies" (paragraph 7)
      4. Repressed emotions will be expressed—if not in nonviolent ways, then through violence (paragraph 8)
   B. Redefines himself as a "creative extremist" (paragraph 9)
      1. Extremism for love, truth, and goodness is creative extremism
      2. Identifies himself with the creative extremists Jesus, Amos, Paul, Martin Luther, John Bunyan, Abraham Lincoln, and Thomas Jefferson
   C. Not all whites are moderates; many are creative extremists (paragraph 10)
      1. Lists names of white writers
      2. Refers to white activists

SUMMARIZING

Summarizing is one of the most widely used strategies for critical reading because it helps you understand and remember what is most important in a text. Another advantage of summarizing is that it creates a condensed version of the reading's ideas and information, which you can refer to later or insert into your own written text. Along with quoting and paraphrasing, summarizing enables you to refer to and integrate other writers' ideas into your own writing.

A summary is a relatively brief restatement, primarily in the reader's own words, of the reading's main ideas. Summaries vary in length. Some are very brief—a sentence or even a subordinate clause. For example, if you were referring to the excerpt from "Letter from Birmingham Jail" and simply needed to indicate how it relates to your other sources, your summary might focus on only one aspect of the reading. It might look something like this:

> There have always been advocates of extremism in politics. Martin Luther King Jr., in "Letter from Birmingham Jail," for instance, defends nonviolent civil disobedience as an extreme but necessary means of bringing about racial justice.

If, however, you were surveying the important texts of the civil rights movement, you might write a longer, more detailed summary, one that not only identifies the reading's main ideas but also shows how the ideas relate to one another.

Many writers find it useful to outline the reading as a preliminary to writing a summary. A paragraph-by-paragraph scratch outline (like the one illustrated in the preceding section) lists the reading's main ideas following the sequence in which they appear in the original. But writing a summary requires more than merely stringing together the entries in an outline. A summary has to make explicit the logical connections between the ideas. Writing a summary shows how reading critically is a truly constructive process of interpretation involving both close analysis and creative synthesis.

To summarize, you need to segregate the main ideas from the supporting material, usually by making an outline of the reading. You want to use your own words for the most part because doing so confirms that you understand the material you have read, but you may also use key words and phrases from the reading. You may also want to cite the title and refer to the author by name, using verbs like *expresses*, *acknowledges*, and *explains* to indicate the writer's purpose and strategy at each point in the argument.

Following is a sample summary of the King excerpt. It is based on the outline on page 563 but is much more detailed. Most important, it fills in connections between the ideas that King left for readers to make:

> King expresses his disappointment with white moderates who, by opposing his program of nonviolent direct action, have blocked progress toward racial justice. He acknowledges that his program has raised tension in the South, but he explains that tension is necessary to bring about

change. Furthermore, he argues that tension already exists. But because it has been unexpressed, it is unhealthy and potentially dangerous.

He defends his actions against the clergymen's criticisms, particularly their argument that he is in too much of a hurry. Responding to charges of extremism, King claims that he has actually prevented racial violence by channeling the natural frustrations of oppressed blacks into nonviolent protest. He asserts that extremism is precisely what is needed now—but it must be creative, rather than destructive, extremism. He concludes by again expressing disappointment with white moderates for not joining his effort as many other whites have.

CHECKLIST

Summarizing

To restate briefly the main ideas in a text,

1. Make an outline.

2. Write one or more paragraphs that present the main ideas largely in your own words. Use the outline as a guide, but reread parts of the original text as necessary.

3. To make the summary coherent, fill in connections between ideas.

PARAPHRASING

Unlike a summary, which is much briefer than the original text, a *paraphrase* is generally as long as the original and often longer. Whereas summarizing seeks to present the gist or essence of the reading and leave out everything else, paraphrasing tries to be comprehensive and leave out nothing that contributes to the meaning. (For more on summarizing, see the preceding section.)

Paraphrasing works as a critical reading strategy for especially complex and obscure passages. Because it requires a word-for-word or phrase-by-phrase rewording of the original text, paraphrasing is too time-consuming and labor-intensive to use with long texts. But it is perfect for making sure you understand the important passages of a difficult reading. To paraphrase, you need to work systematically through the text, looking up in a good college dictionary many of the key words, even those you are somewhat familiar with. If you quote the author's words, put quotation marks around them, and be sure to define them.

Following are two passages. The first is excerpted from paragraph 2 of "Letter from Birmingham Jail." The second passage paraphrases the first.

Original

I had hoped that the white moderate would understand that law and order exist for the purpose of establishing justice and that when they fail in this purpose they become the dangerously structured dams that block the flow of social progress. I had hoped that the white moderate would understand that the present tension in the South is a necessary phase of the transition from an obnoxious negative peace, in which the Negro passively accepted his unjust plight, to a substantive and positive peace, in which all men will respect the dignity and worth of human personality.

Paraphrase

King writes that he had hoped for more understanding from the white moderates—specifically that they would recognize that law and order are not ends in themselves but means to the greater end of establishing justice. When law and order do not serve this greater end, they stand in the way of progress. King expected the white moderates to recognize that the current tense situation in the South is part of a transition that is necessary for progress. The current situation is bad because although there is peace, it is an "obnoxious" and "negative" kind of peace based on blacks passively accepting the injustice of the status quo. A better kind of peace, one that is "substantive," real and not imaginary, as well as "positive," requires that all people, regardless of race, be valued.

When you compare the paraphrase with the original, you can see that the paraphrase tries to remain true to the original by including *all* the important information and ideas. It also tries to be neutral—to avoid inserting the reader's opinions or distorting the original writer's ideas. But because paraphrasing requires the use of different words and putting those words together into different sentences, the resulting paraphrase will be different from the original. The paraphrase always, intentionally or not, expresses the reader's interpretation of the original text's meaning.

CHECKLIST

Paraphrasing

To paraphrase information in a text,

1. Reread the passage to be paraphrased, looking up unfamiliar words in a college dictionary.

2. Relying on key words in the passage, translate the information into your own sentences.

3. Revise to ensure coherence.

SYNTHESIZING

Synthesizing involves combining ideas and information gleaned from different sources. As a critical reading strategy, synthesizing can help you see how different sources relate to one another—for example, by offering supporting details or opposing arguments.

When you synthesize material from different sources, you construct a conversation among your sources, a conversation in which you also participate. Synthesizing contributes most to critical thinking when writers use sources not only to support their ideas but to challenge and extend them as well.

In the following example, the reader uses a variety of sources related to the King passage (pp. 553–57). The synthesis brings the sources together around a central idea. Notice how quotation, paraphrase, and summary are all used to present King's and the other sources' ideas:

> When King defends his campaign of nonviolent direct action against the clergymen's criticism that "our actions, even though peaceful, must be condemned because they precipitate violence" (King excerpt, paragraph 3), he is using what Vinit Haksar calls Mohandas Gandhi's "safety-valve argument" ("Civil Disobedience and Non-Cooperation" 117). According to Haksar, Gandhi gave a "non-threatening warning of worse things to come" if his demands were not met. King similarly makes clear that advocates of actions more extreme than those he advocates are waiting in the wings: "The other force is one of bitterness and hatred, and it comes perilously close to advocating violence" (King excerpt, paragraph 5). King identifies this force with Elijah Muhammad, and although he does not name him, King's contemporary readers would have known that he was referring also to Malcolm X, who, according to Herbert J. Storing, "urged that Negroes take seriously the idea of revolution" ("The Case against Civil Disobedience" 90). In fact, Malcolm X accused King of being a modern-day Uncle Tom, trying "to keep us under control, to keep us passive and peaceful and nonviolent" (*Malcolm X Speaks* 12).

CHECKLIST

Synthesizing

To synthesize ideas and information,

1. Find and read a variety of sources on your topic, annotating the passages that give you ideas about the topic.

2. Look for patterns among your sources, possibly supporting or refuting your ideas or those of other sources.

3. Write one or more paragraphs synthesizing your sources, using quotation, paraphrase, and summary to present what they say on the topic.

QUESTIONING TO UNDERSTAND AND REMEMBER

As a student, you are accustomed to having teachers ask you questions about your reading. These questions are designed to help you understand a reading and respond to it more fully. However, when you need to understand and use new information, it may be more beneficial for *you* to write the questions. This strategy, *questioning to understand and remember*, involves writing questions while you read a text the first time. In difficult academic reading, you will understand the material better and remember it longer if you write a question for every paragraph or brief section.

We can demonstrate how this strategy works by returning to the excerpt from "Letter from Birmingham Jail" and examining, paragraph by paragraph, some questions that might be written about it. Reread the King selection (pp. 553–57). When you finish each paragraph, look at the question numbered to match that paragraph in the following list. Assume for this rereading that your goal is to comprehend the information and ideas. Notice that each question in the list asks about the content of a paragraph and that you can answer the question with information from that paragraph.

Paragraph	*Question*
1	How can white moderates be more of a barrier to racial equality than the Ku Klux Klan?
2	How can community tension resulting from nonviolent direct action benefit the civil rights movement?
3	How can peaceful actions be justified even if they cause violence?
4	Why should civil rights activists take action now instead of waiting for white moderates to support them?
5	How are complacent members of the community different from black nationalist groups?
6	What is King's position in relation to these two forces of complacency and anger?
7	What would have happened if King's nonviolent direct action movement had not started?

8   What is the focus of the protest, and what do King and others who are protesting hope to achieve?

9   What other creative extremists does King associate himself with?

10   Who are the whites who have supported King, and what has happened to some of them?

Each question focuses on the main idea in the paragraph, not on illustrations or details. Note, too, that each question is expressed partly in the reader's own words, not just copied from parts of the paragraph.

How can writing questions during reading help you understand and remember the content—the ideas and information—of the reading? Researchers studying the ways people learn from their reading have found that writing questions during reading enables readers to remember more than they would by reading the selection twice. Researchers who have compared the results of readers who write brief summary sentences for a paragraph with readers who write questions have found that readers who write questions learn more and remember the information longer. These researchers conjecture that writing a question involves reviewing or rehearsing information in a way that allows it to enter long-term memory, where it is more easily recalled. The result is that you clarify and "file" the information as you go along. You can then read more confidently because you have more of a base on which to build your understanding, a base that allows meaning to develop and that enables you to predict what is coming next and add it readily to what you have already learned.

This way of reading informational material is very slow, and at first it may seem inefficient. In those reading situations where you must use the information in an exam or a class discussion, it can be very efficient, however. Because this reading strategy is relatively time-consuming, you will want to use it selectively.

CHECKLIST

Questioning to Understand and Remember

To use questioning to understand and remember a reading, especially one that is unfamiliar or difficult,

1. Pause at the end of each paragraph to review the information.

2. Try to identify the most important information—the main ideas or gist of the discussion.

3. Write a question that can be answered by the main idea or ideas in the paragraph.

4. Move on to the next paragraph, repeating the process.

CONTEXTUALIZING

The texts you read were written in the past and often embody historical and cultural assumptions, values, and attitudes different from your own. To read critically, you need to become aware of these differences. *Contextualizing* is a critical reading strategy that involves making inferences about a reading's historical and cultural contexts and examining the differences between those contexts and your own.

We can divide the process of contextualizing into two steps:

1. Reread the text to see how it represents the historical and cultural situation. Compare the way the text presents the situation with what you know about the situation from other sources—such as what you have read in other books and articles, seen on television or in the movies, and learned in school or from talking with people who were directly involved.

   Write a few sentences describing your understanding of what it was like at that particular time and place. Note how the representation of the time and place in the text differs in significant ways from the other representations with which you are familiar.

2. Consider how much and in what ways the situation has changed. Write another sentence or two exploring the historical and cultural differences.

The excerpt from "Letter from Birmingham Jail" is a good example of a text that benefits from being read contextually. If you knew little about the history of slavery and segregation in the United States, Martin Luther King Jr., or the civil rights movement, it would be very difficult to understand the passion for justice and the impatience with delay expressed in the King selection. Most Americans, however, have read about Martin Luther King Jr. and the civil rights movement, or they have seen films such as Spike Lee's *Malcolm X*.

Here is how one reader contextualized the excerpt from "Letter from Birmingham Jail":

1. I am not old enough to remember what it was like in the early 1960s when Dr. King was leading marches and sit-ins, but I have seen television documentaries of newsclips showing demonstrators being attacked by dogs, doused by fire hoses, beaten and dragged by helmeted police. Such images give me a sense of the violence, fear, and hatred that King was responding to.

The tension King writes about comes across in his writing. He uses his anger and frustration creatively to inspire his critics. He also threatens them, although he denies it. I saw a film on Malcolm X, so I could see that King was giving white people a choice between his nonviolent way and Malcolm's more confrontational way.

2. Things have certainly changed since the sixties. Legal segregation has ended. The term *Negro* is no longer used, but there still are racists

like Don Imus on the radio. African Americans like Oprah Winfrey and Barack Obama are highly respected and powerful. The civil rights movement is over. So when I'm reading King, I'm reading history.

Things seem better than when police officers beat black men like Rodney King or extremists like Ice T threatened violence. Don Imus, after all, lost his job for what he said. But in the ghetto, black children are still dying: where there were riots, there's now gang violence. I don't know who's playing Dr. King's role today.

CHECKLIST

Contextualizing

To contextualize,

1. Describe the historical and cultural situation as it is represented in the reading and in other sources with which you are familiar.

2. Compare the text's historical and cultural contexts with your own historical and cultural situations.

REFLECTING ON CHALLENGES TO YOUR BELIEFS AND VALUES

Reading often challenges our attitudes, our unconsciously held beliefs, or our positions on current issues. We may feel anxious, irritable, or disturbed; threatened or vulnerable; ashamed or combative. We may feel suddenly wary or alert. When we experience these feelings as we read, we are reacting in terms of our personal or family values, religious beliefs, racial or ethnic group, gender, sexual orientation, social class, or regional experience.

You can grow intellectually, emotionally, and in social understanding if you are willing (at least occasionally) to *reflect on challenges to your beliefs and values* instead of simply resisting them. Learning to question your unexamined assumptions and attitudes is an important part of becoming a critical thinker.

This reading strategy involves marking the text where you feel challenged and then reflecting on why you feel challenged. As you read a text for the first time, mark an *X* in the margin at each point where you sense a challenge to your attitudes, beliefs, or values. Make a brief note in the margin about what you feel at that point or about what in the text seems to create the challenge. The challenge you feel may be mild or strong. It may come frequently or only occasionally.

Review the places you have marked in the text where you felt challenged in some way. Consider what connections you can make among these places or among the feelings you experienced at each place. For example, you might notice that you object to only a limited part of a writer's argument, resist nearly all of an authority's quoted statements, or dispute implied judgments about your gender or social class.

Write about what you have learned. Begin by describing briefly the part or parts of the text that make you feel challenged. Then write several sentences, reflecting on your responses. Keep the focus on your feelings. You need not defend or justify your feelings. Instead, try to give them a voice. Where do they come from? Why are they important to you? Although the purpose is to explore why you feel as you do, you may find that thinking about your values, attitudes, and beliefs sends you back to the text for help with defining your own position.

Here, for example, is how one writer responded to the excerpt from "Letter from Birmingham Jail":

> I'm troubled and confused by the way King uses the labels *moderate* and *extremist*. He says he doesn't like being labeled an extremist but he labels the clergymen moderate. How could it be okay for King to be moderate and not okay for the clergymen? What does *moderate* mean anyway? My dictionary defines *moderate* as "keeping within reasonable or proper limits; not extreme, excessive, or intense." Being a moderate sounds a lot better than being an extremist. I was taught not to act rashly or to go off the deep end. I'm also troubled that King makes a threat (although he says he does not).

CHECKLIST

Reflecting on Challenges to Your Beliefs and Values

To reflect on challenges to your beliefs and values,

1. Identify the challenges by marking where in the text you feel your beliefs and values are being opposed, criticized, or unfairly characterized.

2. Select one or two of the most troubling challenges you have identified, and write a few sentences describing why you feel as you do. Do not attempt to defend your feelings; instead, analyze them to see where they come from.

EXPLORING THE SIGNIFICANCE OF FIGURATIVE LANGUAGE

Figurative language—metaphors, similes, and symbols—takes words literally associated with one object or idea and applies them to another object or idea. Because it embodies abstract ideas in vivid images, figurative language can often communicate more dramatically than direct statement. Figurative language also enriches meaning by drawing on a complex of feeling and association, indicating relations of resemblance and likeness. Here are definitions and examples of the most common figures of speech.

Metaphor implicitly compares two things by identifying them with each other. For instance, when King calls the white moderate "the Negro's great stumbling block in his stride toward freedom" (paragraph 1), he does not mean that the white moderate literally trips the Negro who is attempting to walk toward freedom. The sentence makes sense only when it is understood figuratively: the white moderate trips up the Negro by frustrating every effort to eliminate injustice. Similarly, King uses the image of a dam to express the abstract idea of the blockage of justice (paragraph 2).

Simile, a more explicit form of comparison, uses *like* or *as* to signal the relation of two seemingly unrelated things. King uses simile when he says that injustice is "like a boil that can never be cured so long as it is covered up" (paragraph 2). This simile makes several points of comparison between injustice and a boil. It suggests that injustice is a disease of society, just as a boil is a disease of the body, and that injustice, like a boil, must be exposed or it will fester and worsen. A simile with many points of comparison is called an *extended simile* or *conceit*.

A *symbol* is something that stands for or represents something else. Critics do not agree about the differences between a metaphor and a symbol, but one popular line of thought is that a symbol relates two or more items that already have a strong recognized alliance or affinity, whereas metaphor involves a more general association of two related or unrelated items. By this definition, King uses the white moderate as a symbol for supposed liberals and would-be supporters of civil rights who are actually frustrating the cause.

How these figures of speech are used in a text reveals something of the writer's feelings about the subject and attitude toward prospective readers and may even suggest the writer's feelings about the act of writing. Annotating and taking inventory of patterns of figurative language can thus provide insight into the tone and intended emotional effect of the writing.

Exploring the significance of figurative language involves (1) annotating and then listing all the metaphors, similes, and symbols you find in the reading; (2) grouping the figures of speech that appear to express similar feelings and attitudes, and labeling each group; and (3) writing to explore the meaning of the patterns you have found.

The following sample inventory and analysis of the King excerpt demonstrate the process of exploring the significance of figurative language.

Listing Figures of Speech

Step 1 produced the following inventory:

order is a dangerously structured dam that blocks the flow

social progress should flow

stumbling block in the stride toward freedom

injustice is like a boil that can never be cured

the light of human conscience and air of national opinion

time is something to be used, neutral, an ally, ripe

quicksand of racial injustice

the solid rock of human dignity

human progress never rolls in on wheels of inevitability

men are coworkers with God

groups springing up

promised land of racial justice

vital urge engulfed

pent-up resentments

normal and healthy discontent can be channeled into the creative outlet of nonviolent direct action

root out injustice

powerful action is an antidote

disease of segregation

Grouping Figures of Speech

Step 2 yielded three common themes:

Sickness: segregation is a disease; action is healthy, the only antidote; injustice is like a boil

Underground: tension is hidden; injustice must be rooted out; extremist groups are springing up; discontent can be channeled into a creative outlet

Blockage: forward movement is impeded by obstacles—the dam, stumbling block; human progress never rolls in on wheels of inevitability; social progress should flow

Exploring Patterns

Step 3 entailed about ten minutes of writing to explore the themes listed in step 2:

The patterns of *blockage* and *underground* suggest a feeling of frustration. Inertia is a problem; movement forward toward progress or upward toward the promised land is stalled. There seems to be a strong need to break through the resistance, the passivity, the discontent, and to be creative, active, vital. These are probably King's feelings both about his attempt to lead purposeful, effective demonstrations and about his effort to write a convincing letter.

The simile of injustice being like a boil links the two patterns of *underground* and *sickness*, suggesting something bad, a disease, is inside the people or the society. The cure is to expose the blocked hatred and injustice, root it out, and release the tension or emotion that has so long been repressed. This implies that repression itself, not simply what is repressed, is the evil.

CHECKLIST

Exploring the Significance of Figurative Language

To understand how figurative language—metaphors, similes, and symbols—contributes to a reading's meaning,

1. Annotate and then list all the figures of speech you find.

2. Group them, and label each group.

3. Write to explore the meaning of the patterns you have found.

LOOKING FOR PATTERNS OF OPPOSITION

All texts contain *voices* or *patterns of opposition*. These voices may echo the views and values of critical readers the writer anticipates or predecessors to which the writer is responding; they may even reflect the writer's own conflicting values. You may need to look closely for such a dialogue of opposing voices within the text.

When we think of oppositions, we ordinarily think of polarities such as *yes* and *no*, *up* and *down*, *black* and *white*, *new* and *old*. Some oppositions, however, may be more subtle. The excerpt from "Letter from Birmingham Jail" is rich in such oppositions: *moderate* versus *extremist*, *order* versus *justice*, *direct action* versus *passive acceptance*, *expression* versus *repression*. These oppositions are not accidental; they form a significant pattern that gives a critical reader important information about King's letter.

A careful reading shows that one of the two terms in an opposition is nearly always valued over the other. In the King excerpt, for example, *extremist* is valued over *moderate* (paragraph 9). This preference for extremism is surprising. The critical reader should ask why, when white extremists like the Ku Klux Klan have committed so many outrages against black Southerners, King would prefer extremism. If King is trying to convince his readers to accept his point of view, why would he represent himself as an extremist? Moreover, why would a clergyman advocate extremism instead of moderation?

By studying the patterns of opposition, you can answer these questions more fully. You can see that King sets up this opposition to force his readers to examine their own values and realize that they are in fact misplaced. Instead of working toward justice, he says, those who support law and order maintain the unjust status quo. Getting his readers to think of the white moderate as blocking rather than facilitating peaceful change brings them to align themselves with King and perhaps even embrace his strategy of nonviolent resistance.

Looking for patterns of opposition is a four-step method of analysis:

1. Divide a piece of paper in half lengthwise or select two-column formatting in your word-processing program. In the left-hand column, list those words and phrases from the text that you have annotated as indicating oppositions. In the right-hand column, enter the word or phrase that seems, according to this writer, the opposite of each word or phrase in the left-hand column. You may have to paraphrase or even supply this opposite word or phrase if it is not stated directly in the text.

2. For each pair of words or phrases, put an asterisk next to the one that seems to be preferred by the writer.

3. Study the list of preferred words or phrases, and identify what you think is the predominant system of values put forth by the text. Do the same for the other list, identifying the alternative system or systems of values implied in the text. Take about ten minutes to describe the oppositions in writing.

4. To explore these conflicting points of view, write a few sentences presenting one side, and then write a few more sentences presenting the other side. Use as many of the words or phrases from the list as you can—explaining, extending, and justifying the values they imply. You may also, if you wish, quarrel with the choice of words or phrases on the grounds that they are loaded or oversimplify the issue.

The following sample inventory and analysis of the King excerpt demonstrate the method for exploring patterns of opposition in a text.

Listing Oppositions

Steps 1 and 2: This list of oppositions uses asterisks to identify King's preferred word or phrase in each pair:

white moderate	*extremist
order	*justice
negative peace	*positive peace
absence of justice	*presence of justice
goals	*methods
*direct action	passive acceptance
*exposed tension	hidden tension
*robbed	robber
*individual	society
*words	silence
*expression	repression
*extension of justice	preservation of injustice
*extremist for love, truth, and justice	extremist for immorality

Analyzing Oppositions

Step 3 produced the following description of the conflicting points of view:

In this reading, King addresses as "white moderates" the clergymen who criticized him. He sees the moderate position in essentially negative terms, whereas extremism can be either negative or positive. Moderation is equated with passivity, acceptance of the status quo, fear of disorder, perhaps even fear of any change. The moderates believe justice can wait, whereas law and order cannot. Yet, as King points out, there is no law and order for blacks who are victimized and denied their constitutional rights.

The argument King has with the white moderates is basically over means and ends. Both agree on the ends but disagree on the means that should be taken to secure those ends. What means are justified to achieve one's goals? How does one decide? King is willing to risk a certain amount of tension and disorder to bring about justice; he suggests that if progress is not made, more disorder, not less, is bound to result. In a sense, King represents himself as a moderate caught between the two extremes—the white moderates' "do-nothingism" and the black extremists' radicalism.

At the same time, King replaces the opposition between moderation and extremism with an opposition between two kinds of extremism—one for love and the other for hate. In fact, he represents himself as an extremist willing to make whatever sacrifices—and perhaps even to take whatever means—are necessary to reach his goal of justice.

Considering Alternative Points of View

Step 4 entailed a few minutes of exploratory writing about the opposing point of view and then several more minutes of writing about King's possible response to the opposition's argument:

> *The moderates' side:* I can sympathize with the moderates' fear of further disorder and violence. Even though King advocates nonviolence, violence does result. He may not cause it, but it does occur because of him. Moderates do not really advocate passive acceptance of injustice but want to pursue justice through legal means. These methods may be slow, but since ours is a system of law, the only way to make change is through that system. King wants to shake up the system and force it to move quickly for fear of violence. That strikes me as blackmail, as bad as if he were committing violence himself. Couldn't public opinion be brought to bear on the legal system to move more quickly? Can't we elect officials who will change unjust laws and see that the just ones are obeyed? The *vote* should be the weapon in a democracy, shouldn't it?
>
> *King's possible response:* He would probably have argued that the opposing viewpoint was naive. One of the major injustices at that time was that blacks were prevented from voting, and no elected official would risk going against those who voted for him or her. King would probably have agreed that public opinion needed to be changed, that people needed to be educated, but he would also have argued that education was not enough when people were being systematically deprived of their legal rights. The very system of law that should have protected people was being used as a weapon against blacks in the South. The only way to get something done was to shake people up, make them aware of the injustice they were allowing to continue. Seeing their own police officers committing violence should have made people question their own values and begin to take action to right the wrongs.

CHECKLIST

Looking for Patterns of Opposition

To explore and analyze the patterns of opposition in a reading,

1. Annotate the selection to identify the oppositions, and list the pairs on a separate page.

2. Put an asterisk next to the writer's preferred word or phrase in each pair of opposing terms.

3. Examine the pattern of preferred terms to discover the system of values the pattern implies; then do the same for the unpreferred terms.

4. Write to analyze and evaluate the opposing points of view or, in the case of a reading that does not take a position, the alternative systems of value.

EVALUATING THE LOGIC OF AN ARGUMENT

An *argument* has two essential parts—the claim and the support. The *claim* asserts a conclusion—an idea, an opinion, a judgment, or a point of view—that the writer wants readers to accept. The *support* includes *reasons* (shared beliefs, assumptions, and values) and *evidence* (facts, examples, statistics, and authorities) that give readers the basis for accepting the writer's conclusion.

When you *evaluate the logic of an argument*, you are concerned about the process of reasoning as well as the argument's truthfulness. Three conditions must be met for an argument to be considered logically acceptable—what we call the ABC test:

A. The support must be *appropriate* to the claim.

B. All of the statements must be *believable*.

C. The argument must be *consistent* and *complete*.

In addition to the ABC test, you can also use other ways to evaluate the logic of an argument. The next two sections of this appendix explain how to use a specific method called a Toulmin analysis to determine the underlying assumptions in an argument (p. 583) and ways to recognize specific kinds of errors in reasoning, or logical fallacies (p. 587).

A. Testing for Appropriateness

To assess whether a writer's reasoning is *appropriate*, you look to see if all of the evidence is relevant to the claim it supports. For example, if a writer claims that children must be allowed certain legal rights, readers could readily accept as appropriate support quotations from Supreme Court justices' decisions but might question quotations from a writer of popular children's books. Readers could probably accept the reasoning that if women have certain legal rights then so should children, but few readers would agree that all human rights under the law should be extended to animals.

As these examples illustrate, appropriateness of support comes most often into question when the writer is invoking authority or arguing by analogy. For example, in the excerpt from "Letter from Birmingham Jail," King argues by analogy and, at the same time, invokes authority: "Isn't this like condemning Socrates because his unswerving commitment to truth and his philosophical inquiries precipitated the act by the misguided populace in which they made him drink hemlock?" (paragraph 3). Readers must judge the appropriateness (1) of comparing the Greek populace's condemnation of Socrates to the white moderates' condemnation of King's action and (2) also of accepting Socrates as an authority on this subject. Because Socrates is generally respected for his teaching on justice, his words and actions are likely to be considered appropriate to King's situation in Birmingham.

In paragraph 2, King argues that if law and order fail to establish justice, "they become the dangerously structured dams that block the flow of social progress." The analogy asserts a logical relationship—that law and order are to social justice what a dam is to water. If readers do not accept this analogy, then the argument fails the test of appropriateness. Arguing by analogy is usually considered a weak kind of argument because most analogies are parallel only up to a point, beyond which they may fail.

B. Testing for Believability

Believability is a measure of the degree to which readers are willing to accept the assertions supporting the claim. Whereas some assertions are obviously true, most depend on the readers' sharing certain values, beliefs, and assumptions with the writer. Readers who agree with the white moderate that maintaining law and order is more important than establishing justice are not going to accept King's claim that the white moderate is blocking progress.

Other statements, such as those asserting facts, statistics, examples, anecdotes, and authorities, present evidence to support a claim. Readers must put all of these kinds of evidence to the test of believability.

Facts are statements that can be proven objectively to be true. The believability of facts depends on their *accuracy* (they should not distort or misrepresent reality), their *completeness* (they should not omit important details), and the *trustworthiness* of their sources (sources should be qualified and unbiased). In the excerpt from "Letter from Birmingham Jail," for instance, King asserts as fact that African Americans will not wait much longer for racial justice (paragraph 8). His critics might question the factuality of this assertion by asking: Is it true of all African Americans? How much longer will they wait? How does King know what African Americans will and will not do?

Statistics are often assumed to be factual, but they are really only interpretations of numerical data. The believability of statistics depends on the *accuracy* of the methods of gathering and analyzing data (representative samples should be used and variables accounted for), the *trustworthiness* of the sources (sources should be qualified and unbiased), and often the *comparability* of the data (are apples being compared to oranges?).

Examples and *anecdotes* are particular instances that if accepted as believable lead readers to accept the general claim. The power of examples depends on their *representativeness* (whether they are truly typical and thus generalizable) and their *specificity* (whether particular details make them seem true to life). Even if a vivid example or gripping anecdote does not convince readers, it strengthens argumentative writing by bringing home the point dramatically. In paragraph 5, for example, King supports his generalization that there are black nationalist extremists motivated by bitterness and hatred by citing the specific example of Elijah Muhammad's Muslim movement. Conversely, in paragraph 9, he refers to Jesus, Paul, Luther, and others as examples of extremists motivated by love. These examples support his assertions that extremism is not in itself wrong and that any judgment must depend on the cause for which one is an extremist.

Authorities are people whom the writer consults for expertise on a given subject. Such authorities must be not only appropriate, as mentioned earlier, but believable as well. The believability of authorities, their *credibility*, depends on whether the reader accepts them as experts on the topic. King cites authorities repeatedly throughout the essay, referring to religious leaders such as Jesus and Luther and to American political leaders such as Lincoln and Jefferson. These figures are certain to have a high degree of credibility among King's readers.

C. Testing for Consistency and Completeness

Be sure that all the support works together, that no supporting statement contradicts any of the others, and that no important objection or opposing argument is unacknowledged. To test for *consistency* and *completeness*, ask yourself: Are any of the supporting statements contradictory? Are any likely objections or opposing arguments not refuted?

In his essay, a potential contradiction is King's characterizing himself first as a moderate between the forces of complacency and violence and later as an extremist opposed to the forces of violence. King attempts to reconcile this apparent contradiction by explicitly redefining extremism in paragraph 9. Similarly, the fact that King fails to examine and refute every legal recourse available to his cause might allow a critical reader to question the sufficiency of his supporting arguments.

Following is one student's evaluation of the logic of King's argument. The student wrote these paragraphs after applying the ABC test to evaluate the appropriateness, believability, consistency, and completeness of King's supporting reasons and evidence:

> King writes both to the ministers who published the letter in the Birmingham newspaper and to the people of Birmingham. He seems to

want to justify his group's actions. He challenges white moderates, but he also tries to avoid antagonizing them. Given this purpose and his readers, his supporting statements are generally appropriate. He relies mainly on assertions of shared belief with his readers and on memorable analogies. For example, he knows his readers will accept assertions like "law and order exist for the purpose of establishing justice"; it is good to be an extremist for "love, truth, and goodness"; and progress is not inevitable but results from tireless work and creativity. His analogies also seem acceptable and are based on appropriate comparisons. For example, he compares injustice to a boil that nonviolent action must expose to the air if it is to be healed.

Likewise, his support is believable in terms of the well-known authorities he cites (Socrates, Jesus, Amos, Paul, Luther, Bunyan, Lincoln, Jefferson), the facts he asserts (for example, that racial tension results from injustice, not from nonviolent action), and the examples he offers (such as his assertion that extremism is not in itself wrong— as exemplified by Jesus, Paul, and Luther). If there is an inconsistency in the argument, it is the contradiction between King's portraits of himself both as a moderating force and as an "extremist for love," but his redefinition of extremism as a positive value for any social change is central to the overall persuasiveness of his logical appeal to white moderates.

CHECKLIST

Evaluating the Logic of an Argument

To determine whether an argument makes sense, apply the ABC test:

1. *Test for appropriateness* by checking to be sure that each piece of evidence is clearly and directly related to the claim it is supposed to support.

2. *Test for believability* by deciding whether you can accept as true the writer's facts, statistics, and expert testimony and whether you can accept the generalizations based on the examples given.

3. *Test for consistency and completeness* by ascertaining whether there are any contradictions in the argument and whether any important objections or opposing arguments have been ignored.

Then write a few sentences exploring the appropriateness, believability, consistency, and completeness of the argument.

USING A TOULMIN ANALYSIS

In addition to the ways of evaluating the logic of an argument that are discussed in the previous section, scholars have developed various formal systems for doing so. In *The Uses of Argument* (1964), Stephen Toulmin sets out a popular approach to reading, writing, and critical thinking that is widely used to discover and assess the logical structure of arguments. Students of legal writing frequently use Toulmin analysis, and you may find it helpful in your own reading and writing. As a user of this book, you may find that the most useful part of Toulmin's analysis is uncovering the underlying assumptions in an argument (or in any piece of writing)—the focus of the third part of the Reading for Meaning activities that follow the readings in Chapters 2 through 9.

Toulmin's specialized terms—*claim*, *data* and *grounds*, and *warrant*—are defined as follows:

- *Claim:* the thesis or main point of the argument.

- *Data* and *grounds:* the reasons and evidence that support the claim.

- *Warrant:* the beliefs, values, and assumptions that "warrant" or justify the claim based on the evidence. Often the warrant is unstated or implicit.

To find the warrant, you must figure out the belief or value system that enables the author to make the claim or draw the conclusion from the reasons and evidence set forth. The following strategies will help you identify the warrant underlying the argument. Once you uncover the warrant or assumption, you can determine whether the evidence—in Toulmin's words—"authorizes, entitles, or justifies the writer to make the claim based on the data," which basically means that the warrant helps you judge whether the writer's claim is justified by the evidence provided.

Identifying the Warrant

Let's look again at the beginning of the excerpt from King's "Letter from Birmingham Jail":

> . . . I must confess that over the past few years I have been gravely disappointed with the white moderate. I have almost reached the regret-table conclusion that the Negro's great stumbling block in his stride toward freedom is not the White Citizen's Counciler or the Ku Klux Klanner, but the white moderate, who is more devoted to "order" than to justice; who prefers a negative peace which is the absence of tension to a positive peace which is the presence of justice; who constantly says: "I agree with you in the goal you seek, but I cannot agree with your meth-ods of direct action"; who paternalistically believes he can set the timetable for another man's freedom; who lives by a mythical concept of time and who constantly advises the Negro to wait for a "more convenient

season." Shallow understanding from people of good will is more frustrating than absolute misunderstanding from people of ill will. Lukewarm acceptance is much more bewildering than outright rejection.

I had hoped that the white moderate would understand that law and order exist for the purpose of establishing justice and that when they fail in this purpose they become the dangerously structured dams that block the flow of social progress. I had hoped that the white moderate would understand that the present tension in the South is a necessary phase of the transition from an obnoxious negative peace, in which the Negro passively accepted his unjust plight, to a substantive and positive peace, in which all men will respect the dignity and worth of human personality.

Step 1. To apply a Toulmin analysis to King's argument, you first need to *find the claim and reasons* in the passage. What is the author's assertion? What point is the author trying to make? The answer to these questions is the claim. Then ask why the author thinks this claim is true: What reasons are offered to support it? Often you can paraphrase the passage as a *because* statement that is completed by those reasons: This claim is true because of reason one, reason two, and so on. It is helpful to use as much of the writer's own language as possible because the writer's choice of words will be important when you try to analyze the assumptions and discover the warrant. It is also helpful to underline or highlight words and phrases that seem to have a great deal of importance to the author.

A Toulmin analysis of the preceding passage might look like this:

- *Claim:* White moderates impede the African American's progress toward freedom

- *Reason 1:* because they care more for *order* than *justice* and

- *Reason 2:* because they prefer "a *negative peace* which is the *absence of tension* to a *positive peace* which is the *presence of justice*."

Step 2. *Uncover the warrant* by discovering the assumptions of the writer. Write a few sentences exploring the values and beliefs implied by each key term or phrase. Ask yourself these questions: What are the connotations of these words? What do they mean beyond their literal meaning? How does their context in this passage affect my understanding of their meaning?

Let's look first at the argument based on reason 1. King apparently assumes that his readers believe, as he does, that justice is more important than order. Readers would have to ask themselves what these two key terms, *order* and *justice*, mean to King. How would you define these terms as King uses them? After you identify key terms, look up their dictionary meanings (*denotations*). Then write out the emotional or cultural associations (*connotations*) the words carry within the context of the passage. For example, the Dictionary.com definition of *order* is "a state of public peace or conformity to law." Clearly King believes that a state of public peace exists at the expense of African Americans' march toward freedom.

He is troubled that white moderates prefer "a negative peace which is the absence of tension to a positive peace which is the presence of justice." An *order* that does not include justice, then, leads to his connotative definition: that the current *order* means a state of stagnation and a force for inertia (or not making any change or progress). However, in the next few lines, King adds to his connotative definition by criticizing white moderates for "prefer[ring] a negative peace," for "paternalistically believ[ing they] can set the timetable for another man's freedom," for suffering from a "shallow understanding" of the problem and for not understanding "that law and order exist for the purpose of establishing justice and that when they fail in this purpose they become the dangerously structured dams that block the flow of social progress."

The Dictionary.com definition for *justice* is "the quality of conforming to principles of reason, to generally accepted standards of right and wrong, and to the stated terms of laws, rules, agreements, etc. in matters affecting persons who could be wronged or unduly favored." Here King's connotative meaning is complex: he questions the laws that keep order, if the laws are not just. (That is why he later carefully defines just and unjust laws.) When he writes that "law and order exist for the purpose of establishing justice and . . . when they fail in this purpose they become the dangerously structured dams that block the flow of social progress," he is adding to the connotations of the word *justice* (as well as *order*) by arguing how tightly linked order must be to justice—that order for its own sake can prevent society from changing in ways that it needs to change.

Once you define the denotative and connotative meanings of key terms in a passage, write a few sentences summarizing the beliefs and values you have discovered in these meanings. For example, King believes that justice can be achieved only by disturbing the current order or, to put it another way, that a preference for order keeps people from making progress. Order means the status quo, as opposed to change or "progress towards freedom." By uncovering this warrant, you know that King believes that a disturbance of order is necessary to foster African Americans' progress. He does not believe that order is what is most important. Rather, he believes a disturbance of order is justified by the goal of progress toward freedom. King also believes that justice cannot be achieved without disturbing order and that justice is more important than order.

Step 3. *Consider alternative assumptions* readers might have about the key terms in King's argument. If you know anything about the context of the period when the passage was written, or if the author gives you any clues or direct information about the audience, you will be able to figure out these assumptions from the text. For example, whereas King values justice over order, he clearly assumes that white moderates and other readers in 1963 would think the opposite. Write a few sentences exploring the meanings of *order* and *justice* that might lead someone to value order more than justice. King's readers may not feel quite the same way about the concepts embodied in these terms: *order* could mean "safety," or if justice can come only at the price of social chaos, perhaps (as King worries) readers might conclude that it is better to wait for justice than to risk social upheaval.

Step 4. *Restate the warrants underlying the argument (the claim and the reasons)* using the denotations and connotations of the key terms. One way to do this is to phrase the beliefs of the author in *that* clauses. King expects his readers to believe, as he does:

> that justice for African Americans in the 1960s requires progress toward freedom

> that anyone who stops or slows this progress is a stumbling block

> that peace is less important than justice

> that order is less important than justice

> that safety is less important than justice

> that progress is more important than maintaining the status quo

> that social unrest and disorder are necessary to achieve justice

> that although breaking the law (what King calls "direct action" and we know as "civil disobedience") disrupts order, peace, and safety, it is necessary to achieve justice

Step 5. *Explore your own values and beliefs* in relation to those uncovered in your Toulmin analysis. How do you feel about the warrants you identified, given your own experience? Given the difference (if any) between the time the passage was written and the present?

CHECKLIST

Using a Toulmin Analysis

To perform a Toulmin analysis,

1. Identify the author's claim. Identify the reasons and evidence that support that claim.

2. Consider how key terms reflect the author's beliefs and values by defining those terms denotatively and connotatively.

3. Consider alternative assumptions readers might have about the key terms.

4. Restate the author's warrants—the beliefs, values, and assumptions that "warrant" the claim.

5. Compare your own values and beliefs with the author's.

RECOGNIZING LOGICAL FALLACIES

A *logical fallacy* is an error or a distortion in the reasoning process. Sometimes writers are unaware that they have committed a logical fallacy: they believe their logic is correct and don't understand why it is faulty. In many cases, however, writers use a fallacy deliberately because they want to avoid reasoning that might undermine their argument or because they want to divert the reader into a different line of reasoning. As you learn to spot logical fallacies in your reading (and in what you hear on radio and television), you will learn also to avoid them in your writing. Students who study formal debate in a speech course or debate club often learn fallacies so they can call attention to and refute the false logic in an opponent's argument. Ethical writers should beware of using fallacies, but they should know how to recognize them and how to refute them.

Identifying fallacies can be tricky, however. Many of them involve subtle and complex issues of reasoning that require careful thought and analysis. In addition, in many cases reasoning becomes fallacious or false only when it is taken too far—when it has become extreme—and reasonable people can disagree about when that point is reached. In logic, as in life, the line between truth and falsehood is often not clearly defined. In fact, one of the most common logical fallacies is the belief that there are only two choices in particular situations.

In general, though, you should suspect that you might be reading a logical fallacy when you stop to think "wait a minute—that doesn't make sense" or when you believe the writer has "gone too far." Recognizing the following common fallacies is an important step in learning to be a critical reader.

Slippery Slope

A *slippery-slope* fallacy occurs when someone asserts that if one thing happens, then a series of bad related consequences will *necessarily* follow. The name comes from the idea that if a person takes one step down a slippery slope, he or she cannot help sliding all the way to the bottom. Here are a few examples of this type of faulty reasoning:

- Often when people start making improvements to their homes, the work leads to the need for more improvements. If you paint one room, then it makes the rest of the rooms look dingy, so you have to paint them, too; then the windows need replacing; and so on. This is a valid slippery-slope argument because a particular chain of events does often or usually result from the initial action (though not necessarily in every case).

- Antidrug campaigns often claim that if someone smokes marijuana, then he or she will likely become addicted to other illegal drugs. While there is some evidence that marijuana use may lead to additional drug use, this is not true of most people.

- A common argument against euthanasia is that if we allow people to take their own lives (or allow doctors or relatives to help them do so) to avoid extraordinary misery in their final days, then down the line we will allow or encourage assisted suicide for matters that might not be devastating or fatal. Given the relatively brief time in which euthanasia has been practiced legally anywhere in the world, it seems too early to judge whether this argument is based on sound reasoning or is a slippery-slope fallacy.

Post hoc, ergo propter hoc

One of the most common fallacies has the Latin name *post hoc, ergo propter hoc*, which means "after this, therefore because of this." A *post hoc* fallacy wrongly assumes that an event that occurs *after* another event is *caused* by the first event. In many cases, there is no connection at all between the events; in others, a connection does exist, but it is more complicated than the person making it realizes or admits. This fallacy in causal analysis often occurs when writers try to attribute to one cause something that has several or many causes. When complex issues are made to seem simple, look for this fallacy. Here are some examples:

- If you took medicine prescribed by your doctor for a cold and then broke out in hives, you might assume that the medicine caused the hives. However, if you took the medicine with a drink you had never had before, it could have been the drink or the combination of the drink and the medicine that caused the hives. Or the hives might be from a case of nerves or another cause completely unrelated to the medicine, the drink, or anything else you ingested.

- Some people argue that depictions of violence on television and in films cause teenagers to act violently. But most teenagers do not become violent even if they watch a great deal of violence on the screen. To avoid the *post hoc* fallacy, someone making this argument would have to show a clear connection between the amount of violence teenagers watch and the likelihood that they will become violent themselves. The person would also need to consider other possible causes, such as membership in gangs, alienation at school, parental abuse, and so on.

False Dilemma (Either/Or Reasoning)

One of the most common fallacies, the *false dilemma* or *either/or reasoning*, puts readers in the position of having to choose one of two options as if there were no other choices—but rarely in life are options narrowed down to only two. Writers who employ the false dilemma fallacy are usually trying to make the reader choose an option they favor by making the reader believe there are only two choices. Their reasoning avoids the complexities of most issues. Here are some examples:

- Martin Luther King Jr., in paragraph 5 of the excerpt from "Letter from Birmingham Jail" (p. 555), refutes an either/or argument made by others.

Arguing that the choice between a "force of complacency" or a force "of bitterness and hatred" is a false dilemma, King points out that there are other alternatives, among them the option of nonviolent protest that he represents.

- A candidate for governor argues that the way to solve traffic congestion is to turn freeways into toll roads, because building a subway system would be too expensive. This argument sets up a fallacious either/or opposition. In fact, toll roads could help raise funds to pay for a subway system, which would give commuters an alternative means of transportation.

Mistaking the Part for the Whole (Nonrepresentative Sample)

The *nonrepresentative sample* fallacy occurs when a writer assumes that if something is true of a part of a larger whole, then it is true of the whole, or vice versa. Sometimes this is indeed the case, but often it is not because the part is not representative—it does not have the typical characteristics—of the whole. This fallacy often occurs in connection with public opinion polls, especially online polls, when no effort is made to ensure that respondents accurately represent the characteristics of the larger group whose opinion they are said to reflect. Here are some examples of this fallacy:

- One of the best-known examples of a nonrepresentative sample in political polling occurred in the 1936 presidential election, when *Literary Digest* magazine conducted a telephone poll that predicted President Franklin D. Roosevelt would be defeated for reelection by his Republican opponent, Alfred P. Landon. On Election Day, Roosevelt won reelection in a landslide. The main explanation for this faulty forecast was the way in which the poll was conducted: because Republican voters tended to be wealthier than Democratic ones and because during the Depression of the 1930s many Democratic voters could not afford telephones, the magazine surveyed a disproportionately large number of Republicans.

- Suppose that your school has the best football team in its conference. That does not necessarily mean that the quarterback, the kicker, or the defensive line is the best in the conference, because putting the various members of the team together gives the team as a whole qualities that are different from those of the individuals involved.

Hasty Generalization

A *hasty generalization* leaps to a conclusion without providing enough evidence to support the leap. Here are some examples:

- Government leaders think that the appearance of troop maneuvers in a border town of a neighboring country signals an immediate invasion of the nearby territory. However, in the absence of other, confirming information, it could be just as likely that a leader had not planned an invasion but had decided that the border town was a good place to practice troop maneuvers, especially if the goal was to impress the neighbor with his or her military might.

- "Crime in this city is getting worse and worse. Just yesterday, two people were held up at ATMs downtown." Two crimes, no matter how serious, do not indicate that the overall *rate* of crime is rising. This may indeed be the case, but proving it would require statistics, not just a couple of examples.

Bandwagon Appeal

This fallacy can be recognized when someone is appealing to the notion that "since everyone else does it, you should too." *Bandwagon appeals* are probably most common in advertising and political rhetoric. Here are some examples:

- "Join the thousands who've found relief from arthritis pain with Ache-No-More."

- "A powerful new political tide is surging through America. Want to come together with millions of your fellow citizens in a movement to change our nation's priorities? Volunteer for Americans for National Renewal."

Ad hominem (or *ad personam*) Attack

These Latin names mean "to the man" or "to the person." An *ad hominem* or *ad personam attack* occurs when writers attack the person who propounds the ideas with which they disagree, rather than attack the ideas themselves. Certainly the character and credibility of the writer making the argument affect how persuasive a reader finds it, but they do not affect the underlying soundness of the argument. Here are some examples:

- Whenever a writer attacks a person, be alert for a logical fallacy. Martin Luther King Jr. could have attacked the clergy who wrote the letter he is addressing in "Letter from Birmingham Jail." He could have called them intolerant or foolish, for example. Instead, he carefully addresses their arguments step by step and shows how his logic is superior to theirs. Some readers might think King does fall victim to this fallacy when he says that the white moderate has only a "shallow understanding" (paragraph 1) of the problem, but he goes on to show how complex the problem is and how the white moderate needs to become more engaged and active in implementing change.

- "My opponent, one of the richest men in the state, wants to cut taxes for himself and his rich friends." "Of course my opponent favors raising corporate taxes. He's just a political hack who's never had to meet a payroll."

A proposal's value does not depend on whether the person making it will personally benefit from it or has personal experience with the issue involved. Something that benefits the person who proposes it may well (although not necessarily) benefit society in general, and someone with an outsider's perspective on an issue may well (although not necessarily) have better ideas about it than someone with experience. Again, note that sound reasoning is not the same as credibility. Those with something personal to gain from a proposal or with no experience in the issue may carry less credibility with the people they are trying to persuade, but that does not mean that their views are any less logical. An important part of becoming a critical reader is learning to disregard personal attacks on (or ridicule of) the person making an argument and to focus on the logic of the argument.

Straw Man (or Straw Person)

In a straw-man fallacy, the writer portrays an opponent's position as more extreme than it actually is so that it can be refuted more easily, as one would be able to knock down a straw scarecrow more easily than a live human being. As with many other fallacies, however, the line between what is and is not a straw-man argument is not always clear. Sometimes the writer claims that the opponent's position is part of a plan to achieve a more extreme position—and this claim could be considered either a straw-man argument (which would be fallacious) or a slippery-slope argument (which might be fallacious or might not). Here is an example:

- If a political candidate supports partial privatization of Social Security, an opponent who simply claims that the candidate "proposes doing away with Social Security" is creating a straw-man fallacy. If the opponent simply claims that "partial privatization would be a first step toward doing away with Social Security," this would be a slippery-slope argument—which may or may not be fallacious in itself but is not a straw-man argument because it does not actually misrepresent the candidate's position. Finally, if the opponent argues that the candidate "supports partial privatization as a first step toward doing away with Social Security," the reader would have to consider other evidence (such as other positions the candidate has taken or his or her voting record) to judge whether this is a fallacious straw-man argument or a sound slippery-slope one.

Begging the Question (Circular Reasoning)

In *begging the question*, the writer makes an argument that assumes the truth of what is theoretically the point at issue. In other words, to believe what the argument is trying to prove, the reader has to already believe it. Here are some examples:

- "We shouldn't do that because it's a bad idea." This statement essentially just says, "That's a bad idea because it's a bad idea."

- "God created the world in seven days; this has to be true because the Bible says so, and the Bible is the word of God." This example shows why this fallacy is often called *circular reasoning*: the reasoning simply circles back to the original underlying claim that God is all-powerful. If the reader already believes that the Bible is the word of God and therefore is sufficient evidence for God's creation of the world in seven days, then there is no need to make this claim. If not, then he or she will not be convinced by this argument for it.

- When the U.S. Supreme Court was deciding whether to hear the case of *Bush v. Gore*, an appeal of a decision by the Florida Supreme Court after the disputed presidential election of 2000, Justice Antonin Scalia argued that the Court should accept the case to avoid "casting a cloud" over the election of George W. Bush as president. But the point at issue in the case—the claim that was being argued—was whether Bush had indeed been elected president. Gore supporters pointed out that Scalia's argument, based on the assumption that the claim had already been established, was an example of circular reasoning.

Red Herring

You can remember this fallacy by the picture it presents—dragging a dead fish across a trail to distract dogs from pursuing the scent of their real target. In this case, writers use irrelevant arguments to distract readers from the real issue, perhaps because their own argument is weak and they don't want the reader to notice. Red herrings often occur in political debates when one debater does not really want to address an issue raised by the other debater. Here are some examples:

- "My opponent tries to blame my administration for the high price of prescription drugs, but he supports a government takeover of health care." That the opponent supports a government takeover of health care (whether true or false) has nothing to do with whether the policies of the speaker's administration are responsible for the high price of prescription drugs.

- In a U.S. Senate race in 2004, a candidate argued that gay people should not be allowed to adopt children because incest may result if adopted siblings unknowingly marry each other. The risk the candidate mentions is real (if remote), but it is no more likely for children adopted by gay people than for those adopted by heterosexuals. In trying to make an argument against gay adoption, the candidate was making an argument against adoption in general (also implying another kind of incest is likely to occur—between parent and child).

Recognizing Logical Fallacies

To determine whether the writer succumbs to any logical fallacies,

1. Annotate places in the text where you stop to think "wait a minute—that doesn't make sense" or where you think the writer has "gone too far."

2. Analyze these places to see if they represent any of the fallacies discussed in this section.

3. Write a few sentences exploring what you discover.

RECOGNIZING EMOTIONAL MANIPULATION

Writers often try to arouse emotions in readers—to excite their interest, make them care, move them to action. Although nothing is wrong with appealing to readers' emotions, it is wrong to manipulate readers with false or exaggerated emotional appeals.

Many words have connotations, associations that enrich their meaning and give words much of their emotional power. For example, we use the word *manipulation* in naming this particular critical reading strategy to arouse an emotional response in readers like you. No one wants to be manipulated. Everyone wants to feel in control of his or her attitudes and opinions. This is especially true in reading arguments: we want to be convinced, not tricked.

Emotional manipulation often works by distracting readers from relevant reasons and evidence. To keep from being distracted, you want to pay close attention as you read and try to distinguish between emotional appeals that are acceptable and those that you consider manipulative or excessive.

Here is an example of one student's reaction to the emotional appeal of the excerpt from "Letter from Birmingham Jail":

> As someone King would probably identify as a white moderate, I can't help reacting negatively to some of the language he uses in this reading. For example, in the first paragraph, he equates white moderates with members of the Ku Klux Klan even though he admits that white moderates were in favor of racial equality and justice. He also puts down white moderates for being paternalistic. Finally, he uses scare tactics when he threatens "a frightening racial nightmare."

CHECKLIST

Recognizing Emotional Manipulation

To assess whether emotional appeals are unfair and manipulative,

1. Annotate places in the text where you sense emotional appeals are being used.

2. Write a few sentences identifying the kinds of appeals you have found and exploring your responses to them.

JUDGING THE WRITER'S CREDIBILITY

Writers often try to persuade readers to respect and believe them. Because readers may not know them personally or even by reputation, writers must present an image of themselves in their writing that will gain their readers' confidence. This image cannot be made directly but must be made indirectly, through the arguments, language, and system of values and beliefs implied in the writing. Writers establish *credibility* in several ways:

- by showing their knowledge of the subject,

- by building common ground with readers, and

- by responding fairly to objections and opposing arguments.

Testing for Knowledge

Writers demonstrate their knowledge of the subject through the facts and statistics they marshal, the sources they rely on for information, and the scope and depth of their understanding. As a critical reader, you may not be sufficiently expert on the subject yourself to know whether the facts are accurate, the sources reliable, and the understanding sufficient. You may need to do some research to see what others are saying about the subject. You can also check credentials—the writer's educational and professional qualifications, the respectability of the publication in which the selection first appeared, any reviews of the writer's work—to determine whether the writer is a respected authority in the field. King brings with him the authority that comes from being a member of the clergy and a respected leader of the Southern Christian Leadership Conference.

Testing for Common Ground

One way that writers can establish common ground with their readers is by basing their reasoning on shared values, beliefs, and attitudes. They use language that includes their readers (*we*) rather than excludes them (*they*). They qualify their assertions to keep them from being too extreme. Above all, they acknowledge differences of opinion and try to make room in their argument to accommodate reasonable differences. As a reader, you will be affected by such appeals.

King creates common ground with readers by using the inclusive pronoun *we*, suggesting shared concerns between himself and his audience. Notice, however, his use of masculine pronouns and other references ("the Negro . . . he," "our brothers"). Although King intended this letter to be published in the local newspaper, where it would be read by an audience of both men and women, he addressed it to male clergy. By using language that excludes women, King missed the opportunity to build common ground with half his readers.

Testing for Fairness

Writers display their character by how they handle objections to their arguments. As a critical reader, you want to pay particular attention to how writers treat possible differences of opinion. Be suspicious of those who ignore differences and pretend everyone agrees with their viewpoints. When objections or opposing views are represented, you should consider whether they have been distorted in any way; if they are refuted, you want to be sure they are challenged fairly—with sound reasoning and solid evidence.

One way to gauge an author's credibility is to identify the tone of the argument. *Tone*, the writer's attitude toward the subject and toward the reader, is concerned not so much with what is said as with how it is said. By reading sensitively, you should be able to detect the writer's tone. To identify the tone, list whatever descriptive adjectives come to mind in response to either of these questions: How would you characterize the attitude of this selection? What sort of emotion does the writer bring to his or her writing? Judging from this piece of writing, what kind of person does the author seem to be?

Here is one student's answer to the second question, based on the excerpt from "Letter from Birmingham Jail":

> I know something about King from television programs on the civil rights movement. But if I were to talk about my impression of him from this passage, I'd use words like *patient, thoughtful, well educated, moral, confident.* He doesn't lose his temper but tries to convince his readers by making a case that is reasoned carefully and painstakingly. He's trying to change people's attitudes; no matter how annoyed he might be

with them, he treats them with respect. It's as if he believes that their hearts are right, but they're just confused. If he can just set them straight, everything will be fine. Of course, he also sounds a little pompous when he compares himself to Jesus and Socrates, and the threat he appears to make in paragraph 8 seems out of character. Maybe he's losing control of his self-image at those moments.

CHECKLIST

Judging the Writer's Credibility

To decide whether you can trust the writer,

1. As you read and annotate, consider the writer's knowledge of the subject, the ways that the writer establishes common ground with readers, and the ways that the writer deals fairly with objections and opposing arguments.

2. Write a few sentences exploring what you discover.

COMPARING AND CONTRASTING RELATED READINGS

When you *compare* two reading selections, you look for similarities. When you *contrast* them, you look for differences. As critical reading strategies, comparing and contrasting enable you to see both texts more clearly.

Both strategies depend on how imaginative you are in preparing the grounds or basis for comparison. We often hear that it is fruitless, so to speak, to compare apples and oranges. It is true that you cannot add or multiply them, but you can put one against the other and come up with some interesting similarities and differences. For example, comparing apples and oranges in terms of their roles as symbols in Western culture (say, the apple of Adam and Eve compared to the symbol for Apple computers) could be quite productive. The grounds or basis for comparison, like a camera lens, brings some things into focus while blurring others.

To demonstrate how this strategy works, we compare and contrast the excerpt from "Letter from Birmingham Jail" (pp. 553–57) with the following selection by Lewis H. Van Dusen Jr.

Lewis H. Van Dusen Jr.

Legitimate Pressures and Illegitimate Results

A respected attorney and legal scholar, Lewis H. Van Dusen Jr. has served as chair of the American Bar Association Committee on Ethics and Professional Responsibility. This selection comes from the essay "Civil Disobedience: Destroyer of Democracy," which first appeared in the American Bar Association Journal *in 1969. As you read, notice the annotations we made comparing this essay with the one by King.*

1   There are many civil rights leaders who show impatience with the process of democracy. They rely on the sit-in, boycott, or mass picketing to gain speedier solutions to the problems that face every citizen. But we must realize that the legitimate pressures that [won concessions in the past] can easily escalate into the illegitimate power plays that might [extort] demands in the future.] The victories of these civil rights leaders must not shake our confidence in the democratic procedures, as the pressures of demonstration are desirable only if they take place within the limits allowed by law. Civil rights gains should continue to be won by the persuasion of Congress and other legislative bodies and by the decision of courts. Any illegal entreaty for the [rights of some] can be an injury to the [rights of others,] for mass demonstrations often trigger violence.

To get something by force or intimidation

2   Those who advocate [taking the law into their own hands] should reflect that when they are disobeying what they consider to be an immoral law, they are deciding on a possibly immoral course. Their answer is that the process for democratic relief is too slow, that only mass confrontation can bring immediate action, and that any injuries are the inevitable cost of the pursuit of justice. Their answer is, simply put, that the end justifies the means. It is this justification of any form of demonstration as a form of dissent that threatens to destroy a society built on the rule of law.

King's concern with time

*Ends vs. means debate
Any form?*

3   Our Bill of Rights guarantees wide opportunities to use mass meetings, public parades, and organized demonstrations to stimulate sentiment, to dramatize issues, and to cause change. The Washington freedom march of 1963 was such a call for action. But the rights of free expression cannot be mere force cloaked in the garb of free speech. As the courts have decreed in labor cases, free assembly does not mean mass picketing or sit-down

These are legal

strikes. These <u>rights are subject to limitations</u> of time and place
so as to secure the rights of others. When militant students storm
a college president's office to achieve demands, when certain
groups plan rush-hour car stalling to protest discrimination
in employment, these are not dissent, but a <u>denial of rights to
others</u>. Neither is it the lawful use of mass protest, but rather the
unlawful use of mob power.

Justice Black, one of the foremost advocates and defenders   4
of the right of protest and dissent, has said:

> . . . Experience demonstrates that it is not a far step
> from what to many seems to be the earnest, honest,
> patriotic, kind-spirited multitude of today, to the fanati-
> cal, threatening, lawless mob of tomorrow. And the
> crowds that press in the streets for noble goals today
> can be supplanted tomorrow by street mobs pressuring
> the courts for precisely opposite ends.

Society must censure those demonstrators who would tres-   5
pass on the public peace, as it must condemn those rioters
whose pillage would destroy the public peace. But more ambivalent is society's posture toward the civil disobedient. Unlike the
rioter, <u>the true civil disobedient commits no violence</u>. Unlike
the mob demonstrator, <u>he commits no trespass on others' rights</u>.
The civil disobedient, while deliberately violating a law, <u>shows
an oblique respect for the law</u> by voluntarily submitting to its
sanctions. He neither resists arrest nor evades punishment. Thus,
<u>he breaches the law but not the peace</u>.

<u>But</u> civil disobedience, whatever the ethical rationalization,   6
is still an <u>assault</u> on our democratic society, an <u>affront</u> to our
legal order, and an <u>attack</u> on our constitutional government.
To indulge civil disobedience is to invite <u>anarchy</u>, and the per-
missive arbitrariness of anarchy is hardly less tolerable than the
repressive arbitrariness of tyranny. Too often the license of liberty is followed by the loss of liberty, because into the desert of
anarchy comes the man on horseback, a Mussolini or a Hitler.

We had already read and annotated the King excerpt, so we read the Van
Dusen selection looking for a basis for comparison. We decided to base our
contrast on the writers' different views of nonviolent direct action. We carefully reread the Van Dusen selection, annotating aspects of his argument against
the use of nonviolent direct action. These annotations led directly to the first
paragraph of our contrast, which summarizes Van Dusen's argument. Then we

reread the King excerpt, looking for how he justifies nonviolent direct action. The second paragraph of our contrast presents King's defense, plus some of our own ideas on how he could have responded to Van Dusen.

> King and Van Dusen present radically different views of legal, nonviolent direct action, such as parades, demonstrations, boycotts, sit-ins, or pickets. Although Van Dusen acknowledges that direct action is legal, he nevertheless fears it; and he challenges it energetically in these paragraphs. He seems most concerned about the ways direct action disturbs the peace, infringes on others' rights, and threatens violence. He worries that, even though some groups make gains through direct action, the end result is that everyone else begins to doubt the validity of the usual democratic procedures of relying on legislation and the courts. He condemns advocates of direct action like King for believing that the end (in this case, racial justice) justifies the means (direct action). Van Dusen argues that demonstrations often end violently and that an organized movement like King's can in the beginning win concessions through direct action but then end up extorting demands through threats and illegal uses of power.
>
> In contrast, King argues that nonviolent direct action preserves the peace by bringing hidden tensions and prejudices to the surface where they can be acknowledged and addressed. Direct action enhances democracy by changing its unjust laws and thereby strengthening it. Since direct action is entirely legal, to forgo it as a strategy for change would be to turn one's back on a basic democratic principle. Although it may inconvenience people, its end (a more just social order) is entirely justified by its means (direct action). King would no doubt insist that the occasional violence that follows direct action results always from aggressive, unlawful interference with demonstrations—interference sometimes led by police officers. He might also argue that neither anarchy nor extortion followed from his group's actions.

Notice that these paragraphs address each writer's argument separately. An alternative plan would have been to compare and contrast the two writers' arguments point by point.

CHECKLIST

Comparing and Contrasting Related Readings

To compare and contrast two related readings,

1. Read them both to decide on a basis or grounds for comparison or contrast.

2. Reread and annotate one selection to identify points of comparison or contrast.

3. Reread the second selection, annotating for the points you have already identified.

4. Write up your analyses of the two selections, revising your analysis of the first selection to reflect any new insights you have gained. Or write a point-by-point comparison or contrast of the two selections.

Martin Luther King Jr. wrote "Letter from Birmingham Jail" in response to the following public statement by eight Alabama clergymen.

Public Statement by Eight Alabama Clergymen

April 12, 1963

1   We the undersigned clergymen are among those who, in January, issued "An Appeal for Law and Order and Common Sense," in dealing with racial problems in Alabama. We expressed understanding that honest convictions in racial matters could properly be pursued in the courts, but urged that decisions of those courts should in the meantime be peacefully obeyed.

2   Since that time there has been some evidence of increased forebearance and a willingness to face facts. Responsible citizens have undertaken to work on various problems which cause racial friction and unrest. In Birmingham, recent public events have given indication that we all have opportunity for a new constructive and realistic approach to racial problems.

3   However, we are now confronted by a series of demonstrations by some of our Negro citizens, directed and led in part by outsiders. We recognize the natural impatience of people who feel that their hopes are slow in being realized. But we are convinced that these demonstrations are unwise and untimely.

4   We agree rather with certain local Negro leadership which has called for honest and open negotiation of racial issues in our area. And we believe this kind of facing of issues can best be accomplished by citizens of our own metropolitan area, white and Negro, meeting with their knowledge

and experience of the local situation. All of us need to face that responsibility and find proper channels for its accomplishment.

Just as we formerly pointed out that "hatred and violence have no sanction in our religious and political traditions," we also point out that such actions as incite to hatred and violence, however technically peaceful those actions may be, have not contributed to the resolution of our local problems. We do not believe that these days of new hope are days when extreme measures are justified in Birmingham. [5]

We commend the community as a whole, and the local news media and law enforcement officials in particular, on the calm manner in which these demonstrations have been handled. We urge the public to continue to show restraint should the demonstrations continue, and the law enforcement officials to remain calm and continue to protect our city from violence. [6]

We further strongly urge our own Negro community to withdraw support from these demonstrations, and to unite locally in working peacefully for a better Birmingham. When rights are consistently denied, a cause should be pressed in the courts and in negotiations among local leaders, and not in the streets. We appeal to both our white and Negro citizenry to observe the principles of law and order and common sense. [7]

Signed by:

C. C. J. CARPENTER, D.D., LL.D., *Bishop of Alabama*

JOSEPH A. DURICK, D.D., *Auxiliary Bishop, Diocese of Mobile–Birmingham*

Rabbi MILTON L. GRAFMAN, *Temple Emanu-El, Birmingham, Alabama*

Bishop PAUL HARDIN, *Bishop of the Alabama-West Florida Conference of the Methodist Church*

Bishop NOLAN B. HARMON, *Bishop of the North Alabama Conference of the Methodist Church*

GEORGE M. MURRAY, D.D., LL.D., *Bishop Coadjutor, Episcopal Diocese of Alabama*

EDWARD V. RAMAGE, *Moderator, Synod of the Alabama Presbyterian Church in the United States*

EARL STALLINGS, *Pastor, First Baptist Church, Birmingham, Alabama*

2

Strategies for Research and Documentation

A s many of the essays in *Reading Critically, Writing Well* show, writers often rely on research to expand and test their own ideas about a topic. This appendix offers advice on conducting research, evaluating potential sources, integrating source material you decide to use with your own writing, and documenting this material in an acceptable way.

CONDUCTING RESEARCH

In your college career, you may have opportunities to do many different kinds of research, including laboratory experiments and statistical surveys. Here we introduce the three basic types of research you are most likely to use to satisfy the assignments in *Reading Critically, Writing Well* and to fulfill requirements of other lower-division courses: field research using observation and interview, library research, and Internet research.

Doing Field Research

Observation and *interview* are the two major kinds of *field* or *ethnographic research*. The observational essays in Chapter 3 illustrate some of the ways you might use field research. You might also use these research techniques when proposing a solution to a problem (Chapter 9) or when arguing a position on a controversial issue (Chapter 7). You may be asked to read and write essays based on field research in other courses as well, such as in sociology, political science, anthropology, psychology, communication, or business.

Observation

Following are guidelines for planning an observational visit, taking notes on your observations, and reflecting on what you observed.

PLANNING THE VISIT

To ensure that you use your time productively during observational visits, you must plan them carefully.

Getting Access. If the place you propose to visit is public, you probably will have easy access to it. Ask yourself whether everything you need to see is within casual view. If not, you have encountered a potential problem of access. If you require special access or permission, you will need to call ahead or make a get-acquainted visit to introduce yourself and explain your purpose.

Announcing Your Intentions. Explain politely who you are, where you are from, and why you would like access. You may be surprised at how receptive people can be to a student on assignment from a college course. Not every place you wish to visit will welcome you, however. A variety of constraints on outside visitors exist in private businesses as well as public institutions. But generally, if people know your intentions, they may be able to tell you about aspects of a place or an activity you would not have thought to observe.

Bringing Tools. Take a few pens and a notebook with a firm back so that you will have a steady writing surface. If you prefer to use an audio recorder to record your observations, bring along extra tapes and batteries. Also take a notebook in case something goes wrong with the audio recorder.

OBSERVING AND TAKING NOTES

Here are some practical suggestions for making observations and taking notes.

Observing. Some activities invite multiple vantage points, whereas others seem to limit the observer to a single perspective. Explore the space as much as possible, taking advantage of every vantage point available to you. Consider it from different angles, both literally and figuratively. Since your purposes are to analyze as well as to describe your subject, look for its typical and atypical features, how it is like and unlike similar subjects. Think also about what would make the subject interesting to your readers.

Notetaking. You undoubtedly will find your own style of notetaking, but here are a few pointers:

- Take notes in words and phrases. Use abbreviations as much as you like, but use them consistently and clearly.

- Take photos or draw diagrams and sketches that will help you recall the place later on.

- Note any ideas or questions that occur to you.

- Use quotation marks around any overheard conversations you take down.

Because you can later reorganize your observational notes easily, you do not need to record them in any planned or systematic way. Your notes should include information about the place, the people, and your personal reactions to both.

The Place. Begin by listing objects you see. Then add details of some of these objects—color, shape, size, texture, function, relation to similar or dissimilar objects. Although visual details will probably dominate your notes, you might also want to note sounds and smells. Be sure to include some notes about the shape, dimensions, and layout of the place. How big is it? How is it organized?

The People. Note the number of people and their activities, movements, and behavior. Describe their appearance or dress. Record parts of overheard conversations. Note whether you see more men than women, more people of one racial group than of another, more older than younger people. Most important, note anything surprising or unusual about people in the scene and how they interact with one another.

REFLECTING ON YOUR OBSERVATIONS

Immediately after your visit (within a few minutes, if possible), find a quiet place to reflect on what you saw, review your notes, and add any images, details, insights, or questions you now recall. Give yourself at least a half hour to add to your notes and to write a few sentences about your main impressions of the place. What did you learn? How did this visit change or confirm your preconceptions? What impression of the place and people would you like to convey to readers?

Interview

Here are guidelines for planning and setting up an interview, conducting an interview, and reflecting on what you learned.

PLANNING THE INTERVIEW

Choosing an Interview Subject. If you will be interviewing a person who is the focus of your research, consider beginning with one or two background interviews with other people. If several people play important roles in your subject, interview as many of them as possible. Try to be flexible, because you may be unable to speak with the people you targeted initially and may wind up interviewing someone else—an assistant, perhaps. You might even learn more from an assistant than you would from the person in charge.

Arranging an Interview. You may be nervous about phoning or e-mailing a busy person and asking for some of his or her time. Indeed, you may get turned down. If so, do ask if someone else might talk with you: many people are genuinely flattered to be asked about themselves and their work. Moreover, because you are a college student on assignment, some people may feel that they are doing a public service by allowing you to interview them. When arranging the interview, introduce yourself with a short, simple, and enthusiastic description of your project.

Keep in mind that the person you want to interview will be donating time to you. When you call or e-mail ahead to arrange a specific time for the interview, be sure to ask what time is most convenient. Arrive at the appointed time, and bring all the materials you will need to conduct the interview. Remember, too, to express your thanks when the interview has ended.

Preparing for the Interview. Make any necessary observational visits, and do any essential background reading before the interview. Consider your objectives: for example, do you want the "big picture," answers to specific questions, or clarification of something you observed, read, or heard about in another interview?

The key to good interviewing is flexibility. You may be looking for facts, but your interview subject may not have any to offer. In that case, you should be willing to shift gears and go after whatever insight your subject does have to offer.

Composing Interview Questions. You probably will want to mix *specific questions* requesting factual information with *open-ended questions*, which are likely to generate anecdotes and reveal attitudes that could lead to other, more penetrating questions. In interviewing a small-business owner, for example, you might begin with a specific question about when the business was established and then follow up with an open-ended question, such as "Could you take a few minutes to tell me something about your early days in the business? I'd be interested to hear about how you got started, what your hopes were, and what problems you had to face." Also consider asking directly for an anecdote ("What happened when your employees threatened to strike?"), encouraging reflection ("What do you think has helped you most? What has hampered you?"), or soliciting advice ("What advice would you give someone trying to start a new business today?").

The best questions encourage the interview subject to talk freely but to the point. If the answer strays too far from the point, a follow-up question may be necessary to refocus the talk. Another way to direct the conversation is to rephrase the subject's answer, saying something like "Let me see if I have this right . . ." or "Am I correct in saying that you feel . . . ?" Often, the interview subject will take this opportunity to amplify the original response by adding just the anecdote or quotation you have been looking for.

One type of question to avoid during interviewing is the *leading question*. Such questions assume too much. Consider, for example, this question: "Do you think the increase in the occurrence of rape is due to the fact that women are perceived as competitors in a severely depressed economy?" The question makes several assumptions, including that there is an increase in the occurrence of rape, that women are perceived (apparently by rapists) as competitors, and that the economy is severely depressed. A better way of asking the question might be to make the assumptions more explicit by dividing the question into its parts: "Do you think there is an increase in the occurrence of rape? What could have caused it? I've heard some people argue that the economy has something to do with it. Do you think so? Do you think rapists perceive women as competitors? Could the current economic situation have made this competition more severe?" This form of questioning allows you to voice what others have said without bullying your subject into echoing your terms.

Bringing Tools. You will need several pencils or pens and a notebook with a firm back so you can write without a table. We recommend dividing the page into two columns. Use the left-hand column (one-third of the page) to note your impressions and descriptions of the scene, the person, and the mood of the interview. Title this column *Impressions*. Title the wider, right-hand column *Information*. Before the interview, write down a few basic questions to jog your memory. During the interview, however, listen and ask questions based on what your interview subject says. Do not mechanically go through your list of questions.

TAKING NOTES DURING THE INTERVIEW

Your interview notes might include a few full quotations, key words, and phrases to jog your memory, as well as descriptive jottings about the scene, the person, and the mood of the interview. Remember that how something is said may be as important as what is said. Do not try to record everything your subject says during the interview. Except for the occasional quotation that you will cite directly, you do not want to make a verbatim transcript of the interview. You may not have much confidence in your memory, but if you pay close attention to your subject you are likely to recall a good deal of the conversation immediately after the interview, when you should take the time to add to your notes.

REFLECTING ON THE INTERVIEW

Soon after the interview has concluded, find a quiet place to review your notes. Spend at least half an hour adding to your notes and thinking about what you learned. At the end of this time, write a few sentences about your main impressions from the interview:

- What were the highlights of the interview for you?

- Which questions did not get as much of a response as you anticipated or seem less important to you now?

- How did the interview change your attitude toward or understanding of the subject?

- How has this experience influenced your plans to interview others or to reinterview this person?

Doing Library Research

Most college libraries are more complex than typical high school or public libraries, so make a point of getting acquainted with your school's library. Your instructor may arrange a library orientation tour for your composition class. If not, find out whether the library offers tours, and, if so, take one. Otherwise, design your own tour (for suggestions of important resources to look for in your college library, see the table on p. 608.)

DESIGNING YOUR SELF-GUIDED LIBRARY TOUR

Library Resource	What This Resource Does for You
Circulation desk	Check out materials, place holds and recalls, pay fees or fines.
Reference desk/room	Obtain help from reference librarians to locate and use library resources. Find reference materials such as encyclopedias, dictionaries, handbooks, atlases, bibliographies, statistics, and periodical indexes and abstracts.
Reserves	Gain access to books and journal articles that are on reserve for specific classes.
Interlibrary loan	Request materials not available on site. (*Note: Many libraries now offer this service online only.*)
Open-access computers	Gain access to the library catalog, electronic periodical indexes, the campus network, and the Internet.
Periodicals	Locate bound and unbound current issues of newspapers, journals, and magazines. (*Note: Many periodicals are now available electronically through the library databases.*)
Government publications	Locate publications from federal, state, and local government agencies.
Multimedia resources	Locate nonprint materials such as videos, CD-ROMs, and audiotapes.
Microforms	Locate materials on microfilm (reels) and microfiche (cards).
Special collections/ Rare-book room	Find rare or highly specialized materials not readily available in most library collections (*in larger libraries only*).
Archives	Find collections of papers from important individuals and organizations that provide source material for original research (*in larger libraries only*).
Maps and atlases	Locate maps and atlases (housed in a special location because of their size and format).
Copiers, printers, and scanners	Make copies, print, and/or scan material. (*Note: Be aware that you almost always pay for copies by the page, and some libraries charge for printing or require students to supply their own paper.*)

Library Resource	What This Resource Does for You
Reading areas	Read in quiet, comfortable areas.
Study rooms	Study in rooms reserved for individuals or small groups.
Computer labs	Use networked computers for word processing, research, and other functions.

You don't have to visit in person, though, to find out what your college library offers. Most libraries have useful Web sites describing their resources and services, and many offer virtual tours. Many of these sites also offer access to online databases, tutorials for using the library's resources, expert advice on doing research and writing, and more.

Consulting Librarians

Think of college librarians as instructors whose job is to help you understand the library and get your hands on resources you need to complete your research projects. You should not hesitate to approach them with any questions you have about getting started, locating sources, or completing your research project. Remember, however, that they can be most helpful when you can explain your research assignment clearly and ask questions that are as specific as possible. You need not do so face-to-face: Many libraries now offer e-mail, phone, or Internet chat or messaging options to connect library users to a reference librarian.

Finding Out What Your Library Offers

For your library research to be manageable and productive, you will want to work carefully and systematically, and this takes time. Although specific search strategies may vary to fit the needs of individual research tasks, the general process presented on page 610 should help you organize your time. Remember that you will be constantly refining and revising your research strategy as you find out more about your topic.

At this early stage, you need an overview of your topic. Your instructor and/ or a reference librarian can advise you about sources that provide overviews of your topic. If your topic is currently in the news, you will want to consult newspapers, magazines, or Web sites. For all other topics, encyclopedias and bibliographies are often the place to start.

Consulting Encyclopedias

General encyclopedias, such as the *Encyclopaedia Britannica* and the *Columbia Encyclopedia*, provide basic information about many topics. Like

OVERVIEW OF AN INFORMATION SEARCH STRATEGY

Know your research task and your resources.

Find out what your library offers.

Get an overview of your topic.

- Look in encyclopedias and bibliographies.
- Review textbooks and other course materials.
- Explore newspapers, magazines, and Internet sites.
- Consult with your instructor and/or a reference librarian.
- Construct a list of keywords and subject headings.
- Develop a preliminary topic statement.

Keep track of what you learn.

- Keep a working bibliography.
- Take notes.

Search for in-depth information on your topic.

Conduct a preliminary search for sources, using keywords and subject headings.

- Check the online catalog for books.
- Check periodical databases for articles.
- Check Internet sites.

Evaluate and refine your search by asking yourself:

- Is this what I expected to find?
- Am I finding enough?
- Am I finding too much?
- Do I need to modify my keywords?
- Do I need to recheck background sources?
- Do I need to modify my topic statement?

Refine your search based on the answers.

Locate sources.

- Books
- Magazine and journal articles
- Newspaper articles
- Internet sites
- Government and statistical sources
- Other sources appropriate to your topic

Evaluate your sources.

- For information
- For relevance
- For accuracy
- For comprehensiveness
- For bias
- For currency

Continue to evaluate and refine your search strategy based on the research results.

many encyclopedias, these works are available online and in print. Wikipedia is often the first stop for students who are accustomed to consulting the open Internet first for information. Wikipedia is not always a reliable source, however, so you should ask your instructor for advice on consulting it at this stage. Whichever general encyclopedia you consult, bear in mind that general encyclopedias should be used only for an overview of a topic; on their own, they are not adequate resources for college research.

Specialized encyclopedias cover topics in more depth than general encyclopedias do. In addition to providing an overview of a topic, they often include an explanation of issues related to the topic, definitions of specialized terminology, and selective bibliographies of additional sources. The following list identifies some specialized encyclopedias in the major academic disciplines:

Art	*Dictionary of Art*
Biology	*Concise Encyclopedia Biology*
Chemistry	*Concise Encyclopedia Chemistry*
Computers	*Encyclopedia of Computer Science and Technology*
Economics	*Fortune Encyclopedia of Economics*
Education	*Encyclopedia of Educational Research*
Environment	*Encyclopedia of the Environment*
Foreign Relations	*Encyclopedia of U.S. Foreign Relations*
	Encyclopedia of the Third World
History	*Encyclopedia USA*
	New Cambridge Modern History
Law	*Corpus Juris Secundum*
	American Jurisprudence
Literature	*Encyclopedia of World Literature in the Twentieth Century*
	Encyclopedia of Literature and Criticism
Medicine	*American Medical Association's Complete Medical Encyclopedia*
Music	*New Grove Dictionary of Music and Musicians*
Nursing	*Miller-Keane Encyclopedia and Dictionary of Medicine, Nursing, and Allied Health*

Philosophy	*Routledge Encyclopedia of Philosophy*
Psychology	*Encyclopedia of Psychology*
Religion	*Encyclopedia of Religion*
Science	*McGraw-Hill Encyclopedia of Science and Technology*
Social Sciences	*International Encyclopedia of the Social Sciences*
Sociology	*Encyclopedia of Sociology*
Women's Studies	*Women's Studies Encyclopedia*

Consulting Bibliographies

A **bibliography** is simply a list of publications on a given subject. All researched articles and books include bibliographies to document their sources of information. In addition, separately published, book-length bibliographies exist for many subjects that have attracted significant amounts of writing. Some bibliographies are annotated with brief summaries and evaluations of the entries.

Even if you attend a large research university, your library is unlikely to hold every book or journal article that a bibliography might direct you to. If a source looks likely to be useful but your library does not have a copy, ask a reference librarian about the possibility of acquiring it from another library through interlibrary loan.

Keeping Track of Your Research

As you research your topic, you will want to keep a careful record of all the sources you locate by setting up a working bibliography. You will also want to take notes on your sources in some systematic way.

Keeping a Working Bibliography

A **working bibliography** is a preliminary, ongoing record of books, articles, Web sites, and other sources of information you discover as you research your subject. In addition, you can use your working bibliography to keep track of any encyclopedias and bibliographies you consult, even though these general reference tools are usually not cited in an essay.

Each entry in a working bibliography is called a **bibliographic citation**. The information you record in each bibliographic citation will help you to locate the source in the library and then, if you end up using it in your paper, to *cite* or *document* it in the list of references or works cited you provide at the end of an essay. *Recording this information for each possible source as you identify it, rather than reconstructing it later, will save you hours of work.* In addition to the bibliographic information, note the library location where the source is kept, the name of the database or other reference work where you learned about it, and the date you accessed it, just in case you have to track it down again. (See the forms below and on p. 614 for guidelines on what to record for a book or a print periodical article. For guidelines for Internet sources, see the form on p. 629.)

INFORMATION FOR WORKING BIBLIOGRAPHY– BOOKS

Author	
Title	
Place of publication	
Publisher	
Date of publication	
Location	
Notes	

This appendix presents two common documentation styles—one adopted by the Modern Language Association (MLA) and widely used in the humanities, and the other advocated by the American Psychological Association (APA) and used in the social sciences. Other disciplines have their own preferred styles of documentation. Confirm with your instructor which documentation style is required for your assignment so that you can follow that style for all the sources you put into your working bibliography.

Practiced researchers keep their working bibliography in a computer file, in a notebook, or on index cards. Researchers who record the information in a computer file use either standard software (such as Word or Excel) or specialized software (such as RefWorks, EndNote, Zotero, or the Bedford Bibliographer) designed for creating bibliographies. Others find index cards convenient because they are portable and easy to arrange in the alphabetical order required for the list of works

INFORMATION FOR WORKING BIBLIOGRAPHY—
PERIODICAL ARTICLES

Author of article	
Title of article	
Title of journal	
Volume / issue number	
Date of issue	
Page numbers	
Location	
Notes	

cited or references. Still others find cards too easy to lose and prefer instead to keep everything—working bibliography, notes, and drafts—in a notebook.

Whatever method you use for your working bibliography, your entries need to be accurate and complete. If the call number you record for a book is incomplete or inaccurate, for example, you may not be able to find the book easily on the shelves. If you initially get some bibliographic information from a catalog or an index, check it again for accuracy when you examine the source directly.

Taking Notes

When you find a useful **electronic source**, print it out and/or download the material to a flash drive or network drive, if possible. It is also a good idea to e-mail it to yourself. Be sure your electronic version includes all the source information required by the documentation system you are using. To take notes on a document you have downloaded, you can either print it out and annotate by hand, copy and paste relevant passages into a separate document, or (depending on the format in which you download it) annotate it electronically.

When you find a useful **print source**, photocopying it can be helpful, because you can make notes directly on the photocopied page and highlight material you may wish to quote, summarize, or paraphrase. Photocopying also allows you to reread and analyze important sources at your leisure. It can be costly, however, so you will want to be selective. If you do choose to photocopy, be sure to copy title pages or other publication information for each source, or otherwise record this information on your copy of the text.

Some libraries now offer the option of scanning documents. Once you have scanned a document you can print and annotate it, or, depending on the format, annotate it electronically or cut and paste key information into another document. Be sure your scanned version includes all the source information.

If you can neither photocopy, download, nor scan a source, you will have to record source information, notes, and quotations carefully in a separate document. *If you record notes separately, be sure to include the page numbers where you find information, so that you can go back and reread if necessary.* You will also need to give page numbers when you cite sources within your essay and in your list of works cited.

Be sure *never* to copy an author's phrases and sentences without enclosing them in quotation marks and noting the source, and always double-check all your notes for accuracy. Messy or inaccurate notes can lead to **plagiarism**, the unacknowledged and therefore improper use of another's phrases and sentences or ideas.

Searching Library Catalogs and Periodical Databases

Books and periodical articles are the two types of sources most commonly used for academic research projects. Books can be found in the library's **online catalog**. Articles in periodicals are listed in **periodical databases** or **indexes**. Much of the success of your research will depend on your ability to effectively search online library catalogs and periodical databases.

Search Strategies

Computerized library catalogs and periodical databases consist of thousands or even millions of records, each representing an item such as a book, an article, or a government publication. Each record is made up of different fields describing the item.

Basic search strategies include author, title, keyword, and subject searches. When you perform an **author search**, the computer looks for a match between the name you type and the names listed in the author field of all the records in the online catalog or other database. When you perform a **title search**, the computer looks for a match in the title field. Most systems will try to match only the exact terms you enter.

Most online catalogs also permit **keyword** searching, which is an effective way to get started in most cases. Keywords are words or phrases that describe your topic. As you read about your subject in an encyclopedia or other reference book, you should keep a list of keywords that may be useful.

As you review the results of a keyword search, look for the titles that seem to match most closely the topics that you are looking for. (It is usually a good sign, for example, if your keyword(s) appear in the title.) If you get too few relevant returns, try different keywords. When you call up the detailed information for titles that seem promising, look for the section labeled "Subject" or "Subject Heading." **Subject headings** are specific words and phrases used in library catalogs and periodical databases to categorize the contents of books and articles. In many catalogs and databases, these subject headings are links that you can click on to get a list of other materials on the same subject. Here is an example of an online catalog listing for a book on home schooling:

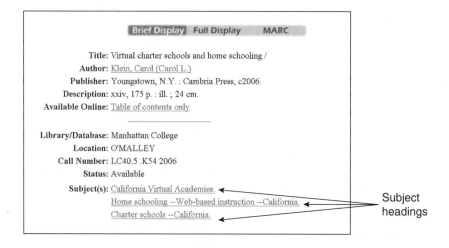

The table on p. 617 describes some search capabilities commonly offered by library catalogs and databases.

Advanced Searches and Boolean Operators. The real power of using online catalogs or other databases is demonstrated when you need to look up books or articles using more than one search term. For example, suppose you want information about home schooling in California. Rather than looking through an index listing all the articles on home schooling and picking out those that mention California, you can ask the computer to do the work for you by linking your two keywords. Most online catalogs and databases offer the option

COMMON SEARCH CAPABILITIES OFFERED BY LIBRARY CATALOGS AND DATABASES

Type of Search	How the Computer Conducts the Search	Things to Know
Author Search (exact) • Individual (*Guterson, David*) • Organization (*U.S. Department of Education*)	Looks in the author field for the words entered	• Names are usually, but not always, entered *last name, first name* (for example, "Shakespeare, William"). • Organizations can be considered authors. Enter the name of the organization in natural word order. • An exact-match author search is useful for finding books and articles by a particular author.
Title Search (exact) • Book title • Magazine or journal title	Looks in the title field for words in the exact order you enter them	An exact-match title search is useful for identifying the location of known items, such as when you are looking for a particular journal or book.
Subject Search (exact)	Looks in the subject heading or descriptor field for words in the exact order you enter them	An exact-match subject search is useful when you are sure about the subject heading.
Keyword Search	Looks in the title, note, subject, abstract, and text fields for the words entered	A keyword search is the broadest kind you can use. It is useful during early exploration of a subject.

of an **advanced search**, sometimes on a separate page from the main search page, that allows you to search for more than one keyword at a time, search for certain keywords while excluding others, or search for an exact phrase.

Most systems also allow you to perform advanced searches by using the **Boolean operators** AND, OR, and NOT. To understand the operation of **Boolean logic** (developed by and named after George Boole, a nineteenth-century mathematician), picture one set of articles about home schooling and another set of articles about California. A third set is formed by articles that are about both home schooling and California. The figures that follow provide an illustration of how each Boolean operator works.

The Boolean Operators: AND, OR, and NOT

AND

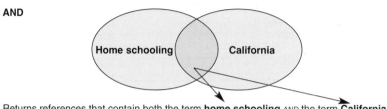

Returns references that contain both the term **home schooling** AND the term **California**

- Narrows the search
- Combines unrelated terms
- Is the default used by most online catalogs and databases

OR

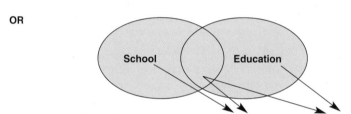

Returns all references that contain either the term **school** OR the term **education** OR both terms

- Broadens the search **("OR is more")**
- Is useful with synonyms and variant spellings: ("home schooling" and "homeschooling")

NOT

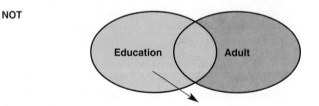

Returns references that include the term **education** but NOT the term **adult**

- Narrows the search
- May eliminate relevant material

Truncation. Another useful search strategy employs **truncation**. With this technique, you drop the ending of a word or term and replace it with a symbol, which indicates you want to retrieve records containing any term that begins the same way as your term. Truncation symbols vary with the catalog or database. The question mark (?), asterisk (*), and pound sign (#) are frequently used. Truncation is useful when you want to retrieve both the plural and singular forms of a word or any word for which you are not sure of the ending. For example, in systems using the asterisk, the term *"home school*"* would return all the records that have terms such as *home school, home schooling, home schools, home schooled,* or *home schoolers.*

The table below offers suggestions for expanding or narrowing an electronic search.

ELECTRONIC SEARCH TIPS

If You Find Too Many Sources on Your Topic	If You Find Insufficient Information on Your Topic
• Use a subject search instead of a keyword search. • Add additional words to your search. • Use a more precise vocabulary to describe your topic. • Use an advanced search to restrict your findings by date, format, language, or other options.	• Use a keyword instead of a subject. • Eliminate words from your search terms. • Try truncated forms of your keyword. • Use different words to describe your topic. • Check the spelling of each term you type.

Finding Articles: Using Periodical Databases or Indexes

Traditionally available in print, in microform, or on CD-ROM, most major periodical indexes are now available online. (Keep in mind, however, that some of these online databases cover only the last fifteen to twenty years; for some research projects, you may need to consult older printed versions of indexes as well.) Some of the general databases serve mainly as indexes. Others, however, include **abstracts** or short summaries of articles, and some give you access to the **full text** of articles.

Beginning on the next page you will find a list of some of the most common periodical databases, divided into three categories: general, newspaper, and subject-specific. Your college library will likely subscribe to some but not all of these databases. Note that many online databases listed here are delivered via one of three major online reference database services—EBSCOhost, InfoTrac, and WilsonWeb—which allow you to search multiple databases in a single search. Many libraries also offer access to a separate **federated search engine**, which allows you to search multiple databases across database services.

General guidelines for searching online databases are given on pp. 615–19. Because online databases contain so much information, however, you may want to consult with a librarian to develop an efficient search strategy.

General Databases and Indexes.   These indexes are a good place to start your research because they cover a broad range of subjects in popular periodicals and scholarly journals.

Academic OneFile (InfoTrac) provides full text for more than 11,000 peer-reviewed journals.

Academic Search Premier (EBSCOhost) provides full text for more than 4,500 academic journals, including more than 3,700 peer-reviewed titles.

CQ Researcher offers an overview, background, and bibliography on news-worthy or controversial topics (e.g., terrorism, global warming, stem-cell research) in public health, social trends, criminal justice, international affairs, education, the environment, technology, and the economy.

General OneFile (InfoTrac) offers full text for more than 11,000 general-interest magazines.

JSTOR offers a high-quality, interdisciplinary archive of over 1,000 academic journals across the humanities, social sciences, and sciences.

MasterFILE (EBSCOhost) provides full text for over 1,800 general-interest, business, consumer health, general science, and multicultural periodicals, in addition to indexing and abstracts for over 2,500 other periodicals.

Project Muse offers scholarly journals in the arts and humanities, social sciences, and mathematics; currently the database includes 385 journals by 91 publishers.

Newspaper Databases and Indexes.   Libraries used to photograph newspapers and store them in miniature form on microfilm (reels) or microfiche (cards) that must be placed in viewing machines to be read. Now much of this material is available online. Newspaper indexes such as the *Los Angeles Times Index, New York Times Index*, and *London Times Index*, which are available online as well as in print, can help you locate specific articles on your topic. Many include the full text of articles going back a number of years. Your library may also subscribe to the following:

Alt-PressWatch offers full-text access to selected newspapers, magazines, and journals of the alternative and independent press.

LexisNexis provides full-text access to documents from over 5,600 news, business, legal, medical, and reference publications, including U.S. and international newspapers, magazines, wire services, newsletters, and broadcast transcripts.

NewsBank provides full-text newspaper articles from the *New York Times, Los Angeles Times, Washington Post, Atlanta Journal-Constitution, Chicago*

Tribune, Christian Science Monitor, and many others. *NewsBank* is especially useful for local and regional (United States) papers.

Newspaper Source provides cover-to-cover full text for 35 national and international newspapers and selective full text for 375 regional (U.S.) newspapers, in addition to full-text television and radio news transcripts.

Proquest Newspapers provides full-text access to articles from U.S. national newspapers, international English-language newspapers, and selected regional/state newspapers.

Subject-Specific Databases and Indexes. These databases list or summarize articles from periodicals devoted to specific fields of study. Here is a list of some of the more common subject-specific periodical databases:

America: History and Life indexes 1,700 journals from 1964 to present, covering the history and culture of the United States and Canada.

Business Source Premier (EBSCOhost) provides full text for more than 2,300 marketing, management, MIS, POM, accounting, finance, and economics journals, including more than 1,100 peer-reviewed titles.

ERIC (Educational Resource Information Center) contains links to more than 224,000 full-text documents and more than 1,243,000 records of education-related literature.

Humanities Index offers full text (starting 1995) plus abstracts and bibliographic indexes (starting 1984) of scholarly sources in the humanities.

MEDLINE allows users to search abstracts from over 4,600 current biomedical journals covering the fields of medicine, nursing, dentistry, veterinary medicine, the healthcare system, preclinical sciences, and more.

MLA (Modern Language Association) International Bibliography indexes 3,000 English-language and foreign periodicals as well as books, book chapters, and dissertations dating back to the 1920s.

PAIS International indexes articles, books, conference proceedings, government documents, book chapters, and statistical directories in the area of public affairs. Topics include business, government, international relations, banking, environment, health, social sciences, demographics, law and legislation, political science, public administration, finance, agriculture, education, and statistics.

PsycINFO contains over 2.5 million citations to and summaries of peer-reviewed articles and other documents in the field of psychology dating as far back as the early 1800s.

Science Full Text offers full text, indexing, and abstracts from over 320 journals in the fields of zoology, biology, earth science, environmental science, genetics, botany, and chemistry.

Social Sciences Index covers concepts, trends, opinions, theories, and methods from more than 350 English-language periodicals in the social sciences.

Distinguishing Scholarly Journals and Popular Magazines

Although they are both called periodicals, journals and magazines have important differences. **Journals** publish articles written by experts in a particular field of study, frequently professors or researchers in academic institutions. Journals are usually specialized in their subject focus, research oriented, and peer reviewed (that is, extensively reviewed by specialists) prior to publication. They are intended to be read by experts and students conducting research. **Magazines**, in contrast, usually publish articles written to entertain and educate the general public. In most college courses requiring research, original research published in journals is preferred to the accounts of research and other trends published in magazines. For this reason, it is important to note that many periodical databases will let you limit a search to scholarly journals.

The table below summarizes some of the important differences between scholarly journals and popular magazines.

HOW TO DISTINGUISH A SCHOLARLY JOURNAL FROM A POPULAR MAGAZINE

Scholarly Journal	Popular Magazine
• It is usually published once every other month or four times per year. • The authors of articles have *Ph.D.* or academic affiliations after their names. • Many articles have more than one author. • A short summary (abstract) of an article may appear on the first page. • Most articles are fairly long, five to twenty pages. • The articles may include charts, tables, figures, and quotations from other scholarly sources. • The articles have a bibliography (list of references to other books and articles) at the end.	• It is published frequently, usually once a week or once a month. • The authors of articles are journalists or reporters. • Most articles have a single author but may quote experts. • A headline or engaging description may precede the article. • Most of the articles are fairly short, one to five pages. • The articles have color pictures and sidebar boxes. • The articles do not include a bibliography.

Locating Periodicals in the Library

Let us say that you have identified a promising magazine, journal, or newspaper article in a periodical index or database. If that article is not available in full text electronically, you must go to the library's online catalog or online periodicals list to learn whether the library subscribes to the periodical, whether the issue is available, and, if so, where you can find it. No library can subscribe to every periodical, so as you go through indexes and databases, be sure to identify more articles than you actually need. This will save you from having to repeat your search later.

Although every library arranges its print periodicals differently, recent issues are usually arranged alphabetically by title on open shelves. Older issues may be bound like books or filmed and available in microform.

Suppose you want to look up the following article from the *Journal for the Scientific Study of Religion* that you found indexed in *Academic Search Premier*:

Alternative Schooling Strategies and *the Religious Lives* of American Adolescents.
By: UECKER, JEREMY E., *Journal for the Scientific Study of Religion*, Dec 2008, Vol. 47 Issue 4, p563-584, 22p;
DOI: 10.1111/j.1468-5906.2008.00427.x; (AN 35052364)
Add to folder | Cited References: (24)

Since the article is not available online, you need to do a bit more digging to find a copy. You start with the library's online catalog or online periodicals list, searching by the title of the journal, and you find the following record:

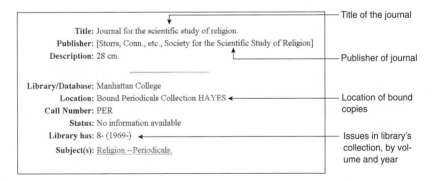

From this record, you would learn that the library does subscribe to the journal and that you could locate the December 2008 issue in the library's periodicals collection. If your library does not subscribe to a journal you are looking for, consult a reference librarian for other ways to access it (interlibrary loan, for example).

Finding Books: Using the Online Library Catalog

Look again at the sample catalog listing for a book on home schooling:

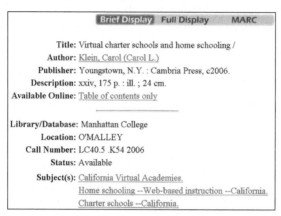

Whether you performed your search by author, title, subject, or keyword, each record you find will provide the following standard information.

1. **Title:** The title appears exactly as it does on the title page of the book, except that only the first word and proper nouns and adjectives are capitalized.

2. **Author:** The author's name usually appears last name first, sometimes followed by birth and (if applicable) death dates. For books with multiple authors, the record includes an author entry under each author's name.

3. **Publication information:** The place of publication, the publisher, and the year of publication are listed. If the book was published simultaneously in the United States and abroad, both places and publishers are indicated.

4. **Physical description:** This section provides information about the book's page length and size. A roman numeral indicates the number of pages devoted to front matter (such as a preface, table of contents, and acknowledgments).

5. **Location:** While a call number explains where a book is shelved in relation to other books, large library systems might be divided across more than one physical location. If that's the case, the name of that location will be listed.

6. **Call number:** Most college libraries use the Library of Congress system, and most public libraries use the Dewey decimal system. Call numbers provide an exact location for every book in the library, and because they are assigned according to subject classifications, they group together books on the same

topic. When you go to the stacks to locate the book, therefore, always browse for other useful material on the shelves around it.

7. *Status:* Most catalogs will tell you whether a book is on the shelf, already checked out, lost, etc. Some will allow you to reserve or hold a book.

8. *Subject headings:* These headings indicate how the book is categorized in terms of subject. Often, these subject headings are active links; clicking on them will bring up a list of other books on the same subject.

If your search for books in your college library yields little that is useful to you, do not give up. Most college libraries belong to one or more **interlibrary networks** that can be useful to you in your search. Known by different names in different regions, these networks allow you to search in the catalogs of colleges and universities in your area and across the country. Also consider using a relatively new Internet source called WorldCat (http://www.worldcat.org), which searches through some ten thousand libraries in the United States. WorldCat links directly to the library's catalog if a specific library has the book. In many cases, you can request a book by interlibrary loan, although it may take several weeks to be delivered to your library.

Finding Government and Statistical Information

Federal, state, and local governments now make many of their publications and reference services available directly through the Web, though most college libraries still maintain print collections of government publications. Ask a reference librarian for assistance in locating governmental sources and other sources of statistical information in the library or on the Web. The following sources can be useful in finding information on political subjects and national trends:

Congressional Quarterly (CQ.com) is a news and analysis service that includes up-to-date summaries of congressional committee actions, congressional votes, and executive branch activities as well as overviews of current policy discussions and other activities of the federal government.

Google U.S. Government Search (www.google.com/unclesam) is a search engine for federal, state, and local government material.

GPO Access, a service of the U.S. Government Printing Office, provides free electronic access to documents produced by the federal government.

Statistical Abstract of the United States is a publication of the Bureau of the Census, providing a variety of social, economic, and political statistics from 1878 to the present, including tables, graphs, charts, and references to additional sources of information.

WorldAlmanac presents information on a variety of subjects drawn from many sources, including a chronology of the year, climatological data, and lists of inventions and awards.

Finding Other Library Sources

Libraries hold vast amounts of useful materials other than books, periodicals, and government documents. Some of the following may be appropriate for your research:

- *Digital collections:* Materials that have been scanned or otherwise saved in digital format and made available online

- *Special collections:* Manuscripts, rare books, and materials of local interest

- *Audio collections:* Records, audiotapes, music CDs, readings, and speeches

- *Video collections:* Slides, filmstrips, videotapes, and DVDs

- *Art collections:* Drawings, paintings, and engravings

- *Computer resources:* Interactive computer programs that combine text, video, and audio resources in history, literature, business, and other disciplines

Determining the Most Promising Sources

As you search for sources in your library's catalog and databases, you will discover many seemingly relevant books and articles. How do you decide which ones to track down? You may have little to go on but author, title, date, and publisher or periodical name, but these details actually provide useful clues. Look

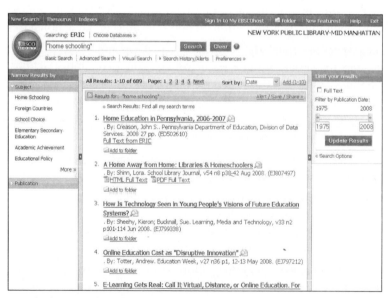

ERIC database search results

again, for example, at the online catalog listing for *Virtual Charter Schools and Home Schooling* (p. 624). Note that the publication date, 2006, is fairly recent. From the subject headings, you can see that the geographic focus of the book is California. Finally, from the title and subject headings, you can see that the book emphasizes online (or virtual) learning.

Now look at the image on the previous page, which shows search results from *ERIC*, an electronic periodical database of education journals, searched through EBSCOhost. The search on the term *home schooling* yielded 689 articles. Looking just at the titles of the article and the journal, you can surmise that the first article is a government publication on home schooling in Pennsylvania between 2006 and 2007; the second expresses a librarian's point of view; and the third and fourth address different technological aspects of the issue. With such variety in only the first four articles, you will clearly have to be careful to stay focused. In fact, it might be a good idea at this point to limit your search by adding another search term.

Each entry contains the information that you will need to locate it in a library, and some databases provide links to the full text of articles from selected periodicals. Here is a typical entry:

Always consider the following points when deciding whether you should track down a particular source:

- **Relevance to your topic:** Examine the title, subtitle, subject headings, and abstract (if provided) to determine whether the source addresses your topic.

- **Publication date:** How recent is the source? For current controversies, emerging trends, and scientific or technological developments, consult recent material. For historical or biographical topics, start with present-day perspectives but consider exploring older sources that offer authoritative perspectives.

- **Description:** Does the length of the source indicate a brief treatment of the topic or an extended treatment? Does the work include illustrations that may illuminate concepts discussed? Does the source include a bibliography that could lead you to other works or an index that could give you an overview of the text?

From among the sources that look promising, select publications that seem to address different aspects of your topic or to approach it from different perspectives. Avoid selecting sources that are mostly by the same author, from the same publisher, or in the same journal.

Using the Web for Research

In this section, we discuss the open Web—the open-access areas of the Internet that exclude proprietary subscription services like the databases available through your library. By now, most of you are familiar with searching the Web. This section introduces you to some tools and strategies that will help you use it more efficiently.

Keep the following concerns and guidelines in mind:

- *Many significant electronic sources require a paid subscription or other fees.* Electronic periodical indexes, full-text article databases, and other valuable electronic resources are often available only by subscription. If your college subscribes to these resources, your tuition grants you access to them. For these reasons (as well as the ones discussed in this section), you should plan to use the resources available via your library's Web site for much of your electronic research.

- *Open-access Web sources may be less reliable than print sources or electronic sources to which your library or campus subscribes.* Depending on your topic, purpose, and audience, the sources you find on the Web may not be as credible or authoritative as print sources or subscription electronic sources, which have usually been screened by publishers, editors, librarians, and authorities on the topic. When in doubt about the reliability of an online source for a particular assignment, check with your instructor. (See Evaluating Sources Critically on pp. 632–34 for more specific suggestions.)

- *Web sources may be less stable than print sources or the electronic sources to which your library or campus subscribes.* A Web site that existed last week may no longer be available today, or its content may have changed.

- *Web sources must be documented.* You will need to follow appropriate conventions for quoting, paraphrasing, summarizing, and documenting the online sources you use, just as you do for print sources. Because a Web source can change or disappear quickly, be sure to record the information for the working-bibliography entry when you first find the source. Whenever possible, download and print out the source to preserve it. Make sure your download or printout includes all the items of information required for the entry, or at least all those you can find. (See the form on the next page for guidelines on what to record for an Internet source.)

INFORMATION FOR WORKING BIBLIOGRAPHY—
INTERNET SOURCES

Author(s) of work	
Title of work	
Title of site	
Sponsor of site	
URL (address)	
Date of electronic publication or of latest update	
Date you accessed source	
Publication information for print version of work (if any)	
Notes	

Finding the Best Information Online

Search tools like Google and Yahoo! are important resources for searching the Web for information on your topic. To use these tools effectively, you should understand their features, strengths, and limitations.

Search engines like Google are based on keywords. They are simply computer programs that scan the open Web—or that part of the Web that is in the particular search engine's database—looking for the keyword(s) you have entered. Search engines are useful whenever you have a good idea of the appropriate keywords for your topic or if you are not sure under what category the topic falls.

Of particular interest to the academic writer are Google Scholar, which searches peer-reviewed articles from scholarly databases including JSTOR,

Project Muse, Wiley, Sage, and Google Book Search, which searches a wide range of general-interest and scholarly books. Both Google Scholar and Google Book Search offer overviews and, in some cases, full text of indexed material.

Subject directories like Yahoo! are based on categories, like the subject headings in a library catalog or periodical index. Beginning with a menu of general subjects, you click on increasingly narrow subjects (for example, going from Science to Biology to Genetics to DNA Mapping), until you reach either a list of specific Web sites or a point where you have to do a keyword search within the narrowest subject you have chosen. Subject directories can help quickly narrow your search to those parts of the Web that are likely to be most productive and thus avoid keyword searches that produce hundreds or thousands of results. Always click on the link called Help, Hints, or Tips on a search tool's home page to find out more about the recognized commands and advanced-search techniques for that specific search tool.

As with searches of library catalogs and databases, the success of a Web search depends to a great extent on the keywords you choose. Remember that many different words often describe the same topic. If your topic is "ecology," for example, you may find information under the keywords *ecosystem, environment, pollution,* and *endangered species,* as well as a number of other related keywords, depending on the focus of your research. When you find a source that seems promising, be sure to create a bookmark for the Web page so that you can return to it easily later on.

No matter how precise your keywords are, search engines can be unreliable, and you may not find the best available resources. You might instead begin your search at the Web site of a relevant and respected organization. If you want photos of constellations, for example, go to the NASA Web page. If you want public laws, go to a government Web page like GPO Access. In addition, be sure to supplement your Internet research with other sources from your library, including books, reference works, and articles from appropriate periodicals.

The following open-access sources can also be of use to you in some research projects:

American Memory from the Library of Congress (memory.loc.gov) is a gateway to the Library of Congress's vast digitized collection of American historical and cultural materials, including manuscripts, prints, photographs, posters, maps, sound recordings, motion pictures, books, pamphlets, and sheet music.

Project Gutenberg (gutenberg.org), a pioneer in the development of and distribution of ebooks, now offers over 25,000 digitized public-domain texts.

Wikimedia Commons (commons.wikimedia.org/wiki/Main_Page) provides over 3.5 million images and other media that are in the public domain.

WorldCat.org is an enormous online network of library content and services that allows you to search for books, DVDs, CDs, audiobooks, research articles, and other content and either download items directly or locate them in a library nearby.

YouTube (youtube.com), a phenomenally popular video-sharing site, offers some resources of interest to academic writers. Be aware that YouTube is an open site that attracts a great deal of material of questionable quality. Also, remember that any YouTube material you do wish to introduce in your projects must be fully cited.

Two other sources of online information are **blogs** and **RSS**. A blog, or Web log, is a Web site, often based on a particular topic, that is maintained by an individual or organization and updated on a regular basis, often many times a day. Blogs may contain postings written by the sponsor(s) of the site; information such as news articles, press releases, and commentary from other sites; and comments posted by readers. Blogs are usually organized chronologically, with the newest post at the top. Because they are not subjected to the same editorial scrutiny as published books or periodical articles and may reflect just one person's opinions and biases, it is a good idea to find several blogs from multiple perspectives about your subject. Some Web sites, such as Blogwise (www.blogwise.com) and Blogger (www.blogger.com), provide directories and search functions to help you find blogs on a particular topic. You can search the content of literally millions of blog posts by using blog search engines such as technorati.com or blogsearch.google.com.

If you are researching a very current topic and need to follow constantly updated news sites and blogs, you can use a program called an **aggregator**, which obtains news automatically from many sources and assembles it through a process called RSS (Really Simple Syndication). Using an aggregator, you can scan the information from a variety of sources by referring to just one Web page or e-mail and then click on links to the news stories to read further. Many aggregators, such as NetNewsWire, NewsGator, and SharpReader, are available as software that you can download to your computer; others are Web sites you can customize to your own preferences, such as Bloglines (www.bloglines .com) and NewsIsFree (www.newsisfree.com). Google Alerts offers Google account holders updates on news, Web pages, blogs, and videos relevant to key terms entered into their Alerts home page.

Using E-mail and Online Communities for Research

You may find it possible to use your computer to do research in ways other than those already discussed in this chapter. In particular, if you can find out the e-mail address of an expert on your topic, you may want to contact the person and ask whether he or she would agree to a brief online (or telephone) interview.

In addition, several kinds of electronic communities available on the Internet may possibly be helpful. Many Web sites consist of or incorporate tools known as **message boards**, in which anyone who registers may post messages to and receive them from other members. Older Internet servers known as news servers also provide access to message boards or variants called **newsgroups**. Another kind of community, **mailing lists**, are groups of people who subscribe to and receive e-mail messages shared among all the members simultaneously. **Chatrooms** allow users to meet together at the same time in a shared message space. Finally, **wikis**—of which Wikipedia is the best-known example—offer content of various kinds contributed and modified collaboratively by a community of users. These can be very useful for background information, but be aware that most teachers will not accept information from wikis as sources for papers.

These different kinds of online communities often focus on a specific field of shared interest, and the people who frequent them are sometimes working professionals or academics with expertise in topics that are obscure or difficult to research otherwise. Such experts are often willing to answer both basic and advanced questions and will sometimes consent to an e-mail or telephone interview. Even if they are not authorities in the field, online community members may stimulate your thinking about the topic in new directions or save you a large amount of research time by pointing you to resources that might otherwise have taken you quite a while to uncover. Many communities provide some kind of indexing or search mechanism so that you can look for "threads" (conversation) related to your topic. As with other sources, however, evaluate the credibility and reliability of online communities.

For most topics, you will be able to find a variety of related newsgroups; www.groups.google.com catalogs many of them (and allows you to start your own). For mailing lists, you have to register for a subscription to the list. Remember that unless a digest option (an option that compiles messages into one daily or weekly e-mail) is available, each subscription means you will be receiving a large amount of e-mail, so think about the implications before you sign up.

Evaluating Sources Critically

From the beginning of your library and Internet search, you should evaluate potential sources that you have tracked down to determine which ones you should take the time to examine more closely and then which of these you should use in your essay. Obviously, you must decide which sources provide information relevant to the topic. But you must also decide how credible or trustworthy the sources are. Just because a book or an essay appears in print or online does not necessarily mean that an author's information or opinions are reliable.

Begin your evaluation of sources by narrowing your working bibliography to the most relevant works. Consider them in terms of scope, date of publication, and viewpoint.

Scope and Approach

To decide how relevant a particular source is to your topic, you need to examine the source in depth. Do not depend on title alone, for it may be misleading. If the source is a book, check its table of contents and index to see how many pages are specifically devoted to the subject you are exploring. In most cases, you will want an in-depth, not a superficial, treatment of the subject. Read the preface or introduction to a book or the abstract or opening paragraphs of an article and any biographical information given about the author to determine the author's basic approach to the subject or special way of looking at it. As you attend to these elements, consider the following questions:

- Does the source provide a general or specialized view? General sources are helpful early in your research, but you will also need the authority or up-to-date coverage of specialized sources. Extremely specialized works, however, may be too technical.

- Is the source long enough to provide adequate detail?

- Is the source written for general readers? Specialists? Advocates? Critics?

- Is the author an expert on the topic? Does the author's way of looking at the topic support or challenge your own views? (The fact that an author's viewpoint challenges your own does not mean that you should reject the author as a source, as you will see from the discussion on viewpoints.)

- Is the information in the source substantiated elsewhere? Does its approach seem to be comparable to, or a significant challenge to, the approaches of other credible sources?

Date of Publication

Although you should always consult the most up-to-date sources available on your subject, older sources often establish the principles, theories, and data on which later work is based and may provide a useful perspective for evaluating it. If older works are considered authoritative, you may want to become familiar with them. To determine which sources are authoritative, note the ones that are cited most often in encyclopedia articles, bibliographies, and recent works on the subject. If your source is on the Web, consider whether it has been regularly updated.

Viewpoint

Your sources should represent multiple viewpoints on the subject. Just as you would not depend on a single author for all of your information, so you do not want to use only authors who belong to the same school of thought. Using sources that represent a variety of different viewpoints is especially important when developing an argument for one of the essay assignments in Chapters 6–9.

During the invention work in those chapters, you may want to research what others have said about your subject to see what positions have been staked out and what arguments have been made. You will then be able to define the issue more carefully, collect arguments supporting your position, and anticipate arguments opposing it.

Although the text of the source will give you the most precise indication of the author's viewpoint, you can often get a good idea of it by looking at the preface or introduction or at the sources the author cites. When you examine a reference, you can often determine the general point of view it represents by considering the following elements.

Title

Does the title or subtitle indicate the text's bias? Watch for loaded words or confrontational phrasing.

Author

What is the author's professional title or affiliation? What is the author's perspective? Is the author in favor of something or at odds with it? What has persuaded the author to take this stance? How might the author's professional affiliation affect his or her perspective? What is the author's tone? Information on the author may be available in the book, article, or Web site itself or in biographical sources available in the library. You could also try entering the author's name into a search engine and see what you learn from sites that discuss him or her.

Presentation

What evidence does the author provide as support for his or her point of view? Is the evidence from authoritative sources? Is the evidence persuasive? Does the author make concessions to or refute opposing arguments?

Publication Information

Is the source published or sponsored by a commercial publisher, another kind of corporation, a government agency, a private organization, an educational institution, or an individual? What is the publisher's or sponsor's position on the topic? Is the author funded by or affiliated with the publisher or sponsor? If you cannot determine the sponsor of a Web site, it is very likely not a credible source. For periodical articles in particular, some background about the publisher can help to determine the viewpoint, because all periodicals have their own editorial slants. Reference sources to help you determine this information include the *Encyclopedia of Associations* (called *Associations Unlimited* online) and the *Gale Directory of Publications and Broadcast Media.*

INTEGRATING SOURCES WITH YOUR OWN WRITING

Writers commonly use sources by quoting directly, by paraphrasing, and by summarizing. This section provides guidelines for deciding when to use each of these three methods and how to do so effectively.

Deciding Whether to Quote, Paraphrase, or Summarize

As a general rule, quote only in these situations: (1) when the wording of the source is particularly memorable or vivid or expresses a point so well that you cannot improve it without destroying the meaning, (2) when the words of reliable and respected authorities would lend support to your position, (3) when you wish to highlight the author's opinions, (4) when you wish to cite an author whose opinions challenge or vary greatly from those of other experts, or (5) when you are going to discuss the source's choice of words. Paraphrase passages whose details you wish to note completely but whose language is not particularly striking. Summarize any long passages whose main points you wish to record selectively as background or general support for a point you are making.

Quoting

A *quotation* duplicates the source exactly, word for word. If the source has an error, copy it and add the notation *sic* (Latin for "thus") in brackets immediately after the error to indicate that it is not your error but your source's:

> According to a recent newspaper article, "Plagirism [*sic*] is a problem among journalists and scholars as well as students" (Berensen 62).

However, you can change quotations (1) by italicizing particular words to emphasize them, (2) by using ellipsis marks to omit irrelevant information or to make the quotation conform grammatically to your sentence, and (3) by using brackets to make the quotation conform grammatically or to insert information.

Use Italics for Emphasis

You may italicize any words in the quotation that you want to emphasize; add a semicolon and the words *emphasis added* (in regular type, not italicized) to the parenthetical citation.

> In her 2001 exposé of the struggles of the working class, Ehrenreich writes, "The wages Winn-Dixie is offering—*$6 and a couple of dimes to start with*—are not enough, I decide, to compensate for this indignity" (14; emphasis added).

Use Ellipsis Marks for Omissions

A writer may decide to leave certain words out of a quotation because they are not relevant to the point being made or because they add information readers will not need in the context in which the quotation is being used. When you omit words from within a quotation, you must use ellipsis marks—three spaced periods (. . .)—in place of the missing words. When the omission occurs within the sentence, include a space before the first ellipsis mark and after the closing mark. There should also be spaces between the three marks.

> Ellen Ruppel Shell claims in "Does Civilization Cause Asthma?" that what asthma "lacks in lethality, it more than makes up for in morbidity: it wears people down . . . and threatens their livelihood" (90).

When the omission falls at the end of a sentence, place a sentence period *directly after* the final word of the sentence, followed by a space and three spaced ellipsis marks.

> But Grimaldi's commentary contends that for Aristotle, rhetoric, like dialectic, had "no limited and unique subject matter upon which it must be exercised. . . . Instead, rhetoric as an art transcends all specific disciplines and may be brought into play in them" (6).

A period plus ellipsis marks can indicate the omission of the rest of the sentence as well as whole sentences, paragraphs, or even pages.

When a parenthetical reference follows the ellipsis marks at the end of a sentence, place the three spaced periods after the quotation, and place the sentence period after the final parenthesis:

> But Grimaldi's commentary contends that for Aristotle, rhetoric, like dialectic, had "no limited and unique subject matter upon which it must be exercised . . ." (6).

When you quote only single words or phrases, you do not need to use ellipsis marks because it will be obvious that you have left out some of the original.

> According to Geoffrey Nunberg, many people believe that the Web is "just one more route along which English will march on an ineluctable course of world conquest" (40).

For the same reason, you need not use ellipsis marks if you omit the beginning of a quoted sentence unless the rest of the sentence begins with a capitalized word and still appears to be a complete sentence.

Use Brackets for Insertions or Changes

Use brackets around an insertion or other change needed to make a quotation conform grammatically to your sentence, such as a change in the form of a verb or pronoun or in the capitalization of the first word of the quotation. In this example from an essay on James Joyce's "Araby," the writer adapts Joyce's phrases "we played till our bodies glowed" and "shook music from the buckled harness" to fit the grammar of her sentences:

> In the dark, cold streets during the "short days of winter," the boys must generate their own heat by "play[ing] till [their] bodies glowed." Music is "[shaken] from the buckled harness" as if it were unnatural, and the singers in the market chant nasally of "the troubles in our native land" (30).

You may also use brackets to add or substitute explanatory material in a quotation:

> Guterson notes that among Native Americans in Florida, "education was in the home; learning by doing was reinforced by the myths and legends which repeated the basic value system of their [the Seminoles'] way of life" (159).

Some changes that make a quotation conform grammatically to another sentence may be made without any signal to readers: (1) A period at the end of a quotation may be changed to a comma if you are using the quotation within your own sentence, and (2) double quotation marks enclosing a quotation are changed to single quotation marks when the quotation is enclosed within a longer quotation.

Integrating Quotations

Depending on its length, a quotation may be incorporated into your text by being enclosed in quotation marks or set off from your text in a block without quotation marks. In either case, be sure to blend the quotation smoothly into your essay rather than just drop it in.

In-Text Quotations

Incorporate brief quotations (no more than four typed lines of prose or three lines of poetry) into your text. You may place the quotation virtually anywhere in your sentence—at the beginning, in the middle, at the end, or with your own words dividing it:

At the Beginning

> "To live a life is not to cross a field," Sutherland quotes Pasternak at the beginning of her narrative (11).

In the Middle

> Anna Quindlen argues that "booze and beer are not the same as illegal drugs. They're worse" (88)—a claim that meets much resistance.

At the End

> In *The Second Sex,* Simone de Beauvoir describes such an experience as one in which the girl "becomes an object, and she sees herself as object" (378).

Divided by Your Own Words

"Science usually prefers the literal to the nonliteral term," Kinneavy writes, "—that is, figures of speech are often out of place in science" (177).

When you quote poetry within your text, use a slash (/) with spaces before and after to signal the end of each line of verse:

Alluding to St. Augustine's distinction between the City of God and the Earthly City, Lowell writes that "much against my will / I left the City of God where it belongs" (4–5).

Block Quotations

In MLA documentation style, use block form for prose quotations of five or more typed lines and poetry quotations of four or more lines. Indent the quotation an inch (ten character spaces) from the left margin, as shown in the following example. In APA style, use block form for quotations of forty words or more. Indent the block quotation one-half inch, keeping your indents consistent throughout your paper.

In a block quotation, double-space between lines just as you do in your text. *Do not* enclose the passage within quotation marks. Use a colon to introduce a block quotation, unless the context calls for another punctuation mark or none at all. When quoting a single paragraph or part of one in MLA style, do not indent the first line of the quotation more than the rest. In quoting two or more paragraphs, indent the first line of each paragraph an extra quarter inch. If you are using APA style, the first line of subsequent paragraphs in the block quotation indents an additional half inch from the block quotation indent.

In "A Literary Legacy from Dunbar to Baraka," Margaret Walker says of Paul Lawrence Dunbar's dialect poems:

He realized that the white world in the United States tolerated his literary genius only because of his "jingles in a broken tongue," and they found the old "darky" tales and speech amusing and within the vein of folklore into which they wished to classify all Negro life. This troubled Dunbar because he realized that white America was denigrating him as a writer and as a man. (70)

Note that in MLA style the parenthetical page reference follows the period in block quotations.

Introducing Quotations

Statements that introduce in-text quotations take a range of punctuation marks and lead-in words. Here are some examples of ways writers typically introduce quotations.

Introducing a Quotation Using a Colon

A colon usually follows an independent clause that introduces a quotation.

> Richard Dyer argues that racism will disappear only when whites stop thinking of themselves as raceless: "White people need to learn to see themselves as white, to see their particularity" (12).

Introducing a Quotation Using a Comma

A comma usually follows an introduction that incorporates the quotation in its sentence structure (an introduction that could not stand on its own as a sentence).

> Similarly, Duncan Turner asserts, "As matters now stand, it is unwise to talk about communication without some understanding of Burke" (259).

Introducing a Quotation Using *that*

No punctuation is generally needed with *that*, and no capital letter is used to begin the quotation.

> Noting this failure, Alice Miller asserts that "the reason for her despair was not her suffering but the impossibility of communicating her suffering to another person" (255).

Punctuating within Quotations

Although punctuation within a quotation should reproduce the original, some adaptations may be necessary. Use single quotation marks for quotations within the quotation:

Original from Guterson (16–17)

E. D. Hirsch recognizes the connection between family and learning, suggesting in his discussion of family background and academic achievement "that the significant part of our children's education has been going on outside rather than inside the schools."

Quoted Version

> Guterson claims that E. D. Hirsch "recognizes the connection between family and learning, suggesting in his discussion of family background and academic achievement 'that the significant part of our children's education has been going on outside rather than inside the schools'" (16–17).

If the quotation ends with a question mark or an exclamation point, retain the original punctuation:

> "Did you think I loved you?" Edith later asks Dombey (566).

If a quotation ending with a question mark or an exclamation point concludes your sentence, retain the question mark or exclamation point, and put the parenthetical reference and sentence period outside the quotation marks:

> Edith later asks Dombey, "Did you think I loved you?" (566).

Avoiding Grammatical Tangles

When you incorporate quotations into your writing, and especially when you omit words from quotations, you run the risk of creating ungrammatical sentences. Three common errors you should try to avoid are *verb incompatibility*, *ungrammatical omissions*, and *sentence fragments*.

Verb Incompatibility

When this error occurs, the verb form in the introductory statement is grammatically incompatible with the verb form in the quotation. When your quotation has a verb form that does not fit in with your text, it is usually possible to use just part of the quotation, thus avoiding verb incompatibility.

The narrator suggests his bitter disappointment when [*he describes seeing himself*] ~~"I saw myself"~~ as a creature driven and derided by vanity" (35).

As this sentence illustrates, use the present tense when you refer to events in a literary work.

Ungrammatical Omission

Sometimes omitting text from a quotation leaves you with an ungrammatical sentence. Two ways of correcting the grammar are (1) to adapt the quotation (with brackets) so that its parts fit together grammatically and (2) to use only one part of the quotation.

From the moment of the boy's arrival in Araby, the bazaar is presented as a commercial enterprise: "I could not find any sixpenny entrance and . . . hand[ed] a shilling to a weary-looking man" (34).

From the moment of the boy's arrival in Araby, the bazaar is presented as a commercial enterprise: [*He*] "I could not find any sixpenny entrance [*so had to*] and . . . ~~handing a shilling to a weary looking man" (34).~~ [*pay a shilling to get in (34).*]

Sentence Fragment

Sometimes when a quotation is a complete sentence, writers neglect the sentence that introduces the quote—for example, by forgetting to include a verb. It is important to make sure that the quotation is introduced by a complete sentence.

The girl's interest in the bazaar [*leads*] ~~leading~~ the narrator to make what amounts to a sacred oath: "If I go . . . I will bring you something" (32).

Paraphrasing and Summarizing

In addition to quoting sources, writers have the option of paraphrasing or summarizing what others have written.

Paraphrasing

In a *paraphrase*, the writer restates primarily in his or her own words all the relevant information from a passage, without offering any additional comments or any suggestion of agreement or disagreement with the source's ideas. Paraphrasing is useful for recording details of the passage when the order of the details is important but the source's wording is not. It also allows you to avoid quoting too much—or at all when the author's choice of words is not worth special attention. Because all the details of the passage are included in a paraphrase, it is often about the same length as the original passage.

Here are a passage from a book on home schooling and an example of an acceptable paraphrase of it:

Original Passage

Bruner and the discovery theorists have also illuminated conditions that apparently pave the way for learning. It is significant that these conditions are unique to each learner, so unique, in fact, that in many cases classrooms can't provide them. Bruner also contends that the more one discovers information in a great variety of circumstances, the more likely one is to develop the inner categories required to organize that information. Yet life at school, which is for the most part generic and predictable, daily keeps many children from the great variety of circumstances they need to learn well.

—David Guterson, *Family Matters:
Why Homeschooling Makes Sense*, p.172

Acceptable Paraphrase

According to Guterson, the "discovery theorists," particularly Bruner, have found that there seem to be certain conditions that help learning to take place. Because each individual requires different conditions, many children are not able to learn in the classroom. When people can explore information in many different situations, Bruner's argument goes on, they learn to classify and order what they discover. The general routine of the school day, however, does not provide children with the diverse activities and situations that would allow them to learn these skills (172).

Readers assume that some words in a paraphrase are taken from the source. Indeed, it would be nearly impossible for paraphrasers to avoid using any key terms from the source, and it would be counterproductive to try to do so because the original and paraphrase necessarily share the same information and concepts. Notice, though, that of the total of eighty-seven words in the paraphrase, the paraphraser uses only a name ("Bruner") and a few key nouns and verbs ("discovery theorists," "conditions," "children," "learn[ing]," "classroom[s]," "information," "situations") for which it would be awkward to substitute other words or phrases. If the paraphraser had wanted to use other kinds of language from the source, such as the description of life at school as "generic and predictable," these adjectives should have been enclosed in quotation marks. In fact, the paraphraser does put quotation marks around the term "discovery theorists," a technical term likely to be unfamiliar to readers.

The source of all the material in the paraphrase is identified by the author's name in the first sentence and by the page number in the last sentence, which indicates where the paraphrased material appears in David Guterson's book. This source citation follows the style of the Modern Language Association (MLA). Notice that placing the citation information in this way indicates clearly to readers where the paraphrase begins and ends, so that they understand where the text is expressing ideas taken from a source and where it is expressing the writer's own ideas (or ideas from a different source). Should readers want to check the accuracy or completeness of the paraphrase, they could turn to the alphabetically arranged list of works cited at the end of the essay, look for Guterson's name, and find there all the information they would need to locate the book and check the source.

Although it is acceptable and often necessary to reuse a few key terms or to quote striking or technical language from a source, paraphrasers must avoid borrowing too many words or repeating the same sentence structure. Notice in the following paraphrase of Guterson's first sentence that the paraphraser repeats too many of the author's own words and phrases:

Unacceptable Paraphrase:
Too Many Borrowed Words and Phrases

> Apparently, some conditions, which have been illuminated by Bruner and other discovery theorists, pave the way for people to learn.

By comparing the source's first sentence and this paraphrase of it, you can see that the paraphraser borrows almost all of the key terms from the original sentence, including the entire phrase "pave the way for." Even if you cite the source, this sort of heavy borrowing is an example of *plagiarism*—using the ideas and words of others as though they were your own (see p. 644).

The following paraphrase of the same sentence is unacceptable because it too closely resembles the structure of the original sentence:

Unacceptable Paraphrase:
Sentence Structure Repeated Too Closely

> Bruner and other researchers have also identified circumstances that seem to ease the path to learning.

Here the paraphraser borrows the phrases and clauses of the source and arranges them in an identical sequence, merely substituting synonyms for Guterson's key terms: "researchers" for "theorists," "identified" for "illuminated," "circumstances" for "conditions," "seem to" for "apparently," and "ease the path to" for "pave the way for." Even though most key terms have been changed, this paraphrase is also an example of plagiarism.

Summarizing

Like a paraphrase, a *summary* may use key terms from the source, but it is made up mainly of words supplied by the writer. A summary presents only the main ideas of the source, leaving out examples and details. Consequently, summaries allow you to bring concisely into your writing large amounts of information from source material.

Here is an example of a summary of five pages from Guterson's book. You can see at a glance how drastically some summaries condense information, in this case from five pages to five sentences. Depending on the summarizer's purpose, however, the same five pages could be summarized in one sentence or in two dozen sentences.

Summary

In looking at different theories of learning that discuss individual-based programs (such as home schooling) versus the public school system, Guterson describes the disagreements among "cognitivist theorists." One group, the "discovery theorists," believes that individual children learn by creating their own ways of sorting the information they take in from their experiences. Schools should help students develop better ways of organizing new material, not just present them with material that is already categorized, as traditional schools do. "Assimilationist theorists," by contrast, believe that children learn by linking what they don't know to information they already know. These theorists claim that traditional schools help students learn when they present information in ways that allow children to fit the new material into categories they have already developed (171–75).

Notice that the source of the summarized material is identified by the author's name in the first sentence and that the page numbers from the source are cited parenthetically in the last sentence, following MLA citation style. As with a paraphrase, putting the citation information at the beginning and the end of the summary in this way makes clear to the reader the boundaries between the ideas in the source and the writer's own ideas (or the ideas in a different source).

Although this summarizer encloses in quotation marks three technical terms from the original source, summaries usually do not include quotations: Their purpose is not to display the source's language but to present its main ideas. Even a lengthy summary is more than a dry list of main ideas from a source; it is a coherent, readable new text composed of the source's main ideas. An effective summary provides balanced coverage of the source, following the same sequence of ideas while avoiding any hint of agreement or disagreement.

ACKNOWLEDGING SOURCES

Notice in the preceding examples that the source is acknowledged by name. Even when you use your own words to present someone else's information, you must acknowledge that you borrowed the information. The only types of information that do not require acknowledgment are common knowledge (John F. Kennedy was assassinated in Dallas), facts widely available in many sources (before 1933, U.S. presidents were inaugurated on March 4 rather than on January 20), well-known quotations ("To be, or not to be, that is the question"), and material you created or gathered yourself, such as your own photographs or survey data. Remember to acknowledge the source of visuals (photographs, tables, charts, graphs, diagrams, drawings, maps, screen shots) that you do not create yourself as well as the source of any information that you use to create your own visuals. (You should also request permission from the source of every visual you want to borrow if your essay will be posted on the Web.) When in doubt about the need to acknowledge a source, it is always safer to include a citation.

The documentation guidelines later in this appendix (pp. 645–66) present various styles for citing sources. Whichever style you use, your readers must be able to tell where words or ideas that are not your own begin and end. You can accomplish this most readily by taking and transcribing notes carefully, by placing parenthetical source citations correctly, and by separating your words from those of the source with *signal phrases*, such as "According to Smith," "Peters claims," and "As Olmos asserts." (When you cite a source for the first time in a signal phrase, you may use the author's full name; after that, use just the last name.)

Avoiding Plagiarism

Writers—students and professionals alike—occasionally fail to acknowledge sources properly. The word *plagiarism*, which derives from the Latin word for "kidnapping," refers to the unacknowledged use of another's words, ideas, sentence structure, or information. Students sometimes get into trouble because they mistakenly assume that plagiarizing occurs only when another writer's exact words are used without acknowledgment. In fact, plagiarism applies to such diverse forms of expression as musical compositions and visual images as well as ideas and statistics. So keep in mind that, with the exceptions listed above, you must indicate the source of any borrowed information or ideas you use in your essay—whether you have paraphrased, summarized, or quoted directly from the source or have reproduced it or referred to it in some other way.

Remember especially the need to document electronic sources fully and accurately. Perhaps because it is so easy to access and distribute text and visuals online and to copy material from one electronic document and paste it into another, many students do not realize—or may forget—that information, ideas, and images from electronic sources require acknowledgment in even more detail than those from print sources do (and are often easier to detect if they are not acknowledged).

Some people plagiarize simply because they do not know the conventions for using and acknowledging sources. This appendix makes clear how to incorporate sources into your writing and how to acknowledge your use of those sources. Others plagiarize because they keep sloppy notes that fail to distinguish between their own and their sources' ideas. Either they neglect to enclose their sources' words in quotation marks, or they fail to indicate when they are paraphrasing or summarizing a source's ideas and information. If you keep a working bibliography and careful notes, you will not make this serious mistake.

Another reason some people plagiarize is that they doubt their ability to write an essay by themselves. They feel intimidated by the writing task, the deadline, or their own and others' expectations. If you experience this same anxiety about your work, speak to your instructor. Do not run the risk of failing a course or being expelled because of plagiarism. If you are confused about what is and what is not plagiarism, be sure to ask your instructor.

Understanding Documentation Styles

Although there are several systems for acknowledging sources, most documentation styles use short in-text citations that are keyed to a separate bibliography. The information required in the in-text citations and the order and content of the bibliography vary across academic disciplines. The following guidelines present the basic features of two styles: the *Modern Language Association (MLA)* system, which is widely used in the humanities, and the *American Psychological Association (APA)* system, which is widely used in the social sciences. Earlier in this book, you can find student-written essays that follow MLA style (Linh Kieu Ngo and Justin Ton, Chapter 5; Tan-Li Hsu and Jessica Statsky, Chapter 7; Jeremy Khella and Joshua Slick, Chapter 8; and Jeff Varley, Chapter 9) and APA style (Patrick O'Malley, Chapter 9).

Documenting Sources Using MLA Style

The following guidelines are sufficient for most college research assignments in English and other humanities courses that call for MLA-style documentation. For additional information, see the *MLA Handbook for Writers of Research Papers*, seventh edition (2009), or check the MLA Web site (http://www.mla.org).

Use In-Text Citations to Show Where You Have Used Material from Sources

The MLA author-page system requires parenthetical in-text citations that are keyed to a list of works cited in the paper. In-text citations generally include the author's last name and the page number of the passage being cited. There is no punctuation between author and page. The parenthetical citation should follow the quoted, paraphrased, or summarized material as closely as possible without disrupting the flow of the sentence.

> Dr. James is described as a "not-too-skeletal Ichabod Crane" (Simon 68).

Note that the parenthetical citation comes before the final period. With block quotations, however, the citation comes after the final period, preceded by a space (see p. 638 for an example).

If you mention the author's name in your text, supply just the page reference in parentheses.

> Simon describes Dr. James as a "not-too-skeletal Ichabod Crane" (68).

USE THE FOLLOWING MODELS FOR IN-TEXT CITATIONS

1. **When the source has more than one author**

   > Dyal, Corning, and Willows identify several types of students, including the "Authority-Rebel" (4).

   > Authority-Rebels see themselves as "superior to other students in the class" (Dyal, Corning, and Willows 4).

   > The drug AZT has been shown to reduce the risk of transmission from HIV-positive mothers to their infants by as much as two-thirds (Van de Perre et al. 4-5).

For four or more authors, use all the authors' names or only the first author's name followed by *et al.* ("and others"), as in the example above.

2. **When the author is not named**

   > In 1992, five years after the Symms legislation, the number of deaths from automobile accidents reached a thirty-year low ("Highways" 51).

3. **When the source has a corporate or government author**

In a parenthetical citation, give the full name of the author if it is brief or a shortened version if it is long. If you name the author in your text, give the full name even if it is long.

   > A tuition increase has been proposed for community and technical colleges to offset budget deficits from Initiative 601 (Washington State Board 4).

   > According to the Washington State Board for Community and Technical Colleges, a tuition increase . . . from Initiative 601 (4).

4. **When two or more works by the same author are cited**

   > When old paint becomes transparent, it sometimes shows the artist's original plans: "A tree will show through a woman's dress" (Hellman, *Pentimento* 1).

Because more than one of Hellman's works is included in the list of works cited, the title follows the author's name in the parentheses.

5. When two or more authors have the same last name

According to Edgar V. Roberts, Chaplin's *Modern Times* provides a good example of montage used to make an editorial statement (246).

Chaplin's *Modern Times* provides a good example of montage used to make an editorial statement (E. V. Roberts 246).

Note that Roberts's first and middle initials are included in the parentheses because another author with the same last name is included in the list of works cited.

6. When a work without page numbers is cited

The average speed on Montana's interstate highways, for example, has risen by only 2 miles per hour since the repeal of the federal speed limit, with most drivers topping out at 75 (Schmid).

There is no page number available for this source because it comes from the Internet.

7. When a quotation is taken from a secondary source

Chancellor Helmut Kohl summed up the German attitude: "For millions of people, a car is part of their personal freedom" (qtd. in Cote 12).

Create a works-cited entry for the secondary source in which you found the quote, rather than for the original source (for this example, an entry for Cote, not Kohl, would appear in the list of works cited).

8. When a citation comes from a multivolume work

"Double meaning," according to Freud, "is one of the most fertile sources for . . . jokes" (8: 56).

In the parentheses, the number *8* indicates the volume and *56* indicates the page. (For a works-cited entry for a single volume in a multivolume work, see p. 650, entry 8.)

9. When the source is a literary work

For a novel or other prose work available in various editions, provide the page numbers from the edition used. To help readers locate the quotation in another edition, add the part and/or chapter number.

In *Hard Times*, Tom reveals his utter narcissism by blaming Louisa for his own failure: "'You have regularly given me up. You never cared for me'" (Dickens 262; bk. 3, ch. 9).

For a play in verse, such as a Shakespearean play, indicate the act, scene, and line numbers instead of the page numbers.

> At the beginning, Regan's fawning rhetoric hides her true attitude toward Lear: "I profess / Myself an enemy to all other joys / . . . / And find I am alone felicitate / In your dear highness' love" (*King Lear* 1.1.74–75, 77–78).

For a poem, indicate the stanzas and line numbers (if they are numbered) instead of the page numbers.

> In "Song of Myself," Whitman finds poetic details in busy urban settings, as when he describes "the blab of the pave, tires of carts . . . / . . . the driver with his interrogating thumb" (8.153–54).

If the source gives only line numbers, use the word *lines* (spelled out) in the first citation; in subsequent citations, give only the numbers.

10. When the citation comes from a work in an anthology

> In "Six Days: Some Rememberings," Grace Paley recalls that when she was in jail for protesting the Vietnam War, her pen and paper were taken away and she felt "a terrible pain in the area of my heart--a nausea" (191).

If you are discussing the editor's preface or introduction, name the editor.

11. When two or more works are cited in the same parentheses

When two or more different sources are used in the same passage, it may be necessary to cite them in the same parentheses. Separate the citations with a semicolon.

> A few studies have considered differences between oral and written discourse production (Scardamalia, Bereiter, and Goelman; Gould).

> The scene registers conflicts in English law as well, for while the medieval Westminster statutes also distinguish between lawful and unlawful exchanges of women, sixteenth-century statutes begin to redefine rape as a violent crime against a woman rather than as a property crime against her guardians (Maitland 2: 490–91; Post; Bashar; Gossett).

12. When an entire work is cited

> In *The Structure of Scientific Revolutions*, Thomas Kuhn discusses how scientists change their thinking.

No parenthetical citation is necessary.

13. When material from the Internet is cited

> In handling livestock, "many people attempt to restrain animals with sheer force instead of using behavioral principles" (Grandin).

Give enough information in the citation to enable readers to locate the Internet source in the list of works cited. If the author is not named, give the document title. Include page, section, paragraph, or screen numbers, if available.

Include All of Your Sources in a Works-Cited List at the End of Your Essay

In MLA style, every source referred to in the text of your essay must have a corresponding entry in the list of works cited at the end of your essay. Conversely, every entry in the works-cited list must correspond to at least one in-text citation in the essay. The MLA recommends that the list of works cited begin on a new page; that the first line of each entry begin flush with the left margin; that subsequent lines of the same entry indent one-half inch (or five character spaces); and that the entire list be double-spaced, between and within entries.

Do not worry about including information that is unavailable within the source, such as the author's middle initial or the issue number for a periodical.

BASIC ENTRY FOR A BOOK

> Author's last name, First name, Middle initial. *Book Title*. City of publication:
> Publisher's name, year published. Medium.

USE THE FOLLOWING MODELS FOR BOOKS

1. A book by a single author

> Ehrenreich, Barbara. *Nickel and Dimed: On (Not) Getting By in America*.
> New York: Metropolitan, 2001. Print.

2. Multiple works by the same author (or same group of authors)

> Kingsolver, Barbara. *High Tide in Tucson: Essays from Now or Never*. New York:
> HarperCollins, 1995. Print.
>
> ---. *Small Wonder*. New York: HarperCollins, 2002. Print.

3. A book by an agency, organization, or corporation

> American Medical Association. *Family Medical Guide*. 4th ed. Hoboken: Wiley,
> 2004. Print.

4. A book by two or more authors

For two or three authors:

> Saba, Laura, and Julie Gattis. *The McGraw-Hill Homeschooling Companion*. New
> York: McGraw, 2002. Print.

For more than three authors, name all the authors *or* only the first author followed by *et al.* ("and others"):

> Hunt, Lynn, Thomas R. Martin, Barbara H. Rosenwein, P. Po-Chia Hsia, and
> Bonnie G. Smith. *The Making of the West: Peoples and Cultures*. Boston:
> Bedford, 2001. Print.
>
> Hunt, Lynn, et al. *The Making of the West: Peoples and Cultures*. Boston: Bedford,
> 2001. Print.

5. **A book with an unlisted author**

   Rand McNally Commercial Atlas and Marketing Guide. Skokie: Rand, 2003. Print.

6. **A book with one or more editors**

   Waldman, Diane, and Janet Walker, eds. *Feminism and Documentary.* Minneapolis: U of Minnesota P, 1999. Print.

7. **A book with an author and an editor**

If you refer to the work itself:

   Arnold, Matthew. *Culture and Anarchy.* Ed. Samuel Lipman. New Haven: Yale UP, 1994. Print.

If you discuss the editor's work in your essay:

   Lipman, Samuel, ed. *Culture and Anarchy.* By Matthew Arnold. 1869. New Haven: Yale UP, 1994. Print.

8. **One volume of a multivolume work**

If only one volume from a multivolume set is used, indicate the volume number after the title:

   Freud, Sigmund. *The Standard Edition of the Complete Psychological Works of Sigmund Freud.* Vol. 8. Trans. and ed. James Strachey. New York: Norton, 2000. Print.

9. **Two or more volumes of a multivolume work**

   Sandburg, Carl. *Abraham Lincoln.* 6 vols. New York: Scribner's, 1939. Print.

10. **A book that is part of a series**

After the medium of publication, include the series title in regular type (not italicized or in quotation marks), followed by the series number and a period. If the word *Series* is part of the name, include *Ser.* before the number. Common abbreviations may be used for selected words in the series title.

   Zigova, Tanya, et al. *Neural Stem Cells: Methods and Protocols.* Totowa: Humana, 2002. Print. Methods in Molecular Biology 198.

11. **A republished book**

Provide the original publication date after the title of the book, followed by normal publication information for the current edition:

   Alcott, Louisa May. *An Old-Fashioned Girl.* 1870. New York: Puffin, 1995. Print.

12. A later edition of a book

> Rottenberg, Annette T., and Donna Haisty Winchell. *The Structure of Argument*. 6th ed. Boston: Bedford, 2009. Print.

13. A book with a title in its title

Do not italicize a title normally italicized when it appears within a book title.

> Hertenstein, Mike. *The Double Vision of* Star Trek: *Half-Humans, Evil Twins, and Science Fiction*. Chicago: Cornerstone, 1998. Print.

> O'Neill, Terry, ed. *Readings on* To Kill a Mockingbird. San Diego: Greenhaven, 2000. Print.

Use quotation marks around a work normally enclosed in quotation marks when it appears within the title of a book.

> Miller, Edwin Haviland. *Walt Whitman's "Song of Myself": A Mosaic of Interpretation*. Iowa City: U of Iowa P, 1989. Print.

14. A work in an anthology or a collection

> Lahiri, Jhumpa. "Nobody's Business." *The Best American Short Stories 2002*. Ed. Sue Miller. Boston: Houghton, 2002. 136–72. Print.

15. A translation

If you refer to the work itself:

> Tolstoy, Leo. *War and Peace*. Trans. Constance Garnett. New York: Modern, 2002. Print.

If you discuss the translation in your essay:

> Garnett, Constance, trans. *War and Peace*. By Leo Tolstoy. 1869. New York: Modern, 2002. Print.

16. A dictionary entry or an article in a reference book

> "Homeopathy." *Webster's New World College Dictionary*. 4th ed. 1999. Print.

> Rowland, Lewis P. "Myasthenia Gravis." *The Encyclopedia Americana*. 2001 ed. Print.

17. An introduction, preface, foreword, or afterword

> Graff, Gerald, and James Phelan. Preface. *Adventures of Huckleberry Finn*. By Mark Twain. 2nd ed. New York: Bedford, 2004. iii-vii. Print.

BASIC ENTRY FOR AN ARTICLE

> Author's last name, First name, Middle initial. "Title of the Article." *Journal Name* Volume number. Issue number (year published): page range. Medium.

USE THE FOLLOWING MODELS FOR ARTICLES

If the article is not on continuous pages, give the first page number followed by a plus sign, as in the following example.

18. An article from a newspaper

> Stoll, John D., et al. "U.S. Squeezes Auto Creditors." *Wall Street Journal* 10 Apr. 2009: A1+. Print.

19. An article from a weekly or biweekly magazine

> Doig, Will. "America's Real First Family." *Advocate* 17 July 2007: 46–50. Print.

20. An article from a monthly or bimonthly magazine

> Shelby, Ashley. "Good Going: Alaska's Glacier Crossroads." *Sierra* Sept.-Oct. 2005: 23. Print.

21. An article in a scholarly journal

Include the volume and issue number even if the journal has continuous pagination throughout the volume.

> Feuerstein, S., and Oliver Grimm. "On the Credibility of Currency Boards." *Review of International Economics* 14.5 (2006): 818–35. Print.

22. An unsigned editorial

> "Addiction behind Bars." Editorial. *New York Times* 12 Apr. 2009: A20. Print.

23. A letter to the editor

> Orent, Wendy, and Alan Zelicoff. Letter. *New Republic* 18 Nov. 2002: 4–5. Print.

24. A review

> Cassidy, John. "Master of Disaster." Rev. of *Globalization and Its Discontents*, by Joseph Stiglitz. *New Yorker* 12 July 2002: 82–86. Print.

> Lane, Anthony. Rev. of *The English Patient*, dir. Anthony Minghella. *New Yorker* 25 Nov. 1996: 118–21. Print.

If the review has no title and no named author, start with the words *Rev. of* (not italicized) and the title of the work being reviewed. Alphabetize the entry under the title of the work being reviewed.

25. An unsigned article

> "A Shot of Reality." *U.S. News & World Report* 1 July 2003: 13. Print.

Although there are many varieties of works-cited entries for Internet sources, the information generally follows this order:

> Author's last name, First name, Middle initial. "Title of Document." *Title of Book, Periodical, or Web Site.* Name of sponsoring institution or organization, Publication date or date of last revision. Medium. Date of access.

Citations of electronic sources require information normally included in citations of print sources (author, document title, and publication date) as well as information specific to electronic sources, including the following:

- The version or edition used.
- The publisher or sponsor of the site; if not available, use *N.p.*
- The date of publication; if not available, use *n.d.*
- The medium of publication (*Web*).
- The date you accessed the source.

If you cannot find some of this information, include what you do find. Always keep your goal in mind: to provide enough information so that your reader could track the source down later.

26. An entire Web site

> Gardner, James Alan. *A Seminar on Writing Prose.* N.p., 2001. Web. 4 June 2008.

Professional Web site:

> *The International Virginia Woolf Society Web Page.* International Virginia Woolf Society, 31 Aug. 2002. Web. 21 Feb. 2008.

Personal Web site:

> Chesson, Frederick W. Home page. N.p., 1 Apr. 2003. Web. 26 Apr. 2008.

27. A scholarly project

> *The Darwin Correspondence Project.* Ed. Duncan Porter. Cambridge U Library, 2 June 2003. Web. 28 Nov. 2008.

Book within a scholarly project:

> Corelli, Marie. *The Treasure of Heaven.* London: Constable, 1906. *Victorian Women Writer's Project.* Ed. Percy Willett. Indiana U, 10 July 1999. Web. 10 Sept. 2008.

Short work within a scholarly project:

> Heims, Marjorie. "The Strange Case of Sarah Jones." *The Free Expression Policy Project*. FEPP, 24 Jan. 2003. Web. 13 Mar. 2006.

28. An article from an online journal

> Cesarini, Paul. "Computers, Technology, and Literacies." *The Journal of Literacy and Technology* 4.1 (2004/2005): n. pag. Web. 12 Oct. 2008.

29. An article accessed from an online periodical database

After the publication information, give the name of the database in italics.

> Braus, Patricia. "Sex and the Single Spender." *American Demographics* 15.11 (1993): 28–34. *Academic Search Premier*. Web. 13 Aug. 2008.

30. A posting to a discussion group or newsgroup

Include the author's name (if you know it), the title or subject line of the posting (in quotation marks), the group name, the sponsor, the posting date, the medium, and the access date.

> Willie, Otis. "In the Heat of the Battle." *soc.history.war.us-revolution*. Google, 27 Sept. 2005. Web. 7 Oct. 2008.

> Martin, Francesca Alys. "Wait—Did Somebody Say 'Buffy'?" *Cultstud-L*. U of S Fl, 8 Mar. 2000. Web. 8 Mar. 2008.

31. An e-mail message

Include the person who sent the message, the subject line (in quotation marks), the person who received the message, the date it was sent, and the medium (*E-mail*), not italicized.

> Olson, Kate. "Update on State Legislative Grants." Message to the author. 5 Nov. 2008. E-mail.

USE THE FOLLOWING MODELS FOR OTHER SOURCES

32. An interview

Published interview:

> Ashrawi, Hanan. "Tanks vs. Olive Branches." Interview with Rose Marie Berger. *Sojourners Magazine* Feb. 2005: 22–26. Print.

Personal interview:

> Ellis, Trey. Personal interview. 3 Sept. 2008.

Broadcast interview:

> Calloway, Cab. Interview by Rich Conaty. *The Big Broadcast*. WFUV, New York. 10 Dec. 1990. Radio.

33. A lecture or public address

> Birnbaum, Jack. "The Domestication of Computers." Conf. of the Usability
> Professionals Association. Hyatt Grand Cypress Resort, Orlando. 10 July
> 2002. Lecture.

34. A government document

> United States. Dept. of Health and Human Services. *Trends in Underage
> Drinking in the United States, 1991–2007.* By Gabriella Newes-Adeyi, et al.
> Washington: GPO, 2009. Print.

If the author is known, the author's name may either come first or be placed after
the title and introduced with the word *By.*

35. A pamphlet

> BoatU.S. Foundation for Boating Safety and Clean Water. *Hypothermia and Cold
> Water Survival.* Alexandria, VA: BoatU.S. Foundation, 2001. Print.

36. A published doctoral dissertation

> Botts, Roderic C. *Influences in the Teaching of English, 1917–1935: An Illusion of
> Progress.* Diss. Northeastern U, 1970. Ann Arbor: UMI, 1971. Print.

37. An unpublished doctoral dissertation

> Bullock, Barbara. "Basic Needs Fulfillment among Less Developed Countries:
> Social Progress over Two Decades of Growth." Diss. Vanderbilt U, 1986.
> Print.

38. A dissertation abstract

> Bernstein, Stephen David. "Fugitive Genre: Gothicism, Ideology, and
> Intertextuality." Diss. Yale U, 1991. *DAI* 51.9 (1991): 3078–79A. Print.

39. Published proceedings of a conference

> Duffett, John, ed. *Against the Crime of Silence: Proceedings of the International
> War Crimes Tribunal.* Nov. 1967, Stockholm. New York: Clarion-Simon,
> 1970. Print.

If the name of the conference is part of the title of the publication, it need not be
repeated. Use the format for a work in an anthology (see entry 14 on p. 651) to
cite an individual presentation.

40. A letter

A published letter in a collection:

> Hamilton, Alexander. "To William Seton." 3 Dec. 1790. *The Papers of Alexander
> Hamilton.* Ed. Harold C. Syrett. Vol. 7. New York: Columbia UP, 1969. 190.
> Print.

Use the designation *MS* for handwritten letters and *TS* for typed letters.

> DuHamel, Grace. Letter to the author. 22 Mar. 2008. TS.

41. A map or chart

> *Map of Afghanistan and Surrounding Territory*. Map. Burlington: GiziMap, 2001. Print.

42. A cartoon or comic strip

Provide the title (if given) in quotation marks directly following the artist's name.

> Cheney, Tom. Cartoon. *New Yorker*. 10 Oct. 2005: 55. Print.

43. An advertisement

> Hospital for Special Surgery. Advertisement. *New York Times* 13 Apr. 2009: A7. Print.

44. A work of art or a musical composition

> De Goya, Francisco. *The Sleep of Reason Produces Monsters*. 1799. Etching with watercolor. Norton Simon Museum, Pasadena.

> Beethoven, Ludwig van. *Violin Concerto in D Major, Op. 61*. 1809. New York: Edwin F. Kalmus, n.d. Print.

> Gershwin, George. *Porgy and Bess*. 1935. New York: Alfred, 1999. Print.

45. A performance

> *Proof*. By David Auburn. Dir. Daniel Sullivan. Perf. Mary-Louise Parker. Walter Kerr Theatre, New York. 9 Sept. 2001. Performance.

Include the names of any performers or other contributors who are relevant to or cited in your essay.

46. A television or radio program

> "Murder of the Century." *American Experience*. Narr. David Ogden Stiers. Writ. and prod. Carl Charlson. PBS. WEDU, Tampa, 14 July 2003. Television.

Include the names of any contributors who are relevant to or cited in your essay. If you are discussing the work of a particular person (for example, the director or writer), begin the entry with that person's name.

47. A film or video recording

> *Space Station*. Prod. and dir. Toni Myers. Narr. Tom Cruise. IMAX, 2002. Film.

> *Casablanca*. Dir. Michael Curtiz. Perf. Humphrey Bogart, Ingrid Bergman, and Paul Henreid. 1942. Warner Home Video, 2003. DVD.

Include the names of any performers or other contributors who are relevant to or cited in your essay. If you are discussing the work of a particular person (for example, an actor), begin the entry with that person's name:

> Bogart, Humphrey, perf. *Casablanca*. Dir. Michael Curtiz. 1942. Warner Home Video, 2003. DVD.

48. A sound recording

> Beethoven, Ludwig van. *Violin Concerto in D Major, Op. 61*. U.S.S.R. State Orchestra. Cond. Alexander Gauk. Perf. David Oistrakh. Allegro, 1980. Audiocassette.

> Springsteen, Bruce. "Dancing in the Dark." *Born in the USA*. Columbia, 1984. CD.

Documenting Sources Using APA Style

The following guidelines are sufficient for most college research reports that call for APA-style documentation. For additional information, see the *Publication Manual of the American Psychological Association*, sixth edition (2010), or check the APA Web site: http://apastyle.apa.org. APA style requires parenthetical in-text citations that are keyed to a list of references mentioned in the paper.

Use In-Text Citations to Show Where You Have Used Material from Sources

The APA author-year system calls for the last name of the author and the year of publication of the original work in the citation. If the cited material is a quotation, you also need to include the page number(s) of the original. If the cited material is not a quotation, the page reference is optional. Use commas to separate author, year, and page in a parenthetical citation. The page number is preceded by $p.$ for a single page or $pp.$ for a range (not italicized). Use an ampersand (&) to join the names of multiple authors.

If you are citing an electronic source without page numbers, give the paragraph number if it is provided, preceded by the abbreviation *para.* If no paragraph number is given, give the heading of the section and the number of the paragraph within it where the material appears, if possible.

> The conditions in the stockyards were so dangerous that workers "fell into the vats; and when they were fished out, there was never enough of them left to be worth exhibiting" (Sinclair, 2005, p. 134).

> Racial bias does not necessarily diminish merely through exposure to individuals of other races (Jamison & Tyree, 2001, Conclusion section, para. 2).

If the author's name is mentioned in your text, cite the year in parentheses directly following the author's name, and place the page reference in parentheses before the final sentence period. Use *and* to join the names of multiple authors. (See examples on p. 658.)

Sinclair (2005) wrote that workers sometimes "fell into the vats; and when they were fished out, there was never enough of them left to be worth exhibiting" (p. 134).

As Jamison and Tyree (2001) have found, racial bias does not diminish merely through exposure to individuals of other races (Conclusion section, para. 2).

USE THE FOLLOWING MODELS FOR IN-TEXT CITATIONS

1. When the source has three or more authors

First citation for a source with three to five authors:

Rosenzweig, Breedlove, and Watson (2005) wrote that biological psychology is an interdisciplinary field that includes scientists from "quite different backgrounds" (p. 3).

Subsequent citations for a source with three to five authors:

Biological psychology is "the field that relates behavior to bodily processes, especially the workings of the brain" (Rosenzweig et al., 2005, p. 3).

For a source with six or more authors, use the last name of the first author and *et al.* in all in-text citations.

2. When the author is not named

As reported in the 1994 *Economist* article "Classless Society," estimates as late as 1993 placed the number of home-schooled children in the 350,000 to 500,000 range.

An international pollution treaty still to be ratified would prohibit all plastic garbage from being dumped at sea ("Awash," 1987).

3. When the author is an agency or a corporation

First in-text or parenthetical citation:

According to the Washington State Board of Community and Technical Colleges (WSBCTC, 1995), a tuition increase has been proposed to offset budget deficits from Initiative 601.

Tuition increases proposed for Washington community and technical colleges would help offset budget deficits brought about by Initiative 601 (Washington State Board of Community and Technical Colleges [WSBCTC], 1995).

Subsequent parenthetical citations for the same source:

The tuition increases would amount to about 3 percent and would still not cover the loss of revenue (WSBCTC, 1995).

4. When two or more authors have the same last name

"Women are more in the public world, the heretofore male world, than at any previous moment in history," transforming "the lives of women and men to an

extent probably unparalleled by any other social or political movement"
(W. Brown, 1988, pp. 1, 3).

If two or more primary authors with the same last name are listed in the references, include the authors' first initial in all in-text citations, even if the year of publication of the authors' works differs.

5. When two or more works by the same author share the
   same publication year

When two or more works by the same author or authors are cited, the years of publication are usually enough to distinguish them. However, when the works share the same publication date, arrange the works (in the list of references) alphabetically by title, and then add *a, b, c,* and so on after the year to distinguish works published in the same year by the same author(s). Include the letter in each in-text citation.

> Middle-class unemployed workers are better off than their lower-class counterparts, because "the white collar unemployed are likely to have some assets to invest in their job search" (Ehrenreich, 2005b, p. 16).

6. When a quotation is taken from a secondary source

> E. M. Forster said "the collapse of all civilization, so realistic for us, sounded in Matthew Arnold's ears like a distant and harmonious cataract" (as cited in Trilling, 1955, p. 11).

Create an entry in the list of references for the secondary source in which you found the quote, not for the original source.

7. When an e-mail or other personal communication is cited

> According to L. Jones (personal communication, May 2, 2001), some parents believe they must maximize their day-care value and leave their children at day-care centers for up to ten hours a day, even on their days off.

In addition to e-mail messages, personal communications include letters, memos, personal interviews, telephone conversations, and online discussion group postings that are not archived. Give the initial(s) as well as the surname of the communicator, and provide as exact a date as possible. Personal communications are cited only in the text; do not include them in the list of references.

Include All of Your Sources in a References List at the End of Your Essay

In APA style, every source referred to in the text of your essay (except personal communications or works such as the Bible or the Qur'an) must have a corresponding entry in the list of references at the end of your essay. Conversely, every entry in the references list must correspond to at least one in-text citation in the essay. The information provided in this list enables readers to find the sources cited in the essay. If you want to show the sources you consulted but did not cite in the essay, list them on a separate page titled *Bibliography*.

The APA recommends that all references be double-spaced and that students use a *hanging indent*: the first line of the entry is not indented, but subsequent lines are indented one-half inch. The examples in this section demonstrate the hanging-indent style. The APA encourages use of italics, as shown in the following model entries.

Copy the author's name and the title from the first or title page of the source, but use only initials, not first names. For the location of the publisher, use the first city listed on the title page. Include state abbreviations for all cities, unless the state appears in the publisher's name (as in some university presses).

BASIC ENTRY FOR A BOOK

> Author's last name, First initial. Middle initial. (year published). *Book title*. City of publication, State: Publisher's name.

USE THE FOLLOWING MODELS FOR BOOKS

1. A book by a single author

> Ehrenreich, B. (2001). *Nickel and dimed: On (not) getting by in America*. New York, NY: Metropolitan.

2. A book by more than one author

> Hunt, L., Po-Chia Hsia, R., Martin, T. R., Rosenwein, B. H., Rosenwein, H., & Smith, B. G. (2001). *The making of the West: Peoples and cultures*. Boston, MA: Bedford/St. Martin's.

> Saba, L., & Gattis, J. (2002). *The McGraw-Hill homeschooling companion*. New York, NY: McGraw-Hill.

If there are more than seven authors, list only the first six, then insert three spaced periods, and add the last author's name.

3. A book by an agency, organization, or corporation

> American Medical Association. (2004). *Family medical guide*. Hoboken, NJ: Wiley.

4. A book with an unlisted author

> *Rand McNally commercial atlas and marketing guide*. (2003). Skokie, IL: Rand McNally.

If the word *Anonymous* appears on the title page, cite the author as *Anonymous*.

5. A later edition of a book

Lewis, I. M. (1996). *Religion in context: Cults and charisma* (2nd ed.). New York, NY: Cambridge University Press.

6. Multiple works by the same author (or same group of authors)

Ritzer, G. (1993). *The McDonaldization of society*. Newbury Park, CA: Pine Forge Press.

Ritzer, G. (1994). *Sociological beginnings: On the origins of key ideas in sociology*. New York, NY: McGraw-Hill.

List the works in chronological order, as shown above. However, when the books also have the same publication year, arrange them alphabetically by title and add a lowercase letter after the year: *1996a, 1996b.* (See item 22 on p. 663 for examples.)

7. A multivolume work

Sandburg, C. (1939). *Abraham Lincoln: Vol. 2. The war years*. New York, NY: Scribner's.

Sandburg, C. (1939). *Abraham Lincoln* (Vols. 1-6). New York, NY: Scribner's.

8. A book with an author and an editor

Baum, L. F. (1996). *Our landlady* (N. T. Koupal, Ed.). Lincoln, NE: University of Nebraska Press.

9. An edited collection

Waldman, D., & Walker, J. (Eds.). (1999). *Feminism and documentary*. Minneapolis: University of Minnesota Press.

10. A work in an anthology or a collection

Fairbairn-Dunlop, P. (1993). Women and agriculture in western Samoa. In J. H. Momsen & V. Kinnaird (Eds.), *Different places, different voices* (pp. 211–226). London, England: Routledge.

11. A republished book

Arnold, M. (1994). *Culture and anarchy* (S. Lipman, Ed.). New Haven, CT: Yale University Press. (Original work published 1869)

Note: Both the original and the republished dates are included in the in-text citation, separated by a slash: *(Arnold, 1869/1994).*

12. A translation

Tolstoy, L. (2002). *War and peace* (C. Garnett, Trans.). New York, NY: Modern Library. (Original work published 1869)

Note: Both the original publication date and the publication date for the translation are included in the in-text citation, separated by a slash: *(Tolstoy, 1869/2002).*

13. An article in a reference book

> Rowland, R. P. (2001). Myasthenia gravis. In *Encyclopedia Americana* (Vol. 19, p. 683). Danbury, CT: Grolier.

14. An introduction, preface, foreword, or afterword

> Graff, G., & Phelan, J. Preface (2004). In M. Twain, *Adventures of Huckleberry Finn* (pp. iii–vii). New York, NY: Bedford/St. Martin's.

BASIC ENTRY FOR AN ARTICLE

> Author's last name, First initial. Middle initial. (publication date). Title of the article. *Journal Name, volume number* (issue number), page range.

USE THE FOLLOWING MODELS FOR ARTICLES

15. An article in a scholarly journal with continuous annual pagination

The volume number follows the title of the journal.

> Shan, J. Z., Morris, A. G., & Sun, F. (2001). Financial development and economic growth: A chicken and egg problem? *Review of Economics, 9,* 443–454.

16. An article in a scholarly journal that paginates each issue separately

The issue number appears in parentheses after the volume number.

> Tran, D. (2002). Personal income by state, second quarter 2002. *Current Business, 82*(11), 55–73.

17. An article from a newspaper

> Peterson, A. (2003, May 20). Finding a cure for old age. *Wall Street Journal,* pp. D1, D5.

18. An article from a magazine

> Fallows, J. (2008, September). Rhetorical questions. *The Atlantic, 302*(2), 34–52.

> Gross, M. J. (2003, April 29). Family life during war time. *The Advocate,* 42–48.

> Shelby, A. (2005, September/October). Good going: Alaska's glacier crossroads. *Sierra, 90*(5), 23.

19. An unsigned article

> Communities blowing whistle on street basketball. (2003, November 9). *USA Today,* p. 20A.

20. A review

> Cassidy, J. (2002, July 12). Master of disaster [Review of the book *Globalization and its discontents* by Joseph Stiglitz]. *The New Yorker*, 82-86.

If the review is untitled, use the bracketed information as the title, retaining the brackets.

21. An editorial or a letter to the editor

> Meader, R. (1997, May 11). Hard to see how consumers will benefit from deregulation [Letter to the editor]. *Seattle Post-Intelligencer*, p. E3.

22. Two or more articles by the same author published in the same year

Arrange the articles alphabetically by title, and add *a, b, c,* and so on after the year in each entry.

> Selimuddin, A. K. (1989a, March 25). The selling of America. *USA Today*, pp. 12–14.

> Selimuddin, A. K. (1989b, September). Will America become #2? *USA Today Magazine*, 14–16.

USE THE FOLLOWING MODELS FOR ELECTRONIC SOURCES

The APA's guidelines require that citations of electronic sources be detailed enough to let readers retrieve the source. For most sources accessed on the Internet, cite the name of the author (if available); date of publication or most recent update (in parentheses; if unavailable, use the abbreviation *n.d.*); title of document; publication information, including volume and issue numbers for periodicals; and retrieval information, including information necessary to locate the document. Note that the APA requires the date of access only for content that is likely to be changed or updated.

23. A journal article with a DOI assigned

For journals that assign each article a Digital Object Identifier (DOI)—a string of computer-generated letters and numbers that serves as a more permanent identifier than a URL—use the article's DOI instead of its URL.

> Konig, A., Lating, J., & Kirkhart, M. W. (2007). Content of disclosure and health: Autonomic response to talking about a stressful event. *Brief Treatment and Crisis Intervention, 7*(3), 176–183. doi:10.1093/brief-treatment/mhm012

> Tharp, R. G. (1989). Psychocultural variables and constants: Effects on teaching and learning in schools. *American Psychologist, 44*(2), 249–359. doi:10.1037/0003-066X.44.2.349

24. A journal article with no DOI assigned

If the article has no DOI assigned, use the URL of the journal's home page.

Houston, R. G., & Toma, F. (2003). Home schooling: An alternative school choice. *Southern Economic Journal, 69*(4), 920–936. Retrieved from http://www.southerneconomic.org

25. An abstract retrieved from a database

Kerlikowske, R. G., & Wilson, M. (2007). NetSmartz: a comprehensive approach to Internet safety and awareness (NCJ No. 219566) [Abstract]. Retrieved from http://www.ncjrs.gov

26. A U.S. government report

U.S. Department of Labor Bureau of Labor Statistics. (n.d.). *Occupational outlook handbook 2000–01*. Retrieved from http://stats.bls.gov/ocohome.htm

27. An online encyclopedia article

Chad. (2007). In *Encyclopædia Britannica*. Retrieved from http://www.britannica .com/eb

Begin the entry with the author if one is listed.

28. A newspaper article

Hauser, C. (2007, September 24). Amid protests, president of Iran speaks at Columbia. *New York Times*. Retrieved from http://www.nytimes.com

29. Online magazine content not available in print

Gordon, P. H. (2007, September 24). Should there be a "War on Terror"? A TNR online debate [Online exclusive]. *The New Republic*. Retrieved from http:// www.tnr.com

30. An article on a Web site

Cite the author (if available), the date of publication or most recent update (in parentheses), the title of the document (in italics), and the URL. List the retrieval date only if the content is likely to change. Name the organization in your retrieval statement if it's not clear from the other information cited.

Manino, L., & Newman, C. (2007, September). *Time is money . . . and dinner!* Retrieved from http://www.ers.usda.gov/AmberWaves/September07/Findings /TimeMoney.htm

American Cancer Society. (2003). *How to fight teen smoking*. Retrieved from http://www.cancer.org/docroot/ped/content/ped_10_14_how_to_fight_teen _smoking.asp

Heins, M. (2003, January 24). *The strange case of Sarah Jones. The Free Expression Policy Project*. Retrieved from http://www.fepproject.org/commentaries /sarahjones.html

31. A posting to an electronic mailing list or newsgroup

> Paikeday, T. (2005, October 10). "Esquivalience" is out [Electronic mailing list message]. Retrieved from http://listserv.linguistlist.org/cgi-bin/wa?A1=ind0510b&L=ads-1#1

> Ditmire, S. (2005, February 10). NJ tea party [Newsgroup message]. Retrieved from http://groups.google.com/group/TeaParty

32. A blog posting

> Frappe. (2007, September 25). Re: Senate Dems reluctant to de-authorize Iraq war. [Web log message]. Retrieved from http://www.huffingtonpost.com

33. An e-mail message

The APA's *Publication Manual* discourages including e-mail messages in the list of references. Cite an e-mail message only in the text as a personal communication (see entry 7 on p. 659).

USE THE FOLLOWING MODELS FOR OTHER SOURCES

34. A government document

> U.S. Department of Health and Human Services. (2009). *Trends in underage drinking in the United States, 1991–2007*. Washington, DC: Government Printing Office.

35. An unpublished doctoral dissertation

> Bullock, B. (1986). *Basic needs fulfillment among less developed countries: Social progress over two decades of growth* (Unpublished doctoral dissertation). Vanderbilt University, Nashville, TN.

36. A television program

> Charlson, C. (Writer/producer). (2003, July 14). Murder of the century [Television series episode]. In M. Samels (Executive producer). *American experience*. Boston, MA: WGBH.

37. A film or video recording

> Myers, T. (Producer/director). (2002). *Space station* [Motion picture]. New York, NY: IMAX.

For a film on DVD or videocassette, list this as the medium in place of "Motion picture" in the brackets.

38. A music recording

> Beethoven, L. van. (1806). Violin concerto in D major, op. 61 [Recorded by USSR State Orchestra]. (Cassette Recording No. ACS 8044). New York, NY: Allegro. (1980)

> Springsteen, B. (1984). Dancing in the dark. On *Born in the U.S.A.* [CD]. New York, NY: Columbia.

If the recording date differs from the copyright date, it should appear in parentheses after the name of the label. When it is necessary to include a number for the recording, use parentheses for the medium; otherwise, use brackets.

39. An interview

Do not list personal interviews in your APA-style references list. Simply cite the person's name (last name and initials) in your text, and in parentheses give the notation *personal communication* (in regular type, not italicized) followed by a comma and the date of the interview. For published interviews, use the appropriate format for an article.

Strategies for Analyzing Visuals

We live in a highly visual world. Every day we are barraged with a seemingly endless stream of images from television, magazines, billboards, books, Web pages, newspapers, flyers, storefront signs, and more, all of them competing for our attention, and all of them loaded with information and ideas. Forms of communication that traditionally used only the written word (letters, books, term papers) or the spoken word (telephone conversations, lectures) are today increasingly enhanced with visual components (PowerPoint slides, cell-phone graphics, video, photos, illustrations, graphs, and the like) for greater impact. And most of us would agree that visuals do, indeed, have an impact: A picture, as the saying goes, is worth a thousand words.

In part because of their potentially powerful effect on us, visuals and visual texts* should be approached the way we approach written texts: analytically and critically. Whether their purpose is to sell us an idea or a car, to spur us to action or inspire us to dream, visuals invite analysis both of their key components and of their rhetorical context. As we "read" a visual, therefore, we should ask ourselves a series of questions: Who created it? Where was it published? What audience is it addressing? What is it trying to get this audience to think and feel about the subject? How does it attempt to achieve this purpose?

Let's look, for example, at the visual text on the next page: a public service announcement (PSA) from the World Wildlife Fund (WWF).

This visual actually includes two images, one superimposed upon the other. The smaller image, in front of the larger one, is made to look like a photograph held in the palm of a hand, suggesting the idea that it was possibly taken by someone on a family vacation. The photo is of a family of polar bears walking on ice. The mother is followed closely by two cubs, so closely that they seem to be

---

*In this appendix, we use the word *image* to refer primarily to photographs. We use the word *visual* as a broader designation for visual elements of texts (including images, but also such components as diagrams, charts, and graphs), and *visual text* for documents such as ads, brochures, and the like, in which visuals are strongly featured, but which consist of more than a single image.

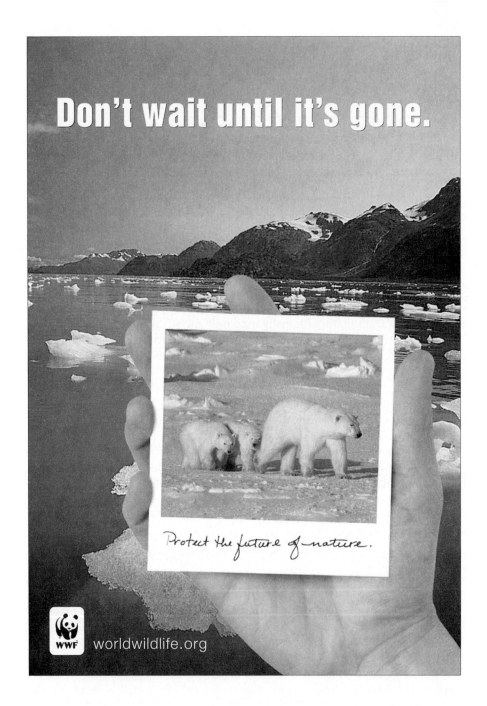

touching the mother and each other. The ice on which they are walking extends as far as the eye can see.

The second image shows a broad expanse of sea water littered with the remains of melted ice. There appears to be more water than ice. In the far distance, a mountain range has only a bit of snow on its otherwise barren hillsides.

These two images are in stark contrast, and the writing makes the message clear. Above the sea of melted ice is written "Don't wait until it's gone." Viewers might initially think that "it" refers simply to the ice. But the writing on the photo of the polar bear family, "Protect the future of nature," makes clear that it also refers to the natural life that depends on a stable environment. The two contrasting images present a startling "before" and "after" comparison, one that brings home the idea that the World Wildlife Fund is needed to help "protect" nature. What is the threat to nature? Clearly it is global warming, which is melting the Arctic ice and endangering species such as polar bears. The reputable, nonprofit WWF's logo and URL, which constitute its "signature," are meant to be an assurance that this threat is real, and not just an idea a profit-seeking ad agency dreamt up to manipulate us.

People continue to argue about how urgent the problem of climate change is and what, if anything, we need to do about it. Not everyone will be convinced by this PSA to support the work of the WWF, and some viewers may feel manipulated by the visual image. They may disagree that the problem is as dire as the depiction implicitly claims it is. They may feel that our resources and energy would be better directed toward other problems facing our nation. Nevertheless, most people would agree that, with two simple images, two brief lines of text, and a logo, the PSA delivers its message clearly and forcefully.

CRITERIA FOR ANALYZING VISUALS

The primary purpose of this appendix is to help you analyze visuals and write about them. In your college courses, some of you will be asked to write entire papers in which you analyze one or more visuals (a painting or a photo, for example). Some of you will write papers in which you include analysis of one or more visual texts within the context of a larger written essay (say, by analyzing the brochures and ads authorized by a political candidate, in an argument about her campaign).

Of course, learning to analyze visuals effectively can also help you gain a more complete understanding of any document that *uses* visuals but that is not entirely or predominantly composed of them. Why did the author of a remembered event essay, for example, choose a particular photo of a person mentioned in the text? If there is a caption under the photo, how does it affect the way we read the essay? In a concept explanation, why are illustrations of one process included, but not another? Understanding what visuals can do for a text can also help you effectively integrate them in your own essays, whatever your topic.

The chart on pp. 670–72 outlines key criteria for analyzing visuals and provides questions for you to ask about documents that include them.

CRITERIA FOR ANALYZING VISUALS

Key Components

Composition

- Of what elements is the visual composed?

- What is the focal point—that is, the place your eyes are drawn to?

- From what perspective do you view the focal point? Are you looking straight ahead at it, down at it, or up at it? If the visual is a photograph, what angle was the image shot from—straight ahead, looking down or up?

- What colors are used? Are there obvious special effects employed? Is there a frame, or are there any additional graphical elements? If so, what do these elements contribute to your "reading" of the visual?

People/Other Main Figures

- If people are depicted, how would you describe their age, gender, subculture, ethnicity, profession, level of attractiveness, and socio-economic class? How do these factors relate to other elements of the image?

- Who is looking at whom? Do the people represented seem conscious of the viewer's gaze?

- What do the facial expressions and body language tell you about power relationships (equal, subordinate, in charge) and attitudes (self-confident, vulnerable, anxious, subservient, angry, aggressive, sad)?

Scene

- If a recognizable scene is depicted, what is its setting? What is in the background and the foreground?

- What has happened just before the image was "shot"? What will happen in the next scene?

- What, if anything, is happening just outside of the visual frame?

Words

- If text is combined with the visual, what role does the text play? Is it a slogan? A famous quote? Lyrics from a well-known song?

- Does the text help you interpret the visual's overall meaning? What interpretive clues does it provide?

- What is the tone of the text? Humorous? Elegiac? Ironic?

Tone

- What tone, or mood, does the visual convey? Is it light-hearted, somber, frightening, shocking, joyful? What elements in the visual (color, composition, words, people, setting, etc.) convey this tone?

Context(s)

Rhetorical Context

- **What is its main purpose?** Are we being asked to buy a product? Form an opinion or judgment about something? Support a political party's candidate? Take some other kind of action?

- **Who is its target audience?** Children? Men? Women? Some sub- or super-set of these groups (e.g., African American men; "tweens"; seniors)?

- **Who is the author? Who sponsored its publication?** What background/associations do the author and the sponsoring publication have? What other works have they produced?

- **Where was it published, and in what form?** Online? On television? In print? In a commercial publication (e.g., a sales brochure, billboard, ad) or an informational one (newspaper, magazine)?

- **If the visual is embedded within a document that is primarily written text, how do the written text and the visual relate to one another?** Do they convey the same message, or are they at odds in any way? Does the image seem subordinate to the written text, or is it the other way around?

- *Social Context.* **What is the immediate social and cultural context within which the visual is operating?** If we are being asked to support a certain candidate, for example, how does the visual reinforce or counter what we already know about this candidate? What other social/cultural knowledge does the visual assume its audience already has?

- *Historical Context*. **What historical knowledge does it assume the audience already possesses?** Does the visual refer to other historical images, figures, events, or stories that the audience would recognize? How do these historical references relate to the visual's audience and purpose?

- *Intertextuality*. **How does the visual connect, relate to, or contrast with any other significant texts, visual or otherwise, that you are aware of?** How do such considerations inform your ideas about this particular visual?

A SAMPLE ANALYSIS

In a composition class, students were asked to do a short written analysis of a photograph of their choosing. In looking for ideas online, one student, Paul Taylor, came across the Library of Congress's *Documenting America*, an exhibit of photographs taken between 1935 and 1945 for the federal government's Farm Security Administration. The work of African American photographer Gordon Parks struck Paul as particularly interesting, especially his photos of Ella Watson, a poorly paid office cleaner employed by the federal government.

After studying the photographs, Paul read what the site had to say about the context from which they emerged:

> Gordon Parks was born in Kansas in 1912. . . . During the Depression a variety of jobs . . . took him to various parts of the northern United States. He took up photography during his travels. . . . In 1942, an opportunity to work for the Farm Security Administration brought the photographer to the nation's capital; Parks later recalled that "discrimination and bigotry were worse there than any place I had yet seen."[1]

The exhibit also quotes Parks's recollection of his first photo session with Watson:

> She began to spill out her life's story. It was a pitiful one. She had struggled alone after her mother had died and her father had been killed by a lynch mob. . . . Her husband was accidentally shot to death two days before their daughter was born. . . . My first photograph of [Watson] was unsubtle. I overdid it and posed her, Grant Wood style, before the American flag, a broom in one hand, a mop in the other, staring straight into the camera.[2]

[1]Martin H. Bush, "A Conversation with Gordon Parks," in *The Photographs of Gordon Parks* (Wichita, Kansas: Wichita State University, 1983), 36.
[2]Gordon Parks, *A Choice of Weapons* (New York: Harper & Row, 1966), 230–31.

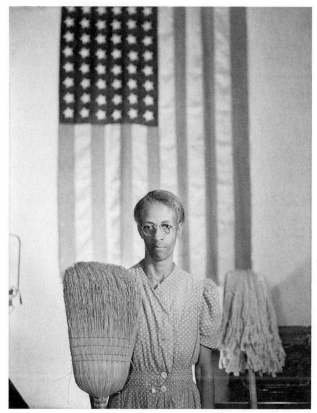

Ella Watson, Gordon Parks (1942)

Paul didn't understand Parks's reference to "Grant Wood" in his description of the photo, so he did an Internet search using the terms *"Grant Wood"* *"Gordon Parks" "Ella Watson"* and discovered that Parks was referring to a classic painting by Wood called *American Gothic* (see p. 674). Reading further about the connection, he discovered that Parks's photo of Watson is itself commonly titled *American Gothic* and discussed as a parody of Grant Wood's painting.

Intrigued by what he had learned so far, Paul decided to delve into Parks's later career. A 2006 obituary of Parks in the *New York Times* reproduced his 1952 photo *Emerging Man* (see p. 674), which Paul decided to analyze for his assignment. First, he did additional research on the photo. Then he made notes on his responses to the photo using the criteria for analysis provided on pp. 670–72.

© Estate of Nan Wood Graham/VAGA, NYC.

American Gothic, Grant Wood (1930)

Emerging Man, Gordon Parks (1952)

Key Components of the Visual

Composition

- **Of what elements is the visual composed?**

  It's a black-and-white photo showing the top three-quarters of a man's face and his hands (mostly fingers). He appears to be emerging out of the ground—out of a sewer? There's what looks like asphalt in the foreground, and buildings (out of focus) in the far background.

- **What is the focal point—that is, the place your eyes are drawn to?**

  The focal point is the face of the man staring directly into the camera's lens. There's a shaft of light angled (slightly from the right?) onto the lower-middle part of his face. His eyes appear to glisten slightly. The rest of his face, his hands, and the foreground are in shadow.

- **From what perspective do you view the focal point?**

  We appear to be looking at him at eye level--weird, since eye level for him is just a few inches from the ground. Was the photographer lying down? The shot is also a close-up—a foot or two from the man's face. Why so close?

- **What colors are used? Are there obvious special effects employed? Is there a frame, or are there any additional graphical elements?**

  There's no visible frame or any graphic elements. The image is in stark black and white, and there's a "graininess" to it: we can see the texture of the man's skin and the asphalt on the street.

People/Other Main Figures

- **If people are depicted, how would you describe their age, gender, subculture, ethnicity, profession, level of attractiveness, and socioeconomic class?**

  The man is African American, and probably middle-aged (or at least not obviously very young or very old). We can't see his clothing or any other marker of class, profession, etc. The fact that he seems to be emerging from a sewer implies that he's not hugely rich or prominent, of course—a "man of the people"?

- **Who is looking at whom? Do the people represented seem conscious of the viewer's gaze?**

  The man seems to be looking directly into the camera, and at the viewer (who's in the position of the photographer). I guess, yes, he seems to look straight at the viewer—perhaps in a challenging or questioning way.

- **What do the facial expressions and body language tell you about power relationships (equal, subordinate, in charge) and attitudes (self-confident, vulnerable, anxious, subservient, angry, aggressive, sad)?**

  We can only see his face from the nose up, and his fingertips. It looks like one eyebrow is slightly raised, which might mean he's questioning or skeptical. The expression in his eyes is definitely serious. The position of his fingers implies that he's clutching the rim of the manhole—that, and the title, indicate that he's pulling himself up out of the hole. But since we see only the fingers, not the whole hand, does his hold seem tenuous—he's "holding on by his fingertips"? Not sure.

Scene

- **If a recognizable scene is depicted, what is its setting? What is in the background and the foreground?**

  It looks like an urban setting (asphalt, manhole cover, buildings, and lights in the blurry distant background). Descriptions of the photo note that Parks shot the image in Harlem. Hazy buildings and objects are in the distance. Only the man's face and fingertips are in focus. The sky behind him is light gray, though—is it dawn?

- **What has happened just before the image was "shot"? What will happen in the next scene?**

  He appears to be coming up and out of the hole in the ground (the sewer).

- **What, if anything, is happening just outside of the visual frame?**

  It's not clear. There's no activity in the background at all. It's deserted, except for him.

Words

- **If text is combined with the visual, what role does the text play?**

  There's no text on or near the image. There is the title, though—*Emerging Man*.

- **Does the text help you interpret the visual's overall meaning?**

  The title is a literal description, but it might also refer to the civil rights movement—the gradual racial and economic integration—of African Americans into American society.

- **What is the tone of the text?**

  Hard to say. I guess, assuming wordplay is involved, it's sort of witty (merging traffic?)?

Tone

- **What tone, or mood, does the image convey? What elements in the image (color, composition, words, people, setting, etc.) convey this tone?**

  The tone is serious, even perhaps a bit spooky. The use of black and white and heavy shadows lends a somewhat ominous feel, though the ray of light on the man's face, the lightness of the sky, and the lights in the background counterbalance this to an extent. The man's expression is somber, though not obviously angry or grief-stricken.

Context(s)

Rhetorical Context

- **What is its main purpose?**

  Given Parks's interest in politics and social justice, it seems fair to assume that the image of the man emerging from underground—from the darkness into the light?—is a reference to social progress (civil rights movement) and suggests rebirth of a sort. The use of black and white, while certainly not unusual in photographs of the era, emphasizes the division between black and white that is in part the photo's subject.

- **Who is its target audience?**

  Because it appeared first in *Life*, the target audience was mainstream—a broad cross-section of the magazine-reading U.S. population at mid-twentieth century.

- **Who is the author? Who sponsored its publication?**

  During this era, Gordon Parks was best known as a photographer whose works documented and commented on social conditions. The fact that this photo was originally published in *Life* magazine (a mainstream periodical read by white Americans throughout the country) is probably significant.

- **Where was it published, and in what form?**

  In *Life*, it accompanied an article on Ralph Ellison's novel *Invisible Man*.

- **If the visual is embedded within a document that is primarily written text, how do the written text and the visual relate to one another?**

  The photo accompanied an article about Ellison's *Invisible Man*, a novel about a man who goes underground to escape racism and conflicts within the early civil rights movement. Now the man is reentering mainstream society?

- *Social Context*. **What is the immediate social and cultural context within which the visual is operating?**

  The civil rights movement was gaining ground in post–World War II society.

- *Historical Context*. **What historical knowledge does it assume the audience already possesses?**

  For a viewer in 1952, the image would call to mind the current and past situation of African Americans. Uncertainty about what the future would hold (Would the emergence be successful? What kind of man would eventually emerge?) would be a big part of the viewer's response. Viewers today obviously feel less suspense about what would happen in the immediate (post-1952) future. The "vintage" feel of the photo's style and even the man's hair, along with the use of black and white, probably have a "distancing" effect on the viewer today. At the same time, the subject continues to be relevant—most viewers will likely think about the progress we've made in race relations, and where we're currently headed.

- *Intertextuality*. **How does the visual connect, relate to, or contrast with any other significant texts, visual or otherwise, that you are aware of?**

  Invisible Man, which I've already discussed, was a best-seller and won the National Book Award in 1953.

After writing and reviewing these notes and doing some further research to fill in gaps in his knowledge about Parks, Ellison, and the civil rights movement, Paul drafted his analysis. He submitted this draft to his peer group for comments, and then revised. His final draft follows.

Paul Taylor

Professor Stevens

Writing Seminar I

4 October 2009

The Rising

Gordon Parks's 1952 photograph *Emerging Man* (Fig. 1) is as historically significant a reflection of the civil rights movement as are the speeches of Martin Luther King and Malcolm X, the music of Mahalia Jackson, and the books of Ralph Ellison and James Baldwin. Through striking use of black and white--a reflection of the racial divisions plaguing American cities and towns throughout much of the nineteenth and twentieth centuries--and a symbolically potent central subject--an African American man we see literally "emerging" from a city manhole--Parks's photo evokes the centuries of racial and economic marginalization of African Americans, at the same time as it projects a spirit of determination and optimism regarding the civil rights movement's eventual success.

In choosing the starkest of urban settings and giving the image a gritty feel, Parks alerts the viewer to the gravity of his subject and gives

Fig. 1. Gordon Parks, *Emerging Man* (1952)

Taylor 2

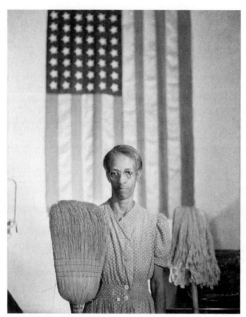

Fig. 2. Gordon Parks, *Ella Watson* (1942)

it a sense of immediacy. As with the documentary photographs Parks took of office cleaner Ella Watson for the Farm Security Administration in the 1940s--see Fig. 2 for one example--the carefully chosen setting and the spareness of the treatment ensure the viewer's focus on the social statement the artist is making (*Documenting*). Whereas the photos of Ella Watson document a particular woman and the actual conditions of her life and work, however, *Emerging Man* strips away any particulars, including any name for the man, with the result that the photo enters the symbolic or even mythic realm.

The composition of *Emerging Man* makes it impossible for us to focus on anything other than the unnamed subject rising from the manhole--we are, for instance, unable to consider what the weather might be, though we might surmise from the relatively light tone of the sky and the emptiness of the street that it is dawn. Similarly, we are not given any specifics of the setting, which is simply urban and, apart from the central figure, unpopulated. Reducing the elements to their outlines in this way keeps the viewer focused on the grand central theme of the piece: the role of race in mid-twentieth-century America and the future of race relations.

The fact that the man is looking directly at the camera, in a way that's challenging and serious but not hostile, speaks to the racial optimism of the period among a large cross-section of the society, African American and white alike. President Truman's creation of the President's Committee on Civil Rights in 1946 and his 1948 Executive Order for the integration of all armed services were significant steps toward the emergence of the full-blown civil rights movement, providing hope that African Americans would be able, for perhaps the first time in American history, to look directly into the eyes of their white counterparts and fearlessly emphasize their shared humanity (Leuchtenburg). The "emerging man" seems to be daring us to try to stop his rise from the manhole, his hands gripping its sides, his eyes focused intently upon the viewer.

According to several sources, Parks planned and executed the photograph as a photographic counterpart to Ralph Ellison's 1952 *Invisible Man*, a breakthrough novel about race and society that was both a best-seller and a critical success. *Invisible Man* is narrated in the first person by an unnamed African American man who traces his experiences from boyhood. The climax of the novel shows the narrator hunted by policemen controlling a Harlem race riot; escaping down a manhole, the narrator is trapped at first, but eventually decides to live permanently underground, hidden from society ("Ralph Ellison"). The correspondences between the photo and the book are apparent. In fact, according to the catalog accompanying an exhibit of Parks's photos selected by the photographer himself before his death in 2006, Ellison actually collaborated on the staging of the photo (*Bare Witness*).

More than just a photographic counterpart, however, it seems that Parks's *Emerging Man* can be read as a sequel to *Invisible Man*,

Taylor 4

with the emphasis radically shifted from resignation to optimism. The man who had decided to live underground now decides to emerge, and does so with determination. In this compelling photograph, Parks--himself an "emerging man," considering he was the first African American photographer to be hired full-time by the widely respected mainstream *Life* magazine--created a photograph that celebrated the changing racial landscape in American society.

Taylor 5

Works Cited

Bare Witness: Photographs by Gordon Parks. Catalog. Milan: Skira;
    Stanford, CA: Iris & B. Gerald Cantor Center for Visual Arts at
    Stanford University, 2006. Traditional Fine Arts Organization.
    Resource Library. Web. 5 Dec. 2008.

Documenting America: Photographers on Assignment. 15 Dec. 1998.
    *America from the Great Depression to World War II: Black-and-
    White Photographs from the FSA-OWI, 1935–1945*. Prints and
    Photographs Div., Lib. of Cong. Web. 3 Dec. 2008.

Leuchtenburg, William E. "The Conversion of Harry Truman."
    American Heritage 42.7 (1991): 55–68. *America: History & Life*.
    Web. 5 Dec. 2008.

Parks, Gordon. *Ella Watson*. Aug. 1942. *America from the Great
    Depression to World War II: Black-and-White Photographs from
    the FSA-OWI, 1935-1945*. Prints and Photographs Div., Lib. of
    Cong. Web. 3 Dec. 2008.

---. *Emerging Man*. 1952. *PhotoMuse*. George Eastman House and
    ICP, n.d. Web. 8 Dec. 2008.

"Ralph Ellison: *Invisible Man*." *Literature and Its Times: Profiles of 300
    Notable Literary Works and the Historical Events That Influenced
    Them*. Ed. Joyce Moss and George Wilson. Vol. 4. Gale Research,
    1997. *Literature Resource Center*. Web. 10 Dec. 2008.

Kornbluh, Karen. Originally published in *New American Foundation*, June 29, 2005. © 2005 New America Foundation. Reprinted with permission of the author.

Kuther, Tara L. "Understanding Bullying." Originally published on the national PTA Website; www.pta.org.

Lemonick, Michael D. "The Bully Blight." *Time*, April 2005. Copyright © 2005. Reprinted with permission of Time, Inc.

Maurstad, Tom. "Review of *Avatar*." Copyright © 2010. Reprinted with permission of The Dallas Morning News.

Nansel, Tonja R. et al. Excerpt from "Bullying Behaviors among US Youth: Prevalence and Association with Psychological Adjustment." *Journal of the American Medical Association* (JAMA), April 2001, pages 2094–2100.

Orenstein, Peggy. Excerpt from *Schoolgirls: Young Women, Self-Esteem and the Confidence Gap*, by Peggy Orenstein. © 1994 by Peggy Orenstein and the American Association of University Women. Used with permission of Doubleday, a Division of Random House, Inc.

Orlean, Susan. "Show Dog" from *The Orchid Thief*. Copyright © 1998. Reprinted with permission of Random House, Inc.

Page, Cristina. "A Mom before the Prom." *Huffington Post*, October 10, 2008. Copyright © 2008. Reprinted with permission of the author.

Rodriguez, Luis J. Excerpt from *Always Running—La Vida Loca, Gang Days in L.A.*, by Luis J. Rodriguez. Copyright © 1990. Reprinted with permission of Northwestern University Press.

Rosen, Christine. "The Myth of Multitasking," *The New Atlantis*, Number 20, Spring, 2008, pp. 105–110. Copyright © 2008. Reprinted with permission of the author.

Shah, Saira. "Longing to Belong." First published in *The New York Times Magazine*, Sept. 21, 2003. Copyright © 2003. Reprinted with permission of Conville & Walsh Limited.

Shughart, William F. "Why Not a Football Degree?" Copyright © 2007. Reprinted with permission of the author.

Stabiner, Karen. "Boys Here, Girls There," *Washington Post*, May 12, 2002. Copyright © 2002. Reprinted with permission of the author.

Staples, Brent. "Black Men and Public Space" from *Harper's*. Copyright © 1987. Reprinted with permission of the author.

Staples, Brent. Excerpt from *Parallel Time: Growing Up Black and White*. New York: HarperCollins Publishers. Copyright © 1994 Brent Staples. Reprinted with permission of the author.

Sunstein, Cass. "To Become an Extremist, Hang Out with People You Agree With" (edited extract from "Going to Extreme"). Copyright © 2009. Reprinted with permission of the author.

Tannen, Deborah. "Wears Jumpsuits, Sensible Shoes, Uses Husband's Last Name" (Originally titled, "Marked Women, Unmarked Men"). *The New York Times Magazine*, June 20, 1993. Copyright © Deborah Tannen. Reprinted with permission.

Van Dusen, Lewis H., Jr. "Civil Disobedience: Destroyer of Democracy." *American Bar Association Journal.* Copyright © 1969. Reprinted with permission.

Wallis, Claudia. "The Multitasking Generation." *Time*, March 19, 2006. Copyright © 2006. Reprinted with permission.

Photo Credits

pp. 47, 49. © Aleksandra Crapanzano. Used by permission.

p. 105. © Shannon Brinkman.

p. 164. © Jonathon Rosen.

pp. 212, 215. Wired/Conde Nast Archives/Copyright © Conde Nast.

p. 295. © TWENTIETH CENTURY-FOX FILM CORPORATION / THE KOBAL COLLECTION

p. 326. SLUMDOG MILLIONAIRE Fox Searchlight 2008 Photo by: Mary Evans/ WORKING TITLE/Ronald Grant/Everett Collection.

p. 391. © James Mulligan/The New Yorker Collection/www.cartoonbank.com.

p. 446. © 2010 Guy Billout. First published in *The Atlantic*.

p. 490. New America Foundation, Ten Big Ideas for a New America, 2 February 2007.

pp. 624, 626, 627. Courtesy of EBSCO publishing.

p. 668. WWF-US 2010 Public Service Campaign.

p. 673. Charwoman by Gordon Parks courtesy Library of Congress.

p. 674. (1) Grant Wood, American, 1891–1942, *American Gothic,* 1930, Oil on beaver board, 30 11/16 × 25 11/16 in. (78 × 65.3 cm) unframed, Friends of American Art Collection, 1930.934, The Art Institute of Chicago. Photography © The Art Institute of Chicago. Art © Figge Art Museum, successors to the Estate of Nan Wood Graham/Licensed by VAGA, New York, NY. (2) © The Gordon Parks Foundation.

p. 679. © The Gordon Parks Foundation.

p. 680. Library of Congress.

Index to Methods of Development

This index lists the readings in the text according to the methods of writing the authors used to develop their ideas. For readings relying predominantly on one method or strategy, we indicate the first page of the reading. If a method plays a minor role in a reading, we provide both the first page of the reading as well as the paragraph number(s) where the method is put to use.

Comparison and Contrast

Narration

Process

Index of Authors, Titles, and Terms